PRINCIPLES OF

MICRO-
ECONOMICS

Fourth Edition

THE McGRAW-HILL SERIES IN ECONOMICS

ESSENTIALS OF ECONOMICS

Brue, McConnell, and Flynn
Essentials of Economics
Second Edition

Mandel
Economics: The Basics
First Edition

Schiller
Essentials of Economics
Seventh Edition

PRINCIPLES OF ECONOMICS

Colander
Economics, Microeconomics, and Macroeconomics
Seventh Edition

Frank and Bernanke
Principles of Economics, Principles of Microeconomics, Principles of Macroeconomics
Fourth Edition

Frank and Bernanke
Brief Editions: Principles of Economics, Principles of Microeconomics, Principles of Macroeconomics
First Edition

McConnell, Brue, and Flynn
Economics, Microeconomics, and Macroeconomics
Eighteenth Edition

McConnell, Brue, and Flynn
Brief Editions: Economics, Microeconomics, Macroeconomics
First Edition

Miller
Principles of Microeconomics
First Edition

Samuelson and Nordhaus
Economics, Microeconomics, and Macroeconomics
Eighteenth Edition

Schiller
The Economy Today, The Micro Economy Today, and The Macro Economy Today
Eleventh Edition

Slavin
Economics, Microeconomics, and Macroeconomics
Ninth Edition

ECONOMICS OF SOCIAL ISSUES

Guell
Issues in Economics Today
Fourth Edition

Sharp, Register, and Grimes
Economics of Social Issues
Eighteenth Edition

ECONOMETRICS

Gujarati and Porter
Basic Econometrics
Fifth Edition

Gujarati and Porter
Essentials of Econometrics
Fourth Edition

MANAGERIAL ECONOMICS

Baye
Managerial Economics and Business Strategy
Sixth Edition

Brickley, Smith, and Zimmerman
Managerial Economics and Organizational Architecture
Fifth Edition

Thomas and Maurice
Managerial Economics
Ninth Edition

INTERMEDIATE ECONOMICS

Bernheim and Whinston
Microeconomics
First Edition

Dornbusch, Fischer, and Startz
Macroeconomics
Tenth Edition

Frank
Microeconomics and Behavior
Seventh Edition

ADVANCED ECONOMICS

Romer
Advanced Macroeconomics
Third Edition

MONEY AND BANKING

Cecchetti
Money, Banking, and Financial Markets
Second Edition

URBAN ECONOMICS

O'Sullivan
Urban Economics
Seventh Edition

LABOR ECONOMICS

Borjas
Labor Economics
Fourth Edition

McConnell, Brue, and Macpherson
Contemporary Labor Economics
Eighth Edition

PUBLIC FINANCE

Rosen and Gayer
Public Finance
Eighth Edition

Seidman
Public Finance
First Edition

ENVIRONMENTAL ECONOMICS

Field and Field
Environmental Economics: An Introduction
Fifth Edition

INTERNATIONAL ECONOMICS

Appleyard, Field, and Cobb
International Economics
Sixth Edition

King and King
International Economics, Globalization, and Policy: A Reader
Fifth Edition

Pugel
International Economics
Fourteenth Edition

PRINCIPLES OF
MICRO-
ECONOMICS
Fourth Edition

ROBERT H. FRANK
Cornell University

BEN S. BERNANKE
Princeton University [affiliated]
Chairman, Board of Governors of the Federal Reserve System

with special contribution by

LOUIS D. JOHNSTON
College of Saint Benedict | Saint John's University

Boston   Burr Ridge, IL   Dubuque, IA   New York   San Francisco   St. Louis
Bangkok   Bogotá   Caracas   Kuala Lumpur   Lisbon   London   Madrid   Mexico City
Milan   Montreal   New Delhi   Santiago   Seoul   Singapore   Sydney   Taipei   Toronto

The McGraw·Hill Companies

McGraw-Hill
Irwin

PRINCIPLES OF MICROECONOMICS

Published by McGraw-Hill/Irwin, a business unit of The McGraw-Hill Companies, Inc., 1221 Avenue of the Americas, New York, NY, 10020. Copyright © 2009, 2007, 2004, 2001 by The McGraw-Hill Companies, Inc. All rights reserved. No part of this publication may be reproduced or distributed in any form or by any means, or stored in a database or retrieval system, without the prior written consent of The McGraw-Hill Companies, Inc., including, but not limited to, in any network or other electronic storage or transmission, or broadcast for distance learning.

Some ancillaries, including electronic and print components, may not be available to customers outside the United States.

This book is printed on acid-free paper.

1 2 3 4 5 6 7 8 9 0 QPD/QPD 0 9 8

ISBN   978-0-07-336266-3
MHID   0-07-336266-2

Design of book: The images in the design of this book are based on elements of the architecture of Frank Lloyd Wright, specifically from the leaded glass windows seen in many of his houses. Wright's design was rooted in nature and based on simplicity and harmony. His windows use elemental geometry to abstract natural forms, complementing and framing the natural world outside. This concept of seeing the world through an elegantly structured framework ties in nicely to the idea of framing one's view of the world through the window of economics.

The typeface used for some of the elements was taken from the Arts and Crafts movement. The typeface, as well as the color palette, bring in the feeling of that movement in a way that complements the geometric elements of Wright's windows. The Economic Naturalist icon is visually set apart from the more geometric elements but is a representation of the inspirational force behind all of Wright's work.

Editor-in-chief: *Brent Gordon*
Publisher: *Douglas Reiner*
Developmental editor: *Angela Cimarolli*
Senior marketing manager: *Melissa Larmon*
Senior project manager: *Susanne Riedell*
Senior production supervisor: *Debra R. Sylvester*
Lead designer: *Matthew Baldwin*
Senior photo research coordinator: *Jeremy Cheshareck*
Photo researcher: *Robin Sand*
Senior media project manager: *Cathy Tepper*
Cover design: *Matt Diamond*
Cover image: © *Jill Braaten*
Typeface: *10/12 Sabon Roman*
Compositor: *Aptara, Inc.*
Printer: *Quebecor World Dubuque Inc.*

Library of Congress Cataloging-in-Publication Data

Frank, Robert H.
   Principles of microeconomics / Robert H. Frank, Ben S. Bernanke ; with special contribution by Louis D. Johnston.—4th ed.
     p. cm.—(The McGraw-Hill series in economics)
   Includes index.
   ISBN-13: 978-0-07-336266-3 (alk. paper)
   ISBN-10: 0-07-336266-2 (alk. paper)
   1. Microeconomics. I. Bernanke, Ben S. II. Johnston, Louis (Louis Dorrance) III. Title.
HB172.F72 2009
338.5—dc22

                            2008026579

www.mhhe.com

DEDICATION

For Ellen

R. H. F.

For Anna

B. S. B.

ROBERT H. FRANK

Professor Frank is the Henrietta Johnson Louis Professor of Management and Professor of Economics at the Johnson Graduate School of Management at Cornell University, where he has taught since 1972. His "Economic View" column appears regularly in *The New York Times*. After receiving his B.S. from Georgia Tech in 1966, he taught math and science for two years as a Peace Corps Volunteer in rural Nepal. He received his M.A. in statistics in 1971 and his Ph.D. in economics in 1972 from The University of California at Berkeley. During leaves of absence from Cornell, he has served as chief economist for the Civil Aeronautics Board (1978–1980), a Fellow at the Center for Advanced Study in the Behavioral Sciences (1992–93), and Professor of American Civilization at l'École des Hautes Études en Sciences Sociales in Paris (2000–01).

Professor Frank is the author of a best-selling intermediate economics textbook—*Microeconomics and Behavior*, Seventh Edition (Irwin/McGraw-Hill, 2008). He has published on a variety of subjects, including price and wage discrimination, public utility pricing, the measurement of unemployment spell lengths, and the distributional consequences of direct foreign investment. His research has focused on rivalry and cooperation in economic and social behavior. His books on these themes, which include *Choosing the Right Pond* (Oxford, 1995), *Passions Within Reason* (W. W. Norton, 1988), and *What Price the Moral High Ground?* (Princeton, 2004), *The Economic Naturalist* (Basic Book, 2007), and *Falling Behind* (The University of California Press, 2007), have been translated into 15 languages. *The Winner-Take-All Society* (The Free Press, 1995), co-authored with Philip Cook, received a Critic's Choice Award, was named a Notable Book of the Year by *The New York Times,* and was included in *BusinessWeek's* list of the 10 best books of 1995. *Luxury Fever* (The Free Press, 1999) was named to the *Knight-Ridder* Best Books list for 1999.

Professor Frank has been awarded an Andrew W. Mellon Professorship (1987–1990), a Kenan Enterprise Award (1993), and a Merrill Scholars Program Outstanding Educator Citation (1991). He is a co-recipient of the 2004 Leontief Prize for Advancing the Frontiers of Economic Thought. He was awarded the Johnson School's Stephen Russell Distinguished Teaching Award in 2004 and the School's Apple Distinguished Teaching Award in 2005. His introductory microeconomics course has graduated more than 7,000 enthusiastic economic naturalists over the years.

BEN S. BERNANKE

Professor Bernanke received his B.A. in economics from Harvard University in 1975 and his Ph.D. in economics from MIT in 1979. He taught at the Stanford Graduate School of Business from 1979 to 1985 and moved to Princeton University in 1985, where he was named the Howard Harrison and Gabrielle Snyder Beck Professor of Economics and Public Affairs, and where he served as Chairman of the Economics Department.

Professor Bernanke was sworn in on February 1, 2006, as Chairman and a member of the Board of Governors of the Federal Reserve System. Professor Bernanke also serves as Chairman of the Federal Open Market Committee, the System's principal monetary policymaking body. He was appointed as a member of the Board to a full 14-year term, which expires January 31, 2020 and to a four-year term as Chairman, which expires January 31, 2010. Before his appointment as Chairman, Dr. Bernanke was Chairman of the President's Council of Economic Advisers from June 2005 to January 2006.

Professor Bernanke's intermediate textbook, with Andrew Abel, *Macroeconomics*, Sixth Edition (Addison-Wesley, 2008), is a best seller in its field. He has authored more than 50 scholarly publications in macroeconomics, macroeconomic history, and finance. He has done significant research on the causes of the Great Depression, the role of financial markets and institutions in the business cycle, and measuring the effects of monetary policy on the economy.

Professor Bernanke has held a Guggenheim Fellowship and a Sloan Fellowship, and he is a Fellow of the Econometric Society and of the American Academy of Arts and Sciences. He served as the Director of the Monetary Economics Program of the National Bureau of Economic Research (NBER) and as a member of the NBER's Business Cycle Dating Committee. In July 2001, he was appointed Editor of the *American Economic Review*. Professor Bernanke's work with civic and professional groups includes having served two terms as a member of the Montgomery Township (N.J.) Board of Education.

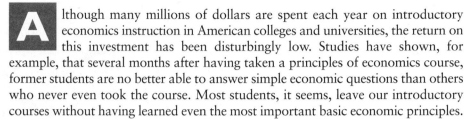

PREFACE

Although many millions of dollars are spent each year on introductory economics instruction in American colleges and universities, the return on this investment has been disturbingly low. Studies have shown, for example, that several months after having taken a principles of economics course, former students are no better able to answer simple economic questions than others who never even took the course. Most students, it seems, leave our introductory courses without having learned even the most important basic economic principles.

The problem, in our view, is that these courses almost always try to teach students far too much. In the process, really important ideas get little more coverage than minor ones, and everything ends up going by in a blur. Many instructors ask themselves, "How much can I cover today?" when instead they should be asking, "How much can my students absorb?"

Our textbook grew out of our conviction that students will learn far more if we attempt to cover much less. Our basic premise is that a small number of basic principles do most of the heavy lifting in economics, and that if we focus narrowly and repeatedly on those principles, students can actually master them in just a single semester.

The enthusiastic reactions of users of our first three editions affirm the validity of this premise. Although recent editions of a few other texts now pay lip service to the less-is-more approach, ours is by consensus the most carefully thought-out and well-executed text in this mold. Avoiding excessive reliance on formal mathematical derivations, we present concepts intuitively through examples drawn from familiar contexts. We rely throughout on a well-articulated list of seven core principles, which we reinforce repeatedly by illustrating and applying each principle in numerous contexts. We ask students periodically to apply these principles themselves to answer related questions, exercises, and problems.

Throughout this process, we encourage students to become "economic naturalists," people who employ basic economic principles to understand and explain what they observe in the world around them. An economic naturalist understands, for example, that infant safety seats are required in cars but not in airplanes because the marginal cost of space to accommodate these seats is typically zero in cars but often hundreds of dollars in airplanes. Scores of such examples are sprinkled throughout the book. Each one, we believe, poses a question that should make any normal, curious person eager to learn the answer. These examples stimulate interest while teaching students to see each feature of their economic landscape as the reflection of one or more of the core principles. Students talk about these examples with their friends and families. Learning economics is like learning a language. In each case, there is no substitute for actually speaking. By inducing students to speak economics, the economic naturalist examples serve this purpose.

For those who are interested in lerning more about the role of examples in learning economics, Bob Frank's lecture on the topic is posted on You Tube's "Authors @ Google" series (**http://www.youtube.com/watch?v=QalNVxeIKEE** or search "Authors @ Google Robert Frank").

FEATURES

- **An emphasis on seven core principles:** As noted, a few core principles do most of the work in economics. By focusing almost exclusively on these principles, the text assures that students leave the course with a deep mastery of them. In contrast, traditional encyclopedic texts so overwhelm students with detail that they often leave the course with little useful working knowledge at all.

Scarcity

Cost-Benefit

Incentive

Comparative Advantage

Increasing Opportunity Cost

Efficiency

Equilibrium

1 **The Scarcity Principle:** Having more of one good thing usually means having less of another.

2 **The Cost-Benefit Principle:** Take no action unless its marginal benefit is at least as great as its marginal cost.

3 **The Incentive Principle:** Cost-benefit comparisons are relevant not only for identifying the decisions that rational people should make, but also for predicting the actual decisions they do make.

4 **The Principle of Comparative Advantage:** Everyone does best when each concentrates on the activity for which he or she is relatively most productive.

5 **The Principle of Increasing Opportunity Cost:** Use the resources with the lowest opportunity cost before turning to those with higher opportunity costs.

6 **The Efficiency Principle:** Efficiency is an important social goal because when the economic pie grows larger, everyone can have a larger slice.

7 **The Equilibrium Principle:** A market in equilibrium leaves no unexploited opportunities for individuals but may not exploit all gains achievable through collective action.

- **Economic naturalism:** Our ultimate goal is to produce economic naturalists—people who see each human action as the result of an implicit or explicit cost-benefit calculation. The economic naturalist sees mundane details of ordinary existence in a new light and becomes actively engaged in the attempt to understand them. Some representative examples:

  - Why are whales and elephants, but not chickens, threatened with extinction?

  - Why do we often see convenience stores located on adjacent street corners?

  - Why do supermarket checkout lines all tend to be roughly the same length?

- **Active learning stressed:** The only way to learn to hit an overhead smash in tennis is through repeated practice. The same is true for learning economics. Accordingly, we consistently introduce new ideas in the context of simple examples and then follow them with applications showing how they work in familiar settings. At frequent intervals, we pose exercises that both test and reinforce the understanding of these ideas. The end-of-chapter questions and problems are carefully crafted to help students internalize and extend core concepts. Experience with our first three editions confirms that this approach really does prepare students to apply basic economic principles to solve economic puzzles drawn from the real world.

- **Modern Microeconomics:** *Economic surplus,* introduced in Chapter 1 and employed repeatedly thereafter, is more fully developed here than in any other text. This concept underlies the argument for economic efficiency as an important social goal. Rather than speak of trade-offs between efficiency and other goals, we stress that maximizing economic surplus facilitates the achievement of *all* goals. *Common decision pitfalls* identified by 2002 Nobel Laureate Daniel Kahneman and others—such as the tendency to ignore implicit costs, the tendency not to ignore sunk costs, and the tendency to confuse average and marginal costs and benefits—are introduced early in Chapter 1 and invoked repeatedly in subsequent chapters.

There is perhaps no more exciting toolkit for the economic naturalist than a few *principles of elementary game theory*. In Chapter 10, we show how these principles enable students to answer a variety of strategic questions that arise in the marketplace and everyday life. We believe that the insights of Nobel Laureate Ronald Coase are indispensable for understanding a host of familiar laws, customs, and social norms. In Chapter 11 we show how such devices function to minimize misallocations that result from externalities. A few simple principles from the *economics of information* form another exciting addition to the economic naturalist's toolkit. In Chapter 12 we show how the insights that earned the 2001 Nobel Prize in economics for George Akerlof, Joseph Stiglitz, and Michael Spence can be employed to answer a variety of questions from everyday experience.

IMPROVEMENTS

Our less-is-more approach is well-suited for a wide spectrum of institutions. Yet it remains a formidable challenge for any single book to fit the needs and capabilities of all students across these diverse institutions. Some students arrive with AP credit in advanced calculus, while others still lack confidence in basic geometry and algebra. Guided by extensive reviewer feedback, our main goal in preparing our fourth edition has been to reorganize our presentation to accommodate the broadest possible range of student preparation. For example, while continuing to emphasize verbal and graphical approaches in the main text, we offer several appendices that allow for more detailed and challenging algebraic treatments of the same material. Among the hundreds of specific refinements we made, the following merit explicit mention.

- **More and clearer emphasis on the core principles:** If we asked a thousand economists to provide their own versions of the most important economic principles, we'd get a thousand different lists. Yet to dwell on their differences would be to miss their essential similarities. It is less important to have exactly the best short list of principles than it is to use some well-thought-out list of this sort.

- **Integrated the outsourcing and international trade material** from (previously) Chapter 9 into the discussions within:
  - Chapter 2: Comparative Advantage
  - Chapter 28: International Trade and Capital Flows

- **Chapter learning objectives:** Students and professors can be confident that the organization of each chapter surrounds common themes outlined by five to seven learning objectives listed on the first page of each chapter. These objectives, along with AACSB and Bloom's Taxonomy Learning Categories, are connected to all test Bank questions and end-of-chapter material to offer a comprehensive, thorough teaching and learning experience.

- **Assurance of learning ready:** Many educational institutions today are focused on the notion of assurance of learning, an important element of some accreditation standards. *Principles of Microeconomics*, 4e is designed specifically to support your assurance of learning initiatives with a simple, yet powerful, solution.

You can use our test bank software, EZTest, to easily query for Learning Objectives that directly relate to the objectives for your course. You can then use the reporting features of EZTest to aggregate student results in a similar fashion, making the collection and presentation of assurance of learning data simple and easy.

THE CHALLENGE

The world is a more competitive place now than it was when we started teaching in the 1970s. In arena after arena, business as usual is no longer good enough. Baseball players used to drink beer and go fishing during the off season, but they now lift weights and ride exercise bicycles. Assistant professors used to work on their houses on weekends, but the current crop can now be found most weekends at the office. The competition for student attention has grown similarly more intense. There are many tempting courses in the typical college curriculum and even more tempting diversions outside the classroom. Students are freer than ever to pick and choose. Yet many of us seem to operate under the illusion that most freshmen arrive with a burning desire to become economics majors. And many of us do not yet seem to have recognized that students' cognitive abilities and powers of concentration are scarce resources. To hold our ground, we must become not only more selective in what we teach, but also more effective as advocates for our discipline. We must persuade students that we offer something of value.

A well-conceived and well-executed introductory course in economics can teach our students more about society and human behavior in a single term than virtually any other course in the university. This course can and should be an intellectual adventure of the first order. Not all students who take the kind of course we envisioned when writing this book will go on to become economics majors, of course. But many will, and even those who do not will leave with a sense of admiration for the power of economic ideas.

A salesperson knows that he or she often gets only one chance to make a good first impression on a potential customer. Analogously, the principles course is often our only shot at persuading most students to appreciate the value of economics. By trying to teach them everything we know—rather than teaching them the most important things we know—we too often squander this opportunity.

SUPPLEMENTS FOR THE INSTRUCTOR

McGraw-Hill's Homework Manager Plus™: McGraw-Hill's Homework Manager Plus is a complete, Web-based solution that includes and expands upon the actual problem sets found at the end of each chapter. It features enhanced technology that provides a varied supply of auto-graded assignments and graphing exercises, tied to the learning objectives in the book. McGraw-Hill's Homework Manager can be used for student practice, graded homework assignments, and formal examinations; the results are easily integrated with your course management system, including WebCT and Blackboard.

Instructor's Manual: Prepared by Louis D. Johnston of the College of Saint Benedict | Saint John's University, this expanded manual will be extremely useful for all teachers. In addition to such general topics as Using the Web Site, Economic Education Resources, and Innovative Ideas, there will be for each chapter: An Overview, Core Principles, Important Concepts Covered, Teaching Objectives, Teaching Tips/Student Stumbling Blocks, More Economic Naturalists, In-Class and Web Activities, Annotated Chapter Outline, Answers to Textbook Problems, Sample Homework, and a Sample Reading Quiz.

Test Bank: Prepared by Kate Krause of the University of New Mexico, this manual contains more than 2,000 questions categorized by chapter Learning Objectives, AACSB learning categories, and Bloom's Taxonomy Objectives. The test bank is available in the latest EZTest test-generating software, ensuring maximum flexibility in test preparation.

PowerPoints: Prepared by Carol Swartz of the University of North Carolina-Charlotte, these slides contain a detailed, chapter-by-chapter review of the important ideas presented in the textbook, accompanied by animated graphs and slide notes.

Customizable Micro Lecture Notes and PowerPoints: One of the biggest hurdles to an instructor considering changing textbooks is the prospect of having to prepare new lecture notes and slides. For the microeconomics chapters, this hurdle no longer exists. A full set of lecture notes for principles of microeconomics, prepared by Bob Frank for his award-winning introductory microeconomics course at Cornell University, is available as Microsoft Word files that instructors are welcome to customize as they see fit. The challenge for any instructor is to reinforce the lessons of the text in lectures without generating student unrest by merely repeating what's in the book. These lecture notes address that challenge by constructing examples that run parallel to those presented in the book, yet are different from them in interesting contextual ways. Also available is a complete set of richly illustrated PowerPoint files to accompany these lecture notes. Instructors are also welcome to customize these files as they wish.

Instructor's CD-ROM: This remarkable Windows software program contains the complete Instructor's Manual with solutions to the end-of-chapter problems, Solman Videos, Computerized Test Bank, PowerPoints, and the complete collection of art from the text.

Online Learning Center (www.mhhe.com/fb4e): The contents of the IRCD are available online at the textbook's Web site for quick download and convenient access for professors anytime.

SUPPLEMENTS FOR THE STUDENT

Study Guide: Revised by Louis D. Johnson of the College of Saint Benedict | Saint John's University, this book contains for each chapter a pre-test; a "Key Point Review" that integrates the learning objectives with the chapter content; a self-test with matching and multiple choice problems; short answer problems; and an Economic Naturalist case study that helps students apply what they learned.

Online Learning Center (www.mhhe.com/fb4e): For students there are such useful features as the Glossary from the textbook; Graphing Exercises, PowerPoints, a set of study and practice quizzes.

Premium Content: The Online Learning Center now offers students the opportunity to purchase premium content. Like an electronic study guide, the OLC Premium Content enables students to take self-grading quizzes for each chapter as well as to download Frank and Bernanke-exclusive iPod content including podcasts by Brad Schiller, narrated lecture slides, and Paul Solman videos—all accessible through the student's MP3 device. In the chapter when

EN 2

you see an iPod icon, there is a podcast that correlates to that material. The label EN stands for Economic Naturalist, and the number represents the chapter number.

A NOTE ON THE WRITING OF THIS EDITION

Ben Bernanke was sworn in on February 1, 2006, as Chairman and a member of the Board of Governors of the Federal Reserve System. From June 2005 until January 2006, he served as chairman of the President's Council of Economic Advisers. These positions have allowed him to play an active role in making U.S. economic policy, but the rules of government service have restricted his ability to participate in the preparation of the Fourth Edition.

Fortunately, we were able to enlist the aid of Louis D. Johnston of the College of Saint Benedict | Saint John's University to take the lead in revising the macro portions of the book and to assist Robert Frank in revising the micro portions of the book. Ben Bernanke and Robert Frank express their deep gratitude to Louis for the energy and creativity he has brought to his work on the book. He has made the book a better tool for students and professors.

ACKNOWLEDGMENTS

Our thanks first and foremost go to our publisher, Douglas Reiner, and our development editor, Angela Cimarolli. Douglas encouraged us to think deeply about how to improve the book and helped us transform our ideas into concrete changes. Angie shepherded us through the revision process in person, on the telephone, through the mail, and via e-mail with intelligence, sound advice, and good humor. We are grateful as well to the production team, whose professionalism (and patience) was outstanding: Susanne Riedell, senior project manager; Matthew Baldwin, designer; Debra Sylvester, senior production supervisor; Jeremy Cheshareck, senior photo research coordinator; and all of those who worked on the production team to turn our manuscript into the book you hold in your hands. Finally, we also thank Melissa Larmon, senior marketing manager, for getting our message into the wider world.

Finally, our sincere thanks to the following teachers and colleagues, whose thorough reviews and thoughtful suggestions led to innumerable substantive improvements.

Adel Abadeer, *Calvin College*

Cynthia Abadie, *Southwest Tennessee Community College*

Hesham Abdel-Rahman, *University of New Orleans*

Teshome Abebe, *Eastern Illinois University*

Roger L. Adkins, *Marshall University*

Richard Agesa, *Marshall University*

Frank Albritton, *Seminole Community College*

Rashid Al-Hmoud, *Texas Tech University*

Farhad Ameen, *SUNY - Westchester Community College*

Mauro C. Amor, *Northwood University*

Nejat Anbarci, *Florida International University*

Giuliana Campanelli Andreopoulos, *William Paterson University*

Michael Applegate, *Oklahoma State University*

Becca Arnold, *Mesa College*

Mohsen Bahmani-Oskooee, *University of Wisconsin-Milwaukee*

Sudeshna Bandyopadhyay, *West Virginia University*

Gyanendra Baral, *Oklahoma City Community College*

James Bartkus, *Xavier University*

Hamid Bastin, *Shippensburg University*

John H. Beck, *Gonzaga University*

Klaus Becker, *Texas Tech University*

Doris Bennett, *Jacksonville State University*

Derek Berry, *Calhoun Community College*

Tom Beveridge, *Durham Technical Community College*

Okmyung Bin, *East Carolina University*

Robert G. Bise, *Orange Coast College*

John Bishop, *East Carolina University*

John L. Brassel, *Southwest Tennessee Community College*

William J. Brennan, *Minnesota State University at Mankato*

Jozell Brister, *Abilene Christian University*

Taggert Brooks, *University of Wisconsin–La Crosse*

Christopher Burkart, *University of West Florida*

Joseph Calhoun, *Florida State University*

Colleen Callahan, *American University*

Denis G. Carter, *University of North Carolina, Wilmington*

Shawn Carter, *Jacksonville State University*

Peter Cashel-Cordo, *University of Southern Indiana*

Andrew Cassey, *University of Minnesota*

Rebecca Chakraborty, *Northwood University*

Joni S. Charles, *Texas State University–San Marcos*

Adhip Chaudhuri, *Georgetown University*

Richard Cherrin, *Delaware Technical & Community College*

Eric P. Chiang, *Florida Atlantic University*

Unk Christiadi, *University of the Pacific, Stockton*

James Cobbe, *Florida State University*

Howard Cochran, *Belmont University*

Jeffrey P. Cohen, *University of Hartford*

Barbara Connolly, *Westchester Community College*

Jim Couch, *University of North Alabama*

Elizabeth Crowell, *University of Michigan–Dearborn*

William Dawes, *SUNY at Stony Brook*

Matthew Dawson, *Charleston Southern University*

Marcelin W. Diagne, *Towson University*

Vernon J. Dobis, *Minnesota State University, Moorhead*

Amrik Singh Dua, *Mt. San Antonio College*

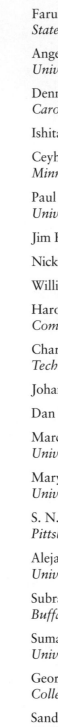

Tran Dung, *Wright State University*

Faruk Eray Duzenli, *Bowling Green State University*

Angela Dzata, *Alabama State University*

Dennis S. Edwards, *Coastal Carolina University*

Ishita Edwards, *Oxnard College*

Ceyhun Elgin, *University of Minnesota*

Paul Emberton, *Texas State University*

Jim Fain, *Oklahoma State University*

Nick Feltovich, *University of Houston*

William J. Field, *DePauw University*

Harold Steven Floyd, *Manatee Community College*

Charles Fraley, *Cincinnati State Technical and Community College*

Johanna Francis, *Fordham University*

Dan Friesner, *Gonzaga University*

Marc Fusaro, *East Carolina University*

Mary N. Gade, *Oklahoma State University*

S. N. Gajanan, *University of Pittsburgh*

Alejandro Gallegos, *Winona State University*

Subrahmanyam Ganti, *University at Buffalo*

Suman Ghosh, *Florida Atlantic University*

George M. Greenlee, *St. Petersburg College*

Sandra Grigg, *East Carolina University*

Sunil Gulati, *Columbia University*

Barnali Gupta, *Miami University*

Richard L. Hannah, *Middle Tennessee State University*

Mehdi Haririan, *Bloomsburg University of Pennsylvania*

Robert Harris, *Indiana University-Purdue University Indianapolis*

Tina J. Harvell, *Blinn College*

Joe Haslag, *University of Missouri*

Philip S. Heap, *James Madison University*

George Heitmann, *Muhlenberg College*

John Hejkal, *University of Iowa*

Mickey Hepner, *University of Central Oklahoma*

Michael J. Hilmer, *San Diego State University*

George E. Hoffer, *Virginia Commonwealth University*

Carol Hogan, *University of Michigan–Dearborn*

James Holcomb, *University of Texas at El Paso*

Lora Holcombe, *Florida State University*

Calvin Hoy, *County College of Morris*

Yu Hsing, *Southeastern Louisiana University*

Eric Isenberg, *DePauw University*

David E. Kalist, *Shippensburg University*

Lillian Kamal, *Northwestern University*

Brad Kamp, *University of South Florida*

Tim D. Kane, *University of Texas at Tyler*

Janis Y. F. Kea, *West Valley College*

Brian Kench, *University of Tampa*

Kamau Kinuthia, *American River College–Sacramento*

Mary Knudson, *University of Iowa*

Janet Koscianski, *Shippensburg University*

Stephan Kroll, *California State University, Sacramento*

Patricia Kuzyk, *Washington State University*

Felix Kwan, *Maryville University*

Katherine Lande, *University of Minnesota*

Gary F. Langer, *Roosevelt University*

Fritz Laux, *Northeastern State University, Oklahoma*

Sang H. Lee, *Southeastern Louisiana University*

Hui Li, *Eastern Illinois University*

Yan Li, *University of Iowa*

Clifford A. Lipscomb, *Valdosta State University*

Donald Liu, *University of Minnesota, Twin Cities*

Teresa Long, *Marymount University*

Alina Luca, *Drexel University*

Brian M. Lynch, *Lake Land College*

Karla Lynch, *North Central Texas College*

Alyson Ma, *University of San Diego*

Rita Madarass, *Westminster College*

Y. Lal Mahajan, *Monmouth University*

John G. Marcis, *Coastal Carolina University*

Dale Matcheck, *Northwood University*

Mike McIlhon, *Metropolitan State University*

Russell McKenzie, *Southeastern Louisiana University*

Matthew McPherson, *Gonzaga University*

Kimberly D. Mencken, *Baylor University*

Lewis E. Metcalf, *Parkland College*

Arthur W. Meyer, *Lincoln Land Community College*

Douglas Miller, *University of Missouri–Columbia*

Norman C. Miller, *Miami University–Oxford*

Ed Miseta, *Penn State University–Erie*

David Mitch, *University of Maryland Baltimore County*

Amlan Mitra, *Purdue University at Calumet*

Robert Moden, *Central Virginia Community College*

James A. Moreno, *Blinn College*

Thaddeaus Mounkurai, *Daytona Beach Community College*

Sudesh Mujumdar, *University of Southern Indiana*

David C. Murphy, *Boston College*

Christopher Mushrush, *Illinois State University*

Annette Najjar, *Lindenwood University*

Helen Naughton, *University of Oregon*

Charles Newton, *Houston Community College*

Daniel Nguyen, *Purdue University*

James Nguyen, *Southeastern Louisiana University*

Sung C. No, *Southern University and A&M College*

Richard Numrich, *Community College of Southern Nevada*

Norman P. Obst, *Michigan State University*

Thomas A. Odegaard, *Baylor University*

Babatunde Odusami, *Southeastern Louisiana University*

Sebastien Oleas, *University of Minnesota Duluth*

Maria P. Olivero, *Drexel University*

Una Okonkwo Osili, *Indiana University-Purdue University Indianapolis*

Stephanie Owings, *Fort Lewis College*

Debashis Pal, *University of Cincinnati*

Michel-Ange Pantal, *University of Missouri*

James M. Payne, *Calhoun Community College*

Richard Peck, *University of Illinois at Chicago*

Robert L. Pennington, *University of Central Florida*

Martin M. Perline, *Wichita State University*

Genevieve Peters, *University of California–San Diego*

Josh Pickrell, *South Plains College*

Rex Pjesky, *Northeastern State University*

Linnea Polgreen, *University of Iowa*

Robert C. Posatko, *Shippensburg University*

Edgar Preugschat, *University of Minnesota*

William Pritchard, *Metropolitan State University*

Farhad Rassekh, *University of Hartford*

Mitchell Redlo, *Monroe Community College*

Jong C. Rhim, *University of Southern Indiana*

Terry L. Riddle, *Central Virginia Community College*

Richard M. Romano, *SUNY/Broome Community College*

Brian Rosario, *University of California–Davis*

Thomas Rossi, *Broome Community College*

Sara Saderion, *Houston Community College–Southwest*

George E. Samuels, *Sam Houston State University*

Jonathan Sandy, *University of San Diego*

George Santopietro, *Radford University*

Samuel Sarri, *University & Community College System of Nevada*

Eric Schansberg, *Indiana University Southeast*

Gerald Scott, *Florida Atlantic University*

Mourad Sebti, *Central Texas College*

Ousmane Seck *California State University at Fullerton*

Anirban Sengupta, *Texas A&M University*

Luis Guillermo Serpa, *University of Illinois at Chicago*

Dennis Shannon, *Southwestern Illinois College*

Rimma Shiptosva, *Utah State University*

Noel S. Smith, *Palm Beach Community College*

Stephen Smith, *Bakersfield College*

Nick Spangenberg, *Ozarks Technical Community College*

Vera Tabakova, *East Carolina University*

Henry S. Terrell, *University of Maryland College Park*

Charles Thompson, *Troy University*

Wendine R. Thompson-Dawson, *University of Utah*

Steve Thorpe, *Phoenix College*

Derek Tittle, *Georgia Institute of Technology*

Elwin Tobing, *California State University at Fullerton*

Brian M. Trinque, *The University of Texas at Austin*

Boone A. Turchi, *University of North Carolina at Chapel Hill*

Markland Tuttle, *Sam Houston State University*

Jesus M. Valencia, *Slippery Rock University*

James Walker, *Indiana University, Bloomington*

Elizabeth Wark, *Worcester State College*

James Wetzel, *Virginia Commonwealth University*

Jennifer Wissink, *Cornell University*

Kristen Wolfe, *St. Johns River Community College*

James Woods, *Portland State University*

J. Christopher Wreh, *North Central Texas College*

Mickey Wu, *Coe College*

Steven Yamarik, *California State University at Long Beach*

Tao Chen Yeh, *University of Alabama*

Andrew M. Yuengert, *Pepperdine University*

Reviewers for previous editions

Ugur Aker, *Hiram College*

Ercument Aksoy, *Los Angeles Valley College*

Rashid Al-Hmoud, *Texas Tech University*

Richard Anderson, *Texas A&M University*

Sudeshna Bandyopadhay, *West Virginia University*

Michael Bar, *University of Minnesota*

Klaus Becker, *Texas Tech University*

Ariel Belason, *Binghamton University*

Daniel Berkowitz, *University of Pittsburgh*

Guatam Bhattacharya, *University of Kansas*

Scott Bierman, *Carleton College*

Calvin Blackwell, *College of Charleston*

Bruce Blonigen, *University of Oregon*

Beth Bogan, *Princeton University*

George Borts, *Brown University*

Nancy Brooks, *University of Vermont*

Clair Brown, *University of California–Berkeley*

Douglas Brown, *Georgetown University*

Andrew Buck, *Temple University*

Marie Bussings-Burk, *Southern Indiana University*

James Butikofer, *Washington University in St. Louis*

Randy Campbell, *Mississippi State University*

Lon Carlson, *Illinois State University*

David Carr, *University of Colorado*

Nevin Cavusoglu, *University of New Hampshire*

Jack Chambless, *Valencia Community College*

Xia Chen, *Tulane University*

Nan-Ting Chou, *University of Louisville*

James Cover, *University of Alabama*

Eleanor Craig, *University of Delaware*

Ward Curran, *Trinity College*

Donald Dale, *Muhlenberg College*

Carl Davidson, *Michigan State University*

Fred Derrick, *Loyola University Maryland*

Lynn Pierson Doti, *Chapman College*

Donald Dutkowsky, *Syracuse University*

Linda Dynan, *Northern Kentucky University*

Michael Enz Western, *New England College*

Belton Fleisher, *The Ohio State University*

Robert Florence, *St. Bonaventure University*

Kent Ford, *Onondaga Community College*

Nancy Fox, *Saint Joseph's College*

Joseph Friedman, *Temple University*

Ynon Gablinger, *City University of New York–Hunter College*

Rob Garnett, *Texas Christian University*

Jonah Gelbach, *University of Maryland*

Linda Ghent, *East Carolina University*

Kirk Gifford, *Ricks College*

Robert Gillette, *University of Kentucky*

Stephen Gohman, *University of Louisville*

Gregory Green, *Idaho State University*

Sunil Gulati, *Columbia University*

Alan Gummerson, *Florida International University*

Refet Gurkaynak, *Princeton University*

Paul Hamilton, *DePauw University*

Mehdi Haririan, *Bloomsburg University of Pennsylvania*

Joe Haslag, *University of Missouri–Columbia*

Jeff Hefel, *Saint Mary's University*

Barry Hirsch, *Trinity University, Texas*

Mary Jean Horney, *Furman University*

Nancy Jianakoplos, *Colorado State University*

Robert Johnson, *University of San Diego*

Brett Katzman, *Kennesaw State University*

Brendan Kennelly, *National University of Ireland*

Herbert Kiesling, *Indiana University*

Bruce Kingma, *State University of New York–Albany*

Frederick Kolb, *University of Wisconsin–Eau Claire*

Stephan Kroll, *California State University–Sacramento*

Christopher Laincz, *Drexel University*

Leonard Lardaro, *University of Rhode Island*

Tom Lehman, *Indiana Wesleyan*

Anthony Lima, *California State University–Hayward*

Patricia Lindsey, *Butte College*

Tom Love, *North Central University*

Alina Luca, *Drexel University*

Jeffrey Macher, *Georgetown University*

Steven McCafferty, *The Ohio State University*

Edward McNertney, *Texas Christian University*

William Merrill, *Iowa State University*

Norman Miller, *Miami University Ohio*

Christopher Mushrush, *Illinois State University*

Paul Nelson, *Northeast Louisiana State University*

Wilhelm Neuefeind, *Washington University in St. Louis*

Neil Niman, *University of New Hampshire*

Norman Obst, *Michigan State University*

Frank O'Connor, *Eastern Kentucky University*

Thomas Odegaard, *Baylor University*

Charles Okeke, *Community College of Southern Nevada*

Ronald Olive, *University of Massachusetts–Lowell*

Terry Olson, *Truman State University*

Duane Oyen, *University of Wisconsin–Eau Claire*

Theodore Palivos, *Louisiana State University*

Santiago Pinto, *West Virginia University*

Michael Potepan, *San Francisco State University*

Robert Rebelein, *Vassar College*

Steve Robinson, *University of North Carolina–Wilmington*

Michael Rolleigh, *University of Minnesota*

Christina Romer, *University of California–Berkeley*

David Romer, *University of California–Berkeley*

Greg Rose, *Sacramento City College*

Robert Rossana, *Wayne State University*

Dan Rubenson, *Southern Oregon University*

Richard Salvucci, *Trinity University*

Edward Scahill, *University of Scranton*

Pamela Schmitt, *Indiana University*

Esther-Mirjam Sent, *University of Notre Dame*

John Solow, *University of Iowa*

Sumati Srinivas, *Radford University*

Dennis Starleaf, *Iowa State University*

Petia Stoytcheva, *Louisiana State University*

Helen Tauchen, *University of North Carolina–Chapel Hill*

Marie Truesdell, *Marian College Indiana*

Nora Underwood, *Central Florida University*

Kay Unger, *University of Montana*

Norman Van Cott, *Ball State University*

Kristin Van Gaasbeck, *California State University–Sacramento*

Stephan Weiler, *Colorado State University*

Jeffrey Weiss, *City University of New York–Baruch College*

William Welch Saginaw, *Valley State University*

Richard Winkelman, *Arizona State University*

Mark Wohar, *University of Nebraska–Omaha*

Louise Wolitz, *University of Texas–Austin*

Paula Worthington, *University of Chicago*

Micky Wu, *Coe College*

Zhenhui Xu, *Georgia College and State University*

Darrel Young, *University of Texas–Austin*

Zenon Zygmont, *Western Oregon University*

AACSB STATEMENT

McGraw-Hill Companies is a proud corporate member of AACSB International. Recognizing the importance and value of AACSB accreditation, the author of *Principles of Microeconomics*, 4e has sought to recognize the curricula guidelines detailed in AACSB standards for business accreditation by connecting questions in the test bank and end-of-chapter material to the general knowledge and skill guidelines found in the AACSB standards. It is important to note that the statements contained in *Principles of Microeconomics*, 4e are provided only as a guide for the users of this text.

BRIEF CONTENTS

Preface vii

PART 1   **Introduction**

   1   Thinking Like an Economist   3

   2   Comparative Advantage   35

   3   Supply and Demand   61

PART 2   **Competition and the Invisible Hand**

   4   Elasticity   97

   5   Demand   125

   6   Perfectly Competitive Supply   150

   7   Efficiency and Exchange   175

   8   The Invisible Hand in Action   203

PART 3   **Market Imperfections**

   9   Monopoly, Oligopoly, and Monopolistic Competition   233

   10   Games and Strategic Behavior   269

   11   Externalities and Property Rights   297

   12   The Economics of Information   325

PART 4   **Economics of Public Policy**

   13   Labor Markets, Poverty, and Income Distribution   349

   14   The Environment, Health, and Safety   375

   15   Public Goods and Tax Policy   397

Glossary   G-1

Index   I-1

CONTENTS

Preface   vii

PART I   **Introduction**

Chapter 1   **Thinking Like an Economist**   3

Economics: Studying Choice in a World of Scarcity   4
Applying the Cost-Benefit Principle   6
    Economic Surplus   6
    Opportunity Cost   7
    The Role of Economic Models   7
Three Important Decision Pitfalls   8
    Pitfall 1: Measuring Costs and Benefits as Proportions Rather
    Than Absolute Dollar Amounts   9
    Pitfall 2: Ignoring Implicit Costs   9
    Pitfall 3: Failure to Think at the Margin   11
Normative Economics versus Positive Economics   15
Economics: Micro and Macro   15
The Approach of This Text   16
Economic Naturalism   17
EXAMPLE 1.1 THE ECONOMIC NATURALIST: Why do many hardware
manufacturers include more than $1,000 worth of "free" software with a
computer selling for only slightly more than that?   17
EXAMPLE 1.2 THE ECONOMIC NATURALIST: Why don't auto manufacturers
make cars without heaters?   18
EXAMPLE 1.3 THE ECONOMIC NATURALIST: Why do the keypad buttons
on drive-up automatic teller machines have Braille dots?   18
Summary   19
Core Principles   20
Key Terms   20
Review Questions   20
Problems   20
Answers to In-Chapter Exercises   22
Appendix: Working with Equations, Graphs, and Tables   23

Chapter 2   **Comparative Advantage**   35

Exchange and Opportunity Cost   36
    The Principle of Comparative Advantage   37
EXAMPLE 2.1 THE ECONOMIC NATURALIST: Where have all the
400 hitters gone?   39
    Sources of Comparative Advantage   40
EXAMPLE 2.2 THE ECONOMIC NATURALIST: Televisions and videocassette
recorders were developed and first produced in the United States, but today the United

States accounts for only a minuscule share of the total world production of these products. Why did the United States fail to retain its lead in these markets? 41

Comparative Advantage and Production Possibilities 41

The Production Possibilities Curve 41

How Individual Productivity Affects the Slope and Position of the PPC 44

The Gains from Specialization and Exchange 46

A Production Possibilities Curve for a Many-Person Economy 47

Factors That Shift the Economy's Production Possibilities Curve 49

Why Have Some Countries Been Slow to Specialize? 51

Can We Have Too Much Specialization? 52

Comparative Advantage and International Trade 53

EXAMPLE 2.3 THE ECONOMIC NATURALIST: If trade between nations is so beneficial, why are free-trade agreements so controversial? 53

Outsourcing 53

EXAMPLE 2.4 THE ECONOMIC NATURALIST: Is PBS economics reporter Paul Solman's job a likely candidate for outsourcing? 54

Summary 56

Core Principles 56

Key Terms 56

Review Questions 57

Problems 57

Answers to In-Chapter Exercises 58

Chapter 3   **Supply and Demand** 61

What, How, and for Whom? Central Planning versus the Market 63

Buyers and Sellers in Markets 64

The Demand Curve 65

The Supply Curve 66

Market Equilibrium 68

Rent Controls Reconsidered 71

Pizza Price Controls? 73

Predicting and Explaining Changes in Prices and Quantities 74

Shifts in Demand 75

EXAMPLE 3.1 THE ECONOMIC NATURALIST: When the federal government implements a large pay increase for its employees, why do rents for apartments located near Washington Metro stations go up relative to rents for apartments located far away from Metro stations? 77

Shifts in the Supply Curve 78

EXAMPLE 3.2 THE ECONOMIC NATURALIST: Why do major term papers go through so many more revisions today than in the 1970s? 80

Four Simple Rules 81

EXAMPLE 3.3 THE ECONOMIC NATURALIST: Why do the prices of some goods, like airline tickets to Europe, go up during the months of heaviest consumption, while others, like sweet corn, go down? 84

Efficiency and Equilibrium 84

Cash on the Table 85

Smart for One, Dumb for All 86

Summary 87

Core Principles 88

Key Terms 89

Review Questions 89

Problems 89

Answers to In-Chapter Exercises   90
Appendix: The Algebra of Supply and Demand   93

PART 2   Competition and the Invisible Hand

Chapter 4   Elasticity   97

Price Elasticity of Demand   98
   Price Elasticity Defined   98
   Determinants of Price Elasticity of Demand   100
   Some Representative Elasticity Estimates   101
   Using Price Elasticity of Demand   102
EXAMPLE 4.1 THE ECONOMIC NATURALIST: Will a higher tax on cigarettes curb teenage smoking?   102
EXAMPLE 4.2 THE ECONOMIC NATURALIST: Why was the luxury tax on yachts such a disaster?   102
A Graphical Interpretation of Price Elasticity   103
   Price Elasticity Changes along a Straight-Line Demand Curve   105
   Two Special Cases   106
Elasticity and Total Expenditure   107
Income Elasticity and Cross-Price Elasticity of Demand   111
The Price Elasticity of Supply   112
   Determinants of Supply Elasticity   114
EXAMPLE 4.3 THE ECONOMIC NATURALIST: Why are gasoline prices so much more volatile than car prices?   116
   Unique and Essential Inputs: The Ultimate Supply Bottleneck   117
Summary   118
Key Terms   119
Review Questions   119
Problems   119
Answers to In-Chapter Exercises   121
Appendix: The Midpoint Formula   123

Chapter 5   Demand   125

The Law of Demand   126
   The Origins of Demand   126
   Needs versus Wants   127
EXAMPLE 5.1 THE ECONOMIC NATURALIST: Why does California experience chronic water shortages?   128
Translating Wants into Demand   128
   Measuring Wants: The Concept of Utility   128
   Allocating a Fixed Income between Two Goods   132
   The Rational Spending Rule   135
   Income and Substitution Effects Revisited   135
Applying the Rational Spending Rule   138
   Substitution at Work   138
EXAMPLE 5.2 THE ECONOMIC NATURALIST: Why do the wealthy in Manhattan live in smaller houses than the wealthy in Seattle?   138
EXAMPLE 5.3 THE ECONOMIC NATURALIST: Why did people turn to four-cylinder cars in the 1970s, only to shift back to six- and eight-cylinder cars in the 1990s?   138
EXAMPLE 5.4 THE ECONOMIC NATURALIST: Why are automobile engines smaller in England than in the United States?   140
   The Importance of Income Differences   140

EXAMPLE 5.5 THE ECONOMIC NATURALIST: Why are waiting lines longer in poorer neighborhoods?   140

Individual and Market Demand Curves   140

Horizontal Addition   141

Demand and Consumer Surplus   142

Calculating Consumer Surplus   142

Summary   145

Key Terms   145

Review Questions   145

Problems   146

Answers to In-Chapter Exercises   147

Chapter 6   Perfectly Competitive Supply   150

Thinking about Supply: The Importance of Opportunity Cost   150

Individual and Market Supply Curves   152

Profit-Maximizing Firms in Perfectly Competitive Markets   153

Profit Maximization   153

The Demand Curve Facing a Perfectly Competitive Firm   154

Production in the Short Run   155

Some Important Cost Concepts   156

Choosing Output to Maximize Profit   157

A Note on the Firm's Shutdown Condition   159

Average Variable Cost and Average Total Cost   159

A Graphical Approach to Profit Maximization   159

Price = Marginal Cost: The Maximum-Profit Condition   161

The "Law" of Supply   163

Determinants of Supply Revisited   164

Technology   164

Input Prices   164

The Number of Suppliers   165

Expectations   165

Changes in Prices of Other Products   165

Applying the Theory of Supply   165

EXAMPLE 6.1 THE ECONOMIC NATURALIST: When recycling is left to private market forces, why are many more aluminum beverage containers recycled than glass ones?   165

Supply and Producer Surplus   168

Calculating Producer Surplus   168

Summary   169

Key Terms   170

Review Questions   170

Problems   170

Answers to In-Chapter Exercises   173

Chapter 7   Efficiency and Exchange   175

Market Equilibrium and Efficiency   176

Efficiency Is Not the Only Goal   179

Why Efficiency Should Be the First Goal   179

The Cost of Preventing Price Adjustments   179

Price Ceilings   180

Price Subsidies   183

First-Come, First-Served Policies   185

EXAMPLE 7.1 THE ECONOMIC NATURALIST: Why does no one complain any longer about being bumped from an overbooked flight? 185

Marginal Cost Pricing of Public Services 188

Taxes and Efficiency 190

  Who Pays a Tax Imposed on Sellers of a Good? 190

EXAMPLE 7.2 THE ECONOMIC NATURALIST: How will a tax on cars affect their prices in the long run? 191

  How a Tax Collected from a Seller Affects Economic Surplus 192

  Taxes, Elasticity, and Efficiency 194

  Taxes, External Costs, and Efficiency 195

Summary 196

Key Terms 197

Review Questions 197

Problems 197

Answers to In-Chapter Exercises 199

Chapter 8   The Invisible Hand in Action 203

The Central Role of Economic Profit 204

  Three Types of Profit 204

The Invisible Hand Theory 207

  Two Functions of Price 207

  Responses to Profits and Losses 208

  The Importance of Free Entry and Exit 214

Economic Rent versus Economic Profit 215

The Invisible Hand in Action 216

  The Invisible Hand at the Supermarket and on the Freeway 216

EXAMPLE 8.1 THE ECONOMIC NATURALIST: Why do supermarket checkout lines all tend to be roughly the same length? 216

  The Invisible Hand and Cost-Saving Innovations 217

  The Invisible Hand in Regulated Markets 217

EXAMPLE 8.2 THE ECONOMIC NATURALIST: Why do New York City taxicab medallions sell for more than $300,000? 218

EXAMPLE 8.3 THE ECONOMIC NATURALIST: Why did major commercial airlines install piano bars on the upper decks of Boeing 747s in the 1970s? 219

  The Invisible Hand in Antipoverty Programs 220

  The Invisible Hand in the Stock Market 220

EXAMPLE 8.4 THE ECONOMIC NATURALIST: Why isn't a stock portfolio consisting of Canada's "50 best-managed companies" a particularly good investment? 223

The Distinction between an Equilibrium and a Social Optimum 224

  Smart for One, Dumb for All 225

EXAMPLE 8.5 THE ECONOMIC NATURALIST: Are there "too many" smart people working as corporate earnings forecasters? 225

Summary 226

Key Terms 227

Review Questions 227

Problems 227

Answers to In-Chapter Exercises 229

PART 3   Market Imperfections

Chapter 9   Monopoly, Oligopoly, and Monopolistic Competition 233

Imperfect Competition 234

Different Forms of Imperfect Competition   234

The Essential Difference between Perfectly and Imperfectly
Competitive Firms   236

Five Sources of Market Power   237

Exclusive Control over Important Inputs   237

Patents and Copyrights   237

Government Licenses or Franchises   237

Economies of Scale and Natural Monopolies   238

Network Economies   238

Economies of Scale and the Importance of Start-Up Costs   239

EXAMPLE 9.1 THE ECONOMIC NATURALIST: Why does Intel sell the
overwhelming majority of all microprocessors used in personal computers?   241

Profit Maximization for the Monopolist   242

Marginal Revenue for the Monopolist   242

The Monopolist's Profit-Maximizing Decision Rule   245

Being a Monopolist Doesn't Guarantee an Economic Profit   246

Why the Invisible Hand Breaks Down under Monopoly   247

Using Discounts to Expand the Market   249

Price Discrimination Defined   249

EXAMPLE 9.2 THE ECONOMIC NATURALIST: Why do many movie theaters
offer discount tickets to students?   250

How Price Discrimination Affects Output   250

The Hurdle Method of Price Discrimination   252

Is Price Discrimination a Bad Thing?   255

Examples of Price Discrimination   255

EXAMPLE 9.3 THE ECONOMIC NATURALIST: Why might an appliance retailer
instruct its clerks to hammer dents into the sides of its stoves and refrigerators?   256

Public Policy toward Natural Monopoly   257

State Ownership and Management   257

State Regulation of Private Monopolies   258

Exclusive Contracting for Natural Monopoly   258

Vigorous Enforcement of Antitrust Laws   259

Summary   260

Key Terms   261

Review Questions   261

Problems   261

Answers to In-Chapter Exercises   264

Appendix: The Algebra of Monopoly Profit Maximization   267

Chapter 10   **Games and Strategic Behavior**   269

Using Game Theory to Analyze Strategic Decisions   270

The Three Elements of a Game   270

Nash Equilibrium   272

The Prisoner's Dilemma   274

The Original Prisoner's Dilemma   274

The Economics of Cartels   275

EXAMPLE 10.1 THE ECONOMIC NATURALIST: Why are cartel agreements
notoriously unstable?   275

Tit-for-Tat and the Repeated Prisoner's Dilemma   277

EXAMPLE 10.2 THE ECONOMIC NATURALIST: How did Congress unwittingly solve
the television advertising dilemma confronting cigarette producers?   278

EXAMPLE 10.3 THE ECONOMIC NATURALIST: Why do people shout at parties?   280

Games in Which Timing Matters   280

Credible Threats and Promises   282

Monopolistic Competition When Location Matters   283

EXAMPLE 10.4 THE ECONOMIC NATURALIST: Why do we often see convenience stores located on adjacent street corners?   284

Commitment Problems   285

The Strategic Role of Preferences   287

Are People Fundamentally Selfish?   288

Preferences as Solutions to Commitment Problems   288

Summary   289

Key Terms   290

Review Questions   290

Problems   290

Answers to In-Chapter Exercises   294

Chapter 11   **Externalities and Property Rights**   297

External Costs and Benefits   298

How Externalities Affect Resource Allocation   298

How Do Externalities Affect Supply and Demand?   299

The Coase Theorem   301

Legal Remedies for Externalities   305

EXAMPLE 11.1 THE ECONOMIC NATURALIST: What is the purpose of free speech laws?   306

EXAMPLE 11.2 THE ECONOMIC NATURALIST: Why does government subsidize private property owners to plant trees on their hillsides?   306

The Optimal Amount of Negative Externalities Is Not Zero   307

Compensatory Taxes and Subsidies   307

Property Rights and the Tragedy of the Commons   309

The Problem of Unpriced Resources   309

The Effect of Private Ownership   311

When Private Ownership Is Impractical   312

EXAMPLE 11.3 THE ECONOMIC NATURALIST: Why do blackberries in public parks get picked too soon?   313

EXAMPLE 11.4 THE ECONOMIC NATURALIST: Why are shared milkshakes consumed too quickly?   313

Positional Externalities   314

Payoffs That Depend on Relative Performance   314

EXAMPLE 11.5 THE ECONOMIC NATURALIST: Why do football players take anabolic steroids?   315

Positional Arms Races and Positional Arms Control Agreements   316

Social Norms as Positional Arms Control Agreements   317

Summary   318

Key Terms   320

Review Questions   320

Problems   320

Answers to In-Chapter Exercises   323

Chapter 12   **The Economics of Information**   325

How the Middleman Adds Value   326

The Optimal Amount of Information   328

The Cost-Benefit Test   328

The Free-Rider Problem   329

EXAMPLE 12.1 THE ECONOMIC NATURALIST: Why is finding a knowledgeable salesclerk often difficult?   329

EXAMPLE 12.2 THE ECONOMIC NATURALIST: Why did Rivergate Books, the last bookstore in Lambertville, New Jersey, go out of business?   329

Two Guidelines for Rational Search   330

The Gamble Inherent in Search   331

The Commitment Problem When Search Is Costly   332

Asymmetric Information   333

The Lemons Model   334

The Credibility Problem in Trading   336

The Costly-to-Fake Principle   336

EXAMPLE 12.3 THE ECONOMIC NATURALIST: Why do firms insert the phrase "As advertised on TV" when they advertise their products in magazines and newspapers?   337

EXAMPLE 12.4 THE ECONOMIC NATURALIST: Why do many companies care so much about elite educational credentials?   337

Conspicuous Consumption as a Signal of Ability   337

EXAMPLE 12.5 THE ECONOMIC NATURALIST: Why do many clients seem to prefer lawyers who wear expensive suits?   338

Statistical Discrimination   338

EXAMPLE 12.6 THE ECONOMIC NATURALIST: Why do males under 25 years of age pay more than other drivers for auto insurance?   339

Adverse Selection   340

Moral Hazard   340

Disappearing Political Discourse   341

EXAMPLE 12.7 THE ECONOMIC NATURALIST: Why do opponents of the death penalty often remain silent?   341

EXAMPLE 12.8 THE ECONOMIC NATURALIST: Why do proponents of legalized drugs remain silent?   342

Summary   342

Key Terms   344

Review Questions   344

Problems   344

Answers to In-Chapter Exercises   346

PART 4   Economics of Public Policy

Chapter 13   Labor Markets, Poverty, and Income Distribution   349

The Economic Value of Work   350

The Equilibrium Wage and Employment Levels   352

The Demand Curve for Labor   352

The Supply Curve of Labor   353

Market Shifts   354

Explaining Differences in Earnings   355

Human Capital Theory   355

Labor Unions   355

EXAMPLE 13.1 THE ECONOMIC NATURALIST: If unionized firms have to pay more, how do they manage to survive in the face of competition from their nonunionized counterparts?   357

Compensating Wage Differentials   357

EXAMPLE 13.2 THE ECONOMIC NATURALIST: Why do some ad–copy writers earn more than others?   357

    Discrimination in the Labor Market   358

    Winner-Take-All Markets   360

EXAMPLE 13.3 THE ECONOMIC NATURALIST: Why does Renée Fleming earn millions more than sopranos of only slightly lesser ability?   360

Recent Trends in Inequality   361

Is Income Inequality a Moral Problem?   362

Methods of Income Redistribution   364

    Welfare Payments and In-Kind Transfers   364

    Means-Tested Benefit Programs   364

    The Negative Income Tax   365

    Minimum Wages   366

    The Earned-Income Tax Credit   367

    Public Employment for the Poor   368

    A Combination of Methods   369

Summary   370

Key Terms   371

Review Questions   371

Problems   371

Answers to In-Chapter Exercises   373

Chapter 14   **The Environment, Health, and Safety**   375

The Economics of Health Care Delivery   376

    Applying the Cost-Benefit Criterion   376

    Designing a Solution   378

    The HMO Revolution   379

EXAMPLE 14.1 THE ECONOMIC NATURALIST: Why is a patient with a sore knee more likely to receive an MRI exam if he has conventional health insurance than if he belongs to a health maintenance organization?   379

    Paying for Health Insurance   380

EXAMPLE 14.2 THE ECONOMIC NATURALIST: In the richest country on Earth, why do so many people lack basic health insurance?   381

Using Price Incentives in Environmental Regulation   382

    Taxing Pollution   382

    Auctioning Pollution Permits   384

Workplace Safety Regulation   385

EXAMPLE 14.3 THE ECONOMIC NATURALIST: Why does the government require safety seats for infants who travel in cars but not for infants who travel in airplanes?   389

Public Health and Security   390

EXAMPLE 14.4 THE ECONOMIC NATURALIST: Why do many states have laws requiring students to be vaccinated against childhood illnesses?   390

EXAMPLE 14.5 THE ECONOMIC NATURALIST: Why do more Secret Service agents guard the president than the vice president, and why do no Secret Service agents guard college professors?   391

Summary   392

Key Terms   393

Review Questions   393

Problems   393

Answers to In-Chapter Exercises   395

Chapter 15   Public Goods and Tax Policy   397

Government Provision of Public Goods   398
    Public Goods versus Private Goods   398
    Paying for Public Goods   400
EXAMPLE 15.1 THE ECONOMIC NATURALIST: Why don't most married couples contribute equally to joint purchases?   402
The Optimal Quantity of a Public Good   403
    The Demand Curve for a Public Good   405
    Private Provision of Public Goods   405
EXAMPLE 15.2 THE ECONOMIC NATURALIST: Why do television networks favor *Jerry Springer* over *Masterpiece Theater*?   406
Additional Functions of Government   408
    Externalities and Property Rights   408
    Local, State, or Federal?   409
Sources of Inefficiency in the Political Process   410
    Pork Barrel Legislation   410
EXAMPLE 15.3 THE ECONOMIC NATURALIST: Why does check-splitting make the total restaurant bill higher?   410
EXAMPLE 15.4 THE ECONOMIC NATURALIST: Why do legislators often support one another's pork barrel spending programs?   411
    Rent-Seeking   411
    Starve the Government?   413
What Should We Tax?   414
Summary   416
Key Terms   417
Review Questions   417
Problems   417
Answers to In-Chapter Exercises   420

Glossary   G-1

Index   I-1

Scarcity

CORE PRINCIPLE 1
The Scarcity Principle (also called "The No-Free-Lunch Principle")
Although we have boundless needs and wants, the resources available to us are limited. So having more of one good thing usually means having less of another.

Cost-Benefit

CORE PRINCIPLE 2
The Cost-Benefit Principle
An individual (or a firm or a society) should take an action if, and only if, the extra benefits from taking the action are at least as great as the extra costs.

Incentive

CORE PRINCIPLE 3
The Incentive Principle
A person (or a firm or a society) is more likely to take an action if the benefit rises and less likely to take it if the cost rises.

Comparative Advantage

CORE PRINCIPLE 4
The Principle of Comparative Advantage
Everyone does best when each person (or each country) concentrates on the activities for which his or her opportunity cost is lowest.

Increasing Opportunity Cost

CORE PRINCIPLE 5
The Principle of Increasing Opportunity Cost (also called "The Low-Hanging-Fruit Principle")
In expanding the production of any good, first employ those resources with the lowest opportunity cost, and only afterward turn to resources with higher opportunity costs.

Efficiency

CORE PRINCIPLE 6
The Efficiency Principle
Efficiency is an important social goal because when the economic pie grows larger, everyone can have a larger slice.

Equilibrium

CORE PRINCIPLE 7
The Equilibrium Principle (also called "The No-Cash-on-the-Table Principle")
A market in equilibrium leaves no unexploited opportunities for individuals but may not exploit all gains achievable through collective action.

PART

I

INTRODUCTION

.

As you begin the study of economics, perhaps the most important thing to realize is that economics is not a collection of settled facts, to be copied down and memorized. Mark Twain said that nothing is older than yesterday's newspaper, and the same can be said of yesterday's economic statistics. Indeed, the only prediction about the economy that can be made with confidence is that there will continue to be large, and largely unpredictable, changes.

If economics is not a set of durable facts, then what is it? Fundamentally, it is a way of thinking about the world. Over many years economists have developed some simple but widely applicable principles that are useful for understanding almost any economic situation, from the relatively simple economic decisions that individuals make every day to the workings of highly complex markets such as international financial markets. The principal objective of this book, and of this course, is to help you learn these principles and how to apply them to a variety of economic questions and issues.

The three chapters in Part 1 lay out the Core Principles that will be used throughout the book. All seven Core Principles are listed on the previous page and on the back of the book for easy reference.

Chapter 1 introduces and illustrates three Core Principles, the first of which is the *Scarcity Principle*—the unavoidable fact that, although our needs and wants are boundless, the resources available to satisfy them are limited. The chapter goes on to show that the *Cost-Benefit Principle*, deciding whether to take an action by comparing the cost and benefit of the action, is a useful approach for dealing with the inevitable trade-offs that scarcity creates. After discussing several important decision pitfalls, the chapter concludes by describing the *Incentive Principle* and introducing the concept of economic naturalism.

Chapter 2 goes beyond individual decision making to consider trade among both individuals and countries. An important reason for trade is the *Principle of Comparative Advantage:* by specializing in the production of particular goods and services, people and countries enhance their productivity and raise standards of living. Further, people and countries expand their production of the goods or services by applying the *Principle of Increasing Opportunity Cost*—first employing those resources with the lowest opportunity cost and only afterward turning to resources with higher opportunity costs.

Chapter 3 presents an overview of the concepts of supply and demand, perhaps the most basic and familiar tools used by economists. These tools are used to show the final two Core Principles: the *Efficiency Principle* (efficiency is an important social goal because when the economics pie grows larger, everyone can have a larger slice) and the *Equilibrium Principle* (a market in equilibrium leaves no unexploited opportunities for individuals but may not exploit all gains achievable through collective action).

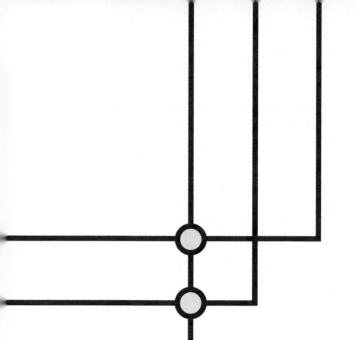

CHAPTER

1

Thinking Like an Economist

LEARNING OBJECTIVES

In this chapter, we'll introduce three simple principles that will help you understand and explain patterns of behavior you observe in the world around you. These principles also will help you avoid three pitfalls that plague decision makers in everyday life. The principles and pitfalls you'll learn about are

1. The Scarcity Principle, which says that having more of any good thing necessarily requires having less of something else.

2. The Cost-Benefit Principle, which says that an action should be taken if, but only if, its benefit is at least as great as its cost.

3. The Incentive Principle, which says that if you want to predict people's behavior, a good place to start is by examining their incentives.

4. The pitfall of measuring costs and benefits as proportions rather than as absolute dollar amounts.

5. The pitfall of ignoring implicit costs.

6. The pitfall of failing to weigh costs and benefits at the margin.

How many students are in your introductory economics class? Some classes have just 20 or so; others average 35, 100, or 200 students. At some schools, introductory economics classes may have as many as 2,000 students. What size is best?

If cost were no object, the best size for an introductory economics course—or any other course, for that matter—might be a single student. Think about it: the whole course, all term long, with just you and your professor! Everything could be custom-tailored to your own background and ability, allowing you to cover the material at just the right pace. The tutorial format also would promote

Are small classes "better" than large ones?

close communication and personal trust between you and your professor. And your grade would depend more heavily on what you actually learned than on your luck when taking multiple-choice exams. We may even suppose, for the sake of discussion, that studies by educational psychologists prove definitively that students learn best in the tutorial format.

Why, then, do so many universities continue to schedule introductory classes with hundreds of students? The simple reason is that costs *do* matter. They matter not just to the university administrators who must build classrooms and pay faculty salaries, but also to *you*. The direct cost of providing you with your own personal introductory economics course—most notably, the professor's salary and the expense of providing a classroom in which to meet—might easily top $50,000. *Someone* has to pay these costs. In private universities, a large share of the cost would be recovered directly from higher tuition payments; in state universities, the burden would be split between higher tuition payments and higher tax payments. But, in either case, the course would be unaffordable for many, if not most, students.

With a larger class size, of course, the cost per student goes down. For example, in a class of 300 students, the cost of an introductory economics course might come to as little as $200 per student. But a class that large would surely compromise the quality of the learning environment. Compared to the custom tutorial format, however, it would be dramatically more affordable.

In choosing what size introductory economics course to offer, then, university administrators confront a classic economic trade-off. In making the class larger, they lower the quality of instruction—a bad thing—but, at the same time, they reduce costs, and hence the tuition students must pay—a good thing.

ECONOMICS: STUDYING CHOICE IN A WORLD OF SCARCITY

economics the study of how people make choices under conditions of scarcity and of the results of those choices for society

Even in rich societies like the United States, *scarcity* is a fundamental fact of life. There is never enough time, money, or energy to do everything we want to do or have everything we would like to have. **Economics** is the study of how people make choices under conditions of scarcity and of the results of those choices for society.

In the class-size example just discussed, a motivated economics student might definitely prefer to be in a class of 20 rather than a class of 100, everything else being equal. But other things, of course, are not equal. Students can enjoy the benefits of having smaller classes, but only at the price of having less money for other activities. The student's choice inevitably will come down to the relative importance of competing activities.

That such trade-offs are widespread and important is one of the core principles of economics. We call it the **scarcity principle** because the simple fact of scarcity makes trade-offs necessary. Another name for the scarcity principle is the **no-free-lunch principle** (which comes from the observation that even lunches that are given to you are never really free—somebody, somehow, always has to pay for them).

Scarcity ⟶ ◯   **The Scarcity Principle (also called the No-Free-Lunch Principle): Although we have boundless needs and wants, the resources available to us are limited. So having more of one good thing usually means having less of another.**

Inherent in the idea of a trade-off is the fact that choice involves compromise between competing interests. Economists resolve such trade-offs by using *cost-benefit analysis*, which is based on the disarmingly simple principle that an action should be taken if, and only if, its benefits exceed its costs. We call this statement the **cost-benefit principle**, and it, too, is one of the core principles of economics:

The Cost-Benefit Principle: An individual (or a firm or a society) should take an action if, and only if, the extra benefits from taking the action are at least as great as the extra costs.

> **Cost-Benefit**

With the Cost-Benefit Principle in mind, let's think about our class-size question again. Imagine that classrooms come in only two sizes—100-seat lecture halls and 20-seat classrooms—and that your university currently offers introductory economics courses to classes of 100 students. Question: Should administrators reduce the class size to 20 students? Answer: Reduce if, and only if, the value of the improvement in instruction outweighs its additional cost.

This rule sounds simple, but to apply it we need some way to measure the relevant costs and benefits—a task that is often difficult in practice. If we make a few simplifying assumptions, however, we can see how the analysis might work. On the cost side, the primary expense of reducing class size from 100 to 20 is that we will now need five professors instead of just one. We'll also need five smaller classrooms rather than a single big one, and this too may add slightly to the expense of the move. For the sake of discussion, suppose that the cost with a class size of 20 turns out to be $1,000 per student more than the cost per student when the class size is 100. Should administrators switch to the smaller class size? If they apply the Cost-Benefit Principle, they will realize that *the reduction in class size makes sense only if the value of attending the smaller class is at least $1,000 per student greater than the value of attending the larger class.*

> **Cost-Benefit**

Would you (or your family) be willing to pay an extra $1,000 for a smaller economics class? If not, and if other students feel the same way, then sticking with the larger class size makes sense. But if you and others would be willing to pay the extra tuition, then reducing the class size to 20 makes good economic sense.

Notice that the "best" class size, from an economic point of view, will generally not be the same as the "best" size from the point of view of an educational psychologist. The difference arises because the economic definition of "best" takes into account both the benefits *and* the costs of different class sizes. The psychologist ignores costs and looks only at the learning benefits of different class sizes.

In practice, of course, different people will feel differently about the value of smaller classes. People with high incomes, for example, tend to be willing to pay more for the advantage, which helps to explain why average class size is smaller, and tuition higher, at private schools whose students come predominantly from high-income families.

The cost-benefit framework for thinking about the class-size problem also suggests a possible reason for the gradual increase in average class size that has been taking place in American colleges and universities. During the last 20 years, professors' salaries have risen sharply, making smaller classes more costly. During the same period, median family income—and hence the willingness to pay for smaller classes—has remained roughly constant. When the cost of offering smaller classes goes up but willingness to pay for smaller classes does not, universities shift to larger class sizes.

Scarcity and the trade-offs that result also apply to resources other than money. Bill Gates is one of the richest men on Earth. His wealth was once estimated at over $100 billion—more than the combined wealth of the poorest 40 percent of Americans. Gates has enough money to buy more houses, cars, vacations, and other consumer goods than he could possibly use. Yet Gates, like the rest of us, has only 24 hours each day and a limited amount of energy. So even he confronts trade-offs, in that any activity he pursues—whether it be building his business empire or redecorating his mansion—uses up time and energy that he could otherwise spend on other things. Indeed, someone once calculated that the value of Gates's time is so great that pausing to pick up a $100 bill from the sidewalk simply wouldn't be worth his while.

If Bill Gates saw a $100 bill lying on the sidewalk, would it be worth his time to pick it up?

APPLYING THE COST-BENEFIT PRINCIPLE

rational person someone with well-defined goals who tries to fulfill those goals as best he or she can

In studying choice under scarcity, we'll usually begin with the premise that people are **rational,** which means they have well-defined goals and try to fulfill them as best they can. The cost-benefit principle illustrated in the class-size example is a fundamental tool for the study of how rational people make choices.

As in the class-size example, often the only real difficulty in applying the cost-benefit rule is to come up with reasonable measures of the relevant benefits and costs. Only in rare instances will exact dollar measures be conveniently available. But the cost-benefit framework can lend structure to your thinking even when no relevant market data are available.

To illustrate how we proceed in such cases, the following example asks you to decide whether to perform an action whose cost is described only in vague, qualitative terms.

Should you walk downtown to save $10 on a $25 computer game?

Imagine you are about to buy a $25 computer game at the nearby campus store when a friend tells you that the same game is on sale at a downtown store for only $15. If the downtown store is a 30-minute walk away, where should you buy the game?

Cost-Benefit

The Cost-Benefit Principle tells us that you should buy it downtown if the benefit of doing so exceeds the cost. The benefit of taking any action is the dollar value of everything you gain by taking it. Here, the benefit of buying downtown is exactly $10, since that is the amount you will save on the purchase price of the game. The cost of taking any action is the dollar value of everything you give up by taking it. Here, the cost of buying downtown is the dollar value you assign to the time and trouble it takes to make the trip. But how do we estimate that dollar value?

One way is to perform the following hypothetical auction. Imagine that a stranger has offered to pay you to do an errand that involves the same walk downtown (perhaps to drop off a letter for her at the post office). If she offered you a payment of, say, $1,000, would you accept? If so, we know that your cost of walking downtown and back must be less than $1,000. Now imagine her offer being reduced in small increments until you finally refuse the last offer. For example, if you would agree to walk downtown and back for $9.00 but not for $8.99, then your cost of making the trip is $9.00. In this case, you should buy the game downtown because the $10 you'll save (your benefit) is greater than your $9.00 cost of making the trip.

But suppose, alternatively, that your cost of making the trip had been greater than $10. In that case, your best bet would have been to buy the game from the nearby campus store. Confronted with this choice, different people may choose differently, depending on how costly they think it is to make the trip downtown. But although there is no uniquely correct choice, most people who are asked what they would do in this situation say they would buy the game downtown. ◆

ECONOMIC SURPLUS

economic surplus the economic surplus from taking any action is the benefit of taking that action minus its cost

Suppose again that in the preceding example your "cost" of making the trip downtown was $9. Compared to the alternative of buying the game at the campus store, buying it downtown resulted in an **economic surplus** of $1, the difference between the benefit of making the trip and its cost. In general, your goal as an economic decision maker is to choose those actions that generate the largest possible economic surplus. This means taking all actions that yield a positive total economic surplus, which is just another way of restating the Cost-Benefit Principle.

Cost-Benefit

Note that the fact that your best choice was to buy the game downtown doesn't imply that you *enjoy* making the trip, any more than choosing a large class means that you prefer large classes to small ones. It simply means that the trip is less unpleasant than the prospect of paying $10 extra for the game. Once again, you've faced a trade-off—in this case, the choice between a cheaper game and the free time gained by avoiding the trip.

OPPORTUNITY COST

Of course, your mental auction could have produced a different outcome. Suppose, for example, that the time required for the trip is the only time you have left to study for a difficult test the next day. Or suppose you are watching one of your favorite movies on cable, or that you are tired and would love a short nap. In such cases, we say that the **opportunity cost** of making the trip—that is, the value of what you must sacrifice to walk downtown and back—is high and you are more likely to decide against making the trip.

Strictly speaking, your opportunity cost of engaging in an activity is the value of everything you must sacrifice to engage in it. For instance, if seeing a movie requires not only that you buy a $10 ticket but also that you give up a $20 babysitting job that you would have been willing to do for free, then the opportunity cost of seeing the film is $30.

Under this definition, *all* costs—both implicit and explicit—are opportunity costs. Unless otherwise stated, we will adhere to this strict definition.

We must warn you, however, that some economists use the term *opportunity cost* to refer only to the implicit value of opportunities forgone. Thus, in the example just discussed, these economists would not include the $10 ticket price when calculating the opportunity cost of seeing the film. But virtually all economists would agree that your opportunity cost of not doing the babysitting job is $20.

In the previous example, if watching the last hour of the cable TV movie is the most valuable opportunity that conflicts with the trip downtown, the opportunity cost of making the trip is the dollar value you place on pursuing that opportunity—that is, the largest amount you'd be willing to pay to avoid missing the end of the movie. Note that the opportunity cost of making the trip is not the combined value of *all* possible activities you could have pursued, but only the value of your *best* alternative—the one you would have chosen had you not made the trip.

Throughout the text we will pose exercises like the one that follows. You'll find that pausing to answer them will help you to master key concepts in economics. Because doing these exercises isn't very costly (indeed, many students report that they are actually fun), the Cost-Benefit Principle indicates that it's well worth your while to do them.

opportunity cost the opportunity cost of an activity is the value of what must be forgone in order to undertake the activity

Cost-Benefit

EXERCISE 1.1

You would again save $10 by buying the game downtown rather than at the campus store, but your cost of making the trip is now $12, not $9. How much economic surplus would you get from buying the game downtown? Where should you buy it?

THE ROLE OF ECONOMIC MODELS

Economists use the cost-benefit principle as an abstract model of how an idealized rational individual would choose among competing alternatives. (By "abstract model" we mean a simplified description that captures the essential elements of a situation and allows us to analyze them in a logical way.) A computer model of a complex phenomenon like climate change, which must ignore many details and includes only the major forces at work, is an example of an abstract model.

Noneconomists are sometimes harshly critical of the economist's cost-benefit model on the grounds that people in the real world never conduct hypothetical mental auctions before deciding whether to make trips downtown. But this criticism betrays a fundamental misunderstanding of how abstract models can help to explain and predict human behavior. Economists know perfectly well that people don't conduct hypothetical mental auctions when they make simple decisions. All the cost-benefit principle really says is that a rational decision is one that is explicitly or implicitly based on a weighing of costs and benefits.

Most of us make sensible decisions most of the time, without being consciously aware that we are weighing costs and benefits, just as most people ride a bike without being consciously aware of what keeps them from falling. Through trial and error, we gradually learn what kinds of choices tend to work best in different contexts, just as bicycle riders internalize the relevant laws of physics, usually without being conscious of them.

Even so, learning the explicit principles of cost-benefit analysis can help us make better decisions, just as knowing about physics can help in learning to ride a bicycle. For instance, when a young economist was teaching his oldest son to ride a bike, he followed the time-honored tradition of running alongside the bike and holding onto his son, then giving him a push and hoping for the best. After several hours and painfully skinned elbows and knees, his son finally got it. A year later, someone pointed out that the trick to riding a bike is to turn slightly in whichever direction the bike is leaning. Of course! The economist passed this information along to his second son, who learned to ride almost instantly. Just as knowing a little physics can help you learn to ride a bike, knowing a little economics can help you make better decisions.

RECAP	**COST-BENEFIT ANALYSIS**

Scarcity is a basic fact of economic life. Because of it, having more of one good thing almost always means having less of another (the Scarcity Principle). The Cost-Benefit Principle holds that an individual (or a firm or a society) should take an action if, and only if, the extra benefit from taking the action is at least as great as the extra cost. The benefit of taking any action minus the cost of taking the action is called the *economic surplus* from that action. Hence, the Cost-Benefit Principle suggests that we take only those actions that create additional economic surplus.

THREE IMPORTANT DECISION PITFALLS*

Rational people will apply the Cost-Benefit Principle most of the time, although probably in an intuitive and approximate way, rather than through explicit and precise calculation. Knowing that rational people tend to compare costs and benefits enables economists to predict their likely behavior. As noted earlier, for example, we can predict that students from wealthy families are more likely than others to attend colleges that offer small classes. (Again, while the cost of small classes is the same for all families, the benefit of small classes, as measured by what people are willing to pay for them, tends to be higher for wealthier families.)

Yet researchers have identified situations in which people tend to apply the cost-benefit principle inconsistently. In these situations, the cost-benefit principle may not predict behavior accurately, but it proves helpful in another way, by identifying specific strategies for avoiding bad decisions.

---

*The examples in this section are inspired by the pioneering research of Daniel Kahneman and the late Amos Tversky. Kahneman was awarded the 2002 Nobel Prize in economics for his efforts to integrate insights from psychology into economics.

PITFALL 1: MEASURING COSTS AND BENEFITS AS PROPORTIONS RATHER THAN ABSOLUTE DOLLAR AMOUNTS

As the next example makes clear, even people who seem to know they should weigh the pros and cons of the actions they are contemplating sometimes don't have a clear sense of how to measure the relevant costs and benefits.

Should you walk downtown to save $10 on a $2,020 laptop computer?

You are about to buy a $2,020 laptop computer at the nearby campus store when a friend tells you that the same computer is on sale at a downtown store for only $2,010. If the downtown store is half an hour's walk away, where should you buy the computer?

Assuming that the laptop is light enough to carry without effort, the structure of this example is exactly the same as that of the earlier example about where to buy the computer game—the only difference being that the price of the laptop is dramatically higher than the price of the computer game. As before, the benefit of buying downtown is the dollar amount you'll save, namely, $10. And since it's exactly the same trip, its cost also must be the same as before. So if you are perfectly rational, you should make the same decision in both cases. Yet when real people are asked what they would do in these situations, the overwhelming majority say they would walk downtown to buy the game but would buy the laptop at the campus store. When asked to explain, most of them say something like "The trip was worth it for the game because you save 40 percent, but not worth it for the laptop because you save only $10 out of $2,020."

This is faulty reasoning. The benefit of the trip downtown is not the *proportion* you save on the original price. Rather, it is the *absolute dollar amount* you save. Since the benefit of walking downtown to buy the laptop is $10—exactly the same as for the computer game—and since the cost of the trip must also be the same in both cases, the economic surplus from making both trips must be exactly the same. And that means that a rational decision maker would make the same decision in both cases. Yet, as noted, most people choose differently. ◆

EXERCISE 1.2

Which is more valuable: saving $100 on a $2,000 plane ticket to Tokyo or saving $90 on a $200 plane ticket to Chicago?

The pattern of faulty reasoning in the decision just discussed is one of several decision pitfalls to which people are often prone. In the discussion that follows, we will identify two additional decision pitfalls. In some cases, people ignore costs or benefits that they ought to take into account, while on other occasions they are influenced by costs or benefits that are irrelevant.

PITFALL 2: IGNORING IMPLICIT COSTS

Sherlock Holmes, Arthur Conan Doyle's legendary detective, was successful because he saw details that most others overlooked. In *Silver Blaze*, Holmes is called on to investigate the theft of an expensive racehorse from its stable. A Scotland Yard inspector assigned to the case asks Holmes whether some particular aspect of the crime requires further study. "Yes," Holmes replies, and describes "the curious incident of the dog in the nighttime." "The dog did nothing in the nighttime," responds the puzzled inspector. But as Holmes realized, that was precisely the problem.

Implicit costs are like dogs that fail to bark in the night.

The watchdog's failure to bark when Silver Blaze was stolen meant that the watchdog knew the thief. This clue ultimately proved the key to unraveling the mystery.

Just as we often don't notice when a dog fails to bark, many of us tend to overlook the implicit value of activities that fail to happen. As discussed earlier, however, intelligent decisions require taking the value of forgone opportunities properly into account.

The opportunity cost of an activity, once again, is the value of all that must be forgone in order to engage in that activity. If buying a computer game downtown means not watching the last hour of a movie, then the value to you of watching the end of that movie is an implicit cost of the trip. Many people make bad decisions because they tend to ignore the value of such forgone opportunities. To avoid overlooking implicit costs, economists often translate questions like "Should I walk downtown?" into ones like "Should I walk downtown or watch the end of the movie?"

Should you use your frequent-flyer coupon to fly to Fort Lauderdale for spring break?

With spring break only a week away, you are still undecided about whether to go to Fort Lauderdale with a group of classmates at the University of Iowa. The round-trip airfare from Cedar Rapids is $500, but you have a frequent-flyer coupon you could use to pay for the trip. All other relevant costs for the vacation week at the beach total exactly $1,000. The most you would be willing to pay for the Fort Lauderdale vacation is $1,350. That amount is your benefit of taking the vacation. Your only alternative use for your frequent-flyer coupon is for your plane trip to Boston the weekend after spring break to attend your brother's wedding. (Your coupon expires shortly thereafter.) If the Cedar Rapids–Boston round-trip airfare is $400, should you use your frequent-flyer coupon to fly to Fort Lauderdale for spring break?

Cost-Benefit ◯

Is your flight to Fort Lauderdale "free" if you travel on a frequent-flyer coupon?

The Cost-Benefit Principle tells us that you should go to Fort Lauderdale if the benefits of the trip exceed its costs. If not for the complication of the frequent-flyer coupon, solving this problem would be a straightforward matter of comparing your benefit from the week at the beach to the sum of all relevant costs. And since your airfare and other costs would add up to $1,500, or $150 more than your benefit from the trip, you would not go to Fort Lauderdale.

But what about the possibility of using your frequent-flyer coupon to make the trip? Using it for that purpose might make the flight to Fort Lauderdale seem free, suggesting you would reap an economic surplus of $350 by making the trip. But doing so also would mean you would have to fork over $400 for your airfare to Boston. So the implicit cost of using your coupon to go to Fort Lauderdale is really $400. If you use it for that purpose, the trip still ends up being a loser because the cost of the vacation, $1,400, exceeds the benefit by $50. In cases like these, you are much more likely to decide sensibly if you ask yourself, "Should I use my frequent-flyer coupon for this trip or save it for an upcoming trip?" ◆

We cannot emphasize strongly enough that the key to using the Cost-Benefit Principle correctly lies in recognizing precisely what taking a given action prevents us from doing. The following exercise illustrates this point by modifying the details of the previous example slightly.

EXERCISE I.3

Same as the previous example, except that now your frequent-flyer coupon expires in a week, so your only chance to use it will be for the Fort Lauderdale trip. Should you use your coupon?

PITFALL 3: FAILURE TO THINK AT THE MARGIN

When deciding whether to take an action, the only costs and benefits that are relevant are those that would occur as a result of taking the action. Sometimes people are influenced by costs they ought to ignore while other times they compare the wrong costs and benefits. *The only costs that should influence a decision about whether to take an action are those that we can avoid by not taking the action. Similarly, the only benefits we should consider are those that would not occur unless the action were taken.* As a practical matter, however, many decision makers appear to be influenced by costs or benefits that would have occurred independently of whether the action was taken. Thus, people are often influenced by **sunk costs**—costs that are beyond recovery at the moment a decision is made. For example, money spent on a nontransferable, nonrefundable airline ticket is a sunk cost.

sunk cost a cost that is beyond recovery at the moment a decision must be made

   As the following example illustrates, sunk costs must be borne *whether or not an action is taken,* so they are irrelevant to the decision of whether to take the action.

How much should you eat at an all-you-can-eat restaurant?

Sangam, an Indian restaurant in Philadelphia, offers an all-you-can-eat lunch buffet for $5. Customers pay $5 at the door, and no matter how many times they refill their plates, there is no additional charge. One day, as a goodwill gesture, the owner of the restaurant tells 20 randomly selected guests that their lunch is on the house. The remaining guests pay the usual price. If all diners are rational, will there be any difference in the average quantity of food consumed by people in these two groups?

   Having eaten their first helping, diners in each group confront the following question: "Should I go back for another helping?" For rational diners, if the benefit of doing so exceeds the cost, the answer is yes; otherwise it is no. Note that at the moment of decision about a second helping, the $5 charge for the lunch is a sunk cost. Those who paid it have no way to recover it. Thus, for both groups, the (extra) cost of another helping is exactly zero. And since the people who received the free lunch were chosen at random, there is no reason to suppose that their appetites or incomes are different from those of other diners. The benefit of another helping thus should be the same, on average, for people in both groups. And since their respective costs and benefits of an additional helping are the same, the two groups should eat the same number of helpings, on average.

   Psychologists and economists have experimental evidence, however, that people in such groups do *not* eat similar amounts.[1] In particular, those for whom the luncheon charge is not waived tend to eat substantially more than those for whom the charge is waived. People in the former group seem somehow determined to "get their money's worth." Their implicit goal is apparently to minimize the average cost per bite of the food they eat. Yet minimizing average cost is not a particularly sensible objective. It brings to mind the man who drove his car on the highway at night, even though he had nowhere to go, because he wanted to boost his average fuel economy. The irony is that diners who are determined to get their money's worth usually end up eating too much, as evidenced later by their regrets about having gone back for their last helpings. ◆

   The fact that the cost-benefit criterion failed the test of prediction in this example does nothing to invalidate its advice about what people *should* do. If you are letting sunk costs influence your decisions, you can do better by changing your behavior. In addition to paying attention to costs and benefits that should be ignored, people often use incorrect measures of the relevant costs and benefits. This error often occurs when we must choose the *extent* to which an activity should be pursued

[1]See, for example, Richard Thaler, "Toward a Positive Theory of Consumer Choice," *Journal of Economic Behavior and Organization* **1,** no. 1 (1980).

(as opposed to choosing whether to pursue it at all). We can apply the Cost-Benefit Principle in such situations by repeatedly asking the question "Should I increase the level at which I am currently pursuing the activity?"

In attempting to answer this question, the focus should always be on the benefit and cost of an *additional* unit of activity. To emphasize this focus, economists refer to the cost of an additional unit of activity as the **marginal cost** of the activity. Similarly, the benefit of an additional unit of the activity is the **marginal benefit** of the activity.

marginal cost the increase in total cost that results from carrying out one additional unit of an activity

marginal benefit the increase in total benefit that results from carrying out one additional unit of an activity

When the problem is to discover the proper level at which to pursue an activity, the cost-benefit rule is to keep increasing the level as long as the marginal benefit of the activity exceeds its marginal cost. As the following example illustrates, however, people often fail to apply this rule correctly.

Should NASA expand the space shuttle program from four launches per year to five?

Professor Kösten Banifoot, a prominent supporter of the National Aeronautics and Space Administration's (NASA) space shuttle program, estimated that the gains from the program are currently $24 billion per year (an average of $6 billion per launch) and that its costs are currently $20 billion per year (an average of $5 billion per launch). On the basis of these estimates, Professor Banifoot testified before Congress that NASA should definitely expand the space shuttle program. Should Congress follow his advice?

average cost the total cost of undertaking n units of an activity divided by n

average benefit the total benefit of undertaking n units of an activity divided by n

To discover whether expanding the program makes economic sense, we must compare the marginal cost of a launch to its marginal benefit. The professor's estimates, however, tell us only the **average cost** and **average benefit** of the program—which are, respectively, the total cost of the program divided by the number of launches and the total benefit divided by the number of launches. Knowing the average benefit and average cost per launch for all shuttles launched thus far is simply not useful for deciding whether to expand the program. Of course, the average cost of the launches undertaken so far *might* be the same as the cost of adding another launch. But it also might be either higher or lower than the marginal cost of a launch. The same statement holds true regarding average and marginal benefits.

Suppose, for the sake of discussion, that the benefit of an additional launch is in fact the same as the average benefit per launch thus far, $6 billion. Should NASA add another launch? Not if the cost of adding the fifth launch would be more than $6 billion. And the fact that the average cost per launch is only $5 billion simply does not tell us anything about the marginal cost of the fifth launch.

Suppose, for example, that the relationship between the number of shuttles launched and the total cost of the program is as described in Table 1.1. The average

TABLE 1.1
How Total Cost Varies with the Number of Launches

Number of launches	Total cost ($ billions)	Average cost ($ billion/launch)
0	0	0
1	3	3
2	7	3.5
3	12	4
4	20	5
5	32	6.4

cost per launch (third column) when there are four launches would then be $20 billion/ 4 = $5 billion per launch, just as Professor Banifoot testified. But note in the second column of the table that adding a fifth launch would raise costs from $20 billion to $32 billion, making the marginal cost of the fifth launch $12 billion. So if the benefit of an additional launch is $6 billion, increasing the number of launches from four to five would make absolutely no economic sense. ◆

The following example illustrates how to apply the Cost-Benefit Principle correctly in this case.

How many space shuttles should NASA launch?

NASA must decide how many space shuttles to launch. The benefit of each launch is estimated to be $6 billion and the total cost of the program again depends on the number of launches in the manner shown in Table 1.1. How many shuttles should NASA launch?

NASA should continue to launch shuttles as long as the marginal benefit of the program exceeds its marginal cost. In this example, the marginal benefit is constant at $6 billion per launch, regardless of the number of shuttles launched. NASA should thus keep launching shuttles as long as the marginal cost per launch is less than or equal to $6 billion.

Applying the definition of marginal cost to the total cost entries in the second column of Table 1.1 yields the marginal cost values in the third column of Table 1.2. (Because marginal cost is the change in total cost that results when we change the number of launches by one, we place each marginal cost entry midway between the rows showing the corresponding total cost entries.) Thus, for example, the marginal cost of increasing the number of launches from one to two is $4 billion, the difference between the $7 billion total cost of two launches and the $3 billion total cost of one launch.

TABLE 1.2
How Marginal Cost Varies with the Number of Launches

Number of launches	Total cost ($ billion)	Marginal cost ($ billion/launch)
0	0	
		3
1	3	
		4
2	7	
		5
3	12	
		8
4	20	
		12
5	32	

As we see from a comparison of the $6 billion marginal benefit per launch with the marginal cost entries in the third column of Table 1.2, the first three launches satisfy the cost-benefit test, but the fourth and fifth launches do not. NASA should thus launch three space shuttles. ◆

EXERCISE 1.4

If the marginal benefit of each launch had been not $6 billion but $9 billion, how many shuttles should NASA have launched?

The cost-benefit framework emphasizes that the only relevant costs and benefits in deciding whether to pursue an activity further are *marginal* costs and benefits—measures that correspond to the *increment* of activity under consideration. In many contexts, however, people seem more inclined to compare the *average* cost and benefit of the activity. As the first shuttle launch example made clear, increasing the level of an activity may not be justified, even though its average benefit at the current level is significantly greater than its average cost.

Here's an exercise that further illustrates the importance of thinking at the margin.

EXERCISE 1.5

Should a basketball team's best player take all the team's shots?

A professional basketball team has a new assistant coach. The assistant notices that one player scores on a higher percentage of his shots than other players. Based on this information, the assistant suggests to the head coach that the star player should take *all* the shots. That way, the assistant reasons, the team will score more points and win more games.

On hearing this suggestion, the head coach fires his assistant for incompetence. What was wrong with the assistant's idea?

RECAP	**THREE IMPORTANT DECISION PITFALLS**

1. **The pitfall of measuring costs or benefits proportionally.** Many decision makers treat a change in cost or benefit as insignificant if it constitutes only a small proportion of the original amount. Absolute dollar amounts, not proportions, should be employed to measure costs and benefits.

2. **The pitfall of ignoring implicit costs.** When performing a cost-benefit analysis of an action, it is important to account for all relevant costs, including the implicit value of alternatives that must be forgone in order to carry out the action. A resource (such as a frequent-flyer coupon) may have a high implicit cost, even if you originally got it "for free," if its best alternative use has high value. The identical resource may have a low implicit cost, however, if it has no good alternative uses.

3. **The pitfall of failing to think at the margin.** When deciding whether to perform an action, the only costs and benefits that are relevant are those that would result from taking the action. It is important to ignore sunk costs—those costs that cannot be avoided even if the action is not taken. Even though a ticket to a concert may have cost you $100, if you have already bought it and cannot sell it to anyone else, the $100 is a sunk cost and should not influence your decision about whether to go to the concert. It is also important not to confuse average costs and benefits with marginal costs and benefits. Decision makers often have ready information about the total cost and benefit of an activity, and from these it is simple to compute the activity's average cost and benefit. A common mistake is to conclude that an activity should be increased if its average benefit exceeds its average cost. The Cost-Benefit Principle tells us that the level of an activity should be increased if, and only if, its *marginal* benefit exceeds its *marginal* cost.

Some costs and benefits, especially marginal costs and benefits and implicit costs, are important for decision making, while others, like sunk costs and average costs and benefits, are essentially irrelevant. This conclusion is implicit in our original statement of the Cost-Benefit Principle (an action should be taken if, and only if, the extra benefits of taking it exceed the extra costs). When we encounter additional examples of decision pitfalls, we will flag them by inserting the icon for the Cost-Benefit Principle in the margin.

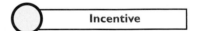

NORMATIVE ECONOMICS VERSUS POSITIVE ECONOMICS

The examples discussed in the preceding section make the point that people *sometimes* choose irrationally. We must stress that our purpose in discussing these examples was not to suggest that people *generally* make irrational choices. On the contrary, most people appear to choose sensibly most of the time, especially when their decisions are important or familiar ones. The economist's focus on rational choice thus offers not only useful advice about making better decisions, but also a basis for predicting and explaining human behavior. We used the cost-benefit approach in this way when discussing how rising faculty salaries have led to larger class sizes. And as we will see, similar reasoning helps to explain human behavior in virtually every other domain.

The Cost-Benefit Principle is an example of a **normative economic principle,** one that provides guidance about how we *should* behave. For example, according to the Cost-Benefit Principle, we should ignore sunk costs when making decisions about the future. As our discussion of the various decision pitfalls makes clear, however, the Cost-Benefit Principle is not always a **positive,** or descriptive, **economic principle,** one that describes how we actually *will* behave. As we saw, the Cost-Benefit Principle can be tricky to implement, and people sometimes fail to heed its prescriptions.

normative economic principle one that says how people should behave

positive economic principle one that predicts how people will behave

That said, we stress that knowing the relevant costs and benefits surely does enable us to predict how people will behave much of the time. If the benefit of an action goes up, it is generally reasonable to predict that people will be more likely to take that action. And conversely, if the cost of an action goes up, the safest prediction will be that people will be less likely to take that action. This point is so important that we designate it as the **Incentive Principle.**

The Incentive Principle: A person (or a firm or a society) is more likely to take an action if its benefit rises, and less likely to take it if its cost rises. In short, incentives matter.

Incentive

The Incentive Principle is a positive economic principle. It stresses that the relevant costs and benefits usually help us predict behavior, but at the same time does not insist that people will behave rationally in each instance. For example, if the price of heating oil were to rise sharply, we would invoke the Cost-Benefit Principle to say that people *should* turn their thermostats down, and invoke the Incentive Principle to predict that average thermostat settings *will* in fact go down in most cases.

microeconomics the study of individual choice under scarcity and its implications for the behavior of prices and quantities in individual markets

macroeconomics the study of the performance of national economies and the policies that governments use to try to improve that performance

ECONOMICS: MICRO AND MACRO

By convention, we use the term **microeconomics** to describe the study of individual choices and of group behavior in individual markets. **Macroeconomics,** by contrast, is the study of the performance of national economies and of the policies that governments use to try to improve that performance. Macroeconomics tries to understand the determinants of such things as the national unemployment rate, the overall price level, and the total value of national output.

Our focus in this chapter is on issues that confront the individual decision maker, whether that individual confronts a personal decision, a family decision, a business decision, a government policy decision, or indeed any other type of decision. Further on, we'll consider economic models of groups of individuals such as all buyers or all sellers in a specific market. Later still we will turn to broader economic issues and measures.

No matter which of these levels is our focus, however, our thinking will be shaped by the fact that although economic needs and wants are effectively unlimited, the material and human resources that can be used to satisfy them are finite. Clear thinking about economic problems must therefore always take into account the idea of trade-offs—the idea that having more of one good thing usually means having less of another. Our economy and our society are shaped to a substantial degree by the choices people have made when faced with trade-offs.

THE APPROACH OF THIS TEXT

Scarcity ⬤

Choosing the number of students to register in each class is just one of many important decisions in planning an introductory economics course. Another decision, to which the Scarcity Principle applies just as strongly, concerns which of many different topics to include on the course syllabus. There is a virtually inexhaustible set of topics and issues that might be covered in an introductory course, but only limited time in which to cover them. There is no free lunch. Covering some topics inevitably means omitting others.

All textbook authors are necessarily forced to pick and choose. A textbook that covered *all* the issues ever written about in economics would take up more than a whole floor of your campus library. It is our firm view that most introductory textbooks try to cover far too much. One reason that each of us was drawn to the study of economics was that a relatively short list of the discipline's core ideas can explain a great deal of the behavior and events we see in the world around us. So rather than cover a large number of ideas at a superficial level, our strategy is to focus on this short list of core ideas, returning to each entry again and again, in many different contexts. This strategy will enable you to internalize these ideas remarkably well in the brief span of a single course. And the benefit of learning a small number of important ideas well will far outweigh the cost of having to ignore a host of other, less important ideas.

So far, we've already encountered three core ideas: the Scarcity Principle, the Cost-Benefit Principle, and the Incentive Principle. As these core ideas reemerge in the course of our discussions, we'll call your attention to them. And shortly after a *new* core idea appears, we'll highlight it by formally restating it.

A second important element in the philosophy of this text is our belief in the importance of active learning. In the same way that you can learn Spanish only by speaking and writing it, or tennis only by playing the game, you can learn economics only by *doing* economics. And because we want you to learn how to do economics, rather than just to read or listen passively as the authors or your instructor does economics, we will make every effort to encourage you to stay actively involved.

For example, instead of just telling you about an idea, we will usually first motivate the idea by showing you how it works in the context of a specific example. Often, these examples will be followed by exercises for you to try, as well as applications that show the relevance of the idea to real life. Try working the exercises *before* looking up the answers (which are at the back of the corresponding chapter).

Think critically about the applications: Do you see how they illustrate the point being made? Do they give you new insight into the issue? Work the problems at the end of the chapters and take extra care with those relating to points that you do not fully understand. Apply economic principles to the world around you. (We'll say more about this when we discuss economic naturalism below.) Finally, when you come across an idea or example that you find interesting, tell a friend about it. You'll be surprised to discover how much the mere act of explaining it helps you understand and remember the underlying principle. The more actively you can become engaged in the learning process, the more effective your learning will be.

ECONOMIC NATURALISM

With the rudiments of the cost-benefit framework under your belt, you are now in a position to become an "economic naturalist," someone who uses insights from economics to help make sense of observations from everyday life. People who have studied biology are able to observe and marvel at many details of nature that would otherwise have escaped their notice. For example, on a walk in the woods in early April, the novice may see only trees whereas the biology student notices many different species of trees and understands why some are already into leaf while others still lie dormant. Likewise, the novice may notice that in some animal species males are much larger than females, but the biology student knows that pattern occurs only in species in which males take several mates. Natural selection favors larger males in those species because their greater size helps them prevail in the often bloody contests among males for access to females. By contrast, males tend to be roughly the same size as females in monogamous species, in which there is much less fighting for mates.

In similar fashion, learning a few simple economic principles enables us to see the mundane details of ordinary human existence in a new light. Whereas the uninitiated often fail even to notice these details, the economic naturalist not only sees them, but becomes actively engaged in the attempt to understand them. Let's consider a few examples of questions economic naturalists might pose for themselves.

Why do many hardware manufacturers include more than $1,000 worth of "free" software with a computer selling for only slightly more than that?

The software industry is different from many others in the sense that its customers care a great deal about product compatibility. When you and your classmates are working on a project together, for example, your task will be much simpler if you all use the same word-processing program. Likewise, an executive's life will be easier at tax time if her financial software is the same as her accountant's.

The implication is that the benefit of owning and using any given software program increases with the number of other people who use that same product. This unusual relationship gives the producers of the most popular programs an enormous advantage and often makes it hard for new programs to break into the market.

Recognizing this pattern, the Intuit Corporation offered computer makers free copies of *Quicken*, its personal financial-management software. Computer makers, for their part, were only too happy to include the program, since it made their new computers more attractive to buyers. *Quicken* soon became the standard for personal financial-management programs. By giving away free copies of the program, Intuit "primed the pump," creating an enormous demand for upgrades of *Quicken* and for more advanced versions of related software. Thus, *TurboTax* and *Macintax,* Intuit's personal income-tax software, have become the standards for tax-preparation programs. ●

Inspired by this success story, other software developers have jumped onto the bandwagon. Most hardware now comes bundled with a host of free software programs. Some software developers are even rumored to *pay* computer makers to include their programs!

Example 1.1

THE ECONOMIC NATURALIST

The free-software example illustrates a case in which the *benefit* of a product depends on the number of other people who own that product. As the next example demonstrates, the *cost* of a product may also depend on the number of others who own it.

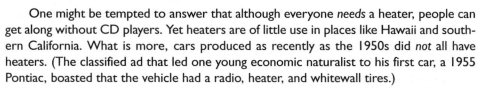

Example 1.2
THE ECONOMIC NATURALIST

Why don't auto manufacturers make cars without heaters?

Virtually every new car sold in the United States today has a heater. But not every car has a CD player. Why this difference?

One might be tempted to answer that although everyone *needs* a heater, people can get along without CD players. Yet heaters are of little use in places like Hawaii and southern California. What is more, cars produced as recently as the 1950s did *not* all have heaters. (The classified ad that led one young economic naturalist to his first car, a 1955 Pontiac, boasted that the vehicle had a radio, heater, and whitewall tires.)

Although heaters cost extra money to manufacture and are not useful in all parts of the country, they do not cost *much* money and are useful on at least a few days each year in most parts of the country. As time passed and people's incomes grew, manufacturers found that people were ordering fewer and fewer cars without heaters. At some point it actually became cheaper to put heaters in *all* cars, rather than bear the administrative expense of making some cars with heaters and others without. No doubt a few buyers would still order a car without a heater if they could save some money in the process, but catering to these customers is just no longer worth it.

Similar reasoning explains why certain cars today cannot be purchased without a CD player. Buyers of the 2009 BMW 750i, for example, got a CD player whether they wanted one or not. Most buyers of this car, which sells for more than $75,000, have high incomes, so the overwhelming majority of them would have chosen to order a CD player had it been sold as an option. Because of the savings made possible when all cars are produced with the same equipment, it would have actually cost BMW more to supply cars for the few who would want them without CD players.

EN 1

Buyers of the least-expensive makes of car have much lower incomes on average than BMW 750i buyers. Accordingly, most of them have more pressing alternative uses for their money than to buy CD players for their cars, and this explains why some inexpensive makes continue to offer CD players only as options. But as incomes continue to grow, new cars without CD players will eventually disappear. ●

The insights afforded by the preceding example suggest an answer to the following strange question:

Example 1.3
THE ECONOMIC NATURALIST

Why do the keypad buttons on drive-up automatic teller machines have Braille dots?

Braille dots on elevator buttons and on the keypads of walk-up automatic teller machines enable blind people to participate more fully in the normal flow of daily activity. But even though blind people can do many remarkable things, they cannot drive automobiles on

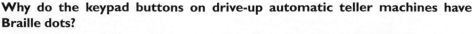

public roads. Why, then, do the manufacturers of automatic teller machines install Braille dots on the machines at drive-up locations?

The answer to this riddle is that once the keypad molds have been manufactured, the cost of producing buttons with Braille dots is no higher than the cost of producing smooth buttons. Making both would require separate sets of molds and two different types of inventory. If the patrons of drive-up machines found buttons with Braille dots harder to use, there might be a reason to incur these extra costs. But since the dots pose no difficulty for sighted users, the best and cheapest solution is to produce only keypads with dots. •

The preceding example was suggested by Cornell student Bill Tjoa, in response to the following assignment:

EXERCISE 1.6

In 500 words or less, use cost-benefit analysis to explain some pattern of events or behavior you have observed in your own environment.

There is probably no more useful step you can take in your study of economics than to perform several versions of the assignment in Exercise 1.6. Students who do so almost invariably become lifelong economic naturalists. Their mastery of economic concepts not only does not decay with the passage of time; it actually grows stronger. We urge you, in the strongest possible terms, to make this investment!

Why do the keypad buttons on drive-up automatic teller machines have Braille dots?

■ SUMMARY ■

- Economics is the study of how people make choices under conditions of scarcity and of the results of those choices for society. Economic analysis of human behavior begins with the assumption that people are rational—that they have well-defined goals and try to achieve them as best they can. In trying to achieve their goals, people normally face trade-offs: Because material and human resources are limited, having more of one good thing means making do with less of some other good thing. **LO1**

- Our focus in this chapter has been on how rational people make choices among alternative courses of action. Our basic tool for analyzing these decisions is cost-benefit analysis. The Cost-Benefit Principle says that a person should take an action if, and only if, the benefit of that action is at least as great as its cost. The benefit of an action is defined as the largest dollar amount the person would be willing to pay in order to take the action. The cost of an action is defined as the dollar value of everything the person must give up in order to take the action. **LO2**

- Often the question is not whether to pursue an activity but rather how many units of it to pursue. In these cases, the rational person pursues additional units as long as the marginal benefit of the activity (the benefit from pursuing an additional unit of it) exceeds its marginal cost (the cost of pursuing an additional unit of it). **LO2**

- In using the cost-benefit framework, we need not presume that people choose rationally all the time. Indeed, we identified three common pitfalls that plague decision makers in all walks of life: a tendency to treat small proportional changes as insignificant, a tendency to ignore implicit costs, and a tendency to fail to think at the margin—for example, by failing to ignore sunk costs or by failing to compare marginal costs and benefits. **LO4, LO5, LO6**

- Microeconomics is the study of individual choices and of group behavior in individual markets, while macroeconomics is the study of the performance of national economics and of the policies that governments use to try to improve economic performance.

▪ CORE PRINCIPLES ▪

Scarcity ◯

The Scarcity Principle (also called the No-Free-Lunch Principle)
Although we have boundless needs and wants, the resources available to us are limited. So having more of one good thing usually means having less of another.

Cost-Benefit ◯

The Cost-Benefit Principle
An individual (or a firm or a society) should take an action if, and only if, the extra benefits from taking the action are at least as great as the extra costs.

Incentive ◯

The Incentive Principle
A person (or a firm or a society) is more likely to take an action if its benefit rises, and less likely to take it if its cost rises.

▪ KEY TERMS ▪

average benefit (12)
average cost (12)
economic surplus (16)
economics (4)
macroeconomics (15)

marginal benefit (12)
marginal cost (12)
microeconomics (15)
normative economic
  principle (15)

opportunity cost (7)
positive economic
  principle (15)
rational person (6)
sunk cost (11)

▪ REVIEW QUESTIONS ▪

1. A friend of yours on the tennis team says, "Private tennis lessons are definitely better than group lessons." Explain what you think he means by this statement. Then use the Cost-Benefit Principle to explain why private lessons are not necessarily the best choice for everyone.   **LO2**

2. True or false: Your willingness to drive downtown to save $30 on a new appliance should depend on what fraction of the total selling price $30 is. Explain.   **LO4**

3. Why might someone who is trying to decide whether to see a movie be more likely to focus on the $10 ticket price than on the $20 she would fail to earn by not babysitting?   **LO5**

4. Many people think of their air travel as being free when they use frequent-flyer coupons. Explain why these people are likely to make wasteful travel decisions.   **LO5**

5. Is the nonrefundable tuition payment you made to your university this semester a sunk cost? How would your answer differ if your university were to offer a full tuition refund to any student who dropped out of school during the first two months of the semester?   **LO6**

▪ PROBLEMS ▪

1. The most you would be willing to pay for having a freshly washed car before going out on a date is $6. The smallest amount for which you would be willing to wash someone else's car is $3.50. You are going out this evening and your car is dirty. How much economic surplus would you receive from washing it?   **LO2**

2. To earn extra money in the summer, you grow tomatoes and sell them at the farmers' market for 30 cents per pound. By adding compost to your garden, you can increase your yield as shown in the table below. If compost costs 50 cents per pound and your goal is to make as much money as possible, how many pounds of compost should you add?   **LO2**

Pounds of compost	Pounds of tomatoes
0	100
1	120
2	125
3	128
4	130
5	131
6	131.5

3. Residents of your city are charged a fixed weekly fee of $6 for garbage collection. They are allowed to put out as many cans as they wish. The average household disposes of three cans of garbage per week under this plan. Now suppose that your city changes to a "tag" system. Each can of refuse to be collected must have a tag affixed to it. The tags cost $2 each and are not reusable. What effect do you think the introduction of the tag system will have on the total quantity of garbage collected in your city? Explain briefly.   **LO2**

4. Once a week, Smith purchases a six-pack of cola and puts it in his refrigerator for his two children. He invariably discovers that all six cans are gone on the first day. Jones also purchases a six-pack of cola once a week for his two children, but unlike Smith, he tells them that each may drink no more than three cans. If the children use cost-benefit analysis each time they decide whether to drink a can of cola, explain why the cola lasts much longer at Jones's house than at Smith's.   **LO2**

5. Tom is a mushroom farmer. He invests all his spare cash in additional mushrooms, which grow on otherwise useless land behind his barn. The mushrooms double in weight during their first year, after which time they are harvested and sold at a constant price per pound. Tom's friend Dick asks Tom for a loan of $200, which he promises to repay after 1 year. How much interest will Dick have to pay Tom in order for Tom to recover his opportunity cost of making the loan? Explain briefly.   **LO2**

6. Suppose that in the last few seconds you devoted to question 1 on your physics exam you earned 4 extra points, while in the last few seconds you devoted to question 2 you earned 10 extra points. You earned a total of 48 and 12 points, respectively, on the two questions and the total time you spent on each was the same. If you could take the exam again, how—if at all—should you reallocate your time between these questions?   **LO2**

7. Martha and Sarah have the same preferences and incomes. Just as Martha arrived at the theater to see a play, she discovered that she had lost the $10 ticket she had purchased earlier. Sarah also just arrived at the theater planning to buy a ticket to see the same play when she discovered that she had lost a $10 bill from her wallet. If both Martha and Sarah are rational and both still have enough money to pay for a ticket, is one of them more likely than the other to go ahead and see the play anyway?   **LO2**

8.* You and your friend Joe have identical tastes. At 2 p.m., you go to the local Ticketmaster outlet and buy a $30 ticket to a basketball game to be played that night in Syracuse, 50 miles north of your home in Ithaca. Joe plans to attend the same game, but because he cannot get to the Ticketmaster outlet, he plans to buy his ticket at the game. Tickets sold at the game cost only $25 because they carry no Ticketmaster surcharge. (Many people nonetheless pay the higher

*Problems marked with an asterisk (*) are more difficult.

price at Ticketmaster, to be sure of getting good seats.) At 4 p.m., an unexpected snowstorm begins, making the prospect of the drive to Syracuse much less attractive than before (but assuring the availability of good seats). If both you and Joe are rational, is one of you more likely to attend the game than the other? **LO2**

9.*For each long-distance call anywhere in the continental United States, a new phone service will charge users 30 cents per minute for the first 2 minutes and 2 cents per minute for additional minutes in each call. Tom's current phone service charges 10 cents per minute for all calls, and his calls are never shorter than 7 minutes. If Tom's dorm switches to the new phone service, what will happen to the average length of his calls? **LO3**

10.*The meal plan at university A lets students eat as much as they like for a fixed fee of $500 per semester. The average student there eats 250 pounds of food per semester. University B charges $500 for a book of meal tickets that entitles the student to eat 250 pounds of food per semester. If the student eats more than 250 pounds, he or she pays $2 for each additional pound; if the student eats less, he or she gets a $2 per pound refund. If students are rational, at which university will average food consumption be higher? Explain briefly. **LO3**

■ ANSWERS TO IN-CHAPTER EXERCISES ■

1.1 The benefit of buying the game downtown is again $10 but the cost is now $12, so your economic surplus from buying it downtown would be $10 − $12 = −$2. Since your economic surplus from making the trip would be negative, you should buy at the campus store.   **LO2**

1.2 Saving $100 is $10 more valuable than saving $90, even though the percentage saved is much greater in the case of the Chicago ticket.   **LO4**

1.3 Since you now have no alternative use for your coupon, the opportunity cost of using it to pay for the Fort Lauderdale trip is zero. That means your economic surplus from the trip will be $1,350 − $1,000 = $350 > 0, so you should use your coupon and go to Fort Lauderdale.   **LO2**

1.4 The marginal benefit of the fourth launch is $9 billion, which exceeds its marginal cost of $8 billion, so the fourth launch should be added. But the fifth launch should not, since its marginal cost ($12 billion) exceeds its marginal benefit ($9 billion).   **LO2**

1.5 If the star player takes one more shot, some other player must take one less. The fact that the star player's *average* success rate is higher than the other players' does not mean that the probability of making his *next* shot (the marginal benefit of having him shoot once more) is higher than the probability of another player making his next shot. Indeed, if the best player took all his team's shots, the other team would focus its defensive effort entirely on him, in which case letting others shoot would definitely pay.   **LO6**

*Problems marked with an asterisk (*) are more difficult.

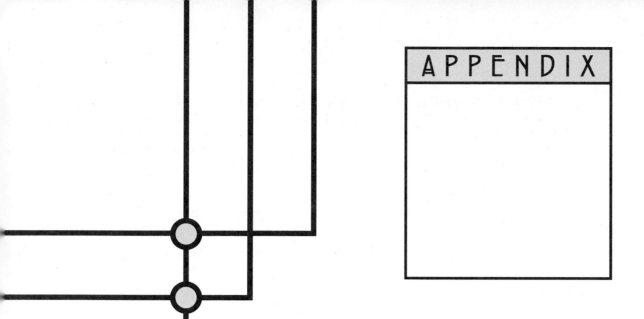

Working with Equations, Graphs, and Tables

Although many of the examples and most of the end-of-chapter problems in this book are quantitative, none requires mathematical skills beyond rudimentary high school algebra and geometry. In this brief appendix, we review some of the skills you'll need for dealing with these examples and problems.

One important skill is to be able to read simple verbal descriptions and translate the information they provide into the relevant equations or graphs. You'll also need to be able to translate information given in tabular form into an equation or graph, and sometimes you'll need to translate graphical information into a table or equation. Finally, you'll need to be able to solve simple systems with two equations and two unknowns. The following examples illustrate all the tools you'll need.

USING A VERBAL DESCRIPTION TO CONSTRUCT AN EQUATION

We begin with an example that shows how to construct a long-distance telephone billing equation from a verbal description of the billing plan.

Your long-distance telephone plan charges you $5 per month plus 10 cents per minute for long-distance calls. Write an equation that describes your monthly telephone bill.

equation a mathematical expression that describes the relationship between two or more variables

variable a quantity that is free to take a range of different values

dependent variable a variable in an equation whose value is determined by the value taken by another variable in the equation

independent variable a variable in an equation whose value determines the value taken by another variable in the equation

constant (or parameter) a quantity that is fixed in value

An **equation** is a simple mathematical expression that describes the relationship between two or more **variables,** or quantities that are free to assume different values in some range. The most common type of equation we'll work with contains two types of variables: **dependent variables** and **independent variables.** In this example, the dependent variable is the dollar amount of your monthly telephone bill and the independent variable is the variable on which your bill depends, namely, the volume of long-distance calls you make during the month. Your bill also depends on the $5 monthly fee and the 10 cents per minute charge. But, in this example, those amounts are **constants,** not variables. A constant, also called a **parameter,** is a quantity in an equation that is fixed in value, not free to vary. As the terms suggest, the dependent variable describes an outcome that depends on the value taken by the independent variable.

Once you've identified the dependent variable and the independent variable, choose simple symbols to represent them. In algebra courses, X is typically used to represent the independent variable and Y the dependent variable. Many people find it easier to remember what the variables stand for, however, if they choose symbols that are linked in some straightforward way to the quantities that the variables represent. Thus, in this example, we might use B to represent your monthly *bill* in dollars and T to represent the total *time* in minutes you spent during the month on long-distance calls.

Having identified the relevant variables and chosen symbols to represent them, you are now in a position to write the equation that links them:

$$B = 5 + 0.10T, \tag{1A.1}$$

where B is your monthly long-distance bill in dollars and T is your monthly total long-distance calling time in minutes. The fixed monthly fee (5) and the charge per minute (0.10) are parameters in this equation. Note the importance of being clear about the units of measure. Because B represents the monthly bill in dollars, we must also express the fixed monthly fee and the per-minute charge in dollars, which is why the latter number appears in Equation 1A.1 as 0.10 rather than 10. Equation 1A.1 follows the normal convention in which the dependent variable appears by itself on the left-hand side while the independent variable or variables and constants appear on the right-hand side.

Once we have the equation for the monthly bill, we can use it to calculate how much you'll owe as a function of your monthly volume of long-distance calls. For example, if you make 32 minutes of calls, you can calculate your monthly bill by simply substituting 32 minutes for T in Equation 1A.1:

$$B = 5 + 0.10(32) = 8.20. \tag{1A.2}$$

Your monthly bill when you make 32 minutes of calls is thus equal to $8.20. ◆

EXERCISE IA.I

Under the monthly billing plan described in the example above, how much would you owe for a month during which you made 45 minutes of long-distance calls?

GRAPHING THE EQUATION OF A STRAIGHT LINE

The next example shows how to portray the billing plan described in the preceding example as a graph.

Construct a graph that portrays the monthly long-distance telephone billing plan described in the preceding example, putting your telephone charges, in dollars per month, on the vertical axis and your total volume of calls, in minutes per month, on the horizontal axis.

The first step in responding to this instruction is the one we just took, namely, to translate the verbal description of the billing plan into an equation. When graphing an equation, the normal convention is to use the vertical axis to represent the dependent variable and the horizontal axis to represent the independent variable. In Figure 1A.1, we therefore put B on the vertical axis and T on the horizontal axis. One way to construct the graph shown in the figure is to begin by plotting the monthly bill values that correspond to several different total amounts of long-distance calls. For example, someone who makes 10 minutes of calls during the month would have a bill of $B = 5 + 0.10(10) = \$6$. Thus, in Figure 1A.1 the value of 10 minutes per month on the horizontal axis corresponds to a bill of \$6 per month on the vertical axis (point A). Someone who makes 30 minutes of long-distance calls during the month will have a monthly bill of $B = 5 + 0.10(30) = \$8$, so the value of 30 minutes per month on the horizontal axis corresponds to \$8 per month on the vertical axis (point C). Similarly, someone who makes 70 minutes of long-distance calls during the month will have a monthly bill of $B = 5 + 0.10(70) = \$12$, so the value of 70 minutes on the horizontal axis corresponds to \$12 on the vertical axis (point D). The line joining these points is the graph of the monthly billing Equation 1A.1.

As shown in Figure 1A.1, the graph of the equation $B = 5 + 0.10T$ is a straight line. The parameter 5 is the **vertical intercept** of the line—the value of B when $T = 0$, or the point at which the line intersects the vertical axis. The parameter 0.10 is the **slope** of the line, which is the ratio of the **rise** of the line to the corresponding **run**. The ratio rise/run is simply the vertical distance between any two points on the line divided by the horizontal distance between those points. For example, if we choose points A and C in Figure 1A.1, the rise is $8 - 6 = 2$ and the corresponding run is $30 - 10 = 20$, so rise/run $= 2/20 = 0.10$. More generally, for the graph of any equation $Y = a + bX$, the parameter a is the vertical intercept and the parameter b is the slope. ◆

vertical intercept in a straight line, the value taken by the dependent variable when the independent variable equals zero

slope in a straight line, the ratio of the vertical distance the straight line travels between any two points (*rise*) to the corresponding horizontal distance (*run*)

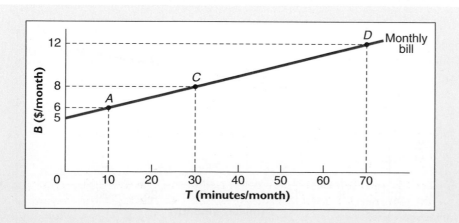

FIGURE 1A.1
The Monthly Telephone Bill in Example 1A.1.
The graph of the equation $B = 5 + 0.10T$ is the straight line shown. Its vertical intercept is 5 and its slope is 0.10.

DERIVING THE EQUATION OF A STRAIGHT LINE FROM ITS GRAPH

The next example shows how to derive the equation for a straight line from a graph of the line.

Figure 1A.2 shows the graph of the monthly billing plan for a new long-distance plan. What is the equation for this graph? How much is the fixed monthly fee under this plan? How much is the charge per minute?

FIGURE 1A.2
Another Monthly Long-Distance Plan.
The vertical distance between points A and C is $12 - 8 = 4$ units, and the horizontal distance between points A and C is $40 - 20 = 20$, so the slope of the line is $4/20 = 1/5 = 0.20$. The vertical intercept (the value of B when $T = 0$) is 4. So the equation for the billing plan shown is $B = 4 + 0.20T$.

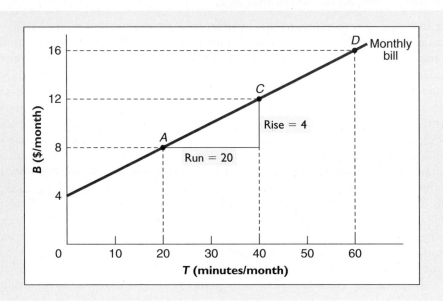

The slope of the line shown is the rise between any two points divided by the corresponding run. For points A and C, rise $= 12 - 8 = 4$ and run $= 40 - 20 = 20$, so the slope equals rise/run $= 4/20 = 1/15 = 0.20$. And since the horizontal intercept of the line is 4, its equation must be given by

$$B = 4 + 0.20T. \tag{1A.3}$$

Under this plan, the fixed monthly fee is the value of the bill when $T = 0$, which is \$4. The charge per minute is the slope of the billing line, 0.20, or 20 cents per minute. ◆

EXERCISE 1A.2

Write the equation for the billing plan shown in the accompanying graph. How much is its fixed monthly fee? Its charge per minute?

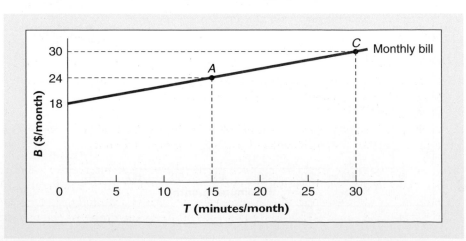

CHANGES IN THE VERTICAL INTERCEPT AND SLOPE

The next two examples and exercises provide practice in seeing how a line shifts with a change in its vertical intercept or slope.

Show how the billing plan whose graph is in Figure 1A.2 would change if the monthly fixed fee were increased from $4 to $8.

An increase in the monthly fixed fee from $4 to $8 would increase the vertical intercept of the billing plan by $4 but would leave its slope unchanged. An increase in the fixed fee thus leads to a parallel upward shift in the billing plan by $4, as shown in Figure 1A.3. For any given number of minutes of long-distance calls, the monthly charge on the new bill will be $4 higher than on the old bill. Thus 20 minutes of

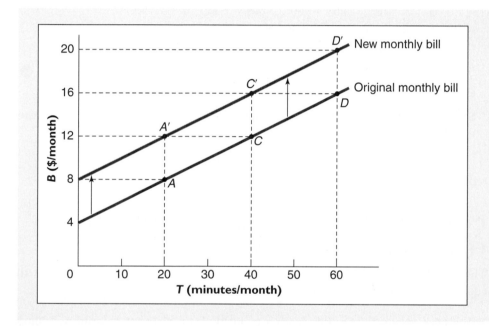

FIGURE 1A.3
The Effect of an Increase in the Vertical Intercept.
An increase in the vertical intercept of a straight line produces an upward parallel shift in the line.

calls per month costs $8 under the original plan (point A) but $12 under the new plan (point A'). And 40 minutes costs $12 under the original plan (point C), $16 under the new plan (point C'); and 60 minutes costs $16 under the original plan (point D), $20 under the new plan (point D'). ◆

EXERCISE 1A.3

Show how the billing plan whose graph is in Figure 1A.2 would change if the monthly fixed fee were reduced from $4 to $2.

Show how the billing plan whose graph is in Figure 1A.2 would change if the charge per minute were increased from 20 cents to 40 cents.

Because the monthly fixed fee is unchanged, the vertical intercept of the new billing plan continues to be 4. But the slope of the new plan, shown in Figure 1A.4, is 0.40, or twice the slope of the original plan. More generally, in the equation $Y = a + bX$, an increase in b makes the slope of the graph of the equation steeper.

FIGURE 1A.4
The Effect of an Increase in the Charge per Minute.
Because the fixed monthly fee continues to be $4, the vertical intercept of the new plan is the same as that of the original plan. With the new charge per minute of 40 cents, the slope of the billing plan rises from 0.20 to 0.40.

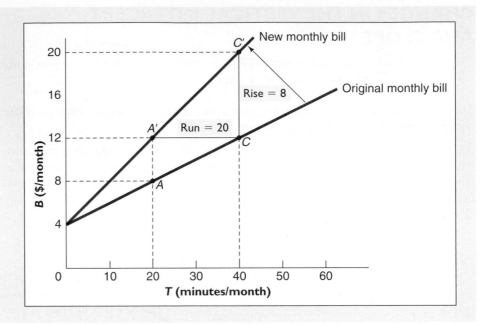

EXERCISE 1A.4

Show how the billing plan whose graph is in Figure 1A.2 would change if the charge per minute were reduced from 20 cents to 10 cents.

Exercise 1A.4 illustrates the general rule that in an equation $Y = a + bX$, a reduction in b makes the slope of the graph of the equation less steep.

CONSTRUCTING EQUATIONS AND GRAPHS FROM TABLES

The next example and exercise show how to transform tabular information into an equation or graph.

Table 1A.1 shows four points from a monthly long-distance telephone billing equation. If all points on this billing equation lie on a straight line, find the vertical intercept of the equation and graph it. What is the monthly fixed fee? What is the charge per minute? Calculate the total bill for a month with 1 hour of long-distance calls.

TABLE 1A.1
Points on a Long-Distance Billing Plan

Long-distance bill ($/month)	Total long-distance calls (minutes/month)
10.50	10
11.00	20
11.50	30
12.00	40

One approach to this problem is simply to plot any two points from the table on a graph. Since we are told that the billing equation is a straight line, that line must be

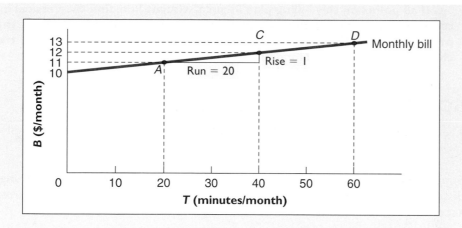

FIGURE 1A.5
Plotting the Monthly Billing Equation from a Sample of Points.
Point A is taken from row 2, Table 1A.1, and point C from row 4. The monthly billing plan is the straight line that passes through these points.

the one that passes through any two of its points. Thus, in Figure 1A.5 we use A to denote the point from Table 1A.1 for which a monthly bill of $11 corresponds to 20 minutes per month of calls (second row) and C to denote the point for which a monthly bill of $12 corresponds to 40 minutes per month of calls (fourth row). The straight line passing through these points is the graph of the billing equation.

Unless you have a steady hand, however, or use extremely large graph paper, the method of extending a line between two points on the billing plan is unlikely to be very accurate. An alternative approach is to calculate the equation for the billing plan directly. Since the equation is a straight line, we know that it takes the general form $B = f + sT$, where f is the fixed monthly fee and s is the slope. Our goal is to calculate the vertical intercept f and the slope s. From the same two points we plotted earlier, A and C, we can calculate the slope of the billing plan as $s = \text{rise/run} = 1/20 = 0.05$.

So all that remains is to calculate f, the fixed monthly fee. At point C on the billing plan, the total monthly bill is $12 for 40 minutes, so we can substitute $B = 12$, $s = 0.05$, and $T = 40$ into the general equation $B = f + sT$ to obtain

$$12 = f + 0.05(40), \tag{1A.4}$$

or

$$12 = f + 2, \tag{1A.5}$$

which solves for $f = 10$. So the monthly billing equation must be

$$B = 10 + 0.05T. \tag{1A.6}$$

For this billing equation, the fixed fee is $10 per month, the calling charge is 5 cents per minute ($0.05/minute), and the total bill for a month with 1 hour of long-distance calls is $B = 10 + 0.05(60) = \$13$, just as shown in Figure 1A.5. ◆

EXERCISE 1A.5

The following table shows four points from a monthly long-distance telephone billing plan.

Long-distance bill ($/month)	Total long-distance calls (minutes/month)
20.00	10
30.00	20
40.00	30
50.00	40

If all points on this billing plan lie on a straight line, find the vertical intercept of the corresponding equation without graphing it. What is the monthly fixed fee? What is the charge per minute? How much would the charges be for 1 hour of long-distance calls per month?

SOLVING SIMULTANEOUS EQUATIONS

The next example and exercise demonstrate how to proceed when you need to solve two equations with two unknowns.

Suppose you are trying to choose between two rate plans for your long-distance telephone service. If you choose Plan 1, your charges will be computed according to the equation

$$B = 10 + 0.04T, \tag{1A.7}$$

where B is again your monthly bill in dollars and T is your monthly volume of long-distance calls in minutes. If you choose Plan 2, your monthly bill will be computed according to the equation

$$B = 20 + 0.02T. \tag{1A.8}$$

How many minutes of long-distance calls would you have to make each month, on average, to make Plan 2 cheaper?

Plan 1 has the attractive feature of a relatively low monthly fixed fee, but also the unattractive feature of a relatively high rate per minute. In contrast, Plan 2 has a relatively high fixed fee but a relatively low rate per minute. Someone who made an extremely low volume of calls (for example, 10 minutes per month) would do better under Plan 1 (monthly bill = $10.40) than under Plan 2 (monthly bill = $20.20) because the low fixed fee of Plan 1 would more than compensate for its higher rate per minute. Conversely, someone who made an extremely high volume of calls (say, 10,000 minutes per month) would do better under Plan 2 (monthly bill = $220) than under Plan 1 (monthly bill = $410) because Plan 2's lower rate per minute would more than compensate for its higher fixed fee.

Our task here is to find the *break-even calling volume*, which is the monthly calling volume for which the monthly bill is the same under the two plans. One way to answer this question is to graph the two billing plans and see where they cross. At that crossing point, the two equations are satisfied simultaneously, which means that the monthly call volumes will be the same under both plans, as will the monthly bills.

In Figure 1A.6, we see that the graphs of the two plans cross at A, where both yield a monthly bill of $30 for 500 minutes of calls per month. The break-even calling volume for these plans is thus 500 minutes per month. If your calling volume is higher than that, on average, you will save money by choosing Plan 2. For example, if you average 700 minutes, your monthly bill under Plan 2 ($34) will be $4 cheaper than under Plan 1 ($38). Conversely, if you average fewer than 500 minutes each month, you will do better under Plan 1. For example, if you average only 200 minutes, your monthly bill under Plan 1 ($18) will be $6 cheaper than under Plan 2 ($24). At 500 minutes per month, the two plans cost exactly the same ($30).

The question posed here also may be answered algebraically. As in the graphical approach just discussed, our goal is to find the point (T, B) that satisfies both billing equations simultaneously. As a first step, we rewrite the two billing equations, one on top of the other, as follows:

$$B = 10 + 0.04T. \quad \text{(Plan 1)}$$

$$B = 20 + 0.02T. \quad \text{(Plan 2)}$$

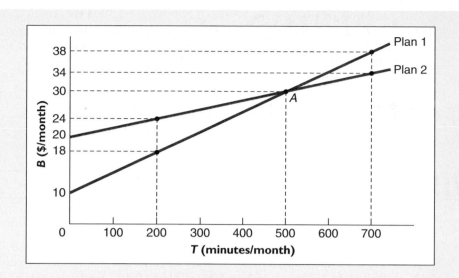

The Break-Even Volume of Long-Distance Calls. When your volume of long-distance calls is 500 minutes per month, your monthly bill will be the same under both plans. For higher calling volumes, Plan 2 is cheaper; Plan 1 is cheaper for lower volumes.

As you'll recall from high school algebra, if we subtract the terms from each side of one equation from the corresponding terms of the other equation, the resulting differences must be equal. So if we subtract the terms on each side of the Plan 2 equation from the corresponding terms in the Plan 1 equation, we get

$$B = 10 + 0.04T \qquad \text{(Plan 1)}$$

$$-B = -20 - 0.02T \qquad \text{(−Plan 2)}$$

$$0 = -10 + 0.02T \qquad \text{(Plan 1 − Plan 2)}.$$

Finally, we solve the last equation (Plan 1 − Plan 2) to get $T = 500$.

Plugging $T = 500$ into either plan's equation, we then find $B = 30$. For example, Plan 1's equation yields $10 + 0.04(500) = 30$, as does Plan 2's: $20 + 0.2(500) = 30$.

Because, the point $(T, B) = (500, 30)$ lies on the equations for both plans simultaneously, the algebraic approach just described is often called *the method of simultaneous equations.* ◆

EXERCISE 1A.6

Suppose you are trying to choose between two rate plans for your long-distance telephone service. If you choose Plan 1, your monthly bill will be computed according to the equation

$$B = 10 + 0.10T \qquad \text{(Plan 1)},$$

where B is again your monthly bill in dollars and T is your monthly volume of long-distance calls in minutes. If you choose Plan 2, your monthly bill will be computed according to the equation

$$B = 100 + 0.01T \qquad \text{(Plan 2)}.$$

Use the algebraic approach described in the preceding example to find the break-even level of monthly call volume for these plans.

▪ KEY TERMS ▪

constant (24)	parameter (24)	variable (24)
dependent variable (24)	rise (25)	vertical intercept (25)
equation (24)	run (25)	
independent variable (24)	slope (25)	

▪ ANSWERS TO IN-APPENDIX EXERCISES ▪

1A.1 To calculate your monthly bill for 45 minutes of calls, substitute 45 minutes for T in equation 1A.1 to get $B = 5 + 0.10(45) = \$9.50$.

1A.2 Calculating the slope using points A and C, we have rise $= 30 - 24 = 6$ and run $= 30 - 15 = 15$, so rise/run $= 6/15 = 2/5 = 0.40$. And since the horizontal intercept of the line is 18, its equation is $B = 18 + 0.40T$. Under this plan, the fixed monthly fee is \$18 and the charge per minute is the slope of the billing line, 0.40, or 40 cents per minute.

1A.3 A \$2 reduction in the monthly fixed fee would produce a downward parallel shift in the billing plan by \$2.

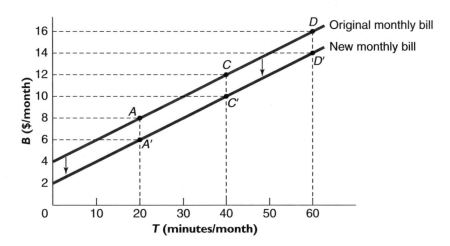

1A.4 With an unchanged monthly fixed fee, the vertical intercept of the new billing plan continues to be 4. The slope of the new plan is 0.10, half the slope of the original plan.

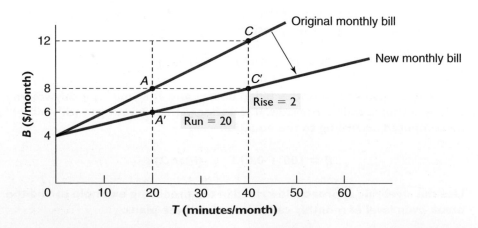

1A.5 Let the billing equation be $B = f + sT$, where f is the fixed monthly fee and s is the slope. From the first two points in the table, calculate the slope $s = \text{rise/run} = 10/10 = 1.0$. To calculate f, we can use the information in row 1 of the table to write the billing equation as $20 = f + 1.0(10)$ and solve for $f = 10$. So the monthly billing equation must be $B = 10 + 1.0T$. For this billing equation, the fixed fee is $10 per month, the calling charge is $1 per minute, and the total bill for a month with 1 hour of long-distance calls is $B = 10 + 1.0(60) = \$70$.

1A.6 Subtracting the Plan 2 equation from the Plan 1 equation yields the equation

$$0 = -90 + 0.09T \qquad \text{(Plan 1} - \text{Plan 2),}$$

which solves for $T = 1{,}000$. So if you average more than 1,000 minutes of long-distance calls each month, you'll do better on Plan 2.

CHAPTER 2

Comparative Advantage

LEARNING OBJECTIVES

In this chapter, you'll master ideas that help explain observed patterns of exchange in the marketplace. These ideas include

1. The principle of comparative advantage

2. The principle of increasing opportunity cost (also called the low-hanging fruit principle)

3. Factors that shift the menu of production possibilities.

4. The role of comparative advantage in international trade.

5. Why some jobs are more vulnerable to outsourcing than others.

During a stint as a Peace Corps volunteer in rural Nepal, a young economic naturalist employed a cook named Birkhaman, who came from a remote Himalayan village in neighboring Bhutan. Although Birkhaman had virtually no formal education, he was spectacularly resourceful. His primary duties, to prepare food and maintain the kitchen, he performed extremely well. But he also had other skills. He could thatch a roof, butcher a goat, and repair shoes. An able tinsmith and a good carpenter, he could sew and fix a broken alarm clock, as well as plaster walls. And he was a local authority on home remedies.

Birkhaman's range of skills was broad even in Nepal, where the least-skilled villager could perform a wide range of services that most Americans hire others to perform. Why this difference in skills and employment?

One might be tempted to answer that the Nepalese are simply too poor to hire others to perform these services. Nepal is indeed a poor country, whose income per person is less than one one-fortieth that of the United States. Few Nepalese have spare cash to spend on outside services. But as reasonable as this poverty explanation may seem, the reverse is actually the case. The Nepalese do not perform their own services because they are poor; rather, they are poor largely *because* they perform their own services.

The alternative to a system in which everyone is a jack of all trades is one in which people *specialize* in particular goods and services, then satisfy their needs by trading among themselves. Economic systems based on specialization and the

Did this man perform most of his own services because he was poor, or was he poor because he performed most of his own services?

exchange of goods and services are generally far more productive than those with less specialization. Our task in this chapter is to investigate why this is so. In doing so, we will explore why people choose to exchange goods and services in the first place, rather than having each person produce his or her own food, cars, clothing, shelter, and the like.

As this chapter will show, the reason that specialization is so productive is the existence of what economists call *comparative advantage*. Roughly, a person has a comparative advantage at producing a particular good or service, say, haircuts, if that person is *relatively* more efficient at producing haircuts than at producing other goods or services. We will see that we can all have more of *every* good and service if each of us specializes in the activities at which we have a comparative advantage.

This chapter also will introduce the *production possibilities curve*, which is a graphical method of describing the combinations of goods and services that an economy can produce. The development of this tool will allow us to see much more precisely how specialization enhances the productive capacity of even the simplest economy.

EXCHANGE AND OPPORTUNITY COST

| Scarcity | ◯ |

The Scarcity Principle (see Chapter 1) reminds us that the opportunity cost of spending more time on any one activity is having less time available to spend on others. As the following example makes clear, this principle helps explain why everyone can do better by concentrating on those activities at which he or she performs best relative to others.

Should a Joe Jamail prepare his own will?

absolute advantage one person has an absolute advantage over another if he or she takes fewer hours to perform a task than the other person

comparative advantage one person has a comparative advantage over another if his or her opportunity cost of performing a task is lower than the other person's opportunity cost

Should Joe Jamail write his own will?

Joe Jamail, known in the legal profession as "The King of Torts," is the most renowned trial lawyer in American history. And at number 317 on the Forbes list of the 400 richest Americans, he is also one of the wealthiest, with net assets totaling more than $1 billion.

But although Mr. Jamail devotes virtually all of his working hours to high-profile litigation, he is also competent to perform a much broader range of legal services. Suppose, for example, that he could prepare his own will in two hours, only half as long as it would take any other attorney. Does that mean that Jamail should prepare his own will?

On the strength of his talent as a litigator, Jamail earns many millions of dollars a year, which means that the opportunity cost of any time he spends preparing his will would be several thousand dollars per hour. Attorneys who specialize in property law typically earn far less than that amount. Jamail would have little difficulty engaging a competent property lawyer who could prepare his will for him for less than $800. So even though Jamail's considerable skills would enable him to perform this task more quickly than another attorney, it would not be in his interest to prepare his own will. ◆

In the preceding example, economists would say that Jamail has an **absolute advantage** at preparing his will but a **comparative advantage** at trial work. He has an absolute advantage at preparing his will because he can perform that task in less time than a property lawyer could. Even so, the property lawyer has a comparative advantage at preparing wills because his opportunity cost of performing that task is lower than Jamail's.

The point of the preceding example is not that people whose time is valuable should never perform their own services. That example made the implicit assumption that Jamail would have been equally happy to spend an hour preparing his will or preparing for a trial. But suppose he was tired of trial preparation and felt it might be enjoyable to refresh his knowledge of property law. Preparing his own will might then have made perfect sense! But unless he expected to gain special satisfaction from performing that task, he would almost certainly do better to hire a property lawyer. The property lawyer would also benefit, or else she wouldn't have offered to prepare wills for the stated price.

THE PRINCIPLE OF COMPARATIVE ADVANTAGE

One of the most important insights of modern economics is that when two people (or two nations) have different opportunity costs of performing various tasks, they can always increase the total value of available goods and services by trading with one another. The following simple example captures the logic behind this insight.

Should Paula update her own Web page?

Consider a small community in which Paula is the only professional bicycle mechanic and Beth is the only professional HTML programmer. Paula also happens to be an even better HTML programmer than Beth. If the amount of time each of them takes to perform these tasks is as shown in Table 2.1, and if each regards the two tasks as equally pleasant (or unpleasant), does the fact that Paula can program faster than Beth imply that Paula should update her own Web page?

The entries in the table show that Paula has an absolute advantage over Beth in both activities. While Paula, the mechanic, needs only 20 minutes to update a Web page, Beth, the programmer, needs 30 minutes. Paula's advantage over Beth is even greater when the task is fixing bikes: She can complete a repair in only 10 minutes, compared to Beth's 30 minutes.

TABLE 2.1
Productivity Information for Paula and Beth

	Time to update a Web page	Time to complete a bicycle repair
Paula	20 minutes	10 minutes
Beth	30 minutes	30 minutes

But the fact that Paula is a better programmer than Beth does *not* imply that Paula should update her own Web page. As with the lawyer who litigates instead of preparing his own will, Beth has a comparative advantage over Paula at programming: She is *relatively* more productive at programming than Paula. Similarly, Paula has a comparative advantage in bicycle repair. (Remember that a person has a comparative advantage at a given task if his or her opportunity cost of performing that task is lower than another person's.)

What is Beth's opportunity cost of updating a Web page? Since she takes 30 minutes to update each page—the same amount of time she takes to fix a bicycle—her opportunity cost of updating a Web page is one bicycle repair. In other words, by taking the time to update a Web page, Beth is effectively giving up the opportunity to do one bicycle repair. Paula, in contrast, can complete two bicycle repairs in the time she takes to update a single Web page. For her, the opportunity cost of updating a Web page is two bicycle repairs. Paula's opportunity cost of programming, measured in terms of bicycle repairs forgone, is twice as high as Beth's. Thus, Beth has a comparative advantage at programming.

TABLE 2.2
Opportunity Costs for Paula and Beth

	Opportunity cost of updating a Web page	Opportunity cost of a bicycle repair
Paula	2 bicycle repairs	0.5 Web page update
Beth	1 bicycle repair	1 Web page update

The interesting and important implication of the opportunity cost comparison summarized in Table 2.2 is that the total number of bicycle repairs and Web updates accomplished if Paula and Beth both spend part of their time at each activity will always be smaller than the number accomplished if each specializes in the activity in which she has a comparative advantage. Suppose, for example, that people in their community demand a total of 16 Web page updates per day. If Paula spent half her time updating Web pages and the other half repairing bicycles, an eight-hour workday would yield 12 Web page updates and 24 bicycle repairs. To complete the remaining 4 updates, Beth would have to spend two hours programming, which would leave her six hours to repair bicycles. And since she takes 30 minutes to do each repair, she would have time to complete 12 of them. So when the two women try to be jacks-of-all-trades, they end up completing a total of 16 Web page updates and 36 bicycle repairs.

Consider what would have happened had each woman specialized in her activity of comparative advantage. Beth could have updated 16 Web pages on her own and Paula could have performed 48 bicycle repairs. Specialization would have created an additional 12 bicycle repairs out of thin air. ◆

"We're a natural, Rachel. I handle intellectual property, and you're a content-provider."

When computing the opportunity cost of one good in terms of another, we must pay close attention to the form in which the productivity information is presented. In the preceding example, we were told how many minutes each person needed to perform each task. Alternatively, we might be told how many units of each task each person can perform in an hour. Work through the following exercise to see how to proceed when information is presented in this alternative format.

EXERCISE 2.1

Should Barb update her own Web page?

Consider a small community in which Barb is the only professional bicycle mechanic and Pat is the only professional HTML programmer. If their productivity rates at the two tasks are as shown in the table, and if each regards the two tasks as equally pleasant (or unpleasant), does the fact that Barb can program faster than Pat imply that Barb should update her own Web page?

	Productivity in programming	Productivity in bicycle repair
Pat	2 Web page updates per hour	1 repair per hour
Barb	3 Web page updates per hour	3 repairs per hour

The principle illustrated by the preceding examples is so important that we state it formally as one of the core principles of the course:

The Principle of Comparative Advantage: Everyone does best when each person (or each country) concentrates on the activities for which his or her opportunity cost is lowest.

Indeed, the gains made possible from specialization based on comparative advantage constitute the rationale for market exchange. They explain why each person does not devote 10 percent of his or her time to producing cars, 5 percent to growing food, 25 percent to building housing, 0.0001 percent to performing brain surgery, and so on. By concentrating on those tasks at which we are relatively most productive, together we can produce vastly more than if we all tried to be self-sufficient.

This insight brings us back to Birkhaman the cook. Though Birkhaman's versatility was marvelous, he was neither as good a doctor as someone who has been trained in medical school, nor as good a repairman as someone who spends each day fixing things. If a number of people with Birkhaman's native talents had joined together, each of them specializing in one or two tasks, together they would have enjoyed more and better goods and services than each could possibly have produced independently. Although there is much to admire in the resourcefulness of people who have learned through necessity to rely on their own skills, that path is no route to economic prosperity.

Specialization and its effects provide ample grist for the economic naturalist. Here's an example from the world of sports.

Where have all the .400 hitters gone?

In baseball, a .400 hitter is a player who averages at least four hits every 10 times he comes to bat. Though never common in professional baseball, .400 hitters used to appear relatively frequently. Early in the twentieth century, for example, a player known as Wee Willie Keeler batted .432, meaning that he got a hit in over 43 percent of his times at bat. But since Ted Williams of the Boston Red Sox batted .406 in 1941, there has not been a single .400 hitter in the major leagues. Why not?

Some baseball buffs argue that the disappearance of the .400 hitter means today's baseball players are not as good as yesterday's. But that claim does not withstand close

Example 2.1

THE ECONOMIC NATURALIST

Why has no major league baseball player batted .400 since Ted Williams did it more than half a century ago?

examination. We can document, for example, that today's players are bigger, stronger, and faster than those of Willie Keeler's day. (Wee Willie himself was just a little over 5 feet, 4 inches, and he weighed only 140 pounds.)

Bill James, a leading analyst of baseball history, argues that the .400 hitter has disappeared because the quality of play in the major leagues has *improved,* not declined. In particular, pitching and fielding standards are higher, which makes batting .400 more difficult.

Why has the quality of play in baseball improved? Although there are many reasons, including better nutrition, training, and equipment, specialization also has played an important role.[1] At one time, pitchers were expected to pitch for the entire game. Now pitching staffs include pitchers who specialize in starting the game ("starters"), others who specialize in pitching two or three innings in the middle of the game ("middle relievers"), and still others who specialize in pitching only the last inning ("closers"). Each of these roles requires different skills and tactics. Pitchers also may specialize in facing left-handed or right-handed batters, in striking batters out, or in getting batters to hit balls on the ground. Similarly, few fielders today play multiple defensive positions; most specialize in only one. Some players specialize in defense (to the detriment of their hitting skills); these "defensive specialists" can be brought in late in the game to protect a lead. Even in managing and coaching, specialization has increased markedly. Relief pitchers now have their own coaches, and statistical specialists use computers to discover the weaknesses of opposing hitters. The net result of these increases in specialization is that even the weakest of today's teams play highly competent defensive baseball. With no "weaklings" to pick on, hitting .400 over an entire season has become a near-impossible task. •

SOURCES OF COMPARATIVE ADVANTAGE

At the individual level, comparative advantage often appears to be the result of inborn talent. For instance, some people seem to be naturally gifted at programming computers while others seem to have a special knack for fixing bikes. But comparative advantage is more often the result of education, training, or experience. Thus, we usually leave the design of kitchens to people with architectural training, the drafting of contracts to people who have studied law, and the teaching of physics to people with advanced degrees in that field.

At the national level, comparative advantage may derive from differences in natural resources or from differences in society or culture. The United States, which has a disproportionate share of the world's leading research universities, has a comparative advantage in the design of electronic computing hardware and software. Canada, which has one of the world's highest per-capita endowments of farm and forest land, has a comparative advantage in the production of agricultural products. Topography and climate explain why Colorado specializes in the skiing industry while Hawaii specializes as an ocean resort.

Seemingly noneconomic factors also can give rise to comparative advantage. For instance, the emergence of English as the de facto world language gives English-speaking countries a comparative advantage over non–English-speaking nations in the production of books, movies, and popular music. Even a country's institutions may affect the likelihood that it will achieve comparative advantage in a particular pursuit. For example, cultures that encourage entrepreneurship will tend to have a comparative advantage in the introduction of new products, whereas those that promote high standards of care and craftsmanship will tend to have a comparative advantage in the production of high-quality variants of established products.

---

[1]For an interesting discussion of specialization and the decline of the .400 hitter from the perspective of an evolutionary biologist, see Stephen Jay Gould, *Full House* (New York: Three Rivers Press, 1996), Part 3.

Televisions and videocassette recorders were developed and first produced in the United States, but today the United States accounts for only a minuscule share of the total world production of these products. Why did the United States fail to retain its lead in these markets?

Example 2.2

THE ECONOMIC NATURALIST

That televisions and VCRs were developed in the United States is explained in part by the country's comparative advantage in technological research, which in turn was supported by the country's outstanding system of higher education. Other contributing factors were high expenditures on the development of electronic components for the military and a culture that actively encourages entrepreneurship. As for the production of these products, America enjoyed an early advantage partly because the product designs were themselves evolving rapidly at first, which favored production facilities located in close proximity to the product designers. Early production techniques also relied intensively on skilled labor, which is abundant in the United States. In time, however, product designs stabilized and many of the more complex manufacturing operations were automated. Both of these changes gradually led to greater reliance on relatively less-skilled production workers. And at that point, factories located in high-wage countries like the United States could no longer compete with those located in low-wage areas overseas. ●

Why was the United States unable to remain competitive as a manufacturer of televisions and other electronic equipment?

RECAP	**EXCHANGE AND OPPORTUNITY COST**

Gains from exchange are possible if trading partners have comparative advantages in producing different goods and services. You have a comparative advantage in producing, say, Web pages if your opportunity cost of producing a Web page—measured in terms of other production opportunities forgone—is smaller than the corresponding opportunity costs of your trading partners. Maximum production is achieved if each person specializes in producing the good or service in which he or she has the lowest opportunity cost (the Principle of Comparative Advantage). Comparative advantage makes specialization worthwhile even if one trading partner is more productive than others, in absolute terms, in every activity.

COMPARATIVE ADVANTAGE AND PRODUCTION POSSIBILITIES

Comparative advantage and specialization allow an economy to produce more than if each person tries to produce a little of everything. In this section, we gain further insight into the advantages of specialization by introducing a graph that can be used to describe the various combinations of goods and services that an economy can produce.

THE PRODUCTION POSSIBILITIES CURVE

We begin with a hypothetical economy in which only two goods are produced: coffee and pine nuts. It is a small island economy and "production" consists either of picking coffee beans that grow on small bushes on the island's central valley floor or of gathering pine nuts that fall from trees on the steep hillsides overlooking the valley. The more time workers spend picking coffee, the less time they have available for gathering nuts. So if people want to drink more coffee, they must make do with a smaller amount of nuts.

If we know how productive workers are at each activity, we can summarize the various combinations of coffee and nuts they can produce each day. This menu of possibilities is known as the **production possibilities curve.**

production possibilities curve
a graph that describes the maximum amount of one good that can be produced for every possible level of production of the other good

To keep matters simple, we begin with an example in which the economy has only a single worker who can divide her time between the two activities.

What is the production possibilities curve for an economy in which Susan is the only worker?

Consider a society consisting only of Susan, who allocates her production time between coffee and nuts. She has nimble fingers, a quality that makes her more productive at picking coffee than at gathering nuts. She can gather 2 pounds of nuts or pick 4 pounds of coffee in an hour. If she works a total of 6 hours per day, describe her production possibilities curve—the graph that displays, for each level of nut production, the maximum amount of coffee that Susan can pick.

The vertical axis in Figure 2.1 shows Susan's daily production of coffee and the horizontal axis shows her daily production of nuts. Let's begin by looking at two extreme allocations of her time. First, suppose she employs her entire workday (6 hours) picking coffee. In that case, since she can pick 4 pounds of coffee per hour, she would pick 24 pounds per day of coffee and gather zero pounds of nuts. That combination of coffee and nut production is represented by point A in Figure 2.1. It is the vertical intercept of Susan's production possibilities curve.

Now suppose, instead, that Susan devotes all her time to gathering nuts. Since she can gather 2 pounds of nuts per hour, her total daily production would be 12 pounds of nuts. That combination is represented by point D in Figure 2.1, the horizontal intercept of Susan's production possibilities curve. Because Susan's production of each good is exactly proportional to the amount of time she devotes to that good, the remaining points along her production possibilities curve will lie on the straight line that joins A and D.

For example, suppose that Susan devotes 4 hours each day to picking coffee and 2 hours to gathering nuts. She will then end up with (4 hours/day) × (4 pounds/hour) = 16 pounds of coffee per day and (2 hours/day) × (2 pounds/hour) = 4 pounds of nuts. This is the point labeled B in Figure 2.1. Alternatively, if she devotes 2 hours to coffee and 4 to nuts, she will get (2 hours/day) × (4 pounds/hour) = 8 pounds of coffee per day and (4 hours/day) × (2 pounds/hour) = 8 pounds of nuts. This alternative combination is represented by point C in Figure 2.1.

FIGURE 2.1
Susan's Production Possibilities.
For the production relationships given, the production possibilities curve is a straight line.

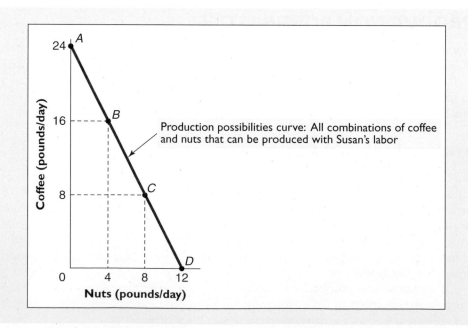

Production possibilities curve: All combinations of coffee and nuts that can be produced with Susan's labor

Since Susan's production possibilities curve (PPC) is a straight line, its slope is constant. The absolute value of the slope of Susan's PPC is the ratio of its vertical intercept to its horizontal intercept: (24 pounds of coffee/day)/(12 pounds of nuts/day) = (2 pounds of coffee)/(1 pound of nuts). (Be sure to keep track of the units of measure on each axis when computing this ratio.) *This ratio means that Susan's opportunity cost of an additional pound of nuts is 2 pounds of coffee.*

Note that Susan's opportunity cost (OC) of nuts can also be expressed as the following simple formula:

$$OC_{nuts} = \frac{\text{loss in coffee}}{\text{gain in nuts}}, \tag{2.1}$$

where "loss in coffee" means the amount of coffee given up and "gain in nuts" means the corresponding increase in nuts. Likewise, Susan's opportunity cost of coffee is expressed by this formula:

$$OC_{coffee} = \frac{\text{loss in nuts}}{\text{gain in coffee}}. \tag{2.2}$$

To say that Susan's opportunity cost of an additional pound of nuts is 2 pounds of coffee is thus equivalent to saying that her opportunity cost of a pound of coffee is ½ pound of nuts. ◆

The downward slope of the production possibilities curve shown in Figure 2.1 illustrates the Scarcity Principle—the idea that because our resources are limited, having more of one good thing generally means having to settle for less of another (see Chapter 1). Susan can have an additional pound of coffee if she wishes, but only if she is willing to give up half a pound of nuts. If Susan is the only person in the economy, her opportunity cost of producing a good becomes, in effect, its price. Thus, the price she has to pay for an additional pound of coffee is half a pound of nuts; or the price she has to pay for an additional pound of nuts is 2 pounds of coffee.

Any point that lies either along the production possibilities curve or within it is said to be an **attainable point,** meaning that it can be produced with currently available resources. In Figure 2.2, for example, points *A, B, C, D,* and *E* are attainable

Scarcity

attainable point any combination of goods that can be produced using currently available resources

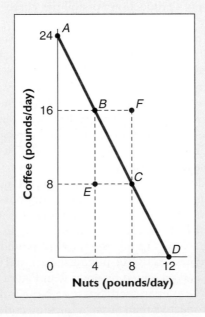

FIGURE 2.2
Attainable and Efficient Points on Susan's Production Possibilities Curve.
Points that lie either along the production possibilities curve (for example, A, B, C, and D) or within it (for example, E) are said to be attainable. Points that lie outside the production possibilities curve (for example, F) are unattainable. Points that lie along the curve are said to be efficient, while those that lie within the curve are said to be inefficient.

unattainable point any combination of goods that cannot be produced using currently available resources

inefficient point any combination of goods for which currently available resources enable an increase in the production of one good without a reduction in the production of the other

efficient point any combination of goods for which currently available resources do not allow an increase in the production of one good without a reduction in the production of the other

points. Points that lie outside the production possibilities curve are said to be **unattainable,** meaning that they cannot be produced using currently available resources. In Figure 2.2, F is an unattainable point because Susan cannot pick 16 pounds of coffee per day *and* gather 8 pounds of nuts. Points that lie within the curve are said to be **inefficient,** in the sense that existing resources would allow for production of more of at least one good without sacrificing the production of any other good. At E, for example, Susan is picking only 8 pounds of coffee per day and gathering 4 pounds of nuts, which means that she could increase her coffee harvest by 8 pounds per day without giving up any nuts (by moving from E to B). Alternatively, Susan could gather as many as 4 additional pounds of nuts each day without giving up any coffee (by moving from E to C). An **efficient** point is one that lies along the production possibilities curve. At any such point, more of one good can be produced only by producing less of the other.

EXERCISE 2.2

For the PPC shown in Figure 2.2, state whether the following points are attainable and/or efficient:

- **a. 20 pounds per day of coffee, 4 pounds per day of nuts.**

- **b. 12 pounds per day of coffee, 6 pounds per day of nuts.**

- **c. 4 pounds per day of coffee, 8 pounds per day of nuts.**

HOW INDIVIDUAL PRODUCTIVITY AFFECTS THE SLOPE AND POSITION OF THE PPC

To see how the slope and position of the production possibilities curve depend on an individual's productivity, let's compare Susan's PPC to that of Tom, who is less productive at picking coffee but more productive at gathering nuts.

How do changes in productivity affect the opportunity cost of nuts?

Tom is short and has keen eyesight, qualities that make him especially well-suited for gathering nuts that fall beneath trees on the hillsides. He can gather 4 pounds of nuts or pick 2 pounds of coffee per hour. If Tom were the only person in the economy, describe the economy's production possibilities curve.

We can construct Tom's PPC the same way we did Susan's. Note first that if Tom devotes an entire workday (6 hours) to coffee picking, he ends up with (6 hours/day) × (2 pounds/hour) = 12 pounds of coffee per day and zero pounds of nuts. So the vertical intercept of Tom's PPC is A in Figure 2.3. If instead he devotes all his time to gathering nuts, he gets (6 hours/day) × (4 pounds/hour) = 24 pounds of nuts per day and no coffee. That means the horizontal intercept of his PPC is D in Figure 2.3. Because Tom's production of each good is proportional to the amount of time he devotes to it, the remaining points on his PPC will lie along the straight line that joins these two extreme points.

For example, if he devotes 4 hours each day to picking coffee and 2 hours to gathering nuts, he will end up with (4 hours/day) × (2 pounds/hour) = 8 pounds of coffee per day and (2 hours/day) × (4 pounds/hour) = 8 pounds of nuts per day. This is the point labeled B in Figure 2.3. Alternatively, if he devotes 2 hours to coffee and 4 to nuts, he will get (2 hours/day) × (2 pounds/hour) = 4 pounds of coffee per day and (4 hours/day) × (4 pounds/hour) = 16 pounds of nuts. This alternative combination is represented by point C in Figure 2.3.

How does Tom's PPC compare with Susan's? Note in Figure 2.4 that because Tom is absolutely less productive than Susan at picking coffee, the vertical intercept

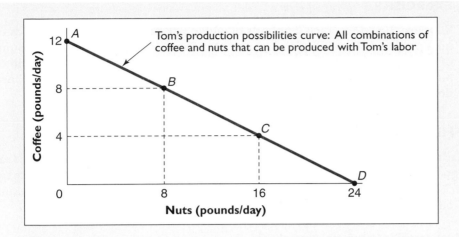

FIGURE 2.3
Tom's Production Possibilities Curve.
Tom's opportunity cost of producing one pound of nuts is only half a pound of coffee.

of his PPC lies closer to the origin than Susan's. By the same token, because Susan is absolutely less productive than Tom at gathering nuts, the horizontal intercept of her PPC lies closer to the origin than Tom's. For Tom, the opportunity cost of an additional pound of nuts is ½ pound of coffee, which is one-fourth Susan's opportunity cost of nuts. This difference in opportunity costs shows up as a difference in the slopes of their PPCs: the absolute value of the slope of Tom's PPC is ½, whereas Susan's is 2.

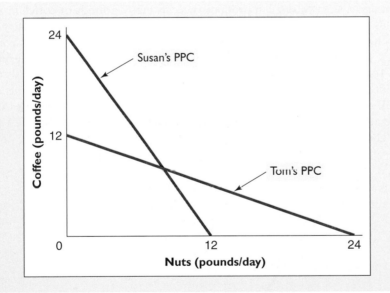

FIGURE 2.4
Individual Production Possibilities Curves Compared.
Tom is less productive in coffee than Susan, but more productive in nuts.

In this example, Tom has both an absolute advantage and a comparative advantage over Susan in gathering nuts. Susan, for her part, has both an absolute advantage and a comparative advantage over Tom in picking coffee. ◆

We cannot emphasize strongly enough that the principle of comparative advantage is a relative concept—one that makes sense only when the productivities of two or more people (or countries) are being compared. To cement this idea, work through the following exercise.

EXERCISE 2.3

Suppose Susan can pick 2 pounds of coffee per hour or gather 4 pounds of nuts per hour; Tom can pick 1 pound of coffee per hour and gather 1 pound of nuts per hour. What is Susan's opportunity cost of gathering a pound of nuts? What is Tom's opportunity cost of gathering a pound of nuts? Where does Susan's comparative advantage now lie?

THE GAINS FROM SPECIALIZATION AND EXCHANGE

Earlier we saw that a comparative advantage arising from disparities in individual opportunity costs creates gains for everyone (see the first two examples in this chapter). The following example shows how the same point can be illustrated using production possibility curves.

How costly is failure to specialize?

Suppose that in the preceding example Susan and Tom had divided their time so that each person's output consisted of half nuts and half coffee. How much of each good would Tom and Susan have been able to consume? How much could they have consumed if each had specialized in the activity for which he or she enjoyed a comparative advantage?

Since Tom can produce twice as many pounds of nuts in an hour as pounds of coffee, to produce equal quantities of each, he must spend 2 hours picking coffee for every hour he devotes to gathering nuts. And since he works a 6-hour day, that means spending 2 hours gathering nuts and 4 hours picking coffee. Dividing his time in this way, he will end up with 8 pounds of coffee per day and 8 pounds of nuts. Similarly, since Susan can produce twice as many pounds of coffee in an hour as pounds of nuts, to pick equal quantities of each, she must spend 2 hours gathering nuts for every hour she devotes to picking coffee. And since she too works a 6-hour day, that means spending 2 hours picking coffee and 4 hours gathering nuts. So, like Tom, she will end up with 8 pounds of coffee per day and 8 pounds of nuts. (See Figure 2.5.) Their combined daily production will thus be 16 pounds of each good. By contrast, had they each specialized in their respective activities of comparative advantage, their combined daily production would have been 24 pounds of each good.

FIGURE 2.5
Production without Specialization.
When Tom and Susan divide their time so that each produces the same number of pounds of coffee and nuts, they can consume a total of 16 pounds of coffee and 16 pounds of nuts each day.

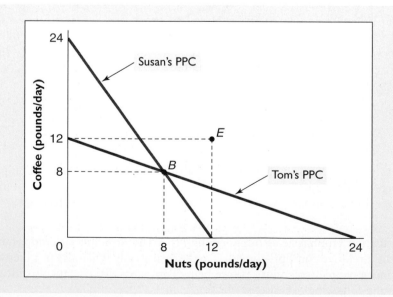

If they exchange coffee and nuts with one another, each can consume a combination of the two goods that would have been unattainable if exchange had not been possible. For example, Susan can give Tom 12 pounds of coffee in exchange for 12 pounds of nuts, enabling each to consume 4 pounds per day more of each good than when each produced and consumed alone. Note that point E in Figure 2.5, which has 12 pounds per day of each good, lies beyond each person's PPC, yet is easily attainable with specialization and exchange. ◆

As the following exercise illustrates, the gains from specialization grow larger as the difference in opportunity costs increases.

EXERCISE 2.4

How do differences in opportunity cost affect the gains from specialization? Susan can pick 5 pounds of coffee or gather 1 pound of nuts in an hour. Tom can pick 1 pound of coffee or gather 5 pounds of nuts in an hour. Assuming they again work 6-hour days and want to consume coffee and nuts in equal quantities, by how much will specialization increase their consumption compared to the alternative in which each produced only for his or her own consumption?

Although the gains from specialization and exchange grow with increases in the differences in opportunity costs among trading partners, these differences alone still seem insufficient to account for the enormous differences in living standards between rich and poor countries. Average income in the 20 richest countries in the year 2000, for example, was over \$27,000 per person, compared to only \$211 per person in the 20 poorest countries.[2] Although we will say more later about specialization's role in explaining these differences, we first discuss how to construct the PPC for an entire economy and examine how factors other than specialization might cause it to shift outward over time.

A PRODUCTION POSSIBILITIES CURVE FOR A MANY-PERSON ECONOMY

Although most actual economies consist of millions of workers, the process of constructing a production possibilities curve for an economy of that size is really no different from the process for a one-person economy. Consider again an economy in which the only two goods are coffee and nuts, with coffee again on the vertical axis and nuts on the horizontal axis. The vertical intercept of the economy's PPC is the total amount of coffee that could be picked if all available workers worked full-time picking coffee. Thus, the maximum attainable amount of coffee production is shown for the hypothetical economy in Figure 2.6 as 100,000 pounds per day (an amount chosen arbitrarily, for illustrative purposes). The horizontal intercept of the PPC is the amount of nuts that could be gathered if all available workers worked full-time gathering nuts, shown for this same economy as 80,000 pounds per day (also an amount chosen arbitrarily). But note that the PPC shown in the diagram is not a straight line—as in the earlier examples involving only a single worker—but rather a curve that is bowed out from the origin.

---

[2]High-income countries: Australia, Austria, Belgium, Canada, China, Hong Kong, Denmark, Finland, France, Germany, Iceland, Ireland, Japan, Luxembourg, Netherlands, Norway, Singapore, Sweden, Switzerland, United Kingdom, and United States. Low-income countries: Burkina Faso, Burundi, Central African Republic, Chad, Ethiopia, Ghana, Guinea-Bisau, Kenya, Madagascar, Malawi, Mali, Mozambique, Myanmar, Nepal, Niger, Nigeria, Rwanda, Sierra Leone, Tanzania, and Uganda. (Source: Global Policy Forum, http://www.globalpolicy.org/).

FIGURE 2.6
Production Possibilities Curve for a Large Economy.
For an economy with millions of workers, the PPC typically has a gentle outward bow shape.

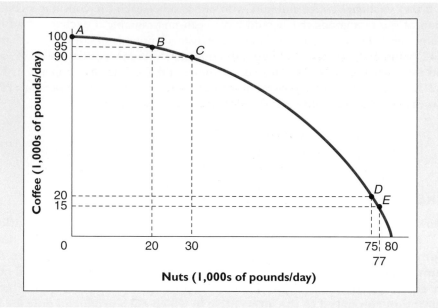

We'll say more in a moment about the reasons for this shape. But first note that a bow-shaped PPC means that the opportunity cost of producing nuts increases as the economy produces more of them. Notice, for example, that when the economy moves from *A*, where it is producing only coffee, to *B*, it gets 20,000 pounds of nuts per day by giving up only 5,000 pounds per day of coffee. When nut production is increased still further, however—for example, by moving from *B* to *C*—the economy again gives up 5,000 pounds per day of coffee, yet this time gets only 10,000 additional pounds of nuts. This pattern of increasing opportunity cost persists over the entire length of the PPC. For example, note that in moving from *D* to *E*, the economy again gives up 5,000 pounds per day of coffee but now gains only 2,000 pounds a day of nuts. Note, finally, that the same pattern of increasing opportunity cost applies to coffee. Thus, as more coffee is produced, the opportunity cost of producing additional coffee—as measured by the amount of nuts that must be sacrificed—also rises.

Why is the PPC for the multiperson economy bow-shaped? The answer lies in the fact that some resources are relatively well-suited for gathering nuts while others are relatively well-suited for picking coffee. If the economy is initially producing only coffee and wants to begin producing some nuts, which workers will it reassign? Recall Susan and Tom, the two workers discussed in the preceding example, in which Tom's comparative advantage was gathering nuts and Susan's comparative advantage was picking coffee. If both workers were currently picking coffee and you wanted to reassign one of them to gather nuts instead, whom would you send? Tom would be the clear choice, because his departure would cost the economy only half as much coffee as Susan's and would augment nut production by twice as much.

The principle is the same in any large multiperson economy, except that the range of opportunity cost differences across workers is even greater than in the earlier two-worker example. As we keep reassigning workers from coffee production to nut production, sooner or later we must withdraw even coffee specialists like Susan from coffee production. Indeed, we must eventually reassign others whose opportunity cost of producing nuts is far higher than hers.

The shape of the production possibilities curve shown in Figure 2.6 illustrates the general principle that when resources have different opportunity costs, we should always exploit the resource with the lowest opportunity cost first. We call this the *low-hanging-fruit principle,* in honor of the fruit picker's rule of picking the most accessible fruit first:

The Principle of Increasing Opportunity Cost (also called "The Low-Hanging-Fruit Principle"): In expanding the production of any good, first employ those resources with the lowest opportunity cost, and only afterward turn to resources with higher opportunity costs.

Increasing
Opportunity Cost

A Note on the Logic of the Fruit Picker's Rule

Why should a fruit picker harvest the low-hanging fruit first? This rule makes sense for several reasons. For one, the low-hanging fruit is easier (and hence cheaper) to pick, and if he planned on picking only a limited amount of fruit to begin with, he would clearly come out ahead by avoiding the less-accessible fruit on the higher branches. But even if he planned on picking all the fruit on the tree, he would do better to start with the lower branches first because this would enable him to enjoy the revenue from the sale of the fruit sooner.

The fruit picker's job can be likened to the task confronting a new CEO who has been hired to reform an inefficient, ailing company. The CEO has limited time and attention, so it makes sense to focus first on problems that are relatively easy to correct and whose elimination will provide the biggest improvements in performance—the low-hanging fruit. Later on, the CEO can worry about the many smaller improvements needed to raise the company from very good to excellent.

Again, the important message of the low-hanging-fruit principle is to be sure to take advantage of your most favorable opportunities first.

RECAP	COMPARATIVE ADVANTAGE AND PRODUCTION POSSIBILITIES

For an economy that produces two goods, the production possibilities curve describes the maximum amount of one good that can be produced for every possible level of production of the other good. Attainable points are those that lie on or within the curve and efficient points are those that lie along the curve. The slope of the production possibilities curve tells us the opportunity cost of producing an additional unit of the good measured along the horizontal axis. The Principle of Increasing Opportunity Cost, or the Low-Hanging-Fruit Principle, tells us that the slope of the production possibilities curve becomes steeper as we move downward to the right. The greater the differences among individual opportunity costs, the more bow-shaped the production possibilities curve will be and the more bow-shaped the production possibilities curve, the greater will be the potential gains from specialization.

FACTORS THAT SHIFT THE ECONOMY'S PRODUCTION POSSIBILITIES CURVE

As its name implies, the production possibilities curve provides a summary of the production options open to any society. At any given moment, the PPC confronts society with a trade-off. The only way people can produce and consume more nuts is to produce and consume less coffee. In the long run, however, it is often possible to increase production of all goods. This is what is meant when people speak of economic growth. As shown in Figure 2.7, economic growth is an outward shift in the economy's production possibilities curve. It can result from increases in the amount of productive resources available or from improvements in knowledge or technology that render existing resources more productive.

FIGURE 2.7
Economic Growth: An Outward Shift in the Economy's PPC.
Increases in productive resources (such as labor and capital equipment) or improvements in knowledge and technology cause the PPC to shift outward. They are the main factors that drive economic growth.

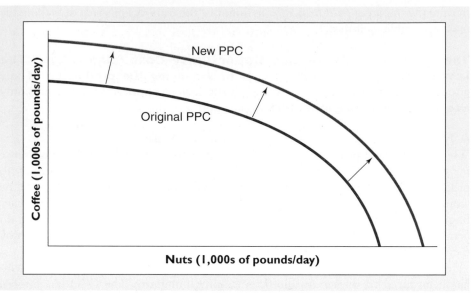

What causes the quantity of productive resources to grow in an economy? One factor is investment in new factories and equipment. When workers have more and better equipment to work with, their productivity increases, often dramatically. This is surely an important factor behind the differences in living standards between rich and poor countries. According to one study, for example, the value of capital investment per worker in the United States is about $30,000, while in Nepal the corresponding figure is less than $1,000.[3]

Such large differences in capital per worker don't occur all at once. They are a consequence of decades, even centuries, of differences in rates of savings and investment. Over time, even small differences in rates of investment can translate into extremely large differences in the amount of capital equipment available to each worker. Differences of this sort are often self-reinforcing: Not only do higher rates of saving and investment cause incomes to grow, but the resulting higher income levels also make it easier to devote additional resources to savings and investment. Over time, then, even small initial productivity advantages from specialization can translate into very large income gaps.

Population growth also causes an economy's PPC curve to shift outward and thus is often listed as one of the sources of economic growth. But because population growth also generates more mouths to feed, it cannot by itself raise a country's standard of living. Indeed it may even cause a decline in the standard of living if existing population densities have already begun to put pressure on available land, water, and other scarce resources.

Perhaps the most important source of economic growth is improvements in knowledge and technology. As economists have long recognized, such improvements often lead to higher output through increased specialization. Improvements in technology often occur spontaneously, but more frequently they are directly or indirectly the result of increases in education.

Earlier we discussed a two-person example in which individual differences in opportunity cost led to a threefold gain from specialization (Exercise 2.4). Real-world gains from specialization often are far more spectacular than those in the example. One reason is that specialization not only capitalizes on preexisting differences in individual skills but also deepens those skills through practice and experience. Moreover, it eliminates many of the switching and start-up costs people incur when they move back and forth among numerous tasks. These gains apply

[3]Alan Heston and Robert Summers, "The Penn World Table (Mark 5): An Expanded Set of International Comparisons, 1950–1988," *Quarterly Journal of Economics*, May 1991, pp. 327–68.

not only to people but also to the tools and equipment they use. Breaking a task down into simple steps, each of which can be performed by a different machine, greatly multiplies the productivity of individual workers.

Even in simple settings, these factors can combine to increase productivity hundreds- or even thousands-fold. Adam Smith, the Scottish philosopher who is remembered today as the founder of modern economics, was the first to recognize the enormity of the gains made possible by the division and specialization of labor. Consider, for instance, his description of work in an eighteenth-century Scottish pin factory:

> One man draws out the wire, another straightens it, a third cuts it, a fourth points it, a fifth grinds it at the top for receiving the head; to make the head requires two or three distinct operations ... I have seen a small manufactory of this kind where only ten men were employed ... [who] could, when they exerted themselves, make among them about twelve pounds of pins in a day. There are in a pound upwards of four thousand pins of middling size. Those ten persons, therefore, could make among them upwards of forty-eight thousand pins in a day. Each person, therefore, making a tenth part of forty-eight thousand pins, might be considered as making four thousand eight hundred pins in a day. But if they had all wrought separately and independently, and without any of them having been educated to this peculiar business, they certainly could not each of them have made twenty, perhaps not one pin in a day.[4]

The gains in productivity that result from specialization are indeed often prodigious. They constitute the single most important explanation for why societies that don't rely heavily on specialization and exchange are rapidly becoming relics.

WHY HAVE SOME COUNTRIES BEEN SLOW TO SPECIALIZE?

You may be asking yourself, "If specialization is such a great thing, why don't people in poor countries like Nepal just specialize?" If so, you are in good company. Adam Smith spent many years attempting to answer precisely the same question. In the end, his explanation was that population density is an important precondition for specialization. Smith, ever the economic naturalist, observed that work tended to be far more specialized in the large cities of England in the eighteenth century than in the rural highlands of Scotland:

> In the lone houses and very small villages which are scattered about in so desert a country as the Highlands of Scotland, every farmer must be butcher, baker and brewer for his own family. . . . A country carpenter . . . is not only a carpenter, but a joiner, a cabinet maker, and even a carver in wood, as well as a wheelwright, a ploughwright, a cart and waggon maker.[5]

In contrast, each of these same tasks was performed by a different specialist in the large English and Scottish cities of Smith's day. Scottish highlanders also would have specialized had they been able to, but the markets in which they participated were simply too small and fragmented. Of course, high population density by itself provides no guarantee that specialization will result in rapid economic growth. But especially before the arrival of modern shipping and electronic communications technology, low population density was a definite obstacle to gains from specialization.

Nepal remains one of the most remote and isolated countries on the planet. As recently as the mid-1960s, its average population density was less than 30 people per square mile (as compared, for example, to more than 1,000 people per square

[4]Adam Smith, *The Wealth of Nations* (New York: Everyman's Library, 1910 (1776)), book 1.
[5]*Id.*, chapter 3.

Can specialization proceed too far?

mile in New Jersey). Specialization was further limited by Nepal's rugged terrain. Exchanging goods and services with residents of other villages was difficult, because the nearest village in most cases could be reached only after trekking several hours, or even days, over treacherous Himalayan trails. More than any other factor, this extreme isolation accounts for Nepal's longstanding failure to benefit from widespread specialization.

Population density is by no means the only important factor that influences the degree of specialization. Specialization may be severely impeded, for example, by laws and customs that limit people's freedom to transact freely with one another. The communist governments of North Korea and the former East Germany restricted exchange severely, which helps explain why those countries achieved far less specialization than South Korea and the former West Germany, whose governments were far more supportive of exchange.

CAN WE HAVE TOO MUCH SPECIALIZATION?

Of course, the mere fact that specialization boosts productivity does not mean that more specialization is always better than less, for specialization also entails costs. For example, most people appear to enjoy variety in the work they do, yet variety tends to be one of the first casualties as workplace tasks become ever more narrowly specialized.

Indeed, one of Karl Marx's central themes was that the fragmentation of workplace tasks often exacts a heavy psychological toll on workers. Thus, he wrote,

> All means for the development of production . . . mutilate the laborer into a fragment of a man, degrade him to the level of an appendage of a machine, destroy every remnant of charm in his work and turn it into hated toil.[6]

Charlie Chaplin's 1936 film *Modern Times* paints a vivid portrait of the psychological costs of repetitive factory work. As an assembly worker, Chaplin's only task, all day every day, is to tighten the nuts on two bolts as they pass before him on the assembly line. Finally, he snaps and staggers from the factory, wrenches in hand, tightening every nutlike protuberance he encounters.

[6]Karl Marx, *Das Kapital* (New York: Modern Library), pp. 708, 709.

Do the extra goods made possible by specialization simply come at too high a price? We must certainly acknowledge at least the *potential* for specialization to proceed too far. Yet specialization need not entail rigidly segmented, mind-numbingly repetitive work. And it is important to recognize that *failure* to specialize entails costs as well. Those who don't specialize must accept low wages or work extremely long hours.

When all is said and done, we can expect to meet life's financial obligations in the shortest time—thereby freeing up more time to do whatever else we wish—if we concentrate at least a significant proportion of our efforts on those tasks for which we have a comparative advantage.

COMPARATIVE ADVANTAGE AND INTERNATIONAL TRADE

The same logic that leads the individuals in an economy to specialize and exchange goods with one another also leads nations to specialize and trade among themselves. As with individuals, each nation can benefit from exchange, even though one may be generally more productive than the other in absolute terms.

If trade between nations is so beneficial, why are free-trade agreements so controversial?

One of the most heated issues in the 1996 presidential campaign was President Clinton's support for the North American Free Trade Agreement (NAFTA), a treaty to sharply reduce trade barriers between the United States and its immediate neighbors north and south. The treaty attracted fierce opposition from third-party candidate Ross Perot, who insisted that it would mean unemployment for millions of American workers. If exchange is so beneficial, why does anyone oppose it?

The answer is that while reducing barriers to international trade increases the total value of all goods and services produced in each nation, it does not guarantee that each individual citizen will do better. One specific concern regarding NAFTA was that it would help Mexico to exploit a comparative advantage in the production of goods made by unskilled labor. Although U.S. consumers would benefit from reduced prices for such goods, many Americans feared that unskilled workers in the United States would lose their jobs to workers in Mexico.

In the end, NAFTA was enacted over the vociferous opposition of American labor unions. So far, however, studies have failed to detect significant overall job losses among unskilled workers in the United States, although there have been some losses in specific industries. •

Example 2.3
THE ECONOMIC NATURALIST

If free trade is so great, why do so many people oppose it?

outsourcing a term increasingly used to connote having services performed by low-wage workers overseas

OUTSOURCING

An issue very much in the news in recent years has been the **outsourcing** of U.S. service jobs. Although the term once primarily meant having services performed by subcontractors anywhere outside the confines of the firm, increasingly it connotes the act of replacing relatively expensive American service workers with much cheaper service workers in overseas locations.

A case in point is the transcription of medical records. In an effort to maintain accurate records, many physicians dictate their case notes for later transcription after examining their patients. In the past, transcription was often performed by the physician's secretary in spare moments. But secretaries also must attend to a variety of other tasks that disrupt concentration. They must answer phones, serve as receptionists, prepare correspondence, and so on. As insurance disputes and malpractice litigation became more frequent during the 1980s and 1990s, errors in medical records became much more costly to physicians. In response, many turned to independent companies that offered transcription services by full-time, dedicated specialists.

These companies typically served physicians whose practices were located in the same community. But while many of the companies that manage transcription services are still located in the United States, an increasing fraction of the actual work itself is now performed outside the United States. For example, Eight Crossings, a company headquartered in northern California, enables physicians to upload voice dictation files securely to the internet, whereupon they are transmitted to transcribers who perform the work in India. The finished documents are then transmitted back, in electronic form, to physicians, who may edit and even sign them online. The advantage for physicians, of course, is that the fee for this service is much lower than for the same service performed domestically because wage rates in India are much lower than in the United States.

In China, Korea, Indonesia, India, and elsewhere, even highly skilled professionals still earn just a small fraction of what their counterparts in the United States are paid. Accordingly, companies face powerful competitive pressure to import not just low-cost goods from overseas suppliers, but also a growing array of professional services.

As Microsoft chairman Bill Gates put it in a 1999 interview,

> As a business manager, you need to take a hard look at your core competencies. Revisit the areas of your company that aren't directly involved in those competencies, and consider whether Web technologies can enable you to spin off those tasks. Let another company take over the management responsibilities for that work, and use modern communication technology to work closely with the people—now partners instead of employees are doing the work. In the Web work style, employees can push the freedom the Web provides to its limits.

EN 2

In economic terms, the outsourcing of services to low-wage foreign workers is exactly analogous to the importation of goods manufactured by low-wage foreign workers. In both cases, the resulting cost savings benefit consumers in the United States. And in both cases, jobs in the United States may be put in jeopardy, at least temporarily. An American manufacturing worker's job is at risk if it is possible to import the good he produces from another country at lower cost. By the same token, an American service worker's job is at risk if a lower-paid worker can perform that same service somewhere else.

Example 2.4
THE ECONOMIC NATURALIST

Is PBS economics reporter Paul Solman's job a likely candidate for outsourcing?

Paul Solman and his associate Lee Koromvokis produce video segments that provide in-depth analysis of current economic issues for the PBS evening news program *The News-Hour with Jim Lehrer*. Is it likely that his job will someday be outsourced to a low-wage reporter from Hyderabad?

In a recent book, the economists Frank Levy and Richard Murnane attempt to identify the characteristics of a job that make it a likely candidate for outsourcing.[7] In their view, any job that is amenable to computerization is also vulnerable to outsourcing. To computerize a task means to break it down into units that can be managed with simple rules. ATM machines, for example, were able to replace many of the tasks that bank tellers once performed because it was straightforward to reduce these tasks to a simple series of questions that a machine could answer. By the same token, the workers in off-shore call centers who increasingly book our airline and hotel reservations are basically following simple scripts much like computer programs.

[7]Frank Levy and Richard Murnane, *The New Division of Labor: How Computers Are Creating the Next Job Market* (Princeton, NJ: Princeton University Press, 2004).

So the less rules-based a job is, the less vulnerable it is to outsourcing. Safest of all are those that Levy and Murnane describe as "face-to-face" jobs. Unlike most rules-based jobs, these jobs tend to involve complex face-to-face communication with other people, precisely the kind of communication that dominates Mr. Solman's economics reporting.

In an interview for the *NewsHour*, Mr. Solman asked Mr. Levy what he meant, exactly, by "complex communication."

> "Suppose I say the word *bill*," Levy responded, "and you hear that. And the question is what does that mean? . . . Am I talking about a piece of currency? Am I talking about a piece of legislation, the front end of a duck? The only way you're going to answer that is to think about the whole context of the conversation. But that's very complicated work to break down into some kind of software."[8]

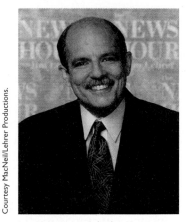

Courtesy MacNeil/Lehrer Productions.

Is a low-wage foreign economics reporter likely to replace Paul Solman?

Levy and Murnane describe a second category of tasks that are less vulnerable to out-sourcing—namely, those that for one reason or another require the worker to be physically present. For example, it is difficult to see how someone in China or India could build an addition to someone's house in a Chicago suburb or repair a blown head gasket on someone's Chevrolet Corvette in Atlanta or fill a cavity in someone's tooth in Los Angeles.

So on both counts, Paul Solman's job appears safe for the time being. Because it involves face-to-face, complex communication, and because many of his interviews can be conducted only in the United States, it is difficult to see how a reporter from Hyderabad could displace him. ●

Of course, the fact that a job is relatively safe does not mean that it is completely sheltered. For example, although most dentists continue to think themselves immune from outsourcing, it is now possible for someone requiring extensive dental work to have the work done in New Delhi and still save enough to cover his airfare and a two-week vacation in India.

There are more than 135 million Americans in the labor force. Every three months or so, approximately 7 million of them lose their jobs and 7 million find new ones. At various points in your life, you are likely to be among this group in transition. In the long run, the greatest security available to you or any other worker is the ability to adapt quickly to new circumstances. Having a good education provides no guarantee against losing your job, but it should enable you to develop a comparative advantage at the kinds of tasks that require more than just executing a simple set of rules.

RECAP	COMPARATIVE ADVANTAGE AND INTERNATIONAL TRADE

Nations, like individuals, can benefit from exchange, even though one trading partner may be more productive than the other in absolute terms. The greater the difference between domestic opportunity costs and world opportunity costs, the more a nation benefits from exchange with other nations. But expansions of exchange do not guarantee that each individual citizen will do better. In particular, unskilled workers in high-wage countries may be hurt in the short run by the reduction of barriers to trade with low-wage nations.

[8]http://www.pbs.org/newshour/bb/economy/july-dec04/jobs_8-16.html.

▪ SUMMARY ▪

- One person has an *absolute* advantage over another in the production of a good if she can produce more of that good than the other person. One person has a *comparative* advantage over another in the production of a good if she is relatively more efficient than the other person at producing that good, meaning that her opportunity cost of producing it is lower than her counterpart's. Specialization based on comparative advantage is the basis for economic exchange. When each person specializes in the task at which he or she is relatively most efficient, the economic pie is maximized, making possible the largest slice for everyone. **LO1**

- At the individual level, comparative advantage may spring from differences in talent or ability or from differences in education, training, and experience. At the national level, sources of comparative advantage include these innate and learned differences, as well as differences in language, culture, institutions, climate, natural resources, and a host of other factors. **LO1**

- The production possibilities curve is a simple device for summarizing the possible combinations of output that a society can produce if it employs its resources efficiently. In a simple economy that produces only coffee and nuts, the PPC shows the maximum quantity of coffee production (vertical axis) possible at each level of nut production (horizontal axis). The slope of the PPC at any point represents the opportunity cost of nuts at that point, expressed in pounds of coffee. **LO3**

- All production possibilities curves slope downward because of the Scarcity Principle, which states that the only way a consumer can get more of one good is to settle for less of another. In economies whose workers have different opportunity costs of producing each good, the slope of the PPC becomes steeper as consumers move downward along the curve. This change in slope illustrates the Principle of Increasing Opportunity Cost (or the Low-Hanging-Fruit Principle), which states that in expanding the production of any good, a society should first employ those resources that are relatively efficient at producing that good, only afterward turning to those that are less efficient. **LO2**

- Factors that cause a country's PPC to shift outward over time include investment in new factories and equipment, population growth, and improvements in knowledge and technology. **LO3**

- The same logic that prompts individuals to specialize in their production and exchange goods with one another also leads nations to specialize and trade with one another. On both levels, each trading partner can benefit from an exchange, even though one may be more productive than the other, in absolute terms, for each good. For both individuals and nations, the benefits of exchange tend to be larger the larger are the differences between the trading partners' opportunity costs. **LO4**

▪ CORE PRINCIPLES ▪

Comparative Advantage ◯

The Principle of Comparative Advantage
Everyone does best when each person (or each country) concentrates on the activities for which his or her opportunity cost is lowest.

Increasing Opportunity Cost ◯

The Principle of Increasing Opportunity Cost (also called "The Low-Hanging-Fruit Principle")
In expanding the production of any good, first employ those resources with the lowest opportunity cost, and only afterward turn to resources with higher opportunity costs.

▪ KEY TERMS ▪

absolute advantage (36)
attainable point (43)
comparative advantage (36)

efficient point (44)
inefficient point (44)
outsourcing (53)

production possibilities
  curve (41)
unattainable point (44)

▪ REVIEW QUESTIONS ▪

---

1. Explain what "having a comparative advantage" at producing a particular good or service means. What does "having an absolute advantage" at producing a good or service mean? **LO1**

2. How will a reduction in the number of hours worked each day affect an economy's production possibilities curve? **LO3**

3. How will technological innovations that boost labor productivity affect an economy's production possibilities curve? **LO3**

4. Why does saying that people are poor because they do not specialize make more sense than saying that people perform their own services because they are poor? **LO1**

5. What factors have helped the United States to become the world's leading exporter of movies, books, and popular music? **LO4**

▪ PROBLEMS ▪

1. Ted can wax 4 cars per day or wash 12 cars. Tom can wax 3 cars per day or wash 6. What is each man's opportunity cost of washing a car? Who has a comparative advantage in washing cars? **LO1**

2. Ted can wax a car in 20 minutes or wash a car in 60 minutes. Tom can wax a car in 15 minutes or wash a car in 30 minutes. What is each man's opportunity cost of washing a car? Who has a comparative advantage in washing cars? **LO1**

3. Toby can produce 5 gallons of apple cider or 2.5 ounces of feta cheese per hour. Kyle can produce 3 gallons of apple cider or 1.5 ounces of feta cheese per hour. Can Toby and Kyle benefit from specialization and trade? Explain. **LO1**

4. Nancy and Bill are auto mechanics. Nancy takes 4 hours to replace a clutch and 2 hours to replace a set of brakes. Bill takes 6 hours to replace a clutch and 2 hours to replace a set of brakes. State whether anyone has an absolute advantage at either task and, for each task, identify who has a comparative advantage. **LO1**

5. Consider a society consisting only of Helen, who allocates her time between sewing dresses and baking bread. Each hour she devotes to sewing dresses yields 4 dresses and each hour she devotes to baking bread yields 8 loaves of bread. If Helen works a total of 8 hours per day, graph her production possibilities curve. **LO3**

6. Refer to the preceding question. Which of the points listed below is efficient? Which is attainable? **LO3**
   a. 28 dresses per day, 16 loaves per day.
   b. 16 dresses per day, 32 loaves per day.
   c. 18 dresses per day, 24 loaves per day.

7. Suppose that in Problem 5 a sewing machine is introduced that enables Helen to sew 8 dresses per hour rather than only 4. Show how this development shifts her production possibilities curve. **LO3**

8. Refer to the preceding question to explain what is meant by the following statement: "An increase in productivity with respect to any one good increases our options for producing and consuming all other goods." **LO3**

9. Susan can pick 4 pounds of coffee in an hour or gather 2 pounds of nuts. Tom can pick 2 pounds of coffee in an hour or gather 4 pounds of nuts. Each works 6 hours per day. **LO2**
   a. What is the maximum number of pounds of coffee the two can pick in a day?
   b. What is the maximum number of pounds of nuts the two can gather in a day?

   c. If Susan and Tom were picking the maximum number of pounds of coffee when they decided that they would like to begin gathering 4 pounds of nuts per day, who would gather the nuts, and how many pounds of coffee would they still be able to pick?

   d. Now suppose Susan and Tom were gathering the maximum number of pounds of nuts when they decided that they would like to begin picking 8 pounds of coffee per day. Who would pick the coffee, and how many pounds of nuts would they still be able to gather?

   e. Would it be possible for Susan and Tom in total to gather 26 pounds of nuts and pick 20 pounds of coffee each day? If so, how much of each good should each person pick?

10.*Refer to the two-person economy described in the preceding problem. **LO1**

   a. Is the point (30 pounds of coffee per day, 12 pounds of nuts per day) an attainable point? Is it an efficient point? What about the point (24 pounds of coffee per day, 24 pounds of nuts per day)?

   b. On a graph with pounds of coffee per day on the vertical axis and pounds of nuts per day on the horizontal axis, show all the points you identified in Problem 9, parts a–e, and Problem 10a. Connect these points with straight lines. Is the result the PPC for the economy consisting of Susan and Tom?

   c. Suppose that Susan and Tom could buy or sell coffee and nuts in the world market at a price of $2 per pound for coffee and $2 per pound for nuts. If each person specialized completely in the good for which he or she had a comparative advantage, how much could they earn by selling all their produce?

   d. At the prices just described, what is the maximum amount of coffee Susan and Tom could buy in the world market? The maximum amount of nuts? Would it be possible for them to consume 40 pounds of nuts and 8 pounds of coffee each day?

   e. In light of their ability to buy and sell in world markets at the stated prices, show on the same graph all combinations of the two goods it would be possible for them to consume.

■ ANSWERS TO IN-CHAPTER EXERCISES ■

2.1

	Productivity in programming	**Productivity in bicycle repair**
Pat	2 Web page updates per hour	1 repair per hour
Barb	3 Web page updates per hour	3 repairs per hour

The entries in the table tell us that Barb has an absolute advantage over Pat in both activities. While Barb, the mechanic, can update 3 Web pages per hour, Pat, the programmer, can update only 2. Barb's absolute advantage over Pat is even greater in the task of fixing bikes—3 repairs per hour versus Pat's 1.

But as in second example in this chapter, the fact that Barb is a better programmer than Pat does not imply that Barb should update her own Web page. Barb's opportunity cost of updating a Web page is 1 bicycle repair, whereas Pat must give up only half a repair to update a Web page. Pat has a comparative advantage over Barb at programming and Barb has a comparative advantage over Pat at bicycle repair. **LO1**

*Problems marked with an asterisk (*) are more difficult.

2.2 In the accompanying graph, *A* (20 pounds per day of coffee, 4 pounds per day of nuts) is unattainable; *B* (12 pounds per day of coffee, 6 pounds per day of nuts) is both attainable and efficient; and *C* (4 pounds per day of coffee, 8 pounds per day of nuts) is both attainable and inefficient. **LO3**

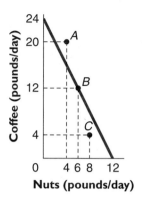

2.3 Susan's opportunity cost of gathering a pound of nuts is now ½ pound of coffee and Tom's opportunity cost of gathering a pound of nuts is now only 1 pound of coffee. So Tom has a comparative advantage at picking coffee and Susan has a comparative advantage at gathering nuts. **LO3**

2.4 Since Tom can produce five times as many pounds of nuts in an hour as pounds of coffee, to produce equal quantities of each, he must spend 5 hours picking coffee for every hour he devotes to gathering nuts. And since he works a 6-hour day, that means spending 5 hours picking coffee and 1 hour gathering nuts. Dividing his time in this way, he will end up with 5 pounds of each good. Similarly, if she is to produce equal quantities of each good, Susan must spend 5 hours gathering nuts and 1 hour picking coffee. So she too produces 5 pounds of each good if she divides her 6-hour day in this way. Their combined daily production will thus be 10 pounds of each good. By working together and specializing, however, they can produce and consume a total of 30 pounds per day of each good. **LO1**

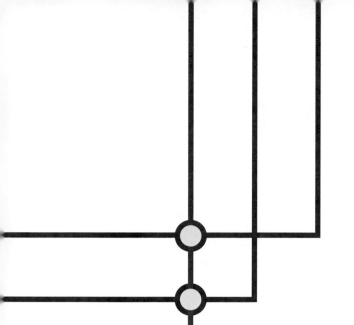

Supply and Demand

LEARNING OBJECTIVES

In this chapter, we will take up the basic supply and demand model. In the process, you will learn

1. How the demand curve summarizes the behavior of buyers in the market-place.

2. How the supply curve summarizes the behavior of sellers in the market-place.

3. How the supply and demand curves interact to determine the equilibrium price and quantity.

4. How shifts in supply and demand curves cause prices and quantities to change.

5. The Efficiency Principle, which says that efficiency is an important social goal because, when the economic pie grows larger, it is always possible for everyone to have a larger slice than before.

6. The Equilibrium Principle (also called the No-Cash-on-the-Table Principle), which says that a market in equilibrium leaves no unexploited opportunities for individuals.

The stock of foodstuffs on hand at any moment in New York City's grocery stores, restaurants, and private kitchens is sufficient to feed the area's 10 million residents for at most a week or so. Since most of these residents have nutritionally adequate and highly varied diets, and since almost no food is produced within the city proper, provisioning New York requires that millions of pounds of food and drink be delivered to locations throughout the city each day.

No doubt many New Yorkers, buying groceries at their favorite local markets or eating at their favorite Italian restaurants, give little or no thought to the nearly miraculous coordination of people and resources that is required to feed city residents on a daily basis. But near-miraculous it is, nevertheless. Even if the supplying of New York City consisted only of transporting a fixed collection of foods to a given list of destinations each day, it would be quite an impressive operation, requiring at least a small (and well-managed) army to carry out.

Yet the entire process is astonishingly more complex than that. For example, the system must somehow ensure that not only *enough* food is delivered to satisfy New Yorkers' discriminating palates, but also the *right kinds* of food. There mustn't be too much pheasant and not enough smoked eel; or too much bacon and not enough eggs; or too much caviar and not enough canned tuna; and so on. Similar judgments must be made *within* each category of food and drink: There must be the right amount of Swiss cheese and the right amounts of provolone, gorgonzola, and feta.

But even this doesn't begin to describe the complexity of the decisions and actions required to provide our nation's largest city with its daily bread. Someone has to decide where each particular type of food gets produced, and how, and by whom. Someone must decide how much of each type of food gets delivered to *each* of the tens of thousands of restaurants and grocery stores in the city. Someone must determine whether the deliveries should be made in big trucks or small ones, arrange that the trucks be in the right place at the right time, and ensure that gasoline and qualified drivers be available.

Thousands of individuals must decide what role, if any, they will play in this collective effort. Some people—just the right number—must choose to drive food-delivery trucks rather than trucks that deliver lumber. Others must become the mechanics who fix these trucks rather than carpenters who build houses. Others must become farmers rather than architects or bricklayers. Still others must become chefs in upscale restaurants, or flip burgers at McDonald's, instead of becoming plumbers or electricians.

Yet despite the almost incomprehensible number and complexity of the tasks involved, somehow the supplying of New York City manages to get done remarkably smoothly. Oh, a grocery store will occasionally run out of flank steak or a diner will sometimes be told that someone else has just ordered the last serving of roast duck. But if episodes like these stick in memory, it is only because they are rare. For the most part, New York's food delivery system—like that of every other city in the country—functions so seamlessly that it attracts virtually no notice.

The situation is strikingly different in New York City's rental housing market. According to one recent estimate, the city needs between 20,000 and 40,000 new housing units each year merely to keep up with population growth and to replace existing housing that is deteriorated beyond repair. The actual rate of new construction in the city, however, is only 6,000 units per year. As a result, America's most densely populated city has been experiencing a protracted housing shortage. Yet, paradoxically, in the midst of this shortage, apartment houses are being demolished; and in the vacant lots left behind, people from the neighborhoods are planting flower gardens!

New York City is experiencing not only a growing shortage of rental housing, but also chronically strained relations between landlords and tenants. In one all-too-typical case, for example, a photographer living in a loft on the Lower East Side waged an eight-year court battle with his landlord that generated literally thousands of pages of legal documents. "Once we put up a doorbell for ourselves," the photographer recalled, "and [the landlord] pulled it out, so we pulled out the wires to his doorbell."[1] The landlord, for his part, accused the photographer of obstructing his efforts to renovate the apartment. According to the landlord, the tenant preferred for the apartment to remain in substandard condition since that gave him an excuse to withhold rent payments.

Same city, two strikingly different patterns: In the food industry, goods and services are available in wide variety and people (at least those with adequate income) are generally satisfied with what they receive and the choices available to them. In contrast, in the rental housing industry, chronic shortages and chronic dissatisfaction are rife among both buyers and sellers. Why this difference?

Why does New York City's food distribution system work so much better than its housing market?

[1]Quoted by John Tierney, "The Rentocracy: At the Intersection of Supply and Demand," *New York Times Magazine*, May 4, 1997, p. 39.

The brief answer is that New York City relies on a complex system of administrative rent regulations to allocate housing units but leaves the allocation of food essentially in the hands of market forces—the forces of supply and demand. Although intuition might suggest otherwise, both theory and experience suggest that the seemingly chaotic and unplanned outcomes of market forces, in most cases, can do a better job of allocating economic resources than can (for example) a government agency, even if the agency has the best of intentions.

In this chapter we'll explore how markets allocate food, housing, and other goods and services, usually with remarkable efficiency despite the complexity of the tasks. To be sure, markets are by no means perfect, and our stress on their virtues is to some extent an attempt to counteract what most economists view as an underappreciation by the general public of their remarkable strengths. But, in the course of our discussion, we'll see why markets function so smoothly most of the time and why bureaucratic rules and regulations rarely work as well in solving complex economic problems.

To convey an understanding of how markets work is a major goal of this course, and in this chapter we provide only a brief introduction and overview. As the course proceeds, we will discuss the economic role of markets in considerably more detail, paying attention to some of the problems of markets as well as their strengths.

WHAT, HOW, AND FOR WHOM? CENTRAL PLANNING VERSUS THE MARKET

No city, state, or society—regardless of how it is organized—can escape the need to answer certain basic economic questions. For example, how much of our limited time and other resources should we devote to building housing, how much to the production of food, and how much to providing other goods and services? What techniques should we use to produce each good? Who should be assigned to each specific task? And how should the resulting goods and services be distributed among people?

In the thousands of different societies for which records are available, issues like these have been decided in essentially one of two ways. One approach is for all economic decisions to be made centrally, by an individual or small number of individuals on behalf of a larger group. For example, in many agrarian societies throughout history, families or other small groups consumed only those goods and services that they produced for themselves and a single clan or family leader made most important production and distribution decisions. On an immensely larger scale, the economic organization of the former Soviet Union (and other communist countries) was also largely centralized. In so-called centrally planned communist nations, a central bureaucratic committee established production targets for the country's farms and factories, developed a master plan for how to achieve the targets (including detailed instructions concerning who was to produce what), and set up guidelines for the distribution and use of the goods and services produced.

Neither form of centralized economic organization is much in evidence today. When implemented on a small scale, as in a self-sufficient family enterprise, centralized decision making is certainly feasible. For the reasons discussed in the preceding chapter, however, the jack-of-all-trades approach was doomed once it became clear how dramatically people could improve their living standards by specialization—that is, by having each individual focus his or her efforts on a relatively narrow range of tasks. And with the fall of the Soviet Union and its satellite nations in the late 1980s, there are now only three communist economies left in the world: Cuba, North Korea, and China. The first two of these appear to be on their last legs, economically speaking, and China has by now largely abandoned any attempt to control production and distribution decisions from the center. The major remaining examples of centralized allocation and control now reside in the bureaucratic agencies that administer programs like New York City's rent controls—programs that are themselves becoming increasingly rare.

At the beginning of the twenty-first century, we are therefore left, for the most part, with the second major form of economic system, one in which production and distribution decisions are left to individuals interacting in private markets. In the so-called capitalist, or free-market, economies, people decide for themselves which careers to pursue and which products to produce or buy. In fact, there are no *pure* free-market economies today. Modern industrial countries are more properly described as "mixed economies," meaning that goods and services are allocated by a combination of free markets, regulation, and other forms of collective control. Still, it makes sense to refer to such systems as free-market economies because people are for the most part free to start businesses, to shut them down, or to sell them. And within broad limits, the distribution of goods and services is determined by individual preferences backed by individual purchasing power, which in most cases comes from the income people earn in the labor market.

In country after country, markets have replaced centralized control for the simple reason that they tend to assign production tasks and consumption benefits much more effectively. The popular press, and the conventional wisdom, often asserts that economists disagree about important issues. (As someone once quipped, "If you lay all the economists in the world end to end, they still wouldn't reach a conclusion.") The fact is, however, that there is overwhelming agreement among economists about a broad range of issues, with the great majority accepting the efficacy of markets as means for allocating society's scarce resources. For example, a recent survey found that more than 90 percent of American professional economists believe that rent regulations like the ones implemented by New York City do more harm than good. That the stated aim of these regulations—to make rental housing more affordable for middle- and low-income families—is clearly benign was not enough to prevent them from wreaking havoc on New York City's housing market. To see why, we must explore how goods and services are allocated in private markets, and why nonmarket means of allocating goods and services often do not produce the expected results.

BUYERS AND SELLERS IN MARKETS

Beginning with some simple concepts and definitions, we will explore how the interactions among buyers and sellers in markets determine the prices and quantities of the various goods and services traded in those markets. We begin by defining a market: The **market** for any good consists of all the buyers and sellers of that good. So, for example, the market for pizza on a given day in a given place is just the set of people (or other economic actors such as firms) potentially able to buy or sell pizza at that time and location.

In the market for pizza, sellers comprise the individuals and companies that either do sell—or might, under the right circumstances, sell—pizza. Similarly, buyers in this market include all individuals who buy—or might buy—pizza.

In most parts of the country, a decent pizza—or some other life-sustaining meal—can still be had for less than $10. Where does the market price of pizza come from? Looking beyond pizza to the vast array of other goods that are bought and sold every day, we may ask, "Why are some goods cheap and others expensive?" Aristotle had no idea. Nor did Plato, or Copernicus, or Newton. On reflection, it is astonishing that, for almost the entire span of human history, not even the most intelligent and creative minds on Earth had any real inkling of how to answer that seemingly simple question. Even Adam Smith, the Scottish moral philosopher whose *Wealth of Nations* launched the discipline of economics in 1776, suffered confusion on this issue.

Smith and other early economists (including Karl Marx) thought that the market price of a good was determined by its cost of production. But although costs surely do affect prices, they cannot explain why one of Pablo Picasso's paintings sells for so much more than one of Jackson Pollock's.

Why do Pablo Picasso's paintings sell for so much more than Jackson Pollock's?

market the market for any good consists of all buyers or sellers of that good

Stanley Jevons and other nineteenth-century economists tried to explain price by focusing on the value people derived from consuming different goods and services. It certainly seems plausible that people will pay a lot for a good they value highly. Yet willingness to pay cannot be the whole story, either. Deprive a person in the desert of water, for example, and he will be dead in a matter of hours, and yet water sells for less than a penny a gallon. By contrast, human beings can get along perfectly well without gold, and yet gold sells for more than $800 an ounce.

Cost of production? Value to the user? Which is it? The answer, which seems obvious to today's economists, is that both matter. Writing in the late nineteenth century, the British economist Alfred Marshall was among the first to show clearly how costs and value interact to determine both the prevailing market price for a good and the amount of it that is bought and sold. Our task in the pages ahead will be to explore Marshall's insights and gain some practice in applying them. As a first step, we introduce the two main components of Marshall's pathbreaking analysis: the demand curve and the supply curve.

THE DEMAND CURVE

In the market for pizza, the **demand curve** for pizza is a simple schedule or graph that tells us how many slices people would be willing to buy at different prices. By convention, economists usually put price on the vertical axis of the demand curve and quantity on the horizontal axis.

A fundamental property of the demand curve is that it is downward-sloping with respect to price. For example, the demand curve for pizza tells us that as the price of pizza falls, buyers will buy more slices. Thus, the daily demand curve for pizza in Chicago on a given day might look like the curve seen in Figure 3.1. (Although economists usually refer to demand and supply "curves," we often draw them as straight lines in examples.)

The demand curve in Figure 3.1 tells us that when the price of pizza is low—say $2 per slice—buyers will want to buy 16,000 slices per day, whereas they will want to buy only 12,000 slices at a price of $3 and only 8,000 at a price of $4. The demand curve for pizza—as for any other good—slopes downward for multiple reasons. Some of these reasons have to do with the individual consumer's reactions to price changes. Thus, as pizza becomes more expensive, a consumer may switch to chicken sandwiches, hamburgers, or other foods that substitute for pizza. This is called the **substitution effect** of a price change. In addition, a price increase reduces the quantity demanded because it reduces purchasing power: A consumer simply can't afford to buy as many slices of pizza at higher prices as at lower prices. This is called the **income effect** of a price change.

demand curve a schedule or graph showing the quantity of a good that buyers wish to buy at each price

substitution effect the change in the quantity demanded of a good that results because buyers switch to or from substitutes when the price of the good changes

income effect the change in the quantity demanded of a good that results because a change in the price of a good changes the buyer's purchasing power

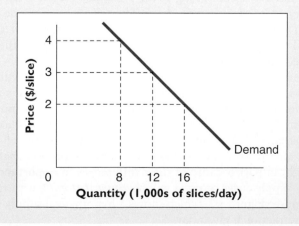

FIGURE 3.1
The Daily Demand Curve for Pizza in Chicago.
The demand curve for any good is a downward-sloping function of its price.

Cost-Benefit

buyer's reservation price the largest dollar amount the buyer would be willing to pay for a good

---

Another reason that the demand curve slopes downward is that consumers differ in terms of how much they are willing to pay for the good. The Cost-Benefit Principle tells us that a given person will buy the good if the benefit he expects to receive from it exceeds its cost. The benefit is the **buyer's reservation price**, the highest dollar amount he would be willing to pay for the good. The cost of the good is the actual amount that the buyer actually must pay for it, which is the market price of the good. In most markets, different buyers have different reservation prices. Thus, when the good sells for a high price, it will satisfy the cost-benefit test for fewer buyers than when it sells for a lower price.

To put this same point another way, the fact that the demand curve for a good is downward-sloping reflects the fact that the reservation price of the marginal buyer declines as the quantity of the good bought increases. Here the marginal buyer is the person who purchases the last unit of the good that is sold. If buyers are currently purchasing 12,000 slices of pizza a day in Figure 3.1, for example, the reservation price for the buyer of the 12,000th slice must be $3. (If someone had been willing to pay more than that, the quantity demanded at a price of $3 would have been more than 12,000 to begin with.) By similar reasoning, when the quantity sold is 16,000 slices per day, the marginal buyer's reservation price must be only $2.

We defined the demand curve for any good as a schedule telling how much of it consumers wish to purchase at various prices. This is called the *horizontal interpretation* of the demand curve. Using the horizontal interpretation, we start with price on the vertical axis and read the corresponding quantity demanded on the horizontal axis. Thus, at a price of $4 per slice, the demand curve in Figure 3.1 tells us that the quantity of pizza demanded will be 8,000 slices per day.

The demand curve also can be interpreted in a second way, which is to start with quantity on the horizontal axis and then read the marginal buyer's reservation price on the vertical axis. Thus, when the quantity of pizza sold is 8,000 slices per day, the demand curve in Figure 3.1 tells us that the marginal buyer's reservation price is $4 per slice. This second way of reading the demand curve is called the *vertical interpretation*.

EXERCISE 3.1

In Figure 3.1, what is the marginal buyer's reservation price when the quantity of pizza sold is 10,000 slices per day? For the same demand curve, what will be the quantity of pizza demanded at a price of $2.50 per slice?

THE SUPPLY CURVE

supply curve a graph or schedule showing the quantity of a good that sellers wish to sell at each price

In the market for pizza, the **supply curve** is a simple schedule or graph that tells us, for each possible price, the total number of slices that all pizza vendors would be willing to sell at that price. What does the supply curve of pizza look like? The answer to this question is based on the logical assumption that suppliers should be willing to sell additional slices as long as the price they receive is sufficient to cover their opportunity costs of supplying them. Thus, if what someone could earn by selling a slice of pizza is insufficient to compensate her for what she could have earned if she had spent her time and invested her money in some other way, she will not sell that slice. Otherwise, she will.

Just as buyers differ with respect to the amounts they are willing to pay for pizza, sellers also differ with respect to their opportunity costs of supplying pizza. For those with limited education and work experience, the opportunity cost of selling pizza is relatively low (because such individuals typically do not have a lot of high-paying alternatives). For others, the opportunity cost of selling pizza is of moderate value, and for still others—like rock stars and professional athletes—it is prohibitively high. In part because of these differences in opportunity cost among people, the daily supply curve of pizza will be *upward-sloping* with respect to price. As an illustration, see Figure 3.2, which shows a hypothetical supply curve for pizza in the Chicago market on a given day.

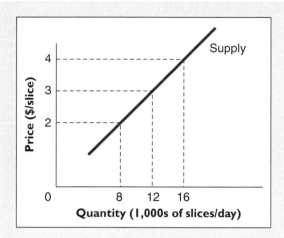

FIGURE 3.2
The Daily Supply Curve of Pizza in Chicago.
At higher prices, sellers generally offer more units for sale.

The fact that the supply curve slopes upward may be seen as a consequence of the Low-Hanging-Fruit Principle, discussed in the preceding chapter. This principle tells us that as we expand the production of pizza, we turn first to those whose opportunity costs of producing pizza are lowest, and only then to others with higher opportunity costs.

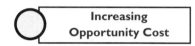

Like the demand curve, the supply curve can be interpreted either horizontally or vertically. Under the horizontal interpretation, we begin with a price, then go over to the supply curve to read the quantity that sellers wish to sell at that price on the horizontal axis. For instance, at a price of $2 per slice, sellers in Figure 3.2 wish to sell 8,000 slices per day.

Under the vertical interpretation, we begin with a quantity, then go up to the supply curve to read the corresponding marginal cost on the vertical axis. Thus, if sellers in Figure 3.2 are currently supplying 12,000 slices per day, the opportunity cost of the marginal seller is $3 per slice. In other words, the supply curve tells us that the marginal cost of producing the 12,000th slice of pizza is $3. (If someone could produce a 12,001st slice for less than $3, she would have an incentive to supply it, so the quantity of pizza supplied at $3 per slice would not have been 12,000 slices per day to begin with.) By similar reasoning, when the quantity of pizza supplied is 16,000 slices per day, the marginal cost of producing another slice must be $4. The **seller's reservation price** for selling an additional unit of a good is her marginal cost of producing that good. It is the smallest dollar amount for which she would not be worse off if she sold an additional unit.

seller's reservation price the smallest dollar amount for which a seller would be willing to sell an additional unit, generally equal to marginal cost

EXERCISE 3.2

In Figure 3.2, what is the marginal cost of a slice of pizza when the quantity of pizza sold is 10,000 slices per day? For the same supply curve, what will be the quantity of pizza supplied at a price of $3.50 per slice?

RECAP	DEMAND AND SUPPLY CURVES

The *market* for a good consists of the actual and potential buyers and sellers of that good. For any given price, the *demand curve* shows the quantity that demanders would be willing to buy and the *supply curve* shows the quantity that suppliers of the good would be willing to sell. Suppliers are willing to sell more at higher prices (supply curves slope upward) and demanders are willing to buy less at higher prices (demand curves slope downward).

MARKET EQUILIBRIUM

equilibrium a system is in equilibrium when there is no tendency for it to change

The concept of **equilibrium** is employed in both the physical and social sciences, and it is of central importance in economic analysis. In general, a system is in equilibrium when all forces at work within the system are canceled by others, resulting in a balanced or unchanging situation. In physics, for example, a ball hanging from a spring is said to be in equilibrium when the spring has stretched sufficiently that the upward force it exerts on the ball is exactly counterbalanced by the downward force of gravity. In economics, a market is said to be in equilibrium when no participant in the market has any reason to alter his or her behavior, so that there is no tendency for production or prices in that market to change.

equilibrium price and ***equilibrium quantity*** the values of price and quantity for which quantity supplied and quantity demanded are equal

If we want to determine the final position of a ball hanging from a spring, we need to find the point at which the forces of gravity and spring tension are balanced and the system is in equilibrium. Similarly, if we want to find the price at which a good will sell (which we will call the **equilibrium price**) and the quantity of it that will be sold (the **equilibrium quantity**), we need to find the equilibrium in the market for that good. The basic tools for finding the equilibrium in a market for a good are the supply and demand curves for that good. For reasons that we will explain, the equilibrium price and equilibrium quantity of a good are the price and quantity at which the supply and demand curves for the good intersect. For the hypothetical supply and demand curves shown earlier for the pizza market in Chicago, the equilibrium price will therefore be $3 per slice, and the equilibrium quantity of pizza sold will be 12,000 slices per day, as shown in Figure 3.3.

In Figure 3.3, note that at the equilibrium price of $3 per slice, both sellers and buyers are "satisfied" in the following sense: Buyers are buying exactly the quantity of pizza they wish to buy at that price (12,000 slices per day) and sellers are selling exactly the quantity of pizza they wish to sell (also 12,000 slices per day). And since they are satisfied in this sense, neither buyers nor sellers face any incentives to change their behavior.

market equilibrium occurs in a market when all buyers and sellers are satisfied with their respective quantities at the market price

Note the limited sense of the term "satisfied" in the definition of **market equilibrium**. It doesn't mean that sellers would not be pleased to receive a price higher than the equilibrium price. Rather, it means only that they're able to sell all they wish to sell at that price. Similarly, to say that buyers are satisfied at the equilibrium price doesn't mean that they would not be happy to pay less than the equilibrium price. Rather, it means only that they're able to buy exactly as many units of the good as they wish to at the equilibrium price.

Note also that if the price of pizza in our Chicago market were anything other than $3 per slice, either buyers or sellers would be frustrated. Suppose, for example, that the price of pizza were $4 per slice, as shown in Figure 3.4. At that price, buyers wish to buy only 8,000 slices per day, but sellers wish to sell 16,000. And since no one can force someone to buy a slice of pizza against her wishes, this means that

FIGURE 3.3
The Equilibrium Price and Quantity of Pizza in Chicago.
The equilibrium quantity and price of a product are the values that correspond to the intersection of the supply and demand curves for that product.

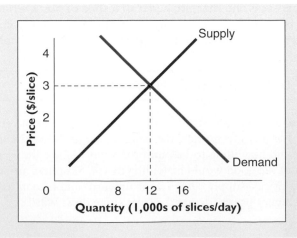

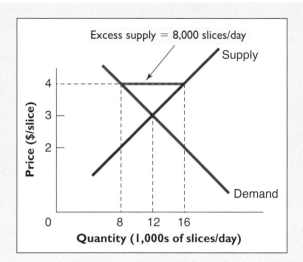

FIGURE 3.4
Excess Supply.
When price exceeds the equilibrium price, there is excess supply, or surplus, the difference between quantity supplied and quantity demanded.

buyers will buy only the 8,000 slices they wish to buy. So when the price exceeds the equilibrium price, it is sellers who end up being frustrated. At a price of $4 in this example, they are left with an **excess supply** of 8,000 slices per day.

Conversely, suppose that the price of pizza in our Chicago market were less than the equilibrium price—say, $2 per slice. As shown in Figure 3.5, buyers want to buy 16,000 slices per day at that price, whereas sellers want to sell only 8,000. And since sellers cannot be forced to sell pizza against their wishes, this time it is the buyers who end up being frustrated. At a price of $2 per slice in this example, they experience an **excess demand** of 8,000 slices per day.

An extraordinary feature of private markets for goods and services is their automatic tendency to gravitate toward their respective equilibrium prices and quantities. This tendency is a simple consequence of the Incentive Principle. The mechanisms by which the adjustment happens are implicit in our definitions of excess supply and excess demand. Suppose, for example, that the price of pizza in our hypothetical market was $4 per slice, leading to excess supply as shown in Figure 3.4. Because sellers are frustrated in the sense of wanting to sell more pizza than buyers wish to buy, sellers have an incentive to take whatever steps they can to increase their sales. The simplest strategy available to them is to cut their price slightly. Thus, if one seller reduced his price from $4 to, say, $3.95 per slice, he would attract many of the buyers who had been paying $4 per slice for pizza supplied by other sellers. Those sellers, in order to recover their lost business, would then have an incentive to match the price cut. But notice that if all sellers lowered

excess supply the amount by which quantity supplied exceeds quantity demanded when the price of a good exceeds the equilibrium price

excess demand the amount by which quantity demanded exceeds quantity supplied when the price of a good lies below the equilibrium price

Incentive

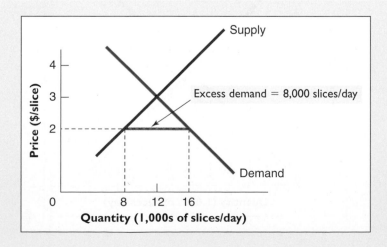

FIGURE 3.5
Excess Demand.
When price lies below the equilibrium price, there is excess demand, the difference between quantity demanded and quantity supplied.

their prices to $3.95 per slice, there would still be considerable excess supply. So sellers would face continuing incentives to cut their prices. This pressure to cut prices will not go away until price falls all the way to $3 per slice.

Conversely, suppose that price starts out less than the equilibrium price—say, $2 per slice. This time it is buyers who are frustrated. A person who can't get all the pizza he wants at a price of $2 per slice has an incentive to offer a higher price, hoping to obtain pizza that would otherwise have been sold to other buyers. And sellers, for their part, will be only too happy to post higher prices as long as queues of frustrated buyers remain.

The upshot is that price has a tendency to gravitate to its equilibrium level under conditions of either excess supply or excess demand. And when price reaches its equilibrium level, both buyers and sellers are satisfied in the technical sense of being able to buy or sell precisely the amounts of their choosing.

Samples of points on the demand and supply curves of a pizza market are provided in Table 3.1. Graph the demand and supply curves for this market and find its equilibrium price and quantity.

TABLE 3.1
Points along the Demand and Supply Curves of a Pizza Market

Demand for Pizza		Supply of Pizza	
Price ($/slice)	Quantity demanded (1,000s of slices/day)	Price ($/slice)	Quantity supplied (1,000s of slices/day)
1	8	1	2
2	6	2	4
3	4	3	6
4	2	4	8

The points in the table are plotted in Figure 3.6 and then joined to indicate the supply and demand curves for this market. These curves intersect to yield an equilibrium price of $2.50 per slice and an equilibrium quantity of 5,000 slices per day.

FIGURE 3.6
Graphing Supply and Demand and Finding the Equilibrium Price and Quantity.
To graph the demand and supply curves, plot the relevant points given in the table and then join them with a line. The equilibrium price and quantity occur at the intersection of these curves.

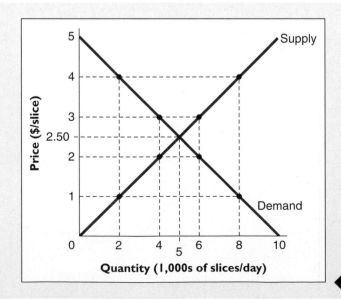

We emphasize that market equilibrium does not necessarily produce an ideal outcome for all market participants. Thus, in the example just considered, market participants are satisfied with the amount of pizza they buy and sell at a price of $2.50 per slice, but for a poor buyer this may signify little more than that he *can't* buy additional pizza without sacrificing other more highly valued purchases.

Indeed, buyers with extremely low incomes often have difficulty purchasing even basic goods and services, which has prompted governments in almost every society to attempt to ease the burdens of the poor. Yet the laws of supply and demand cannot simply be repealed by an act of the legislature. In the next section, we will see that when legislators attempt to prevent markets from reaching their equilibrium prices and quantities, they often do more harm than good.

RENT CONTROLS RECONSIDERED

Consider again the market for rental housing units in New York City and suppose that the demand and supply curves for one-bedroom apartments are as shown in Figure 3.7. This market, left alone, would reach an equilibrium monthly rent of $1,600, at which 2 million one-bedroom apartments would be rented. Both landlords and tenants would be satisfied, in the sense that they would not wish to rent either more or fewer units at that price.

This would not necessarily mean, of course, that all is well and good. Many potential tenants, for example, might simply be unable to afford a rent of $1,600 per month and thus be forced to remain homeless (or to move out of the city to a cheaper location). Suppose that, acting purely out of benign motives, legislators made it unlawful for landlords to charge more than $800 per month for one-bedroom apartments. Their stated aim in enacting this law was that no person should have to remain homeless because decent housing was unaffordable.

But note in Figure 3.8 that when rents for one-bedroom apartments are prevented from rising above $800 per month, landlords are willing to supply only 1 million apartments per month, 1 million fewer than at the equilibrium monthly rent of $1,600. Note also that at the controlled rent of $800 per month, tenants want to rent 3 million one-bedroom apartments per month. (For example, many people who would have decided to live in New Jersey rather than pay $1,600 a month in New York will now choose to live in the city.) So when rents are prevented from rising above $800 per month, we see an excess demand for one-bedroom apartments of 2 million units each month. Put another way, the rent controls result in a housing shortage of 2 million units each month. What is more, the number of apartments actually available *declines* by 1 million units per month.

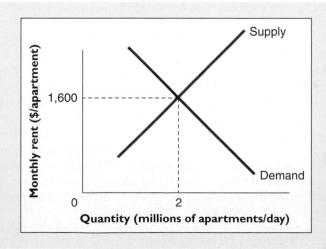

FIGURE 3.7
An Unregulated Housing Market.
For the supply and demand curves shown, the equilibrium monthly rent is $1,600 and 2 million apartments will be rented at that price.

FIGURE 3.8
Rent Controls.
When rents are prohibited from rising to the equilibrium level, the result is excess demand in the housing market.

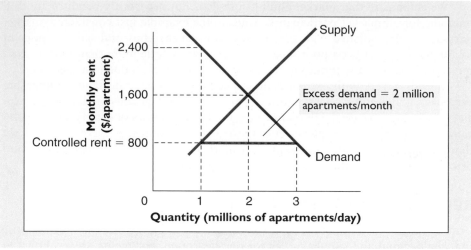

If the housing market were completely unregulated, the immediate response to such a high level of excess demand would be for rents to rise sharply. But here the law prevents them from rising above $800. Many other ways exist, however, in which the pressures of excess demand can make themselves felt. For instance, owners will quickly learn that they are free to spend less on maintaining the quality of their rental units. After all, if there are scores of renters knocking at the door of each vacant apartment, a landlord has considerable room to maneuver. Leaking pipes, peeling paint, broken furnaces, and other problems are less likely to receive prompt attention—or, indeed, any attention at all—when rents are set well below market-clearing levels.

Nor are reduced availability of apartments and poorer maintenance of existing apartments the only difficulties. With an offering of only 1 million apartments per month, we see in Figure 3.8 that there are renters who would be willing to pay as much as $2,400 per month for an apartment. As the Incentive Principle suggests, this pressure will almost always find ways, legal or illegal, of expressing itself. In New York City, for example, it is not uncommon to see "finder's fees" or "key deposits" as high as several thousand dollars. Owners who cannot charge a market-clearing rent for their apartments also have the option of converting them to condominiums or co-ops, which enables them to sell their assets for prices much closer to their true economic value.

Even when rent-controlled apartment owners do not hike their prices in these various ways, serious misallocations result. For instance, ill-suited roommates often remain together despite their constant bickering because each is reluctant to reenter the housing market. Or a widow might steadfastly remain in her seven-room apartment even after her children have left home because it is much cheaper than alternative dwellings not covered by rent control. It would be much better for all concerned if she relinquished that space to a larger family that valued it more highly. But under rent controls, she has no economic incentive to do so.

There is also another more insidious cost of rent controls. In markets without rent controls, landlords cannot discriminate against potential tenants on the basis of race, religion, sexual orientation, physical disability, or national origin without suffering an economic penalty. Refusal to rent to members of specific groups would reduce the demand for their apartments, which would mean having to accept lower rents. When rents are artificially pegged below their equilibrium level, however, the resulting excess demand for apartments enables landlords to engage in discrimination with no further economic penalty.

Rent controls are not the only instance in which governments have attempted to repeal the law of supply and demand in the interest of helping the poor. During the late 1970s, for example, the federal government tried to hold the price of gasoline below its equilibrium level out of concern that high gasoline prices imposed unacceptable hardships on low-income drivers. As with controls in the rental housing market, unintended consequences of price controls in the gasoline market made the policy an extremely costly way of trying to aid the poor. For example, gasoline shortages resulted in long lines at the pumps, a waste not only of valuable time, but also of gasoline as cars sat idling for extended periods.

In their opposition to rent controls and similar measures, are economists revealing a total lack of concern for the poor? Although this claim is sometimes made by those who don't understand the issues, or who stand to benefit in some way from government regulations, there is little justification for it. *Economists simply realize that there are much more effective ways to help poor people than to try to give them apartments and other goods at artificially low prices.*

One straightforward approach would be to give the poor additional income and let them decide for themselves how to spend it. True, there are also practical difficulties involved in transferring additional purchasing power into the hands of the poor—most importantly, the difficulty of targeting cash to the genuinely needy without weakening others' incentives to fend for themselves. But there are practical ways to overcome this difficulty. For example, for far less than the waste caused by price controls, the government could afford generous subsidies to the wages of the working poor and could sponsor public-service employment for those who are unable to find jobs in the private sector.

Regulations that peg prices below equilibrium levels have far-reaching effects on market outcomes. The following exercise asks you to consider what happens when a price control is established at a level above the equilibrium price.

EXERCISE 3.3

In the rental housing market whose demand and supply curves are shown below, what will be the effect of a law that prevents rents from rising above $1,200 per month?

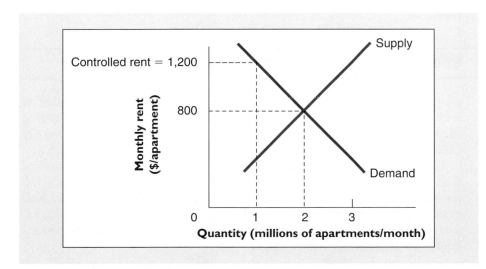

PIZZA PRICE CONTROLS?

The sources of the contrast between the rent-controlled housing market and the largely unregulated food markets in New York City can be seen more vividly by trying to imagine what would happen if concern for the poor led the city's leaders to implement price controls on pizza. Suppose, for example, that the supply and

FIGURE 3.9
Price Controls in the Pizza Market.
A price ceiling below the equilibrium price of pizza would result in excess demand for pizza.

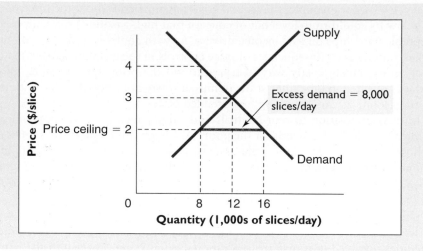

price ceiling a maximum allowable price, specified by law

EN 3

demand curves for pizza are as shown in Figure 3.9 and that the city imposes a **price ceiling** of $2 per slice, making it unlawful to charge more than that amount. At $2 per slice, buyers want to buy 16,000 slices per day, but sellers want to sell only 8,000.

At a price of $2 per slice, every pizza restaurant in the city will have long queues of buyers trying unsuccessfully to purchase pizza. Frustrated buyers will behave rudely to clerks, who will respond in kind. Friends of restaurant managers will begin to get preferential treatment. Devious pricing strategies will begin to emerge (such as the $2 slice of pizza sold in combination with a $5 cup of Coke). Pizza will be made from poorer-quality ingredients. Rumors will begin to circulate about sources of black-market pizza. And so on.

The very idea of not being able to buy a pizza seems absurd, yet precisely such things happen routinely in markets in which prices are held below the equilibrium levels. For example, prior to the collapse of communist governments, it was considered normal in those countries for people to stand in line for hours to buy basic goods, while the politically connected had first choice of those goods that were available.

RECAP	MARKET EQUILIBRIUM

Market equilibrium, the situation in which all buyers and sellers are satisfied with their respective quantities at the market price, occurs at the intersection of the supply and demand curves. The corresponding price and quantity are called the *equilibrium price* and the *equilibrium quantity*.

Unless prevented by regulation, prices and quantities are driven toward their equilibrium values by the actions of buyers and sellers. If the price is initially too high, so that there is excess supply, frustrated sellers will cut their price in order to sell more. If the price is initially too low, so that there is excess demand, competition among buyers drives the price upward. This process continues until equilibrium is reached.

PREDICTING AND EXPLAINING CHANGES IN PRICES AND QUANTITIES

If we know how the factors that govern supply and demand curves are changing, we can make informed predictions about how prices and the corresponding quantities will change. But when describing changing circumstances in the marketplace,

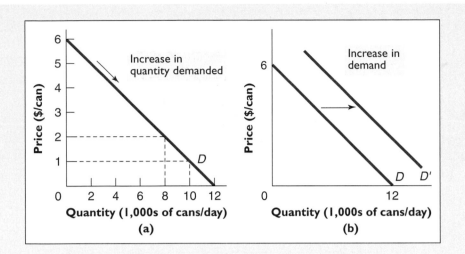

FIGURE 3.10
An Increase in the Quantity Demanded versus an Increase in Demand.
(a) An increase in quantity demanded describes a downward movement along the demand curve as price falls. (b) An increase in demand describes an outward shift of the demand curve.

we must take care to recognize some important terminological distinctions. For example, we must distinguish between the meanings of the seemingly similar expressions **change in the quantity demanded** and **change in demand**. When we speak of a "change in the quantity demanded," this means the change in the quantity that people wish to buy that occurs in response to a change in price. For instance, Figure 3.10(a) depicts an increase in the quantity demanded that occurs in response to a reduction in the price of tuna. When the price falls from $2 to $1 per can, the quantity demanded rises from 8,000 to 10,000 cans per day. By contrast, when we speak of a "change in demand," this means a *shift in the entire demand curve*. For example, Figure 3.10(b) depicts an increase in demand, meaning that at every price the quantity demanded is higher than before. In summary, a "change in the quantity demanded" refers to a movement *along* the demand curve and a "change in demand" means a *shift* of the entire curve.

A similar terminological distinction applies on the supply side of the market. A **change in supply** means a shift in the entire supply curve, whereas a **change in the quantity supplied** refers to a movement along the supply curve.

Alfred Marshall's supply and demand model is one of the most useful tools of the economic naturalist. Once we understand the forces that govern the placements of supply and demand curves, we are suddenly in a position to make sense of a host of interesting observations in the world around us.

SHIFTS IN DEMAND

To get a better feel for how the supply and demand model enables us to predict and explain price and quantity movements, it is helpful to begin with a few simple examples. The first one illustrates a shift in demand that results from events outside the particular market itself.

What will happen to the equilibrium price and quantity of tennis balls if court rental fees decline?

Let the initial supply and demand curves for tennis balls be as shown by the curves *S* and *D* in Figure 3.11, where the resulting equilibrium price and quantity are $1 per ball and 40 million balls per month, respectively. Tennis courts and tennis balls are what economists call **complements**, goods that are more valuable when used in combination than when used alone. Tennis balls, for example, would be of little value if there were no tennis courts on which to play. (Tennis balls would still have *some* value even without courts—for example, to the parents who pitch them to their children for batting practice.) As tennis courts become cheaper to use, people

change in the quantity demanded a movement along the demand curve that occurs in response to a change in price

change in demand a shift of the entire demand curve

change in supply a shift of the entire supply curve

change in the quantity supplied a movement along the supply curve that occurs in response to a change in price

complements two goods are complements in consumption if an increase in the price of one causes a leftward shift in the demand curve for the other (or if a decrease causes a rightward shift)

FIGURE 3.11

The Effect on the Market for Tennis Balls of a Decline in Court-Rental Fees.

When the price of a complement falls, demand shifts right, causing equilibrium price and quantity to rise.

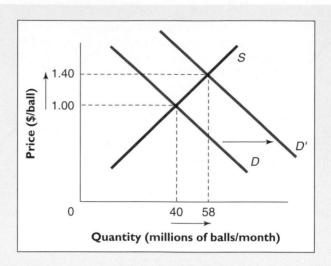

will respond by playing more tennis, and this will increase their demand for tennis balls. A decline in court-rental fees will thus shift the demand curve for tennis balls rightward to D'. (A "rightward shift" of a demand curve also can be described as an "upward shift." These distinctions correspond, respectively, to the horizontal and vertical interpretations of the demand curve.)

Note in Figure 3.11 that for the illustrative demand shift shown, the new equilibrium price of tennis balls, $1.40, is higher than the original price and the new equilibrium quantity, 58 million balls per month, is higher than the original quantity. ◆

What will happen to the equilibrium price and quantity of overnight letter delivery service as the price of internet access falls?

Suppose the initial supply and demand curves for overnight letter deliveries are as shown by the curves S and D in Figure 3.12 and that the resulting equilibrium price and quantity are denoted P and Q. E-mail messages and overnight letters are examples of what economists call **substitutes**, meaning that, in many applications at least, the two serve similar functions for people. (Many noneconomists would call them substitutes, too. Economists don't *always* choose obscure terms for important concepts!) When two goods or services are substitutes, a decrease in the price of one will cause a leftward shift in the demand curve for the other. (A "leftward shift" in

substitutes two goods are substitutes in consumption if an increase in the price of one causes a rightward shift in the demand curve for the other (or if a decrease causes a leftward shift).

FIGURE 3.12

The Effect on the Market for Overnight Letter Delivery of a Decline in the Price of Internet Access.

When the price of a substitute falls, demand shifts left, causing equilibrium price and quantity to fall.

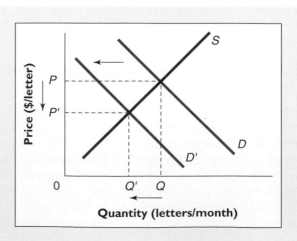

a demand curve can also be described as a "downward shift.") Diagrammatically, the demand curve for overnight delivery service shifts from D to D' in Figure 3.12.

As the figure shows, both the new equilibrium price, P', and the new equilibrium quantity, Q', are lower than the initial values, P and Q. Cheaper internet access probably won't put Federal Express and UPS out of business, but it will definitely cost them many customers. ◆

To summarize, economists define goods as substitutes if an increase in the price of one causes a rightward shift in the demand curve for the other. By contrast, goods are complements if an increase in the price of one causes a leftward shift in the demand curve for the other.

The concepts of substitutes and complements enable you to answer questions like the one posed in the following exercise.

EXERCISE 3.4

How will a decline in airfares affect intercity bus fares and the price of hotel rooms in resort communities?

Demand curves are shifted not just by changes in the prices of substitutes and complements but also by other factors that change the amounts that people are willing to pay for a given good or service. One of the most important such factors is income.

When the federal government implements a large pay increase for its employees, why do rents for apartments located near Washington Metro stations go up relative to rents for apartments located far away from Metro stations?

For the citizens of Washington, D.C., a substantial proportion of whom are government employees, it is more convenient to live in an apartment located one block from the nearest subway station than to live in one that is 20 blocks away. Conveniently located apartments thus command relatively high rents. Suppose the initial demand and supply curves for such apartments are as shown in Figure 3.13. Following a federal pay raise, some government employees who live in less convenient apartments will be willing and able to use part of their extra income to bid for more conveniently located apartments, and those who already live in such apartments will be willing and able to pay more to keep them. The effect of the pay raise is thus to shift the demand curve for conveniently located apartments to the right, as indicated by the demand curve labeled D' in Figure 3.13. As a result, both the equilibrium price and quantity of such apartments, P' and Q', will be higher than before.

Example 3.1
THE ECONOMIC NATURALIST

Who gets to live in the most conveniently located apartments?

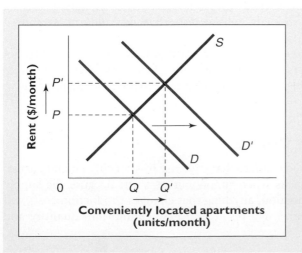

**FIGURE 3.13
The Effect of a Federal Pay Raise on the Rent for Conveniently Located Apartments in Washington, D.C.**
An increase in income shifts demand for a normal good to the right, causing equilibrium price and quantity to rise.

Incentive

It might seem natural to ask how there could be an increase in the number of conveniently located apartments, which might appear to be fixed by the constraints of geography. But the Incentive Principle reminds us never to underestimate the ingenuity of sellers when they confront an opportunity to make money by supplying more of something that people want. For example, if rents rose sufficiently, some landlords might respond by converting warehouse space to residential use. Or perhaps people with cars who do not place high value on living near a subway station might sell their apartments to landlords, thereby freeing them for people eager to rent them. (Note that these responses constitute movements along the supply curve of conveniently located apartments, as opposed to shifts in that supply curve.)

When incomes increase, the demand curves for most goods will behave like the demand curve for conveniently located apartments, and in recognition of that fact, economists have chosen to call such goods **normal goods**.

normal good one whose demand curve shifts rightward when the incomes of buyers increase and leftward when the incomes of buyers decrease

Not all goods are normal goods, however. In fact, the demand curves for some goods actually shift leftward when income goes up; such goods are called **inferior goods**.

When would having more money tend to make you want to buy less of something? In general, this will happen in the case of goods for which there exist attractive substitutes that sell for only slightly higher prices. Apartments in an unsafe, inconveniently located neighborhood are an example. Most residents would choose to move out of such neighborhoods as soon as they could afford to, which means that an increase in income would cause the demand for such apartments to shift leftward.

inferior good one whose demand curve shifts leftward when the incomes of buyers increase and rightward when the incomes of buyers decrease

EXERCISE 3.5

How will a large pay increase for federal employees affect the rents for apartments located far away from Washington Metro stations?

Ground beef with high fat content is another example of an inferior good. For health reasons, most people prefer grades of meat with low fat content, and when they do buy high-fat meats it is usually a sign of budgetary pressure. When people in this situation receive higher incomes, they usually switch quickly to leaner grades of meat.

Cost-Benefit

Preferences, or tastes, are another important factor that determines whether the purchase of a given good will satisfy the Cost-Benefit Principle. Steven Spielberg's film *Jurassic Park* appeared to kindle a powerful, if previously latent, preference among children for toy dinosaurs. When this film was first released, the demand for such toys shifted sharply to the right. And the same children who couldn't find enough dinosaur toys suddenly seemed to lose interest in toy designs involving horses and other present-day animals, whose respective demand curves shifted sharply to the left.

Expectations about the future are another factor that may cause demand curves to shift. If Apple Macintosh users hear a credible rumor, for example, that a cheaper or significantly upgraded model will be introduced next month, the demand curve for the current model is likely to shift leftward.

SHIFTS IN THE SUPPLY CURVE

The preceding examples involved changes that gave rise to shifts in demand curves. Next, we'll look at what happens when supply curves shift. Because the supply curve is based on costs of production, anything that changes production costs will shift the supply curve, and hence will result in a new equilibrium quantity and price.

What will happen to the equilibrium price and quantity of skateboards if the price of fiberglass, a substance used for making skateboards, rises?

Suppose the initial supply and demand curves for skateboards are as shown by the curves *S* and *D* in Figure 3.14, resulting in an equilibrium price and quantity of

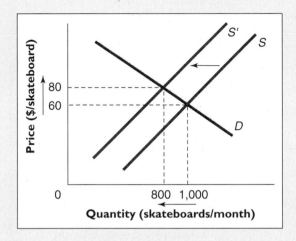

FIGURE 3.14
The Effect on the Skateboard Market of an Increase in the Price of Fiberglass.
When input prices rise, supply shifts left, causing equilibrium price to rise and equilibrium quantity to fall.

$60 per skateboard and 1,000 skateboards per month, respectively. Since fiberglass is one of the ingredients used to produce skateboards, the effect of an increase in the price of fiberglass is to raise the marginal cost of producing skateboards. How will this affect the supply curve of skateboards? Recall that the supply curve is upward-sloping because when the price of skateboards is low, only those potential sellers whose marginal cost of making skateboards is low can sell boards profitably, whereas at higher prices, those with higher marginal costs also can enter the market profitably (again, the Low-Hanging-Fruit Principle). So if the cost of one of the ingredients used to produce skateboards rises, the number of potential sellers who can profitably sell skateboards at any given price will fall. And this, in turn, implies a leftward shift in the supply curve for skateboards. Note that a "leftward shift" in a supply curve also can be viewed as an "upward shift" in the same curve. The first corresponds to the horizontal interpretation of the supply curve, while the second corresponds to the vertical interpretation. We will use these expressions to mean exactly the same thing. The new supply curve (after the price of fiberglass rises) is the curve labeled *S'* in Figure 3.14.

Increasing Opportunity Cost

Does an increase in the cost of fiberglass have any effect on the demand curve for skateboards? The demand curve tells us how many skateboards buyers wish to purchase at each price. Any given buyer is willing to purchase a skateboard if his reservation price for it exceeds its market price. And since each buyer's reservation price, which is based on the benefits of owning a skateboard, does not depend on the price of fiberglass, there should be no shift in the demand curve for skateboards.

In Figure 3.14, we can now see what happens when the supply curve shifts leftward and the demand curve remains unchanged. For the illustrative supply curve shown, the new equilibrium price of skateboards, $80, is higher than the original price and the new equilibrium quantity, 800 per month, is lower than the original quantity. (These new equilibrium values are merely illustrative. There is insufficient information provided in the example to determine their exact values.) People who don't place a value of at least $80 on owning a skateboard will choose to spend their money on something else. ◆

The effects on equilibrium price and quantity run in the opposite direction whenever marginal costs of production decline, as illustrated in the next example.

What will happen to the equilibrium price and quantity of new houses if the wage rate of carpenters falls?

Suppose the initial supply and demand curves for new houses are as shown by the curves S and D in Figure 3.15, resulting in an equilibrium price of $120,000 per

FIGURE 3.15
The Effect on the Market for New Houses of a Decline in Carpenters' Wage Rates.
When input prices fall, supply shifts right, causing equilibrium price to fall and equilibrium quantity to rise.

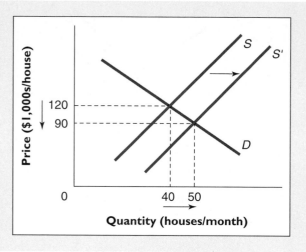

house and an equilibrium quantity of 40 houses per month. A decline in the wage rate of carpenters reduces the marginal cost of making new houses, and this means that, for any given price of houses, more builders can profitably serve the market than before. Diagrammatically, this means a rightward shift in the supply curve of houses, from S to S'. (A "rightward shift" in the supply curve also can be described as a "downward shift.")

Does a decrease in the wage rate of carpenters have any effect on the demand curve for houses? The demand curve tells us how many houses buyers wish to purchase at each price. Because carpenters are now earning less than before, the maximum amount that they are willing to pay for houses may fall, which would imply a leftward shift in the demand curve for houses. But because carpenters make up only a tiny fraction of all potential home buyers, we may assume that this shift is negligible. Thus, a reduction in carpenters' wages produces a significant rightward shift in the supply curve of houses, but no appreciable shift in the demand curve.

We see from Figure 3.15 that the new equilibrium price, $90,000 per house, is lower than the original price and the new equilibrium quantity, 50 houses per month, is higher than the original quantity. ◆

Both of the preceding examples involved changes in the cost of an ingredient, or input, in the production of the good in question—fiberglass in the production of skateboards and carpenters' labor in the production of houses. As the following example illustrates, supply curves also shift when technology changes.

Example 3.2
THE ECONOMIC NATURALIST

Why do major term papers go through so many more revisions today than in the 1970s?

Students in the dark days before word processors were in widespread use could not make even minor revisions in their term papers without having to retype their entire manuscripts from scratch. The availability of word-processing technology has, of course, radically changed the picture. Instead of having to retype the entire draft, now only the changes need be entered.

In Figure 3.16, the curves labeled S and D depict the supply and demand curves for re-visions in the days before word processing, and the curve S' depicts the supply curve for revisions today. As the diagram shows, the result is not only a sharp decline in the price per revision, but also a corresponding increase in the equilibrium number of revisions.

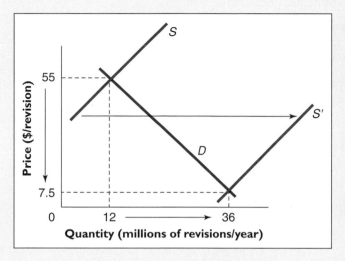

FIGURE 3.16
The Effect of Technical Change on the Market for Term-Paper Revisions.
When a new technology reduces the cost of production, supply shifts right, causing equilibrium price to fall and equilibrium quantity to rise.

Why does written work go through so many more revisions now than in the 1970s?

Note that in the preceding discussion we implicitly assumed that students pur-chased typing services in a market. In fact, however, many students type their own term papers. Does that make a difference? Even if no money actually changes hands, students pay a price when they revise their term papers—namely, the oppor-tunity cost of the time it takes to perform that task. Because technology has radi-cally reduced that cost, we would expect to see a large increase in the number of term-paper revisions even if most students type their own work.

Changes in input prices and technology are two of the most important factors that give rise to shifts in supply curves. In the case of agricultural commodities, weather may be another important factor, with favorable conditions shifting the supply curves of such products to the right and unfavorable conditions shifting them to the left. (Weather also may affect the supply curves of nonagricultural products through its effects on the national transportation system.) Expectations of future price changes also may shift current supply curves, as when the expectation of poor crops from a current drought causes suppliers to withhold supplies from ex-isting stocks in the hope of selling at higher prices in the future. Changes in the number of sellers in the market also can cause supply curves to shift.

FOUR SIMPLE RULES

For supply and demand curves that have the conventional slopes (upward-sloping for supply curves, downward-sloping for demand curves), the preceding examples illustrate the four basic rules that govern how shifts in supply and demand affect equilibrium prices and quantities. These rules are summarized in Figure 3.17.

RECAP	FACTORS THAT SHIFT SUPPLY AND DEMAND

Factors that cause an increase (rightward or upward shift) in demand:

1. A decrease in the price of complements to the good or service.

2. An increase in the price of substitutes for the good or service.

3. An increase in income (for a normal good).

4. An increased preference by demanders for the good or service.

5. An increase in the population of potential buyers.

6. An expectation of higher prices in the future.

When these factors move in the opposite direction, demand will shift left.

Factors that cause an increase (rightward or downward shift) in supply:

1. A decrease in the cost of materials, labor, or other inputs used in the production of the good or service.

2. An improvement in technology that reduces the cost of producing the good or service.

3. An improvement in the weather (especially for agricultural products).

4. An increase in the number of suppliers.

5. An expectation of lower prices in the future.

When these factors move in the opposite direction, supply will shift left.

FIGURE 3.17
Four Rules Governing the Effects of Supply and Demand Shifts.

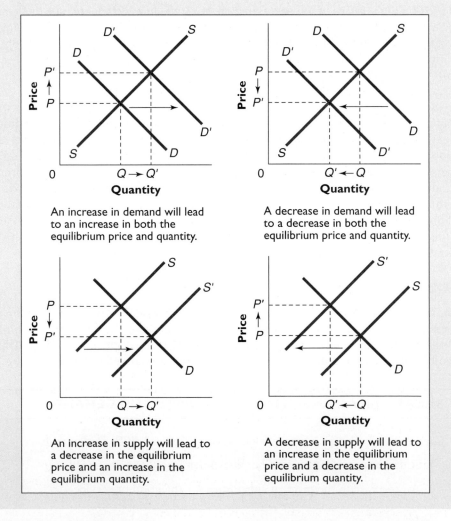

An increase in demand will lead to an increase in both the equilibrium price and quantity.

A decrease in demand will lead to a decrease in both the equilibrium price and quantity.

An increase in supply will lead to a decrease in the equilibrium price and an increase in the equilibrium quantity.

A decrease in supply will lead to an increase in the equilibrium price and a decrease in the equilibrium quantity.

The qualitative rules summarized in Figure 3.17 hold for supply or demand shifts of any magnitude, provided the curves have their conventional slopes. But as the next example demonstrates, when both supply and demand curves shift at the same time, the direction in which equilibrium price or quantity changes will depend on the relative magnitudes of the shifts.

How do shifts in *both* demand and supply affect equilibrium quantities and prices?

What will happen to the equilibrium price and quantity in the corn tortilla chip market if both of the following events occur: (1) researchers prove that the oils in which tortilla chips are fried are harmful to human health and (2) the price of corn harvesting equipment falls?

The conclusion regarding the health effects of the oils will shift the demand for tortilla chips to the left because many people who once bought chips in the belief that they were healthful will now switch to other foods. The decline in the price of harvesting equipment will shift the supply of chips to the right because additional farmers will now find it profitable to enter the corn market. In Figures 3.18(a) and 3.18(b), the original supply and demand curves are denoted by S and D, while the new curves are denoted by S' and D'. Note that in both panels, the shifts lead to a decline in the equilibrium price of chips.

But note also that the effect of the shifts on equilibrium quantity cannot be determined without knowing their relative magnitudes. Taken separately, the demand shift causes a decline in equilibrium quantity, whereas the supply shift causes an increase in equilibrium quantity. The net effect of the two shifts thus depends on which of the individual effects is larger. In Figure 3.18(a), the demand shift dominates, so equilibrium quantity declines. In Figure 3.18(b), the supply shift dominates, so equilibrium quantity goes up.

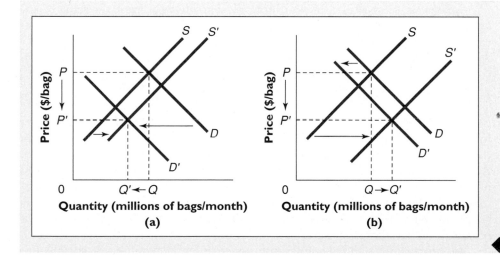

FIGURE 3.18
The Effects of Simultaneous Shifts in Supply and Demand. When demand shifts left and supply shifts right, equilibrium price falls, but equilibrium quantity may either rise (b) or fall (a).

The following exercise asks you to consider a simple variation on the problem posed in the previous example.

EXERCISE 3.6

What will happen to the equilibrium price and quantity in the corn tortilla chip market if both of the following events occur: (1) researchers discover that a vitamin found in corn helps protect against cancer and heart disease and (2) a swarm of locusts destroys part of the corn crop?

Example 3.3

THE ECONOMIC NATURALIST

Why are some goods cheapest during the months of heaviest consumption, while others are most expensive during those months?

Why do the prices of some goods, like airline tickets to Europe, go up during the months of heaviest consumption, while others, like sweet corn, go down?

Seasonal price movements for airline tickets are primarily the result of seasonal variations in demand. Thus, ticket prices to Europe are highest during the summer months because the demand for tickets is highest during those months, as shown in Figure 3.19(a), where the w and s subscripts denote winter and summer values, respectively.

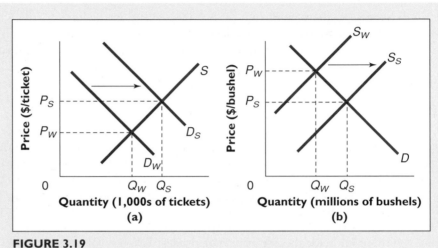

FIGURE 3.19
Seasonal Variation in the Air Travel and Corn Markets.
(a) Prices are highest during the period of heaviest consumption when heavy consumption is the result of high demand. (b) Prices are lowest during the period of heaviest consumption when heavy consumption is the result of high supply.

By contrast, seasonal price movements for sweet corn are primarily the result of seasonal variations in supply. The price of sweet corn is lowest in the summer months because its supply is highest during those months, as seen in Figure 3.19(b). ●

EFFICIENCY AND EQUILIBRIUM

Markets represent a highly effective system of allocating resources. When a market for a good is in equilibrium, the equilibrium price conveys important information to potential suppliers about the value that potential demanders place on that good. At the same time, the equilibrium price informs potential demanders about the opportunity cost of supplying the good. This rapid, two-way transmission of information is the reason that markets can coordinate an activity as complex as supplying New York City with food and drink, even though no one person or organization oversees the process.

But are the prices and quantities determined in market equilibrium socially optimal, in the sense of maximizing total economic surplus? That is, does equilibrium in unregulated markets always maximize the difference between the total benefits and total costs experienced by market participants? As we will see, the answer is "it depends": A market that is out of equilibrium, such as the rent-controlled New York housing market, always creates opportunities for individuals to arrange transactions that will increase their individual economic surplus. As we will see, however, a market for a good that is in equilibrium makes the largest possible contribution to total economic surplus only when its supply and demand curves fully reflect all costs and benefits associated with the production and consumption of that good.

CASH ON THE TABLE

In economics we assume that all exchange is purely voluntary. This means that a transaction cannot take place unless the buyer's reservation price for the good exceeds the seller's reservation price. When that condition is met and a transaction takes place, both parties receive an economic surplus. The **buyer's surplus** from the transaction is the difference between his reservation price and the price he actually pays. The **seller's surplus** is the difference between the price she receives and her reservation price. The **total surplus** from the transaction is the sum of the buyer's surplus and the seller's surplus. It is also equal to the difference between the buyer's reservation price and the seller's reservation price.

Suppose there is a potential buyer whose reservation price for an additional slice of pizza is $4 and a potential seller whose reservation price is only $2. If this buyer purchases a slice of pizza from this seller for $3, the total surplus generated by this exchange is $4 − $2 = $2, of which $4 − $3 = $1 is the buyer's surplus and $3 − $2 = $1 is the seller's surplus.

A regulation that prevents the price of a good from reaching its equilibrium level unnecessarily prevents exchanges of this sort from taking place, and in the process reduces total economic surplus. Consider again the effect of price controls imposed in the market for pizza. The demand curve in Figure 3.20 tells us that if a price ceiling of $2 per slice were imposed, only 8,000 slices of pizza per day would be sold. At that quantity, the vertical interpretations of the supply and demand curves tell us that a buyer would be willing to pay as much as $4 for an additional slice and that a seller would be willing to sell one for as little as $2. The difference— $2 per slice—is the additional economic surplus that would result if an additional slice were produced and sold. As noted earlier, an extra slice sold at a price of $3 would result in an additional $1 of economic surplus for both buyer and seller.

buyer's surplus the difference between the buyer's reservation price and the price he or she actually pays

seller's surplus the difference between the price received by the seller and his or her reservation price

total surplus the difference between the buyer's reservation price and the seller's reservation price

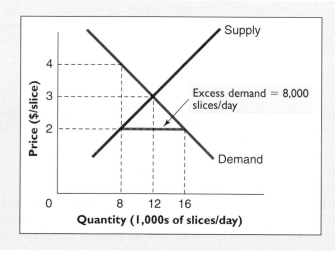

FIGURE 3.20
Price Controls in the Pizza Market.
A price ceiling below the equilibrium price of pizza would result in excess demand for pizza.

When a market is out of equilibrium, it is always possible to identify mutually beneficial exchanges of this sort. When people have failed to take advantage of all mutually beneficial exchanges, we often say that there is "**cash on the table**"—the economist's metaphor for unexploited opportunities. When the price in a market is below the equilibrium price, there is cash on the table because the reservation price of sellers (marginal cost) will always be lower than the reservation price of buyers. In the absence of a law preventing buyers paying more than $2 per slice, restaurant owners would quickly raise their prices and expand their production until the equilibrium price of $3 per slice was reached. At that price, buyers would be able to get precisely the 12,000 slices of pizza they want to buy each day. All mutually beneficial opportunities for exchange would have been exploited, leaving no more cash on the table.

cash on the table economic metaphor for unexploited gains from exchange

Incentive

With the Incentive Principle in mind, it should be no surprise that buyers and sellers in the marketplace have an uncanny ability to detect the presence of cash on the table. It is almost as if unexploited opportunities gave off some exotic scent triggering neurochemical explosions in the olfactory centers of their brains. The desire to scrape cash off the table and into their pockets is what drives sellers in each of New York City's thousands of individual food markets to work diligently to meet their customers' demands. That they succeed to a far higher degree than participants in the city's rent-controlled housing market is plainly evident. Whatever flaws it might have, the market system moves with considerably greater speed and agility than any centralized allocation mechanisms yet devised. But as we emphasize in the following section, this does not mean that markets *always* lead to the greatest good for all.

SMART FOR ONE, DUMB FOR ALL

The **socially optimal quantity** of any good is the quantity that maximizes the total economic surplus that results from producing and consuming the good. From the Cost-Benefit Principle, we know that we should keep expanding production of the good as long as its marginal benefit is at least as great as its marginal cost. This means that the socially optimal quantity is that level for which the marginal cost and marginal benefit of the good are the same.

Cost-Benefit

socially optimal quantity the quantity of a good that results in the maximum possible economic surplus from producing and consuming the good

efficiency (also called *economic efficiency*) occurs when all goods and services are produced and consumed at their respective socially optimal levels

When the quantity of a good is less than the socially optimal quantity, boosting its production will increase total economic surplus. By the same token, when the quantity of a good exceeds the socially optimal quantity, reducing its production will increase total economic surplus. **Economic efficiency**, or **efficiency**, occurs when all goods and services in the economy are produced and consumed at their respective socially optimal levels.

Efficiency is an important social goal. Failure to achieve efficiency means that total economic surplus is smaller than it could have been. Movements toward efficiency make the total economic pie larger, making it possible for everyone to have a larger slice. The importance of efficiency will be a recurring theme as we move forward, and we state it here as one of the core principles:

The Efficiency Principle: Efficiency is an important social goal because when the economic pie grows larger, everyone can have a larger slice.

Efficiency

Is the market equilibrium quantity of a good efficient? That is, does it maximize the total economic surplus received by participants in the market for that good? When the private market for a given good is in equilibrium, we can say that the cost *to the seller* of producing an additional unit of the good is the same as the benefit *to the buyer* of having an additional unit. If all costs of producing the good are borne directly by sellers, and if all benefits from the good accrue directly to buyers, it follows that the market equilibrium quantity of the good will equate the marginal cost and marginal benefit of the good. And this means that the equilibrium quantity also maximizes total economic surplus.

But sometimes the production of a good entails costs that fall on people other than those who sell the good. This will be true, for instance, for goods whose production generates significant levels of environmental pollution. As extra units of these goods are produced, the extra pollution harms other people besides sellers. In the market equilibrium for such goods, the benefit *to buyers* of the last good produced is, as before, equal to the cost incurred by sellers to produce that good. But since producing that good also imposed pollution costs on others, we know that the *full* marginal cost of the last unit produced—the seller's private marginal cost plus the marginal pollution cost borne by others—must be higher than the benefit of the last unit produced. So in this case the market equilibrium quantity of the good will be larger than the socially optimal quantity. Total economic surplus would be higher if output of the good were lower. Yet neither sellers nor buyers have any incentive to alter their behavior.

Another possibility is that people other than those who buy a good may receive significant benefits from it. For instance, when someone purchases a vaccination against measles from her doctor, she not only protects herself against measles, but she also makes it less likely that others will catch this disease. From the perspective of society as a whole, we should keep increasing the number of vaccinations until their marginal cost equals their marginal benefit. The marginal benefit of a vaccination is the value of the protection it provides the person vaccinated *plus* the value of the protection it provides all others. Private consumers, however, will choose to be vaccinated only if the marginal benefit *to them* exceeds the price of the vaccination. In this case, then, the market equilibrium quantity of vaccinations will be smaller than the quantity that maximizes total economic surplus. Again, however, individuals would have no incentive to alter their behavior.

Situations like the ones just discussed provide examples of behaviors that we may call "smart for one but dumb for all." In each case, the individual actors are behaving rationally. They are pursuing their goals as best they can, and yet there remain unexploited opportunities for gain from the point of view of the whole society. The difficulty is that these opportunities cannot be exploited by individuals acting alone. In subsequent chapters, we will see how people can often organize collectively to exploit such opportunities. For now, we simply summarize this discussion in the form of the following core principle:

The Equilibrium Principle (also called the "No-Cash-on-the-Table" Principle): A market in equilibrium leaves no unexploited opportunities for individuals but may not exploit all gains achievable through collective action.

Equilibrium

RECAP	MARKETS AND SOCIAL WELFARE

When the supply and demand curves for a good reflect all significant costs and benefits associated with the production and consumption of that good, the market equilibrium will result in the largest possible economic surplus. But if people other than buyers benefit from the good, or if people other than sellers bear costs because of it, market equilibrium need not result in the largest possible economic surplus.

▪ SUMMARY ▪

- Eighteenth-century economists tried to explain differences in the prices of goods by focusing on differences in their cost of production. But this approach cannot explain why a conveniently located house sells for more than one that is less conveniently located. Early nineteenth-century economists tried to explain price differences by focusing on differences in what buyers were willing to pay. But this approach cannot explain why the price of a lifesaving appendectomy is less than that of a surgical facelift. **LO3**

- Alfred Marshall's model of supply and demand explains why neither cost of production nor value to the

purchaser (as measured by willingness to pay) is, by itself, sufficient to explain why some goods are cheap and others are expensive. To explain variations in price, we must examine the interaction of cost and willingness to pay. As we've seen in this chapter, goods differ in price because of differences in their respective supply and demand curves. **LO3**

- The demand curve is a downward-sloping line that tells what quantity buyers will demand at any given price. The supply curve is an upward-sloping line that tells what quantity sellers will offer at any given price. Market equilibrium occurs when the quantity buyers demand at the market price is exactly the same as the quantity that sellers offer. The equilibrium price-quantity pair is the one at which the demand and supply curves intersect. In equilibrium, market price measures both the value of the last unit sold to buyers and the cost of the resources required to produce it.   **LO1, LO2**

- When the price of a good lies above its equilibrium value, there is an excess supply of that good. Excess supply motivates sellers to cut their prices and price continues to fall until the equilibrium price is reached. When price lies below its equilibrium value, there is excess demand. With excess demand, frustrated buyers are motivated to offer higher prices and the upward pressure on prices persists until equilibrium is reached. A remarkable feature of the market system is that, relying only on the tendency of people to respond in self-interested ways to market price signals, it somehow manages to coordinate the actions of literally billions of buyers and sellers worldwide. When excess demand or excess supply occurs, it tends to be small and brief, except in markets where regulations prevent full adjustment of prices.   **LO3**

- The efficiency of markets in allocating resources does not eliminate social concerns about how goods and services are distributed among different people. For example, we often lament the fact many buyers enter the market with too little income to buy even the most basic goods and services. Concern for the well-being of the poor has motivated many governments to intervene in a variety of ways to alter the outcomes of market forces. Sometimes these interventions take the form of laws that peg prices below their equilibrium levels. Such laws almost invariably generate harmful, if unintended, consequences. Programs like rent-control laws, for example, lead to severe housing shortages, black marketeering, and a rapid deterioration of the relationship between landlords and tenants.   **LO5**

- If the difficulty is that the poor have too little money, the best solution is to discover ways of boosting their incomes directly. The law of supply and demand can-

not be repealed by the legislature. But legislatures do have the capacity to alter the underlying forces that govern the shape and position of supply and demand schedules.   **LO5**

- The basic supply and demand model is a primary tool of the economic naturalist. Changes in the equilibrium price of a good, and in the amount of it traded in the marketplace, can be predicted on the basis of shifts in its supply or demand curves. The following four rules hold for any good with a downward-sloping demand curve and an upward-sloping supply curve:
  - An increase in demand will lead to an increase in equilibrium price and quantity.
  - A reduction in demand will lead to a reduction in equilibrium price and quantity.
  - An increase in supply will lead to a reduction in equilibrium price and an increase in equilibrium quantity.
  - A decrease in supply will lead to an increase in equilibrium price and a reduction in equilibrium quantity.   **LO4**

- Incomes, tastes, population, expectations, and the prices of substitutes and complements are among the factors that shift demand schedules. Supply schedules, in turn, are primarily governed by such factors as technology, input prices, expectations, the number of sellers, and, especially for agricultural products, the weather.   **LO4**

- When the supply and demand curves for a good reflect all significant costs and benefits associated with the production and consumption of that good, the market equilibrium price will guide people to produce and consume the quantity of the good that results in the largest possible economic surplus. This conclusion, however, does not apply if others, besides buyers, benefit from the good (as when someone benefits from his neighbor's purchase of a vaccination against measles) or if others besides sellers bear costs because of the good (as when its production generates pollution). In such cases, market equilibrium does not result in the greatest gain for all.   **LO6**

▪ CORE PRINCIPLES ▪

Efficiency

The Efficiency Principle
Efficiency is an important social goal because when the economic pie grows larger, everyone can have a larger slice.

Equilibrium

The Equilibrium Principle (also called the "No-Cash-on-the-Table" Principle)
A market in equilibrium leaves no unexploited opportunities for individuals but may not exploit all gains achievable through collective action.

▪ KEY TERMS ▪

buyer's reservation price (66)
buyer's surplus (85)
cash on the table (85)
change in demand (75)
change in the quantity
   demanded (75)
change in the quantity
   supplied (75)
change in supply (75)
complements (75)
demand curve (65)

economic efficiency (86)
efficiency (86)
equilibrium (68)
equilibrium price (68)
equilibrium quantity (68)
excess demand (69)
excess supply (69)
income effect (65)
inferior good (78)
market (64)
market equilibrium (68)

normal good (78)
price ceiling (74)
seller's reservation price (67)
seller's surplus (85)
socially optimal quantity (86)
substitutes (76)
substitution effect (65)
supply curve (66)
total surplus (85)

▪ REVIEW QUESTIONS ▪

1. Why isn't knowing the cost of producing a good sufficient to predict its market price? **LO3**

2. Distinguish between the meaning of the expressions "change in demand" and "change in the quantity demanded." **LO4**

3. Last year a government official proposed that gasoline price controls be imposed to protect the poor from rising gasoline prices. What evidence could you consult to discover whether this proposal was enacted? **LO3**

4. Explain the distinction between the horizontal and vertical interpretations of the demand curve. **LO1**

5. Give an example of behavior you have observed that could be described as "smart for one but dumb for all." **LO6**

▪ PROBLEMS ▪

1. State whether the following pairs of goods are complements or substitutes. (If you think a pair is ambiguous in this respect, explain why.) **LO1**
   a. Tennis courts and squash courts.
   b. Squash racquets and squash balls.
   c. Ice cream and chocolate.
   d. Cloth diapers and paper diapers.

2. How would each of the following affect the U.S. market supply curve for corn? **LO2**
   a. A new and improved crop rotation technique is discovered.
   b. The price of fertilizer falls.
   c. The government offers new tax breaks to farmers.
   d. A tornado sweeps through Iowa.

3. Indicate how you think each of the following would shift demand in the indicated market: **LO1**
   a. Incomes of buyers in the market for Adirondack vacations increase.
   b. Buyers in the market for pizza read a study linking hamburger consumption to heart disease.
   c. Buyers in the market for CDs learn of an increase in the price of audiocassettes (a substitute for CDs).
   d. Buyers in the market for CDs learn of an increase in the price of CDs.

4. An Arizona student claims to have spotted a UFO over the desert outside of Tucson. How will his claim affect the *supply* (not the quantity supplied) of binoculars in Tucson stores? **LO2**

5. What will happen to the equilibrium price and quantity of oranges if the wage paid to orange pickers rises? **LO4**

6. How will an increase in the birth rate affect the equilibrium price of land?   **LO4**

7. What will happen to the equilibrium price and quantity of fish if fish oils are found to help prevent heart disease?   **LO4**

8. What will happen to the equilibrium price and quantity of beef if the price of chickenfeed increases?   **LO4**

9. Use supply and demand analysis to explain why hotel room rental rates near your campus during parents' weekend and graduation weekend might differ from the rates charged during the rest of the year.   **LO4**

10. How will a new law mandating an increase in required levels of automobile insurance affect the equilibrium price and quantity in the market for new automobiles?   **LO4**

11. Suppose the current issue of the *New York Times* reports an outbreak of mad cow disease in Nebraska, as well as the discovery of a new breed of chicken that gains more weight than existing breeds that consume the same amount of food. How will these developments affect the equilibrium price and quantity of chickens sold in the United States?   **LO4**

12. What will happen to the equilibrium quantity and price of potatoes if population increases and a new, higher-yielding variety of potato plant is developed?   **LO4**

13. What will happen to the equilibrium price and quantity of apples if apples are discovered to help prevent colds and a fungus kills 10 percent of existing apple trees?   **LO4**

14. What will happen to the equilibrium quantity and price of corn if the price of butter (a complement) increases and the price of fertilizer decreases?   **LO4**

15. Twenty-five years ago, tofu was available only from small businesses operating in predominantly Asian sections of large cities. Today tofu has become popular as a high-protein health food and is widely available in supermarkets throughout the United States. At the same time, tofu production has evolved to become factory-based using modern food-processing technologies. Draw a diagram with demand and supply curves depicting the market for tofu 25 years ago and the market for tofu today. Given the information above, what does the demand-supply model predict about changes in the volume of tofu sold in the United States between then and now? What does it predict about changes in the price of tofu?   **LO4**

■ ANSWERS TO IN-CHAPTER EXERCISES ■

3.1 At a quantity of 10,000 slices per day, the marginal buyer's reservation price is $3.50 per slice. At a price of $2.50 per slice, the quantity demanded will be 14,000 slices per day.   **LO1**

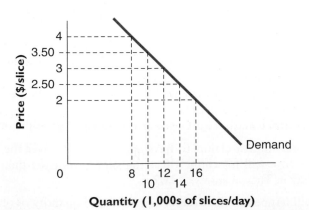

3.2 At a quantity of 10,000 slices per day, the marginal cost of pizza is $2.50 per slice. At a price of $3.50 per slice, the quantity supplied will be 14,000 slices per day. **LO2**

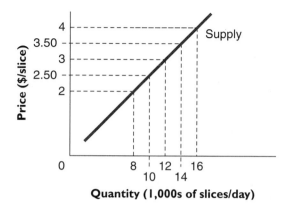

3.3 Since landlords are permitted to charge less than the maximum rent established by rent-control laws, a law that sets the maximum rent at $1,200 will have no effect on the rents actually charged in this market, which will settle at the equilibrium value of $800 per month. **LO3**

3.4 Travel by air and travel by intercity bus are substitutes, so a decline in airfares will shift the demand for bus travel to the left, resulting in lower bus fares and fewer bus trips taken. Travel by air and the use of resort hotels are complements, so a decline in airfares will shift the demand for resort hotel rooms to the right, resulting in higher hotel rates and an increase in the number of rooms rented. **LO4**

3.5 Apartments located far from Washington Metro stations are an inferior good. A pay increase for federal workers will thus shift the demand curve for such apartments downward, which will lead to a reduction in their equilibrium rent. **LO4**

3.6 The vitamin discovery shifts the demand for chips to the right and the crop losses shift the supply of chips to the left. Both shifts result in an increase in the equilibrium price of chips. But depending on the relative magnitude of the shifts, the equilibrium quantity of chips may either rise (left panel) or fall (right panel). **LO4**

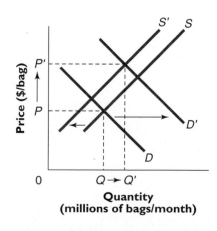

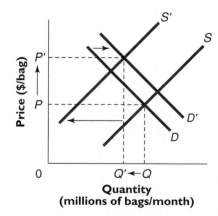

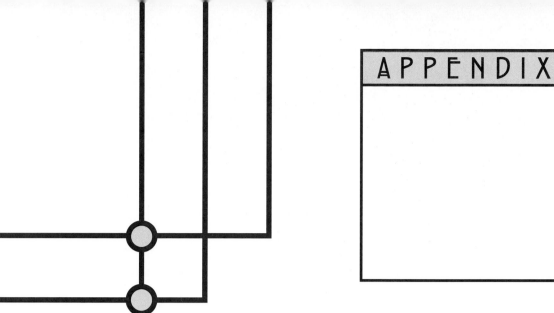

The Algebra of Supply and Demand

In the text of this chapter, we developed supply and demand analysis in a geometric framework. The advantage of this framework is that many find it an easier one within which to visualize how shifts in either curve affect equilibrium price and quantity.

It is a straightforward extension to translate supply and demand analysis into algebraic terms. In this brief appendix, we show how this is done. The advantage of the algebraic framework is that it greatly simplifies computing the numerical values of equilibrium prices and quantities.

Consider, for example, the supply and demand curves in Figure 3A.1, where P denotes the price of the good and Q denotes its quantity. What are the equations of these curves?

Recall from the appendix to Chapter 1 that the equation of a straight-line demand curve must take the general form $P = a + b\,Q^d$, where P is the price of the product (as measured on the vertical axis), Q^d is the quantity demanded at that price (as measured on the horizontal axis), a is the vertical intercept of the demand curve, and b is its slope. For the demand curve shown in Figure 3A.1, the vertical intercept is 16 and the slope is -2. So the equation for this demand curve is

$$P = 16 - 2Q^d. \tag{3A.1}$$

Similarly, the equation of a straight-line supply curve must take the general form $P = c + dQ^s$, where P is again the price of the product, Q^s is the quantity supplied at that price, c is the vertical intercept of the supply curve, and d is its slope. For the supply curve shown in Figure 3A.1, the vertical intercept is 4 and the slope is also 4. So the equation for this supply curve is

$$P = 4 + 4Q^s. \tag{3A.2}$$

If we know the equations for the supply and demand curves in any market, it is a simple matter to solve them for the equilibrium price and quantity using the method of simultaneous equations described in the appendix to Chapter 1. The following example illustrates how to apply this method.

FIGURE 3A.1
Supply and Demand
Curves

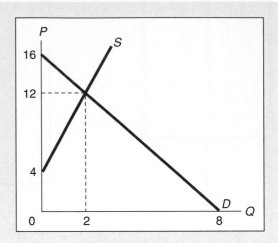

If the supply and demand curves for a market are given by $P = 4 + 4Q^s$ and $P = 16 - 2Q^d$, respectively, find the equilibrium price and quantity for this market.

In equilibrium, we know that $Q^s = Q^d$. Denoting this common value as Q^*, we may then equate the right-hand sides of Equations 3A.1 and 3A.2 and solve:

$$4 + 4Q^* = 16 - 2Q^*, \tag{3A.3}$$

which yields $Q^* = 2$. Substituting $Q^* = 2$ back into either the supply or demand equation gives the equilibrium price $P^* = 12$. ◆

Of course, having already begun with the graphs of Equations 3A.1 and 3A.2 in hand, we could have identified the equilibrium price and quantity by a simple glance at Figure 3A.1. (That is why it seems natural to say that the graphical approach helps us visualize the equilibrium outcome.) As the following exercise illustrates, the advantage of the algebraic approach to finding the equilibrium price and quantity is that it is much less painstaking than having to produce accurate drawings of the supply and demand schedules.

EXERCISE 3A.1

Find the equilibrium price and quantity in a market whose supply and demand curves are given by $P = 2Q^s$ and $P = 8 - 2Q^d$, respectively.

■ ANSWER TO IN-APPENDIX EXERCISE ■

3A.1 Let Q^* denote the equilibrium quantity. Since the equilibrium price and quantity lie on both the supply and demand curves, we equate the right-hand sides of the supply and demand equations to obtain

$$2Q^* = 8 - 2Q^*,$$

which solves for $Q^* = 2$. Substituting $Q^* = 2$ back into either the supply or demand equation gives the equilibrium price $P^* = 4$.

PART

2

COMPETITION AND THE INVISIBLE HAND

■

Having grasped the basic core principles of economics, you are now in a position to sharpen your understanding of how consumers and firms behave. In Part 2 our focus will be on how things work in an idealized, perfectly competitive economy in which consumers are perfectly informed and no firm has market power.

We begin in Chapter 4 by exploring the concept of elasticity, which describes the sensitivity of demand and supply to variations in prices, incomes, and other economic factors. In our discussion of supply and demand in Part 1, we asked you simply to assume the law of demand, which says that demand curves are downward-sloping. In Chapter 5 we will see that this law is a simple consequence of the fact that people spend their limited incomes in rational ways. In Chapter 6 our focus will shift to the seller's side of the market, where our task will be to see why upward-sloping supply curves are a consequence of production decisions taken by firms whose goal is to maximize profit.

Our agenda in Chapter 7 is to develop more carefully and fully the concept of economic surplus introduced in Part 1 and to investigate the conditions under which unregulated markets generate the largest possible economic surplus. We will also explore why attempts to interfere with market outcomes often lead to unintended and undesired consequences.

In Chapter 8 we will investigate the economic forces by which the invisible hand of the marketplace guides profit-seeking firms and satisfaction-seeking consumers in ways that, to a surprising degree, serve society's ends. These forces encourage aggressive cost cutting by firms, even though the resulting gains will eventually take the form of lower prices rather than higher profits. We will also see why misunderstanding of competitive forces often results in costly errors, both in everyday decision making and in government policy.

Elasticity

LEARNING OBJECTIVES

After reading this chapter, you should be able to:

1. Define the price elasticity of demand and explain what determines whether demand is elastic or inelastic.

2. Calculate the price elasticity of demand using information from a demand curve.

3. Understand how changes in the price of a good affect total revenue and total expenditure depending on the price elasticity of demand for the good.

4. Define the cross-price elasticity of demand and the income elasticity of demand.

5. Define the price elasticity of supply and explain what determines whether supply is elastic or inelastic.

6. Calculate the price elasticity of supply using information from a supply curve.

Many illicit drug users commit crimes to finance their addiction. The connection between drugs and crime has led to calls for more vigorous efforts to stop the smuggling of illicit drugs. But can such efforts reduce the likelihood that your iPod or laptop computer will be stolen in the next month? If attempts to reduce the supply of illicit drugs are successful, our basic supply and demand analysis tells us that the supply curve for drugs will shift to the left and the market price of drugs will increase. Given that demand curves are downward-sloping, drug users will respond by consuming a smaller quantity of drugs. But the amount of crime drug users commit depends not on the *quantity* of drugs they consume, but rather on their *total expenditure* on drugs. Depending on the specific characteristics of the demand curve for illicit drugs, a price increase might reduce total expenditure on drugs, but it also could raise total expenditure.

FIGURE 4.1
The Effect of Extra Border Patrols on the Market for Illicit Drugs.
Extra patrols shift supply leftward and reduce the quantity demanded, but they may actually increase the total amount spent on drugs.

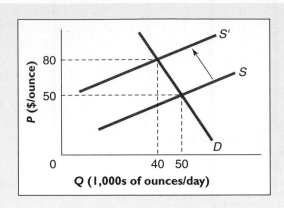

Could reducing the supply of illegal drugs cause an increase in drug-related burglaries?

Suppose, for example, that extra border patrols shift the supply curve in the market for illicit drugs to the left, as shown in Figure 4.1. As a result, the equilibrium quantity of drugs would fall from 50,000 to 40,000 ounces per day and the price of drugs would rise from $50 to $80 per ounce. The total amount spent on drugs, which was $2,500,000 per day (50,000 ounces/day × $50/ounce), would rise to $3,200,000 per day (40,000 ounces/day × $80/ounce). In this case, then, efforts to stem the supply of drugs would actually increase the likelihood of your laptop being stolen.

Other benefits from stemming the flow of illicit drugs might still outweigh the resulting increase in crime. But knowing that the policy might increase drug-related crime would clearly be useful to law-enforcement authorities.

Our task in this chapter will be to introduce the concept of elasticity, a measure of the extent to which quantity demanded and quantity supplied respond to variations in price, income, and other factors. In the preceding chapter, we saw how shifts in supply and demand curves enabled us to predict the direction of change in the equilibrium values of price and quantity. An understanding of price elasticity will enable us to make even more precise statements about the effects of such changes. In the illicit-drug example just considered, the decrease in supply led to an increase in total spending. In many other cases, a decrease in supply will lead to a reduction in total spending. Why this difference? The underlying phenomenon that explains this pattern, we will see, is price elasticity of demand. We will explore why some goods have higher price elasticity of demand than others and the implications of that fact for how total spending responds to changes in prices. We also will discuss price elasticity of supply and examine the factors that explain why it takes different values for different goods.

PRICE ELASTICITY OF DEMAND

When the price of a good or service rises, the quantity demanded falls. But to predict the effect of the price increase on total expenditure, we also must know by how much quantity falls. The quantity demanded of some goods such as salt is not very sensitive to changes in price. Indeed, even if the price of salt were to double, or to fall by half, most people would hardly alter their consumption of it. For other goods, however, the quantity demanded is extremely responsive to changes in price. For example, when a luxury tax was imposed on yachts in the early 1990s, purchases of yachts plummeted sharply.

PRICE ELASTICITY DEFINED

price elasticity of demand
percentage change in quantity demanded that results from a 1 percent change in price

The **price elasticity of demand** for a good is a measure of the responsiveness of the quantity demanded of that good to changes in its price. Formally, the price elasticity of demand for a good is defined as the percentage change in the quantity demanded that results from a 1 percent change in its price. For example, if the price of beef falls by 1 percent and the quantity demanded rises by 2 percent, then the price elasticity of demand for beef has a value of −2.

Although the definition just given refers to the response of quantity demanded to a 1 percent change in price, it also can be adapted to other variations in price, provided they are relatively small. In such cases, we calculate the price elasticity of demand as the percentage change in quantity demanded divided by the corresponding percentage change in price. Thus, if a 2 percent reduction in the price of pork led to a 6 percent increase in the quantity of pork demanded, the price elasticity of demand for pork would be

$$\frac{\text{Percentage change in quantity demanded}}{\text{Percentage change in price}} = \frac{6 \text{ percent}}{-2 \text{ percent}} = -3. \quad (4.1)$$

elastic demand is elastic with respect to price if price elasticity of demand is greater than 1

Strictly speaking, the price elasticity of demand will always be negative (or zero) because price changes are always in the opposite direction from changes in quantity demanded. So for convenience, we drop the negative sign and speak of price elasticities in terms of absolute value. The demand for a good is said to be **elastic** with respect to price if the absolute value of its price elasticity is greater than 1. It is said to be **inelastic** if the absolute value of its price elasticity is less than 1. Finally, demand is said to be **unit elastic** if the absolute value of its price elasticity is equal to 1. (See Figure 4.2.)

inelastic demand is inelastic with respect to price if price elasticity of demand is less than 1

unit elastic demand is unit elastic with respect to price if price elasticity of demand equals 1

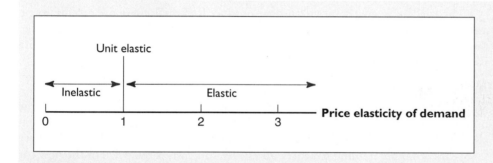

**FIGURE 4.2
Elastic and Inelastic Demand.**
Demand for a good is called elastic, unit elastic, or inelastic with respect to price if the price elasticity is greater than 1, equal to 1, or less than 1, respectively.

What is the elasticity of demand for pizza?

When the price of pizza is $1 per slice, buyers wish to purchase 400 slices per day, but when price falls to $0.97 per slice, the quantity demanded rises to 404 slices per day. At the original price, what is the price elasticity of demand for pizza? Is the demand for pizza elastic with respect to price?

The fall in price from $1 to $0.97 is a decrease of 3 percent. The rise in quantity demanded from 400 slices to 404 slices is an increase of 1 percent. The price elasticity of demand for pizza is thus (1 percent)/(3 percent) = 1/3. So when the initial price of pizza is $1, the demand for pizza is not elastic with respect to price; it is inelastic. ◆

EXERCISE 4.1

What is the elasticity of demand for season ski passes?

When the price of a season ski pass is $400, buyers wish to purchase 10,000 passes per year, but when price falls to $380, the quantity demanded rises to 12,000 passes per year. At the original price, what is the price elasticity of demand for ski passes? Is the demand for ski passes elastic with respect to price?

DETERMINANTS OF PRICE ELASTICITY OF DEMAND

What factors determine the price elasticity of demand for a good or service? To answer this question, recall that before a rational consumer buys any product, the purchase decision must first satisfy the Cost-Benefit Principle. For instance, consider a good (such as a dorm refrigerator) that you buy only one unit of (if you buy it at all). Suppose that, at the current price, you have decided to buy it. Now imagine that the price goes up by 10 percent. Will a price increase of this magnitude be likely to make you change your mind? The answer will depend on factors like the following.

Cost-Benefit

If the price of salt were to double, would you use less of it?

Substitution Possibilities

When the price of a product you want to buy goes up significantly, you are likely to ask yourself, "Is there some other good that can do roughly the same job, but for less money?" If the answer is yes, then you can escape the effect of the price increase by simply switching to the substitute product. But if the answer is no, you are more likely to stick with your current purchase.

These observations suggest that demand will tend to be more elastic with respect to price for products for which close substitutes are readily available. Salt, for example, has no close substitutes, which is one reason that the demand for it is highly inelastic. Note, however, that while the quantity of salt people demand is highly insensitive to price, the same cannot be said of the demand for any *specific brand* of salt. After all, despite what salt manufacturers say about the special advantages of their own labels, consumers tend to regard one brand of salt as a virtually perfect substitute for another. Thus, if Morton were to raise the price of its salt significantly, many people would simply switch to some other brand.

The vaccine against rabies is another product for which there are essentially no attractive substitutes. A person who is bitten by a rabid animal and does not take the vaccine faces a certain and painful death. Most people in that position would pay any price they could afford rather than do without the vaccine.

Budget Share

Suppose the price of key rings suddenly were to double. How would that affect the number of key rings you buy? If you're like most people, it would have no effect at all. Think about it—a doubling of the price of a $1 item that you buy only every few years is simply nothing to worry about. By contrast, if the price of the new car you were about to buy suddenly doubled, you would definitely want to check out possible substitutes such as a used car or a smaller new model. You also might consider holding on to your current car a little longer. The larger the share of your budget an item accounts for, the greater is your incentive to look for substitutes when the price of the item rises. Big-ticket items, therefore, tend to have higher price elasticities of demand.

Time

Home appliances come in a variety of models, some more energy-efficient than others. As a general rule, the more efficient an appliance is, the higher its price. Suppose that you were about to buy a new air conditioner and electric rates suddenly rose sharply. It would probably be in your interest to buy a more efficient machine than you had originally planned. However, what if you had already bought a new air conditioner before you learned of the rate increase? You would not think it worthwhile to discard the machine right away and replace it with a more efficient model. Rather, you would wait until the machine wore out, or until you moved, before making the switch.

As this example illustrates, substitution of one product or service for another takes time. Some substitutions occur in the immediate aftermath of a price increase, but many others take place years or even decades later. For this reason, the price elasticity of demand for any good or service will be higher in the long run than in the short run.

RECAP	FACTORS THAT INFLUENCE PRICE ELASTICITY

The price elasticity of demand for a good or service tends to be larger when substitutes for the good are more readily available, when the good's share in the consumer's budget is larger, and when consumers have more time to adjust to a change in price.

SOME REPRESENTATIVE ELASTICITY ESTIMATES

The entries in Table 4.1 show that the price elasticities of demand for different products often differ substantially—in this sample, ranging from a high of 2.8 for green peas to a low of 0.18 for theater and opera tickets. This variability is explained in part by the determinants of elasticity just discussed. Patrons of theater and opera, for example, tend to have high incomes, implying that the shares of their budgets devoted to these items are likely to be small. What is more, theater and opera patrons are often highly knowledgeable and enthusiastic about these art forms; for many of them, there are simply no acceptable substitute forms of entertainment.

TABLE 4.1
Historical Price Elasticity of Demand Estimates for Selected Products

Good or service	Price elasticity of demand
Green peas	2.80
Restaurant meals	1.63
Automobiles	1.35
Electricity	1.20
Beer	1.19
Movies	0.87
Air travel (foreign)	0.77
Shoes	0.70
Coffee	0.25
Theater, opera	0.18

SOURCE: These short-run elasticity estimates are taken from the following sources: Ronald Fisher, *State and Local Public Finance,* Chicago: Irwin, 1996; H. S. Houthakker and Lester Taylor, *Consumer Demand in the United States: Analyses and Projections,* 2nd ed., Cambridge, MA: Harvard University Press, 1970; L. Taylor, "The Demand for Electricity: A Survey," *Bell Journal of Economics,* Spring 1975; K. Elzinga, "The Beer Industry," in *The Structure of American Industry,* Walter Adams, ed., New York: Macmillan, 1977.

Why is the price elasticity of demand more than 14 times larger for green peas than for theater and opera performances? The answer cannot be that income effects loom larger for green peas than for theater tickets. Even though the average consumer of green peas earns much less than the average theater or opera patron, the share of a typical family's budget devoted to green peas is surely very small. What differentiates green peas from theater and opera performances is that there are so many more close substitutes for peas than for opera and theater. The lowly green pea, which is mostly found in the canned goods or frozen foods sections of supermarkets, does not seem to have inspired a loyal consumer following.

USING PRICE ELASTICITY OF DEMAND

An understanding of the factors that govern price elasticity of demand is necessary not only to make sense of consumer behavior, but also to design effective public policy. Consider, for example, the debate about how taxes affect smoking among teenagers.

Example 4.1
THE ECONOMIC NATURALIST

Do high cigarette prices discourage teen smoking?

Will a higher tax on cigarettes curb teenage smoking?

Consultants hired by the tobacco industry have testified in Congress against higher cigarette taxes aimed at curbing teenage smoking. The main reason teenagers smoke is that their friends smoke, these consultants testified, and they concluded that higher taxes would have little effect. Does the consultants' testimony make economic sense?

The consultants are almost certainly right that peer influence is the most important determinant of teen smoking. But that does not imply that a higher tax on cigarettes would have little impact on adolescent smoking rates. Because most teenagers have little money to spend at their own discretion, cigarettes constitute a significant share of a typical teenage smoker's budget. The price elasticity of demand is thus likely to be far from negligible. For at least some teenage smokers, a higher tax would make smoking unaffordable. And even among those who could afford the higher prices, at least some others would choose to spend their money on other things rather than pay the higher prices.

Given that the tax would affect at least *some* teenage smokers, the consultants' argument begins to unravel. If the tax deters even a small number of smokers directly through its effect on the price of cigarettes, it will also deter others indirectly, by reducing the number of peer role models who smoke. And those who refrain because of these indirect effects will in turn no longer influence others to smoke, and so on. So even if the direct effect of higher cigarette taxes on teen smoking is small, the cumulative effects may be extremely large. The mere fact that peer pressure may be the primary determinant of teen smoking therefore does not imply that higher cigarette taxes will have no significant impact on the number of teens who smoke. ●

Example 4.2
THE ECONOMIC NATURALIST

Why was the luxury tax on yachts such a disaster?

In 1990, Congress imposed a luxury tax on yachts costing more than $100,000, along with similar taxes on a handful of other luxury goods. Before these taxes were imposed, the Joint Committee on Taxation estimated that they would yield more than $31 million in revenue in 1991. However, the tax actually generated a bit more than half that amount, $16.6 million.[1] Several years later, the Joint Economic Committee estimated that the tax on yachts had led to a loss of 7,600 jobs in the U.S. boating industry. Taking account of lost income taxes and increased unemployment benefits, the U.S. government actually came out $7.6 million behind in fiscal 1991 as a result of its luxury taxes—almost $39 million worse than the initial projection. What went wrong?

Why did the luxury tax on yachts backfire?

The 1990 law imposed no luxury taxes on yachts built and purchased outside the United States. What Congress failed to consider was that foreign-built yachts are almost perfect substitutes for yachts built and purchased in the United States. And, no surprise, when prices on domestic yachts went up because of the tax, yacht buyers switched in droves to foreign models. A tax imposed on a good with a high price elasticity of demand stimulates large rearrangements of consumption but yields little revenue. Had Congress done the economic analysis properly, it would have predicted that this particular tax would be a big loser. Facing angry protests from unemployed New England shipbuilders, Congress repealed the luxury tax on yachts in 1993. ●

[1]For an alternative view, see Dennis Zimmerman, "The Effect of the Luxury Excise Tax on the Sale of Luxury Boats." Congressional Research Service, February 10, 1992.

A GRAPHICAL INTERPRETATION OF PRICE ELASTICITY

For small changes in price, price elasticity of demand is the proportion by which quantity demanded changes divided by the corresponding proportion by which price changes. This formulation enables us to construct a simple expression for the price elasticity of demand for a good using only minimal information about its demand curve.

Look at Figure 4.3. P represents the current price of a good and Q the quantity demanded at that price. ΔP represents a small change in the current price and the resulting change in quantity demanded is given by ΔQ. The expression $\Delta P/P$ will

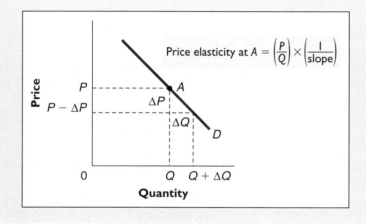

FIGURE 4.3
A Graphical Interpretation of Price Elasticity of Demand.
Price elasticity of demand at any point along a straight-line demand curve is the ratio of price to quantity at that point times the reciprocal of the slope of the demand curve.

then stand for the proportion by which price changes and $\Delta Q/Q$ will stand for the corresponding proportion by which quantity changes. These two expressions, along with our definition of the price elasticity of demand (Equation 4.1), give us the formula for price elasticity:

$$\text{Price elasticity} = \epsilon = \frac{\Delta Q/Q}{\Delta P/P}. \tag{4.2}$$

Suppose, for example, that 20 units were sold at the original price of 100 and that when price rose to 105, quantity demanded fell to 15 units. Neglecting the negative sign of the quantity change, we would then have $\Delta Q/Q = 5/20$ and $\Delta P/P = 5/100$, which yields $\epsilon = (5/20)/(5/100) = 5$.

One attractive feature of this formula is that it has a straightforward graphical interpretation. Thus, if we want to calculate the price elasticity of demand at point A on the demand curve shown in Figure 4.3, we can begin by rewriting the right-hand side of Equation 4.2 as $(P/Q) \times (\Delta Q/\Delta P)$. And since the slope of the demand curve is equal to $\Delta P/\Delta Q$, $\Delta Q/\Delta P$ is the reciprocal of that slope: $\Delta Q/\Delta P = 1/\text{slope}$. The price elasticity of demand at point A, denoted ϵ_A, therefore has the following simple formula:

$$\epsilon_A = \frac{P}{Q} \times \frac{1}{\text{slope}}. \tag{4.3}$$

To demonstrate how convenient this graphical interpretation of elasticity can be, suppose we want to find the price elasticity of demand at point A on the demand curve in Figure 4.4. The slope of this demand curve is the ratio of its vertical intercept to its horizontal intercept: $20/5 = 4$. So $1/\text{slope} = 1/4$. (Actually, the

FIGURE 4.4
Calculating Price
Elasticity of Demand.
The price elasticity of
demand at A is given by
$(P/Q) \times (1/slope) = (8/3)$
$\times (1/4) = 2/3.$

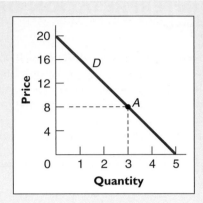

slope is -4, but we again ignore the minus sign for convenience, since price elasticity of demand always has the same sign.) The ratio P/Q at point A is 8/3, so the price elasticity at point A is equal to $(P/Q) \times (1/slope) = (8/3) \times (1/4) = 2/3$. This means that when the price of the good is 8, a 3 percent reduction in price will lead to a 2 percent increase in quantity demanded.

EXERCISE 4.2

What is the price elasticity of demand when $P = 4$ on the demand curve in Figure 4.4?

For the demand curves D_1 and D_2 shown in Figure 4.5, calculate the price elasticity of demand when $P = 4$. What is the price elasticity of demand on D_2 when $P = 1$?

FIGURE 4.5
Price Elasticity and the
Steepness of the Demand
Curve.
When price and quantity are
the same, price elasticity of
demand is always greater for
the less steep of two demand
curves.

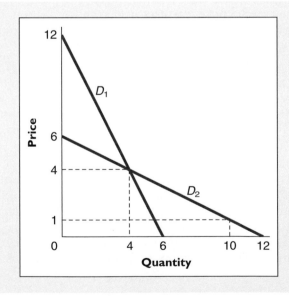

These elasticities can be calculated easily using the formula $\epsilon = (P/Q) \times (1/slope)$. The slope of D_1 is the ratio of its vertical intercept to its horizontal intercept: $12/6 = 2$. So $(1/slope)$ is 1/2 for D_1. Similarly, the slope of D_2 is the ratio of its vertical intercept to its horizontal intercept: $6/12 = 1/2$. So the reciprocal of the slope of D_2 is 2. For both demand curves, $Q = 4$ when $P = 4$, so $(P/Q) = 4/4 = 1$ for each. Thus the price elasticity of demand when $P = 4$ is $(1) \times (1/2) = 1/2$ for D_1

and $(1) \times (2) = 2$ for D_2. When $P = 1$, $Q = 10$ on D_2, so $(P/Q) = 1/10$. Thus price elasticity of demand $= (1/10) \times (2) = 1/5$ when $P = 1$ on D_2. ◆

This example illustrates a general rule: if two demand curves have a point in common, the steeper curve must be the less price elastic of the two with respect to price at that point. However, this does not mean that the steeper curve is less elastic at *every* point. Thus, we saw that at $P = 1$, price elasticity of demand on D_2 was only $1/5$, or less than half the corresponding elasticity on the steeper D_1 at $P = 4$.

PRICE ELASTICITY CHANGES ALONG A STRAIGHT-LINE DEMAND CURVE

As a glance at our elasticity formula makes clear, price elasticity has a different value at every point along a straight-line demand curve. The slope of a straight-line demand curve is constant, which means that 1/slope is also constant. But the price-quantity ratio P/Q declines as we move down the demand curve. The elasticity of demand thus declines steadily as we move downward along a straight-line demand curve.

Since price elasticity is the percentage change in quantity demanded divided by the corresponding percentage change in price, this pattern makes sense. After all, a price movement of a given absolute size is small in percentage terms when it occurs near the top of the demand curve, where price is high, but large in percentage terms when it occurs near the bottom of the demand curve, where price is low. Likewise, a quantity movement of a given absolute value is large in percentage terms when it occurs near the top of the demand curve, where quantity is low, and small in percentage terms when it occurs near the bottom of the curve, where quantity is high.

The graphical interpretation of elasticity also makes it easy to see why the price elasticity of demand at the midpoint of any straight-line demand curve must always be 1. Consider, for example, the price elasticity of demand at point A on the demand curve D shown in Figure 4.6. At that point, the ratio P/Q is equal to $6/3 = 2$. The slope of this demand curve is the ratio of its vertical intercept to its horizontal intercept, $12/6 = 2$. So $(1/\text{slope}) = 1/2$ (again, we neglect the negative sign for simplicity). Inserting these values into the graphical elasticity formula yields $\epsilon_A = (P/Q) \times (1/\text{slope}) = (2) \times (1/2) = 1$.

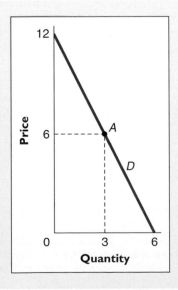

FIGURE 4.6
Elasticity at the Midpoint of a Straight-Line Demand Curve.
The price elasticity of demand at the midpoint of any straight-line demand curve always takes the value 1.

FIGURE 4.7
Price Elasticity Regions along a Straight-Line Demand Curve.
Demand is elastic on the top half, unit elastic at the midpoint, and inelastic on the bottom half of a straight-line demand curve.

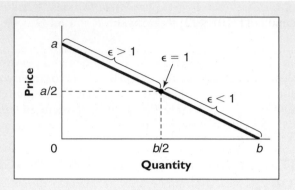

This result holds not just for Figure 4.6, but also for any other straight-line demand curve.[2] A glance at the formula also tells us that since P/Q declines as we move downward along a straight-line demand curve, price elasticity of demand must be less than 1 at any point below the midpoint. By the same token, price elasticity must be greater than 1 for any point above the midpoint. Figure 4.7 summarizes these findings by denoting the elastic, inelastic, and unit elastic portions of any straight-line demand curve.

TWO SPECIAL CASES

There are two important exceptions to the general rule that elasticity declines along straight-line demand curves. First, the horizontal demand curve in Figure 4.8(a) has a slope of zero, which means that the reciprocal of its slope is infinite. Price elasticity of demand is thus infinite at every point along a horizontal demand curve. Such demand curves are said to be **perfectly elastic**.

Second, the demand curve in Figure 4.8(b) is vertical, which means that its slope is infinite. The reciprocal of its slope is thus equal to zero. Price elasticity of

perfectly elastic demand
demand is perfectly elastic with respect to price if price elasticity of demand is infinite

FIGURE 4.8
Perfectly Elastic and Perfectly Inelastic Demand Curves.
The horizontal demand curve (a) is perfectly elastic, or infinitely elastic, at every point. Even the slightest increase in price leads consumers to desert the product in favor of substitutes. The vertical demand curve (b) is perfectly inelastic at every point. Consumers do not, or cannot, switch to substitutes even in the face of large increases in price.

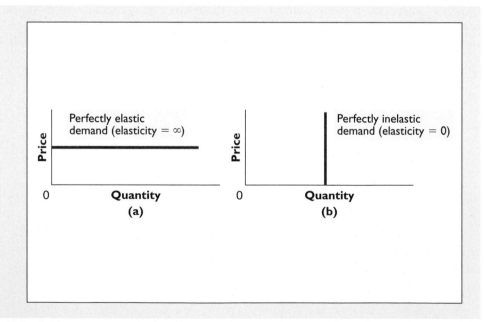

[2]To see why, note that at the midpoint of any such curve, P is exactly half the vertical intercept of the demand curve and Q is exactly half the horizontal intercept. Since the ratio of the vertical intercept to the horizontal intercept is the slope of the demand curve, the ratio (P/Q) must also be equal to the slope of the demand curve. And this means that $(1/\text{slope})$ will always be equal to (Q/P). Thus, the product $(P/Q) \times (1/\text{slope}) = (P/Q) \times (Q/P)$ will always be exactly 1 at the midpoint of any straight-line demand curve.

demand is thus exactly zero at every point along the curve. For this reason, vertical demand curves are said to be **perfectly inelastic**.

perfectly inelastic demand demand is perfectly inelastic with respect to price if price elasticity of demand is zero

RECAP	CALCULATING PRICE ELASTICITY OF DEMAND

The price elasticity of demand for a good is the percentage change in the quantity demanded that results from a 1 percent change in its price. Mathematically, the elasticity of demand at a point along a demand curve is equal to $(P/Q) \times (1/\text{slope})$, where P and Q represent price and quantity and $(1/\text{slope})$ is the reciprocal of the slope of the demand curve at that point. Demand is elastic with respect to price if the absolute value of its price elasticity exceeds 1; inelastic if price elasticity is less than 1; and unit elastic if price elasticity is equal to 1.

ELASTICITY AND TOTAL EXPENDITURE

Sellers of goods and services have a strong interest in being able to answer questions like "Will consumers spend more on my product if I sell more units at a lower price or fewer units at a higher price?" As it turns out, the answer to this question depends critically on the price elasticity of demand. To see why, let us first examine how the total amount spent on a good varies with the price of the good.

The total daily expenditure on a good is simply the daily number of units bought times the price for which it sells. The market demand curve for a good tells us the quantity that will be sold at each price. We can thus use the information on the demand curve to show how the total amount spent on a good will vary with its price.

To illustrate, let's calculate how much moviegoers will spend on tickets each day if the demand curve is as shown in Figure 4.9 and the price is $2 per ticket (a). The demand curve tells us that at a price of $2 per ticket, 500 tickets per day will be sold, so total expenditure at that price will be $1,000 per day. If tickets sell not for $2 but for $4 apiece, 400 tickets will be sold each day (b), so total expenditure at the higher price will be $1,600 per day.

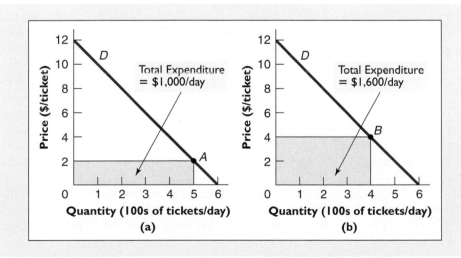

FIGURE 4.9
The Demand Curve for Movie Tickets.
An increase in price from $2 to $4 per ticket increases total expenditure on tickets.

Note that the total amount consumers spend on a product each day must equal the total amount sellers of the product receive. That is to say, the terms **total expenditure** and **total revenue** are simply two sides of the same coin:

> **Total Expenditure = Total Revenue:** The dollar amount that consumers spend on a product $(P \times Q)$ is equal to the dollar amount that sellers receive.

It might seem that an increase in the market price of a product should always result in an increase in the total revenue received by sellers. Although that happened in the case we just saw, it needn't always be so. The law of demand tells us that when the price of a good rises, people will buy less of it. The two factors that govern total revenue—price and quantity—will thus always move in opposite directions as we move along a demand curve. When price goes up and quantity goes down, the product of the two may go either up or down.

Note, for example, that for the demand curve shown in Figure 4.10 (which is the same as the one in Figure 4.9), a rise in price from $8 per ticket (a) to $10 per ticket (b) will cause total expenditure on tickets to go down. Thus people will spend $1,600 per day on tickets at a price of $8, but only $1,000 per day at a price of $10.

FIGURE 4.10

The Demand Curve for Movie Tickets.

An increase in price from $8 to $10 per ticket results in a fall in total expenditure on tickets.

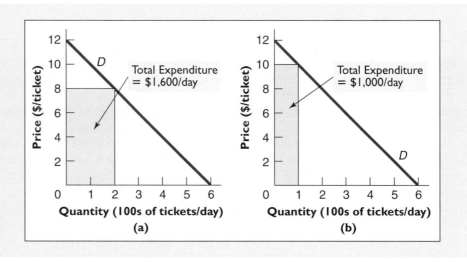

The general rule illustrated by Figures 4.9 and 4.10 is that a price increase will produce an increase in total revenue whenever it is greater, in percentage terms, than the corresponding percentage reduction in quantity demanded. Although the two price increases (from $2 to $4 and from $8 to $10) were of the same absolute value—$2 in each case—they are much different when expressed as a percentage of the original price. An increase from $2 to $4 represents a 100 percent increase in price, whereas an increase from $8 to $10 represents only a 25 percent increase in price. And although the quantity reductions caused by the two price increases were also equal in absolute terms, they too are very different when expressed as percentages of the quantities originally sold. Thus, although the decline in quantity demanded was 100 tickets per day in each case, it was just a 20 percent reduction in the first case (from 500 units to 400 in Figure 4.9) but a 50 percent reduction in the second (from 200 units to 100 in Figure 4.10). In the second case, the negative effect on total expenditure of the 50 percent quantity reduction outweighed the positive effect of the 25 percent price increase. The reverse happened in the first case: the 100 percent increase in price (from $2 to $4) outweighed the 20 percent reduction in quantity (from 5 units to 4 units).

The following example provides further insight into the relationship between total revenue and price.

For the demand curve shown in Figure 4.11, draw a separate graph showing how total expenditure varies with the price of movie tickets.

The first step in constructing this graph is to calculate total expenditure for each price shown in the graph and record the results, as in Table 4.2. The next step is to

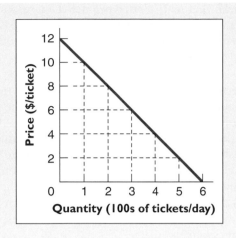

FIGURE 4.11
The Demand Curve for
Movie Tickets.

plot total expenditure at each of the price points on a graph, as in Figure 4.12. Finally, sketch the curve by joining these points. (If greater accuracy is required, you can use a larger sample of points than the one shown in Table 4.2.)

TABLE 4.2
Total Expenditure as a Function of Price

Price ($/ticket)	Total expenditure ($/day)
12	0
10	1,000
8	1,600
6	1,800
4	1,600
2	1,000
0	0

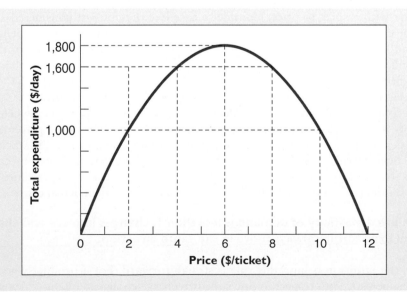

FIGURE 4.12
Total Expenditure as a Function of Price.
For a good whose demand curve is a straight line, total expenditure reaches a maximum at the price corresponding to the midpoint of the demand curve.

Note in Figure 4.12 that as the price per ticket increases from 0 to $6, total expenditure increases. But as the price rises from $6 to $12, total expenditure decreases. Total expenditure reaches a maximum of $1,800 per day at a price of $6. ◆

The pattern observed in the preceding example holds true in general. For a straight-line demand curve, total expenditure is highest at the price that lies on the midpoint of the demand curve.

Bearing in mind these observations about how expenditure varies with price, let's return to the question of how the effect of a price change on total expenditure depends on the price elasticity of demand. Suppose, for example, that the business manager of a rock band knows he can sell 5,000 tickets to the band's weekly summer concerts if he sets the price at $20 per ticket. If the elasticity of demand for tickets is equal to 3, will total ticket revenue go up or down in response to a 10 percent increase in the price of tickets?

Total revenue from tickets sold is currently ($20/ticket) × (5,000 tickets/week) = $100,000 per week. The fact that the price elasticity of demand for tickets is 3 implies that a 10 percent increase in price will produce a 30 percent reduction in the number of tickets sold, which means that quantity will fall to 3,500 tickets per week. Total expenditure on tickets will therefore fall to (3,500 tickets/week) × ($22/ticket) = $77,000 per week, which is significantly less than the current spending total.

What would have happened to total expenditure if the band manager had *reduced* ticket prices by 10 percent, from $20 to $18? Again assuming a price elasticity of 3, the result would have been a 30 percent increase in tickets sold—from 5,000 per week to 6,500 per week. The resulting total expenditure would have been ($18/ticket) × (6,500 tickets/week) = $117,000 per week, significantly more than the current total.

These examples illustrate the following important rule about how price changes affect total expenditure for an elastically demanded good:

When price elasticity of demand is greater than 1, changes in price and changes in total expenditure always move in opposite directions.

Let's look at the intuition behind this rule. Total expenditure is the product of price and quantity. For an elastically demanded product, the percentage change in quantity will be larger than the corresponding percentage change in price. Thus the change in quantity will more than offset the change in revenue per unit sold.

Now let's see how total spending responds to a price increase when demand is *inelastic* with respect to price. Consider a case like the one just considered except that the elasticity of demand for tickets is not 3 but 0.5. How will total expenditure respond to a 10 percent increase in ticket prices? This time the number of tickets sold will fall by only 5 percent to 4,750 tickets per week, which means that total expenditure on tickets will rise to (4,750 tickets/week) × ($22/ticket) = $104,500 per week, or $4,500 per week more than the current expenditure level.

In contrast, a 10 percent price reduction (from $20 to $18 per ticket) when price elasticity is 0.5 would cause the number of tickets sold to grow by only 5 percent, from 5,000 per week to 5,250 per week, resulting in total expenditure of ($18/ticket) × (5,250 tickets/week) = $94,500 per week, significantly less than the current total.

As these examples illustrate, the effect of price changes on total expenditure when demand is inelastic is precisely the opposite of what it was when demand was elastic:

When price elasticity of demand is less than 1, changes in price and changes in total expenditure always move in the same direction.

Again, the intuition behind this rule is straightforward. For a product whose demand is inelastic with respect to price, the percentage change in quantity demanded will be smaller than the corresponding percentage change in price. The change in revenue per unit sold (price) will thus more than offset the change in the number of units sold.

The relationship between elasticity and the effect of a price change on total revenue is summarized in Table 4.3, where the symbol is used to denote elasticity.

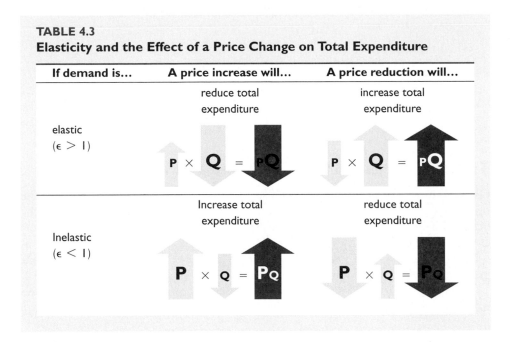

TABLE 4.3
Elasticity and the Effect of a Price Change on Total Expenditure

If demand is...	A price increase will...	A price reduction will...
elastic ($\epsilon > 1$)	reduce total expenditure	increase total expenditure
Inelastic ($\epsilon < 1$)	Increase total expenditure	reduce total expenditure

Recall that in the example with which we began this chapter, an increase in the price of drugs led to an increase in the total amount spent on drugs. That will happen whenever the demand for drugs is inelastic with respect to price, as it was in that example. Had the demand for drugs instead been elastic with respect to price, the drug supply interruption would have led to a reduction in total expenditure on drugs.

INCOME ELASTICITY AND CROSS-PRICE ELASTICITY OF DEMAND

The elasticity of demand for a good can be defined not only with respect to its own price but also with respect to the prices of substitutes or complements, or even to income. For example, the elasticity of demand for peanuts with respect to the price of cashews—also known as the **cross-price elasticity of demand** for peanuts with respect to cashew prices—is the percentage by which the quantity of peanuts demanded changes in response to a 1 percent change in the price of cashews. The **income elasticity of demand** for peanuts is the percentage by which the quantity demanded of peanuts changes in response to a 1 percent change in income.

Unlike the elasticity of demand for a good with respect to its own price, these other elasticities may be either positive or negative, so it is important to note their algebraic signs carefully. The income elasticity of demand for inferior goods, for example, is negative, whereas the income elasticity of demand for normal goods is positive. When the cross-price elasticity of demand for two goods is positive—as in the peanuts/cashews example—the two goods are substitutes. When it is negative, the two goods are complements. The elasticity of demand for tennis racquets with respect to court rental fees, for example, is less than zero.

cross-price elasticity of demand the percentage by which quantity demanded of the first good changes in response to a 1 percent change in the price of the second

income elasticity of demand the percentage by which quantity demanded changes in response to a 1 percent change in income

If a 10 percent increase in income causes the number of students who choose to attend private universities to go up by 5 percent, what is the income elasticity of demand for private universities?

RECAP	CROSS-PRICE AND INCOME ELASTICITIES

When the cross-price elasticity of demand for one good with respect to the price of another good is positive, the two goods are substitutes; when the cross-price elasticity of demand is negative, the two goods are complements. A normal good has positive income elasticity of demand and an inferior good has negative income elasticity of demand.

THE PRICE ELASTICITY OF SUPPLY

price elasticity of supply the percentage change in quantity supplied that occurs in response to a 1 percent change in price

On the buyer's side of the market, we use price elasticity of demand to measure the responsiveness of quantity demanded to changes in price. On the seller's side of the market, the analogous measure is **price elasticity of supply**. It is defined as the percentage change in quantity supplied that occurs in response to a 1 percent change in price. For example, if a 1 percent increase in the price of peanuts leads to a 2 percent increase in the quantity supplied, the price elasticity of supply of peanuts would be 2.

The mathematical formula for price elasticity of supply at any point is the same as the corresponding expression for price elasticity of demand:

$$\text{Price elasticity of supply} = \frac{\Delta Q/Q}{\Delta P/P}. \tag{4.4}$$

where P and Q are the price and quantity at that point, ΔP is a small change in the initial price, and ΔQ the resulting change in quantity.

As with the corresponding expression for price elasticity of demand, Equation 4.4 can be rewritten as $(P/Q) \times (\Delta Q/\Delta P)$. And since $(\Delta Q/\Delta P)$ is the reciprocal of the slope of the supply curve, the right-hand side of Equation 4.4 is equal to $(P/Q) \times (1/\text{slope})$—the same expression we saw in Equation 4.3 for price elasticity of demand. Price and quantity are always positive, as is the slope of the typical supply curve, so price elasticity of supply will be a positive number at every point.

Consider the supply curve shown in Figure 4.13. The slope of this supply curve is 2, so the reciprocal of this slope is 1/2. Using the formula, this means that the price elasticity of supply at A is $(8/2) \times (1/2) = 2$. The corresponding expression at B is $(10/3) \times (1/2) = 5/3$, a slightly smaller value.

FIGURE 4.13
A Supply Curve for Which Price Elasticity Declines as Quantity Rises.
For the supply curve shown, (1/slope) is the same at every point, but the ratio P/Q declines as Q increases. So elasticity = $(P/Q) \times (1/\text{slope})$ declines as quantity increases.

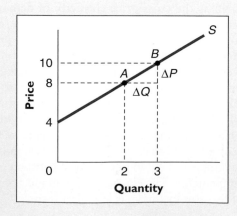

EXERCISE 4.4

For the supply curve shown in Figure 4.13, calculate the elasticity of supply when $P = 6$.

Not all supply curves, however, have the property that price elasticity declines as quantity rises. Consider, for example, the supply curve shown in Figure 4.14. Because the ratio P/Q is the same at every point along this supply curve, and because the slope of the supply curve is also constant, price elasticity of supply will take exactly the same value at every point along this curve. At A, for example, price elasticity of supply = $(P/Q) \times (1/\text{slope}) = (4/12) \times (12/4) = 1$. Similarly, at B price elasticity of supply = $(4/12) \times (12/4) = 1$ again.

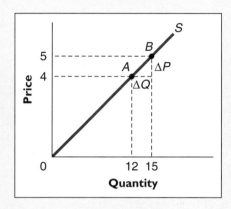

FIGURE 4.14
Calculating the Price Elasticity of Supply Graphically.
Price elasticity of supply is $(P/Q) \times (1/\text{slope})$, which at A is $(4/12) \times (12/4) = 1$, exactly the same as at B. The price elasticity of supply is equal to 1 at any point along a straight-line supply curve that passes through the origin.

Indeed, the price elasticity of supply will always be equal to 1 at any point along a straight-line supply curve that passes through the origin. The reason is that for movements along any such line, both price and quantity always change in exactly the same proportion.

On the buyer's side of the market, two important polar cases were demand curves with infinite price elasticity and zero price elasticity. As the next two examples illustrate, analogous polar cases exist on the seller's side of the market.

What is the elasticity of supply of land within the borough limits of Manhattan?

Land in Manhattan sells in the market for a price, just like aluminum or corn or automobiles or any other product. And the demand for land in Manhattan is a downward-sloping function of its price. For all practical purposes, however, its supply is completely fixed. No matter whether its price is high or low, the same amount of it is available in the market. The supply curve of such a good is vertical, and its price elasticity is zero at every price. Supply curves like the one shown in Figure 4.15 are said to be **perfectly inelastic**.

perfectly inelastic supply
supply is perfectly inelastic with respect to price if elasticity is zero

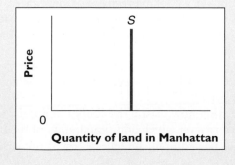

FIGURE 4.15
A Perfectly Inelastic Supply Curve.
Price elasticity of supply is zero at every point along a vertical supply curve.

What is the elasticity of supply of lemonade?

Suppose that the ingredients required to bring a cup of lemonade to market and their respective costs are as follows:

Paper cup	2.0 cents
Lemon	3.8 cents
Sugar	2.0 cents
Water	0.2 cent
Ice	1.0 cent
Labor (30 seconds @ $6/hour)	5.0 cents

If these proportions remain the same no matter how many cups of lemonade are made, and the inputs can be purchased in any quantities at the stated prices, draw the supply curve of lemonade and compute its price elasticity.

Since each cup of lemonade costs exactly 14¢ to make, no matter how many cups are made, the marginal cost of lemonade is constant at 14¢ per cup. And since each point on a supply curve is equal to marginal cost (see Chapter 3), this means that the supply curve of lemonade is not upward-sloping but is instead a horizontal line at 14¢ per cup (Figure 4.16). The price elasticity of supply of lemonade is infinite.

FIGURE 4.16
A Perfectly Elastic Supply Curve.
The elasticity of supply is infinite at every point along a horizontal supply curve.

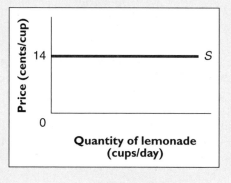

perfectly elastic supply supply is perfectly elastic with respect to price if elasticity of supply is infinite

Whenever additional units of a good can be produced by using the same combination of inputs, purchased at the same prices, as have been used so far, the supply curve of that good will be horizontal. Such supply curves are said to be **perfectly elastic.** ◆

DETERMINANTS OF SUPPLY ELASTICITY

The two preceding examples suggest some of the factors that govern the elasticity of supply of a good or service. The lemonade case was one whose production process was essentially like a cooking recipe. For such cases, we can exactly double our output by doubling each ingredient. If the price of each ingredient remains fixed, the marginal cost of production for such goods will be constant—and hence their horizontal supply curves.

The Manhattan land example is a contrast in the extreme. The inputs that were used to produce land in Manhattan—even if we knew what they were—could not be duplicated at any price.

The key to predicting how elastic the supply of a good will be with respect to price is to know the terms on which additional units of the inputs involved in producing that good can be acquired. In general, the more easily additional units of these inputs can be acquired, the higher price elasticity of supply will be. The following factors (among others) govern the ease with which additional inputs can be acquired by a producer.

Flexibility of Inputs

To the extent that production of a good requires inputs that are also useful for the production of other goods, it is relatively easy to lure additional inputs away from their current uses, making supply of that good relatively elastic with respect to price. Thus the fact that lemonade production requires labor with only minimal skills means that a large pool of workers could shift from other activities to lemonade production if a profitable opportunity arose. Brain surgery, by contrast, requires elaborately trained and specialized labor, which means that even a large price increase would not increase available supplies, except in the very long run.

Mobility of Inputs

If inputs can be easily transported from one site to another, an increase in the price of a product in one market will enable a producer in that market to summon inputs from other markets. For example, the supply of agricultural products is made more elastic with respect to price by the fact that thousands of farm workers are willing to migrate northward during the growing season. The supply of entertainment is similarly made more elastic by the willingness of entertainers to hit the road. Circus performers, lounge singers, comedians, and even exotic dancers often spend a substantial fraction of their time away from home. For instance, according to a 1996 *New York Times* article, the top exotic dancers "basically follow the action, so the same entertainers who worked the Indianapolis 500 now head to Atlanta for the Olympics."

For most goods, the price elasticity of supply increases each time a new highway is built, or when the telecommunications network improves, or indeed when any other development makes it easier to find and transport inputs from one place to another.

Ability to Produce Substitute Inputs

The inputs required to produce finished diamond gemstones include raw diamond crystal, skilled labor, and elaborate cutting and polishing machinery. In time, the number of people with the requisite skills can be increased, as can the amount of specialized machinery. The number of raw diamond crystals buried in the earth is probably fixed in the same way that Manhattan land is fixed, but unlike Manhattan land, rising prices will encourage miners to spend the effort required to find a larger proportion of those crystals. Still, the supply of natural gemstone diamonds tends to be relatively inelastic because of the difficulty of augmenting the number of diamond crystals.

The day is close at hand, however, when gemstone makers will be able to produce synthetic diamond crystals that are indistinguishable from real ones. Indeed, there are already synthetic crystals that fool even highly experienced jewelers. The introduction of a perfect synthetic substitute for natural diamond crystals would increase the price elasticity of supply of diamonds (or, at any rate, the price elasticity of supply of gemstones that look and feel just like diamonds).

Time

Because it takes time for producers to switch from one activity to another, and because it takes time to build new machines and factories and train additional skilled workers, the price elasticity of supply will be higher for most goods in the long run than in the short run. In the short run, a manufacturer's inability to augment existing stocks of equipment and skilled labor may make it impossible to expand output beyond a certain limit. But if a shortage of managers was the bottleneck, new MBAs can be trained in only two years. Or if a shortage of legal staff is the problem, new lawyers can be trained in three years. In the long run, firms can always buy new equipment, build new factories, and hire additional skilled workers.

The conditions that gave rise to the perfectly elastic supply curve for lemonade in the example we discussed earlier are satisfied for many other products in the long run. If a product can be copied (in the sense that any company can acquire the design and other technological information required to produce it), and if the inputs needed for its production are used in roughly fixed proportions and are available at fixed market prices, then the long-run supply curve for that product will be horizontal. But many products do not satisfy these conditions, and their supply curves remain steeply upward-sloping, even in the very long run.

Example 4.3

THE ECONOMIC NATURALIST

EN 4

Why are gasoline prices so much more volatile than car prices?

Automobile price changes in the United States usually occur just once a year, when manufacturers announce an increase of only a few percentage points. In contrast, gasoline prices often fluctuate wildly from day to day. As shown in Figure 4.17, for example, the highest daily gasoline prices in California's two largest cities were three times higher than the lowest daily prices in 2001 and early 2002. Why this enormous difference in volatility?

With respect to price volatility, at least two important features distinguish the gasoline market from the market for cars. One is that the short-run price elasticity of demand for gasoline is much smaller than the corresponding elasticity for cars. The other is that

FIGURE 4.17
Gasoline Prices in Two California Cities.

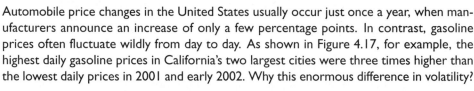

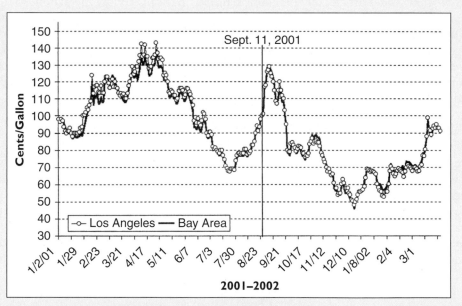

SOURCE: Oil Price Information Service (http://www.opisnet.com).

supply shifts are much more pronounced and frequent in the gasoline market than in the car market. (See Figure 4.18.)

Why are the two markets different in these ways? Consider first the difference in price elasticities of demand. The quantity of gasoline we demand depends largely on the kinds of cars we own and the amounts we drive them. In the short run, car ownership and commuting patterns are almost completely fixed, so even if the price of gasoline were to change sharply, the quantity we demand would not change by much. In contrast, if there were a sudden dramatic change in the price of cars, we could always postpone or accelerate our next car purchases.

To see why the supply curve in the gasoline market experiences larger and more frequent shifts than the supply curve in the car market, we need only examine the relative

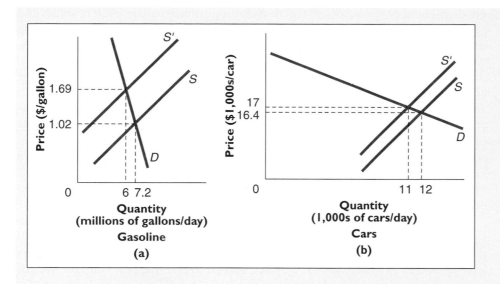

FIGURE 4.18
Greater Volatility in Gasoline Prices Than in Car Prices.
Gasoline prices are more volatile prices because supply shifts are larger and more frequent in the gasoline market (a) than in the car market (b), and also because supply and demand are less elastic in the short run in the gasoline market.

stability of the inputs employed by sellers in these two markets. Most of the inputs used in producing cars—steel, glass, rubber, plastics, electronic components, labor, and others—are reliably available to car makers. In contrast, the key input used in making gasoline—crude oil—is subject to profound and unpredictable supply interruptions.

This is so in part because much of the world's supply of crude oil is controlled by OPEC, a group of oil-exporting countries that has sharply curtailed its oil shipments to the United States on several previous occasions. Even in the absence of formal OPEC action, however, large supply curtailments often occur in the oil market—for example, whenever producers fear that political instability might engulf the major oil-producing countries of the Middle East.

Note in Figure 4.17 the sharp spike in gasoline prices that occurred just after the terrorist attacks on the World Trade Center and Pentagon on September 11, 2001. Because many believed that the aim of these attacks was to provoke large-scale war between Muslim societies and the West, fears of an impending oil supply interruption were perfectly rational. Such fears alone can trigger a temporary supply interruption, even if war is avoided. The prospect of war creates the expectation of oil supply cutbacks that would cause higher prices in the future, which leads producers to withdraw some of their oil from current markets (in order to sell it at higher prices later). But once the fear of war recedes, the supply curve of gasoline reverts with equal speed to its earlier position. Given the low short-run price elasticity of demand for gasoline, that's all it takes to generate the considerable price volatility we see in this market. ●

Why are gasoline prices so much less stable than automobile prices?

Price volatility is also common in markets in which demand curves fluctuate sharply and supply curves are highly inelastic. One such market was California's unregulated market for wholesale electricity during the summer of 2000. The supply of electrical generating capacity was essentially fixed in the short run. And because air conditioning accounts for a large share of demand, several spells of unusually warm weather caused demand to shift sharply to the right. Price at one point reached more than four times its highest level from the previous summer.

UNIQUE AND ESSENTIAL INPUTS: THE ULTIMATE SUPPLY BOTTLENECK

Fans of professional basketball are an enthusiastic bunch. Directly through their purchases of tickets and indirectly through their support of television advertisers, they spend literally billions of dollars each year on the sport. But these dollars are not distributed evenly across all teams. A disproportionate share of all revenues and product endorsement fees accrue to the people associated with consistently winning teams, and at the top of this pyramid generally stands the National Basketball Association's championship team.

Consider the task of trying to produce a championship team in the NBA. What are the inputs you would need? Talented players, a shrewd and dedicated coach and assistants, trainers, physicians, an arena, practice facilities, means for transporting players to away games, a marketing staff, and so on. And whereas some of these inputs can be acquired at reasonable prices in the marketplace, many others cannot. Indeed, the most important input of all—highly talented players—is in extremely limited supply. *This is so because the very definition of talented player is inescapably relative—simply put, such a player is one who is better than most others.*

Given the huge payoff that accrues to the NBA championship team, it is no surprise that the bidding for the most talented players has become so intense. If there were a long list of 7-foot, 1-inch, 325-pound centers, the Phoenix Suns wouldn't have agreed to pay Shaquille O'Neal $20 million over a five-year contract. But, of course, the supply of such players is extremely limited. There are many hungry organizations that would like nothing better than to claim the NBA championship each year, yet no matter how much each is willing to spend, only one can succeed. The supply of NBA championship teams is perfectly inelastic with respect to price even in the very long run.

Sports champions are by no means the only important product whose supply elasticity is constrained by the inability to reproduce unique and essential inputs. In the movie industry, for example, although the supply of movies starring Jim Carrey is not perfectly inelastic, there are only so many films he can make each year. Because his films consistently generate huge box office revenues, scores of film producers want to sign him for their projects. But because there isn't enough of him to go around, his salary per film is more than $20 million.

In the long run, unique and essential inputs are the only truly significant supply bottleneck. If it were not for the inability to duplicate the services of such inputs, most goods and services would have extremely high price elasticities of supply in the long run.

▪ SUMMARY ▪

- The price elasticity of demand is a measure of how strongly buyers respond to changes in price. It is the percentage change in quantity demanded that occurs in response to a 1 percent change in price. The demand for a good is called elastic with respect to price if the absolute value of its price elasticity is more than 1, inelastic if its price elasticity is less than 1, and unit elastic if its price elasticity is equal to 1. **LO1**

- Goods such as salt, which occupy only a small share of the typical consumer's budget and have few or no good substitutes, tend to have low price elasticity of demand. Goods like new cars of a particular make and model, which occupy large budget shares and have many attractive substitutes, tend to have high price elasticity of demand. Price elasticity of demand is higher in the long run than in the short run because people often need time to adjust to price changes. **LO1**

- The price elasticity of demand at a point along a demand curve also can be expressed as the formula $\epsilon = (\Delta Q/Q)/(\Delta P/P)$. Here, P and Q represent price and quantity at that point and ΔQ and ΔP represent small changes in price and quantity. For straight-line demand curves, this formula can also be expressed as $\epsilon = (P/Q) \times (1/\text{slope})$. These formulations tell us that price elasticity declines in absolute terms as we move down a straight-line demand curve. **LO2**

- A cut in price will increase total spending on a good if demand is elastic but reduce it if demand is inelastic. An increase in price will increase total spending on a good if demand is inelastic but reduce it if demand is elastic. Total expenditure on a good reaches a maximum when price elasticity of demand is equal to 1. **LO3**

• Analogous formulas are used to define the elasticity of demand for a good with respect to income and the prices of other goods. In each case, elasticity is the percentage change in quantity demanded divided by the corresponding percentage change in income or price. **LO4**

• Price elasticity of supply is defined as the percentage change in quantity supplied that occurs in response to a 1 percent change in price. The mathematical formula for the price elasticity of supply at any point is $(\Delta Q/Q)/(\Delta P/P)$, where P and Q are the price and quantity at that point, ΔP is a small change in the initial price, and ΔQ is the resulting change in quantity. This formula also can be expressed as $(P/Q) \times$ (1/slope) where (1/slope) is the reciprocal of the slope of the supply curve. **LO5**

• The price elasticity of supply of a good depends on how difficult or costly it is to acquire additional units of the inputs involved in producing that good. In general, the more easily additional units of these inputs can be acquired, the higher price elasticity of supply will be. It is easier to expand production of a product if the inputs used to produce that product are similar to inputs used to produce other products, if inputs are relatively mobile, or if an acceptable substitute for existing inputs can be developed. And like the price elasticity of demand, the price elasticity of supply is greater in the long run than in the short run. **LO6**

▪ KEY TERMS ▪

---

cross-price elasticity of
  demand (111)
elastic (99)
income elasticity of
  demand (111)

inelastic (99)
perfectly elastic demand (106)
perfectly elastic supply (114)
perfectly inelastic demand (107)
perfectly inelastic supply (113)

price elasticity of demand (98)
price elasticity of supply (112)
total expenditure (107)
total revenue (107)
unit elastic (99)

▪ REVIEW QUESTIONS ▪

---

1. Why does a consumer's price elasticity of demand for a good depend on the fraction of the consumer's income spent on that good? **LO1**

2. Why does the price elasticity of demand for a good decline as we move down along a straight-line demand curve? **LO2**

3. Under what conditions will an increase in the price of a product lead to a reduction in total spending for that product? **LO3**

4. Why do economists pay little attention to the algebraic sign of the elasticity of demand for a good with respect to its own price, yet pay careful attention to the algebraic sign of the elasticity of demand for a good with respect to another good's price? **LO4**

5. Why is supply elasticity higher in the long run than in the short run? **LO5**

▪ PROBLEMS ▪

---

1. Calculate the price elasticity of demand at points A, B, C, D, and E on the demand curve below. **LO2**

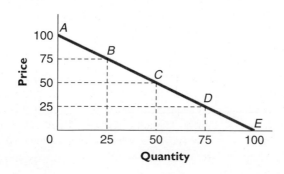

2. The schedule below shows the number of packs of bagels bought in Davis, California, each day at a variety of prices. **LO2, LO3**

Price of bagels ($/pack)	Number of packs purchased per day
6	0
5	3,000
4	6,000
3	9,000
2	12,000
1	15,000
0	18,000

a. Graph the daily demand curve for packs of bagels in Davis.

b. Calculate the price elasticity of demand at the point on the demand curve at which the price of bagels is $3 per pack.

c. If all bagel shops increased the price of bagels from $3 per pack to $4 per pack, what would happen to total revenues?

d. Calculate the price elasticity of demand at a point on the demand curve where the price of bagels is $2 per pack.

e. If bagel shops increased the price of bagels from $2 per pack to $3 per pack, what would happen to total revenues?

3. Suppose, while rummaging through your uncle's closet, you found the original painting of *Dogs Playing Poker*, a valuable piece of art. You decide to set up a display in your uncle's garage. The demand curve to see this valuable piece of art is as shown in the diagram. What price should you charge if your goal is to maximize your revenues from tickets sold? On a graph, show the inelastic and elastic regions of the demand curve. **LO2, LO3**

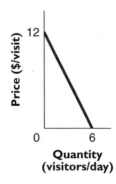

4. Is the demand for a particular brand of car, like a Chevrolet, likely to be more or less price-elastic than the demand for all cars? Explain. **LO1**

5. Among the following groups—senior executives, junior executives, and students—which is likely to have the most and which is likely to have the least price-elastic demand for membership in the Association of Business Professionals? **LO1**

6. A 2 percent increase in the price of milk causes a 4 percent reduction in the quantity demanded of chocolate syrup. What is the cross-price elasticity of demand for chocolate syrup with respect to the price of milk? Are the two goods complements or substitutes? **LO4**

7. What are the respective price elasticities of supply at *A* and *B* on the supply curve shown in the accompanying figure? **LO5**

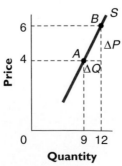

8. Suppose that the ingredients required to bring a slice of pizza to market and their respective costs are as listed in the table:

Paper plate	2 cents
Flour	8 cents
Tomato sauce	20 cents
Cheese	30 cents
Labor (3 minutes @ $12/hour)	60 cents

If these proportions remain the same no matter how many slices are made, and the inputs can be purchased in any quantities at the stated prices, draw the supply curve of pizza slices and compute its price elasticity.   **LO5**

9.* At point A on the demand curve shown, by what percentage will a 1 percent increase in the price of the product affect total expenditure on the product?   **LO3**

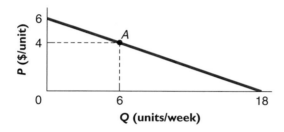

10.* Suppose that, in an attempt to induce citizens to conserve energy, the government enacted regulations requiring that all air conditioners be more efficient in their use of electricity. After this regulation was implemented, government officials were then surprised to discover that people used even more electricity than before. Using the concept of price elasticity, explain how this increase might have occurred.   **LO1, LO4**

*Problems marked with an asterisk (*) are more difficult.

■ ANSWERS TO IN-CHAPTER EXERCISES ■

4.1 In response to a 5 percent reduction in the price of ski passes, the quantity demanded increased by 20 percent. The price elasticity of demand for ski passes is thus (20 percent)/(5 percent) = 4, and that means that at the initial price of $400, the demand for ski passes is elastic with respect to price.   **LO1, LO2**

4.2 At point A in the accompanying diagram, $P/Q = 4/4 = 1$. The slope of this demand curve is 20/5 = 4, so $\epsilon = 1 \times (1/\text{slope}) = 1/4$.   **LO2**

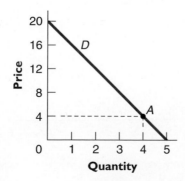

4.3 Income elasticity = percentage change in quantity demanded/percentage change in income = 5 percent/10 percent = 0.5.   **LO4**

4.4 For the supply curve below, $Q = 1$ when $P = 6$, so elasticity of supply = $(P/Q) \times (1/\text{slope}) = (6) \times (1/2) = 3$.   **LO6**

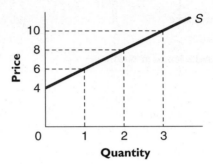

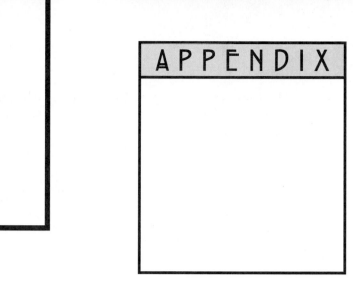

The Midpoint Formula

Suppose you encounter a question like the following on a standardized test in economics:

> At a price of 3, quantity demanded of a good is 6, while at a price of 4, quantity demanded is 4. What is the price elasticity of demand for this good?

Let's attempt to answer this question by using the formula $\epsilon = (\Delta Q/Q)(\Delta P/P)$. In Figure 4A.1 we first plot the two price–quantity pairs given in the question and then draw the straight-line demand curve that connects them. From the graph, it is clear that $\Delta P = 1$ and $\Delta Q = 2$. But what values do we use for P and Q? If we use $P = 4$ and $Q = 4$ (point A), we get an elasticity of 2. But if we use $P = 3$ and $Q = 6$ (point B), we get an elasticity of 1. Thus, if we reckon price and quantity changes as proportions of their values at point A we get one answer, but if we compute them as proportions of their values at point B we get another. Neither of these answers is incorrect. The fact that they differ is merely a reflection of the fact that the elasticity of demand differs at every point along a straight-line demand curve.

Strictly speaking, the original question ("What is the price elasticity of demand for this good?") was not well posed. To have elicited a uniquely correct answer, it should have been "What is the price elasticity of demand at point A?" or "What is the price elasticity of demand at point B?" Economists have nonetheless developed a convention, which we call the *midpoint formula*, for answering ambiguous questions like the one originally posed. If the two points in question are (Q_A, P_A) and (Q_B, P_B), this formula is given by

$$\epsilon = \frac{\Delta Q/[(Q_A + Q_B)/2]}{\Delta P/[(P_A + P_B)/2]}. \tag{4A.1}$$

The midpoint formula thus sidesteps the question of which price–quantity pair to use by using averages of the new and old values. The formula reduces to

$$\epsilon = \frac{\Delta Q/(Q_A + Q_B)}{\Delta P/(P_A + P_B)}. \tag{4A.2}$$

FIGURE 4A.1
Two Points on a Demand Curve.

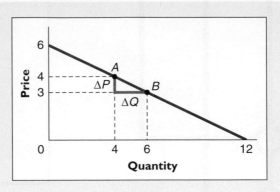

For the two points shown in Figure 4A.1, the midpoint formula yields $\epsilon = [2/(4 + 6)]/[1/(4 + 3)] = 1.4$, which lies between the values for price elasticity at A and B.

We will not employ the midpoint formula again in this text. Hereafter, all questions concerning elasticity will employ the measure discussed in the text of this chapter, which is called *point elasticity*.

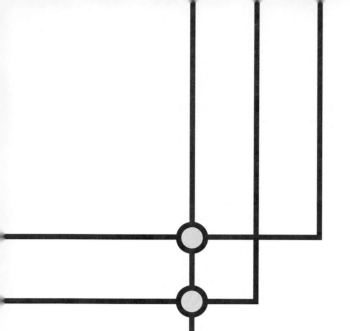

CHAPTER 5

Demand

LEARNING OBJECTIVES

After reading this chapter, you should be able to:

1. Relate the Law of Demand to the Cost-Benefit Principle (Core Principle 2).

2. Discuss how individual wants are translated into demand.

3. Explain the reasoning behind the Rational Spending Rule and apply it to consumer decision making.

4. Show how the Rational Spending Rule is related to substitution and income effects.

5. Discuss the relationship between the individual demand curve and the market demand curve.

6. Define and calculate consumer surplus.

On the northern border of a large university in the East, a creek widens to form a picturesque lake, fondly remembered by generations of alumni as a popular recreation spot. Over the years, the lake had gradually silted in, and by the late 1980s, even paddling a canoe across it had become impossible. A generous alumnus then sponsored an effort to restore the lake. Heavy dredging equipment hauled out load after load of mud, and months later the lake was silt-free.

To mark the occasion, the university held a ceremony. Bands played, the president spoke, a chorus sang, and distinguished visitors applauded the donor's generosity. Hundreds of faculty and students turned out for the festivities. Spotting a good opportunity to promote their product, the proprietors of a local ice cream store set up a temporary stand at the water's edge, with a large sign: "Free Ice Cream."

Word spread. Soon scores of people were lined up waiting to try Vanilla Almond Delight, Hazelnut Cream, and Fudge Faire. The ice cream was plentiful, and because it was free, everyone could obviously afford it—or so it seemed. In fact, many people who wanted ice cream that day never got any. The reason, of course, was that they found waiting in a long line too steep a price to pay for ice cream.

When a good or service is scarce, it must somehow be rationed among competing users. In most markets, monetary prices perform that task. But in the case of a stand offering free ice cream, waiting time becomes the effective rationing device. Having to stand in line is a cost, no less so than having to part with some money.

This example drives home the point that although the demand curve is usually described as a relationship between the quantity demanded of a good and its monetary price, the relationship is really a much more general one. At bottom, the demand curve is a relationship between the quantity demanded and *all* costs—monetary and nonmonetary—associated with acquiring a good.

Our task in this chapter will be to explore the demand side of the market in greater depth than was possible in Chapter 3. There we merely asked you to accept as an intuitively plausible claim that the quantity demanded of a good or service declines as its price rises. This relationship is known as the Law of Demand, and we will see how it emerges as a simple consequence of the assumption that people spend their limited incomes in rational ways. In the process, we will see more clearly the dual roles of income and substitution as factors that account for the Law of Demand. We also will see how to generate market demand curves by adding the demand curves for individual buyers horizontally. Finally, we will see how to use the demand curve to generate a measure of the total benefit that buyers reap from their participation in a market.

THE LAW OF DEMAND

With our discussion of the free ice cream offer in mind, let us restate the law of demand as follows:

Law of Demand: People do less of what they want to do as the cost of doing it rises.

Cost-Benefit ○

By stating the law of demand this way, we can see it as a direct consequence of the Cost-Benefit Principle, which says that an activity should be pursued if (and only if) its benefits are at least as great as its costs. Recall that we measure the benefit of an activity by the highest price we'd be willing to pay to pursue it—namely, our reservation price for the activity. When the cost of an activity rises, it is more likely to exceed our reservation price, and we are therefore less likely to pursue that activity.

The law of demand applies to BMWs, cheap key rings, and "free" ice cream, not to mention compact discs, manicures, medical care, and acid-free rain. It stresses that a "cost" is the sum of *all* the sacrifices—monetary and nonmonetary, implicit and explicit—we must make to engage in an activity.

THE ORIGINS OF DEMAND

How much are you willing to pay for the latest Amy Winehouse CD? The answer will clearly depend on how you feel about her music. To her diehard fans, buying the new release might seem absolutely essential; they'd pay a steep price indeed. But those who don't like her music may be unwilling to buy it at any price.

Wants (also called "preferences" or "tastes") are clearly an important determinant of a consumer's reservation price for a good. But that begs the question of where wants come from. Many tastes—such as the taste for water on a hot day or for a comfortable place to sleep at night—are largely biological in origin. But many others are heavily shaped by culture, and even basic cravings may be socially molded. For example, people raised in southern India develop a taste for hot curry dishes, while those raised in England generally prefer milder foods.

Tastes for some items may remain stable for many years, but tastes for others may be highly volatile. Although books about the *Titanic* disaster have been continuously available since the vessel sank in the spring of 1912, not until the appearance of James Cameron's blockbuster film did these books begin to sell in large quantities. In the spring of 1998, five of the 15 books on the *New York Times* paperback bestseller list were about the *Titanic* itself or one of the actors in the film. Yet none of these books, or any other book about the *Titanic*, made the bestseller list in the years since then. Still, echoes of the film continued to reverberate in the marketplace. In the years since its release, for example, demand for ocean cruises has grown sharply and several television networks have introduced shows set on cruise ships.

EN 5

Peer influence provides another example of how social forces often influence demand. Indeed, it is often the most important single determinant of demand. For instance, if our goal is to predict whether a young man will purchase an illegal recreational drug, knowing how much income he has is not very helpful. Knowing the prices of whiskey and other legal substitutes for illicit drugs also tells us little. Although these factors do influence purchase decisions, by themselves they are weak predictors. But if we know that most of the young man's best friends are heavy drug users, there is a reasonably good chance that he will use drugs as well.

Another important way in which social forces shape demand is in the relatively common desire to consume goods and services that are recognized as the best of their kind. For instance, many people want to hear Placido Domingo sing, not just because of the quality of his voice, but because he is widely regarded as the world's best—or at least the world's best known—living tenor.

Consider, too, the decision of how much to spend on an interview suit. Employment counselors never tire of reminding us that making a good first impression is extremely important when you go for a job interview. At the very least, that means showing up in a suit that looks good. But looking good is a relative concept. If everyone else shows up in a $200 suit, you'll look good if you show up in a $300 suit. But you won't look as good in that same $300 suit if everyone else shows up in suits costing $1,000. The amount you'll choose to spend on an interview suit, then, clearly depends on how much others in your circle are spending.

NEEDS VERSUS WANTS

In everyday language, we distinguish between goods and services people need and those they merely want. For example, we might say that someone wants a ski vacation in Utah, but what he really needs is a few days off from his daily routine; or that someone wants a house with a view, but what she really needs is shelter from the elements. Likewise, since people need protein to survive, we might say that a severely malnourished person needs more protein. But it would strike us as odd to say that anyone—even a malnourished person—needs more prime filet of beef, since health can be restored by consuming far less expensive sources of protein.

Economists like to emphasize that once we have achieved bare subsistence levels of consumption—the amount of food, shelter, and clothing required to maintain our health—we can abandon all reference to needs and speak only in terms of wants. This linguistic distinction helps us to think more clearly about the true nature of our choices.

For instance, someone who says, "Californians don't have nearly as much water as they need" will tend to think differently about water shortages than someone who says, "Californians don't have nearly as much water as they want when the price of water is low." The first person is likely to focus on regulations to prevent people from watering their lawns, or on projects to capture additional runoff from the Sierra Nevada mountains. The second person is more likely to focus on the artificially low price of water in California. Whereas remedies of the first sort are often costly and extremely difficult to implement, raising the price of water is both simple and effective.

Example 5.1

THE ECONOMIC NATURALIST

Why do farmers grow water-intensive crops like rice in an arid state like California?

Why does California experience chronic water shortages?

Some might respond that the state must serve the needs of a large population with a relatively low average annual rainfall. Yet other states, like New Mexico, have even less rainfall per person and do not experience water shortages nearly as often as California. California's problem exists because local governments sell water at extremely low prices, which encourages Californians to use water in ways that make no sense for a state with low rainfall. For instance, rice, which is well suited for conditions in high-rainfall states like South Carolina, requires extensive irrigation in California. But because California farmers can obtain water so cheaply, they plant and flood hundreds of thousands of acres of rice paddies each spring in the Central Valley. Two thousand tons of water are needed to produce one ton of rice, but many other grains can be produced with only half that amount. If the price of California water were higher, farmers would simply switch to other grains.

Likewise, cheap water encourages homeowners in Los Angeles and San Diego to plant water-intensive lawns and shrubs, like the ones common in the East and Midwest. By contrast, residents of cities like Santa Fe, New Mexico, where water prices are high, choose native plantings that require little or no watering. ●

TRANSLATING WANTS INTO DEMAND

It's a simple fact of life that although our resources are finite, our appetites for good things are boundless. Even if we had unlimited bank accounts, we'd quickly run out of the time and energy needed to do all the things we wanted to do. Our challenge is to use our limited resources to fulfill our desires to the greatest possible degree. That leaves us with a practical question: How should we allocate our incomes among the various goods and services that are available? To answer this question, it's helpful to begin by recognizing that the goods and services we buy are not ends in themselves, but rather means for satisfying our desires.

MEASURING WANTS: THE CONCEPT OF UTILITY

Economists use the concept of *utility* to represent the satisfaction people derive from their consumption activities. The assumption is that people try to allocate their incomes so as to maximize their satisfaction, a goal that is referred to as *utility maximization*.

Early economists imagined that the utility associated with different activities might someday be subject to precise measurement. The nineteenth-century British economist Jeremy Bentham, for example, wrote of a "utilometer," a device that could be used to measure the amount of utility provided by different consumption activities. Although no such device existed in Bentham's day, contemporary neuropsychologists now have equipment that can generate at least crude measures of satisfaction.

Figure 5.1, for example, shows a subject who is connected to an apparatus that measures the intensity of electrical waves emanating from his brain. University of Wisconsin psychologist Richard Davidson and his colleagues documented that subjects with relatively heavy brain-wave measures emanating from the left prefrontal cortex tend to be happier (as assessed by a variety of other measures) than subjects with relatively heavy brain-wave measures emanating from the right prefrontal cortex.

Jeremy Bentham would have been thrilled to learn that a device like the one pictured in Figure 5.1 might exist some day. His ideal utilometer would measure utility in utils, much as a thermometer measures temperature in degrees Fahrenheit or Celsius. It would assign a numerical utility value to every activity—watching a movie, eating a cheeseburger, and so on. Unfortunately, even sophisticated devices like the one shown in Figure 5.1 are far from capable of such fine-grained assessments.

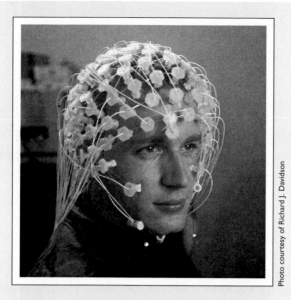

FIGURE 5.1
Can Utility Be Measured Electronically?
Scientists have shown that higher levels of electrical activity on the brain's left side are strongly associated with higher levels of satisfaction.

For Bentham's intellectual enterprise, however, the absence of a real utilometer was of no practical significance. Even without such a machine, he could continue to envision the consumer as someone whose goal was to maximize the total utility she obtained from the goods she consumed. Bentham's "utility maximization model," we will see, affords important insights about how a rational consumer ought to spend her income.

To explore how the model works, we begin with a very simple problem, the one facing a consumer who reaches the front of the line at a free ice cream stand. How many cones of ice cream should this person, whom we'll call Sarah, ask for? Table 5.1 shows the relationship between the total number of ice cream cones Sarah eats per hour and the total utility, measured in utils per hour, she derives from them. Note that the measurements in the table are stated in terms of cones per hour and utils per hour. Why "per hour"? Because without an explicit time dimension, we would have no idea whether a given quantity was a lot or a little. Five ice cream cones in a lifetime isn't much, but five in an hour would be more than most of us would care to eat.

As the entries in Table 5.1 show, Sarah's total utility increases with each cone she eats, up to the fifth cone. Eating five cones per hour makes her happier than eating four, which makes her happier than eating three, and so on. But beyond five cones per hour, consuming more ice cream actually makes Sarah less happy. Thus, the sixth cone reduces her total utility from 150 utils per hour to 140 utils per hour.

TABLE 5.1
Sarah's Total Utility from Ice Cream Consumption

Cone quantity (cones/hour)	Total utility (utils/hour)
0	0
1	50
2	90
3	120
4	140
5	150
6	140

FIGURE 5.2
Sarah's Total Utility from Ice Cream Consumption.
For most goods, utility rises at a diminishing rate with additional consumption.

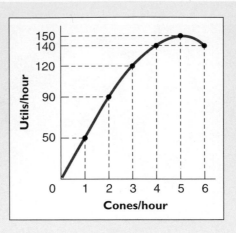

We can display the utility information in Table 5.1 graphically, as in Figure 5.2. Note in the graph that the more cones per hour Sarah eats, the more utils she gets—but again only up to the fifth cone. Once she moves beyond five, her total utility begins to decline. Sarah's happiness reaches a maximum of 150 utils when she eats five cones per hour. At that point she has no incentive to eat the sixth cone, even though it's absolutely free. Eating it would actually make her worse off.

Table 5.1 and Figure 5.2 illustrate another important aspect of the relationship between utility and consumption—namely, that the additional utility from additional units of consumption declines as total consumption increases. Thus, whereas one cone per hour is a *lot* better—by 50 utils—than zero, five cones per hour is just a *little* better than four (just 10 utils' worth).

marginal utility the additional utility gained from consuming an additional unit of a good

The term **marginal utility** denotes the amount by which total utility changes when consumption changes by one unit. In Table 5.2, the third column shows the marginal utility values that correspond to changes in Sarah's level of ice cream consumption. For example, the second entry in that column represents the increase in

TABLE 5.2
Sarah's Total and Marginal Utility from Ice Cream Consumption

Cone quantity (cones/hour)	Total utility (utils/hour)	Marginal utility (utils/cone)
0	0	—
		50
1	50	
		40
2	90	
		30
3	120	
		20
4	140	
		10
5	150	
		−10
6	140	

Marginal utility
$$= \frac{\text{change in utility}}{\text{change in consumption}}$$
$$= \frac{90 \text{ utils} - 50 \text{ utils}}{2 \text{ cones} - 1 \text{ cone}}$$
$$= 40 \text{ utils/cone}$$

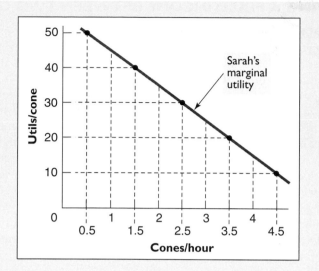

FIGURE 5.3
Diminishing Marginal Utility.
The more cones Sarah consumes each hour, the smaller her marginal utility will be. For Sarah, consumption of ice cream cones satisfies the law of diminishing marginal utility.

total utility (measured in utils per cone) when Sarah's consumption rises from one cone per hour to two. Note that the marginal utility entries in the third column are placed midway between the rows of the preceding columns. We do this to indicate that marginal utility corresponds to the movement from one consumption quantity to the next. Thus, we would say that the marginal utility of moving from one to two cones per hour is 40 utils per cone.

Because marginal utility is the change in utility that occurs as we move from one quantity to another, when we graph marginal utility, we normally adopt the convention of plotting each specific marginal utility value halfway between the two quantities to which it corresponds. Thus, in Figure 5.3, we plot the marginal utility value of 40 utils per cone midway between one cone per hour and two cones per hour, and so on. (In this example, the marginal utility graph is a downward-sloping straight line for the region shown, but this need not always be the case.)

The tendency for marginal utility to decline as consumption increases beyond some point is called the **law of diminishing marginal utility**. It holds not just for Sarah's consumption of ice cream in this illustration, but also for most other goods for most consumers. If we have one brownie or one Ferrari, we're happier than we are with none; if we have two, we'll be even happier—but not twice as happy—and so on. Though this pattern is called a law, there are exceptions. Indeed, some consumption activities even seem to exhibit *increasing* marginal utility. For example, an unfamiliar song may seem irritating the first time you hear it, then gradually become more tolerable the next few times you hear it. Before long, you may discover that you *like* the song, and you may even find yourself singing it in the shower. Notwithstanding such exceptions, the law of diminishing marginal utility is a plausible characterization of the relationship between utility and consumption for many goods. Unless otherwise stated, we'll assume that it holds for the various goods we discuss.

What will Sarah do when she gets to the front of the line? At that point, the opportunity cost of the time she spent waiting is a sunk cost and is hence irrelevant to her decision about how many cones to order. And since there is no monetary charge for the cones, the cost of ordering an additional one is zero. According to the Cost-Benefit Principle, Sarah should therefore continue to order cones as long as the marginal benefit (here, the marginal utility she gets from an additional cone) is greater than or equal to zero. As we can see from the entries in Table 5.2, marginal utility is positive up to and including the fifth cone but becomes negative after five cones. Thus, as noted earlier, Sarah should order five cones.

law of diminishing marginal utility the tendency for the additional utility gained from consuming an additional unit of a good to diminish as consumption increases beyond some point

Cost-Benefit

ALLOCATING A FIXED INCOME BETWEEN TWO GOODS

Most of the time we face considerably more complex purchase decisions than the one Sarah faced. For one thing, we generally must make decisions about many goods, not just a single one like ice cream. Another complication is that the cost of consuming additional units of each good will rarely be zero.

To see how to proceed in more complex cases, let's suppose Sarah must decide how to spend a fixed sum of money on two different goods, each with a positive price. Should she spend all of it on one of the goods or part of it on each? The law of diminishing marginal utility suggests that spending it all on a single good isn't a good strategy. Rather than devote more and more money to the purchase of a good we already consume in large quantities (and whose marginal utility is therefore relatively low), we generally do better to spend that money on other goods we don't have much of, whose marginal utility will likely be higher.

The simplest way to illustrate how economists think about the spending decisions of a utility-maximizing consumer is to work through a series of examples, beginning with the following:

Is Sarah maximizing her utility from consuming chocolate and vanilla ice cream (I)?

Chocolate ice cream sells for $2 per pint and vanilla sells for $1. Sarah has a budget of $400 per year to spend on ice cream and her marginal utility from consuming each type varies with the amount consumed, as shown in Figure 5.4. If she is currently buying 200 pints of vanilla and 100 pints of chocolate each year, is she maximizing her utility?

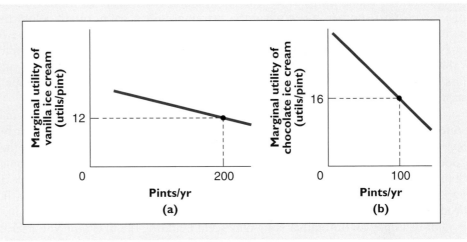

FIGURE 5.4
Marginal Utility Curves for Two Flavors of Ice Cream (I).
At Sarah's current consumption levels, her marginal utility of chocolate ice cream is 25 percent higher than her marginal utility of vanilla. But chocolate is twice as expensive as vanilla.

Note first that with 200 pints per year of vanilla and 100 pints of chocolate, Sarah is spending $200 per year on each type of ice cream, for a total expenditure of $400 per year on ice cream, exactly the amount in her budget. By spending her money in this fashion, is she getting as much utility as possible? Note in Figure 5.4(b) that her marginal utility from chocolate ice cream is 16 utils per pint. Since chocolate costs $2 per pint, her current spending on chocolate is yielding additional utility at the rate of (16 utils/pint)/($2/pint) = 8 utils per dollar. Similarly, note in Figure 5.4(a) that Sarah's marginal utility for vanilla is 12 utils per pint. And since vanilla costs only $1 per pint, her current spending on vanilla is yielding (12 utils/pint)/($1/pint) = 12 utils per dollar. In other words, at her current rates of consumption of the two flavors, her spending yields higher marginal utility per dollar for vanilla than for chocolate. And this means that Sarah cannot possibly be maximizing her total utility.

To see why, note that if she spent $2 less on chocolate (that is, if she bought one pint less than before), she would lose about 16 utils;[1] but with the same $2, she could buy two additional pints of vanilla, which would boost her utility by about 24 utils,[2] for a net gain of about 8 utils. Under Sarah's current budget allocation, she is thus spending too little on vanilla and too much on chocolate. ◆

In the next example, we'll see what happens if Sarah spends $100 per year less on chocolate and $100 per year more on vanilla.

Is Sarah maximizing her utility from consuming chocolate and vanilla ice cream (II)?

Sarah's total ice cream budget and the prices of the two flavors are the same as in the earlier example. If her marginal utility from consuming each type varies with the amount consumed, as shown in Figure 5.5, and if she is currently buying 300 pints of vanilla and 50 pints of chocolate each year, is she maximizing her utility?

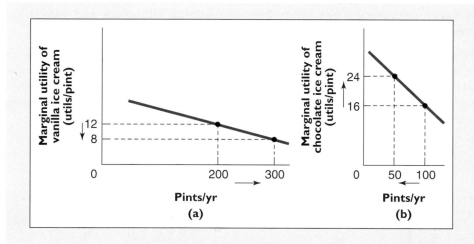

FIGURE 5.5
Marginal Utility Curves for Two Flavors of Ice Cream (II).
When Sarah increases her consumption of vanilla (a), her marginal utility of vanilla falls. Conversely, when she reduces her consumption of chocolate (b), her marginal utility of chocolate rises.

Note first that the direction of Sarah's rearrangement of her spending makes sense in light of the original example, in which we saw that she was spending too much on chocolate and too little on vanilla. Spending $100 less on chocolate ice cream causes her marginal utility from that flavor to rise from 16 to 24 utils per pint [Figure 5.5(b)]. By the same token, spending $100 more on vanilla ice cream causes her marginal utility from that flavor to fall from 12 to 8 utils per pint [Figure 5.5(a)]. Both movements are a simple consequence of the law of diminishing marginal utility.

Since chocolate still costs $2 per pint, her spending on chocolate now yields additional utility at the rate of (24 utils/pint)/($2/pint) = 12 utils per dollar. Similarly, since vanilla still costs $1 per pint, her spending on vanilla now yields additional utility at the rate of only (8 utils/pint)/($1/pint) = 8 utils per dollar. So at her new rates of consumption of the two flavors, her spending yields higher marginal utility per dollar for chocolate than for vanilla—precisely the opposite of the ordering we saw in the original example.

Sarah has thus made too big an adjustment in her effort to remedy her original consumption imbalance. Starting from the new combination of flavors (300 pints per year of vanilla and 50 pints per year of chocolate), for example, if she then

---

[1] The actual reduction would be slightly larger than 16 utils because her marginal utility of chocolate rises slightly as she consumes less of it.
[2] The actual increase will be slightly smaller than 24 utils because her marginal utility of vanilla falls slightly as she buys more of it.

bought two fewer pints of vanilla (which would reduce her utility by about 16 utils) and used the $2 she saved to buy an additional pint of chocolate (which would boost her utility by about 24 utils), she would experience a net gain of about 8 utils. So again, her current combination of the two flavors fails to maximize her total utility. This time, she is spending too little on chocolate and too much on vanilla. ◆

EXERCISE 5.1

In the preceding examples, verify that the stated combination of flavors costs exactly the amount that Sarah has budgeted for ice cream.

optimal combination of goods
the affordable combination that
yields the highest total utility

What is Sarah's **optimal combination** of the two flavors? In other words, among all the combinations of vanilla and chocolate ice cream that Sarah can afford, which one provides the maximum possible total utility? The following example illustrates the condition that this optimal combination must satisfy.

Is Sarah maximizing her utility from consuming chocolate and vanilla ice cream (III)?

Sarah's total ice cream budget and the prices of the two flavors are the same as in the previous examples. If her marginal utility from consuming each type varies with the amounts consumed, as shown in Figure 5.6, and if she is currently buying 250 pints of vanilla and 75 pints of chocolate each year, is she maximizing her utility?

FIGURE 5.6
Marginal Utility Curves for Two Flavors of Ice Cream (III).
At her current consumption levels, marginal utility per dollar is exactly the same for each flavor.

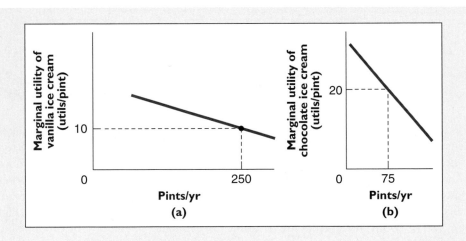

As you can easily verify, the combination of 250 pints per year of vanilla and 75 pints per year of chocolate again costs a total of $400, exactly the amount of Sarah's ice cream budget. Her marginal utility from chocolate is now 20 utils per pint [Figure 5.6(b)], and since chocolate still costs $2 per pint, her spending on chocolate now yields additional utility at the rate of (20 utils/pint)/($2/pint) = 10 utils per dollar. Sarah's marginal utility for vanilla is now 10 utils per pint [Figure 5.6(a)], and since vanilla still costs $1 per pint, her last dollar spent on vanilla now also yields (10 utils/pint)/($1/pint) = 10 utils per dollar. So at her new rates of consumption of the two flavors, her spending yields precisely the same marginal utility per dollar for each flavor. Thus, if she spent a little less on chocolate and a little more on vanilla (or vice versa), her total utility would not change at all. For example, if she bought two more pints of vanilla (which would increase her utility by 20 utils) and one fewer pint of chocolate (which would reduce her utility by 20 utils), both her total expenditure on ice cream and her total utility would remain the same as before. *When her marginal utility per dollar is the same for each flavor, it is impossible for Sarah to rearrange her spending to increase total utility.* Therefore, 250 pints of vanilla and 75 pints of chocolate per year form the optimal combination of the two flavors. ◆

THE RATIONAL SPENDING RULE

The examples we have worked through illustrate the **Rational Spending Rule** for solving the problem of how to allocate a fixed budget across different goods. The optimal, or utility-maximizing, combination must satisfy this rule.

The Rational Spending Rule: Spending should be allocated across goods so that the marginal utility per dollar is the same for each good.

The rational spending rule can be expressed in the form of a simple formula. If we use MU_C to denote marginal utility from chocolate ice cream consumption (again measured in utils per pint) and P_C to denote the price of chocolate (measured in dollars per pint), then the ratio MU_C/P_C will represent the marginal utility per dollar spent on chocolate, measured in utils per dollar. Similarly, if we use MU_V to denote the marginal utility from vanilla ice cream consumption and P_V to denote the price of vanilla, then MU_V/P_V will represent the marginal utility per dollar spent on vanilla. The marginal utility per dollar will be exactly the same for the two types— and hence total utility will be maximized—when the following simple equation for the rational spending rule for two goods is satisfied:

$$MU_C/P_C = MU_V/P_V.$$

The rational spending rule is easily generalized to apply to spending decisions regarding large numbers of goods. In its most general form, it says that the ratio of marginal utility to price must be the same for each good the consumer buys. If the ratio were higher for one good than for another, the consumer could always increase her total utility by buying more of the first good and less of the second.

Strictly speaking, the rational spending rule applies to goods that are perfectly divisible, such as milk or gasoline. Many other goods, such as bus rides and television sets, can be consumed only in whole-number amounts. In such cases, it may not be possible to satisfy the rational spending rule exactly. For example, when you buy one television set, your marginal utility per dollar spent on televisions may be somewhat higher than the corresponding ratio for other goods, yet if you bought a second set, the reverse might well be true. Your best alternative in such cases is to allocate each additional dollar you spend to the good for which your marginal utility per dollar is highest.[3]

Notice that we have not chosen to classify the rational spending rule as one of the core principles of economics. We omit it from this list not because the rule is unimportant, but because it follows directly from the Cost-Benefit Principle. As we noted earlier, there is considerable advantage in keeping the list of core principles as small as possible.

Cost-Benefit

INCOME AND SUBSTITUTION EFFECTS REVISITED

In Chapter 3, we saw that the quantity of a good that consumers wish to purchase depends on its own price, on the prices of substitutes and complements, and on consumer incomes. We also saw that when the price of a good changes, the quantity of

---

[3]See Problems 6 and 10 at the end of the chapter for examples.

it demanded changes for two reasons: the substitution effect and the income effect. The substitution effect refers to the fact that when the price of a good goes up, substitutes for that good become relatively more attractive, causing some consumers to abandon the good for its substitutes.

The income effect refers to the fact that a price change makes the consumer either poorer or richer in real terms. Consider, for instance, the effect of a change in the price of one of the ice cream flavors in the preceding examples. At the original prices ($2 per pint for chocolate, $1 per pint for vanilla), Sarah's $400 annual ice cream budget enabled her to buy at most 200 pints per year of chocolate or 400 pints per year of vanilla. If the price of vanilla rose to $2 per pint, that would reduce not only the maximum amount of vanilla she could afford (from 400 to 200 pints per year) but also the maximum amount of chocolate she could afford in combination with any given amount of vanilla. For example, at the original price of $1 per pint for vanilla, Sarah could afford to buy 150 pints of chocolate while buying 100 pints of vanilla; but when the price of vanilla rises to $2, she can buy only 100 pints of chocolate while buying 100 pints of vanilla. As noted in Chapter 3, a reduction in real income shifts the demand curves for normal goods to the left.

The rational spending rule helps us see more clearly why a change in the price of one good affects demands for other goods. The rule requires that the ratio of marginal utility to price be the same for all goods. This means that if the price of one good goes up, the ratio of its current marginal utility to its new price will be lower than for other goods. Consumers can then increase their total utility by devoting smaller proportions of their incomes to that good and larger proportions to others.

How should Sarah respond to a reduction in the price of chocolate ice cream?

Suppose that Sarah's total ice cream budget is still $400 per year and the prices of the two flavors are again $2 per pint for chocolate and $1 per pint for vanilla. Her marginal utility from consuming each type varies with the amounts consumed, as shown in Figure 5.7. As we showed in the previous examples, she is currently buying 250 pints of vanilla and 75 pints of chocolate each year, which is the optimal combination for her at these prices. How should she reallocate her spending among the two flavors if the price of chocolate ice cream falls to $1 per pint?

FIGURE 5.7
Marginal Utility Curves for Two Flavors of Ice Cream (IV).
At the current combination of flavors, marginal utility per dollar is the same for each flavor. When the price of chocolate falls, marginal utility per dollar becomes higher for chocolate than for vanilla. To redress this imbalance, Sarah should buy more chocolate and less vanilla.

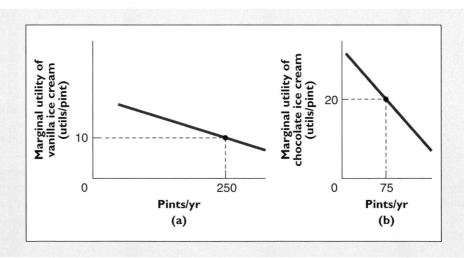

Because the quantities shown in Figure 5.7 constitute the optimal combination of the two flavors for Sarah at the original prices, they must exactly satisfy the rational spending rule:

$$MU_C/P_C = (20 \text{ utils/pint})/(\$2/\text{pint}) = 10 \text{ utils/dollar}$$
$$= MU_V/P_V = (10 \text{ utils/pint})/(\$1/\text{pint}).$$

When the price of chocolate falls to \$1 per pint, the original quantities will no longer satisfy the rational spending rule because the marginal utility per dollar for chocolate will suddenly be twice what it was before:

$$MU_C/P_C = (20 \text{ utils/pint})/(\$1/\text{pint}) = 20 \text{ utils/dollar}$$
$$> MU_V/P_V = 10 \text{ utils/dollar}.$$

To redress this imbalance, Sarah must rearrange her spending on the two flavors in such a way as to increase the marginal utility per dollar for vanilla relative to the marginal utility per dollar for chocolate. And as we see in Figure 5.7, that will happen if she buys a larger quantity than before of chocolate and a smaller quantity than before of vanilla. ◆

EXERCISE 5.2

John spends all of his income on two goods: food and shelter. The price of food is \$5 per pound and the price of shelter is \$10 per square yard. At his current consumption levels, his marginal utilities for the two goods are 20 utils per pound and 30 utils per square yard, respectively. Is John maximizing his utility? If not, how should he reallocate his spending?

In Chapter 1 we saw that people often make bad decisions because they fail to appreciate the distinction between average and marginal costs and benefits. As the following example illustrates, this pitfall also arises when people attempt to apply the economist's model of utility maximization.

Should Eric consume more apples?

Eric gets a total of 1,000 utils per week from his consumption of apples and a total of 400 utils per week from his consumption of oranges. The price of apples is \$2 each, the price of oranges is \$1 each, and he consumes 50 apples and 50 oranges each week. True or false: Eric should consume more apples and fewer oranges.

Eric spends \$100 per week on apples and \$50 on oranges. He thus averages (1,000 utils/week)/(\$100/week) = 10 utils per dollar from his consumption of apples and (400 utils/week)/(\$50/week) = 8 utils per dollar from his consumption of oranges. Many might be tempted to respond that because Eric's average utility per dollar for apples is higher than for oranges, he should consume more apples. But knowing only his *average* utility per dollar for each good does not enable us to say whether his current combination is optimal. To make that determination, we need to compare Eric's *marginal* utility per dollar for each good. The information given simply doesn't permit us to make that comparison. ◆

RECAP	TRANSLATING WANTS INTO DEMAND

The Scarcity Principle challenges us to allocate our incomes among the various goods that are available so as to fulfill our desires to the greatest possible degree. The optimal combination of goods is the affordable combination that yields the highest total utility. For goods that are perfectly divisible, the rational spending rule tells us that the optimal combination is one for which the marginal utility per dollar is the same for each good. If this condition were not satisfied, the consumer could increase her utility by spending less on goods for which the marginal utility per dollar was lower and more on goods for which her marginal utility was higher.

Scarcity

APPLYING THE RATIONAL SPENDING RULE

The real payoff from learning the law of demand and the rational spending rule lies in using these abstract concepts to make sense of the world around you. To encourage you in your efforts to become an economic naturalist, we turn now to a sequence of examples in this vein.

SUBSTITUTION AT WORK

In the first of these examples, we focus on the role of substitution. When the price of a good or service goes up, rational consumers generally turn to less expensive substitutes. Can't meet the payments on a new car? Then buy a used one, or rent an apartment on a bus or subway line. French restaurants too pricey? Then go out for Chinese, or eat at home more often. National Football League tickets too high? Watch the game on television, or read a book. Can't afford a book? Check one out of the library, or download some reading matter from the internet. Once you begin to see substitution at work, you will be amazed by the number and richness of the examples that confront you every day.

Example 5.2

THE ECONOMIC NATURALIST

Why do the wealthy in Manhattan live in smaller houses than the wealthy in Seattle?

Microsoft cofounder Bill Gates lives in a 45,000-square-foot house in Seattle, Washington. His house is large even by the standards of Seattle, many of whose wealthy residents live in houses with more than 10,000 square feet of floor space. By contrast, persons of similar wealth in Manhattan rarely live in houses larger than 5,000 square feet. Why this difference?

For people trying to decide how large a house to buy, the most obvious difference between Manhattan and Seattle is the huge difference in housing prices. The cost of land alone is several times higher in Manhattan than in Seattle, and construction costs are also much higher. Although plenty of New Yorkers could *afford* to build a 45,000-square-foot mansion, Manhattan housing prices are so high that they simply choose to live in smaller houses and spend what they save in other ways—on lavish summer homes in eastern Long Island, for instance. New Yorkers also eat out and go to the theater more often than their wealthy counterparts in other U.S. cities. •

Would Bill Gates build a 45,000-square-foot house if he lived in Manhattan?

An especially vivid illustration of substitution occurred during the late 1970s, when fuel shortages brought on by interruptions in the supply of oil from the Middle East led to sharp increases in the price of gasoline and other fuels. In a variety of ways—some straightforward, others remarkably ingenious—consumers changed their behavior to economize on the use of energy. They formed car pools; switched to public transportation; bought four-cylinder cars; moved closer to work; took fewer trips; turned down their thermostats; installed insulation, storm windows, and solar heaters; and bought more efficient appliances. Many people even moved farther south to escape high winter heating bills.

As the next example points out, consumers not only abandon a good in favor of substitutes when it gets more expensive, but they also return to that good when prices return to their original levels.

Example 5.3

THE ECONOMIC NATURALIST

Why did people turn to four-cylinder cars in the 1970s, only to shift back to six- and eight-cylinder cars in the 1990s?

In 1973, the price of gasoline was 38 cents per gallon. The following year the price shot up to 52 cents per gallon in the wake of a major disruption of oil supplies. A second disruption in 1979 drove the 1980 price to $1.19 per gallon. These sharp increases in the price of gasoline led to big increases in the demand for cars with four-cylinder engines, which delivered much better fuel economy than the six- and eight-cylinder cars most people had owned. After 1980, however, fuel supplies stabilized, and prices rose only slowly, reaching $1.40 per gallon by 1999. Yet despite the continued rise in the price of gasoline, the switch to smaller engines did not continue. By the late 1980s, the proportion of cars sold with six- and eight-cylinder engines began rising again. Why this reversal?

The key to explaining these patterns is to focus on changes in the **real price** of gasoline. When someone decides how big an automobile engine to choose, what matters is not the **nominal price** of gasoline, but the price of gasoline *relative* to all other goods. After all, for a consumer faced with a decision of whether to spend $1.40 for a gallon of gasoline, the important question is how much utility she could get from other things she could purchase with the same money. Even though the price of gasoline continued to rise slowly in nominal, or dollar, terms through the 1980s and 1990s, it declined sharply relative to the price of other goods. Indeed, in terms of real purchasing power, the 1999 price was actually slightly lower than the 1973 price. (That is, in 1999 $1.40 bought slightly fewer goods and services than 38 cents bought in 1973.) It is this decline in the real price of gasoline that accounts for the reversal of the trend toward smaller engines. ●

real price the dollar price of a good relative to the average dollar price of all other goods

nominal price the absolute price of a good in dollar terms

A sharp decline in the real price of gasoline also helps account for the explosive growth in sport utility vehicles in the 1990s. Almost 4 million SUVs were sold in the United States in 2001, up from only 750,000 in 1990. Some of them—like the Ford Excursion—weigh more than 7,500 pounds (three times as much as a Honda Civic) and get less than 10 miles per gallon on city streets. Vehicles like these would have been dismal failures during the 1970s, but they were by far the hottest sellers in the cheap-energy environment of 2001.

"We motored over to say hi!"

In 2004, gasoline prices yet again began to rise sharply in real terms, and by the summer of 2008 had reached almost $4 per gallon in some parts of the country. Just as expected, the patterns of vehicle purchases began to shift almost immediately. Large SUVs, in high demand just months earlier, began selling at deep discounts. And with long waiting lists for fuel-efficient hybrids such as the Toyota Prius, buyers not only seldom received discounts, they frequently paid even more than the sticker price.

Here's another closely related example of the influence of price on spending decisions.

Example 5.4

THE ECONOMIC NATURALIST

Does the quantity of horsepower demanded depend on gasoline prices?

Example 5.5

THE ECONOMIC NATURALIST

Why are lines longer in low-income neighborhoods?

Why are automobile engines smaller in England than in the United States?

In England, the most popular model of BMW's 5-series car is the 516i, whereas in the United States it is the 530i. The engine in the 516i is almost 50 percent smaller than the engine in the 530i. Why this difference?

In both countries, BMWs appeal to professionals with roughly similar incomes, so the difference cannot be explained by differences in purchasing power. Rather, it is the direct result of the heavy tax the British levy on gasoline. With tax, a gallon of gasoline sells for more than $8 in England—about two times the price in the United States. This difference encourages the British to choose smaller, more fuel-efficient engines. ●

THE IMPORTANCE OF INCOME DIFFERENCES

The most obvious difference between the rich and the poor is that the rich have higher incomes. To explain why the wealthy generally buy larger houses than the poor, we need not assume that the wealthy feel more strongly about housing than the poor. A much simpler explanation is that the total utility from housing, as with most other goods, increases with the amount that one consumes.

As the next example illustrates, income influences the demand not only for housing and other goods, but also for quality of service.

Why are waiting lines longer in poorer neighborhoods?

As part of a recent promotional campaign, a Baskin-Robbins retailer offered free ice cream at two of its franchise stores. The first was located in a high-income neighborhood, the second in a low-income neighborhood. Why was the queue for free ice cream longer in the low-income neighborhood?

Residents of both neighborhoods must decide whether to stand in line for free ice cream or go to some other store and avoid the line by paying the usual price. If we make the plausible assumption that people with higher incomes are more willing than others to pay to avoid standing in line, we should expect to see shorter lines in the high-income neighborhood. ●

Similar reasoning helps explain why lines are shorter in grocery stores that cater to high-income consumers. Keeping lines short at *any* grocery store means hiring more clerks, which means charging higher prices. High-income consumers are more likely than others to be willing to pay for shorter lines.

RECAP	APPLYING THE RATIONAL SPENDING RULE

Application of the rational spending rule highlights the important roles of income and substitution in explaining differences in consumption patterns—among individuals, among communities, and across time. The rule also highlights the fact that real, as opposed to nominal, prices and income are what matter. The demand for a good falls when the real price of a substitute falls or the real price of a complement rises.

INDIVIDUAL AND MARKET DEMAND CURVES

If we know what each individual's demand curve for a good looks like, how can we use that information to construct the market demand curve for the good? We must add the individual demand curves together, a process that is straightforward but requires care.

HORIZONTAL ADDITION

Suppose that there are only two buyers—Smith and Jones—in the market for canned tuna and that their demand curves are as shown in Figure 5.8(a) and (b). To construct the market demand curve for canned tuna, we simply announce a sequence of prices and then add the quantity demanded by each buyer at each price. For example, at a price of 40 cents per can, Smith demands six cans per week (a) and Jones demands two cans per week (b), for a market demand of eight cans per week (c).

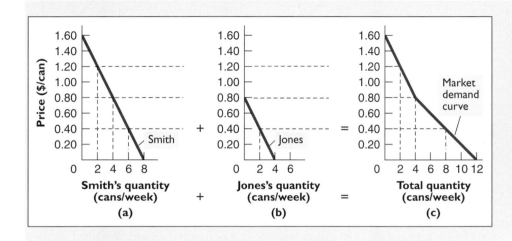

FIGURE 5.8
Individual and Market Demand Curves for Canned Tuna.
The quantity demanded at any price on the market demand curve (c) is the sum of the individual quantities demanded at that price, (a) and (b).

The process of adding individual demand curves to get the market demand curve is known as *horizontal addition*, a term used to emphasize that we are adding quantities, which are measured on the horizontal axes of individual demand curves.

EXERCISE 5.3

The buyers' side of the market for movie tickets consists of two consumers whose demands are as shown in the diagram below. Graph the market demand curve for this market.

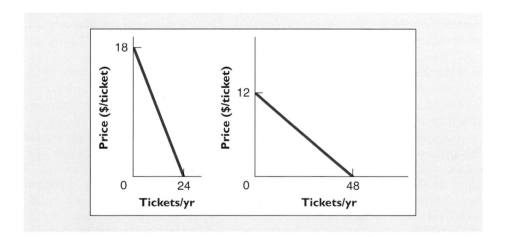

Figure 5.9 illustrates the special case in which each of 1,000 consumers in the market has the same demand curve (a). To get the market demand curve (b) in this case, we simply multiply each quantity on the representative individual demand curve by 1,000.

FIGURE 5.9
The Individual and Market Demand Curves When All Buyers Have Identical Demand Curves. When individual demand curves are identical, we get the market demand curve (b) by multiplying each quantity on the individual demand curve (a) by the number of consumers in the market.

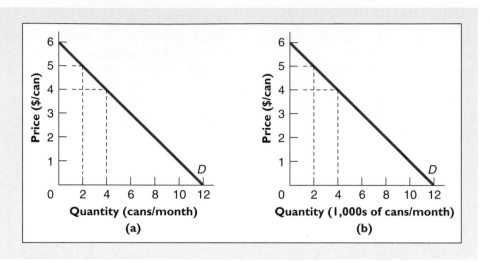

DEMAND AND CONSUMER SURPLUS

In Chapter 1 we first encountered the concept of economic surplus, which in a buyer's case is the difference between the most she would have been willing to pay for a product and the amount she actually pays for it. The economic surplus received by buyers is often referred to as **consumer surplus.**

The term *consumer surplus* sometimes refers to the surplus received by a single buyer in a transaction. On other occasions, it is used to denote the total surplus received by all buyers in a market or collection of markets.

consumer surplus the difference between a buyer's reservation price for a product and the price actually paid

CALCULATING CONSUMER SURPLUS

For performing cost-benefit analysis, it is often important to be able to measure the total consumer surplus received by all buyers who participate in a given market. For example, a road linking a mountain village and a port city would create a new market for fresh fish in the mountain village; in deciding whether the road should be built, analysts would want to count as one of its benefits the gains that would be reaped by buyers in this new market.

To illustrate how economists actually measure consumer surplus, we'll consider a hypothetical market for a good with 11 potential buyers, each of whom can buy a maximum of one unit of the good each day. The first potential buyer's reservation price for the product is $11; the second buyer's reservation price is $10; the third buyer's reservation price is $9; and so on. The demand curve for this market will have the staircase shape shown in Figure 5.10. We can think of this curve as the digital counterpart of traditional analog demand curves. (If the units shown on the horizontal axis were fine enough, this digital curve would be visually indistinguishable from its analog counterparts.)

Suppose the good whose demand curve is shown in Figure 5.10 were available at a price of $6 per unit. How much total consumer surplus would buyers in this market reap? At a price of $6, six units per day would be sold in this market. The buyer of the sixth unit would receive no economic surplus since his reservation price for that unit was exactly $6, the same as its selling price. But the first five buyers would reap a surplus for their purchases. The buyer of the first unit, for example, would have been willing to pay as much as $11 for it, but since she would pay only $6, she would receive a surplus of exactly $5. The buyer of the second unit, who would have been willing to pay as much as $10, would receive a surplus of $4. The surplus would be $3 for the buyer of the third unit, $2 for the buyer of the fourth unit, and $1 for the buyer of the fifth unit.

If we add all the buyers' surpluses together, we get a total of $15 of consumer surplus each day. That surplus corresponds to the shaded area shown in Figure 5.11.

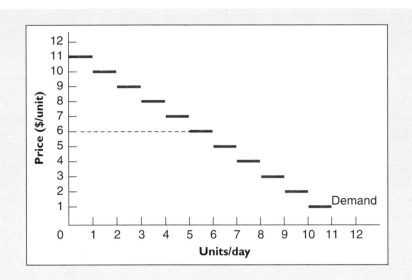

FIGURE 5.10
A Market with a "Digital" Demand Curve.
When a product can be sold only in whole-number amounts, its demand curve has the stair-step shape shown.

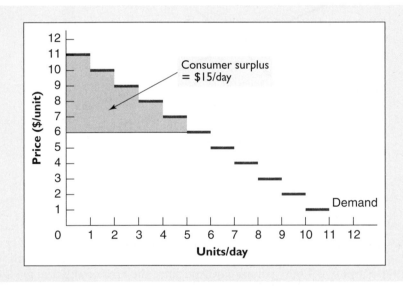

FIGURE 5.11
Consumer Surplus.
Consumer surplus (shaded region) is the cumulative difference between the most that buyers are willing to pay for each unit and the price they actually pay.

EXERCISE 5.4

Calculate consumer surplus for a demand curve like the one just described except that the buyers' reservation prices for each unit are $2 higher than before, as shown in the graph below.

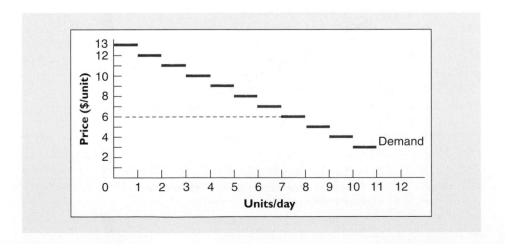

Now suppose we want to calculate consumer surplus in a market with a conventional straight-line demand curve. As the following example illustrates, this task is a simple extension of the method used for digital demand curves.

How much do buyers benefit from their participation in the market for milk?

Consider the market for milk whose demand and supply curves are shown in Figure 5.12, which has an equilibrium price of $2 per gallon and an equilibrium quantity of 4,000 gallons per day. How much consumer surplus do the buyers in this market reap?

In Figure 5.12, note first that, as in Figure 5.11, the last unit exchanged each day generates no consumer surplus at all. Note also that for all milk sold up to 4,000 gallons per day, buyers receive consumer surplus, just as in Figure 5.11. For these buyers, consumer surplus is the cumulative difference between the most they would be willing to pay for milk (as measured on the demand curve) and the price they actually pay.

FIGURE 5.12
Supply and Demand in the Market for Milk.
For the supply and demand curves shown, the equilibrium price of milk is $2 per gallon and the equilibrium quantity is 4,000 gallons per day.

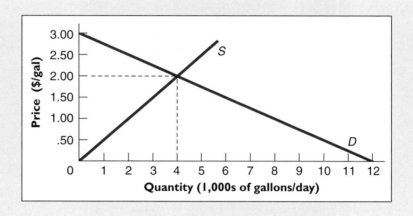

Total consumer surplus received by buyers in the milk market is thus the shaded triangle between the demand curve and the market price in Figure 5.13. Note that this area is a right triangle whose vertical arm is $h = \$1/\text{gallon}$ and whose horizontal arm is $b = 4,000$ gallons/day. And since the area of any triangle is equal to $(1/2)bh$, consumer surplus in this market is equal to

$$(1/2)(4,000 \text{ gallons/day})(\$1/\text{gallon}) = \$2,000/\text{day}.$$

FIGURE 5.13
Consumer Surplus in the Market for Milk.
Consumer surplus is the area of the shaded triangle ($2,000/day).

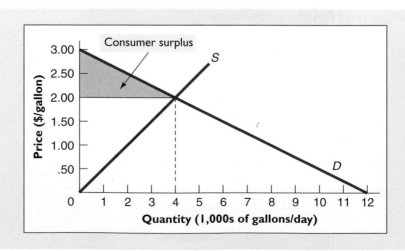

A useful way of thinking about consumer surplus is to ask what is the highest price consumers would pay, in the aggregate, for the right to continue participating in this milk market. The answer is $2,000 per day, since that is the amount by which their combined benefits exceed their combined costs. ◆

As discussed in Chapter 3, the demand curve for a good can be interpreted either horizontally or vertically. The horizontal interpretation tells us, for each price, the total quantity that consumers wish to buy at that price. The vertical interpretation tells us, for each quantity, the most a buyer would be willing to pay for the good at that quantity. For the purpose of computing consumer surplus, we rely on the vertical interpretation of the demand curve. The value on the vertical axis that corresponds to each point along the demand curve corresponds to the marginal buyer's reservation price for the good. Consumer surplus is the cumulative sum of the differences between these reservation prices and the market price. It is the area bounded above by the demand curve and bounded below by the market price.

■ SUMMARY ■

- The rational consumer allocates income among different goods so that the marginal utility gained from the last dollar spent on each good is the same. This rational spending rule gives rise to the law of demand, which states that people do less of what they want to do as the cost of doing it rises. Here, "cost" refers to the sum of all monetary and nonmonetary sacrifices—explicit and implicit—that must be made in order to engage in the activity. **LO1, LO3**

- The ability to substitute one good for another is an important factor behind the law of demand. Because virtually every good or service has at least some substitutes, economists prefer to speak in terms of wants rather than needs. We face choices, and describing our demands as needs is misleading because it suggests we have no options. **LO2**

- For normal goods, the income effect is a second important reason that demand curves slope downward. When the price of such a good falls, not only does it be-

come more attractive relative to its substitutes, but the consumer also acquires more real purchasing power, and this, too, augments the quantity demanded. **LO4**

- The demand curve is a schedule that shows the amounts of a good people want to buy at various prices. Demand curves can be used to summarize the price–quantity relationship for a single individual, but more commonly we employ them to summarize that relationship for an entire market. At any quantity along a demand curve, the corresponding price represents the amount by which the consumer (or consumers) would benefit from having an additional unit of the product. For this reason, the demand curve is sometimes described as a summary of the benefit side of the market. **LO5**

- Consumer surplus is a quantitative measure of the amount by which buyers benefit as a result of their ability to purchase goods at the market price. It is the area between the demand curve and the market price. **LO6**

■ KEY TERMS ■

consumer surplus (142)
law of demand (126)
law of diminishing marginal
  utility (131)

marginal utility (130)
nominal price (139)
optimal combination of
  goods (134)

rational spending rule (135)
real price (139)

■ REVIEW QUESTIONS ■

1. Why do economists prefer to speak of demands arising out of "wants" rather than "needs"? **LO2**

2. Explain why economists consider the concept of utility useful, even if psychologists cannot measure it precisely. **LO2**

3. Why does the law of diminishing marginal utility encourage people to spread their spending across many different types of goods? **LO3**

4. Explain why a good or service that is offered at a monetary price of zero is unlikely to be a truly "free" good from an economic perspective. **LO3**

5. Give an example of a good that you have consumed for which your marginal utility increased with the amount of it you consumed. **LO3**

▪ PROBLEMS ▪

1. In which type of restaurant do you expect the service to be more prompt and courteous: an expensive gourmet restaurant or an inexpensive diner? Explain. **LO4**

2. You are having lunch at an all-you-can-eat buffet. If you are rational, what should be your marginal utility from the last morsel of food you swallow? **LO2**

3. Martha's current marginal utility from consuming orange juice is 75 utils per ounce and her marginal utility from consuming coffee is 50 utils per ounce. If orange juice costs 25 cents per ounce and coffee costs 20 cents per ounce, is Martha maximizing her total utility from the two beverages? If so, explain how you know. If not, how should she rearrange her spending? **LO3**

4. Toby's current marginal utility from consuming peanuts is 100 utils per ounce and his marginal utility from consuming cashews is 200 utils per ounce. If peanuts cost 10 cents per ounce and cashews cost 25 cents per ounce, is Toby maximizing his total utility from the kinds of nuts? If so, explain how you know. If not, how should he rearrange his spending? **LO3**

5. Sue gets a total of 20 utils per week from her consumption of pizza and a total of 40 utils per week from her consumption of yogurt. The price of pizza is $1 per slice, the price of yogurt is $1 per cup, and she consumes 10 slices of pizza and 20 cups of yogurt each week. True or false: Sue is consuming the optimal combination of pizza and yogurt. **LO3**

6. Ann lives in Princeton, New Jersey, and commutes by train each day to her job in New York City (20 round trips per month). When the price of a round trip goes up from $10 to $20, she responds by consuming exactly the same number of trips as before, while spending $200 per month less on restaurant meals. **LO3, LO4**
   a. Does the fact that her quantity of train travel is completely unresponsive to the price increase imply that Ann is not a rational consumer?
   b. Explain why an increase in train travel might affect the amount she spends on restaurant meals.

7. For the demand curve shown, find the total amount of consumer surplus that results in the gasoline market if gasoline sells for $2 per gallon. **LO6**

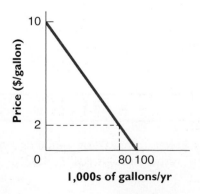

8. Tom has a weekly allowance of $24, all of which he spends on pizza and movie rentals, whose prices are $6 per slice and $3 per rental, respectively. If slices of pizza and movie rentals are available only in whole-number amounts, list all possible combinations of the two goods that Tom can purchase each week with his allowance. **LO3**

9.*Refer to problem 8. Tom's total utility is the sum of the utility he derives from pizza and movie rentals. If these utilities vary with the amounts consumed as shown in the table, and pizzas and movie rentals are again consumable only in whole-number amounts, how many pizzas and how many movie rentals should Tom consume each week? **LO3**

Pizzas/week	Utils/week from pizza	Movie rentals/ week	Utils/week from rentals
0	0	0	0
1	20	1	40
2	38	2	46
3	54	3	50
4	68	4	54
5	80	5	56
6	90	6	57
7	98	7	57
8	104	8	57

10.*The buyers' side of the market for amusement park tickets consists of two consumers whose demands are as shown in the diagram below. **LO5, LO6**
   a. Graph the market demand curve for this market.
   b. Calculate the total consumer surplus in the amusement park market if tickets sell for $12 each.

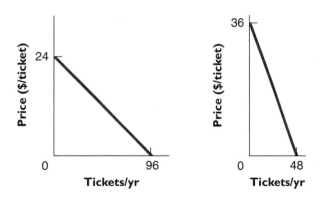

*Problems marked with an asterisk (*) are more difficult.

■ ANSWERS TO IN-CHAPTER EXERCISES ■

5.1 The combination of 300 pints per year of vanilla ($300) and 50 pints of chocolate ($100) costs a total of $400, which is exactly equal to Sarah's ice cream budget. **LO3**

5.2 The rational spending rule requires $MU_F/P_F = MU_S/P_S$ where MU_F and MU_S are John's marginal utilities from food and shelter and P_F and P_S are the prices of food and shelter, respectively. At John's original combination,

$MU_F/P_F = 4$ utils per dollar and $MU_S/P_S = 3$ utils per dollar. John should thus spend more of his income on food and less on shelter.   **LO3**

5.3   Adding the two individual demand curves, (a) and (b), horizontally yields the market demand curve (c):   **LO5**

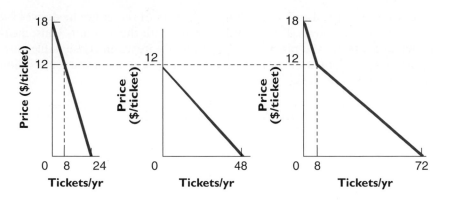

5.4   Consumer surplus is now the new shaded area, $28 per day.   **LO6**

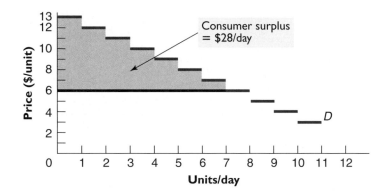

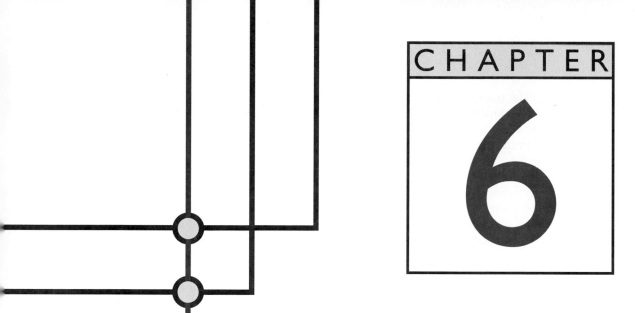

CHAPTER

6

Perfectly Competitive Supply

LEARNING OBJECTIVES

After reading this chapter, you should be able to:

1. Explain how opportunity cost is related to the supply curve.
2. Discuss the relationship between the supply curve for an individual firm and the market supply curve for an industry.
3. Determine a perfectly competitive firm's profit-maximizing output level and profit in the short run.
4. Connect the determinants of supply with the factors that affect individual firms' costs.
5. Define and calculate producer surplus.

Cars that took more than 50 hours to assemble in the 1970s are now built in less than 8 hours. Similar productivity growth has occurred in many other manufacturing industries. Yet in many service industries, productivity has grown only slowly, if at all. For example, the London Philharmonic Orchestra performs Beethoven's Fifth Symphony with no fewer musicians today than it did in 1850. And it still takes a barber about half an hour to cut someone's hair, just as it always has.

Given the spectacular growth in manufacturing workers' productivity, it is no surprise that their real wages have risen more than fivefold during the last century. But why have real wages for service workers risen just as much? If barbers and musicians are no more productive than they were at the turn of the century, why are they now paid five times as much?

An answer is suggested by the observation that the opportunity cost of pursuing any given occupation is the most one could have earned in some other occupation. Most people who become barbers or musicians could instead have chosen jobs in manufacturing. If workers in service industries were not paid roughly as much as they could have earned in other occupations, many of them would not have been willing to work in service industries in the first place.

The trajectories of wages in manufacturing and service industries illustrate the intimate link between the prices at which goods and services are offered for sale in the market and the opportunity cost of the resources required to produce them.

In the previous chapter, we saw that the demand curve is a schedule that tells how many units buyers wish to purchase at different prices. Our task here is to gain insight into the factors that shape the supply curve, the schedule that tells how many units suppliers wish to sell at different prices.

Although the demand side and the supply side of the market are different in several ways, many of these differences are superficial. Indeed, the behavior of both buyers and sellers is, in an important sense, fundamentally the same. After all, the two groups confront essentially similar questions—in the buyer's case, "Should I buy another unit?" and in the seller's, "Should I sell another unit?" What is more, buyers and sellers use the same criterion for answering these questions. Thus, a rational consumer will buy another unit if its benefit exceeds its cost and a rational seller will sell another unit if the cost of making it is less than the extra revenue he can get from selling it (the familiar Cost-Benefit Principle again).

| Cost-Benefit |

THINKING ABOUT SUPPLY: THE IMPORTANCE OF OPPORTUNITY COST

Do you live in a state that requires refundable soft drink container deposits? If so, you've probably noticed that some people always redeem their own containers while other people pass up this opportunity, leaving their used containers to be recycled by others. Recycling used containers is a service and its production obeys the same logic that applies to the production of other goods and services. The following sequence of recycling examples shows how the supply curve for a good or service is rooted in the individual's choice of whether to produce it.

How much time should Harry spend recycling soft drink containers?

Harry is trying to decide how to divide his time between his job as a dishwasher in the dining hall, which pays $6 an hour for as many hours as he chooses to work, and gathering soft drink containers to redeem for deposit, in which case his pay depends on both the deposit per container and the number of containers he finds. Earnings aside, Harry is indifferent between the two tasks, and the number of containers he will find depends, as shown in the table below, on the number of hours per day he searches:

Why are barbers paid five times as much now as in 1900, even though they can't cut hair any faster than they could then?

Search time (hours/day)	Total number of containers found	Additional number of containers found
0	0	
		600
1	600	
		400
2	1,000	
		300
3	1,300	
		200
4	1,500	
		100
5	1,600	

If the containers may be redeemed for 2 cents each, how many hours should Harry spend searching for containers?

For each additional hour Harry spends searching for soft drink containers, he loses the $6 he could have earned as a dishwasher. This is his hourly opportunity cost of searching for soft drink containers. His benefit from each hour spent searching for containers is the number of additional containers he finds (shown in column 3 of the table) times the deposit he collects per container. Since he can redeem each container for 2 cents, his first hour spent collecting containers will yield earnings of 600($0.02) = $12, or $6 more than he could have earned as a dishwasher.

By the Cost-Benefit Principle, then, Harry should spend his first hour of work each day searching for soft drink containers rather than washing dishes. A second hour searching for containers will yield 400 additional containers, for additional earnings of $8, so it too satisfies the cost-benefit test. A third hour spent searching yields 300 additional containers, for 300($0.02) = $6 of additional earnings. Since this is exactly what Harry could have earned washing dishes, he is indifferent between spending his third hour of work each day on one task or the other. For the sake of discussion, however, we'll assume that he resolves ties in favor of searching for containers, in which case he will spend three hours each day searching for containers. ◆

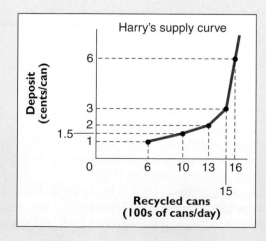

Cost-Benefit

What is the lowest redemption price that would induce Harry to spend at least one hour per day recycling? Since he will find 600 containers in his first hour of search, a one-cent deposit on each container would enable him to match his $6 per hour opportunity cost. More generally, if the redemption price is p, and the next hour spent searching yields ΔQ additional containers, then Harry's additional earnings from searching the additional hour will be $p(\Delta Q)$. This means that the smallest redemption price that will lead Harry to search another hour must satisfy the equation

$$p(\Delta Q) = \$6. \qquad (6.1)$$

How high would the redemption price of containers have to be to induce Harry to search for a second hour? Since he can find $\Delta Q = 400$ additional containers if he searches for a second hour, the smallest redemption price that will lead him to do so must satisfy $p(400) = \$6$, which solves for $p = 1.5$ cents.

EXERCISE 6.1

In the example above, calculate the lowest container redemption prices that will lead Harry to search a third, fourth, and fifth hour.

By searching for soft drink containers, Harry becomes, in effect, a supplier of container-recycling services. In Exercise 6.1, we saw that Harry's reservation prices for his third, fourth, and fifth hours of container search are 2, 3, and 6 cents, respectively. Having calculated these reservation prices, we can now plot his supply curve of container-recycling services. This curve, which plots the redemption price per container on the vertical axis and the number of containers recycled each day on the horizontal axis, is shown in Figure 6.1. Harry's individual supply curve of

FIGURE 6.1

An Individual Supply Curve for Recycling Services.

When the deposit price increases, it becomes attractive to abandon alternative pursuits to spend more time searching for soft drink containers.

container-recycling services tells us the number of containers he is willing to recycle at various redemption prices.

The supply curve shown in Figure 6.1 is upward-sloping, just like those we saw in Chapter 3. There are exceptions to this general rule, but sellers of most goods will offer higher quantities at higher prices.

INDIVIDUAL AND MARKET SUPPLY CURVES

The relationship between the individual and market supply curves for a product is analogous to the relationship between the individual and market demand curves. The quantity that corresponds to a given price on the market demand curve is the sum of the quantities demanded at that price by all individual buyers in the market. Likewise, the quantity that corresponds to any given price on the market supply curve is the sum of the quantities supplied at that price by all individual sellers in the market.

Suppose, for example, that the supply side of the recycling-services market consists only of Harry and his identical twin, Barry, whose individual supply curve is the same as Harry's. To generate the market supply curve, we first put the individual supply curves side by side, as shown in Figure 6.2(a) and (b). We then announce a price, and for that price add the individual quantities supplied to obtain the total quantity supplied in the market. Thus, at a price of 3 cents per container, both Harry and Barry wish to recycle 1,500 cans per day, so the total market supply at that price is 3,000 cans per day. Proceeding in like manner for a sequence of prices, we generate the market supply curve for recycling services shown in Figure 6.2(c). This is the same process of horizontal summation by which we generated market demand curves from individual demand curves in the previous chapter.

FIGURE 6.2
The Market Supply Curve for Recycling Services.
To generate the market supply curve (c) from the individual supply curves (a) and (b), we add the individual supply curves horizontally.

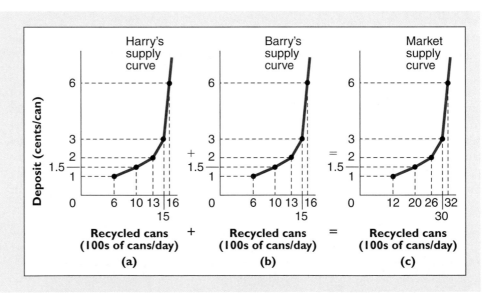

Alternatively, if there were many suppliers with individual supply curves identical to Harry's, we could generate the market supply curve by simply multiplying each quantity value on the individual supply curve by the number of suppliers. For instance, Figure 6.3 shows the supply curve for a market in which there are 1,000 suppliers with individual supply curves like Harry's.

Why do individual supply curves tend to be upward-sloping? One explanation is suggested by the Principle of Increasing Opportunity Cost, or the Low-Hanging-Fruit Principle. Container recyclers should always look first for the containers that

Increasing Opportunity Cost

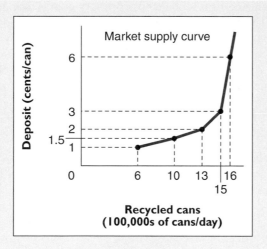

FIGURE 6.3
The Market Supply Curve with 1,000 Identical Sellers.
To generate the market supply curve for a market with 1,000 identical sellers, we simply multiply each quantity value on the individual supply curve by 1,000.

are easiest to find—such as those in plain view in readily accessible locations. As the redemption price rises, it will pay to incur the additional cost of searching farther from the beaten path.

If all individuals have identical upward-sloping supply curves, the market supply curve will be upward-sloping as well. But there is an important additional reason for the positive slope of market supply curves: Individual suppliers generally differ with respect to their opportunity costs of supplying the product. (The Principle of Increasing Opportunity Cost applies not only to each individual searcher, but also *across* individuals.) Thus, whereas people facing unattractive employment opportunities in other occupations may be willing to recycle soft drink containers even when the redemption price is low, those with more attractive options will recycle only if the redemption price is relatively high.

In summary, then, the upward slope of the supply curve reflects the fact that costs tend to rise at the margin when producers expand production, partly because each individual exploits her most attractive opportunities first, but also because different potential sellers face different opportunity costs.

Increasing Opportunity Cost

PROFIT-MAXIMIZING FIRMS IN PERFECTLY COMPETITIVE MARKETS

To explore the nature of the supply curve of a product more fully, we must say more about the goals of the organizations that supply the product and the kind of economic environment in which they operate. In virtually every economy, goods and services are produced by a variety of organizations that pursue a host of different motives. The Red Cross supplies blood because its organizers and donors want to help people in need; the local government fixes potholes because the mayor was elected on a promise to do so; karaoke singers perform because they like public attention; and car-wash employees are driven primarily by the hope of making enough money to pay their rent.

PROFIT MAXIMIZATION

Notwithstanding this rich variety of motives, *most* goods and services that are offered for sale in a market economy are sold by private firms whose main reason for existing is to earn **profit** for their owners. A firm's profit is the difference between the total revenue it receives from the sale of its product and all costs it incurs in producing it.

profit the total revenue a firm receives from the sale of its product minus all costs—explicit and implicit—incurred in producing it

profit-maximizing firm a firm whose primary goal is to maximize the difference between its total revenues and total costs

perfectly competitive market a market in which no individual supplier has significant influence on the market price of the product

price taker a firm that has no influence over the price at which it sells its product

A **profit-maximizing firm** is one whose primary goal is to maximize the amount of profit it earns. The supply curves that economists use in standard supply and demand theory are based on the assumption that goods are sold by profit-maximizing firms in **perfectly competitive markets**, which are markets in which individual firms have no influence over the market prices of the products they sell. Because of their inability to influence market price, perfectly competitive firms are often described as **price takers**.

The following four conditions are characteristic of markets that are perfectly competitive:

1. *All firms sell the same standardized product.* Although this condition is almost never literally satisfied, it holds as a rough approximation for many markets. Thus, the markets for concrete building blocks of a given size, or for apples of a given variety, may be described in this way. This condition implies that buyers are willing to switch from one seller to another if by so doing they can obtain a lower price.

2. *The market has many buyers and sellers, each of which buys or sells only a small fraction of the total quantity exchanged.* This condition implies that individual buyers and sellers will be price takers, regarding the market price of the product as a fixed number beyond their control. For example, a single farmer's decision to plant fewer acres of wheat would have no appreciable impact on the market price of wheat, just as an individual consumer's decision to become a vegetarian would have no perceptible effect on the price of beef.

3. *Productive resources are mobile.* This condition implies that if a potential seller identifies a profitable business opportunity in a market, he or she will be able to obtain the labor, capital, and other productive resources necessary to enter that market. By the same token, sellers who are dissatisfied with the opportunities they confront in a given market are free to leave that market and employ their resources elsewhere.

4. *Buyers and sellers are well informed.* This condition implies that buyers and sellers are aware of the relevant opportunities available to them. If that were not so, buyers would be unable to seek out sellers who charge the lowest prices, and sellers would have no means of deploying their resources in the markets in which they would earn the most profit.

The market for wheat closely approximates a perfectly competitive market. The market for operating systems for desktop computers, however, does not. More than 90 percent of desktop operating systems are sold by Microsoft, giving the company enough influence in that market to have significant control over the price it charges. For example, if it were to raise the price of its latest edition of Windows by, say, 20 percent, some consumers might switch to Macintosh or Linux, and others might postpone their next upgrade; but many—perhaps even most—would continue with their plans to buy Windows.

By contrast, if an individual wheat farmer were to charge even a few cents more than the current market price for a bushel of wheat, he wouldn't be able to sell any of his wheat at all. And since he can sell as much wheat as he wishes at the market price, he has no motive to charge less.

THE DEMAND CURVE FACING A PERFECTLY COMPETITIVE FIRM

From the perspective of an individual firm in a perfectly competitive market, what does the demand curve for its product look like? Since it can sell as much or as little as it wishes at the prevailing market price, the demand curve for its product is

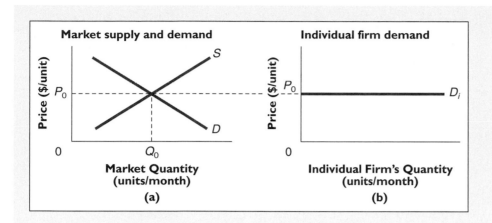

FIGURE 6.4

The Demand Curve Facing a Perfectly Competitive Firm. The market demand and supply curves intersect to determine the market price of the product (a). The individual firm's demand curve, D_i (b), is a horizontal line at the market price.

perfectly elastic at the market price. Figure 6.4(a) shows the market demand and supply curves intersecting to determine a market price of P_0. Figure 6.4(b) shows the product demand curve, D_i, as seen by any individual firm in this market, a horizontal line at the market price level P_0.

Many of the conclusions of the standard supply and demand model also hold for **imperfectly competitive firms**—those firms, like Microsoft, that have at least some ability to vary their own prices. But certain other conclusions do not, as we shall see when we examine the behavior of such firms more closely in Chapter 9.

Since a perfectly competitive firm has no control over the market price of its product, it needn't worry about choosing the level at which to set that price. As we've seen, the equilibrium market price in a competitive market comes from the intersection of the industry supply and demand curves. The challenge confronting the perfectly competitive firm is to choose its output level so that it makes as much profit as it can at that price. As we investigate how the competitive firm responds to this challenge, we'll see that some costs are more important than others.

PRODUCTION IN THE SHORT RUN

To gain a deeper understanding of the origins of the supply curve, it is helpful to consider a perfectly competitive firm confronting the decision of how much to produce. The firm in question is a small company that makes glass bottles. To keep things simple, suppose that the silica required for making bottles is available free of charge from a nearby desert and that the only costs incurred by the firm are the wages it pays its employees and the lease payment on its bottle-making machine. The employees and the machine are the firm's only two **factors of production**—inputs used to produce goods and services. In more complex examples, factors of production also might include land, structures, entrepreneurship, and possibly others, but for the moment we consider only labor and capital.

When we refer to the **short run**, we mean a period of time during which at least some of the firm's factors of production cannot be varied. For our bottle maker, we will assume that the number of employees can be varied on short notice but that the capacity of its bottle-making machine can be altered only with significant delay. For this firm, then, the short run is simply that period of time during which the firm cannot alter the capacity of its bottle-making machine. By contrast, when we speak of the **long run**, we refer to a time period of sufficient length that all the firm's factors of production are variable.

Table 6.1 shows how the company's bottle production depends on the number of hours its employees spend on the job each day. The output–employment relationship described in Table 6.1 exhibits a pattern that is common to many such

imperfectly competitive firm a firm that has at least some control over the market price of its product

factor of production an input used in the production of a good or service

short run a period of time sufficiently short that at least some of the firm's factors of production are fixed

long run a period of time of sufficient length that all the firm's factors of production are variable

TABLE 6.1
Employment and Output for a Glass Bottle Maker

Total number of employees per day	Total number of bottles per day
0	0
1	80
2	200
3	260
4	300
5	330
6	350
7	362

law of diminishing returns a property of the relationship between the amount of a good or service produced and the amount of a variable factor required to produce it; it says that when some factors of production are fixed, increased production of the good eventually requires ever-larger increases in the variable factor

fixed factor of production an input whose quantity cannot be altered in the short run

variable factor of production an input whose quantity can be altered in the short run

fixed cost the sum of all payments made to the firm's fixed factors of production

variable cost the sum of all payments made to the firm's variable factors of production

total cost the sum of all payments made to the firm's fixed and variable factors of production

marginal cost as output changes from one level to another, the change in total cost divided by the corresponding change in output

relationships. Each time we add an additional unit of labor, output grows, but beyond some point the additional output that results from each additional unit of labor begins to diminish. Note in the right column, for example, that output gains begin to diminish with the third employee. Economists refer to this pattern as the **law of diminishing returns,** and it always refers to situations in which at least some factors of production are fixed. Here, the **fixed factor** is the bottle-making machine, and the **variable factor** is labor. In the context of this example, the law of diminishing returns says simply that successive increases in the labor input eventually yield smaller and smaller increments in bottle output. (Strictly speaking, the law ought to be called the law of *eventually* diminishing returns because output may initially grow at an increasing rate with additional units of the variable factor.)

Typically, returns from additional units of the variable input eventually diminish because of some form of congestion. For instance, in an office with three secretaries and only a single desktop computer, we would not expect to get three times as many letters typed per hour as in an office with only one secretary because only one person can use a computer at a time.

SOME IMPORTANT COST CONCEPTS

For the bottle-making firm described in Table 6.1, suppose the lease payment for the company's bottle-making machine is $40 per day, which must be paid whether the company makes any bottles or not. This payment is both a **fixed cost** (since it does not depend on the number of bottles per day the firm makes) and, for the duration of the lease, a sunk cost. The first two columns of Table 6.2 reproduce the employment and output entries from Table 6.1, and the firm's fixed cost appears in column 3.

The company's payment to its employees is called **variable cost** because, unlike fixed cost, it varies with the number of bottles the company produces. The variable cost of producing 200 bottles per day, for example, is shown in column 4 of Table 6.2 as $24 per day. Column 5 shows the firm's **total cost,** which is the sum of its fixed and variable costs. Column 6, finally, shows the firm's **marginal cost,** a measure of how its total cost changes when its output changes. Specifically, marginal cost is defined as the change in total cost divided by the corresponding change in output. Note, for example, that when the firm expands production from 80 to 200 bottles per day, its total cost goes up by $12, which gives rise to the marginal cost entry of ($12/day)/(120 bottles/day) = $0.10 per bottle. To emphasize that marginal cost refers to the change in total cost when quantity changes, we place the marginal cost entries between the corresponding quantity rows of the table.

TABLE 6.2
Fixed, Variable, and Total Costs of Bottle Production

Employees per day	Bottles per day	Fixed cost ($/day)	Variable cost ($/day)	Total cost ($/day)	Marginal cost ($/bottle)
0	0	40	0	40	
					0.15
1	80	40	12	52	
					0.10
2	200	40	24	64	
					0.20
3	260	40	36	76	
					0.30
4	300	40	48	88	
					0.40
5	330	40	60	100	
					0.60
6	350	40	72	112	
					1.00
7	362	40	84	124	

CHOOSING OUTPUT TO MAXIMIZE PROFIT

In the following examples and exercises, we'll explore how the company's decision about how many bottles to produce depends on the price of bottles, the wage, and the cost of capital. Again, our starting assumption is that the firm's basic goal is to maximize the amount of profit it earns from the production and sale of bottles, where profit is the difference between its total revenue and its total cost.

$$\begin{aligned} \text{Profit} &= \text{Total revenue} - \text{Total cost} \\ &= \text{Total revenue} - \text{Variable cost} - \text{Fixed cost} \end{aligned} \qquad (6.2)$$

If bottles sell for 35 cents each, how many bottles should the company described in Table 6.2 produce each day?

To answer this question, we need simply apply the Cost-Benefit Principle to the question "Should the firm expand its level of output?" If its goal is to maximize its profit, the answer to this question will be to expand as long as the marginal benefit from expanding is at least as great as the marginal cost. Since the perfectly competitive firm can sell as many bottles as it wishes at the market price of $0.35 per bottle, its marginal benefit from selling an additional bottle is $0.35. If we compare this marginal benefit with the marginal cost entries shown in column 6 of Table 6.2, we see that the firm should keep expanding until it reaches 300 bottles per day (four employees per day). To expand beyond that level, it would have to hire a fifth employee, and the resulting marginal cost ($0.40 per bottle) would exceed the marginal benefit.

To confirm that the cost-benefit principle thus applied identifies the profit-maximizing number of bottles to produce, we can calculate profit levels directly, as in Table 6.3. Column 3 of this table reports the firm's revenue from the sale of bottles, which is calculated as the product of the number of bottles produced per day and the price of $0.35 per bottle. Note, for example, that in the third row of that column, total revenue is (200 bottles/day)($0.35/bottle) = $70 per day. Column 5 reports the firm's total daily profit, which is just the difference between its total revenue (column 3) and its total cost (column 4). Note that the largest profit entry in column 5, $17 per day, occurs at an output of 300 bottles per day, just as suggested by our earlier application of the cost-benefit principle.

Cost-Benefit

TABLE 6.3
Output, Revenue, Costs, and Profit

Employees per day	Output (bottles/day)	Total revenue ($/day)	Total cost ($/day)	Profit ($/day)
0	0	0	40	−40
1	80	28	52	−24
2	200	70	64	6
3	260	91	76	15
4	300	105	88	17
5	330	115.50	100	15.50
6	350	122.50	112	10.50
7	362	126.70	124	2.70

As the following exercise demonstrates, an increase in the price of the product gives rise to an increase in the profit-maximizing level of output.

EXERCISE 6.2

How would the profit-maximizing level of bottle production change in the example above if bottles sell for 62 cents each?

The following exercise illustrates that a fall in the wage rate leads to a decline in marginal cost, which also causes an increase in the profit-maximizing level of output.

EXERCISE 6.3

How would the profit-maximizing level of bottle production change in the example above if bottles sell for 35 cents each, but wages fall to $6 per day?

Suppose that in the example the firm's fixed cost had been not $40 per day but $45 per day. How, if at all, would that have affected the firm's profit-maximizing level of output? The answer is "not at all." Each entry in the profit column of Table 6.3 would have been $5 per day smaller than before, but the maximum profit entry still would have been 300 bottles per day.

The observation that the profit-maximizing quantity does not depend on fixed costs is not an idiosyncrasy of this example. That it holds true in general is an immediate consequence of the Cost-Benefit Principle, which says that a firm should increase its output if, and only if, the *marginal* benefit exceeds the *marginal* cost. Neither the marginal benefit of expanding (which is the market price of bottles) nor the marginal cost of expanding is affected by a change in the firm's fixed cost.

When the law of diminishing returns applies (that is, when some factors of production are fixed), marginal cost goes up as the firm expands production beyond some point. Under these circumstances, the firm's best option is to keep expanding output as long as marginal cost is less than price.

Note that if the bottle company's fixed cost had been any more than $57 per day, it would have made a loss at *every* possible level of output. As long as it still had to pay its fixed cost, however, its best bet would have been to continue producing 300 bottles per day. It is better, after all, to experience a smaller loss than a larger one. If a firm in that situation expected conditions to remain the same, though, it would want to get out of the bottle business as soon as its equipment lease expired.

Cost-Benefit

A NOTE ON THE FIRM'S SHUTDOWN CONDITION

It might seem that a firm that can sell as much output as it wishes at a constant market price would *always* do best in the short run by producing and selling the output level for which price equals marginal cost. But there are exceptions to this rule. Suppose, for example, that the market price of the firm's product falls so low that its revenue from sales is smaller than its variable cost at all possible levels of output. The firm should then cease production for the time being. By shutting down, it will suffer a loss equal to its fixed costs. But by remaining open, it would suffer an even larger loss.

More formally, if P denotes the market price of the product and Q denotes the number of units produced and sold, then $P \times Q$ is the firm's total revenue from sales, and if we use VC to denote the firm's variable cost, the rule is that the firm should shut down in the short run if $P \times Q$ is less than VC for every level of Q:

Short-run shutdown condition: $\quad P \times Q < VC \quad$ for all levels of Q. (6.3)

EXERCISE 6.4

Using the bottle company example, suppose bottles sold not for $0.35 but only $0.10. Calculate the profit corresponding to each level of output, as in Table 6.3, and verify that the firm's best option is to cease operations in the short run.

AVERAGE VARIABLE COST AND AVERAGE TOTAL COST

Suppose that the firm is unable to cover its variable cost at any level of output—that is, suppose that $P \times Q < VC$ for all levels of Q. It must then also be true that $P < VC/Q$ for all levels of Q, since we obtain the second inequality by simply dividing both sides of the first one by Q. VC/Q is the firm's **average variable cost**—its variable cost divided by its output. The firm's short-run shutdown condition may thus be restated a second way: Discontinue operations in the short run if the product price is less than the minimum value of its average variable cost (AVC). Thus

average variable cost (AVC) variable cost divided by total output

Short-run shutdown condition (alternate version): $\quad P <$ minimum value of AVC. (6.4)

As we'll see in the next section, this version of the shutdown condition often enables us to tell at a glance whether the firm should continue operations.

A related cost concept that facilitates assessment of the firm's profitability is **average total cost** (ATC), which is total cost (TC) divided by output (Q): $ATC = TC/Q$. The firm's profit, again, is the difference between its total revenue ($P \times Q$) and its total cost. And since total cost is equal to average total cost times quantity, the firm's profit is also equal to $(P \times Q) - (ATC \times Q)$. A firm is said to be **profitable** if its revenue ($P \times Q$) exceeds its total cost ($ATC \times Q$). A firm can thus be profitable only if the price of its product price (P) exceeds its ATC for some level of output.

average total cost (ATC) total cost divided by total output

profitable firm a firm whose total revenue exceeds its total cost

Keeping track of all these cost concepts may seem tedious. In the next section, however, we will see that the payoff from doing so is that they enable us to recast the profit-maximization decision in a simple graphical framework.

A GRAPHICAL APPROACH TO PROFIT MAXIMIZATION

For the bottle-making firm we have been discussing, average variable cost and average total cost values are shown in columns 4 and 6 of Table 6.4. Using the entries in this table, we plot the firm's average total cost, average variable cost, and marginal cost curves in Figure 6.5. (Because marginal cost corresponds to the change in total cost as we move between two output levels, each marginal cost value in Table 6.4 is plotted at an output level midway between those in the adjacent rows.)

TABLE 6.4
Average Variable Cost and Average Total Cost of Bottle Production

Employees per day	Bottles per day	Variable cost ($/day)	Average variable cost ($/unit of output)	Total cost ($/day)	Average total cost ($/unit of output)	Marginal cost ($/bottle)
0	0	0		40		
						0.15
1	80	12	0.15	52	0.65	
						0.10
2	200	24	0.12	64	0.32	
						0.20
3	260	36	0.138	76	0.292	
						0.30
4	300	48	0.16	88	0.293	
						0.40
5	330	60	0.182	100	0.303	
						0.60
6	350	72	0.206	112	0.32	
						1.00
7	362	84	0.232	124	0.343	

FIGURE 6.5
The Marginal, Average Variable, and Average Total Cost Curves for a Bottle Manufacturer.
The *MC* curve cuts both the *AVC* and *ATC* curves at their minimum points. The upward-sloping portion of the marginal cost curve corresponds to the region of diminishing returns.

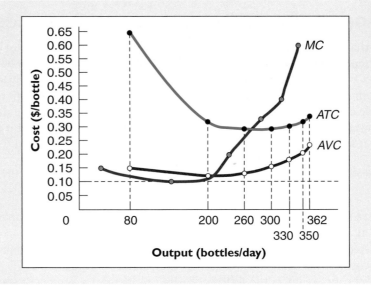

We call your attention to several features of the cost curves in Figure 6.5. Note, for example, that the upward-sloping portion of the marginal cost curve (*MC*) corresponds to the region of diminishing returns discussed earlier. Thus, as the firm moves beyond two employees per day (200 bottles per day), the increments to total output become smaller with each additional employee, which means that the cost of producing additional bottles (*MC*) must be increasing in this region.

Note also that the definition of marginal cost implies that the marginal cost curve must intersect both the average variable cost curve (*AVC*) and the average to-tal cost curve (*ATC*) at their respective minimum points. To see why, consider the logic that explains what happens to the average weight of children in a third-grade class when a new student joins the class. If the new (marginal) student is lighter than the previous average weight for the class, average weight will fall, but if the new student is heavier than the previous average, average weight will rise. By the same token, when marginal cost is below average total cost or average variable cost, the corresponding average cost must be falling, and vice versa. And this ensures that the marginal cost curve must pass through the minimum points of both average cost curves.

Seeing the bottle maker's *AVC* curve displayed graphically makes the question posed in Exercise 6.4 much easier to answer. The question, recall, was whether the firm should shut down in the short run if the price per bottle was only $0.10. A glance at Figure 6.5 reveals that the firm should indeed shut down because this price lies below the minimum value of its *AVC* curve, making it impossible for the firm to cover its variable costs at any output level.

PRICE = MARGINAL COST: THE MAXIMUM-PROFIT CONDITION

So far, we have implicitly assumed that the bottle maker could employ workers only in whole-number amounts. Under these conditions, we saw that the profit-maximizing output level was one for which marginal cost was somewhat less than price (because adding yet another employee would have pushed marginal cost higher than price). In the next example, we will see that when output and employment can be varied continuously, the maximum-profit condition is that price be equal to marginal cost.

For the bottle maker whose cost curves are shown in Figure 6.6, find the profit-maximizing output level if bottles sell for $0.20 each. How much profit will this firm earn? What is the lowest price at which this firm would continue to operate in the short run?

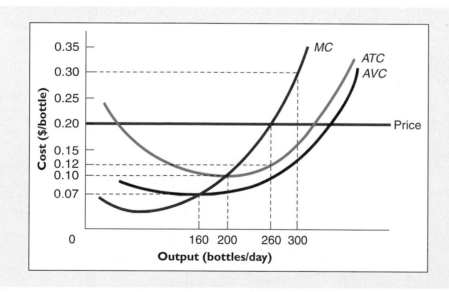

FIGURE 6.6
Price = Marginal Cost: The Perfectly Competitive Firm's Profit-Maximizing Supply Rule.
If price is greater than marginal cost, the firm can increase its profit by expanding production and sales. If price is less than marginal cost, the firm can increase its profit by producing and selling less output.

The Cost-Benefit Principle tells us that this firm should continue to expand as long as price is at least as great as marginal cost. In Figure 6.6 we see that if the firm follows this rule, it will produce 260 bottles per day, the quantity at which price and marginal cost are equal. To gain further confidence that 260 must be the profit-maximizing quantity when the price is $0.20 per bottle, first suppose that the firm had sold some amount less than that—say, only 200 bottles per day. Its benefit from expanding output by one bottle would then be the bottle's market price, here 20 cents. The cost of expanding output by one bottle is equal (by definition) to the firm's marginal cost, which at 200 bottles per day is only 10 cents (see Figure 6.6). So by selling the 201st bottle for 20 cents and producing it for an extra cost of only 10 cents, the firm will increase its profit by 20 − 10 = 10 cents per day. In a similar

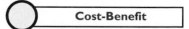
Cost-Benefit

way, we can show that for *any* quantity less than the level at which price equals marginal cost, the seller can boost profit by expanding production.

Conversely, suppose that the firm was currently selling more than 260 bottles per day—say, 300—at a price of 20 cents each. In Figure 6.6 we see that marginal cost at an output of 300 is 30 cents per bottle. If the firm then contracted its output by one bottle per day, it would cut its costs by 30 cents while losing only 20 cents in revenue. As a result, its profit would grow by 10 cents per day. The same argument can be made regarding any quantity larger than 260, so if the firm is currently selling an output at which price is less than marginal cost, it can always do better by producing and selling fewer bottles.

We have thus established that if the firm sold fewer than 260 bottles per day, it could earn more profit by expanding; and if it sold more than 260, it could earn more by contracting. It follows that at a market price of 20 cents per bottle, the seller maximizes its profit by selling 260 units per day, the quantity for which price and marginal cost are exactly the same.

At that quantity the firm will collect total revenue of $P \times Q = (\$0.20/\text{bottle})$ $(260 \text{ bottles/day}) = \$52$ per day. Note in Figure 6.6 that at 260 bottles per day the firm's average total cost is $ATC = \$0.12$ per bottle, which means that its total cost is $ATC \times Q = (\$0.12/\text{bottle})(260 \text{ bottles/day}) = \$31.20$ per day. The firm's profit is the difference between its total revenue and its total cost, or $20.80 per day. Note, finally, that the minimum value of the firm's *AVC* curve is $0.07. So if the price of bottles fell below 7 cents each, the firm would shut down in the short run. ◆

Another attractive feature of the graphical method of finding the profit-maximizing output level is that it permits us to calculate the firm's profit graphically. Thus, for the firm in the preceding example, daily profit is simply the difference between price and *ATC* times the number of units sold: ($0.20/bottle − $0.12/bottle)(260 bottles/day) = $20.80 per day, which is the area of the shaded rectangle in Figure 6.7.

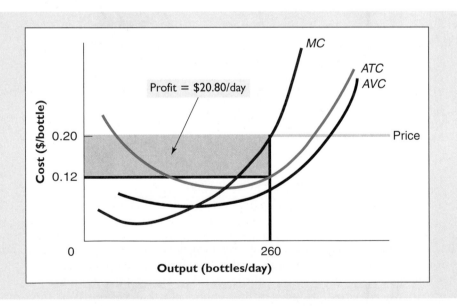

FIGURE 6.7
Measuring Profit Graphically.
Profit is equal to $(P - ATC) \times Q$, which is equal to the area of the shaded rectangle.

Not all firms are as fortunate as the one shown in Figure 6.7. Suppose, for example, that the price of bottles had been not 20 cents but only 8 cents. Since that price is greater than the minimum value of *AVC* (see Figure 6.8), the firm should continue to operate in the short run by producing the level of output for which price equals marginal cost (180 bottles per day). But because price is less than *ATC* at that level of output, the firm will now experience a loss, or negative profit, on

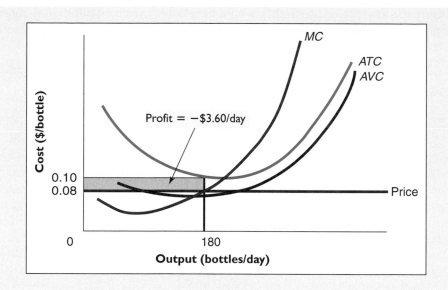

FIGURE 6.8
A Negative Profit.
When price is less than *ATC* at the profit-maximizing quantity, the firm experiences a loss, which is equal to the area of the shaded rectangle.

its operations. This profit is calculated as $(P - ATC) \times Q =$ ($0.08/bottle $-$ $0.10/bottle$) \times$ (180 bottles/day) $= -$3.60$ per day, which is equal to the area of the shaded rectangle in Figure 6.8.

In Chapter 8, we will see how firms move resources from one market to another in response to the incentives implicit in profits and losses. But such movements occur in the long run, and our focus here is on production decisions in the short run.

THE "LAW" OF SUPPLY

The law of demand tells us that consumers buy less of a product when its price rises. If there were an analogous law of supply, it would say that producers offer more of a product for sale when its price rises. Is there such a law? We know that supply curves are essentially marginal cost curves and that because of the law of diminishing returns, marginal cost curves are upward-sloping in the short run. And so there is indeed a law of supply that applies as stated in the short run.

In the long run, however, the law of diminishing returns does not apply. (Recall that it holds only if at least some factors of production are fixed.) Because firms can vary the amounts of *all* factors of production they use in the long run, they can often double their production by simply doubling the amount of each input they use. In such cases, costs would be exactly proportional to output and the firm's marginal cost curve in the long run would be horizontal, not upward-sloping. So for now we'll say only that the "law" of supply holds as stated in the short run but not necessarily in the long run. For both the long run and the short run, however, *the perfectly competitive firm's supply curve is its marginal cost curve.*[1]

Every quantity of output along the market supply curve represents the summation of all the quantities individual sellers offer at the corresponding price. So the correspondence between price and marginal cost exists for the market supply curve as well as for the individual supply curves that lie behind it. That is, *for every price–quantity pair along the market supply curve, price will be equal to each seller's marginal cost of production.*

This is why we sometimes say that the supply curve represents the cost side of the market, whereas the demand curve represents the benefit side of the market. At every point along a market demand curve, price represents what buyers would be willing to pay for an additional unit of the product—and this, in turn, is how we

---

[1]Again, this rule holds subject to the provision that total revenue exceed variable production cost at the output level for which price equals marginal cost.

measure the amount by which they would benefit by having an additional unit of the product. Likewise, at every point along a market supply curve, price measures what it would cost producers to expand production by one unit.

RECAP	PROFIT-MAXIMIZING FIRMS IN PERFECTLY COMPETITIVE MARKETS

The perfectly competitive firm faces a horizontal demand curve for its product, meaning that it can sell any quantity it wishes at the market price. In the short run, the firm's goal is to choose the level of output that maximizes its profits. It will accomplish this by choosing the output level for which its marginal cost is equal to the market price of its product, provided that price exceeds average variable cost. The perfectly competitive firm's supply curve is the portion of its marginal cost curve that lies above its average variable cost curve. At the profit-maximizing quantity, the firm's profit is the product of that quantity and the difference between price and average total cost.

DETERMINANTS OF SUPPLY REVISITED

What factors give rise to changes in supply? (Again, remember that a "change in supply" refers to a shift in the entire supply curve, as opposed to a movement along the curve, which we call a "change in the quantity supplied.") A seller will offer more units if the benefit of selling extra output goes up relative to the cost of producing it. And since the benefit of selling output in a perfectly competitive market is a fixed market price that is beyond the seller's control, our search for factors that influence supply naturally focuses on the cost side of the calculation. The preceding examples suggest why the following factors, among others, will affect the likelihood that a product will satisfy the cost-benefit test for a given supplier.

TECHNOLOGY

Perhaps the most important determinant of production cost is technology. Improvements in technology make it possible to produce additional units of output at lower cost. This shifts each individual supply curve downward (or, equivalently, to the right) and hence shifts the market supply curve downward as well. Over time, the introduction of more sophisticated machinery has resulted in dramatic increases in the number of goods produced per hour of effort expended. Every such development gives rise to a rightward shift in the market supply curve.

But how do we know technological change will reduce the cost of producing goods and services? Might not new equipment be so expensive that producers who used it would have higher costs than those who relied on earlier designs? If so, then rational producers simply would not use the new equipment. The only technological changes that rational producers will adopt are those that will reduce their cost of production.

INPUT PRICES

Whereas technological change generally (although not always) leads to gradual shifts in supply, changes in the prices of important inputs can give rise to large supply shifts literally overnight. As discussed in Chapter 4, for example, the price of crude oil, which is the most important input in the production of gasoline, often fluctuates sharply, and the resulting shifts in supply cause gasoline prices to exhibit corresponding fluctuations.

Similarly, when wage rates rise, the marginal cost of any business that employs labor also rises, shifting supply curves to the left (or, equivalently, upward). When interest rates fall, the opportunity cost of capital equipment also falls, causing supply to shift to the right.

THE NUMBER OF SUPPLIERS

Just as demand curves shift to the right when population grows, supply curves also shift to the right as the number of individual suppliers grows. For example, if container recyclers die or retire at a higher rate than new recyclers enter the industry, the supply curve for recycling services will shift to the left. Conversely, if a rise in the unemployment rate leads more people to recycle soft drink containers (by reducing the opportunity cost of time spent recycling), the supply curve of recycling services will shift to the right.

EXPECTATIONS

Expectations about future price movements can affect how much sellers choose to offer in the current market. Suppose, for example, that recyclers expect the future price of aluminum to be much higher than the current price because of growing use of aluminum components in cars. The rational recycler would then have an incentive to withhold aluminum from the market at today's lower price, thereby to have more available to sell at the higher future price. Conversely, if recyclers expected next year's price of aluminum to be lower than this year's, their incentive would be to offer more aluminum for sale in today's market.

CHANGES IN PRICES OF OTHER PRODUCTS

Apart from technological change, perhaps the most important determinant of supply is variation in the prices of other goods and services that sellers might produce. Prospectors, for example, search for those precious metals for which the surplus of benefits over costs is greatest. When the price of silver rises, many stop looking for gold and start looking for silver. Conversely, when the price of platinum falls, many platinum prospectors shift their attention to gold.

RECAP	THE DETERMINANTS OF SUPPLY

Among the relevant factors causing supply curves to shift are new technologies, changes in input prices, changes in the number of sellers, expectations of future price changes, and changes in the prices of other products that firms might produce.

APPLYING THE THEORY OF SUPPLY

Whether the activity is producing new soft drink containers or recycling used ones, or indeed any other production activity at all, the same logic governs all supply decisions in perfectly competitive markets (and in any other setting in which sellers can sell as much as they wish to at a constant price): Keep expanding output until marginal cost is equal to the price of the product. This logic helps us understand why recycling efforts are more intensive for some products than others.

When recycling is left to private market forces, why are many more aluminum beverage containers recycled than glass ones?

In both cases, recyclers gather containers until their marginal costs are equal to the containers' respective redemption prices. When recycling is left to market forces, the redemption price for a container is based on what companies can sell it (or the materials in it) for. Aluminum containers can be easily processed into scrap aluminum, which commands a high price, and this leads profit-seeking companies to offer a high redemption price for aluminum cans. By contrast, the glass from which glass

Example 6.1
THE ECONOMIC NATURALIST

containers are made has only limited resale value, primarily because the raw materials required to make new glass containers are so cheap. This difference leads profit-seeking companies to offer much lower redemption prices for glass containers than for aluminum ones.

The high redemption prices for aluminum cans induce many people to track these cans down, whereas the low redemption prices for glass containers leads most people to ignore them. If recycling is left completely to market forces, then, we would expect to see aluminum soft drink containers quickly recycled, whereas glass containers would increasingly litter the landscape. This is in fact the pattern we do see in states without recycling laws. (More on how these laws work in a moment.) This pattern is a simple consequence of the fact that the supply curves of container-recycling services are upward-sloping. ●

In states that don't have beverage container deposit laws, why are aluminum cans more likely to be recycled than glass bottles?

The acquisition of valuable raw materials is only one of two important benefits from recycling. The second is that, by removing litter, recycling makes the environment more pleasant for everyone. As the next example suggests, this second benefit might easily justify the cost of recycling substantial numbers of glass containers.

EN 6

What is the socially optimal amount of recycling of glass containers?

Suppose that the 60,000 citizens of Burlington, Vermont, would collectively be willing to pay 6 cents for each glass container removed from their local environment. If the local market supply curve of glass container recycling services is as shown in Figure 6.9, what is the socially optimal level of glass container recycling?

FIGURE 6.9
The Supply Curve of Container Recycling Services for Burlington, Vermont.

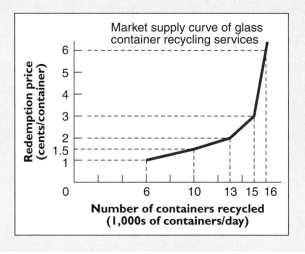

Suppose the citizens of Burlington authorize their city government to collect tax money to finance litter removal. If the benefit of each glass container removed, as measured by what residents are collectively willing to pay, is 6 cents, the government should offer to pay 6 cents for each glass container recycled. To maximize the total economic surplus from recycling, we should recycle that number of containers for which the marginal cost of recycling is equal to the 6-cent marginal benefit. Given the market supply curve shown, the optimal quantity is 16,000 containers per day, and that is how many will be redeemed when the government offers 6 cents per container. ◆

Although 16,000 containers per day will be removed from the environment in the preceding example, others will remain. After all, some are discarded in remote locations, and a redemption price of 6 cents per container is simply not high enough to induce people to track them all down.

So why not offer an even higher price and get rid of *all* glass container litter? For the example given, the reason is that the marginal cost of removing the 16,001st glass container each day is greater than the benefit of removing it. Total economic surplus is largest when we remove litter only up to the point that the marginal benefit of litter removal is equal to its marginal cost, which occurs when 16,000 containers per day are recycled. To proceed past that point is actually wasteful.

Many people become upset when they hear economists say that the socially optimal amount of litter is greater than zero. In the minds of these people, the optimal amount of litter is *exactly* zero. But this position completely ignores the Scarcity Principle. Granted, there would be benefits from reducing litter further, but there also would be costs. Spending more on litter removal therefore means spending less on other useful things. No one would insist that the optimal amount of dirt in his own home is zero. (If someone does make this claim, ask him why he doesn't stay home all day vacuuming the dust that is accumulating in his absence.) If it doesn't pay to remove all the dust from your house, it doesn't pay to remove all the bottles from the environment. Precisely the same logic applies in each case.

If 16,000 containers per day is the optimal amount of litter removal, can we expect the individual spending decisions of private citizens to result in that amount of litter removal? Unfortunately we cannot. The problem is that anyone who paid for litter removal individually would bear the full cost of those services while reaping only a tiny fraction of the benefit. In the previous example, the 60,000 citizens of Burlington reaped a total benefit of 6 cents per container removed, which means a benefit of only $(6/60,000) = 0.0001$ cent per person! Someone who paid 6 cents for someone else to remove a container would thus be incurring a cost 60,000 times greater than his share of the resulting benefit.

© PhotoAlto

Is the socially optimal quantity of litter zero?

Note that the incentive problem here is similar to the one discussed in Chapter 3 for the person deciding whether to be vaccinated against an illness. The problem was that the incentive to be vaccinated was too weak because, even though the patient bears the full cost of the vaccination, many of the resulting benefits accrue to others. Thus, an important part of the extra benefit from any one person being vaccinated is that others also become less likely to contract the illness.

The case of glass container litter is an example in which private market forces do not produce the best attainable outcome for society as a whole. Even people who carelessly toss containers on the ground, rather than recycle them, are often offended by the unsightly landscape to which their own actions contribute. Indeed, this is why they often support laws mandating adequate redemption prices for glass containers.

Activities that generate litter are a good illustration of the Equilibrium Principle described in Chapter 3. People who litter do so not because they don't care about the environment, but because their private incentives make littering misleadingly attractive. Recycling requires some effort, after all, yet no individual's recycling efforts have a noticeable effect on the quality of the environment. The soft-drink-container deposit laws enacted by numerous states were a simple way to bring individual interests more closely into balance with the interests of society as a whole. The vast majority of container litter disappeared almost literally overnight in states that enacted these laws.

EXERCISE 6.5

If the supply curve of glass container recycling services is as shown in the diagram, and each of the city's 60,000 citizens would be willing to pay 0.00005 cent for each glass container removed from the landscape, at what level should the city government set the redemption price for glass containers, and how many will be recycled each day?

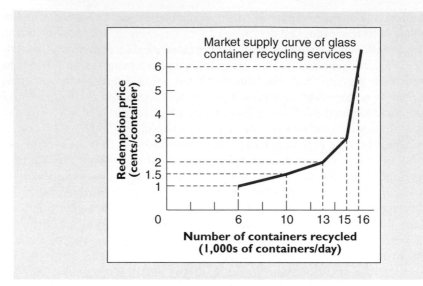

SUPPLY AND PRODUCER SURPLUS

The economic surplus received by a buyer is called *consumer surplus*. The analogous construct for a seller is **producer surplus**, the difference between the price a seller actually receives for the product and the lowest price for which she would have been willing to sell it (her reservation price, which in general will be her marginal cost).

producer surplus the amount by which price exceeds the seller's reservation price

As in the case of consumer surplus, the term *producer surplus* sometimes refers to the surplus received by a single seller in a transaction, while on other occasions it describes the total surplus received by all sellers in a market or collection of markets.

CALCULATING PRODUCER SURPLUS

In the preceding chapter, we saw that consumer surplus in a market is the area bounded above by the demand curve and bounded below by the market price. Producer surplus in a market is calculated in an analogous way. As the following example illustrates, it is the area bounded above by the market price and bounded below by the market supply curve.

How much do sellers benefit from their participation in the market for milk?

Consider the market for milk, whose demand and supply curves are shown in Figure 6.10, which has an equilibrium price of $2 per gallon and an equilibrium quantity of 4,000 gallons per day. How much producer surplus do the sellers in this market reap?

FIGURE 6.10
Supply and Demand in the Market for Milk.
For the supply and demand curves shown, the equilibrium price of milk is $2 per gallon and the equilibrium quantity is 4,000 gallons per day.

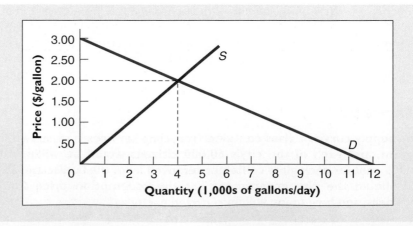

In Figure 6.10, note first that for all milk sold up to 4,000 gallons per day, sellers receive a surplus equal to the difference between the market price of $2 per gallon and their reservation price as given by the supply curve. Total producer surplus received by buyers in the milk market is thus the shaded triangle between the supply curve and the market price in Figure 6.11. Note that this area is a right triangle whose vertical arm is $h = \$2$/gallon and whose horizontal arm is $b = 4,000$ gallons/day. And since the area of any triangle is equal to $(1/2)bh$, producer surplus in this market is equal to

$$(1/2)(4,000 \text{ gallons/day})(\$2/\text{gallon}) = \$4,000/\text{day}.$$

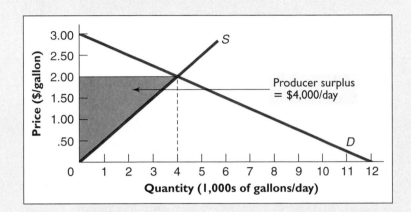

FIGURE 6.11
Producer Surplus in the Market for Milk.
Producer surplus is the area of the shaded triangle ($4,000/day).

Producer surplus in this example may be thought of as the highest price sellers would pay, in the aggregate, for the right to continue participating in the milk market. It is $4,000 per day, since that is the amount by which their combined benefits exceed their combined costs. ◆

As discussed in Chapter 3, the supply curve for a good can be interpreted either horizontally or vertically. The horizontal interpretation tells us, for each price, the total quantity that producers wish to sell at that price. The vertical interpretation tells us, for each quantity, the smallest amount a seller would be willing to accept for the good. For the purpose of computing producer surplus, we rely on the vertical interpretation of the supply curve. The value on the vertical axis that corresponds to each point along the supply curve corresponds to the marginal seller's reservation price for the good, which is the marginal cost of producing it. Producer surplus is the cumulative sum of the differences between the market price and these reservation prices. It is the area bounded above by market price and bounded below by the supply curve.

■ SUMMARY ■

• The demand curve facing a perfectly competitive firm is a horizontal line at the price for which industry supply and demand intersect. **LO1**

• The supply curve for a good or service is a schedule that, for any price, tells us the quantity that sellers wish to supply at that price. The prices at which goods and services are offered for sale in the market depend, in turn, on the opportunity cost of the resources required to produce them. **LO1**

• Supply curves tend to be upward-sloping, at least in the short run, in part because of the Increasing Opportunity Cost Principle. In general, rational producers will always take advantage of their best opportunities first, moving on to more difficult or costly opportunities only after their best ones have been exhausted. Reinforcing this tendency is the law of diminishing returns, which says that when some factors of production are held fixed, the amount of additional variable factors required to produce successive increments in output grows larger.   **LO2**

- For perfectly competitive markets—or, more generally, for markets in which individual sellers can sell whatever quantity they wish at constant price—the seller's best option is to sell that quantity of output for which price equals marginal cost, provided price exceeds the minimum value of average variable cost. The supply curve for the seller thus coincides with the portion of his marginal cost curve that exceeds average variable cost. This is why we sometimes say the supply curve represents the cost side of the market (in

contrast to the demand curve, which represents the benefit side of the market).   **LO3**

- The industry supply curve is the horizontal summation of the supply curves of individual firms in the industry.   **LO2**

- Producer surplus is a measure of the economic surplus reaped by a seller or sellers in a market. It is the cumulative sum of the differences between the market price and their reservation prices, which is the area bounded above by market price and bounded below by the supply curve.   **LO5**

■ KEY TERMS ■

average total cost (*ATC*) (159)
average variable cost (*AVC*) (159)
factor of production (155)
fixed cost (156)
fixed factor of production (156)
imperfectly competitive firm (155)
law of diminishing returns (156)

long run (155)
marginal cost (156)
perfectly competitive
  market (154)
price taker (154)
producer surplus (168)
profit (153)

profit-maximizing firm (154)
profitable firm (159)
short run (155)
total cost (156)
variable cost (156)
variable factor of
  production (156)

■ REVIEW QUESTIONS ■

1. Explain why you would expect supply curves to slope upward on the basis of the Principle of Increasing Opportunity Cost.   **LO1**

2. Which do you think is more likely to be a fixed factor of production for an ice cream producer during the next two months: its factory building or its workers who operate the machines? Explain.   **LO4**

3. Economists often stress that congestion helps account for the law of diminishing returns. With this

in mind, explain why it would be impossible to feed all the people on Earth with food grown in a single flowerpot, even if unlimited water, labor, seed, fertilizer, sunlight, and other inputs were available.   **LO4**

4. True or false: The perfectly competitive firm should *always* produce the output level for which price equals marginal cost.   **LO3**

5. Why do we use the vertical interpretation of the supply curve when we measure producer surplus?   **LO5**

■ PROBLEMS ■

1. Zoe is trying to decide how to divide her time between her job as a wedding photographer, which pays $27 per hour for as many hours as she chooses to work, and as a fossil collector, in which her pay depends on both the price of fossils and the number of them she finds. Earnings aside, Zoe is indifferent between the two tasks, and the number of fossils she can find depends on the number of hours a day she searches, as shown in the table below: **LO3**

Hours per day	Total fossils per day
1	5
2	9
3	12
4	14
5	15

a. Derive a table with price in dollar increments from $0 to $30 in the first column and the quantity of fossils Zoe is willing to supply per day at that price in the second.

b. Plot these points in a graph with price on the vertical axis and quantity per day on the horizontal. What is this curve called?

2. A price-taking firm makes air conditioners. The market price of one of their new air conditioners is $120. Its total cost information is given in the table below:

Air conditioners per day	Total cost ($ per day)
1	100
2	150
3	220
4	310
5	405
6	510
7	650
8	800

How many air conditioners should the firm produce per day if its goal is to maximize its profit? **LO3**

3. The Paducah Slugger Company makes baseball bats out of lumber supplied to it by Acme Sporting Goods, which pays Paducah $10 for each finished bat. Paducah's only factors of production are lathe operators and a small building with a lathe. The number of bats per day it produces depends on the number of employee-hours per day, as shown in the table below. **LO3, LO4**

Number of bats per day	Number of employee-hours per day
0	0
5	1
10	2
15	4
20	7
25	11
30	16
35	22

a. If the wage is $15 per hour and Paducah's daily fixed cost for the lathe and building is $60, what is the profit-maximizing quantity of bats?

b. What would be the profit-maximizing number of bats if the firm's fixed cost were not $60 per day but only $30?

4. In the preceding question, how would Paducah's profit-maximizing level of output be affected if the government imposed a tax of $10 per day on the company? (Hint: Think of this tax as equivalent to a $10 increase in fixed cost.) What would Paducah's profit-maximizing level of output be if the government imposed a tax of $2 per bat? (Hint: Think of this tax as a $2-per-bat increase in the firm's marginal cost.) Why do these two taxes have such different effects? **LO3, LO4**

5. The supply curves for the only two firms in a competitive industry are given by $P = 2Q_1$ and $P = 2 + Q_2$, where Q_1 is the output of firm 1 and Q_2 is the output of firm 2. What is the market supply curve for this industry? (Hint: Graph the two curves side by side, then add their respective quantities at a sample of different prices.) **LO2**

6. Calculate daily producer surplus for the market for pizza whose demand and supply curves are shown in the graph.   **LO5**

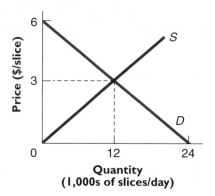

7. For the pizza seller whose marginal, average variable, and average total cost curves are shown in the accompanying diagram, what is the profit-maximizing level of output and how much profit will this producer earn if the price of pizza is $2.50 per slice? **LO3**

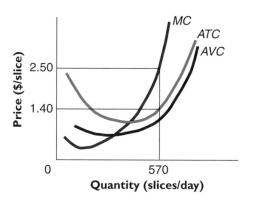

8. For the pizza seller whose marginal, average variable, and average total cost curves are shown in the accompanying diagram, what is the profit-maximizing level of output and how much profit will this producer earn if the price of pizza is $0.80 per slice? **LO3**

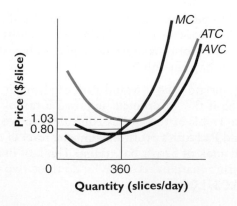

9.* For the pizza seller whose marginal, average variable, and average total cost curves are shown in the accompanying diagram, what is the profit-maximizing level of output and how much profit will this producer earn if the price of pizza is $0.50 per slice?   **LO3**

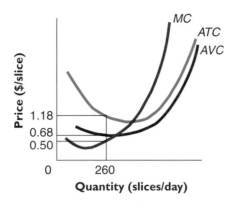

10.* For the pizza seller whose marginal, average variable, and average total cost curves are shown in the accompanying diagram (who is the same seller as in problem 9), what is the profit-maximizing level of output and how much profit will this producer earn if the price of pizza is $1.18 per slice?   **LO3**

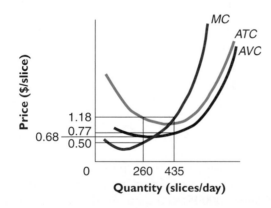

■ ANSWERS TO IN-CHAPTER EXERCISES ■

6.1 Since Harry will find 300 containers if he searches a third hour, we find his reservation price for searching a third hour by solving $p(300) = \$6$ for $p = 2$ cents. His reservation prices for additional hours of search are calculated in an analogous way.   **LO1**

Fourth hour: $p(200) = \$6$, so $p = 3$ cents.
Fifth hour: $p(100) = \$6$, so $p = 6$ cents.

6.2 If bottles sell for 62 cents each, the firm should continue to expand up to and including the sixth employee (350 bottles per day).   **LO3**

6.3 The relevant costs are now as shown in the table on the next page. With each variable and marginal cost entry half what it was in the original example, the firm should now hire six employees and produce 350 bottles per day.   **LO3**

*Problems marked with an asterisk (*) are more difficult.

Employees per day	Bottles per day	Fixed cost ($/day)	Variable cost ($/day)	Total cost ($/day)	Marginal cost ($/bottle)
0	0	40	0	40	
					0.075
1	80	40	6	46	
					0.05
2	200	40	12	52	
					0.10
3	260	40	18	58	
					0.167
4	300	40	24	64	
					0.20
5	330	40	30	70	
					0.30
6	350	40	36	76	
					0.50
7	362	40	42	82	

6.4 Because the firm makes its smallest loss when it hires zero employees, it should shut down in the short run. **LO3**

Employees per day	Output (bottles/day)	Total revenue ($/day)	Total cost ($/day)	Profit ($/day)
0	0	0	40	−40
1	80	8	52	−44
2	200	20	64	−44
3	260	26	76	−50
4	300	30	88	−58
5	330	33	100	−67
6	350	35	112	−77
7	362	36.20	124	−87.80

6.5 The fact that each of the city's 60,000 residents is willing to pay 0.00005 cent for each bottle removed means that the collective benefit of each bottle removed is (60,000)(0.00005) = 3 cents. So the city should set the redemption price at 3 cents, and from the supply curve we see that 15,000 bottles per day will be recycled at that price. **LO3**

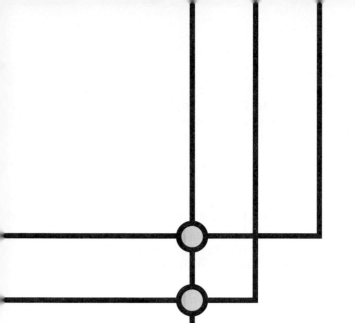

Efficiency and Exchange

LEARNING OBJECTIVES

After reading this chapter, you should be able to:

1. Define efficiency as economists use this term.

2. Analyze how consumer surplus, producer surplus, total economic surplus, and efficiency are affected by public and private policies.

3. Explain how the concept of efficiency helps determine the "right" price for public services.

4. Examine the ways in which the imposition of taxes affects efficiency.

Armando Lopez sat watching one of the national political conventions on television one August night as one orator after another extolled the virtues of the free enterprise system. "The greatest engine of progress mankind has ever witnessed," one of the speakers called it. "A rising tide that will lift all boats," said another.

Lopez, however, was skeptical, for though he had worked hard and played by society's rules, his standard of living had been deteriorating rather than improving. Downsized from his draftsman's position at an aircraft plant the year before, Lopez was working as a janitor for a local office-cleaning company, the best job he had been able to find after months of searching. He could not afford to repair the leaky roof and faulty plumbing at his house in East Los Angeles. Indeed, his two older children had dropped out of college because he could no longer afford their tuition bills. Though his commute to work was only six miles each way, freeway congestion made it a 90-minute trip most mornings. His wife's recurrent asthma attacks, triggered by local air pollution, had recently worsened. Without health insurance, the family's medical bills had been mounting rapidly. And there had been four deaths from drive-by shootings in their neighborhood in the last year.

Given the stark contrast between his own experience and the lofty claims of the orators he was listening to, Lopez's skepticism about the virtues of the free enterprise system was understandable. Yet informed students of the market system understand that it could never have been expected to prevent Lopez's problems in the first place. *In certain domains*—indeed, in very broad domains—markets are every bit as remarkable as their strongest proponents assert. Yet there are many problems they simply cannot be expected to solve. For example, private markets cannot by themselves guarantee an income distribution that most people regard as fair. Nor can they ensure clean air, uncongested highways, or safe neighborhoods for all.

In virtually all successful societies, markets are supplemented by active political coordination in at least some instances. We will almost always achieve our goals more effectively if we know what tasks private markets can do well, and then allow them to perform those tasks. Unfortunately, the discovery that markets cannot solve *every* problem seems to have led some critics to conclude that markets cannot solve *any* problems. This misperception is a dangerous one because it has prompted attempts to prevent markets from doing even those tasks for which they are ideally suited.

Our task in this chapter will be to explore why many tasks are best left to the market. We will explore the conditions under which unregulated markets generate the largest possible economic surplus. We also will discuss why attempts to interfere with market outcomes often lead to unintended and undesired consequences. We will see why public utilities can more efficiently serve their customers if they set prices in a way that closely mimics the market. And we also will discuss why the economic burden of a tax does not always fall most heavily on the parties from whom it is directly collected.

MARKET EQUILIBRIUM AND EFFICIENCY

As noted in Chapter 3, the mere fact that markets coordinate the production of a large and complex list of goods and services is reason enough to marvel at them. But economists make an even stronger claim—namely, that markets not only produce these goods, but also produce them as efficiently as possible.

efficient (or Pareto efficient) a situation is efficient if no change is possible that will help some people without harming others

The term **efficient**, as economists use it, has a narrow technical meaning. When we say that market equilibrium is efficient, we mean simply this: *If price and quantity take anything other than their equilibrium values, a transaction that will make at least some people better off without harming others can always be found.* This conception of efficiency is also known as **Pareto efficiency**, after Vilfredo Pareto, the nineteenth-century Italian economist who introduced it.

Why is market equilibrium efficient in this sense? The answer is that it is always possible to construct an exchange that helps some without harming others whenever a market is out of equilibrium. Suppose, for example, that the supply and demand curves for milk are as shown in Figure 7.1 and that the current price of milk is $1 per gallon. At that price, sellers offer only 2,000 gallons of milk a day. At that quantity, the marginal buyer values an extra gallon of milk at $2. This is the price that corresponds to 2,000 gallons a day on the demand curve, which represents what the

FIGURE 7.1
A Market in Which Price Is Below the Equilibrium Level.
In this market, milk is currently selling for $1 per gallon, $0.50 below the equilibrium price of $1.50 per gallon.

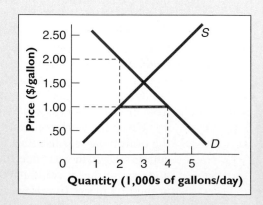

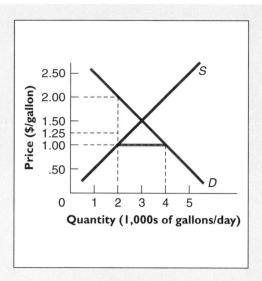

FIGURE 7.2
How Excess Demand Creates an Opportunity for a Surplus-Enhancing Transaction.
At a market price of $1 per gallon, the most intensely dissatisfied buyer is willing to pay $2 for an additional gallon, which a seller can produce at a cost of only $1. If this buyer pays the seller $1.25 for the extra gallon, the buyer gains an economic surplus of $0.75 and the seller gains an economic surplus of $0.25.

marginal buyer is willing to pay for an additional gallon (another application of the vertical interpretation of the demand curve). We also know that the cost of producing an extra gallon of milk is only $1. This is the price that corresponds to 2,000 gallons a day on the supply curve, which equals marginal cost (another application of the vertical interpretation of the supply curve).

Furthermore, a price of $1 per gallon leads to excess demand of 2,000 gallons per day, which means that many frustrated buyers cannot buy as much milk as they want at the going price. Now suppose a supplier sells an extra gallon of milk to the most eager of these buyers for $1.25, as in Figure 7.2. Since the extra gallon cost only $1 to produce, the seller is $0.25 better off than before. And since the most eager buyer values the extra gallon at $2, that buyer is $0.75 better off than before. In sum, the transaction creates an extra $1 of economic surplus out of thin air!

Note that none of the other buyers or sellers is harmed by this transaction. Thus, milk selling for only $1 per gallon cannot be efficient. As the following exercise illustrates, there was nothing special about the price of $1 per gallon. Indeed, if milk sells for *any* price below $1.50 per gallon (the market equilibrium price), we can design a similar transaction, which means that selling milk for any price less than $1.50 per gallon cannot be efficient.

EXERCISE 7.1

In Figure 7.1, suppose that milk initially sells for 50 cents per gallon. Describe a transaction that will create additional economic surplus for both buyer and seller without causing harm to anyone else.

What is more, it is always possible to describe a transaction that will create additional surplus for both buyer and seller whenever the price lies above the market equilibrium level. Suppose, for example, that the current price is $2 per gallon in the milk market shown in Figure 7.1. At that price, we have excess supply of 2,000 gallons per day (see Figure 7.3). Suppose the most dissatisfied producer sells a gallon of milk for $1.75 to the buyer who values it most highly. This buyer, who would have been willing to pay $2, will be $0.25 better off than before. Likewise the producer, who would have been willing to sell milk for as little as $1 per gallon (the marginal cost of production at 2,000 gallons per day), will be $0.75 better off than before. As when the price was $1 per gallon, the new transaction creates $1 of additional economic surplus without harming any other buyer or seller. Since we

FIGURE 7.3
How Excess Supply Creates an Opportunity for a Surplus-Enhancing Transaction.
At a market price of $2 per gallon, dissatisfied sellers can produce an additional gallon of milk at a cost of only $1, which is $1 less than a buyer would be willing to pay for it. If the buyer pays the seller $1.75 for an extra gallon, the buyer gains an economic surplus of $0.25 and the seller gains an economic surplus of $0.75.

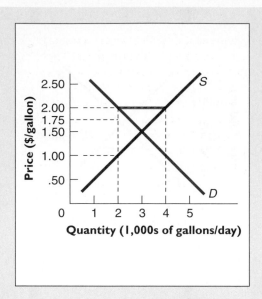

could design a similar surplus-enhancing transaction at any price above the equilibrium level, selling milk for more than $1.50 per gallon cannot be efficient.

The vertical interpretations of the supply and demand curves thus make it clear why only the equilibrium price in a market can be efficient. When the price is either higher or lower than the equilibrium price, the quantity exchanged in the market will always be lower than the equilibrium quantity. If the price is below equilibrium, the quantity sold will be the amount that sellers offer. If the price is above equilibrium, the quantity sold will be the amount that buyers wish to buy. In either case, the vertical value on the demand curve at the quantity exchanged, which is the value of an extra unit to buyers, must be larger than the vertical value on the supply curve, which is the marginal cost of producing that unit.

So the market equilibrium price is the *only* price at which buyers and sellers cannot design a surplus-enhancing transaction. The market equilibrium price leads, in other words, to the largest possible total economic surplus. In this specific, limited sense, free markets are said to produce and distribute goods and services efficiently.

Actually, to claim that market equilibrium is always efficient even in this limited sense is an overstatement. The claim holds only if buyers and sellers are well informed, if markets are perfectly competitive, and if the demand and supply curves satisfy certain other restrictions. For example, market equilibrium will not be efficient if the individual marginal cost curves that add up to the market supply curve fail to include all relevant costs of producing the product. Thus, as we saw in Chapter 3, the true cost of expanding output will be higher than indicated by the market supply curve if production generates pollution that harms others. The equilibrium output will then be inefficiently large and the equilibrium price inefficiently low.

Likewise, market equilibrium will not be efficient if the individual demand curves that make up the market demand curve do not capture all the relevant benefits of buying additional units of the product. For instance, if a homeowner's willingness to pay for ornamental shrubs is based only on the enjoyment she herself gains from them, and not on any benefits that may accrue to her neighbors, the market demand curve for shrubs will understate their value to the neighborhood. The equilibrium quantity of ornamental shrubs will be inefficiently small and the market price for shrubs will be inefficiently low.

We will take up such market imperfections in greater detail in later chapters. For now, we will confine our attention to perfectly competitive markets whose demand curves capture all relevant benefits and whose supply curves capture all relevant costs. For such goods, market equilibrium will always be efficient in the limited sense described earlier.

EFFICIENCY IS NOT THE ONLY GOAL

The fact that market equilibrium maximizes economic surplus is an attractive feature, to be sure. Bear in mind, however, that "efficient" does not mean the same thing as "good." For example, the market for milk may be in equilibrium at a price of $1.50 per gallon, yet many poor families may be unable to afford milk for their children at that price. Still others may not even have a place for their children to sleep.

Efficiency is a concept that is based on predetermined attributes of buyers and sellers—their incomes, tastes, abilities, knowledge, and so on. Through the combined effects of individual cost-benefit decisions, these attributes give rise to the supply and demand curves for each good produced in an economy. If we are concerned about inequality in the distribution of attributes like income, we should not be surprised to discover that markets do not always yield outcomes we like.

Most of us could agree, for example, that the world would be a better one if all people had enough income to feed their families adequately. The claim that equilibrium in the market for milk is efficient means simply that *taking people's incomes as given*, the resulting allocation of milk cannot be altered so as to help some people without at the same time harming others.

To this a critic of the market system might respond: So what? As such critics rightly point out, imposing costs on others may be justified if doing so will help those with sufficiently important unmet demands. For example, most people would prefer to fund homeless shelters with their tax dollars rather than let the homeless freeze to death. Arguing in these terms, American policymakers responded to rapid increases in the price of oil in the late 1970s by imposing price controls on home heating oil. Many of us might agree that if the alternative had been to take no action at all, price controls might have been justified in the name of social justice.

The economist's concept of market efficiency makes clear that there *must* be a better alternative policy. Price controls on oil prevent the market from reaching equilibrium, and as we've seen, that means forgoing transactions that would benefit some people without harming others.

WHY EFFICIENCY SHOULD BE THE FIRST GOAL

Efficiency is important not because it is a desirable end in itself, but because it enables us to achieve all our other goals to the fullest possible extent. It is always possible to generate additional economic surplus when a market is out of equilibrium. To gain additional economic surplus is to gain more of the resources we need to do the things we want to do.

RECAP	EQUILIBRIUM AND EFFICIENCY

A market in equilibrium is said to be efficient, or Pareto efficient, meaning that no reallocation is possible that will benefit some people without harming others.

When a market is not in equilibrium—because price is either above the equilibrium level or below it—the quantity exchanged is always less than the equilibrium level. At such a quantity, a transaction can always be made in which both buyer and seller benefit from the exchange of an additional unit of output.

Total economic surplus in a market is maximized when exchange occurs at the equilibrium price. But the fact that equilibrium is "efficient" in this sense does not mean that it is "good." All markets can be in equilibrium, yet many people may lack sufficient income to buy even basic goods and services. Still, permitting markets to reach equilibrium is important because, when economic surplus is maximized, it is possible to pursue every goal more fully.

THE COST OF PREVENTING PRICE ADJUSTMENTS

PRICE CEILINGS

During 1979, an interruption in oil supplies from the Middle East caused the price of home heating oil to rise by more than 100 percent. Concern about the hardship this sudden price increase would impose on poor families in northern states led the government to impose a price ceiling in the market for home heating oil. This price ceiling prohibited sellers from charging more than a specified amount for heating oil.

The following example illustrates why imposing a price ceiling on heating oil, though well intended, was a bad idea.

How much waste does a price ceiling on heating oil cause?

Suppose the demand and supply curves for home heating oil are as shown in Figure 7.4, in which the equilibrium price is $1.40 per gallon. Suppose that at that price, many poor families cannot heat their homes adequately. Out of concern for the poor, legislators pass a law setting the maximum price at $1 per gallon. How much lost economic surplus does this policy cost society?

FIGURE 7.4

Economic Surplus in an Unregulated Market for Home Heating Oil.

For the supply and demand curves shown, the equilibrium price of home heating oil is $1.40 per gallon and the equilibrium quantity is 3,000 gallons per day. Consumer surplus is the area of the upper shaded triangle ($900 per day). Producer surplus is the area of the lower shaded triangle (also $900 per day).

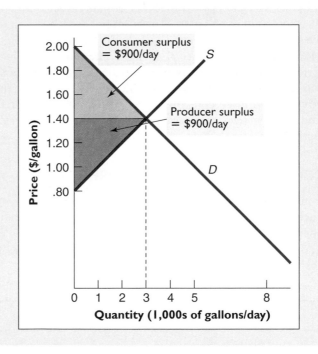

First, let's calculate total economic surplus without price controls. If this market is not regulated, 3,000 gallons per day will be sold at a price of $1.40 per gallon. In Figure 7.4, the economic surplus received by buyers is the area of the upper shaded triangle. Since the height of this triangle is $0.60 per gallon and its base is 3,000 gallons per day, its area is equal to (1/2)(3,000 gallons/day)($0.60/gallon) = $900 per day. The economic surplus received by producers is the area of the lower shaded triangle. Since this triangle also has an area of $900 per day, total economic surplus in this market will be $1,800 per day.

If the price of heating oil is prevented from rising above $1 per gallon, only 1,000 gallons per day will be sold and the total economic surplus will be reduced by the area of the lined triangle shown in Figure 7.5. Since the height of this triangle is $0.80 per gallon and its base is 2,000 gallons per day, its area is

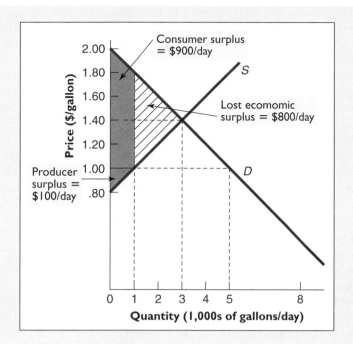

FIGURE 7.5
The Waste Caused by Price Controls.
By limiting output in the home heating oil market to 1,000 gallons per day, price controls cause a loss in economic surplus of $800 per day (area of the lined triangle).

$(1/2)(2,000 \text{ gallons/day})(\$0.80/\text{gallon}) = \$800$ per day. Producer surplus falls from $900 per day in the unregulated market to the area of the lower shaded triangle, or $(1/2)(1,000 \text{ gallons/day})(\$0.20/\text{gallon}) = \$100$ per day, which is a loss of $800 per day. Thus, the loss in total economic surplus is equal to the loss in producer surplus, which means that the new consumer surplus must be the same as the original consumer surplus. To verify this, note that consumer surplus with the price ceiling is the area of the upper shaded figure, which is again $900 per day. (Hint: To compute this area, first split the figure into a rectangle and a triangle.) By preventing the home heating oil market from reaching equilibrium, price controls waste $800 of producer surplus per day without creating any additional surplus for consumers! ◆

EXERCISE 7.2

In the heating oil example, by how much would total economic surplus have been reduced if the price ceiling had been set not at $1 but at $1.20 per gallon?

For several reasons, the reduction in total economic surplus shown in Figure 7.5 is a conservative estimate of the waste caused by attempts to hold price below its equilibrium level. For one thing, the analysis assumes that each of the 1,000 gallons per day that are sold in this market will end up in the hands of the consumers who value them most—in the diagram, those whose reservation prices are above $1.80 per gallon. But since any buyer whose reservation price is above $1 per gallon will want to buy at the ceiling price, much of the oil actually sold is likely to go to buyers whose reservation prices are below $1.80. Suppose, for example, that a buyer whose reservation price was $1.50 per gallon made it into the line outside a heating oil supplier just ahead of a buyer whose reservation price was $1.90 per gallon. If each buyer had a 20-gallon tank to fill, and if the first buyer got the last of the day's available oil, then total surplus would be smaller by $8 that day than if the oil had gone to the second buyer.

A second reason that the reduction in surplus shown in Figure 7.5 is likely to be an underestimate is that shortages typically prompt buyers to take costly actions to enhance their chances of being served. For example, if the heating oil distributor begins selling its available supplies at 6:00 a.m., many buyers may arrive several hours early to ensure a place near the front of the line. Yet when all buyers incur the cost of arriving earlier, no one gets any more oil than before.

Notwithstanding the fact that price ceilings reduce total economic surplus, their defenders might argue that controls are justified because they enable at least some low-income families to buy heating oil at affordable prices. Yes, but the same objective could have been accomplished in a much less costly way—namely, by giving the poor more income with which to buy heating oil.

It may seem natural to wonder whether the poor, who have limited political power, can really hope to receive income transfers that would enable them to heat their homes. On reflection, the answer to this question would seem to be yes, *if the alternative is to impose price controls that would be even more costly than the income transfers*. After all, the price ceiling as implemented ends up costing heating oil sellers $800 per day in lost economic surplus. So they ought to be willing to pay some amount less than $800 a day in additional taxes in order to escape the burden of controls. The additional tax revenue could finance income transfers that would be far more beneficial to the poor than price controls.

This point is so important, and so often misunderstood by voters and policy-makers, that we will emphasize it by putting it another way. Think of the economic surplus from a market as a pie to be divided among the various market participants. Figure 7.6(a) represents the $1,000 per day of total economic surplus available to participants in the home heating oil market when the government limits the price of oil to $1 per gallon. We divided this pie into two slices, labeled *R* and *P*, to denote the surpluses received by rich and poor participants. Figure 7.6(b) represents the $1,800 per day of total economic surplus available when the price of home heating oil is free to reach its equilibrium level. This pie is divided among rich and poor participants in the same proportion as the pie in the left panel.

The important point to notice is this: *Because the pie on the right side is larger, both rich and poor participants in the home heating oil market can get a bigger slice of the pie than they would have had under price controls.* Rather than tinker with the market price of oil, it is in everyone's interest to simply transfer additional income to the poor.

With the Incentive Principle in mind, supporters of price controls may object that income transfers to the poor might weaken people's incentive to work, and thus might prove extremely costly in the long run. Difficult issues do indeed arise in the design of programs for transferring income to the poor—issues we will consider in some detail in later chapters. But for now, suffice it to say that ways exist to transfer

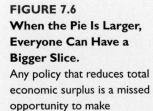

FIGURE 7.6
When the Pie Is Larger, Everyone Can Have a Bigger Slice.
Any policy that reduces total economic surplus is a missed opportunity to make everyone better off.

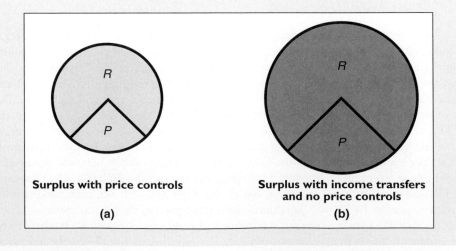

Surplus with price controls

(a)

Surplus with income transfers and no price controls

(b)

income without undermining work incentives significantly. One such method is the Earned Income Tax Credit, a program that supplements the wages of low-income workers. Given such programs, transferring income to the poor will always be more efficient than trying to boost their living standard through price controls.

PRICE SUBSIDIES

Sometimes governments try to assist low-income consumers by subsidizing the prices of "essential" goods and services. France and Russia, for example, have taken this approach at various points by subsidizing the price of bread. As the following example illustrates, such subsidies are like price ceilings in that they reduce total economic surplus.

By how much do subsidies reduce total economic surplus in the market for bread?

A small island nation imports bread for its population at the world price of $2 per loaf. If the domestic demand curve for bread is as shown in Figure 7.7, by how much will total economic surplus decline in this market if the government provides a $1 per loaf subsidy?

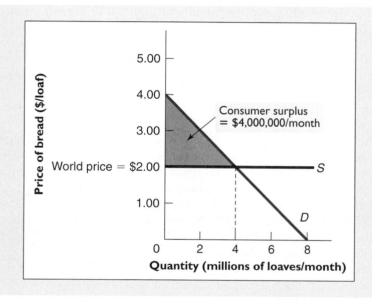

FIGURE 7.7
Economic Surplus in a Bread Market without Subsidy.
For the demand curve shown, consumer surplus (area of the shaded triangle) is $4,000,000 per month. This amount is equal to total economic surplus in the domestic bread market, since no bread is produced domestically.

With no subsidy, the equilibrium price of bread in this market would be the world price of $2 per loaf and the equilibrium quantity would be 4,000,000 loaves per month. The shaded triangle in Figure 7.7 represents consumer economic surplus for buyers in the domestic bread market. The height of this triangle is $2 per loaf, and its base is 4,000,000 loaves per month, so its area is equal to (1/2)(4,000,000 loaves/month)($2/loaf) = $4,000,000 per month. Because the country can import as much bread as it wishes at the world price of $2 per loaf, supply is perfectly elastic in this market. Because the marginal cost of each loaf of bread to sellers is exactly the same as the price buyers pay, producer surplus in this market is zero. So total economic surplus is exactly equal to consumer surplus, which, again, is $4,000,000 per month.

Now suppose that the government administers its $1 per loaf subsidy program by purchasing bread in the world market at $2 per loaf and reselling it in the domestic market for only $1 per loaf. At the new lower price, buyers will now

FIGURE 7.8

The Reduction in Economic Surplus from a Subsidy.

Since the marginal cost of bread is $2 per loaf, total economic surplus is maximized at 4,000,000 loaves per month, the quantity for which the marginal buyer's reservation price is equal to marginal cost. The reduction in economic surplus from consuming an additional 2,000,000 loaves per month is $1,000,000 per month, the area of the smaller shaded triangle.

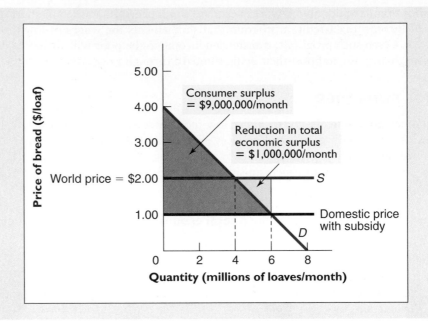

consume not 4,000,000 loaves per month but 6,000,000. Consumer surplus for buyers in the bread market is now the area of the larger shaded triangle in Figure 7.8: (1/2)($3/loaf)(6,000,000 loaves/month) = $9,000,000 per month, or $5,000,000 per month more than before. The catch is that the subsidy wasn't free. Its cost, which must be borne by taxpayers, is ($1/loaf)(6,000,000 loaves/month) = $6,000,000 per month. So even though consumer surplus in the bread market is larger than before, the net effect of the subsidy program is actually to reduce total economic surplus by $1,000,000 per month.

Another way to see why the subsidy reduces total economic surplus by that amount is to note that total economic surplus is maximized at 4,000,000 loaves per month, the quantity for which the marginal buyer's reservation price is equal to marginal cost, and that the subsidy induces additional consumption of 2,000,000 loaves per month. Each additional loaf has a marginal cost of $2 but is worth less than that to the buyer (as indicated by the fact that the vertical coordinate of the demand curve lies below $2 for consumption beyond 4,000,000). As monthly consumption expands from 4,000,000 to 6,000,000 loaves per month, the cumulative difference between the marginal cost of bread and its value to buyers is the area of the smaller shaded triangle in Figure 7.8, which is $1,000,000 per month.

This reduction in economic surplus constitutes pure waste—no different, from the perspective of participants in this market, than if someone had siphoned that much cash out of their bank accounts each month and thrown it into a bonfire. ◆

EXERCISE 7.3

How much total economic surplus would have been lost if the bread subsidy had been set at $0.50 per loaf instead of $1.00?

Compared to a bread subsidy, a much better policy would be to give low-income people some additional income and then let them buy bread on the open market. Subsidy advocates who complain that taxpayers would be unwilling to give low-income people income transfers must be asked to explain why people would be willing to tolerate subsidies, which are *more* costly than income transfers. Logically, if voters are willing to support subsidies, they should be even more eager to support income transfers to low-income persons.

This is not to say that the poor reap no benefit at all from bread subsidies. Since they get to buy bread at lower prices and since the subsidy program is financed by taxes collected primarily from middle- and upper-income families, poor families probably come out ahead on balance. *The point is that for the same expense, we could do much more to help the poor.* Their problem is that they have too little income. The simplest and best solution is not to try to peg the prices of the goods they and others buy below equilibrium levels, but rather to give them some additional money.

FIRST-COME, FIRST-SERVED POLICIES

Governments are not the only institutions that attempt to promote social goals by preventing markets from reaching equilibrium. Some universities, for example, attempt to protect access by low-income students to concerts and sporting events by selling a limited number of tickets below the market-clearing price on a first-come, first-served basis.

The commercial airline industry was an early proponent of the use of the first-come, first-served allocation method, which it employed to ration seats on over-booked flights. Throughout the industry's history, most airlines have routinely accepted more reservations for their flights than there are seats on those flights. Most of the time, this practice causes no difficulty because many reservation holders don't show up to claim their seats. Indeed, if airlines did not overbook their flights, most flights would take off with many more empty seats, forcing airlines to charge higher ticket prices to cover their costs.

The only real difficulty is that every so often, more people actually do show up for a flight than there are seats on the plane. Until the late 1970s, airlines dealt with this problem by boarding passengers on a first-come, first-served basis. For example, if 120 people showed up for a flight with 110 seats, the last 10 to arrive were "bumped," or forced to wait for the next available flight.

The bumped passengers often complained bitterly, and no wonder, since many of them ended up missing important business meetings or family events. As the following example illustrates, there was fortunately a simple solution to this problem.

Why does no one complain any longer about being bumped from an over-booked flight?

In 1978, airlines abandoned their first-come, first-served policy in favor of a new procedure. Since then, their practice has been to solicit volunteers to give up their seats on oversold flights in return for a cash payment or free ticket. Now, the only people who give up their seats are those who volunteer to do so in return for compensation. And hence complaints about being bumped from overbooked flights have completely disappeared. ●

Example 7.1

THE ECONOMIC NATURALIST

Which of the two policies—first-come, first-served or compensation for volunteers—is more efficient? The difficulty with the first-come, first-served policy is that it gives little weight to the interests of passengers with pressing reasons for arriving at their destination on time. Such passengers can sometimes avoid losing their seats by showing up early, but passengers coming in on connecting flights often cannot control when they arrive. And the cost of showing up early is likely to be highest for precisely those people who place the highest value on not missing a flight (such as business executives, whose opportunity cost of waiting in airports is high).

For the sake of illustration, suppose that 37 people show up for a flight with only 33 seats. One way or another, four people will have to wait for another flight. Suppose we ask each of them, "What is the most you would be willing to pay to fly now rather than wait?" Typically, different passengers will have different reservation prices for avoiding the wait. Suppose that the person who is most willing to pay would pay up to $60 rather than miss the flight; that the person second-most willing to pay would pay up to $59; that the person third-most willing to pay would pay up to $58; and so on. In that case, the person with the smallest reservation price for avoiding the wait would have a reservation price of $24. For the entire group of 37 passengers, the average reservation price for avoiding the wait would be ($60 + $59 + $58 + ⋯ + $24)/37 = $42.

Given the difficulty of controlling airport arrival times, the passengers who get bumped under the first-come, first-served policy are not likely to differ systematically from others with respect to their reservation price for not missing the flight. On average, then, the total cost imposed on the four bumped passengers would be four times the average reservation price of $42, or $168. As far as those four passengers are concerned, that total is a pure loss of consumer surplus.

How does this cost compare with the cost imposed on bumped passengers when the airline compensates volunteers? Suppose the airline solicits volunteers by conducting an informal auction, increasing its cash compensation offer by $1 increments until it has the desired number of volunteers. As the incentive to stay behind rises, more people will volunteer; those whose reservation prices are the lowest will volunteer first. In this example, offers below $24 would generate no volunteers. An offer of $24 would generate one volunteer; an offer of $25 would generate two volunteers; and so on. A compensation payment of $27 would generate the necessary four volunteers.

How does switching from the first-come, first-served policy to the policy of compensating volunteers affect total economic surplus? The compensation payments themselves have no net effect since the dollars paid out by the airline are exactly offset by the receipt of those same dollars by passengers who volunteer to wait. Yet switching to the compensation method does increase total economic surplus because those who volunteer have much lower reservation prices for not missing their flight than those who are bumped involuntarily. In this example, we saw that the four passengers bumped under the first-come, first-served policy had an average reservation price of $42, for a total waiting cost of $168. In contrast, the four passengers who volunteered under the compensation policy incurred a total waiting cost of only $27 + $26 + $25 + $24 = $102. Switching to the compensation policy thus produced a gain in total economic surplus of $66.

The compensation policy is more efficient than the first-come, first-served policy because it establishes a market for a scarce resource that would otherwise be allocated by nonmarket means. Figure 7.9 shows the supply and demand curves for seats

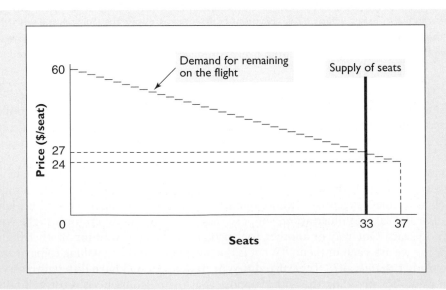

FIGURE 7.9
Equilibrium in the Market for Seats on Oversold Flights.
The demand curve for remaining on the flight is generated by plotting the reservation prices in descending order. The equilibrium compensation payment for volunteers who give up their seats is $27— the price at which 4 passengers volunteer to wait and the remaining 33 choose not to wait.

under the compensation policy. In this market, the equilibrium price of not having to wait is $27. People who choose not to volunteer at that price incur an opportunity cost of $27 in order not to miss the flight. The four people who do volunteer accept $27 as ample compensation—indeed, more than ample for three of them.

An interesting footnote to this example is that the airlines' policy change evoked a fierce protest from the Aviation Consumer Action Project (ACAP), a group that portrayed itself as a watchdog for the interests of airline passengers. ACAP's concern was that the shift to a system of compensation payments would mean that poor people would most often end up waiting for the next flight. This was a curious objection, for several reasons. Although the people who volunteer to wait in return for a compensation payment probably have lower incomes, on average, than those who don't volunteer, the income distributions of the two groups overlap considerably. Many financially comfortable persons with no pressing appointments will gladly volunteer to wait, while many people with lower incomes will choose not to. But more important, the previous policy of first-come, first-served was manifestly less attractive to the poor than the new policy. After all, passengers give up their seats under the volunteer policy only when they find the payment offered sufficient to compensate for the inconvenience of waiting. We may suspect that few poor persons would be grateful if ACAP had succeeded in persuading the government to block the switch to compensation payments.

How should a tennis pro handle the overbooking problem?

Anticipating a high proportion of no-shows, a tennis pro routinely books five people for each of his group lesson slots, even though he is able to teach only three people at a time. One day, all five people show up for their lessons at 10 a.m., the first lesson slot of the morning. Their respective arrival times and the maximum amounts each would be willing to pay to avoid postponing his or her lesson are as given in the table.

Player	Arrival time	Reservation price
Ann	9:50 a.m.	$ 4
Bill	9:52 a.m.	3
Carrie	9:55 a.m.	6
Dana	9:56 a.m.	10
Earl	9:59 a.m.	2

If the tennis pro accommodates the players on a first-come, first-served basis, by how much will total economic surplus be smaller than if he had offered cash compensation to induce two volunteers to reschedule? Which system is more efficient?

The result of using a first-come, first-served policy will be that Dana and Earl, the last two to arrive, will have to postpone their lessons. Since the cost of waiting is $10 for Dana and $2 for Earl, the total waiting cost of the first-come, first-served policy is $12.

Suppose that the pro had instead offered cash compensation payments to elicit volunteers. If he offered a payment of $3, both Bill and Earl would be willing to wait. The total waiting cost of the cash compensation policy would therefore be only $3 + $2 = $5, or $7 less than under the first-come, first-served policy. So the cash compensation policy is more efficient. (Again, the compensation payments themselves have no net effect on total economic surplus because the dollars paid out by the tennis pro are exactly offset by the dollars received by the volunteers.) ◆

You might feel tempted to ask why the tennis pro would bother to offer cash compensation when he has the option of saving the $5 by continuing with his current policy of first-come, first-served. Or you might wonder why an airline would bother to offer cash compensation to elicit volunteers to wait for the next flight. But we know that it is possible for *everyone* to do better under an efficient policy than under an inefficient one. (When the pie is bigger, everyone can have a larger slice.) The following exercise asks you to design such a transaction for the tennis-lesson example.

EXERCISE 7.4

Using the information from the previous example, describe a set of cash transfers that would make each of the five students and the tennis pro better off than under the first-come, first-served policy. (Hint: Imagine that the tennis pro tells his students that he will stick with first-come, first served unless they agree to contribute to the compensation pool as he requests.)

In practice, transactions like the one called for in Exercise 7.4 would be cumbersome to administer. Typically, the seller is in a position to solve such problems more easily by offering cash payments to elicit volunteers, and then financing those cash payments by charging slightly higher prices. Buyers, for their part, are willing to pay the higher prices because they value the seller's promise not to cancel their reservations without compensation.

RECAP	THE COST OF BLOCKING PRICE ADJUSTMENTS

In an effort to increase the economic welfare of disadvantaged consumers, governments often implement policies that attempt to prevent markets from reaching equilibrium. Price ceilings and subsidies attempt to make housing and other basic goods more affordable for poor families. Private organizations also implement policies that prevent markets from reaching equilibrium, such as allocation on a first-come, first-served basis. Such policies always reduce total economic surplus relative to the alternative of letting prices seek their equilibrium levels. It is always possible to design alternative policies under which rich and poor alike fare better.

MARGINAL COST PRICING OF PUBLIC SERVICES

The largest possible total economic surplus is achieved in private markets when goods are exchanged at equilibrium prices, where the value of the last unit to the buyer is exactly equal to the seller's marginal cost of producing it. Suppose the government has decided to become the provider of a good or service such as water or electricity. If the government's goal is to maximize the resulting total economic surplus, how much should it charge its customers? The theory of market exchange, normally applied to perfectly competitive firms that can sell any quantity they choose at a constant market price, helps to answer this question. Consider the following example, in which a local government supplies water to its residents.

What is the marginal cost of water in Gainesville?

The municipal water supply company in Gainesville, Florida, has three potential sources of water: an underground spring, a nearby lake, and the Atlantic Ocean. The spring can supply up to 1 million gallons per day at a cost of 0.2 cent per gallon. The lake can supply an additional 2 million gallons per day at a cost of 0.8 cent per gallon. Additional water must be distilled from the ocean at a cost of 4.0 cents per gallon. Draw the marginal cost curve for water in Gainesville.

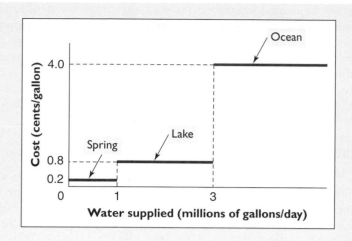

FIGURE 7.10
The Marginal Cost Curve for Water.
The current marginal cost of water is the cost of producing an extra gallon by means of the most expensive production source currently in use.

The Low-Hanging-Fruit Principle tells us that the city will use the cheapest source of water first (the spring). Only when the quantity demanded exceeds the spring's capacity will the city turn to the next least expensive source, the lake; and only when the lake's capacity is exhausted will the city supply water from the ocean. The marginal cost curve will thus be as shown in Figure 7.10. ◆

> **Increasing Opportunity Cost**

As the next example illustrates, total economic surplus is maximized when the government charges each customer exactly the marginal cost of the water he or she consumes.

How much should the government charge for water?

In the preceding example, suppose that if the price of water were 4.0 cents per gallon, citizens of Gainesville would consume 4 million gallons per day. Given the marginal cost curve shown in Figure 7.10, how much should the city charge a citizen whose water comes from the underground spring? How much should it charge someone whose water comes from the lake?

The citizens of Gainesville will enjoy the largest possible economic surplus if the price they pay for water exactly equals the marginal cost of providing it. Since the total amount of water demanded at 4.0 cents per gallon exceeds 3 million gallons per day, the city will have to supply at least some households with water distilled from the Atlantic Ocean, at a cost of 4.0 cents per gallon. At 4 million gallons per day, the marginal cost of water is thus 4.0 cents per gallon, and *this is true no matter where the water comes from.* As long as the city must get *some* of its water from the ocean, the marginal cost of water taken from the underground spring is also 4.0 cents per gallon. Water taken from the lake has a marginal cost of 4.0 cents per gallon as well.

This statement might seem to contradict the claim that water drawn from the spring costs only 0.2 cent per gallon and water drawn from the lake, only 0.8 cent per gallon. But there is no contradiction. To see why, ask yourself how much the city would save if a family that currently gets its water from the spring were to reduce its consumption by 1 gallon per day. The cutback would enable the city to divert that gallon of spring water to some other household that currently gets its water from the ocean, which in turn would reduce consumption of ocean water by 1 gallon. So if a family currently served by the spring were to reduce its daily consumption by 1 gallon, the cost savings would be exactly 4.0 cents. And that, by definition, is the marginal cost of water.

To encourage the efficient use of water, the city should charge every household 4.0 cents per gallon for all the water it consumes. As the Incentive Principle reminds

> **Incentive**

us, charging any household less than that would encourage households to use water whose marginal benefit is less than its marginal cost. For example, suppose the city charged households who get their water from the spring only 0.2 cent per gallon. Those households would then expand their use of water until the benefit they received from the last gallon used equaled 0.2 cent. Because that gallon could have been used to serve someone who is currently using water distilled from the ocean, for whom the value of the marginal gallon is 4 cents, its use would entail a loss in economic surplus of 3.8 cents. ◆

EXERCISE 7.5

Suppose that at a price of 0.8 cent per gallon of water, the citizens of Gainesville would consume a total of only 2 million gallons per day. If the marginal cost of water is as shown in Figure 7.10, how much should the city charge for water? Should that same charge apply to people who get their water from the spring?

EN 7

RECAP	MARGINAL COST PRICING OF PUBLIC SERVICES

When a good is provided by a public utility from several sources, the marginal cost of serving a customer is the cost associated with the least efficient source in use. A public utility should set price equal to marginal cost if its goal is to maximize economic surplus.

TAXES AND EFFICIENCY

WHO PAYS A TAX IMPOSED ON SELLERS OF A GOOD?

Politicians of all stripes seem loath to propose new taxes. But when additional public revenue must be raised, most seem to feel more comfortable proposing taxes paid by sellers than taxes paid by consumers. When pressed to explain why, many respond that businesses can more easily afford to pay extra taxes. Yet the burden of a tax collected from the sellers of a good need not fall exclusively on sellers. Suppose, for example, that a tax of $1 per pound is collected from avocado farmers in the market whose demand and supply curves are shown as D and S in Figure 7.11.

In this market, the initial equilibrium price and quantity are $3 per pound and 3 million pounds per month, respectively. From the farmers' perspective, the imposition

FIGURE 7.11

The Effect of a Tax on the Equilibrium Quantity and Price of Avocados.

With no tax, 3 million pounds of avocados are sold each month at a price of $3 per pound. With a tax of $1 per pound collected from sellers, consumers end up paying $3.50 per pound (including tax), while sellers receive only $2.50 per pound (net of tax). Equilibrium quantity falls from 3 million pounds per month to 2.5 million.

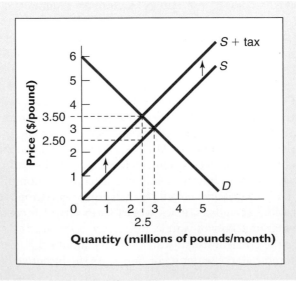

of a tax of $1 per pound is essentially the same as a $1 increase in the marginal cost of producing each pound of avocados, and hence the tax results in an upward shift in the supply curve by $1 per pound.

As shown in Figure 7.11, the new equilibrium price (including the tax) will be $3.50 and the new equilibrium quantity will be 2.5 million pounds per month. The net price per pound received by producers is one dollar less than the price paid by the consumer, or $2.50. Even though the tax was collected entirely from avocado sellers, the burden of the tax fell on both buyers and sellers—on buyers because they pay $0.50 per pound more than before the tax and on sellers because they receive $0.50 per pound less than before the tax.

The burden of the tax need not fall equally on buyers and sellers, as in the illustration just discussed. Indeed, as the following example illustrates, a tax levied on sellers may end up being paid entirely by buyers.

How will a tax on cars affect their prices in the long run?

Suppose that, given sufficient time, all the inputs required to produce cars can be acquired in unlimited quantities at fixed market prices. If the inputs required to produce each car cost $20,000, how will the long-run equilibrium price of automobiles be affected if a tax of $100 per car is levied on manufacturers?

The fact that all the inputs needed to build cars can be acquired at constant prices suggests that the long-run marginal cost of making cars is constant—in other words, that the long-run supply curve of cars is horizontal at $20,000 per car. A tax of $100 per car effectively raises marginal cost by $100 per car, and thus shifts the supply curve upward by exactly $100. If the demand curve for cars is as shown by curve *D* in Figure 7.12, the effect is to raise the equilibrium price of cars by exactly $100, to $20,100. The equilibrium quantity of cars falls from 2 million per month to 1.9 million.

Example 7.2
THE ECONOMIC NATURALIST

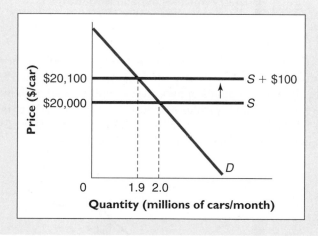

FIGURE 7.12
The Effect of a Tax on Sellers of a Good with Infinite Price Elasticity of Supply.
When the supply curve for a good is perfectly elastic, the burden of a tax collected from sellers falls entirely on buyers.

Although the long-run supply curve shown in Figure 7.12 is in one sense an extreme case (since its price elasticity is infinite), it is by no means an unrepresentative one. As we discussed in Chapter 4, the long-run supply curve will tend to be horizontal when it is possible to acquire more of all the necessary inputs at constant prices. As a first approximation, this can be accomplished for many—perhaps even most—goods and services in a typical economy.

For goods with perfectly elastic supply curves, the entire burden of any tax is borne by the buyer.[1] That is, the increase in the equilibrium price is exactly equal to the tax. For this empirically relevant case, then, there is special irony in the common

---

[1]In the example given, the tax was collected from sellers. If you go on to take intermediate microeconomics, you will see that the same conclusions apply when a tax is collected from buyers.

political practice of justifying taxes on business by saying that businesses have greater ability to pay than consumers.

HOW A TAX COLLECTED FROM A SELLER AFFECTS ECONOMIC SURPLUS

We saw earlier that perfectly competitive markets distribute goods and services efficiently if demand curves reflect all relevant benefits and supply curves reflect all relevant costs. If a tax is imposed on sellers in such a market, will the new market equilibrium still be efficient? Consider again the avocado market discussed earlier, whose supply and demand curves are reproduced in Figure 7.13. In the absence of a tax, 3 million pounds of avocados a month would be sold in this market at a price of $3 per pound, and the resulting total economic surplus would be $9 million per month (the area of the shaded triangle).

FIGURE 7.13
The Market for Avocados without Taxes.
Without taxes, total surplus in the avocado market equals the area of the shaded triangle, $9 million per month.

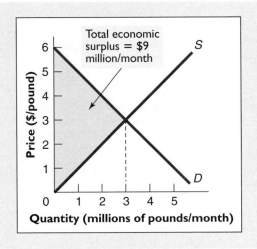

With a tax of $1 per pound collected from avocado sellers, the new equilibrium price of avocados would be $3.50 per pound (of which sellers receive $2.50, net of tax), and only 2.5 millions pounds of avocados would be sold each month (see Figure 7.14). The total economic surplus reaped by buyers and sellers in the avocado market would be the area of the shaded triangle shown in Figure 7.14, which is $6.25 million per month—or $2.75 million less than before.

FIGURE 7.14
The Effect of a $1 per Pound Tax on Avocados.
A $1 per pound tax on avocados would cause an upward shift in the supply curve by $1. The sum of producer and consumer surplus would shrink to the area of the shaded triangle, $6.25 million per month.

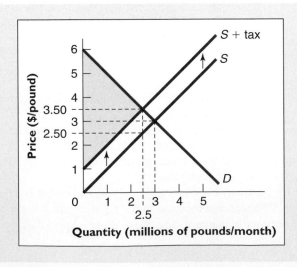

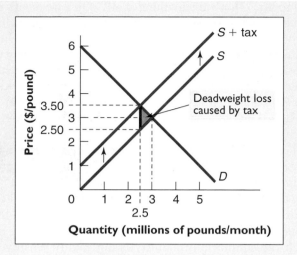

FIGURE 7.15
The Deadweight Loss Caused by a Tax.
For the market shown, the loss in economic surplus caused by a tax of $1 per pound of avocados equals the area of the small shaded triangle, or $250,000 per month.

This drop in surplus may sound like an enormous loss. But it is a misleading figure because it fails to take account of the value of the additional tax revenue collected, which is equal to $2.5 million per month ($1 per pound on 2.5 million pounds of avocados). If the government needs to collect no more than a given total amount of tax revenue in order to pay for the services it provides, then the avocado tax revenue should enable it to reduce other taxes by $2.5 million per month. So although buyers and sellers lose $2.75 million per month in economic surplus from their participation in the avocado market, they also enjoy a $2.5 million reduction in the other taxes they pay. On balance, then, the net reduction in total economic surplus is only $0.25 million.

Graphically, the loss in total economic surplus caused by the imposition of the tax can be shown as the small shaded triangle in Figure 7.15. This loss in surplus is often described as the **deadweight loss** from the tax.

Still, a loss in economic surplus, however small, is something people would prefer to avoid, and taxes like the one just described undoubtedly reduce economic surplus in the markets on which they are imposed. As former Federal Reserve Board chairman Alan Greenspan remarked, "All taxes are a drag on economic growth. It's only a question of degree."[2]

A tax reduces economic surplus because it distorts the basic cost-benefit criterion that would ordinarily guide efficient decisions about production and consumption. In the example just considered, the Cost-Benefit Principle tells us that we should expand avocado production up to the point at which the benefit of the last pound of avocados consumed (as measured by what buyers are willing to pay for it) equals the cost of producing it (as measured by the producer's marginal cost). That condition was satisfied in the avocado market before the tax, but it is not satisfied once the tax is imposed. In Figure 7.15, for example, note that when avocado consumption is 2.5 million pounds per month, the value of an additional pound of avocados to consumers is $3.50, whereas the cost to producers is only $2.50, not including the tax. (The cost to producers, including the tax, is $3.50 per pound, but again we note that this tax is not a cost to society as a whole because it offsets other taxes that would otherwise have to be collected.)

Is a tax on avocados necessarily "bad"? (When economists say that a policy such as a tax is "bad," they mean that it lowers total economic surplus.) To answer this question, we must first identify the best alternative to taxing avocados. You

deadweight loss the reduction in total economic surplus that results from the adoption of a policy

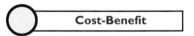

Cost-Benefit

[2]*The Wall Street Journal,* March 26, 1997, p. A1.

may be tempted to say, "Don't tax anything at all!" On a moment's reflection, however, you will realize that this is surely not the best option. After all, a country that taxed nothing could not pay for even the most minimal public services such as road maintenance, fire protection, and national defense. And a country without at least minimal defense capability could not hope to maintain its independence for long. (We will consider why we often empower government to provide public goods in Chapter 15.) On balance, if taxing avocados were the best way to avoid doing without highly valued public services, then a small deadweight loss in the avocado market would be a small price indeed.

So the real question is whether there are other things we could tax that would be better than taxing avocados. The problem with a tax on any activity is that if market incentives encourage people to pursue the "right" amount of the activity (that is, the surplus-maximizing amount), then a tax will encourage them to pursue too little of it. As economists have long recognized, this observation suggests that taxes will cause smaller deadweight losses if they are imposed on goods for which the equilibrium quantity is not highly sensitive to changes in production costs.

TAXES, ELASTICITY, AND EFFICIENCY

Suppose the government put a tax of 50 cents per pound on table salt. How would this affect the amount of salt you and others use? In Chapter 4, we saw that the demand for salt is highly inelastic with respect to price because salt has few substitutes and occupies only a minuscule share in most family budgets. Because the imposition of a tax on table salt would not result in a significant reduction in the amount of it consumed, the deadweight loss from this tax would be relatively small. More generally, the deadweight loss from a per-unit tax imposed on the seller of a good will be smaller the smaller is the price elasticity of demand for the good.

Figure 7.16 illustrates how the deadweight loss from a tax declines as the demand for a good becomes less elastic with respect to price. In both (a) and (b), the original supply and demand curves yield an equilibrium price of $2 per unit and an equilibrium quantity of 24 units per day. The deadweight loss from a tax of $1 per unit imposed on the good shown in Figure 7.16(a) is the area of the shaded triangle in (a), which is $2.50 per day. The demand curve in Figure 7.16(b), D_2,

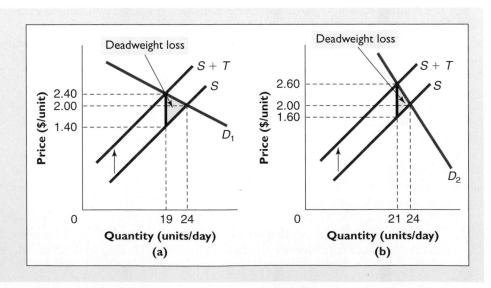

FIGURE 7.16
Elasticity of Demand and the Deadweight Loss from a Tax.
At the equilibrium price and quantity, price elasticity of demand is smaller for the good shown in (b) than for the good shown in (a). The area of the deadweight loss triangle in (b), $1.50 per day, is smaller than the area of the deadweight loss triangle in (a), $2.50 per day.

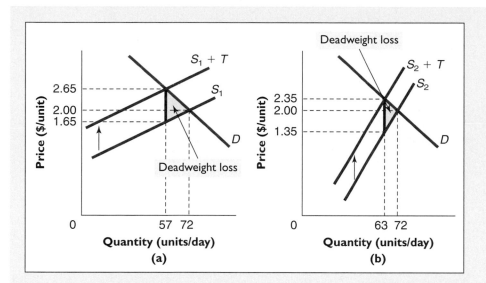

is less elastic at the equilibrium price of $2 than the demand curve in (a), D_1 [this follows from the fact that P/Q is the same in both cases, whereas 1/slope is smaller in (b)]. The deadweight loss from the same $1 per unit tax imposed on the good in Figure 7.16(b) is the area of the shaded triangle in (b), which is only $1.50 per day.

The reduction in equilibrium quantity that results from a tax on a good will also be smaller the smaller is the elasticity of supply of the good. In Figure 7.17, for example, the original supply and demand curves for the markets portrayed in each part yield an equilibrium price of $2 per unit and an equilibrium quantity of 72 units per day. The deadweight loss from a tax of $1 per unit imposed on the good shown in Figure 7.17(a) is the area of the shaded triangle in (a), which is $7.50 per day. The supply curve in Figure 7.17(b), S_2, is less elastic at the equilibrium price than the supply curve in (a), S_1 [again because P/Q is the same in both cases, whereas 1/slope is smaller in (b)]. The deadweight loss from the same $1 per unit tax imposed on the good in Figure 7.17(b) is the area of the shaded triangle in (b), which is only $4.50 per day.

The deadweight loss from a tax imposed on a good whose supply curve is perfectly inelastic will be zero. This explains why many economists continue to favor the tax advocated by Henry George in the nineteenth century. George proposed that all taxes on labor and goods be abolished and replaced by a single tax on land. Such a tax, he argued, would cause no significant loss in economic surplus because the supply of land is almost perfectly inelastic.

TAXES, EXTERNAL COSTS, AND EFFICIENCY

From an efficiency standpoint, taxing activities that people tend to pursue to excess is even more attractive than taxing land. We have mentioned activities that generate environmental pollution as one example; in later chapters, we will discuss others. Whereas a tax on land does not reduce economic surplus, a tax on pollution can actually increase total economic surplus. Taxes on activities that cause harm to others kill two birds with one stone: They generate revenue to pay for useful public services and, at the same time, discourage people from pursuing the harmful activities. The notion that taxes always and everywhere constitute an obstacle to efficiency simply does not withstand careful scrutiny.

RECAP	TAXES AND EFFICIENCY

A per-unit tax levied on the seller of a product has the same effect on equilibrium quantity and price as a rise in marginal cost equal to the amount of the tax. The burden of a tax imposed on sellers will generally be shared among both buyers and sellers. In the case of a good whose elasticity of supply is infinite, the entire burden of the tax is borne by buyers.

A tax imposed on a product whose supply and demand curves embody all relevant costs and benefits associated with its production and use will result in a deadweight loss—a reduction in total economic surplus in the market for the taxed good. Such taxes may nonetheless be justified if the value of the public services financed by the tax outweighs this deadweight loss. In general, the deadweight loss from a tax on a good will be smaller the smaller are the good's price elasticities of supply and demand. Taxes on activities that generate harm to others may produce a net gain in economic surplus, even apart from the value of public services they finance.

■ SUMMARY ■

- When the supply and demand curves for a product capture all the relevant costs and benefits of producing that product, then market equilibrium for that product will be efficient. In such a market, if price and quantity do not equal their equilibrium values, a transaction can be found that will make at least some people better off without harming others. **LO1**

- Total economic surplus is a measure of the amount by which participants in a market benefit by participating in it. It is the sum of total consumer surplus and total producer surplus in the market. One of the attractive properties of market equilibrium is that it maximizes the value of total economic surplus. **LO1**

- Efficiency should not be equated with social justice. If we believe that the distribution of income among people is unjust, we won't like the results produced by the intersection of the supply and demand curves based on that income distribution, even though those results are efficient. **LO1**

- Even so, we should always strive for efficiency because it enables us to achieve all our other goals to the fullest possible extent. Whenever a market is out of equilibrium, the economic pie can be made larger. And with a larger pie, everyone can have a larger slice. **LO1**

- Regulations or policies that prevent markets from reaching equilibrium—such as price ceilings, price subsidies, and first-come, first-served allocation schemes—are often defended on the grounds that they help the poor. But such schemes reduce economic surplus, meaning that we can find alternatives under which both rich and poor would be better off. The main difficulty of the poor is that they have too little income. Rather than trying to control the prices of the goods they buy, we could do better by enacting policies that raise the incomes of the poor and then letting prices seek their equilibrium levels. Those who complain that the poor lack the political power to obtain such income transfers must explain why the poor have the power to impose regulations that are far more costly than income transfers. **LO2**

- Even when a good is provided by a public utility rather than a private firm, the theory of competitive supply has important implications for how to provide the good most efficiently. The general rule is that a public utility maximizes economic surplus by charging its customers the marginal cost of the goods it provides. **LO3**

- Critics often complain that taxes make the economy less efficient. A tax will indeed reduce economic surplus if the supply and demand curves in the market for the taxed good reflect all the relevant costs and benefits of its production and consumption. But this decline in surplus may be more than offset by the increase in economic surplus made possible by public goods financed with the proceeds of the tax. The best taxes are imposed on activities that would otherwise be pursued to excess, such as activities that generate environmental pollution. Such taxes not only do not reduce economic surplus; they actually increase it. **LO4**

▪ KEY TERMS ▪

deadweight loss (193)   efficient (or Pareto efficient) (176)

▪ REVIEW QUESTIONS ▪

1. Why do economists emphasize efficiency as an important goal of public policy? **LO1**

2. You are a senator considering how to vote on a policy that would increase the economic surplus of workers by $100 million per year but reduce the economic surplus of retirees by $1 million per year. What additional measure might you combine with the policy to ensure that the overall result is a better outcome for everyone? **LO2**

3. Why does the loss in total economic surplus directly experienced by participants in the market for a good that is taxed overstate the overall loss in economic surplus that results from the tax? **LO4**

4. Why is compensating volunteers to relinquish their seats on overbooked flights more efficient than a policy of first-come, first-served? **LO3**

5. Why do price ceilings reduce economic surplus? **LO3**

▪ PROBLEMS ▪

1. Suppose the weekly demand and supply curves for used DVDs in Lincoln, Nebraska, are as shown in the diagram. Calculate **LO1**
   a. The weekly consumer surplus.
   b. The weekly producer surplus.
   c. The maximum weekly amount that producers and consumers in Lincoln would be willing to pay to be able to buy and sell used DVDs in any given week.

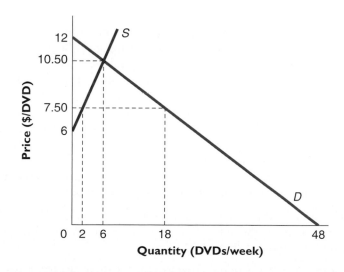

2. Refer to problem 1. Suppose a coalition of students from Lincoln High School succeeds in persuading the local government to impose a price ceiling of $7.50 on used DVDs, on the grounds that local suppliers are taking advantage of teenagers by charging exorbitant prices. **LO2**
   a. Calculate the weekly shortage of used DVDs that will result from this policy.
   b. Calculate the total economic surplus lost every week as a result of the price ceiling.

3. The Kubak crystal caves are renowned for their stalactites and stalagmites. The warden of the caves offers a tour each afternoon at 2 p.m. sharp. The caves can be shown to only four people per day without disturbing their fragile ecology. Occasionally, however, more than four people want to see the caves on the same day. The following table lists the people who wanted to see the caves on September 24, 2003, together with their respective times of arrival and reservation prices for taking the tour that day.   **LO2**

	Arrival time	Reservation price ($)
Herman	1:48	20
Jon	1:50	14
Kate	1:53	30
Jack	1:56	15
Penny	1:57	40
Fran	1:59	12
Faith	2:00	17

a. If the tour is "free" and the warden operates it on a first-come, first-served basis, what will the total consumer surplus be for the four people who get to go on the tour on that day?

b. Suppose the warden solicits volunteers to postpone their tour by offering increasing amounts of cash compensation until only four people still wish to see the caves that day. If he gives each volunteer the same compensation payment, how much money will he have to offer to generate the required number of volunteers? What is the total economic surplus under this policy?

c. Why is the compensation policy more efficient than the first-come, first-served policy?

d. Describe a way of financing the warden's compensation payments that will make everyone, including the warden, either better off or no worse off than under the first-come, first-served approach.

4. Suppose the weekly demand for a certain good, in thousands of units, is given by the equation $P = 8 - Q$ and the weekly supply of the good is given by the equation $P = 2 + Q$, where P is the price in dollars.   **LO4**

a. Calculate the total weekly economic surplus generated at the market equilibrium.

b. Suppose a per-unit tax of $2, to be collected from sellers, is imposed in this market. Calculate the direct loss in economic surplus experienced by participants in this market as a result of the tax.

c. How much government revenue will this tax generate each week? If the revenue is used to offset other taxes paid by participants in this market, what will be their net reduction in total economic surplus?

5. Is a company's producer surplus the same as its profit? (Hint: A company's total cost is equal to the sum of all marginal costs incurred in producing its output, plus any fixed costs.)   **LO1**

6. In Charlotte, North Carolina, citizens can get their electric power from two sources: a hydroelectric generator and a coal-fired steam generator. The hydroelectric generator can supply up to 100 units of power per day at a constant marginal cost of 1 cent per unit. The steam generator can supply any additional power that is needed at a constant marginal cost of 10 cents per unit. When electricity costs 10 cents per unit, residents of Charlotte demand 200 units per day.   **LO3**

a. Draw the marginal cost curve of electric power production in Charlotte.

    b. How much should the city charge for electric power? Explain. Should it charge the same price for a family whose power comes from the hydroelectric generator as it does for a family whose power comes from the steam generator?

7. The municipal water works of Cortland draws water from two sources: an underground spring and a nearby lake. Water from the spring costs 2 cents per 100 gallons to deliver and the spring has a capacity of 1 million gallons per day. Water from the lake costs 4 cents per 100 gallons to deliver and is available in unlimited quantities. The demand for water in the summer months in Cortland is $P = 20 - 0.001Q$, where P is the price of water in cents per 100 gallons and Q is quantity demanded in hundreds of gallons per day. The demand curve for water in the winter months is $P = 10 - 0.001Q$. If the water works wants to encourage efficient water use, how much should it charge for water in the summer months? In the winter months? **LO3**

8.* Phil's demand curve for visits to the Gannett walk-in medical clinic is given by $P = 48 - 8Q$, where P is the price per visit in dollars and Q is the number of visits per semester. The marginal cost of providing medical services at Gannett is $24 per visit. Phil has a choice between two health policies, A and B. Both policies cover all the costs of any serious illness from which Phil might suffer. Policy A also covers the cost of visits to the walk-in clinic, whereas policy B does not. Thus, if Phil chooses policy B, he must pay $24 per visit to the walk-in clinic. **LO2**

    a. If the premiums the insurance company charges for policies A and B must cover their respective costs, by how much will the two premiums differ and what will be the difference in Phil's total expenditure for medical care under the two policies?

    b. Which policy will Phil choose?

    c. What is the most Phil would be willing to pay for the right to continue buying that policy?

9.* The government of Islandia, a small island nation, imports heating oil at a price of $2 per gallon and makes it available to citizens at a price of $1 per gallon. If Islandians' demand curve for heating oil is given by $P = 6 - Q$, where P is the price per gallon in dollars and Q is the quantity in millions of gallons per year, how much economic surplus is lost as a result of the government's policy? **LO2**

10.* Refer to problem 9. Suppose each of the 1 million Islandian households has the same demand curve for heating oil. **LO2**

    a. What is the household demand curve?

    b. How much consumer surplus would each household lose if it had to pay $2 per gallon instead of $1 per gallon for heating oil, assuming there were no other changes in the household budget?

    c. With the money saved by not subsidizing oil, by how much could the Islandian government afford to cut each family's annual taxes?

    d. If the government abandoned its oil subsidy and implemented the tax cut, by how much would each family be better off?

    e. How does the resulting total gain for the 1 million families compare with your calculation of the lost surplus in problem 9?

■ ANSWERS TO IN-CHAPTER EXERCISES ■

7.1 At a price of 50 cents per gallon, there is excess demand of 4,000 gallons per day. Suppose a seller produces an extra gallon of milk (marginal cost = 50 cents) and sells it to the buyer who values it most (reservation price = $2.50) for $1.50. Both buyer and seller will gain additional economic surplus of $1, and no other buyers or sellers will be hurt by the transaction. **LO1**

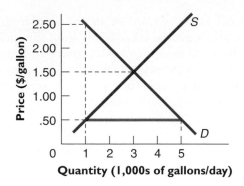

7.2 As shown in the accompanying diagram, the new loss in total economic surplus is $200 per day. **LO1**

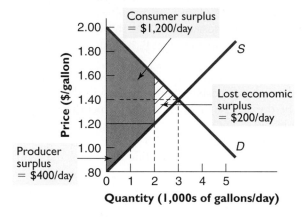

7.3 With a $0.50 per loaf subsidy, the new domestic price becomes $1.50 per loaf. The new lost surplus is the area of the small shaded triangle in the diagram: (1/2)($0.50/loaf)(1,000,000 loaves/month) = $250,000 per month. **LO2**

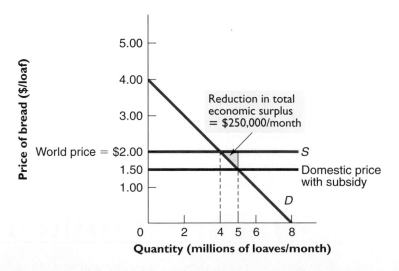

7.4 Under first-come, first-served, Dana will have to postpone his lesson. Since Dana would be willing to pay up to $10 to avoid postponing it, he will be better off if the pro asks for a contribution of, say, $8, and then lets him take

Bill's place at the scheduled time. The pro could then give $4 to Bill, which would make him $1 better off than if he had not postponed his lesson. The remaining $4 of Dana's payment could be distributed by giving $1 each to Ann, Carrie, Earl, and the tennis pro.   **L02**

Player	Arrival time	Reservation price ($)
Ann	9:50 a.m.	4
Bill	9:52 a.m.	3
Carrie	9:55 a.m.	6
Dana	9:56 a.m.	10
Earl	9:59 a.m.	3

7.5 At a consumption level of 2 million gallons per day, the marginal source of water is the lake, which has a marginal cost of 0.8 cent per gallon. The city should charge everyone 0.8 cent per gallon, including those who get their water from the spring.   **L03**

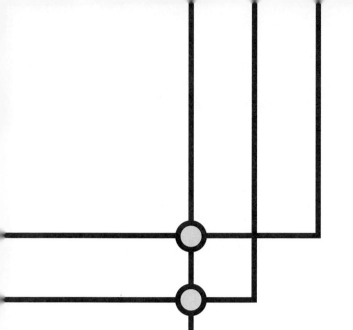

The Invisible Hand in Action

LEARNING OBJECTIVES

After reading this chapter, you should be able to:

1. Define and explain the differences between accounting profit and economic profit.

2. Show how economic profit and economic loss affect the allocation of resources across industries.

3. Explain the difference between economic profit and economic rent.

4. Use the theory of the invisible hand to analyze events in everyday life.

5. Understand and explain the relationship between a market equilibrium and a social optimum.

The market for ethnic cuisine in Ithaca, New York, offered few choices in the early 1970s: the city had one Japanese, two Greek, four Italian, and three Chinese restaurants. Today, more than 30 years later and with essentially the same population, Ithaca has one Sri Lankan, two Indian, one French, one Spanish, six Thai, two Korean, two Vietnamese, four Mexican, three Greek, seven Italian, two Caribbean, two Japanese, and nine Chinese restaurants. In some of the city's other markets, however, the range of available choices has narrowed. For example, several companies provided telephone answering service in 1972, but only one does so today.

Rare indeed is the marketplace in which the identities of the buyers and sellers remain static for extended periods. New businesses enter, established ones leave. There are more body-piercing studios in Ithaca now and fewer watch-repair shops; more marketing consultants and fewer intercity bus companies; and more appliances in stainless steel or black finishes, fewer in avocado or coppertone.

Driving these changes is the businessowner's quest for profit. Businesses migrate to industries and locations in which profit opportunities abound and desert those whose prospects appear bleak. In perhaps the most widely quoted

Why do most American cities now have more tattoo parlors and fewer watch repair shops than in 1972?

Incentive

passage from his landmark treatise, *The Wealth of Nations*, Adam Smith wrote,

> It is not from the benevolence of the butcher, the brewer, or the baker that we expect our dinner, but from their regard of their own interest. We address ourselves not to their humanity, but to their self-love, and never talk to them of our necessities, but of their advantage.

Smith went on to argue that although the entrepreneur "intends only his own gain," he is "led by an invisible hand to promote an end which was no part of his intention." As Smith saw it, even though self-interest is the prime mover of economic activity, the end result is an allocation of goods and services that serves society's collective interests remarkably well. If producers are offering "too much" of one product and "not enough" of another, profit opportunities alert entrepreneurs to that fact and provide incentives for them to take remedial action. All the while, the system exerts relentless pressure on producers to hold the price of each good close to its cost of production, and indeed to reduce that cost in any ways possible. The invisible hand, in short, is about all the good things that can happen because of the Incentive Principle.

Our task in this chapter is to gain deeper insight into the nature of the forces that guide the invisible hand. What exactly does "profit" mean? How is it measured, and how does the quest for it serve society's ends? And if competition holds price close to the cost of production, why do so many entrepreneurs become fabulously wealthy? We will also discuss cases in which misunderstanding of Smith's theory results in costly errors, both in everyday decision making and in the realm of government policy.

THE CENTRAL ROLE OF ECONOMIC PROFIT

The economic theory of business behavior is built on the assumption that the firm's goal is to maximize its profit. So we must be clear at the outset about what, exactly, profit means.

THREE TYPES OF PROFIT

The economist's understanding of profit is different from the accountant's, and the distinction between the two is important to understanding how the invisible hand works. Accountants define the annual profit of a business as the difference between the revenue it takes in and its **explicit costs** for the year, which are the actual payments the firm makes to its factors of production and other suppliers. Profit thus defined is called **accounting profit**.

explicit costs the actual payments a firm makes to its factors of production and other suppliers

accounting profit the difference between a firm's total revenue and its explicit costs

implicit costs the opportunity costs of the resources supplied by the firm's owners

economic profit (or excess profit) the difference between a firm's total revenue and the sum of its explicit and implicit costs

$$\text{Accounting profit} = \text{total revenue} - \text{explicit costs}.$$

Accounting profit is the most familiar profit concept in everyday discourse. It is the one that companies use, for example, when they provide statements about their profits in press releases or annual reports.[1]

Economists, by contrast, define profit as the difference between the firm's total revenue and not just its explicit costs, but also its **implicit costs**, which are the opportunity costs of all the resources supplied by the firm's owners. Profit thus defined is called **economic profit**, or **excess profit**.

$$\text{Economic profit} = \text{total revenue} - \text{explicit costs} - \text{implicit costs}.$$

To illustrate the difference between accounting profit and economic profit, consider a firm with $400,000 in total annual revenue whose only explicit costs are workers' salaries, totaling $250,000 per year. The owners of this firm have supplied

---

[1]For simplicity, this discussion ignores any costs associated with depreciation of the firm's capital equipment. Because the buildings and machines owned by a firm tend to wear out over time, the government allows the firm to consider a fraction of their value each year as a current cost of doing business. For example, a firm that employs a $1,000 machine with a 10-year lifespan might be allowed to record $100 as a current cost of doing business each year.

machines and other capital equipment with a total resale value of $1 million. This firm's accounting profit then is $150,000, or the difference between its total revenue of $400,000 per year and its explicit costs of $250,000 per year.

To calculate the firm's economic profit, we must first calculate the opportunity cost of the resources supplied by the firm's owners. Suppose the current annual interest rate on savings accounts is 10 percent. Had owners not invested in capital equipment, they could have earned an additional $100,000 per year interest by depositing their $1 million in a savings account. So the firm's economic profit is $400,000 per year − $250,000 per year − $100,000 per year = $50,000 per year.

Note that this economic profit is smaller than the accounting profit by exactly the amount of the firm's implicit costs—the $100,000 per year opportunity cost of the resources supplied by the firm's owners. This difference between a business's accounting profit and its economic profit is called its **normal profit**. Normal profit is simply the opportunity cost of the resources supplied to a business by its owners.

Figure 8.1 illustrates the difference between accounting and economic profit. Figure 8.1(a) represents a firm's total revenues, while (b) and (c) show how these revenues are apportioned among the various cost and profit categories.

normal profit the opportunity cost of the resources supplied by a firm's owners, equal to accounting profit minus economic profit

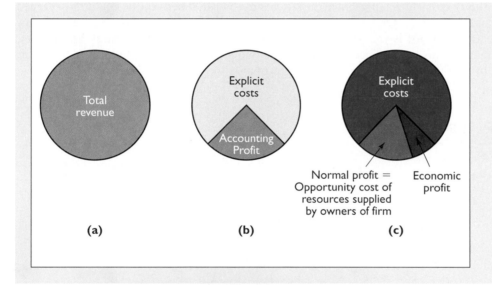

(a)   (b)   (c)

FIGURE 8.1
The Difference between Accounting Profit and Economic Profit.
Accounting profit (b) is the difference between total revenue and explicit costs. Normal profit (c) is the opportunity cost of all resources supplied by a firm's owners. Economic profit (c) is the difference between total revenue and all costs, explicit and implicit (also equal to the difference between accounting profit and normal profit).

"All I know, Harrison, is that I've been on the board forty years and have yet to see an excess profit."

The following examples illustrate why the distinction between accounting and economic profit is so important.

Should Pudge Buffet stay in the farming business?

Pudge Buffet is a corn farmer who lives near Lincoln, Nebraska. His payments for land and equipment rental and for other supplies come to $10,000 per year. The only input he supplies is his own labor, and he considers farming just as attractive as his only other employment opportunity, managing a retail store at a salary of $11,000 per year. Apart from the matter of pay, Pudge is indifferent between farming and being a manager. Corn sells for a constant price per bushel in an international market too large to be affected by changes in one farmer's corn production. Pudge's revenue from corn sales is $22,000 per year. What is his accounting profit? His economic profit? His normal profit? Should he remain a corn farmer?

As shown in Table 8.1, Pudge's accounting profit is $12,000 per year, the difference between his $22,000 annual revenue and his $10,000 yearly payment for land, equipment, and supplies. His economic profit is that amount less the opportunity cost of his labor. Since the latter is the $11,000 per year he could have earned as a store manager, he is making an economic profit of $1,000 per year. Finally, his normal profit is the $11,000 opportunity cost of the only resource he supplies, namely, his labor. Since Pudge likes the two jobs equally well, he will be better off by $1,000 per year if he remains in farming.

TABLE 8.1
Revenue, Cost, and Profit Summary

Total revenue ($/year)	Explicit costs ($/year)	Implicit costs ($/year)	Accounting profit (= total revenue − explicit costs) ($/year)	Economic profit (= total revenue − explicit costs − implicit costs) ($/year)	Normal profit (= implicit cost) ($/year)
22,000	10,000	11,000	12,000	1,000	11,000

◆

EXERCISE 8.1

In the example above, how will Pudge's economic profit change if his annual revenue from corn production is not $22,000, but $20,000? Should he continue to farm?

economic loss an economic profit that is less than zero

When revenue falls from $22,000 to $20,000, Pudge has an economic profit of −$1,000 per year. A negative economic profit is also called an **economic loss**. If Pudge expects to sustain an economic loss indefinitely, his best bet would be to abandon farming in favor of managing a retail store.

You might think that if Pudge could just save enough money to buy his own land and equipment, his best option would be to remain a farmer. But as the following example illustrates, that impression is based on a failure to perceive the difference between accounting profit and economic profit.

Does owning one's own land make a difference?

Let's build on the previous example. Suppose Pudge's Uncle Warren, who owns the farmland Pudge has been renting, dies and leaves Pudge that parcel of land. If the land could be rented to some other farmer for $6,000 per year, should Pudge remain in farming?

TABLE 8.2
Revenue, Cost, and Profit Summary

Total revenue ($/year)	Explicit costs ($/year)	Implicit costs ($/year)	Accounting profit (= total revenue − explicit costs) ($/year)	Economic profit (= total revenue − explicit costs − implicit costs) ($/year)	Normal profit (= implicit costs) ($/year)
20,000	4,000	17,000	16,000	−1,000	17,000

As shown in Table 8.2, if Pudge continues to farm his own land, his accounting profit will be $16,000 per year, or $6,000 more than in Exercise 8.1. But his economic profit will still be the same as before—that is, −$1,000 per year—because Pudge must deduct the $6,000 per year opportunity cost of farming his own land, even though he no longer must make an explicit payment to his uncle for it. The normal profit from owning and operating his farm will be $17,000 per year—the opportunity cost of the land and labor he provides. But since Pudge earns an accounting profit of only $16,000, he will again do better to abandon farming for the managerial job. ◆

Pudge obviously would be wealthier as an owner than he was as a renter. But the question of whether to remain a farmer is answered the same way whether Pudge rents his farmland or owns it. He should stay in farming only if that is the option that yields the highest economic profit.

RECAP	THE CENTRAL ROLE OF ECONOMIC PROFIT

A firm's accounting profit is the difference between its revenue and the sum of all explicit costs it incurs. Economic profit is the difference between the firm's revenue and *all* costs it incurs—both explicit and implicit. Normal profit is the opportunity cost of the resources supplied by the owners of the firm. When a firm's accounting profit is exactly equal to the opportunity cost of the inputs supplied by the firm's owners, the firm's economic profit is zero. For a firm to remain in business in the long run, it must earn an economic profit greater than or equal to zero.

THE INVISIBLE HAND THEORY
TWO FUNCTIONS OF PRICE

In the free enterprise system, market prices serve two important and distinct functions. The first, the **rationing function of price**, is to distribute scarce goods among potential claimants, ensuring that those who get them are the ones who value them most. Thus, if three people want the only antique clock for sale at an auction, the clock goes home with the person who bids the most for it. The second function, the **allocative function of price**, is to direct productive resources to different sectors of the economy. Resources leave markets in which price cannot cover the cost of production and enter those in which price exceeds the cost of production.

Both the allocative and rationing functions of price underlie Adam Smith's celebrated theory of the **invisible hand** of the market. Recall that Smith thought the market system channels the selfish interests of individual buyers and sellers so as to promote the greatest good for society. The carrot of economic profit and the stick of

rationing function of price to distribute scarce goods to those consumers who value them most highly

allocative function of price to direct resources away from overcrowded markets and toward markets that are underserved

invisible hand theory Adam Smith's theory that the actions of independent, self-interested buyers and sellers will often result in the most efficient allocation of resources

economic loss, he argued, were the only forces necessary to ensure that existing sup-plies in any market would be allocated efficiently and that resources would be allo-cated across markets to produce the most efficient possible mix of goods and services.

RESPONSES TO PROFITS AND LOSSES

To get a feel for how the invisible hand works, we begin by looking at how firms re-spond to economic profits and losses. If a firm is to remain in business in the long run, it must cover all its costs, both explicit and implicit. A firm's normal profit is just a cost of doing business. Thus, the owner of a firm that earns no more than a normal profit has managed only to recover the opportunity cost of the resources in-vested in the firm. By contrast, the owner of a firm that makes a positive economic profit earns more than the opportunity cost of the invested resources; she earns a normal profit and then some.

Naturally, everyone would be delighted to earn more than a normal profit, and no one wants to earn less. The result is that those markets in which firms are earn-ing an economic profit tend to attract additional resources, whereas markets in which firms are experiencing economic losses tend to lose resources.

To see how this happens, we'll examine the workings of the market for corn, whose short-run supply and demand curves are shown in Figure 8.2(a). Figure 8.2(b) depicts the marginal and average total cost curves for a representative farm. The equilibrium price of $2 per bushel is determined by the supply–demand intersection in (a). The representative farm whose *MC* and *ATC* curves are shown in (b) then maximizes its profit by producing the quantity for which price equals marginal cost, 130,000 bushels of corn per year.

FIGURE 8.2
Economic Profit in the Short Run in the Corn Market.
At an equilibrium price of $2 per bushel (a), the typical farm earns an economic profit of $104,000 per year (b).

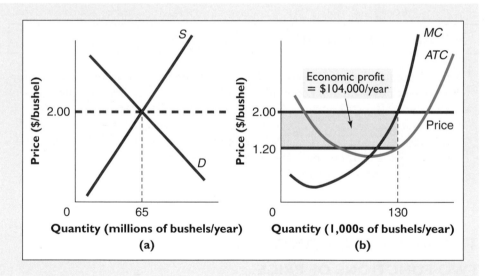

Recall from Chapter 6 that average total cost at any output level is the sum of all costs, explicit and implicit, divided by output. The difference between price and *ATC* is thus equal to the average amount of economic profit earned per unit sold. In Figure 8.2(b), that difference is $0.80 per unit. With 130,000 bushels per year sold, the representative farm earns an economic profit of $104,000 per year.

The existence of positive economic profit in the corn market means that pro-ducers in that market are earning more than their opportunity cost of farming. For simplicity, we assume that the inputs required to enter the corn market—land, labor, equipment, and the like—are available at constant prices and that anyone is free to enter this market if he or she chooses. The key point is that since price exceeds the opportunity cost of the resources required to enter the market, others *will* want to

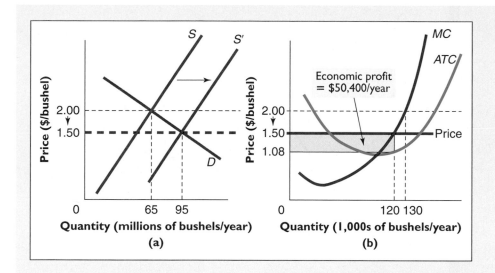

FIGURE 8.3
The Effect of Entry on Price and Economic Profit.
At the original price of $2 per bushel, existing farmers earned economic profit, prompting new farmers to enter. With entry, supply shifts right [from S to S′ in (a)] and equilibrium price falls, as does economic profit (b).

enter. And as they add their corn production to the amount already on offer, supply shifts to the right, causing the market equilibrium price to fall, as shown in Figure 8.3(a). At the new price of $1.50 per bushel, the representative farm now earns much less economic profit than before, only $50,400 per year [Figure 8.3(b)].

For simplicity, we assume that all farms employ the same standard production method, so that their *ATC* curves are identical. Entry will then continue until price falls all the way to the minimum value of *ATC*. (At any price higher than that, economic profit would still be positive, and entry would continue, driving price still lower.) Recall from Chapter 6 that the short-run marginal cost curve intersects the *ATC* curve at the minimum point of the *ATC* curve. This means that once price reaches the minimum value of *ATC*, the profit-maximizing rule of setting price equal to marginal cost results in a quantity for which price and *ATC* are the same. And when that happens, economic profit for the representative farm will be exactly zero, as shown in Figure 8.4(b).

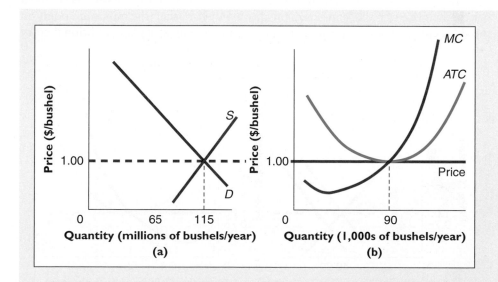

FIGURE 8.4
Equilibrium when Entry Ceases.
Further entry ceases once price falls to the minimum value of *ATC*. At that point, all firms earn a normal economic profit. Equivalently, each earns an economic profit of zero.

In the adjustment process just considered, the initial equilibrium price was above the minimum value of *ATC*, giving rise to positive economic profits. Suppose instead that the market demand curve for corn had intersected the short-run supply curve at a price below the minimum value of each firm's *ATC* curve, as shown in

FIGURE 8.5

A Short-Run Economic Loss in the Corn Market. When price is below the minimum value of *ATC* (a), each farm sustains an economic loss (b).

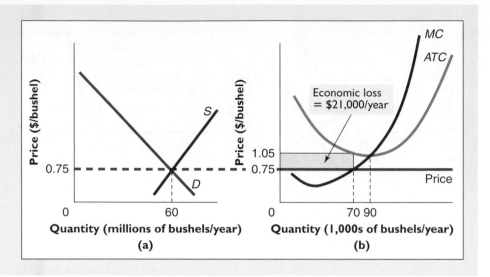

Figure 8.5(a). As long as this price is above the minimum value of average variable cost,[2] each farm will supply that quantity of corn for which price equals marginal cost, shown as 70,000 bushels per year in Figure 8.5(b). Note, however, that at that quantity, the farm's average total cost is $1.05 per bushel, or $0.30 more than the price for which it sells each bushel. As shown in (b), the farm thus sustains an economic loss of $21,000 per year.

If the demand curve that led to the low price and resulting economic losses in Figure 8.5 is expected to persist, farmers will begin to abandon farming for other activities that promise better returns. This means that the supply curve for corn will shift to the left, resulting in higher prices and smaller losses. Exit from corn farming will continue, in fact, until price has again risen to $1 per bushel, at which point there will be no incentive for further exit. Once again we see a stable equilibrium in which price is $1 per bushel, as shown in Figure 8.6.

Given our simplifying assumptions that all corn farms employ a standardized production method and that inputs can be purchased in any quantities at fixed prices, the price of corn cannot remain above $1 per bushel (the minimum point on the *ATC* curve) in the long run. Any higher price would stimulate additional entry

FIGURE 8.6

Equilibrium when Exit Ceases. Further exit ceases once price rises to the minimum value of *ATC*. At that point, all firms earn a normal economic profit. Equivalently, each earns an economic profit of zero.

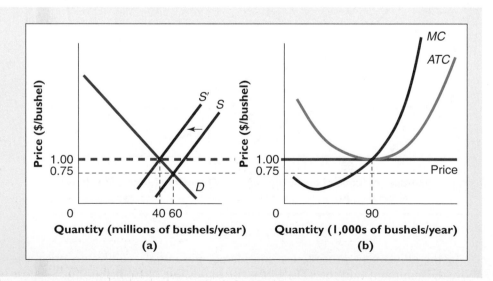

---

[2]This qualification refers to the firm's shutdown condition, discussed in Chapter 6.

until price again fell to that level. Further, the price of corn cannot remain below $1 per bushel in the long run because any lower price would stimulate exit until the price of corn again rose to $1 per bushel.

The fact that firms are free to enter or leave an industry at any time ensures that, in the long run, all firms in the industry will tend to earn zero economic profit. Their *goal* is not to earn zero profit. Rather, the zero-profit tendency is a consequence of the price movements associated with entry and exit. As the Equilibrium Principle— also called the No-Cash-On-the-Table Principle (see Chapter 3)—predicts, when people confront an opportunity for gain, they are almost always quick to exploit it.

What does the long-run supply curve look like in the corn market just discussed? This question is equivalent to asking, "What is the marginal cost of producing additional bushels of corn in the long run?" In general, adjustment in the long run may entail not just entry and exit of standardized firms, but also the ability of firms to alter the mix of capital equipment and other fixed inputs they employ. Explicit consideration of this additional step would complicate the analysis considerably but would not alter the basic logic of the simpler account we present here, which assumes that all firms operate with the same standard mix of fixed inputs in the short run. Under this assumption, the long-run adjustment process consists exclusively of the entry and exit of firms that use a single standardized production method.

The fact that a new firm could enter or leave this corn market at any time means that corn production can always be augmented or reduced in the long run at a cost of $1 per bushel. And this, in turn, means that the long-run supply curve of corn will be a horizontal line at a price equal to the minimum value of the *ATC* curve, $1 per bushel. Since the long-run marginal cost (*LMC*) of producing corn is constant, so is the long-run average cost (*LAC*) and it, too, is $1 per bushel, as shown in Figure 8.7(a). Figure 8.7(b) shows the *MC* and *ATC* curves of a representative corn farm. At a price of $1 per bushel, this corn market is said to be in long-run equilibrium. The representative farm produces 90,000 bushels of corn each year, the quantity for which price equals its marginal cost. And since price is exactly equal to *ATC*, this farm also earns an economic profit of zero.

These observations call attention to two attractive features of the invisible hand theory. One is that the market outcome is efficient in the long run. Note, for example, that when the corn market is in long-run equilibrium, the value to buyers of the last unit of corn sold is $1 per bushel, which is exactly the same as the long-run marginal cost of producing it. Thus, there is no possible rearrangement of resources that would make some participants in this market better off without causing harm to some others. If farmers were to expand production, for example,

Equilibrium

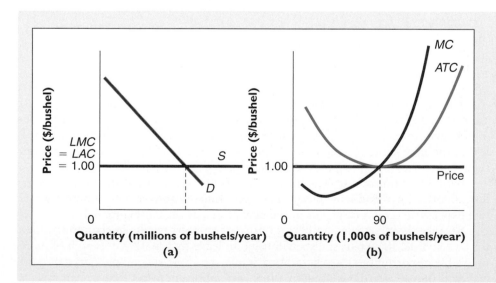

FIGURE 8.7
Long-Run Equilibrium in a Corn Market with Constant Long-Run Average Cost.
When each producer has the same *ATC* curve, the industry can supply as much or as little output as buyers wish to buy at a price equal to the minimum value of *ATC* (a). At that price, the representative producer (b) earns zero economic profit.

the added costs incurred would exceed the added benefits; and if they were to contract production, the cost savings would be less than the benefits forgone.

A second attractive feature of long-run competitive equilibrium is the market outcome can be described as fair, in the sense that the price buyers must pay is no higher than the cost incurred by suppliers. That cost includes a normal profit, the opportunity cost of the resources supplied by owners of the firm.

We must emphasize that Smith's invisible hand theory does not mean that market allocation of resources is optimal in every way. It simply means that markets are efficient in the limited technical sense discussed in the preceding chapter. Thus, if the current allocation differs from the market-equilibrium allocation, the invisible hand theory implies that we can reallocate resources in a way that makes some people better off without harming others.

The following example affords additional insight into how Smith's invisible hand works in practice.

What happens in a city with "too many" hair stylists and "too few" aerobics instructors?

At the initial equilibrium quantities and prices in the markets for haircuts and aerobics classes shown in Figure 8.8, all suppliers are currently earning zero economic profit. Now suppose that styles suddenly change in favor of longer hair and increased physical fitness. If the long-run marginal cost of altering current production levels is constant in both markets, describe how prices and quantities will change in each market, in both the short run and the long run. Are the new equilibrium quantities socially optimal?

FIGURE 8.8

Initial Equilibrium in the Markets for (a) Haircuts and (b) Aerobics Classes. MC_H and ATC_H are the marginal cost and average total cost curves for a representative hair stylist and MC_A and ATC_A are the marginal cost and average total cost curves for a representative aerobics instructor. Both markets are initially in long-run equilibrium, with sellers in each market earning zero economic profit.

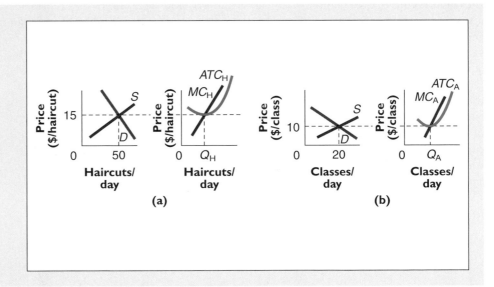

The shift to longer hair styles means a leftward shift in the demand for haircuts, while the increased emphasis on physical fitness implies a rightward shift in the demand curve for aerobics classes, as seen in Figure 8.9. As a result of these demand shifts, the new short-run equilibrium prices change. For the sake of illustration, these new prices are shown as $12 per haircut and $15 per aerobics class.

Because each producer was earning zero economic profit at the original equilibrium prices, hair stylists will experience economic losses and aerobics instructors will experience economic profits at the new prices, as seen in Figure 8.10.

Because the short-run equilibrium price of haircuts results in economic losses for hair stylists, some hair stylists will begin to leave that market in search of more favorable opportunities elsewhere. As a result, the short-run supply curve of haircuts will shift leftward, resulting in a higher equilibrium price. Exit of hair stylists

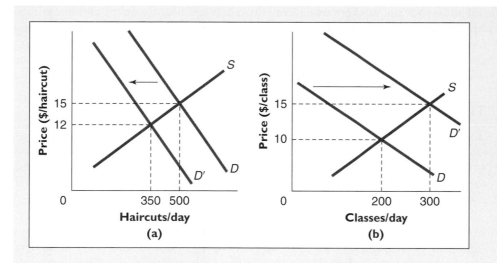

FIGURE 8.9
The Short-Run Effect of Demand Shifts in Two Markets.
(a) The decline in demand for haircuts causes the price of haircuts to fall from $15 to $12 in the short run.
(b) The increase in demand for aerobics classes causes the price of classes to rise from $10 to $15 in the short run.

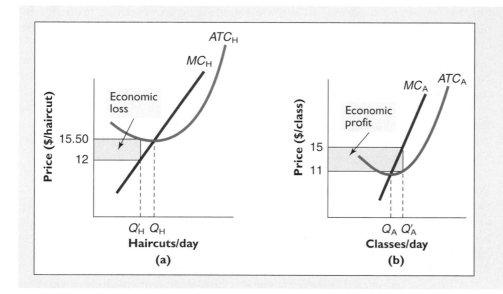

FIGURE 8.10
Economic Profit and Loss in the Short Run.
The assumed demand shifts result in an economic loss for the representative hair stylist (a) and an economic profit for the representative aerobics instructor (b).

will continue until the price of haircuts rises sufficiently to cover the long-run opportunity cost of providing them, which by assumption is $15.

By the same token, because the short-run equilibrium price of aerobics classes results in economic profits for instructors, outsiders will begin to enter that market, causing the short-run supply curve of classes to shift rightward. New instructors will continue to enter until the price of classes falls to the long-run opportunity cost of providing them. By assumption, that cost is $10. Once all adjustments have taken place, there will be fewer haircuts and more aerobics classes than before. But because marginal costs in both markets were assumed constant in the long run, the prices of the two goods will again be at their original levels.

It bears mention that those stylists who leave the hair-cutting market will not necessarily be the same people who enter the aerobics teaching market. Indeed, given the sheer number of occupations a former hair stylist might choose to pursue, the likelihood of such a switch is low. Movements of resources will typically involve several indirect steps. Thus, a former hair stylist might become a secretary, and a former postal worker might become an aerobics instructor.

We also note that the invisible hand theory says nothing about how long these adjustments might take. In some markets, especially labor markets, the required movements might take months or even years. But if the supply and demand curves remain stable, the markets will eventually reach equilibrium prices and quantities. And the new prices and quantities will be socially optimal in the same sense as before. Because the value to buyers of the last unit sold will be the same as the marginal cost of producing it, no additional transactions will be possible that benefit some without harming others. ◆

THE IMPORTANCE OF FREE ENTRY AND EXIT

The allocative function of price cannot operate unless firms can enter new markets and leave existing ones at will. If new firms could not enter a market in which existing firms were making a large economic profit, economic profit would not tend to fall to zero over time, and price would not tend to gravitate toward the marginal cost of production.

barrier to entry any force that prevents firms from entering a new market

Forces that inhibit firms from entering new markets are called **barriers to entry**. In the book publishing market, for example, the publisher of a book enjoys copyright protection granted by the government. Copyright law forbids other publishers from producing and selling their own editions of protected works. This barrier allows the price of a popular book to remain significantly above its cost of production for an extended period, all the while generating an economic profit for its publisher. (A copyright provides no *guarantee* of a profit, and indeed most new books actually generate an economic loss for their publishers.)

Barriers to entry may result from practical as well as legal constraints. Some economists, for example, have argued that the compelling advantages of product compatibility have created barriers to entry in the computer software market. Since more than 90 percent of new desktop computers come with Microsoft's Windows software already installed, rival companies have difficulty selling other operating systems that may prevent users from exchanging files with friends and colleagues. This fact, more than any other, explains Microsoft's spectacular profit history.

No less important than the freedom to enter a market is the freedom to leave. When the airline industry was regulated by the federal government, air carriers were often required to serve specific markets, even though they were losing money in them. When firms discover that a market, once entered, is difficult or impossible to leave, they become reluctant to enter new markets. Barriers to exit thus become barriers to entry. Without reasonably free entry and exit, then, the implications of Adam Smith's invisible hand theory cannot be expected to hold.

All things considered, producers enjoy a high degree of freedom of entry in most U.S. markets. Because free entry is one of the defining characteristics of perfectly competitive markets, unless otherwise stated, we'll assume its existence.

RECAP	THE INVISIBLE HAND THEORY

In market economies, the allocative and rationing functions of prices guide resources to their most highly valued uses. Prices influence how much of each type of good gets produced (the allocative function). Firms enter industries in which prices are sufficiently high to sustain an economic profit and leave those in which low prices result in an economic loss. Prices also direct existing supplies of goods to the buyers who value them most (the rationing function).

Industries in which firms earn a positive economic profit tend to attract new firms, shifting industry supply to the right. Firms tend to leave industries in which they sustain an economic loss, shifting supply curves to the left. In each case, the supply movements continue until economic profit reaches zero. In long-run equilibrium, the value of the last unit produced to buyers is equal to its marginal cost of production, leaving no possibility for additional mutually beneficial transactions.

ECONOMIC RENT VERSUS ECONOMIC PROFIT

Microsoft chairman Bill Gates is the wealthiest man on the planet, largely because the problem of compatibility prevents rival suppliers from competing effectively in the many software markets dominated by his company. Yet numerous people have become fabulously rich even in markets with no conspicuous barriers to entry. If market forces push economic profit toward zero, how can that happen?

The answer to this question hinges on the distinction between economic profit and **economic rent**. Most people think of rent as the payment they make to a landlord or the supplier of a dorm refrigerator, but the term *economic rent* has a different meaning. Economic rent is that portion of the payment for an input that is above the supplier's reservation price for that input. Suppose, for example, that a landowner's reservation price for an acre of land is $100 per year. That is, suppose he would be willing to lease it to a farmer as long as he received an annual payment of at least $100, but for less than that amount he would rather leave it fallow. If a farmer gives him an annual payment not of $100 but of $1,000, the landowner's economic rent from that payment will be $900 per year.

Economic profit is like economic rent in that it, too, may be seen as the difference between what someone is paid (the businessowner's total revenue) and her reservation price for remaining in business (the sum of all her costs, explicit and implicit). But whereas competition pushes economic profit toward zero, it has no such effect on the economic rent for inputs that cannot be replicated easily. For example, although the lease payments for land may remain substantially above the landowner's reservation price, year in and year out, new land cannot come onto the market to reduce or eliminate the economic rent through competition. There is, after all, only so much land to be had.

As the following example illustrates, economic rent can accrue to people as well as land.

economic rent that part of the payment for a factor of production that exceeds the owner's reservation price

How much economic rent will a talented chef get?

A community has 100 restaurants, 99 of which employ chefs of normal ability at a salary of $30,000 per year, the same as the amount they could earn in other occupations that are equally attractive to them. But the 100th restaurant has an unusually talented chef. Because of her reputation, diners are willing to pay 50 percent more for the meals she cooks than for those prepared by ordinary chefs. Owners of the 99 restaurants with ordinary chefs each collect $300,000 per year in revenue, which is just enough to ensure that each earns exactly a normal profit. If the talented chef's opportunities outside the restaurant industry are the same as those of ordinary chefs, how much will she be paid by her employer at equilibrium? How much of her pay will be economic rent? How much economic profit will her employer earn?

Because diners are willing to pay 50 percent more for meals cooked by the talented chef, the owner who hires her will take in total receipts not of $300,000 per year but of $450,000. In the long run, competition should assure that the talented chef's total pay each year will be $180,000 per year, the sum of the $30,000 that ordinary chefs get and the $150,000 in extra revenues for which she is solely responsible. Since the talented chef's reservation price is the amount she could earn outside the restaurant industry—by assumption, $30,000 per year, the same as for ordinary chefs—her economic rent is $150,000 per year. The economic profit of the owner who hires her will be exactly zero. ◆

Since the talented chef's opportunities outside the restaurant industry are no better than an ordinary chef's, why is it necessary to pay the talented chef so much? Suppose her employer were to pay her only $60,000, which they both would consider a generous salary since it is twice what ordinary chefs earn. The employer would then earn an economic profit of $120,000 per year since his annual revenue would be $150,000 more than that of ordinary restaurants, but his costs would be only $30,000 more.

But this economic profit would create an opportunity for the owner of some other restaurant to bid the talented chef away. For example, if the owner of a competing restaurant were to hire the talented chef at a salary of $70,000, the chef would be $10,000 per year better off and the rival owner would earn an economic profit of $110,000 per year, rather than his current economic profit of zero. Furthermore, if the talented chef is the sole reason that a restaurant earns a positive economic profit, the bidding for that chef should continue as long as any economic profit remains. Some other owner will pay her $80,000, still another $90,000, and so on. Equilibrium will be reached only when the talented chef's salary has been bid up to the point that no further economic profit remains—in our example, at an annual paycheck of $180,000.

This bidding process assumes, of course, that the reason for the chef's superior performance is that she possesses some personal talent that cannot be copied. If instead it were the result of, say, training at a culinary institute in France, then her privileged position would erode over time, as other chefs sought similar training.

RECAP	**ECONOMIC RENT VERSUS ECONOMIC PROFIT**

Economic rent is the amount by which the payment to a factor of production exceeds the supplier's reservation price. Unlike economic profit, which is driven toward zero by competition, economic rent may persist for extended periods, especially in the case of factors with special talents that cannot easily be duplicated.

THE INVISIBLE HAND IN ACTION

To help develop your intuition about how the invisible hand works, we will examine how it helps us gain insight into patterns we observe in a wide variety of different contexts. In each case, the key idea we want you to focus on is that opportunities for private gain seldom remain unexploited for very long. Perhaps more than any other, this idea encapsulates the essence of that distinctive mindset known as "thinking like an economist."

THE INVISIBLE HAND AT THE SUPERMARKET AND ON THE FREEWAY

Equilibrium ⊶

As the following example illustrates, the No-Cash-on-the-Table Principle refers not just to opportunities to earn economic profits in cash, but also to any other opportunity to achieve a more desirable outcome.

Example 8.1

THE ECONOMIC NATURALIST

Why do supermarket checkout lines all tend to be roughly the same length?

Pay careful attention the next few times you go grocery shopping and you'll notice that the lines at all the checkout stations tend to be roughly the same length. Suppose you saw one line that was significantly shorter than the others as you wheeled your cart toward the checkout area. Which line would you choose? The shorter one, of course; and because most shoppers would do the same, the short line seldom remains shorter for long. ●

EXERCISE 8.2

Use the No-Cash-on-the-Table Principle to explain why all lanes on a crowded, multilane freeway move at about the same speed.

Equilibrium

THE INVISIBLE HAND AND COST-SAVING INNOVATIONS

When economists speak of perfectly competitive firms, they have in mind businesses whose contribution to total market output is too small to have a perceptible impact on market price. As explained in Chapter 6, such firms are often called price takers: They take the market price of their product as given and then produce that quantity of output for which marginal cost equals that price.

This characterization of the competitive firm gives the impression that the firm is essentially a passive actor in the marketplace. Yet for most firms, that is anything but the case. As the next example illustrates, even those firms that cannot hope to influence the market prices of their products have very powerful incentives to develop and introduce cost-saving innovations.

Why do you seldom see one supermarket checkout line that is substantially shorter than all the others?

How do cost-saving innovations affect economic profit in the short run? In the long run?

Forty merchant marine companies operate supertankers that carry oil from the Middle East to the United States. The cost per trip, including a normal profit, is $500,000. An engineer at one of these companies develops a more efficient propeller design that results in fuel savings of $20,000 per trip. How will this innovation affect the company's accounting and economic profits? Will these changes persist in the long run?

In the short run, the reduction in a single firm's costs will have no impact on the market price of transoceanic shipping services. The firm with the more efficient propeller will thus earn an economic profit of $20,000 per trip (since its total revenue will be the same as before, while its total cost will now be $20,000 per trip lower). As other firms learn about the new design, however, they will begin to adopt it, causing their individual supply curves to shift downward (since the marginal cost per trip at these firms will drop by $20,000). The shift in these individual supply curves will cause the market supply curve to shift, which in turn will result in a lower market price for shipping and a decline in economic profit at the firm where the innovation originated. When all firms have adopted the new, efficient design, the long-run supply curve for the industry will have shifted downward by $20,000 per trip and each company will again be earning only a normal profit. At that point, any firm that did *not* adopt the new propeller design would suffer an economic loss of $20,000 per trip. ◆

The incentive to come up with cost-saving innovations in order to reap economic profit is one of the most powerful forces on the economic landscape. Its beauty, in terms of the invisible hand theory, is that competition among firms ensures that the resulting cost savings will be passed along to consumers in the long run.

THE INVISIBLE HAND IN REGULATED MARKETS

The Incentive Principle is not confined to unregulated markets. The carrot of economic profit and the stick of economic loss also guide resource movements in regulated markets. Consider the taxi industry, which many cities regulate by licensing

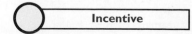

Incentive

cabs. These licenses are often called medallions because they are issued in the form of a metal shield that must be affixed to the hood of the cab, where enforcement officials can easily see it. Cities that regulate cabs in this fashion typically issue fewer medallions than the equilibrium number of taxicabs in similar markets that are not regulated. Officials then allow the medallions to be bought and sold in the marketplace. As the next example demonstrates, the issuance of taxi medallions alters the equilibrium quantity of taxicabs but does not change the fundamental rule that resources flow in response to profit and loss signals.

Example 8.2
THE ECONOMIC NATURALIST

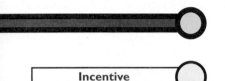

Incentive

Why would a cab driver pay $360,000 for a New York City taxi medallion?

Why do New York City taxicab medallions sell for more than $300,000?

Because New York City issues far fewer taxi medallions than would-be taxi owners could employ profitably, the equilibrium passenger fare is higher than the direct cost of operating a taxicab. Suppose the cost of operating a cab full time—including car, fuel, maintenance, depreciation, and the opportunity cost of the driver's time, but excluding the purchase price of a medallion—is $40,000 per year and a cab in full-time operation will collect $60,000 per year in fares. If the annual interest rate on savings accounts is 6 percent, how much will a medallion cost in equilibrium? Will the owner of a medallion earn an economic profit?

If the medallion were free and could not be sold to others, its owner would earn an economic profit of $20,000 per year—the difference between his $60,000 in fares and his $40,000 in operating cost. But as the Incentive Principle reminds us, the lure of this economic profit would induce outsiders to enter the taxi industry, which could be done by purchasing an owner's medallion.

How much would the entrant be willing to pay for a medallion? If one were available for, say, $100,000, would it be a good buy? Since $100,000 in the bank would earn only $6,000 per year in interest but would bring $20,000 in earnings if used to purchase a taxi medallion, the answer must be yes. In fact, when the annual interest rate is 6 percent, a rational buyer's reservation price for a stream of economic profits of $20,000 per year is the amount of money he would have to put in the bank to earn that much interest each year—$333,333. At any amount less than that, medallions would be underpriced.

Clearly, the owner of a $333,333 medallion has a valuable asset. The opportunity cost of using it to operate a taxi is forgone interest of $20,000 per year. So the medallion owner who takes in $60,000 in fares actually covers only the cost of the resources he has invested in his operation. His economic profit is zero. From the perspective of the medallion owner, the $20,000 difference between his fares and his explicit costs is the implicit cost of the medallion. ●

EXERCISE 8.3

How much would the medallion in the preceding example sell for if the annual interest rate were not 6 percent but 4 percent?

The Present Value of a Permanent Annual Payment

In the taxi cab example, the owner and the entrant both have a critical question to answer: what is the present economic value of a $20,000 payment that would be received each year forever? To say that the **present value of a perpetual annual payment** of $20,000 is $500,000 when the annual interest rate is 4 percent means that a rationally managed bank or other financial institution would be indifferent between receiving either a lump-sum payment of $500,000 right away or a payment of $20,000 per year forever.

Suppose we use the notation PV to represent the present value of a perpetual annual payment of M dollars. How can we calculate that present value? As we saw in the earlier example and exercise, the solution is the answer to the following question: How much money would we have to put in the bank to generate annual interest earnings equal to M dollars? In Exercise 8.3 we saw that if the annual interest

present value of a perpetual annual payment for an annual interest rate r, the present value (PV) of a perpetual annual payment (M) is the amount that would have to be deposited today at that interest rate to generate annual interest earnings of M: $PV = M/r$

rate, expressed as a decimal, is $r = 0.04$ and $M = \$20,000$, we can solve the following equation:

$$PV \times (0.04/\text{year}) = \$20,000/\text{year} \qquad (8.1)$$

for $PV = (\$20,000/\text{year})/(0.04/\text{year}) = \$500,000$. More generally, the present value of a perpetual annual payment of M dollars when the annual interest rate is r is given by the formula

$$PV = M/r. \qquad (8.2)$$

Another regulated market in which the invisible hand was very much in evidence was the regulated commercial airline industry. Until late 1978, airlines were heavily regulated by the Civil Aeronautics Board (CAB), an agency of the federal government. Carriers could not provide air service between two cities unless they were given explicit permission to do so. The CAB also prescribed the fares carriers could charge. The standard practice was to set fares well above the cost of providing service on most routes and then require carriers to use some of the resulting economic profit to pay for service on sparsely traveled routes. But as the following example illustrates, the CAB failed to reckon with the invisible hand.

Why did major commercial airlines install piano bars on the upper decks of Boeing 747s in the 1970s?

At the high airfares the CAB established on the New York to Los Angeles and other popular transcontinental routes in the 1970s, any air carrier that managed to fill a flight with passengers would have earned tens of thousands of dollars in economic profit on that one flight alone. The invisible hand theory tells us that resources will flow into any market in which economic profit is positive and out of any market in which economic profit is negative, eventually driving economic profit to zero. But although an influx of resources will normally cause prices to fall in an unregulated market, the CAB's rules prevented fares from falling. The rules could not prohibit carriers from competing with one another in other ways, however. Because passengers care not only about fares, but also about the frequency of service, a carrier can steal business from rivals simply by adding another flight. Carriers did so, adding flights to their routes until economic profit disappeared. The CAB's goal of generating surplus revenue to pay for service on sparsely traveled routes was doomed from the start.

Adding insult to injury, the policy of setting high fares on heavily traveled routes was wasteful, insofar as it resulted in so many flights on such routes that each flight left with a substantial number of empty seats. Carrier executives quickly realized that they could fill many of those seats by offering service enhancements that would lure passengers away from other airlines. For instance, one carrier converted the upper deck of its 747s to a piano bar, and other airlines quickly followed suit. Others offered elaborate meals. Recognizing this difficulty, the CAB responded by trying to regulate the kinds of food carriers could serve, leading in one case to a protracted legal squabble over the definition of a sandwich.

The problem is not that the extra amenities carriers offered were of *no* value whatever to passengers. Piano bars and more frequent flights were obviously of value to many travelers. But for efficiency's sake, additional amenities should be offered only if their benefit exceeds their cost, and most passengers would not voluntarily have paid for the high level of amenities air carriers offered in the 1970s. Evidence for this claim comes from the operations of several intrastate airlines, which were exempt from federal regulation. Unregulated carriers in California provided service on the San Francisco to San Diego route for about half the fare charged by regulated carriers on the Washington to Boston route of the same distance. Though the California carriers were free to offer more frequent service and more elaborate in-flight amenities, passengers voted with their dollars to sacrifice those amenities for lower airfares. ●

Example 8.3
THE ECONOMIC NATURALIST

Why did commercial airlines once install piano bars in passenger airplanes?

THE INVISIBLE HAND IN ANTIPOVERTY PROGRAMS

As the next example shows, failure to understand the logic of the invisible hand can lead not only to inefficient government regulation, but also to antipoverty programs that are doomed to fail.

How will an irrigation project affect the incomes of poor farmers?

Suppose unskilled workers must choose between working in a textile mill at $8,000 per year and growing rice on a rented parcel of farmland. One worker can farm an 80-acre rice parcel, which rents for $5,000 a year. Such farms yield $16,000 per year in revenue, and the total nonlabor costs of bringing the crop to market are $3,000 per year. The net incomes of rice farmers are thus $8,000 per year—the same as those of textile workers. A state legislator has introduced a bill to fund an irrigation project that would double the output of rice on farms operated by tenant farmers. If the state's contribution to the total supply of rice is too small to affect the price, how will the project affect the incomes of tenant farmers over the long run?

The direct effect of the project will be to double rice yields, which means that each farmer will sell $32,000 worth of rice per year rather than $16,000. If nothing else changed, farmers' incomes would rise from $8,000 per year to $24,000 per year. But the No-Cash-on-the-Table Principle tells us that farmers cannot sustain this income level. From the perspective of textile workers, there is cash on the table in farming. Seeing an opportunity to triple their incomes, many will want to switch to farming. But since the supply of land is fixed, farm rents will rise as textile workers begin bidding for them. They will continue to rise as long as farmers can earn more than textile workers. The long-run effect of the project, then, will be to raise the rent on rice farms, from $5,000 per year to $21,000 (since at the higher rent the incomes of rice farmers and textile workers will again be the same). Thus, the irrigation project will increase the wealth of landowners but will have no long-run effect on the incomes of tenant farmers. ◆

Equilibrium

THE INVISIBLE HAND IN THE STOCK MARKET

One of the most competitive markets on the planet is the market for stocks and bonds on Wall Street in New York. And as we will see, public understanding of how the invisible hand works in this market is often no better than the state legislator's understanding of how the rice market works.

Calculating the Value of a Share of Stock

A share of stock in a company is a claim to a share of the current and future accounting profits of that company. Thus, if you own 1 percent of the total number of shares of a company's stock, you effectively own 1 percent of the company's annual accounting profit, both now and in the future. (We say "effectively" because companies generally do not distribute their accounting profit to shareholders each year; many reinvest their earnings in the company's operations. Such reinvestment benefits the stockholder by enlarging the company and increasing its future accounting profit.) The price of a share of stock depends not only on a company's accounting profit, however, but also on the market rate of interest, as the next example illustrates.

How much will a share of stock sell for?

Suppose we know with certainty that a company's accounting profit will be $1 million this year and every year. If the company has issued a total of 1,000 shares of stock, and the annual interest rate is 5 percent, at what price will each share sell?

Because there are 1,000 shares of stock, each share entitles its owner to one-thousandth of the company's annual accounting profit, or $1,000 per year. Owning this stock is like having a bank deposit that earns $1,000 per year in interest. To calculate the economic value of the stock, therefore, we need only ask how much an investor would need to deposit in the bank at 5 percent interest to generate an annual interest payment of $1,000. The answer is $20,000, and that is the price that each share will command in the stock market. ◆

Calculating the Present Value of Future Costs and Benefits

Someone who is trying to estimate how much a business is worth must take account of the fact that earnings received in the future are less valuable than earnings received today. Consider a company whose only accounting profit, $14,400, will occur exactly two years from now. At all other times its accounting profit will be exactly zero. How much is ownership of this company worth?

To answer this question, we need to employ the concept of the **time value of money**—the fact that money deposited in an interest-bearing account today will grow in value over time.

Our goal is to compute the present value of a $14,400 payment to be received in two years. We can think of this present value as the amount that would have to be deposited in an interest-bearing bank account today to generate a balance of $14,400 two years from today. Let PV denote present value and r the market rate of interest. If we put $100 in an account today at 10 percent annual interest, we will have $100(1.10) = $110 in the account after one year. If we leave $100 in the same account for two years, we will have $100(1.10)(1.10) = $100(1.10)^2 = $121. More generally, if we put PV in the bank today at the interest rate r, we will have $PV(1 + r)$ one year from now and $PV(1 + r)^2$ two years from now. So to find the present value of a $14,400 payment to be received two years from now, we simply solve the equation $14,400 = PV(1 + r)^2$ and get $PV = $14,400/(1 + r)^2$. If the interest rate is 20 percent, then $PV = $14,400/(1.2)^2 = $10,000. To verify this answer, note that $10,000 deposited at 20 percent interest today would grow to $10,000(1 + 0.2) = $12,000 by the end of one year, and that amount left on deposit for a second year would grow to $12,000(1 + 0.2) = $14,400.

More generally, when the interest rate is r, the present value of a payment M to be received T years from now is given by the equation[3]

$$PV = \frac{M}{(1 + r)^T}. \tag{8.3}$$

time value of money the fact that a given dollar amount today is equivalent to a larger dollar amount in the future because the money can be invested in an interest-bearing account in the meantime

EXERCISE 8.4

What is the present value of a payment of $1,728 to be received three years from now if the annual interest rate is 20 percent?

The Efficient Markets Hypothesis

In practice, of course, no one knows with certainty what a company's future profits will be. So the current price of a share of stock will depend not on the actual amount of future profits, but on investors' estimates of them. These estimates incorporate information about current profits, prospects for the company's industry, the state of the economy, demographic trends, and a host of other factors. As this information changes, investors' estimates of future profits change with it, along with the prices of a share of stock.

[3]Notice the difference between Equations 8.3 and 8.2. Equation 8.3 applies to a period of T years while Equation 8.2 applies to an "infinite" stream of payments. The reasoning behind the two equations is, however, exactly the same.

efficient markets hypothesis
the theory that the current price of stock in a corporation reflects all relevant information about its current and future earnings prospects

How fast does new information affect the price of a stock? With blazing speed, according to the **efficient markets hypothesis**. The theory says that the current price of a stock incorporates all available information relevant to the company's earnings. The plausibility of this theory is evident if we think for a moment about what might happen if it were false. Suppose, for example, that at 9:00 a.m. on Monday, October 14, some investors acquire new information to the effect that the company in the example above will realize accounting profits not of $1 million per year, but of $2 million. This information implies that the new equilibrium price for each share of its stock should be $40,000. Now suppose that the price were to remain at its current level ($20,000) for 24 hours before rising gradually to $40,000 over the next two weeks. If so, an investor privy to this information could double her wealth in two weeks without working hard, taking any risk, or even being lucky. All she would have to do is invest all her wealth in the stock at today's price of $20,000 per share.

The Incentive Principle tells us that we may safely assume that there is no shortage of investors who would be delighted to double their wealth without having to work hard or take risks. But in the example just described, they would have to buy shares of the stock within 24 hours of learning of the new profit projections. As eager investors rushed to buy the stock, its price would rise quickly, so that those who waited until the end of the day to buy would miss much of the opportunity for gain. To get the full advantage of the new information, they would have to make their purchases earlier in the day. As more and more investors rushed to buy shares, the window of opportunity would grow narrower and narrower. In the end, the duration of the opportunity to profit from the new information may be just a few minutes long.

In practice, of course, new information often takes time to interpret, and different investors may have different beliefs about exactly what it means. Early information may signal an impending change that is far from certain. As time passes, events may confirm or contradict the implications of the earlier information. The usual pattern is for information to emerge in bits and pieces, and for stock prices to adjust in small increments as each new bit of information emerges. But this does not mean that the price of a stock adjusts gradually to new information. Rather, it means that new information usually emerges gradually. And as each piece of new information emerges, the market reacts almost instantly.

For example, when a Florida jury awarded a lung cancer patient $750,000 in damages in July 1996, the price of tobacco stocks plummeted roughly 20 percent *within minutes*. The award broke a long series of legal precedents in which tobacco companies were not held liable for the illnesses suffered by smokers. When the verdict was announced, no one knew whether it would be reversed on appeal or whether it would influence future verdicts in such cases. Yet investors who had been monitoring the case carefully knew instantly that massive new financial liabilities had become much more likely.

Despite such persuasive evidence in favor of the efficient markets hypothesis, many investors seem to believe that information about the next sure investment bonanza is as close as their broker's latest newsletter. Securities salespersons in New York routinely call investors to offer the latest tips on how to invest their money. The difficulty is that by the time information reaches investors in this way, days, weeks, or even months will have gone by, and the information will have already been incorporated into any stock prices for which it might have been relevant.

The Wall Street Journal publishes a feature in which a group of leading investment advisers predict which stocks will increase most in price during the coming months. The *Journal* then compares the forecasts with the performance of a randomly selected set of stocks. The usual finding is that the randomly selected portfolios perform little differently from those chosen by the "experts." Some of the experts do better than average, others worse. This pattern is consistent with the economist's theory that the invisible hand moves with unusual speed to eliminate profit opportunities in financial markets.

Incentive

Why isn't a stock portfolio consisting of Canada's "50 best-managed companies" a particularly good investment?

Each year since 1993, a panel of distinguished judges has convened to identify the 50 best-managed companies in the country. In their January 2005 press release announcing the companies chosen for the previous year, the judges had this to say:

> Key traits that the 2004 50 Best Managed winners share include their ability to differentiate from their peers by providing exceptional or unique products or services, as well [as] maintain a culture of continued encouragement of employee innovation. Other key determinants which contributed towards companies achieving recognition on this year's 50 Best Managed winners list include a passion to create and retain the right leadership and vision to drive the company forward, and a commitment to maintain an optimal supportive sales culture.

Imagine that you have just read this press release and immediately purchase 100 shares of stock in each of the companies on the list. How well might you expect those stocks to perform relative to a randomly selected portfolio?

A stock is said to "perform well" if its price rises more rapidly than the prices of other stocks. Changes in the price of a company's stock depend not on investors' current beliefs about the company's accounting profit, but on changes in those beliefs. Suppose, for the sake of argument, that the "best-managed" companies had higher accounting profits than other companies at the time of the press release. Because the prices you paid for their stocks would have reflected those higher earnings, there would be no reason to expect their prices to rise more rapidly than those of other stocks.

But won't the accounting profits of a well-managed company be likely to grow more rapidly than those of other companies? Perhaps, but even if so, beliefs to that effect would also be reflected in current stock prices. Indeed, the stocks of many software, biotechnology, and internet commerce companies sell at high prices years before they ever post their first dollar of accounting profit.

An understanding of the invisible hand theory might even lead us to question whether a "well-managed" company will have higher accounting profit than other companies. After all, if an unusually competent manager were known to be the reason a company consistently posted a positive economic profit, other companies could be expected to bid for the manager's services, causing her salary to rise. And the market for the manager's services will not reach equilibrium until her salary has captured all the gains for which her talent is responsible. ●

Example 8.4

THE ECONOMIC NATURALIST

Are the stock prices of the best-managed companies likely to grow faster than stock prices in general?

EN 8

We must stress that our point in the preceding example is *not* that good management doesn't matter. Good management is obviously better than bad management, for it increases total economic surplus. The point is that the reward for good performance tends to be captured by those who provide that performance. And that is a good thing, insofar as it provides powerful incentives for everyone to perform well.

RECAP	**THE INVISIBLE HAND IN ACTION**

Because individuals and firms are generally eager to improve their position, opportunities for gain seldom remain unexploited for long. Early adopters of cost-saving innovations enjoy temporary economic profits. But as additional firms adopt the innovations, the resulting downward supply shift causes price to fall. In the long run, economic profit returns to zero and all cost savings are passed on to consumers.

The quest for advantage guides resources not only in perfectly competitive markets, but also in heavily regulated markets. Firms can almost always find ways to expand sales in markets in which the regulated price permits an economic profit or withdraw service from markets in which the regulated price results in an economic loss.

An understanding of invisible hand theory is also important for the design of antipoverty programs. An irrigation program that makes land more productive, for example, will raise the incomes of tenant farmers only temporarily. In the long run, the gains from such projects tend to be captured as higher rents to landowners.

The efficient markets hypothesis says that the price of a firm's stock at any moment reflects all available information that is relevant for predicting the firm's future earnings. This hypothesis identifies several common beliefs as false—among them that stocks in well-managed companies perform better than stocks in poorly managed ones and that ordinary investors can make large financial gains by trading stocks on the basis of information reported in the news media.

THE DISTINCTION BETWEEN AN EQUILIBRIUM AND A SOCIAL OPTIMUM

Equilibrium

The Equilibrium, or No-Cash-on-the-Table, Principle tells us that when a market reaches equilibrium, no further opportunities for gain are available to individuals. This principle implies that the market prices of resources that people own will eventually reflect their economic value. (As we will see in later chapters, the same cannot be said of resources that are not owned by anyone, such as fish in international waters.)

The No-Cash-on-the-Table Principle is sometimes misunderstood to mean that there are *never* any valuable opportunities to exploit. For example, the story is told of two economists on their way to lunch when they spot what appears to be a $100 bill lying on the sidewalk. When the younger economist stoops to pick up the bill, his older colleague restrains him, saying, "That can't be a $100 bill." "Why not?" asks the younger colleague. "If it were, someone would have picked it up by now," the older economist replies.

Equilibrium

The No-Cash-on-the-Table Principle means not that there *never* are any unexploited opportunities, but that there are none when the market is *in equilibrium*. Occasionally a $100 bill does lie on the sidewalk, and the person who first spots it and picks it up gains a windfall. Likewise, when a company's earnings prospects improve, *somebody* must be the first to recognize the opportunity, and that person can make a lot of money by purchasing the stock quickly.

Still, the No-Cash-on-the-Table Principle is important. It tells us, in effect, that there are only three ways to earn a big payoff: to work especially hard; to have some unusual skill, talent, or training; or simply to be lucky. The person who finds a big bill on the sidewalk is lucky, as are many of the investors whose stocks perform better than average. Other investors whose stocks do well achieve their gains through hard work or special talent. For example, the legendary investor Warren

Buffett, whose portfolio has grown in value at almost three times the stock market average for the last 40 years, spends long hours studying annual financial reports and has a remarkably keen eye for the telling detail. Thousands of others work just as hard yet fail to beat the market averages.

It is important to stress, however, that a market being in equilibrium implies only that no additional opportunities are available *to individuals*. It does not imply that the resulting allocation is necessarily best from the point of view of society as a whole.

SMART FOR ONE, DUMB FOR ALL

Adam Smith's profound insight was that the individual pursuit of self-interest often promotes the broader interests of society. But unlike some of his modern disciples, Smith was under no illusion that this is *always* the case. Note, for example, Smith's elaboration on his description of the entrepreneur led by the invisible hand "to promote an end which was no part of his intention":

> Nor is it *always* the worse for society that it was no part of it. By pursuing his own interest he *frequently* promotes that of society more effectively than when he really intends to promote it. (Emphasis added.)

Smith was well aware that the individual pursuit of self-interest often does not coincide with society's interest. In Chapter 3 we cited activities that generate environmental pollution as an example of conflicting economic interests, noting that behavior in those circumstances may be described as smart for one but dumb for all. As the following example suggests, extremely high levels of investment in earnings forecasts also can be smart for one, dumb for all.

Are there "too many" smart people working as corporate earnings forecasters?

Stock analysts use complex mathematical models to forecast corporate earnings. The more analysts invest in the development of these models, the more accurate the models become. Thus, the analyst whose model produces a reliable forecast sooner than others can reap a windfall by buying stocks whose prices are about to rise. Given the speed with which stock prices respond to new information, however, the results of even the second-fastest forecasting model may come too late to be of much use. Individual stock analysts thus face a powerful incentive to invest more and more money in their models, in the hope of generating the fastest forecast. Does this incentive result in the socially optimal level of investment in forecast models?

Beyond some point, increased speed of forecasting is of little benefit to society as a whole, whose interests suffer little when the price of a stock moves to its proper level a few hours more slowly. If *all* stock analysts spent less money on their forecasting models, *someone's* model would still produce the winning forecast, and the resources that might otherwise be devoted to fine-tuning the models could be put to more valued uses. Yet if any one individual spends less, he can be sure the winning forecast will not be his.

The invisible hand went awry in the situation just described because the benefit of an investment to the individual who made it was larger than the benefit of that investment to society as a whole. In later chapters we will discuss a broad class of investments with this property. In general, the efficacy of the invisible hand depends on the extent to which the individual costs and benefits of actions taken in the marketplace coincide with the respective costs and benefits of those actions to society. These exceptions notwithstanding, some of the most powerful forces at work in competitive markets clearly promote society's interests. ●

Example 8.5
THE ECONOMIC NATURALIST

"Hi, Dad. Investment banking wasn't that great after all."

RECAP	EQUILIBRIUM VERSUS SOCIAL OPTIMUM

A market in equilibrium is one in which no additional opportunities for gain remain available to individual buyers or sellers. The No-Cash-on-the-Table Principle describes powerful forces that help push markets toward equilibrium. But even if all markets are in equilibrium, the resulting allocation of resources need not be socially optimal. Equilibrium will not be socially optimal when the costs or benefits to individual participants in the market differ from those experienced by society as a whole.

■ SUMMARY ■

- Accounting profit is the difference between a firm's revenue and its explicit expenses. It differs from economic profit, which is the difference between revenue and the sum of the firm's explicit and implicit costs. Normal profit is the difference between accounting profit and economic profit. It is the opportunity cost of the resources supplied to a business by its owners. **LO1**

- The quest for economic profit is the invisible hand that drives resource allocation in market economies. Markets in which businesses earn an economic profit tend to attract additional resources, whereas markets in which businesses experience an economic loss tend to lose resources. If new firms enter a market with economic profits, that market's supply curve shifts to the right, causing a reduction in the price of the product. Prices will continue to fall until economic profits are eliminated. By contrast, the departure of firms from markets with economic losses causes the supply curve in such markets to shift left, increasing the price of the product. Prices will continue to rise until economic losses are eliminated. In the long run, market forces drive economic profits and losses toward zero. **LO2**

- When market supply and demand curves reflect the underlying costs and benefits to society of the production of a good or service, the quest for economic profit ensures not only that existing supplies are allocated efficiently among individual buyers, but also that resources are allocated across markets in the most efficient way possible. In any allocation other than the one generated by the market, resources could be rearranged to benefit some people without harming others. **LO2**

- Economic rent is the portion of the payment for an input that exceeds the reservation price for that input. If a professional baseball player who is willing to play for as little as $100,000 per year is paid $15 million, he earns an economic rent of $14,900,000 per year. Whereas the invisible hand drives economic profit toward zero over the long run, economic rent can per-

sist indefinitely because replicating the services of players like Derek Jeter is impossible. Talented individuals who are responsible for the superior performance of a business will tend to capture the resulting financial gains as economic rents. **LO3**

- Failure to understand the logic of Adam Smith's invisible hand often compromises the design of regulatory programs. For instance, when regulation prevents firms from lowering prices to capture business from rivals, firms generally find other ways in which to compete. Thus, if airline regulators set passenger fares above cost, air carriers will try to capture additional business by offering extra amenities and more frequent service. Likewise, many antipoverty programs have been compromised by failure to consider how incentives change people's behavior. **LO4**

- A share of stock in a company is a claim to a share of the current and future accounting profits of that company. The price of a share of stock depends not only on its accounting profits, but on the market rate of interest, since the interest rate affects the present value of future costs and benefits. When the annual interest rate is r, the present value (PV) of a payment M to be received (or paid) T years from now is the amount that would have to be deposited in an account today at interest rate r to generate a balance of M after T years: $PV = M/(1 + r)^T$. **LO4**

- According to the efficient markets hypothesis, the market price of a stock incorporates all currently available information that is relevant to that company's earnings. If this hypothesis were untrue, people could earn large sums of money without working hard, having talent, or being lucky. **LO4**

- The No-Cash-on-the-Table Principle implies that if someone owns a valuable resource, the market price of that resource will fully reflect its economic value. The implication of this principle is not that lucrative opportunities never exist, but rather that such opportunities cannot exist when markets are in equilibrium. **LO4**

• The benefit of an investment to an individual sometimes differs from its benefit to society as a whole. Such conflicting incentives may give rise to behavior that is smart for one but dumb for all. Despite such

exceptions, the invisible hand of the market works remarkably well much of the time. One of the market system's most important contributions to social well-being is the pressure it creates to adopt cost-saving innovations. Competition among firms ensures that the resulting cost savings get passed along to consumers in the long run. **LO5**

▪ KEY TERMS ▪

accounting profit (204)
allocative function of price (207)
barrier to entry (214)
economic loss (206)
economic profit (204)

economic rent (215)
efficient markets hypothesis (222)
explicit costs (204)
implicit costs (204)
invisible hand theory (207)

normal profit (205)
present value of a perpetual
  annual payment (218)
rationing function of price (207)
time value of money (221)

▪ REVIEW QUESTIONS ▪

1. Why do most cities in the United States now have more radios but fewer radio repair shops than they did in 1960? **LO2**

2. How can a businessowner who earns $10 million per year from his business credibly claim to earn zero economic profit? **LO1**

3. Why do market forces drive economic profit but not economic rent toward zero? **LO3**

4. Why did airlines that once were regulated by the government generally fail to earn an economic profit, even on routes with relatively high fares? **LO4**

5. Why is a payment of $10,000 to be received one year from now more valuable than a payment of $10,000 to be received two years from now? **LO4**

▪ PROBLEMS ▪

1. True or False: Explain why the following statements are true or false:
   a. The economic maxim "There's no cash on the table" means that there are never any unexploited economic opportunities. **LO5**
   b. Firms in competitive environments make no accounting profit when the market is in long-run equilibrium. **LO1, LO2**
   c. Firms that can introduce cost-saving innovations can make an economic profit in the short run. **LO2**

2. Explain why new software firms that give away their software products at a short-run economic loss are nonetheless able to sell their stock at positive prices. **LO4**

3. John Jones owns and manages a café in Collegetown whose annual revenue is $5,000. Annual expenses are as follows: **LO1, LO2**

Labor	$2,000
Food and drink	500
Electricity	100
Vehicle lease	150
Rent	500
Interest on loan for equipment	1,000

a. Calculate John's annual accounting profit.

b. John could earn $1,000 per year as a recycler of aluminum cans. However, he prefers to run the café. In fact, he would be willing to pay up to $275 per year to run the café rather than to recycle. Is the café making an economic profit? Should John stay in the café business? Explain.

c. Suppose the café's revenues and expenses remain the same, but recyclers' earnings rise to $1,100 per year. Is the café still making an economic profit? Explain.

d. Suppose John had not had to get a $10,000 loan at an annual interest rate of 10 percent to buy equipment, but instead had invested $10,000 of his own money in equipment. How would your answer to parts a and b change?

e. If John can earn $1,000 a year as a recycler, and he likes recycling just as well as running the café, how much additional revenue would the café have to collect each year to earn a normal profit?

4. The city of New Orleans has 200 advertising companies, 199 of which employ designers of normal ability at a salary of $100,000 a year. Paying this salary, each of the 199 firms makes a normal profit on $500,000 in revenue. However, the 200th company employs Janus Jacobs, an unusually talented designer. This company collects $1,000,000 in revenues because of Jacobs's talent. **LO3**

a. How much will Jacobs earn? What proportion of his annual salary will be economic rent?

b. Why won't the advertising company for which Jacobs works be able to earn an economic profit?

5. Explain carefully why, in the absence of a patent, a technical innovation invented and pioneered in one tofu factory will cause the supply curve for the entire tofu industry to shift to the right. What will finally halt the rightward shift? **LO2**

6. The government of the Republic of Self-Reliance has decided to limit imports of machine tools in order to encourage development of locally made machine tools. To do so, the government offers to sell a small number of machine-tool import licenses. To operate a machine-tool import business costs $30,000, excluding the cost of the import license. An importer of machine tools can expect to earn $50,000 per year. If the annual interest rate is 10 percent, for how much will the government be able to auction the import licenses? Will the owner of a license earn an economic profit? **LO4**

7. Unskilled workers in a poor cotton-growing region must choose between working in a factory for $6,000 a year and being a tenant cotton farmer. One farmer can work a 120-acre farm, which rents for $10,000 a year. Such farms yield $20,000 worth of cotton each year. The total nonlabor cost of producing and marketing the cotton is $4,000 a year. A local politician whose motto is "working people come first" has promised that if he is elected, his administration will fund a fertilizer, irrigation, and marketing scheme that will triple cotton yields on tenant farms at no charge to tenant farmers. **LO4**

a. If the market price of cotton would be unaffected by this policy and no new jobs would be created in the cotton-growing industry, how would the project affect the incomes of tenant farmers in the short run? In the long run?

b. Who would reap the benefit of the scheme in the long run? How much would they gain each year?

8. You have a friend who is a potter. He holds a permanent patent on an indestructible teacup whose sale generates $30,000 a year more revenue than production costs. If the annual interest rate is 20 percent, what is the market value of his patent? **LO4**

9. You have an opportunity to buy an apple orchard that produces $25,000 per year in total revenue. To run the orchard, you would have to give up your current job, which pays $10,000 per year. If you would find both jobs equally satisfying, and the annual interest rate is 10 percent, what is the highest price you would be willing to pay for the orchard?   **LO4**

10.*Louisa, a renowned chef, owns one of the 1,000 spaghetti restaurants in Sicily. Each restaurant, including her own, currently serves 100 plates of spaghetti a night at $5 per plate. Louisa knows she can develop a new sauce, at the same cost as the current sauce, that would be so tasty that all 100,000 spaghetti eaters would want to buy her spaghetti at $10 per plate. There are two problems: developing the new sauce would require some experimental cost and the other spaghetti producers could figure out the recipe after one day.   **LO4**

   a. Assuming that Louisa could accommodate as many additional customers as she chose at no extra cost through her take-out window, what is the highest experimental cost Louisa would be willing to incur?

   b. How would your answer change if Louisa could enforce a year-long patent on her new sauce? (Assume that the interest rate is zero.)

■ ANSWERS TO IN-CHAPTER EXERCISES ■

8.1 As shown in the table below, Pudge's accounting profit is now $10,000, the difference between his $20,000 annual revenue and his $10,000-per-year payment for land, equipment, and supplies. His economic profit is that amount minus the opportunity cost of his labor—again, the $11,000 per year he could have earned as a store manager. So Pudge is now earning a negative economic profit, −$1,000 per year. As before, his normal profit is the $11,000-per-year opportunity cost of his labor. Although an accountant would say Pudge is making an annual profit of $10,000, that amount is less than a normal profit for his activity. An economist would therefore say that he is making an economic loss of $1,000 per year. Since Pudge likes the two jobs equally well, he will be better off by $1,000 per year if he leaves farming to become a manager.   **LO1, LO2**

Total revenue ($/year)	Explicit costs ($/year)	Implicit costs ($/year)	Accounting profit (= total revenue − explicit costs) ($/year)	Economic profit (= total revenue − explicit costs− implicit costs) ($/year)	Normal profit (= implicit costs) ($/year)
20,000	10,000	11,000	10,000	−1,000	11,000

8.2 If each lane did not move at about the same pace, any driver in a slower lane could reduce his travel time by simply switching to a faster one. People will exploit these opportunities until each lane moves at about the same pace.   **LO4**

8.3 If the taxi medallion were available for free, it would still command an economic profit of $20,000 per year. So its value is still the answer to the question "How much would you need to put in the bank to generate interest earnings of $20,000 per year?" When the interest rate is 4 percent a year, the answer is $500,000.   **LO4**

8.4 $PV = \$1,728/(1.2)^3 = \$1,000.$ **LO4**

*Problems marked with an asterisk (*) are more difficult.

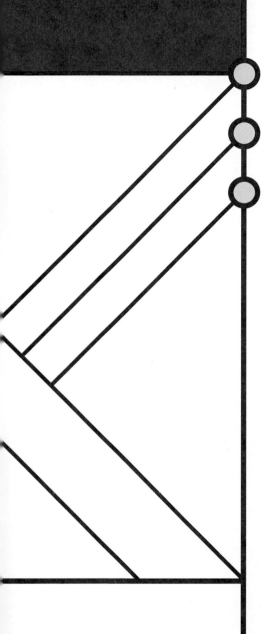

PART

3

MARKET IMPERFECTIONS

We now abandon Adam Smith's frictionless world to investigate what happens when people and firms interact in markets plagued by a variety of imperfections. Not surprisingly, the invisible hand that served society so well in the perfectly competitive world often goes astray in this new environment.

Our focus in Chapter 9 will be on how markets served by only one or a small number of firms differ from those served by perfectly competitive firms. We will see that although monopolies often escape the pressures that constrain the profits of their perfectly competitive counterparts, the two types of firms have many important similarities.

In Chapters 1 to 9 economic decision makers confronted an environment that was essentially fixed. In Chapter 10, however, we will discuss cases in which people expect their actions to alter the behavior of others, as when a firm's decision to advertise or launch a new product induces a rival to follow suit. Interdependencies of this sort are the rule rather than the exception, and we will explore how to take them into account using simple theories of games.

In Chapter 11 we will investigate how the allocation of resources is affected when activities generate costs or benefits that accrue to people not directly involved in those activities. We will see that if parties cannot easily negotiate with one another, the self-serving actions of individuals will not lead to efficient outcomes.

Although the invisible hand theory assumes that buyers and sellers are perfectly informed about all relevant options, this assumption is almost never satisfied in practice. In Chapter 12 we will explore how basic economic principles can help imperfectly informed individuals and firms make the best use of the limited information they possess.

CHAPTER
9

Monopoly, Oligopoly, and Monopolistic Competition

LEARNING OBJECTIVES

After reading this chapter, you should be able to:

1. Define imperfect competition and describe how it differs from perfect competition.

2. Define market power and show how this affects the demand curve facing the firm.

3. Explain how start-up costs affect economics of scale and market power.

4. Understand and use the concepts of marginal cost and marginal revenue to find the output level and price that maximize a monopolist's profit.

5. Show how monopoly alters consumer surplus, producer surplus, and to-tal economic surplus relative to perfect competition.

6. Describe price discrimination and its effects.

7. Discuss public policies that are often applied to natural monopolies.

S ome years ago, schoolchildren around the country became obsessed with the game of Magic. To play, you need a deck of Magic Cards, available only from the creators of the game. But unlike ordinary play-ing cards, which can be bought in most stores for only a dollar or two, a deck of Magic Cards sells for upward of $10. And since Magic Cards cost no more to manufacture than ordinary playing cards, their producer earns an enormous eco-nomic profit.

In a perfectly competitive market, entrepreneurs would see this economic profit as cash on the table. It would entice them to offer Magic Cards at slightly lower prices so that eventually the cards would sell for roughly their cost of pro-duction, just as ordinary playing cards do. But Magic Cards have been on the market for years now, and that hasn't happened. The reason is that the cards are

Why do Magic Cards sell for 10 times as much as ordinary playing cards, even though they cost no more to produce?

imperfectly competitive firm or price setter a firm with at least some latitude to set its own price

pure monopoly the only supplier of a unique product with no close substitutes

monopolistic competition an industry structure in which a large number of firms produce slightly differentiated products that are reasonably close substitutes for one another

copyrighted, which means the government has granted the creators of the game an exclusive license to sell them.

The holder of a copyright is an example of an **imperfectly competitive firm,** or **price setter,** that is, a firm with at least some latitude to set its own price. The competitive firm, by contrast, is a price taker, a firm with no influence over the price of its product.

Our focus in this chapter will be on the ways in which markets served by imperfectly competitive firms differ from those served by perfectly competitive firms. One salient difference is the imperfectly competitive firm's ability, under certain circumstances, to charge more than its cost of production. But if the producer of Magic Cards could charge any price it wished, why does it charge only $10? Why not $100, or even $1,000? We'll see that even though such a company may be the only seller of its product, its pricing freedom is far from absolute. We'll also see how some imperfectly competitive firms manage to earn an economic profit, even in the long run, and even without government protections like copyright. And we'll explore why Adam Smith's invisible hand is less in evidence in a world served by imperfectly competitive firms.

IMPERFECT COMPETITION

The perfectly competitive market is an ideal; the actual markets we encounter in everyday life differ from the ideal in varying degrees. Economics texts usually distinguish among three types of imperfectly competitive market structures. The classifications are somewhat arbitrary, but they are quite useful in analyzing real-world markets.

DIFFERENT FORMS OF IMPERFECT COMPETITION

Farthest from the perfectly competitive ideal is the **pure monopoly,** a market in which a single firm is the lone seller of a unique product. The producer of Magic Cards is a pure monopolist, as are many providers of electric power. If the residents of Miami don't buy their electricity from the Florida Power and Light Company, they simply do without. In between these two extremes are many different types of imperfect competition. We focus on two of them here: monopolistic competition and oligopoly.

Monopolistic Competition

Recall from the chapter on perfectly competitive supply that in a perfectly competitive industry, a large number of firms typically sell products that are essentially perfect substitutes for one another. In contrast, **monopolistic competition** is an industry structure in which a large number of rival firms sell products that are close, but not quite perfect, substitutes. Rival products may be highly similar in many respects, but there are always at least some features that differentiate one product from another in the eyes of some consumers. Monopolistic competition has in common with perfect competition the feature that there are no significant barriers preventing firms from entering or leaving the market.

Local gasoline retailing is an example of a monopolistically competitive industry. The gas sold by different stations may be nearly identical in chemical terms, but a station's particular location is a feature that matters for many consumers. Convenience stores are another example. Although most of the products found on any given store's shelves are also carried by most other stores, the product lists of different stores are not identical. Some offer small stocks of rental DVDs, for example, while others do not. And even more so than in the case of gasoline retailing, location is an important differentiating feature of convenience stores.

Recall that if a perfectly competitive firm were to charge even just slightly more than the prevailing market price for its product, it would not sell any output at all. Things are different for the monopolistically competitive firm. The fact that its offering is not a perfect substitute for those of its rivals means that it can charge a slightly higher price than they do and not lose all its customers.

But that does not mean that monopolistically competitive firms can expect to earn positive economic profits in the long run. On the contrary, because new firms are able to enter freely, a monopolistically competitive industry is essentially the same as a perfectly competitive industry in this respect. If existing monopolistically competitive firms were earning positive economic profits at prevailing prices, new firms would have an incentive to enter the industry. Downward pressure on prices would then result as the larger number of firms competed for a limited pool of potential customers.[1] As long as positive economic profits remained, entry would continue and prices would be driven ever lower. Conversely, if firms in a monopolistically competitive industry were initially suffering economic losses, some firms would begin leaving the industry. As long as economic losses remained, exit and the resulting upward pressure on prices would continue. So in long-run equilibrium, monopolistically competitive firms are in this respect essentially like perfectly competitive firms: All expect to earn zero economic profit.

Although monopolistically competitive firms have some latitude to vary the prices of their product in the short run, pricing is not the most important strategic decision they confront. A far more important issue is how to differentiate their products from those of existing rivals. Should a product be made to resemble a rival's product as closely as possible? Or should the aim be to make it as different as possible? Or should the firm strive for something in between? We will consider these questions in the next chapter, where we will focus on this type of strategic decision making.

Oligopoly

Further along the continuum between perfect competition and pure monopoly lies **oligopoly,** a structure in which the entire market is supplied by a small number of large firms. Cost advantages associated with large size are one of the primary reasons for pure monopoly, as we will discuss presently. Oligopoly is also typically a consequence of cost advantages that prevent small firms from being able to compete effectively.

oligopoly an industry structure in which a small number of large firms produce products that are either close or perfect substitutes

In some cases, oligopolists sell undifferentiated products. In the market for wireless phone service, for example, the offerings of AT&T, Verizon, and Sprint are essentially identical. The cement industry is another example of an oligopoly selling an essentially undifferentiated product. The most important strategic decisions facing firms in such cases are more likely to involve pricing and advertising than specific features of their product. Here, too, we postpone more detailed discussion of such decisions until the next chapter.

In other cases, such as the automobile and tobacco industries, oligopolists are more like monopolistic competitors than pure monopolists, in the sense that differences in their product features have significant effects on consumer demand. Many long-time Ford buyers, for example, would not even consider buying a Chevrolet, and very few smokers ever switch from Camels to Marlboros. As with oligopolists who produce undifferentiated products, pricing and advertising are important strategic decisions for firms in these industries, but so, too, are those related to specific product features.

Because cost advantages associated with large size are usually so important in oligopolies, there is no presumption that entry and exit will push economic profit

---

[1] See Edward Chamberlin, *The Theory of Monopolistic Competition* (Cambridge, MA: Harvard University Press, first edition 1933, 8th edition 1962), and Joan Robinson, *The Economics of Imperfect Competition* (London: Macmillan, first edition 1933, second edition 1969).

to zero. Consider, for example, an oligopoly served by two firms, each of which currently earns an economic profit. Should a new firm enter this market? Possibly, but it also might be that a third firm large enough to achieve the cost advantages of the two incumbents would effectively flood the market, driving price so low that all three firms would suffer economic losses. There is no guarantee, however, that an oligopolist will earn a positive economic profit.

As we'll see in the next section, the essential characteristic that differentiates imperfectly competitive firms from perfectly competitive firms is the same in each of the three cases. So for the duration of this chapter, we'll use the term *monopolist* to refer to any of the three types of imperfectly competitive firms. In the next chapter, we will consider the strategic decisions confronting oligopolists and monopolistically competitive firms in greater detail.

RECAP	MONOPOLISTIC COMPETITION AND OLIGOPOLY

Monopolistic competition is the industry structure in which a large number of small firms offer products that are similar in many respects, yet not perfect substitutes in the eyes of at least some consumers. Monopolistically competitive industries resemble perfectly competitive industries in that entry and exit cause economic profits to tend toward zero in the long run.

Oligopoly is the industry structure in which a small number of large firms supply the entire market. Cost advantages associated with large-scale operations tend to be important. Oligopolists may produce either standardized products or differentiated products.

THE ESSENTIAL DIFFERENCE BETWEEN PERFECTLY AND IMPERFECTLY COMPETITIVE FIRMS

In advanced economics courses, professors generally devote much attention to the analysis of subtle differences in the behavior of different types of imperfectly competitive firms. Far more important for our purposes, however, will be to focus on the single, common feature that differentiates all imperfectly competitive firms from their perfectly competitive counterparts—namely, that *whereas the perfectly competitive firm faces a perfectly elastic demand curve for its product, the imperfectly competitive firm faces a downward-sloping demand curve.*

In the perfectly competitive industry, the supply and demand curves intersect to determine an equilibrium market price. At that price, the perfectly competitive firm can sell as many units as it wishes. It has no incentive to charge more than the market price because it won't sell anything if it does so. Nor does it have any incentive to charge less than the market price because it can sell as many units as it wants to at the market price. The perfectly competitive firm's demand curve is thus a horizontal line at the market price, as we saw in Chapters 6 and 8.

By contrast, if a local gasoline retailer—an imperfect competitor—charges a few pennies more than its rivals for a gallon of gas, some of its customers may desert it. But others will remain, perhaps because they are willing to pay a little extra to continue stopping at their most convenient location. An imperfectly competitive firm thus faces a negatively sloped demand curve. Figure 9.1 summarizes this contrast between the demand curves facing perfectly competitive and imperfectly competitive firms.

If the Sunoco station at State and Meadow Streets raised its gasoline prices by 3 cents per gallon, would all its customers shop elsewhere?

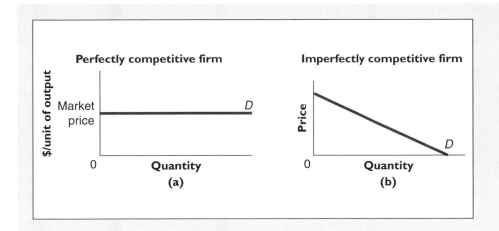

FIGURE 9.1
The Demand Curves Facing Perfectly and Imperfectly Competitive Firms.
(a) The demand curve confronting a perfectly competitive firm is perfectly elastic at the market price.
(b) The demand curve confronting an imperfectly competitive firm is downward-sloping.

FIVE SOURCES OF MARKET POWER

Firms that confront downward-sloping demand curves are said to enjoy **market power,** a term that refers to their ability to set the prices of their products. A common misconception is that a firm with market power can sell any quantity at any price it wishes. It cannot. All it can do is pick a price–quantity combination on its demand curve. If the firm chooses to raise its price, it must settle for reduced sales.

Why do some firms have market power while others do not? Since market power often carries with it the ability to charge a price above the cost of production, such power tends to arise from factors that limit competition. In practice, the following five factors often confer such power: exclusive control over inputs, patents and copyrights, government licenses or franchises, economies of scale, and network economies.

market power a firm's ability to raise the price of a good without losing all its sales

EXCLUSIVE CONTROL OVER IMPORTANT INPUTS

If a single firm controls an input essential to the production of a given product, that firm will have market power. For example, to the extent that some tenants are willing to pay a premium for office space in the country's tallest building, the Sears Tower, the owner of that building has market power.

PATENTS AND COPYRIGHTS

Patents give the inventors or developers of new products the exclusive right to sell those products for a specified period of time. By insulating sellers from competition for an interval, patents enable innovators to charge higher prices to recoup their product's development costs. Pharmaceutical companies, for example, spend millions of dollars on research in the hope of discovering new drug therapies for serious illnesses. The drugs they discover are insulated from competition for an interval—currently 20 years in the United States—by government patents. For the life of the patent, only the patent holder may legally sell the drug. This protection enables the patent holder to set a price above the marginal cost of production to recoup the cost of the research on the drug. In the same way, copyrights protect the authors of movies, software, music, books, and other published works.

GOVERNMENT LICENSES OR FRANCHISES

The Yosemite Concession Services Corporation has an exclusive license from the U.S. government to run the lodging and concession operations at Yosemite National Park. One of the government's goals in granting this monopoly was to preserve the wilderness character of the area to the greatest degree possible. And indeed, the inns

constant returns to scale a production process is said to have constant returns to scale if, when all inputs are changed by a given proportion, output changes by the same proportion

increasing returns to scale a production process is said to have increasing returns to scale if, when all inputs are changed by a given proportion, output changes by more than that proportion; also called ***economies of scale***

natural monopoly a monopoly that results from economies of scale

and cabins offered by the Yosemite Concession Services Company blend nicely with the valley's scenery. No garish neon signs mar the national park as they do in places where rivals compete for the tourist's dollars.

ECONOMIES OF SCALE AND NATURAL MONOPOLIES

When a firm doubles all its factors of production, what happens to its output? If output exactly doubles, the firm's production process is said to exhibit **constant returns to scale.** If output more than doubles, the production process is said to exhibit **increasing returns to scale,** or **economies of scale.** When production is subject to economies of scale, the average cost of production declines as the number of units produced increases. For example, in the generation of electricity, the use of larger generators lowers the unit cost of production. The markets for such products tend to be served by a single seller, or perhaps only a few sellers, because having a large number of sellers would result in significantly higher costs. A monopoly that results from economies of scale is called a **natural monopoly.**

NETWORK ECONOMIES

Although most of us don't care what brand of dental floss others use, many products do become much more valuable to us as more people use them. In the case of home videotape recorders, for instance, the VHS format's defeat of the competing Beta format was explained not by its superior picture quality—indeed, on most important technical dimensions, Beta was regarded by experts as superior to VHS. Rather, VHS won simply because it managed to gain a slight sales edge on the initial version of Beta, which could not record programs longer than one hour. Although Beta later corrected this deficiency, the VHS lead proved insuperable. Once the fraction of consumers owning VHS passed a critical threshold, the reasons for choosing it became compelling—variety and availability of tape rental, access to repair facilities, the capability to exchange tapes with friends, and so on.

A similar network economy helps to account for the dominant position of Microsoft's Windows operating system, which, as noted earlier, is currently installed in more than 90 percent of all personal computers. Because Microsoft's initial sales advantage gave software developers a strong incentive to write for the Windows format, the inventory of available software in the Windows format is now vastly larger than that for any competing operating system. And although general-purpose software such as word processors and spreadsheets continues to be available for multiple operating systems, specialized professional software and games usually appear first—and often only—in the Windows format. This software gap and the desire to achieve compatibility for file sharing gave people a good reason for choosing Windows, even if, as in the case of many Apple Macintosh users, they believed a competing system was otherwise superior.

By far the most important and enduring of these sources of market power are economies of scale and network economies. Lured by economic profit, firms almost always find substitutes for exclusive inputs. Thus, real estate developer Donald Trump has proposed a building taller than the Sears Tower, to be built in Chicago. Likewise, firms can often evade patent laws by making slight changes in design of products. Patent protection is only temporary, in any case. Finally, governments grant very few franchises each year. But economies of scale are both widespread and enduring.

Firmly entrenched network economies can be as persistent a source of natural monopoly as economies of scale. Indeed, network economies are essentially similar to economies of scale. When network economies are of value to the consumer, a product's quality increases as the number of users increases, so we can say that any given quality level can be produced at lower cost as sales volume increases. Thus network economies may be viewed as just another form of economies of scale in production, and that's how we'll treat them here.

RECAP	FIVE SOURCES OF MARKET POWER

A firm's power to raise its price without losing its entire market stems from exclusive control of important inputs, patents and copyrights, government licenses, economies of scale, or network economies. By far the most important and enduring of these are economies of scale and network economies.

ECONOMIES OF SCALE AND THE IMPORTANCE OF START-UP COSTS

As we saw in the previous chapter, variable costs are those that vary with the level of output produced, while fixed costs are independent of output. Strictly speaking, there are no fixed costs in the long run because all inputs can be varied. But as a practical matter, start-up costs often loom large for the duration of a product's useful life. Most of the costs involved in the production of computer software, for example, are start-up costs of this sort, one-time costs incurred in writing and testing the software. Once those tasks are done, additional copies of the software can be produced at a very low marginal cost. A good such as software, whose production entails large fixed start-up costs and low variable costs, will be subject to significant economies of scale. Because by definition fixed costs don't increase as output increases, the average total cost of production for such goods will decline sharply as output increases.

To illustrate, consider a production process for which total cost is given by the equation $TC = F + M*Q$, where F is fixed cost, M is marginal cost (assumed constant in this illustration), and Q is the level of output produced. For the production process with this simple total cost function, variable cost is simply $M*Q$, the product of marginal cost and quantity. Average total cost, TC/Q, is equal to $F/Q + M$. As Q increases, average cost declines steadily because the fixed costs are spread out over more and more units of output.

Figure 9.2 shows the total production cost [part (a)] and average total cost [part (b)] for a firm with the total cost curve $TC = F + M*Q$ and the corresponding average total cost curve $ATC = F/Q + M$. The average total cost curve [part (b)] shows the decline in per-unit cost as output grows. Though average total cost is always higher than marginal cost for this firm, the difference between the two diminishes as

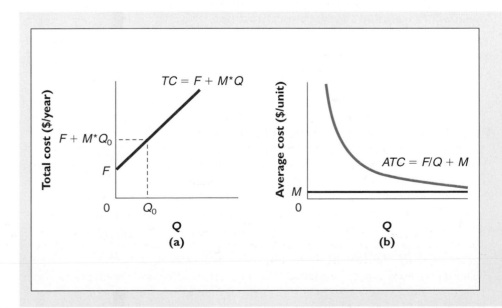

FIGURE 9.2
Total and Average Total Costs for a Production Process with Economies of Scale.
For a firm whose total cost curve of producing Q units of output per year is $TC = F + M*Q$, total cost (a) rises at a constant rate as output grows, while average total cost (b) declines. Average total cost is always higher than marginal cost for this firm, but the difference becomes less significant at high output levels.

output grows. At extremely high levels of output, average total cost becomes very close to marginal cost *(M)*. Because the firm is spreading out its fixed cost over an extremely large volume of output, fixed cost per unit becomes almost insignificant.

As the following examples illustrate, the importance of economies of scale depends on how large fixed cost is in relation to marginal cost.

Two video game producers, Nintendo and Playstation, each have fixed costs of $200,000 and marginal costs of $0.80 per game. If Nintendo produces 1 million units per year and Playstation produces 1.2 million, how much lower will Playstation's average total production cost be?

Table 9.1 summarizes the relevant cost categories for the two firms. Note in the bottom row that Playstation enjoys only a 3-cent average cost advantage over Nintendo. Even though Nintendo produces 20 percent fewer copies of its video game than Playstation, it does not suffer a significant cost disadvantage because fixed cost is a relatively small part of total production cost.

TABLE 9.1
Costs for Two Computer Game Producers (1)

	Nintendo	Playstation
Annual production	1,000,000	1,200,000
Fixed cost	$200,000	$200,000
Variable cost	$800,000	$960,000
Total cost	$1,000,000	$1,160,000
Average total cost per game	$1.00	$0.97

In the next example, note how the picture changes when fixed cost looms large relative to marginal cost.

Two video game producers, Nintendo and Playstation, each have fixed costs of $10,000,000 and marginal costs of $0.20 per video game. If Nintendo produces 1 million units per year and Playstation produces 1.2 million, how much lower will Playstation's average total cost be?

The relevant cost categories for the two firms are now summarized in Table 9.2. The bottom row shows that Playstation enjoys a $1.67 average total cost advantage over Nintendo, substantially larger than in the previous example.

TABLE 9.2
Costs for Two Computer Game Producers (2)

	Nintendo	Playstation
Annual production	1,000,000	1,200,000
Fixed cost	$10,000,000	$10,000,000
Variable cost	$200,000	$240,000
Total cost	$10,200,000	$10,240,000
Average total cost per game	$10.20	$8.53

TABLE 9.3
Costs for Two Computer Game Producers (3)

	Nintendo	Playstation
Annual production	500,000	1,700,000
Fixed cost	$10,000,000	$10,000,000
Variable cost	$100,000	$340,000
Total cost	$10,100,000	$10,340,000
Average total cost per game	$20.20	$6.08

If the video games the two firms produce are essentially similar, the fact that Playstation can charge significantly lower prices and still cover its costs should enable it to attract customers away from Nintendo. As more and more of the market goes to Playstation, its cost advantage will become self-reinforcing. Table 9.3 shows how a shift of 500,000 units from Nintendo to Playstation would cause Nintendo's average total cost to rise to $20.20 per unit, while Playstation's average total cost would fall to $6.08 per unit. The fact that a firm cannot long survive at such a severe disadvantage explains why the video game market is served now by only a small number of firms. ◆

EXERCISE 9.1

How big will Playstation's unit cost advantage be if it sells 2,000,000 units per year, while Nintendo sells only 200,000?

An important worldwide economic trend during recent decades is that an increasing share of the value embodied in the goods and services we buy stems from fixed investment in research and development. For example, in 1984 some 80 percent of the cost of a computer was in its hardware (which has relatively high marginal cost); the remaining 20 percent was in its software. But by 1990 those proportions were reversed. Fixed cost now accounts for about 85 percent of total costs in the computer software industry, whose products are included in a growing share of ordinary manufactured goods.

Why does Intel sell the overwhelming majority of all microprocessors used in personal computers?

The fixed investment required to produce a new leading-edge microprocessor such as the Intel Pentium chip currently runs upward of $2 billion. But once the chip has been designed and the manufacturing facility built, the marginal cost of producing each chip is only pennies. This cost pattern explains why Intel currently sells more than 80 percent of all microprocessors. ●

As fixed cost becomes more and more important, the perfectly competitive pattern of many small firms, each producing only a small share of its industry's total output, becomes less common. For this reason, we must develop a clear sense of how the behavior of firms with market power differs from that of the perfectly competitive firm.

Example 9.1

THE ECONOMIC NATURALIST

Why are most personal computers equipped with Intel microprocessors?

RECAP	ECONOMIES OF SCALE AND THE IMPORTANCE OF START-UP COSTS

Research, design, engineering, and other fixed costs account for an increasingly large share of all costs required to bring products successfully to market. For products with large fixed costs, marginal cost is lower, often substantially, than average total cost, and average total cost declines, often sharply, as output grows. This cost pattern explains why many industries are dominated by either a single firm or a small number of firms.

PROFIT MAXIMIZATION FOR THE MONOPOLIST

Cost-Benefit ⭕

Regardless of whether a firm is a price taker or a price setter, economists assume that its basic goal is to maximize its profit. In both cases, the firm expands output as long as the benefit of doing so exceeds the cost. Further, the calculation of marginal cost is also the same for the monopolist as for the perfectly competitive firm.

The profit-maximizing decision for a monopolist differs from that of a perfectly competitive firm when we look at the benefits of expanding output. For both the perfectly competitive firm and the monopolist, the marginal benefit of expanding output is the additional revenue the firm will receive if it sells one additional unit of output. In both cases, this marginal benefit is called the firm's **marginal revenue.** For the perfectly competitive firm, marginal revenue is exactly equal to the market price of the product. If that price is $6, for example, then the marginal benefit of selling an extra unit is exactly $6.

marginal revenue the change in a firm's total revenue that results from a one-unit change in output

MARGINAL REVENUE FOR THE MONOPOLIST

The situation is different for a monopolist. *To a monopolist, the marginal benefit of selling an additional unit is strictly less than the market price.* As the following discussion will make clear, the reason is that while the perfectly competitive firm can

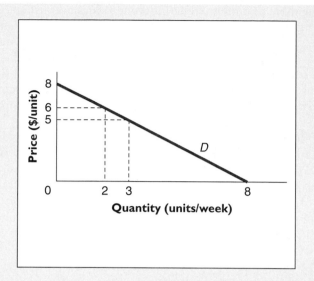

FIGURE 9.3
The Monopolist's Benefit from Selling an Additional Unit.
The monopolist shown receives $12 per week in total revenue by selling 2 units per week at a price of $6 each. This monopolist could earn $15 per week by selling 3 units per week at a price of $5 each. In that case, the benefit from selling the third unit would be $15 − $12 = $3, less than its selling price of $5.

sell as many units as it wishes at the market price, the monopolist can sell an additional unit only if it cuts the price—and it must do so not just for the additional unit but for the units it is currently selling.

Suppose, for example, that a monopolist with the demand curve shown in Figure 9.3 is currently selling 2 units of output at a price of $6 per unit. What would be its marginal revenue from selling an additional unit?

This monopolist's total revenue from the sale of 2 units per week is ($6 per unit)(2 units per week) = $12 per week. Its total revenue from the sale of 3 units per week would be $15 per week. The difference—$3 per week—is the marginal revenue from the sale of the third unit each week. Note that this amount is not only smaller than the original price ($6) but smaller than the new price ($5) as well.

EXERCISE 9.2

Calculate marginal revenue for the monopolist in Figure 9.3 as it expands output from 3 to 4 units per week, and then from 4 to 5 units per week.

For the monopolist whose demand curve is shown in Figure 9.3, a sequence of increases in output—from 2 to 3, from 3 to 4, and from 4 to 5—will yield marginal revenue of $3, $1, and −$1, respectively. We display these results in tabular form in Table 9.4.

TABLE 9.4
Marginal Revenue for a Monopolist ($ per unit)

Quantity	Marginal revenue
2	
	3
3	
	1
4	
	−1
5	

Note in the table that the marginal revenue values are displayed between the two quantity figures to which they correspond. For example, when the firm expanded its output from 2 units per week to 3, its marginal revenue was $3 per unit. Strictly speaking, this marginal revenue corresponds to neither quantity but to the movement between those quantities, hence its placement in the table. Likewise, in moving from 3 to 4 units per week, the firm earned marginal revenue of $1 per unit, so that figure is placed midway between the quantities of 3 and 4, and so on.

To graph marginal revenue as a function of quantity, we would plot the marginal revenue for the movement from 2 to 3 units of output per week ($3) at a quantity value of 2.5, because 2.5 lies midway between 2 and 3. Similarly, we would plot the marginal revenue for the movement from 3 to 4 units per week ($1) at a quantity of 3.5 units per week, and the marginal revenue for the movement from 4 to 5 units per week (−$1) at a quantity of 4.5. The resulting marginal revenue curve, MR, is shown in Figure 9.4.

FIGURE 9.4

Marginal Revenue in Graphical Form.

Because a monopolist must cut price to sell an extra unit, not only for the extra unit sold but also for all existing units, marginal revenue from the sale of the extra unit is less than its selling price.

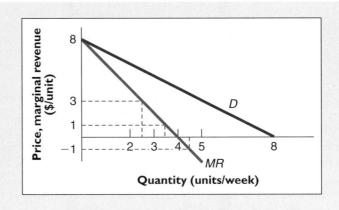

More generally, consider a monopolist with a straight-line demand curve whose vertical intercept is a and whose horizontal intercept is Q_0, as shown in Figure 9.5. This monopolist's marginal revenue curve also will have a vertical intercept of a, and it will be twice as steep as the demand curve. Thus, its horizontal intercept will be not Q_0, but $Q_0/2$, as shown in Figure 9.5.

Marginal revenue curves also can be expressed algebraically. If the formula for the monopolist's demand curve is $P = a - bQ$, then the formula for its marginal

FIGURE 9.5

The Marginal Revenue Curve for a Monopolist with a Straight-Line Demand Curve.

For a monopolist with the demand curve shown, the corresponding marginal revenue curve has the same vertical intercept as the demand curve, and a horizontal intercept only half as large as that of the demand curve.

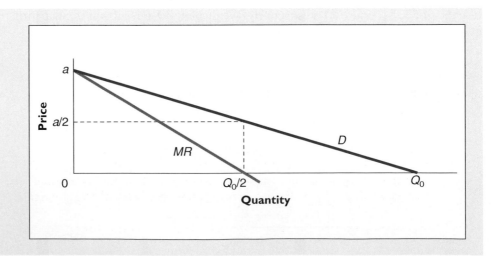

revenue curve will be $MR = a - 2bQ$. If you have had calculus, this relationship is easy to derive,[2] but even without calculus you can verify it by working through a few numerical examples. First, translate the formula for the demand curve into a diagram, and then construct the corresponding marginal revenue curve graphically. Reading from the graph, write the formula for that marginal revenue curve.

THE MONOPOLIST'S PROFIT-MAXIMIZING DECISION RULE

Having derived the monopolist's marginal revenue curve, we are now in a position to describe how the monopolist chooses the output level that maximizes profit. As in the case of the perfectly competitive firm, the Cost-Benefit Principle says that the monopolist should continue to expand output as long as the gain from doing so exceeds the cost. At the current level of output, the benefit from expanding output is the marginal revenue value that corresponds to that output level. The cost of expanding output is the marginal cost at that level of output. Whenever marginal revenue exceeds marginal cost, the firm should expand. Conversely, whenever marginal revenue falls short of marginal cost, the firm should reduce its output. *Profit is maximized at the level of output for which marginal revenue precisely equals marginal cost.*

When the monopolist's profit-maximizing rule is stated in this way, we can see that the perfectly competitive firm's rule is actually a special case of the monopolist's rule. When the perfectly competitive firm expands output by one unit, its marginal revenue exactly equals the product's market price (because the perfectly competitive firm can expand sales by a unit without having to cut the price of existing units). So when the perfectly competitive firm equates price with marginal cost, it is also equating marginal revenue with marginal cost. *Thus, the only significant difference between the two cases concerns the calculation of marginal revenue.*

What is the monopolist's profit-maximizing output level?

Consider a monopolist with the demand and marginal cost curves shown in Figure 9.6. If this firm is currently producing 12 units per week, should it expand or contract production? What is the profit-maximizing level of output?

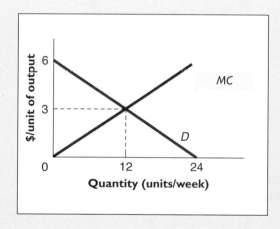

In Figure 9.7, we begin by constructing the marginal revenue curve that corresponds to the monopolist's demand curve. It has the same vertical intercept as the demand curve, and its horizontal intercept is half as large. Note that the monopolist's marginal revenue at 12 units per week is zero, which is clearly less than its marginal

Cost-Benefit

FIGURE 9.6
The Demand and Marginal Cost Curves for a Monopolist.
At the current output level of 12 units per week, price equals marginal cost. Since the monopolist's price is always greater than marginal revenue, marginal revenue must be less than marginal cost, which means this monopolist should produce less.

---

[2]For those who have had an introductory course in calculus, marginal revenue can be expressed as the derivative of total revenue with respect to output. If $P = a - bQ$, then total revenue will be given by $TR = PQ = aQ - bQ^2$, which means that $MR = dTR/dQ = a - 2bQ$.

FIGURE 9.7
The Monopolist's Profit-Maximizing Output Level.
This monopolist maximizes profit by selling 8 units per week, the output level at which marginal revenue equals marginal cost. The profit-maximizing price is $4 per unit, the price that corresponds to the profit-maximizing quantity on the demand curve.

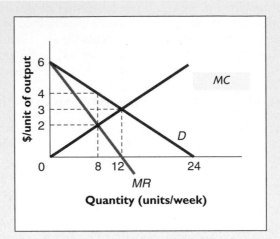

cost of $3 per unit. This monopolist will therefore earn a higher profit by contracting production until marginal revenue equals marginal cost, which occurs at an output level of 8 units per week. At this profit-maximizing output level, the firm will charge $4 per unit, the price that corresponds to 8 units per week on the demand curve. ◆

EXERCISE 9.3

For the monopolist with the demand and marginal cost curves shown, find the profit-maximizing price and level of output.

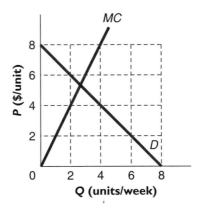

BEING A MONOPOLIST DOESN'T GUARANTEE AN ECONOMIC PROFIT

The fact that the profit-maximizing price for a monopolist will always be greater than marginal cost provides no assurance that the monopolist will earn an economic profit. Consider, for example, the long-distance telephone service provider whose demand, marginal revenue, marginal cost, and average total cost curves are shown in Figure 9.8(a). This monopolist maximizes its daily profit by selling 20 million minutes per day of calls at a price of $0.10 per minute. At that quantity, $MR = MC$, yet price is $0.02 per minute less than the company's average total cost of $0.12 per minute. As a result, the company sustains an economic loss of $0.02 per minute on all calls provided, or a total loss of ($0.02 per minute)(20,000,000 minutes per day) = $400,000 per day.

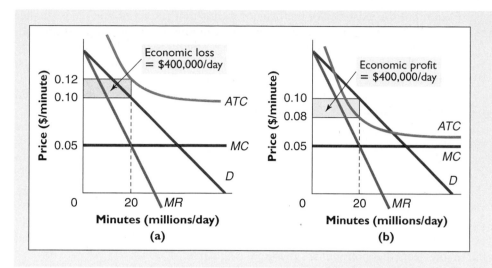

The monopolist in Figure 9.8(a) suffered a loss because its profit-maximizing price was lower than its *ATC*. If the monopolist's profit-maximizing price exceeds its average total cost, however, the company will, of course, earn an economic profit. Consider, for example, the long-distance provider shown in Figure 9.8(b). This firm has the same demand, marginal revenue, and marginal cost curves as the firm shown in Figure 9.8(a). But because the firm in part (b) has lower fixed costs, its *ATC* curve is lower at every level of output than the *ATC* curve in (a). At the profit-maximizing price of $0.10 per minute, the firm in Figure 9.8(b) earns an economic profit of $0.02 per minute, for a total economic profit of $400,000 per day.

RECAP	PROFIT MAXIMIZATION FOR THE MONOPOLIST

Both the perfectly competitive firm and the monopolist maximize profit by choosing the output level at which marginal revenue equals marginal cost. But whereas marginal revenue equals the market price for the perfectly competitive firm, it is always less than the market price for the monopolist. A monopolist will earn an economic profit only if price exceeds average total cost at the profit-maximizing level of output.

WHY THE INVISIBLE HAND BREAKS DOWN UNDER MONOPOLY

In our discussion of equilibrium in perfectly competitive markets in Chapters 7 and 8, we saw conditions under which the self-serving pursuits of consumers and firms were consistent with the broader interests of society as a whole. Let's explore whether the same conclusion holds true for the case of imperfectly competitive firms.

Consider the monopolist in Figures 9.6 and 9.7. Is this firm's profit-maximizing output level efficient from society's point of view? For any given level of output, the corresponding price on the demand curve indicates the amount buyers would be willing to pay for an additional unit of output. When the monopolist is producing 8 units per week, the marginal benefit to society of an additional unit of output is thus $4 (see Figure 9.7). And since the marginal cost of an additional unit at that output level is only $2 (again, see Figure 9.7), society would gain a net benefit of $2 per unit if the monopolist were to expand production by one unit above the profit-maximizing level. Because this economic surplus is not realized, the profit-maximizing monopolist is socially inefficient.

Recall that the existence of inefficiency means that the economic pie is smaller than it might be. If that is so, why doesn't the monopolist simply expand production? The answer is that the monopolist would gladly do so, if only there were some way to maintain the price of existing units and cut the price of only the extra units. As a practical matter, however, that is not always possible.

Now, let's look at this situation from a different angle. For the market served by this monopolist, what *is* the socially efficient level of output?

At any output level, the cost to society of an additional unit of output is the same as the cost to the monopolist, namely, the amount shown on the monopolist's marginal cost curve. The marginal benefit *to society* (not to the monopolist) of an extra unit of output is simply the amount people are willing to pay for it, which is the amount shown on the monopolist's demand curve. To achieve social efficiency, the monopolist should expand production until the marginal benefit to society equals the marginal cost, which in this case occurs at a level of 12 units per week. Social efficiency is thus achieved at the output level at which the market demand curve intersects the monopolist's marginal cost curve.

The fact that marginal revenue is less than price for the monopolist results in a deadweight loss. For the monopolist just discussed, the size of this deadweight loss is equal to the area of the pale blue triangle in Figure 9.9, which is (½)($2 per unit)(4 units per week) = $4 per week. That is the amount by which total economic surplus is reduced because the monopolist produces too little.

FIGURE 9.9

The Deadweight Loss from Monopoly.

A loss in economic surplus results because the profit-maximizing level of output (8 units per week) is less than the socially optimal level of output (12 units per week). This deadweight loss is the area of the pale blue triangle, $4 per week.

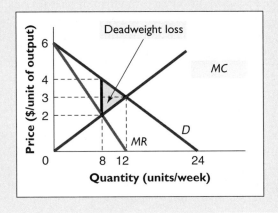

For a monopolist, profit maximization occurs when marginal cost equals marginal revenue. Since the monopolist's marginal revenue is always less than price, the monopolist's profit-maximizing output level is always below the socially efficient level. Under perfect competition, by contrast, profit maximization occurs when marginal cost equals the market price—the same criterion that must be satisfied for social efficiency. This difference explains why the invisible hand of the market is less evident in monopoly markets than in perfectly competitive markets.

If perfect competition is socially efficient and monopoly is not, why isn't monopoly against the law? Congress has, in fact, tried to limit the extent of monopoly through the antitrust laws. But even the most enthusiastic proponents of those laws recognize the limited usefulness of the legislative approach since the alternatives to monopoly often entail problems of their own.

Suppose, for example, that a monopoly results from a patent that prevents all but one firm from manufacturing some highly valued product. Would society be better off without patents? Probably not because eliminating such protection would discourage innovation. Virtually all successful industrial nations grant some form of patent protection, which gives firms a chance to recover the research and development costs without which new products would seldom reach the market.

Or suppose that the market in question is a natural monopoly—one that, because of economies of scale, is most cheaply served by a single firm. Would society do better to require this market to be served by many small firms, each with significantly higher average costs of production? Such a requirement would merely replace one form of inefficiency with another.

In short, we live in an imperfect world. Monopoly is socially inefficient, and that, needless to say, is bad. But the alternatives to monopoly aren't perfect either.

RECAP	WHY THE INVISIBLE HAND BREAKS DOWN UNDER MONOPOLY

The monopolist maximizes profit at the output level for which marginal revenue equals marginal cost. Because its profit-maximizing price exceeds marginal revenue, and hence also marginal cost, the benefit to society of the last unit produced (the market price) must be greater than the cost of the last unit produced (the marginal cost). So the output level for an industry served by a profit-maximizing monopolist is smaller than the socially optimal level of output.

USING DISCOUNTS TO EXPAND THE MARKET

The source of inefficiency in monopoly markets is the fact that the benefit to the monopolist of expanding output is less than the corresponding benefit to society. From the monopolist's point of view, the price reduction the firm must grant existing buyers to expand output is a loss. But from the point of view of those buyers, each dollar of price reduction is a gain—one dollar more in their pockets.

Note the tension in this situation, which is similar to the tension that exists in all other situations in which the economic pie is smaller than it might otherwise be. As the Efficiency Principle reminds us, when the economic pie grows larger, everyone can have a larger slice. To say that monopoly is inefficient means that steps could be taken to make some people better off without harming others. If people have a healthy regard for their own self-interest, why doesn't someone take those steps? Why, for example, doesn't the monopolist from the earlier examples sell 8 units of output at a price of $4, and then once those buyers are out the door, cut the price for more price-sensitive buyers?

Efficiency

PRICE DISCRIMINATION DEFINED

Sometimes the monopolist does precisely that. Charging different buyers different prices for the same good or service is a practice known as **price discrimination.** Examples of price discrimination include senior citizens' and children's discounts on movie tickets, supersaver discounts on air travel, and rebate coupons on retail merchandise.

Attempts at price discrimination seem to work effectively in some markets, but not in others. Buyers are not stupid, after all; if the monopolist periodically offered a 50 percent discount on the $8 list price, those who were paying $8 might anticipate the next price cut and postpone their purchases to take advantage of it. In some markets, however, buyers may not know, or simply may not take the trouble to find out, how the price they pay compares to the prices paid by other buyers. Alternatively, the monopolist may be in a position to prevent some groups from buying at the discount prices made available to others. In such cases, the monopolist can price-discriminate effectively.

price discrimination the practice of charging different buyers different prices for essentially the same good or service

Example 9.2

THE ECONOMIC NATURALIST

Why do students pay lower ticket prices at many movie theaters?

Why do many movie theaters offer discount tickets to students?

Whenever a firm offers a discount, the goal is to target that discount to buyers who would not purchase the product without it. People with low incomes generally have lower reservation prices for movie tickets than people with high incomes. Because students generally have lower disposable incomes than working adults, theater owners can expand their audiences by charging lower prices to students than to adults. Student discounts are one practical way of doing so. Offering student discounts also entails no risk of some people buying the product at a low price and then reselling it to others at a higher price. ●

HOW PRICE DISCRIMINATION AFFECTS OUTPUT

In the following examples, we will see how the ability to price-discriminate affects the monopolist's profit-maximizing level of output. First we will consider a baseline case in which the monopolist must charge the same price to every buyer.

How many manuscripts should Carla edit?

Carla supplements her income as a teaching assistant by editing term papers for undergraduates. There are eight students per week for whom she might edit, each with a reservation price as given in the following table.

Student	Reservation price
A	$40
B	38
C	36
D	34
E	32
F	30
G	28
H	26

Carla is a profit maximizer. If the opportunity cost of her time to edit each paper is $29 and she must charge the same price to each student, how many papers should she edit? How much economic profit will she make? How much accounting profit?

Table 9.5 summarizes Carla's total and marginal revenue at various output levels. To generate the amounts in the total revenue column, we simply multiplied the corresponding reservation price by the number of students whose reservation prices were at least that high. For example, to edit 4 papers per week (for students *A*, *B*, *C*, and *D*), Carla must charge a price no higher than *D*'s reservation price ($34). So her total revenue when she edits 4 papers per week is (4)($34) = $136 per week. Carla should keep expanding the number of students she serves as long as her marginal revenue exceeds the opportunity cost of her time. Marginal revenue, or the difference in total revenue that results from adding another student, is shown in the last column of Table 9.5.

Note that if Carla were editing 2 papers per week, her marginal revenue from editing a third paper would be $32. Since that amount exceeds her $29 opportunity cost, she should take on the third paper. But since the marginal revenue of taking on a fourth paper would be only $28, Carla should stop at 3 papers per week. The total opportunity cost of the time required to edit the 3 papers is (3)($29) = $87, so

TABLE 9.5
Total and Marginal Revenue from Editing

Student	Reservation price ($ per paper)	Total revenue ($ per week)	Marginal revenue ($ per paper)
A	40	40	40
B	38	76	36
C	36	108	32
D	34	136	28
E	32	160	24
F	30	180	20
G	28	196	16
H	26	208	12

Carla's economic profit is $108 − $87 = $21 per week. Since Carla incurs no explicit costs, her accounting profit will be $108 per week. ◆

What is the socially efficient number of papers for Carla to edit?

Again, suppose that Carla's opportunity cost of editing is $29 per paper and that she could edit as many as 8 papers per week for students whose reservation prices are again as listed in the following table.

Student	Reservation price
A	$40
B	38
C	36
D	34
E	32
F	30
G	28
H	26

What is the socially efficient number of papers for Carla to edit? If she must charge the same price to each student, what will her economic and accounting profits be if she edits the socially efficient number of papers?

Students *A* to *F* are willing to pay more than Carla's opportunity cost, so serving these students is socially efficient. But students *G* and *H* are unwilling to pay at least $29 for Carla's services. The socially efficient outcome, therefore, is for Carla to edit 6 papers per week. To attract that number, she must charge a price no higher than $30 per paper. Her total revenue will be (6)($30) = $180 per week, slightly more than her total opportunity cost of (6)($29) = $174 per week. Her economic profit will thus be only $6 per week. Again, because Carla incurs no explicit costs, her accounting profit will be the same as her total revenue, $180 per week. ◆

If Carla can price-discriminate, how many papers should she edit?

Suppose Carla is a shrewd judge of human nature. After a moment's conversation with a student, she can discern that student's reservation price. The reservation prices of her potential customers are again as given in the following table. If Carla confronts the same market as before, but can charge students their respective reservation prices, how many papers should she edit, and how much economic and accounting profit will she make?

Student	Reservation price
A	$40
B	38
C	36
D	34
E	32
F	30
G	28
H	26

Carla will edit papers for students A to F and charge each exactly his or her reservation price. Because students G and H have reservation prices below $29, Carla will not edit their papers. Carla's total revenue will be $40 + $38 + $36 + $34 + $32 + $30 = $210 per week, which is also her accounting profit. Her total opportunity cost of editing 6 papers is (6)($29) = $174 per week, so her economic profit will be $210 − $174 = $36 per week, $30 per week more than when she edited six papers but was constrained to charge each customer the same price. ◆

perfectly discriminating monopolist a firm that charges each buyer exactly his or her reservation price

A monopolist who can charge each buyer exactly his or her reservation price is called a **perfectly discriminating monopolist.** Notice that when Carla was discriminating among customers in this way, her profit-maximizing level of output was exactly the same as the socially efficient level of output: 6 papers per week. With a perfectly discriminating monopoly, there is no loss of efficiency. All buyers who are willing to pay a price high enough to cover marginal cost will be served.

Note that although total economic surplus is maximized by a perfectly discriminating monopolist, consumers would have little reason to celebrate if they found themselves dealing with such a firm. After all, consumer surplus is exactly zero for the perfectly discriminating monopolist. In this instance, total economic surplus and producer surplus are one and the same.

In practice, of course, perfect price discrimination can never occur because no seller knows each and every buyer's precise reservation price. But even if some sellers did know, practical difficulties would stand in the way of their charging a separate price to each buyer. For example, in many markets the seller could not prevent buyers who bought at low prices from reselling to other buyers at higher prices, capturing some of the seller's business in the process. Despite these difficulties, price discrimination is widespread. But it is generally *imperfect price discrimination*, that is, price discrimination in which at least some buyers are charged less than their reservation prices.

THE HURDLE METHOD OF PRICE DISCRIMINATION

The profit-maximizing seller's goal is to charge each buyer the highest price that buyer is willing to pay. Two primary obstacles prevent sellers from achieving this goal. First, sellers don't know exactly how much each buyer is willing to pay. And second, they need some means of excluding those who are willing to pay a high price from buying at a low price. These are formidable problems, which no seller can hope to solve completely.

One common method by which sellers achieve a crude solution to both problems is to require buyers to overcome some obstacle to be eligible for a discount price. This method is called the **hurdle method of price discrimination.** For example, the seller might sell a product at a standard list price and offer a rebate to any buyer who takes the trouble to mail in a rebate coupon.

The hurdle method solves both of the seller's problems, provided that buyers with low reservation prices are more willing than others to jump the hurdle. Because a decision to jump the hurdle must satisfy the Cost-Benefit Principle, such a link seems to exist. As noted earlier, buyers with low incomes are more likely than others to have low reservation prices (at least in the case of normal goods). Because of the low opportunity cost of their time, they are more likely than others to take the trouble to send in rebate coupons. Rebate coupons thus target a discount toward those buyers whose reservation prices are low and who therefore might not buy the product otherwise.

A **perfect hurdle** is one that separates buyers precisely according to their reservation prices, and in the process imposes no cost on those who jump the hurdle. With a perfect hurdle, the highest reservation price among buyers who jump the hurdle will be lower than the lowest reservation price among buyers who choose not to jump the hurdle. In practice, perfect hurdles do not exist. Some buyers will always jump the hurdle, even though their reservation prices are high. And hurdles will always exclude at least some buyers with low reservation prices. Even so, many commonly used hurdles do a remarkably good job of targeting discounts to buyers with low reservation prices. In the examples that follow, we will assume for convenience that the seller is using a perfect hurdle.

hurdle method of price discrimination the practice by which a seller offers a discount to all buyers who overcome some obstacle

perfect hurdle a threshold that completely segregates buyers whose reservation prices lie above it from others whose reservation prices lie below it, imposing no cost on those who jump the hurdle

How much should Carla charge for editing if she uses a perfect hurdle?

Suppose Carla again has the opportunity to edit as many as 8 papers per week for the students whose reservation prices are as given in the following table. This time she can offer a rebate coupon that gives a discount to any student who takes the trouble to mail it back to her. Suppose further that students whose reservation prices are at least $36 never mail in the rebate coupons, while those whose reservation prices are below $36 always do so.

Student	Reservation price
A	$40
B	38
C	36
D	34
E	32
F	30
G	28
H	26

If Carla's opportunity cost of editing each paper is again $29, what should her list price be, and what amount should she offer as a rebate? Will her economic profit be larger or smaller than when she lacked the discount option?

The rebate coupon allows Carla to divide her original market into two submarkets in which she can charge two different prices. The first submarket consists of students *A*, *B*, and *C*, whose reservation prices are at least $36 and who therefore will not bother to mail in a rebate coupon. The second submarket consists of students *D* to *H*, whose lower reservation prices indicate a willingness to use rebate coupons.

In each submarket, Carla must charge the same price to every buyer, just like an ordinary monopolist. She should therefore keep expanding output in each submarket as long as marginal revenue in that market exceeds her marginal cost. The relevant data for the two submarkets are displayed in Table 9.6.

TABLE 9.6
Price Discrimination with a Perfect Hurdle

Student	Reservation price ($ per paper)	Total revenue ($ per week)	Marginal revenue ($ per paper)
List Price Submarket			
			40
A	40	40	
			36
B	38	76	
			32
C	36	108	
Discount Price Submarket			
			34
D	34	34	
			30
E	32	64	
			26
F	30	90	
			22
G	28	112	
			18
H	26	130	

On the basis of the entries in the marginal revenue column for the list price submarket, we see that Carla should serve all three students *(A, B,* and *C)* since marginal revenue for each exceeds $29. Her profit-maximizing price in the list price submarket is $36, the highest price she can charge in that market and still sell her services to students *A*, *B*, and *C*. For the discount price submarket, marginal revenue exceeds $29 only for the first two students *(D* and *E)*. So the profit-maximizing price in this submarket is $32, the highest price Carla can charge and still sell her services to *D* and *E*. (A discount price of $32 means that students who mail in the coupon will receive a rebate of $4 on the $36 list price.)

Note that the rebate offer enables Carla to serve a total of five students per week, compared to only three without the offer. Carla's combined total revenue for the two markets is (3)($36) + 2($32) = $172 per week. Since her opportunity cost is $29 per paper, or a total of (5)($29) = $145 per week, her economic profit is $172 per week − $145 per week = $27 per week, $6 more than when she edited three papers and did not offer the rebate. ◆

EXERCISE 9.4

In the previous example, how much should Carla charge in each submarket if she knows that only those students whose reservation prices are below $34 will use rebate coupons?

IS PRICE DISCRIMINATION A BAD THING?

We are so conditioned to think of discrimination as bad that we may be tempted to conclude that price discrimination must run counter to the public interest. In the example above, however, both consumer and producer surplus were actually enhanced by the monopolist's use of the hurdle method of price discrimination. To show this, let's compare consumer and producer surplus when Carla employs the hurdle method to the corresponding values when she charges the same price to all buyers.

When Carla had to charge the same price to every customer, she edited only the papers of students A, B, and C, each of whom paid a price of $36. We can tell at a glance that the total surplus must be larger under the hurdle method because not only are students A, B, and C served at the same price ($36), but also students D and E are now served at a price of $32.

To confirm this intuition, we can calculate the exact amount of the surplus. For any student who hires Carla to edit her paper, consumer surplus is the difference between her reservation price and the price actually paid. In both the single price and discount price examples, student A's consumer surplus is thus $40 − $36 = $4; student B's consumer surplus is $38 − $36 = $2; and student C's consumer surplus is $36 − $36 = 0. Total consumer surplus in the list price submarket is thus $4 + $2 = $6 per week, which is the same as total consumer surplus in the original situation. But now the discount price submarket generates additional consumer surplus. Specifically, student D receives $2 per week of consumer surplus since this student's reservation price of $34 is $2 more than the discount price of $32. So total consumer surplus is now $6 + $2 = $8 per week, or $2 per week more than before.

Carla's producer surplus also increases under the hurdle method. For each paper she edits, her producer surplus is the price she charges minus her reservation price ($29). In the single-price case, Carla's surplus was (3)($36 − $29) = $21 per week. When she offers a rebate coupon, she earns the same producer surplus as before from students A, B, and C and additional (2)($32 − $29) = $6 per week from students D and E. Total producer surplus with the discount is thus $21 + $6 = $27 per week. Adding that amount to the total consumer surplus of $8 per week, we get a total economic surplus of $35 per week with the rebate coupons, $8 per week more than without the rebate.

Note, however, that even with the rebate, the final outcome is not socially efficient because Carla does not serve student F, even though this student's reservation price of $30 exceeds her opportunity cost of $29. But though the hurdle method is not perfectly efficient, it is still more efficient than charging a single price to all buyers.

EXAMPLES OF PRICE DISCRIMINATION

Once you grasp the principle behind the hurdle method of price discrimination, you will begin to see examples of it all around you. Next time you visit a grocery, hardware, or appliance store, for instance, notice how many different product promotions include cash rebates. Temporary sales are another illustration of the hurdle method. Most of the time, stores sell most of their merchandise at the "regular" price but periodically offer special sales at a significant discount. The hurdle in this instance is taking the trouble to find out when and where the sales occur and then going to the store during that period. This technique works because buyers who care most about price (mainly, those with low reservation prices) are more likely to monitor advertisements carefully and buy only during sale periods.

To give another example, book publishers typically launch a new book in hardcover at a price from $20 to $30, and a year later they bring out a paperback edition priced between $5 and $15. In this instance, the hurdle involves having to wait the extra year and accepting a slight reduction in the quality of the finished product.

People who are strongly concerned about price end up waiting for the paperback edition, while those with high reservation prices usually spring for the hardback.

Or take the example of automobile producers, who typically offer several different models with different trim and accessories. Although GM's actual cost of producing a Cadillac may be only $2,000 more than its cost of producing a Chevrolet, the Cadillac's selling price may be $10,000 to $15,000 higher than the Chevrolet's. Buyers with low reservation prices purchase the Chevrolet, while those with high reservation prices are more likely to choose the Cadillac.

Commercial air carriers have perfected the hurdle method to an extent matched by almost no other seller. Their supersaver fares are often less than half their regular coach fares. To be eligible for these discounts, travelers must purchase their tickets 7 to 21 days in advance and their journey must include a Saturday night stayover. Vacation travelers can more easily satisfy these restrictions than business travelers, whose schedules often change at the last moment and whose trips seldom involve Saturday stayovers. And—no surprise—the business traveler's reservation price tends to be much higher than the vacation traveler's.

Many sellers employ not just one hurdle but several by offering deeper discounts to buyers who jump successively more difficult hurdles. For example, movie producers release their major films to first-run theaters at premium prices, then several months later to neighborhood theaters at a few dollars less. Still later they make the films available on pay-per-view cable channels, then release them on DVD, and finally permit them to be shown on network television. Each successive hurdle involves waiting a little longer, and in the case of the televised versions, accepting lower quality. These hurdles are remarkably effective in segregating movie-goers according to their reservation prices.

Recall that the efficiency loss from single-price monopoly occurs because to the monopolist, the benefit of expanding output is smaller than the benefit to society as a whole. The hurdle method of price discrimination reduces this loss by giving the monopolist a practical means of cutting prices for price-sensitive buyers only. In general, the more finely the monopolist can partition a market using the hurdle method, the smaller the efficiency loss. Hurdles are not perfect, however, and some degree of efficiency will inevitably be lost.

EN 9

Example 9.3
THE ECONOMIC NATURALIST

Would a profit-maximizing appliance retailer ever deliberately damage its own merchandise?

Why might an appliance retailer instruct its clerks to hammer dents into the sides of its stoves and refrigerators?

The Sears "Scratch 'n' Dent Sale" is another example of how retailers use quality differentials to segregate buyers according to their reservation prices. Many Sears stores hold an annual sale in which they display appliances with minor scratches and blemishes in the parking lot at deep discounts. People who don't care much about price are unlikely to turn out for these events, but those with very low reservation prices often get up early to be first in line. Indeed, these sales have proven so popular that it might even be in a retailer's interest to put dents in some of its sale items deliberately. ●

RECAP	USING DISCOUNTS TO EXPAND THE MARKET

A price-discriminating monopolist is one who charges different prices to different buyers for essentially the same good or service. A common method of price discrimination is the hurdle method, which involves granting a discount to buyers who jump over a hurdle such as mailing in a rebate coupon. An effective hurdle is one that is more easily cleared by buyers with low reservation prices than by buyers with high reservation prices. Such a hurdle enables the monopolist to expand output and thereby reduce the deadweight loss from monopoly pricing.

PUBLIC POLICY TOWARD NATURAL MONOPOLY

Monopoly is problematic not only because of the loss in efficiency associated with restricted output but also because the monopolist earns an economic profit at the buyer's expense. Many people are understandably uncomfortable about having to purchase from the sole provider of any good or service. For this reason, voters in many societies have empowered government to adopt policies aimed at controlling natural monopolists.

There are several ways to achieve this aim. A government may assume ownership and control of a natural monopoly, or it may merely attempt to regulate the prices it charges. In some cases, government solicits competitive bids from private firms to produce natural monopoly services. In still other cases, governments attempt to dissolve natural monopolies into smaller entities that compete with one another. But many of these policies create economic problems of their own. In each case, the practical challenge is to come up with the solution that yields the greatest surplus of benefits over costs. Natural monopoly may be inefficient and unfair, but, as noted earlier, the alternatives to natural monopoly are far from perfect.

STATE OWNERSHIP AND MANAGEMENT

Natural monopoly is inefficient because the monopolist's profit-maximizing price is greater than its marginal cost. But even if the natural monopolist *wanted* to set price equal to marginal cost, it could not do so and hope to remain in business. After all, the defining feature of a natural monopoly is economies of scale in production, which means that marginal cost will always be less than average total cost. Setting price equal to marginal cost would fail to cover average total cost, which implies an economic loss.

Consider the case of a local cable television company. Once an area has been wired for cable television, the marginal cost of adding an additional subscriber is very low. For the sake of efficiency, all subscribers should pay a price equal to that marginal cost. Yet a cable company that priced in this manner would never be able to recover the fixed cost of setting up the network. This same problem applies not just to cable television companies but to all other natural monopolies. Even if such firms wanted to set price equal to marginal cost (which, of course, they do not since they will earn more by setting marginal revenue equal to marginal cost), they cannot do so without suffering an economic loss.

One way to attack the efficiency and fairness problems is for the government to take over the industry, set price equal to marginal cost, and then absorb the resulting losses out of general tax revenues. This approach has been followed with good results in the state-owned electric utility industry in France, whose efficient pricing methods have set the standard for electricity pricing worldwide.

But state ownership and efficient management do not always go hand in hand. Granted, the state-owned natural monopoly is free to charge marginal cost, while the private natural monopoly is not. Yet the Incentive Principle directs our attention to the fact that private natural monopolies often face a much stronger incentive to cut costs than their government-owned counterparts. When the private monopolist figures out a way to cut $1 from the cost of production, its profit goes up by $1. But when the government manager of a state-owned monopoly cuts $1 from the cost of production, the government typically cuts the monopoly's budget by $1. Think back to your last visit to the Department of Motor Vehicles. Did it strike you as an efficiently managed organization?

Whether the efficiency that is gained by being able to set price equal to marginal cost outweighs the inefficiency that results from a weakened incentive to cut costs is an empirical question.

Incentive

STATE REGULATION OF PRIVATE MONOPOLIES

In the United States, the most common method of curbing monopoly profits is for government to regulate the natural monopoly rather than own it. Most states, for example, take this approach with electric utilities, natural gas providers, local telephone companies, and cable television companies. The standard procedure in these cases is called **cost-plus regulation**: Government regulators gather data on the monopolist's explicit costs of production and then permit the monopolist to set prices that cover those costs, plus a markup to assure a normal return on the firm's investment.

While it may sound reasonable, cost-plus regulation has several pitfalls. First, it generates costly administrative proceedings in which regulators and firms quarrel over which of the firm's expenditures can properly be included in the costs it is allowed to recover. This question is difficult to answer even in theory. Consider a firm like AT&T, whose local telephone service is subject to cost-plus regulation but whose other products and services are unregulated. Many AT&T employees, from the president on down, are involved in both regulated and unregulated activities. How should their salaries be allocated between the two? The company has a strong incentive to argue for greater allocation to the regulated activities, which allows it to capture more revenue from captive customers in the local telephone market.

A second problem with cost-plus regulation is that it blunts the firm's incentive to adopt cost-saving innovations, for when it does, regulators require the firm to cut its rates. The firm gets to keep its cost savings in the current period, which is a stronger incentive to cut costs than the one facing a government-owned monopoly. But the incentive to cut costs would be stronger still if the firm could retain its cost savings indefinitely. Furthermore, in cases in which regulators set rates by allowing the monopolist to add a fixed markup to costs incurred, the regulated monopolist may actually have an incentive to *increase* costs rather than reduce them. Outrageous though the thought may be, the monopolist may earn a higher profit by installing gold-plated faucets in the company rest rooms.

Finally, cost-plus regulation does not solve the natural monopolist's basic problem: the inability to set price equal to marginal cost without losing money. Although these are all serious problems, governments seem to be in no hurry to abandon cost-plus regulation.

EXCLUSIVE CONTRACTING FOR NATURAL MONOPOLY

One of the most promising methods for dealing with natural monopoly is for the government to invite private firms to bid for the natural monopolist's market. The government specifies in detail the service it wants—cable television, fire protection, garbage collection—and firms submit bids describing how much they will charge for the service. The low bidder wins the contract.

The incentive to cut costs under such an arrangement is every bit as powerful as that facing ordinary competitive firms. Competition among bidders should also eliminate any concerns about the fairness of monopoly profits. And if the government is willing to provide a cash subsidy to the winning bidder, exclusive contracting even allows the monopolist to set price equal to marginal cost.

Contracting has been employed with good results in municipal fire protection and garbage collection. Communities that employ private companies to provide these services often spend only half as much as adjacent communities served by municipal fire and sanitation departments.

Despite these attractive features, however, exclusive contracting is not without problems, especially when the service to be provided is complex or requires a large fixed investment in capital equipment. In such cases, contract specifications may be so detailed and complicated that they become tantamount to regulating the firm directly. And in cases involving a large fixed investment—electric power generation

cost-plus regulation a method of regulation under which the regulated firm is permitted to charge prices that cover explicit costs of production plus a markup to cover the opportunity cost of resources provided by the firm's owners

and distribution, for example—officials face the question of how to transfer the assets if a new firm wins the contract. The winning firm naturally wants to acquire the assets as cheaply as possible, but the retiring firm is entitled to a fair price for them. What, in such cases, is a fair price?

Fire protection and garbage collection are simple enough that the costs of contracting out these functions are not prohibitive. But in other cases, such costs might easily outweigh any savings made possible by exclusive contracting.

VIGOROUS ENFORCEMENT OF ANTITRUST LAWS

The nineteenth century witnessed the accumulation of massive private fortunes, the likes of which had never been seen in the industrialized world. Public sentiment ran high against the so-called robber barons of the period—the Carnegies, Rockefellers, Mellons, and others. In 1890, Congress passed the Sherman Act, which declared illegal any conspiracy "to monopolize, or attempt to monopolize . . . any part of the trade or commerce among the several States." And in 1914, Congress passed the Clayton Act, whose aim was to prevent corporations from acquiring shares in a competitor if the transaction would "substantially lessen competition or create a monopoly."

Antitrust laws have helped to prevent the formation of cartels, or coalitions of firms that collude to raise prices above competitive levels. But they also have caused some harm. For example, federal antitrust officials spent more than a decade trying to break up the IBM Corporation in the belief that it had achieved an unhealthy dominance in the computer industry. That view was proved comically wrong by IBM's subsequent failure to foresee and profit from the rise of the personal computer. By breaking up large companies and discouraging mergers between companies in the same industry, antitrust laws may help to promote competition, but they also may prevent companies from achieving economies of scale.

A final possibility is simply to ignore the problem of natural monopoly: to let the monopolist choose the quantity to produce and sell it at whatever price the market will bear. The obvious objections to this policy are the two we began with, namely, that a natural monopoly is not only inefficient but also unfair. But just as the hurdle method of price discrimination mitigates efficiency losses, it also lessens the concern about taking unfair advantage of buyers.

Consider first the source of the natural monopolist's economic profit. This firm, recall, is one with economies of scale, which means that its average production cost declines as output increases. Efficiency requires that price be set at marginal cost, but because the natural monopolist's marginal cost is lower than its average cost, it cannot charge all buyers the marginal cost without suffering an economic loss.

The depth and prevalence of discount pricing suggest that whatever economic profit a natural monopolist earns generally will not come out of the discount buyer's pocket. Although discount prices are higher than the monopolist's marginal cost of production, in most cases they are lower than the average cost. Thus, the monopolist's economic profit, if any, must come from buyers who pay list price. And since those buyers have the option, in most cases, of jumping a hurdle and paying a discount price, their contribution, if not completely voluntary, is at least not strongly coerced.

So much for the source of the monopolist's economic profit. What about its disposition? Who gets it? A large chunk—some 35 percent, in many cases—goes to the federal government via the corporate income tax. The remainder is paid out to shareholders, some of whom are wealthy and some of whom are not. These shareholder profits are also taxed by state and even local governments. In the end, two-thirds or more of a monopolist's economic profit may fund services provided by governments of various levels.

Both the source of the monopolist's economic profit (the list-price buyer) and the disposition of that profit (largely, to fund public services) cast doubt on the claim that monopoly profit constitutes a social injustice on any grand scale. Nevertheless, the hurdle method of differential pricing cannot completely eliminate the fairness and efficiency problems that result from monopoly pricing. In the end, then, we are left with a choice among imperfect alternatives. As the Cost-Benefit Principle emphasizes, the best choice is the one for which the balance of benefits over costs is largest. But which choice that is will depend on the circumstances at hand.

Cost-Benefit

RECAP	PUBLIC POLICY TOWARD NATURAL MONOPOLY

The natural monopolist sets price above marginal cost, resulting in too little output from society's point of view (the efficiency problem). The natural monopolist also may earn an economic profit at buyers' expense (the fairness problem). Policies for dealing with the efficiency and fairness problems include state ownership and management, state regulation, exclusive contracting, and vigorous enforcement of antitrust laws. Each of these remedies entails problems of its own.

■ SUMMARY ■

- Our concern in this chapter was the conduct and performance of the imperfectly competitive firm, a firm that has at least some latitude to set its own price. Economists often distinguish among three different types of imperfectly competitive firms: the pure monopolist, the lone seller of a product in a given market; the oligopolist, one of only a few sellers of a given product; and the monopolistic competitor, one of a relatively large number of firms that sell similar though slightly differentiated products. **LO1**

- Although advanced courses in economics devote much attention to differences in behavior among these three types of firms, our focus was on the common feature that differentiates them from perfectly competitive firms. Whereas the perfectly competitive firm faces an infinitely elastic demand curve for its product, the imperfectly competitive firm faces a downward-sloping demand curve. For convenience, we use the term *monopolist* to refer to any of the three types of imperfectly competitive firms. **LO1**

- Monopolists are sometimes said to enjoy market power, a term that refers to their power to set the price of their product. Market power stems from exclusive control over important inputs, from economies of scale, from patents and government licenses or franchises, and from network economies. The most important and enduring of these five sources of market power are economies of scale and network economies. **LO2**

- Research, design, engineering, and other fixed costs account for an increasingly large share of all costs required to bring products successfully to market. For products with large fixed costs, marginal cost is lower, often substantially, than average total cost and average total cost declines, often sharply, as output grows. This cost pattern explains why many industries are dominated by either a single firm or a small number of firms. **LO3**

- Unlike the perfectly competitive firm, for which marginal revenue exactly equals market price, the monopolist realizes a marginal revenue that is always less than its price. This shortfall reflects the fact that to sell more output, the monopolist must cut the price not only to additional buyers but to existing buyers as well. For the monopolist with a straight-line demand curve, the marginal revenue curve has the same vertical intercept and a horizontal intercept that is half as large as the intercept for the demand curve. **LO4**

- Whereas the perfectly competitive firm maximizes profit by producing at the level at which marginal cost equals the market price, the monopolist maximizes profit by equating marginal cost with marginal revenue, which is significantly lower than the market price. The result is an output level that is best for the monopolist but smaller than the level that would be best for society as a whole. At the profit-maximizing level of output, the benefit of an extra unit of output (the market price) is greater than its cost (the marginal cost). At the socially efficient level of output, where the monopolist's marginal cost curve intersects the demand curve, the benefit and cost of an extra unit are the same. **LO5**

- Both the monopolist and its potential customers can do better if the monopolist can grant discounts to price-sensitive buyers. The extreme example is the perfectly discriminating monopolist, who charges each buyer exactly his or her reservation price. Such producers are socially efficient because they sell to every buyer whose reservation price is at least as high as the marginal cost. **LO6**

- The various policies that governments employ to mitigate concerns about fairness and efficiency losses arising from natural monopoly include state ownership and management of natural monopolies, state regulation, private contracting, and vigorous enforcement of antitrust laws. Each of these remedies entails costs as well as benefits. In some cases, a combination of policies will produce a better outcome than simply allowing natural monopolists to do as they please. But in other cases, a hands-off policy may be the best available option. **LO7**

▪ KEY TERMS ▪

constant returns to scale (238)
cost-plus regulation (258)
economies of scale (238)
hurdle method of price
  discrimination (253)
imperfectly competitive
  firm (234)

increasing returns to scale (238)
marginal revenue (242)
market power (237)
monopolistic competition (234)
natural monopoly (238)
oligopoly (235)

perfect hurdle (253)
perfectly discriminating
  monopolist (252)
price discrimination (249)
price setter (234)
pure monopoly (234)

▪ REVIEW QUESTIONS ▪

1. What important characteristic do all three types of imperfectly competitive firms share? **LO1**

2. True or false: A firm with market power can sell whatever quantity it wishes at whatever price it chooses. **LO2**

3. Why do most successful industrial societies offer patents and copyright protection, even though these protections enable sellers to charge higher prices? **LO2**

4. Why is marginal revenue always less than price for a monopolist but equal to price for a perfectly competitive firm? **LO4**

5. True or false: Because a natural monopolist charges a price greater than marginal cost, it necessarily earns a positive economic profit. **LO7**

▪ PROBLEMS ▪

1. Two car manufacturers, Saab and Volvo, have fixed costs of $1 billion and marginal costs of $10,000 per car. If Saab produces 50,000 cars per year and Volvo produces 200,000, calculate the average production cost for each company. On the basis of these costs, which company's market share do you think will grow in relative terms? **LO3**

McGraw-Hill's
HOMEWORK
MANAGER®

2. State whether the following statements are true or false, and explain why. **LO1, LO7**

  a. In a perfectly competitive industry, the industry demand curve is horizontal, whereas for a monopoly it is downward-sloping.

  b. Perfectly competitive firms have no control over the price they charge for their product.

c. For a natural monopoly, average cost declines as the number of units produced increases over the relevant output range.

3. A single-price, profit-maximizing monopolist: **LO4**
   a. Causes excess demand, or shortages, by selling too few units of a good or service.
   b. Chooses the output level at which marginal revenue begins to increase.
   c. Always charges a price above the marginal cost of production.
   d. Also maximizes marginal revenue.
   e. None of the above statements is true.

4. If a monopolist could perfectly price-discriminate: **LO6**
   a. The marginal revenue curve and the demand curve would coincide.
   b. The marginal revenue curve and the marginal cost curve would coincide.
   c. Every consumer would pay a different price.
   d. Marginal revenue would become negative at some output level.
   e. The resulting pattern of exchange would still be socially inefficient.

5. Explain why price discrimination and the existence of slightly different variants of the same product tend to go hand in hand. Give an example from your own experience. **LO2, LO6**

6. What is the socially desirable price for a natural monopoly to charge? Why will a natural monopoly that attempts to charge the socially desirable price invariably suffer an economic loss? **LO7**

7. TotsPoses, Inc., a profit-maximizing business, is the only photography business in town that specializes in portraits of small children. George, who owns and runs TotsPoses, expects to encounter an average of eight customers per day, each with a reservation price shown in the following table. **LO5, LO6**

Customer	Reservation price ($ per photo)
A	50
B	46
C	42
D	38
E	34
F	30
G	26
H	22

   a. If the total cost of each photo portrait is $12, how much should George charge if he must charge a single price to all customers? At this price, how many portraits will George produce each day? What will be his economic profit?
   b. How much consumer surplus is generated each day at this price?
   c. What is the socially efficient number of portraits?
   d. George is very experienced in the business and knows the reservation price of each of his customers. If he is allowed to charge any price he likes to any consumer, how many portraits will he produce each day and what will his economic profit be?
   e. In this case, how much consumer surplus is generated each day?
   f. Suppose George is permitted to charge two prices. He knows that customers with a reservation price above $30 never bother with coupons, whereas

those with a reservation price of $30 or less always use them. At what level should George set the list price of a portrait? At what level should he set the discount price? How many photo portraits will he sell at each price?

g. In this case, what is George's economic profit and how much consumer surplus is generated each day?

8. Serena is a single-price, profit-maximizing monopolist in the sale of her own patented perfume, whose demand and marginal cost curves are as shown. Relative to the consumer surplus that would result at the socially optimal quantity and price, how much consumer surplus is lost from her selling at the monopolist's profit-maximizing quantity and price?   **LO5**

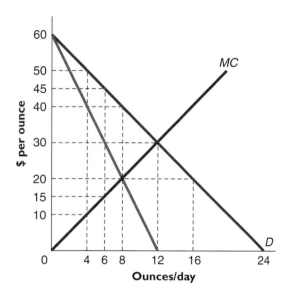

9. In the preceding question, how much total surplus would result if Serena could act as a perfectly price-discriminating monopolist?   **LO6**

10. Beth is a second-grader who sells lemonade on a street corner in your neighborhood. Each cup of lemonade costs Beth 20 cents to produce; she has no fixed costs. The reservation prices for the 10 people who walk by Beth's lemonade stand each day are listed in the following table.

Person	A	B	C	D	E	F	G	H	I	J
Reservation price	$1.00	$0.90	$0.80	$0.70	$0.60	$0.50	$0.40	$0.30	$0.20	$0.10

Beth knows the distribution of reservation prices (that is, she knows that one person is willing to pay $1, another $0.90, and so on), but she does not know any specific individual's reservation price.   **LO4, LO5, LO6**

a. Calculate the marginal revenue of selling an additional cup of lemonade. (Start by figuring out the price Beth would charge if she produced only one cup of lemonade, and calculate the total revenue; then find the price Beth would charge if she sold two cups of lemonade; and so on.)

b. What is Beth's profit-maximizing price?

c. At that price, what are Beth's economic profit and total consumer surplus?

d. What price should Beth charge if she wants to maximize total economic surplus?

e. Now suppose Beth can tell the reservation price of each person. What price would she charge each person if she wanted to maximize profit? Compare her profit to the total surplus calculated in part *d*.

■ ANSWERS TO IN-CHAPTER EXERCISES ■

9.1 The relevant cost figures are as shown in the following table, which shows that the Playstation's unit-cost advantage is now $50.20 − $5.20 = $45.00.   **LO3**

	Nintendo	Playstation
Annual production	200,000	2,000,000
Fixed cost	$10,000,000	$10,000,000
Variable cost	$40,000	$400,000
Total cost	$10,040,000	$10,400,000
Average total cost per game	$50.20	$5.20

9.2 When the monopolist expands from 3 to 4 units per week, total revenue rises from $15 to $16 per week, which means that the marginal revenue from the sale of the fourth unit is only $1 per week. When the monopolist expands from 4 to 5 units per week, total revenue drops from $16 to $15 per week, which means that the marginal revenue from the sale of the fifth unit is actually negative, or −$1 per week.   **LO4**

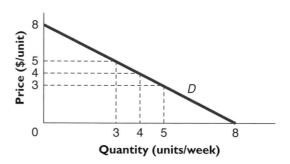

9.3 The profit-maximizing price and quantity are $P^* = \$6$/unit and $Q^* = 2$ units/week.   **LO4**

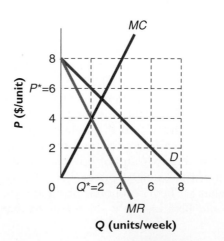

9.4 As the marginal revenue column in the following table shows, Carla should again serve students *A, B,* and *C* in the list price submarket (at a price of $36) and only student *E* in the discount submarket (at a price of $32). **LO6**

Student	Reservation price ($ per paper)	Total revenue ($ per week)	Marginal revenue ($ per paper)
List Price Submarket			
			40
A	40	40	
			36
B	38	76	
			32
C	36	108	
			28
D	34	136	
Discount Price Submarket			
			32
E	32	32	
			28
F	30	60	
			24
G	28	84	
			20
H	26	104	

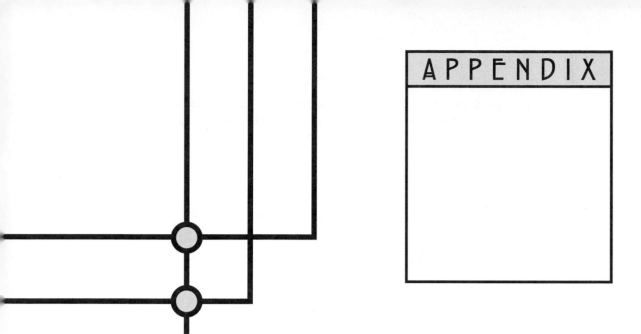

The Algebra of Monopoly Profit Maximization

In the text of this chapter, we developed the profit-maximization analysis for monopoly in a geometric framework. In this brief appendix, we show how this analysis can be done in an algebraic framework. The advantage of the algebraic framework is that it greatly simplifies computing the numerical values of the profit-maximizing prices and quantities.

Find the profit-maximizing price and quantity for a monopolist with the demand curve $P = 15 - 2Q$ and the marginal cost curve $MC = Q$, where P is the product price in dollars per unit and Q is the quantity in units of output per week.

The first step is to find the equation for the marginal revenue curve associated with the monopolist's demand curve. Recall that in the case of a straight-line demand curve, the associated marginal revenue curve has the same vertical intercept as the demand curve and twice the slope of the demand curve. So the equation for this monopolist's marginal revenue curve is $MR = 15 - 4Q$. Letting Q^* denote the profit-maximizing output level, setting $MR = MC$ then yields

$$15 - 4Q^* = Q^*,$$

which solves for $Q^* = 3$. The profit-maximizing price, P^*, is then found by substituting $Q^* = 3$ into the demand equation:

$$P^* = 15 - 2Q^* = 15 - 6 = 9.$$

Thus, the profit-maximizing price and quantity are $9 per unit and 3 units per week, respectively. ◆

EXERCISE 9A.1

Find the profit-maximizing price and level of output for a monopolist with the demand curve $P = 12 - Q$ and the marginal cost curve $MC = 2Q$, where P is the price of the product in dollars per unit and Q is output in units per week.

▪ PROBLEMS ▪

1. Suppose that the University of Michigan Cinema is a local monopoly whose demand curve for adult tickets on Saturday night is $P = 12 - 2Q$, where P is the price of a ticket in dollars and Q is the number of tickets sold in hundreds. The demand for children's tickets on Sunday afternoon is $P = 8 - 3Q$, and for adult tickets on Sunday afternoon, $P = 10 - 4Q$. On both Saturday night and Sunday afternoon, the marginal cost of an additional patron, child or adult, is $2. **LO4**
   a. What is the marginal revenue curve in each of the three submarkets?
   b. What price should the cinema charge in each of the three markets if its goal is to maximize profit?

2. Suppose you are a monopolist in the market for a specific video game. Your demand curve is given by $P = 80 - Q/2$; your marginal cost curve is $MC = Q$. Your fixed costs equal $400. **LO4, LO5**
   a. Graph the demand and marginal cost curves.
   b. Derive and graph the marginal revenue curve.
   c. Calculate and indicate on the graph the equilibrium price and quantity.
   d. What is your profit?
   e. What is the level of consumer surplus?

▪ ANSWER TO IN-APPENDIX EXERCISE ▪

9A.1 For the demand curve $P = 12 - Q$, the corresponding marginal revenue curve is $MR = 12 - 2Q$. Equating MR and MC, we solve the equation $12 - 2Q = 2Q$ for $Q = 3$. Substituting $Q = 3$ into the demand equation, we solve for the profit-maximizing price, $P = 12 - 3 = 9$. **LO4**

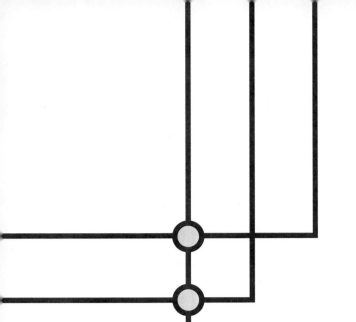

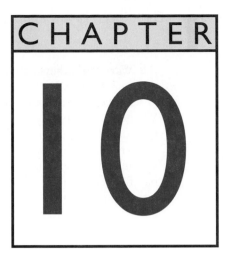

CHAPTER

10

Games and Strategic Behavior

LEARNING OBJECTIVES

After reading this chapter, you should be able to:

1. Describe the basic elements of a game.

2. Define and find an equilibrium for a game.

3. Recognize and show the effects of dominant strategies.

4. Define and explain the Prisoner's Dilemma and how it applies to real-world situations.

5. Show how games in which timing matters differ from games in which it does not.

6. Discuss commitment problems and explain how altering preferences can solve commitment problems.

At a Christmas Eve dinner party in 1997, actor Robert DeNiro pulled singer Tony Bennett aside for a moment. "Hey, Tony—there's a film I want you in," DeNiro said. He was referring to the project that became the 1999 Warner Brothers hit comedy *Analyze This,* in which the troubled head of a crime family, played by DeNiro, seeks the counsel of a psychotherapist, played by Billy Crystal. In the script, both the mob boss and his therapist are big fans of Bennett's music.

Bennett heard nothing further about the project for almost a year. Then his son and financial manager, Danny Bennett, got a phone call from Warner Brothers, in which the studio offered Tony $15,000 to sing "Got the World on a String" in the movie's final scene. As Danny described the conversation, ". . . they made a fatal mistake. They told me they had already shot the film. So I'm like: 'Hey, they shot the whole film around Tony being the end gag and they're offering me $15,000?'"[1]

[1]As quoted by Geraldine Fabrikant, "Talking Money with Tony Bennett," *The New York Times,* May 2, 1999, Money & Business, p. 1.

Warner Brothers wound up paying $200,000 for Bennett's performance.

In business negotiations, as in life, timing can be everything. If executives at Warner Brothers had thought the problem through carefully, they would have negotiated with Bennett *before* shooting the movie. At that point, Bennett would have realized that the script could be rewritten if he asked too high a fee. By waiting, studio executives left themselves with no attractive option other than to pay Bennett's price.

The payoff to many actions depends not only on the actions themselves, but also on when they are taken and how they relate to actions taken by others. In previous chapters, economic decision makers confronted an environment that was essentially fixed. This chapter will focus on cases in which people must consider the effect of their behavior on others. For example, an imperfectly competitive firm will want to weigh the likely responses of rivals when deciding whether to cut prices or to increase its advertising budget. Interdependencies of this sort are the rule rather than the exception in economic and social life. To make sense of the world we live in, then, we must take these interdependencies into account.

Our focus in Chapter 9 was on the pure monopolist. In this chapter, we will explore how a few simple principles from the theory of games can help us better understand the behavior of oligopolists and monopolistic competitors—the two types of imperfectly competitive firms for which strategic interdependencies are most important. Along the way, we also will see how the same principles enable us to answer a variety of interesting questions drawn from everyday social interaction.

USING GAME THEORY TO ANALYZE STRATEGIC DECISIONS

In chess, tennis, or any other game, the payoff to a given move depends on what your opponent does in response. In choosing your move, therefore, you must anticipate your opponent's responses, how you might respond, and what further moves your own response might elicit. Economists and other behavioral scientists have devised the theory of games to analyze situations in which the payoffs to different actors depend on the actions their opponents take.

THE THREE ELEMENTS OF A GAME

basic elements of a game the players, the strategies available to each player, and the payoffs each player receives for each possible combination of strategies

A game has three **basic elements:** the players, the list of possible actions (or strategies) available to each player, and the payoffs the players receive for each possible combination of strategies. We will use a series of examples to illustrate how these elements combine to form the basis of a theory of behavior.

The first example focuses on an important strategic decision confronting two oligopolists who produce an undifferentiated product and must decide how much to spend on advertising.

Should United Airlines spend more money on advertising?

Suppose that United Airlines and American Airlines are the only air carriers that serve the Chicago–St. Louis market. Each currently earns an economic profit of $6,000 per flight on this route. If United increases its advertising spending in this market by $1,000 per flight, and American spends no more on advertising than it does now, United's profit will rise to $8,000 per flight and American's will fall to $2,000. If both spend $1,000 more on advertising, each will earn an economic profit of $5,500 per flight. These payoffs are symmetric, so that if United stands pat while American increases its spending by $1,000, United's economic profit will fall to $2,000 per flight and American's will rise to $8,000. The payoff structure is also common knowledge—that is, each company knows what the relevant payoffs will be for both parties under each of the possible combinations of choices. If each must decide independently whether to increase spending on advertising, what should United do?

Think of this situation as a game. What are its three elements? The players are the two airlines. Each airline must choose one of two strategies: to raise ad spending by $1,000 or leave it the same. The payoffs are the economic profits that correspond to the four possible scenarios resulting from their choices. One way to summarize the relevant information about this game is to display the players, strategies, and payoffs in the form of a simple table called a **payoff matrix** (see Table 10.1).

Confronted with the payoff matrix in Table 10.1, what should United Airlines do? The essence of strategic thinking is to begin by looking at the situation from the other party's point of view. Suppose United assumes that American will raise its spending on advertising (the left column in Table 10.1). In that case, United's best bet would be to follow suit (the top row in Table 10.1). Why is the top row United's best response when American chooses the left column? United's economic profits, given in the upper-left cell of Table 10.1, will be $5,500, compared to only $2,000 if it keeps spending the same (see the lower-left cell).

Alternatively, suppose United assumes that American will keep ad spending the same (that is, that American will choose the right column in Table 10.1). In that case, United would still do better to increase spending because it would earn $8,000 (the upper-right cell), compared to only $6,000 if it keeps spending the same (the lower-right cell). In this particular game, no matter which strategy American chooses, United will earn a higher economic profit by increasing its spending on advertising. And since this game is perfectly symmetric, a similar conclusion holds for American: No matter which strategy United chooses, American will do better by increasing its spending on ads.

When one player has a strategy that yields a higher payoff no matter which choice the other player makes, that player is said to have a **dominant strategy.** Not all games involve dominant strategies, but both players in this game have one, and that is to increase spending on ads. For both players, to leave ad spending the same

payoff matrix a table that describes the payoffs in a game for each possible combination of strategies

dominant strategy one that yields a higher payoff no matter what the other players in a game choose

---

TABLE 10.1
The Payoff Matrix for an Advertising Game

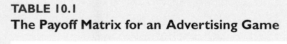

	American's Choices	
	Raise ad spending	Leave ad spending the same
United's Choices — Raise ad spending	$5,500 for United $5,500 for American	$8,000 for United $2,000 for American
United's Choices — Leave ad spending the same	$2,000 for United $8,000 for American	$6,000 for United $6,000 for American

Both airlines do better if both leave ad spending the same than if both raise spending. Yet if one holds spending the same, the other always does better to raise spending.

dominated strategy any other strategy available to a player who has a dominant strategy

is a **dominated strategy**—one that leads to a lower payoff than an alternative choice, regardless of the other player's choice.

Notice, however, that when each player chooses the dominant strategy, the resulting payoffs are smaller than if each had left spending unchanged. When United and American increase their spending on ads, each earns only $5,500 in economic profits, compared to the $6,000 each would have earned without the increase. ◆

NASH EQUILIBRIUM

A game is said to be in equilibrium if each player's strategy is the best he or she can choose, given the other players' choices. This definition of equilibrium is sometimes called a **Nash equilibrium,** after the mathematician John Nash, who developed the concept in the early 1950s. Nash was awarded the Nobel Prize in Economics in 1994 for his contributions to game theory.[2] When a game is in equilibrium, no player has any incentive to deviate from his current strategy.

Nash equilibrium any combination of strategies in which each player's strategy is his or her best choice, given the other players' choices

If each player in a game has a dominant strategy, as in the advertising example, equilibrium occurs when each player follows that strategy. But even in games in which not every player has a dominant strategy, we can often identify an equilibrium outcome. Consider, for instance, the following variation on the advertising game.

Should Americans spend more money on advertising?

Suppose United Airlines and American are the only carriers that serve the Chicago–St. Louis market. Their payoff matrix for advertising decisions is shown in Table 10.2. Does United have a dominant strategy? Does American? If each firm does the best it can, given the incentives facing the other, what will be the outcome of this game?

In this game, no matter what United does, American will do better to raise its ad spending, so raising the advertising budget is a dominant strategy for American. United, however, does not have a dominant strategy. If American raises its spending, United will do better to stand pat; if American stands pat, however, United will do

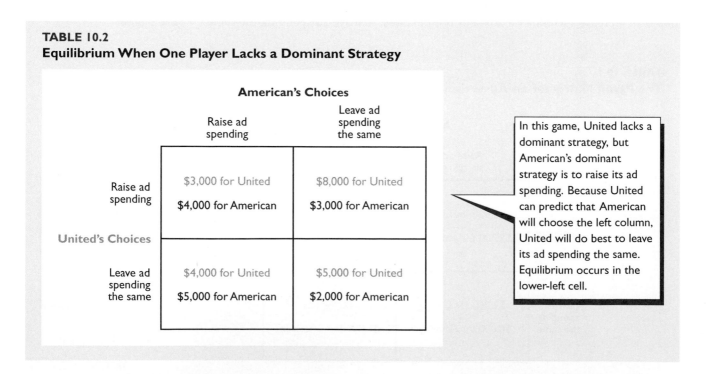

TABLE 10.2
Equilibrium When One Player Lacks a Dominant Strategy

	American's Choices	
	Raise ad spending	Leave ad spending the same
Raise ad spending	$3,000 for United / $4,000 for American	$8,000 for United / $3,000 for American
Leave ad spending the same	$4,000 for United / $5,000 for American	$5,000 for United / $2,000 for American

United's Choices

In this game, United lacks a dominant strategy, but American's dominant strategy is to raise its ad spending. Because United can predict that American will choose the left column, United will do best to leave its ad spending the same. Equilibrium occurs in the lower-left cell.

[2]Nash was also the subject of the Academy Award–winning film *A Beautiful Mind.*

better to spend more. Even though United does not have a dominant strategy, we can employ the Incentive Principle to predict what is likely to happen in this game. United's managers are assumed to know what the payoff matrix is, so they can predict that American will spend more on ads since that is American's dominant strategy. Thus the best strategy for United, given the prediction that American will spend more on ads, is to keep its own spending unchanged. If both players do the best they can, taking account of the incentives each faces, this game will end in the lower-left cell of the payoff matrix: American will raise its spending on ads and United will not. ◆

┌─────────────────┐
◯ │   **Incentive** │
└─────────────────┘

Note that the choices corresponding to the lower-left cell in Table 10.2 satisfy the definition of a Nash equilibrium. If United found itself in that cell, its alternative would be to raise its ad spending, a move that would reduce its payoff from $4,000 to $3,000. So United has no incentive to abandon the lower-left cell. Similarly, if American found itself in the lower-left cell of Table 10.2, its alternative would be to leave ad spending the same, a move that would reduce its payoff from $5,000 to $2,000. So American also has no incentive to abandon the lower-left cell. The lower left cell of Table 10.2 is a Nash equilibrium—a combination of strategies for which each player's choice is the best available option, given the choice made by the other player.

EXERCISE 10.1

What should United and American do if their payoff matrix is modified as follows?

<table>
<tr><th></th><th colspan="2" align="center">American</th></tr>
<tr><th></th><th align="center">Raise ad
spending</th><th align="center">Leave
spending
the same</th></tr>
<tr><td align="right">Raise ad
spending</td><td align="center">$3,000 for United

$8,000 for American</td><td align="center">$4,000 for United

$5,000 for American</td></tr>
<tr><td align="right">United

Leave
spending
the same</td><td align="center">$8,000 for United

$4,000 for American</td><td align="center">$5,000 for United

$2,000 for American</td></tr>
</table>

RECAP	USING GAME THEORY TO ANALYZE STRATEGIC DECISIONS

The three elements of any game are the players, the list of strategies from which they can choose, and the payoffs to each combination of strategies. This information can be summarized in a payoff matrix.

Equilibrium in a game occurs when each player's strategy choice yields the highest payoff available, given the strategies chosen by other players. Such a combination of strategies is called a Nash equilibrium.

THE PRISONER'S DILEMMA

prisoner's dilemma a game in which each player has a dominant strategy, and when each plays it, the resulting payoffs are smaller than if each had played a dominated strategy

The first advertising example we discussed above belongs to an important class of games called the **prisoner's dilemma**. In the prisoner's dilemma, when each player chooses his dominant strategy, the result is unattractive to the group of players as a whole.

THE ORIGINAL PRISONER'S DILEMMA

The next example recounts the original scenario from which the prisoner's dilemma drew its name.

Should the prisoners confess?

Two prisoners, Horace and Jasper, are being held in separate cells for a serious crime that they did in fact commit. The prosecutor, however, has only enough hard evidence to convict them of a minor offense, for which the penalty is a year in jail. Each prisoner is told that if one confesses while the other remains silent, the confessor will go scot-free, and the other will spend 20 years in prison. If both confess, they will get an intermediate sentence of five years. These payoffs are summarized in Table 10.3. The two prisoners are not allowed to communicate with one another. Do they have a dominant strategy? If so, what is it?

In this game, the dominant strategy for each prisoner is to confess. No matter what Jasper does, Horace will get a lighter sentence by speaking out. If Jasper confesses, Horace will get five years (upper-left cell) instead of 20 (lower-left cell). If Jasper remains silent, Horace will go free (upper-right cell) instead of spending a year in jail (lower-right cell). Because the payoffs are perfectly symmetric, Jasper will also do better to confess, no matter what Horace does. The difficulty is that when each follows his dominant strategy and confesses, both will do worse than if each had shown restraint. When both confess, they each get five years (upper-left cell), instead of the one year they would have gotten by remaining silent (lower-right cell). Hence the name of this game, the prisoner's dilemma.

TABLE 10.3
The Payoff Matrix for a Prisoner's Dilemma

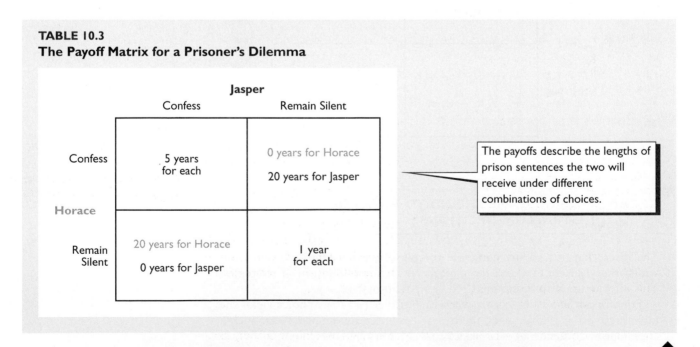

	Jasper Confess	Jasper Remain Silent
Horace Confess	5 years for each	0 years for Horace / 20 years for Jasper
Horace Remain Silent	20 years for Horace / 0 years for Jasper	1 year for each

The payoffs describe the lengths of prison sentences the two will receive under different combinations of choices.

EXERCISE 10.2

GM and Chrysler must both decide whether to invest in a new process. Games 1 and 2 below show how their profits depend on the decisions they might make. Which of these games is a prisoner's dilemma?

Game 1

Chrysler

	Don't invest	Invest
Don't invest	10 for each	4 for GM 12 for Chrysler
Invest	12 for GM 4 for Chrysler	5 for each

GM (labels rows Don't invest / Invest)

Game 2

Chrysler

	Don't invest	Invest
Don't invest	4 for GM 12 for Chrysler	5 for each
Invest	10 for each	12 for GM 4 for Chrysler

GM (labels rows Don't invest / Invest)

The prisoner's dilemma is one of the most powerful metaphors in all of human behavioral science. Countless social and economic interactions have payoff structures analogous to the one confronted by the two prisoners. Some of those interactions occur between only two players, as in the examples just discussed; many others involve larger groups. Games of the latter sort are called *multiplayer prisoner's dilemmas*. But regardless of the number of players involved, the common thread is one of conflict between the narrow self-interest of individuals and the broader interests of larger communities.

THE ECONOMICS OF CARTELS

A **cartel** is any coalition of firms that conspires to restrict production for the purpose of earning an economic profit. As we will see in the next example, the problem confronting oligopolists who are trying to form a cartel is a classic illustration of the prisoner's dilemma.

cartel a coalition of firms that agree to restrict output for the purpose of earning an economic profit

Why are cartel agreements notoriously unstable?

Consider a market for bottled water served by two oligopolists, Aquapure and Mountain Spring. Each firm can draw water free of charge from a mineral spring located on its own land. Customers supply their own bottles. Rather than compete with one another, the two firms decide to collude by selling water at the price a profit-maximizing pure monopolist would charge. Under their agreement (which constitutes a cartel), each firm would produce and sell half the quantity of water demanded by the market at the monopoly price (see Figure 10.1). The agreement is not legally enforceable, however, which means that each firm has the option of charging less than the agreed price. If one firm sells water for less than the other firm, it will capture the entire quantity demanded by the market at the lower price.

Why is this agreement likely to collapse?

Since the marginal cost of mineral water is zero, the profit-maximizing quantity for a monopolist with the demand curve shown in Figure 10.1 is 1,000 bottles per day, the

Example 10.1

THE ECONOMIC NATURALIST

FIGURE 10.1
The Market Demand for Mineral Water.
Faced with the demand curve shown, a monopolist with zero marginal cost would produce 1,000 bottles per day (the quantity at which marginal revenue equals zero) and sell them at a price of $1.00 per bottle.

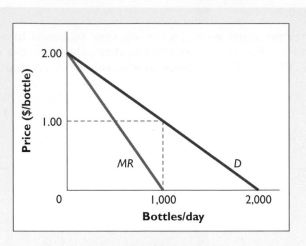

Why is it so difficult for companies to enforce agreements against price cutting?

quantity for which marginal revenue equals marginal cost. At that quantity, the monopoly price is $1 per bottle. If the firms abide by their agreement, each will sell half the market total, or 500 bottles per day, at a price of $1 per bottle, for an economic profit of $500 per day.

But suppose Aquapure reduced its price to 90 cents per bottle. By underselling Mountain Spring, it would capture the entire quantity demanded by the market, which, as shown in Figure 10.2, is 1,100 bottles per day. Aquapure's economic profit would rise from $500 per day to ($0.90 per bottle)(1,100 bottles per day) = $990 per day—almost twice as much as before. In the process, Mountain Spring's economic profit would fall from $500 per day to zero. Rather than see its economic profit disappear, Mountain Spring would match Aquapure's price cut, recapturing its original 50-percent share of the market. But when each firm charges $0.90 per bottle and sells 550 bottles per day, each earns an economic profit of ($.90 per bottle)(550 bottles per day) = $495 per day, or $5 less per day than before.

Suppose we view the cartel agreement as an economic game in which the two available strategies are to sell for $1 per bottle or to sell for $0.90 per bottle. The payoffs are the economic profits that result from these strategies. Table 10.4 shows the payoff matrix for this game. Each firm's dominant strategy is to sell at the lower price, yet in following that strategy, each earns a lower profit than if each had sold at the higher price.

The game does not end with both firms charging $0.90 per bottle. Each firm knows that if it cuts the price a little further, it can recapture the entire market, and in the process earn a substantially higher economic profit. At every step, the rival firm

FIGURE 10.2
The Temptation to Violate a Cartel Agreement.
By cutting its price from $1 per bottle to 90 cents per bottle, Aquapure can sell the entire market quantity demanded at that price, 1,100 bottles per day, rather than half the monopoly quantity of 1,000 bottles per day.

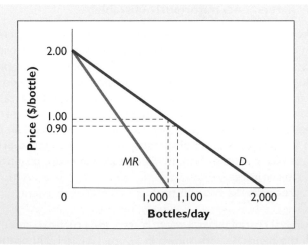

TABLE 10.4
The Payoff Matrix for a Cartel Agreement

	Mountain Spring	
	Charge $1/bottle	Charge $0.90/bottle
Aquapure Charge $1/bottle	$500/day for each	$0 for Aquapure $990/day for Mt. Spring
Charge $0.90/bottle	$990/day Aquapure 0 for Mt. Spring	$495/day for each

> The dominant strategy for each firm is to charge $0.90 per bottle, or 10 cents per bottle less than called for by the cartel agreement. Hence the notorious instability of cartel agreements.

will match any price cut, until the price falls all the way to the marginal cost—in this example, zero.

Cartel agreements confront participants with the economic incentives inherent in the prisoner's dilemma, which explains why such agreements have historically been so unstable. Usually a cartel involves not just two firms, but several, an arrangement that can make retaliation against price cutters extremely difficult. In many cases, discovering which parties have broken the agreement is difficult. For example, the Organization of Petroleum Exporting Countries (OPEC), a cartel of oil producers formed in the 1970s to restrict oil production, has no practical way to prevent member countries from secretly pumping oil offshore in the dead of night. •

TIT-FOR-TAT AND THE REPEATED PRISONER'S DILEMMA

When all players cooperate in a prisoner's dilemma, each gets a higher payoff than when all defect. So people who confront prisoner's dilemmas will be on the lookout for ways to create incentives for mutual cooperation. What they need is some way to penalize players who defect. When players interact with one another only once, this turns out to be difficult. But when they expect to interact repeatedly, new possibilities emerge.

A **repeated prisoner's dilemma** is a standard prisoner's dilemma that confronts the same players not just once but many times. Experimental research on repeated prisoner's dilemmas in the 1960s identified a simple strategy that proves remarkably effective at limiting defection. The strategy is called **tit-for-tat**, and here is how it works: The first time you interact with someone, you cooperate. In each subsequent interaction, you simply do what that person did in the previous interaction. Thus, if your partner defected on your first interaction, you would then defect on your next interaction with her. If she then cooperates, your move next time will be to cooperate as well.

On the basis of elaborate computer simulations, University of Michigan political scientist Robert Axelrod showed that tit-for-tat was a remarkably effective strategy, even when pitted against a host of ingenious counterstrategies that had been designed for the explicit purpose of trying to exploit it. The success of tit-for-tat requires a reasonably stable set of players, each of whom can remember what other players have done in previous interactions. It also requires that players have a significant stake in what happens in the future, for it is the fear of retaliation that deters people from defecting.

repeated prisoner's dilemma a standard prisoner's dilemma that confronts the same players repeatedly

tit-for-tat a strategy for the repeated prisoner's dilemma in which players cooperate on the first move, then mimic their partner's last move on each successive move

Since rival firms in the same industry interact with one another repeatedly, it might seem that the tit-for-tat strategy would assure widespread collusion to raise prices. And yet, as noted earlier, cartel agreements are notoriously unsuccessful. One difficulty is that tit-for-tat's effectiveness depends on there being only two players in the game. In competitive and monopolistically competitive industries, there are generally many firms, and even in oligopolies there are often several. When there are more than two firms, and one defects now, how do the cooperators selectively punish the defector later? By cutting price? That will penalize everyone, not just the defector. Even if there are only two firms in an industry, these firms realize that other firms may enter their industry. So the would-be cartel members have to worry not only about each other, but also about the entire list of firms that might decide to compete with them. Each firm may see this as a hopeless task and decide to defect now, hoping to reap at least some economic profit in the short run. What seems clear, in any event, is that the practical problems involved in implementing tit-for-tat have made it difficult to hold cartel agreements together for long.

Example 10.2
THE ECONOMIC NATURALIST

Why were cigarette manufacturers happy when Congress made it illegal for them to advertise on television?

How did Congress unwittingly solve the television advertising dilemma confronting cigarette producers?

In 1970, Congress enacted a law making cigarette advertising on television illegal after January 1, 1971. As evidenced by the steadily declining proportion of Americans who smoke, this law seems to have achieved its stated purpose of protecting citizens against a proven health hazard. But the law also had an unintended effect, which was to increase the economic profit of cigarette makers, at least in the short run. In the year before the law's passage, manufacturers spent more than $300 million on advertising—about $60 million more than they spent during the year after the law was enacted. Much of the saving in advertising expenditures in 1971 was reflected in higher cigarette profits at year end. But if eliminating television advertising made companies more profitable, why didn't the manufacturers eliminate the ads on their own?

When an imperfectly competitive firm advertises its product, its demand curve shifts rightward, for two reasons. First, people who have never used that type of product learn about it, and some buy it. Second, people who consume a different brand of the product may switch brands. The first effect boosts sales industrywide; the second merely redistributes existing sales among brands.

Although advertising produces both effects in the cigarette industry, its primary effect is brand switching. Thus, the decision of whether to advertise confronts the individual firm with a prisoner's dilemma. Table 10.5 shows the payoffs facing a pair of cigarette producers trying to decide whether to advertise. If both firms advertise on TV (upper-left cell), each earns a profit of only $10 million per year, compared to a profit of $20 million per year for each if neither advertises (lower-right cell). Clearly, both will benefit if neither advertises.

Yet note the powerful incentive that confronts each firm. RJR sees that if Philip Morris doesn't advertise, RJR can earn higher profits by advertising ($35 million per year) than by not advertising ($20 million per year). RJR also sees that if Philip Morris does advertise, RJR will again earn more by advertising ($10 million per year) than by not advertising ($5 million per year). Thus, RJR's dominant strategy is to advertise. And because the payoffs are symmetric, Philip Morris's dominant strategy is also to advertise. So when each firm behaves rationally from its own point of view, the two together do worse than if they had both shown restraint. The congressional ad ban forced cigarette manufacturers to do what they could not have accomplished on their own. ●

As the following example makes clear, understanding the prisoner's dilemma can help the economic naturalist to make sense of human behavior not only in the world of business, but also in other domains of life as well.

TABLE 10.5
Cigarette Advertising as a Prisoner's Dilemma

		Philip Morris	
		Advertise on TV	Don't advertise on TV
RJR	Advertise on TV	$10 million/yr for each	$35 million/yr for RJR $5 million/yr for Philip Morris
	Don't advertise on TV	$5 million/yr for RJR $35 million/yr for Philip Morris	$20 million/yr for each

In many industries, the primary effect of advertising is to encourage consumers to switch brands. In such industries, the dominant strategy is to advertise heavily (upper-left cell), even though firms as a group would do better by not advertising (lower-right cell).

Why do people shout at parties?

Whenever large numbers of people gather for conversation in a closed space, the ambient noise level rises sharply. After attending such gatherings, people often complain of sore throats and hoarse voices. If everyone spoke at a normal volume at parties, the overall noise level would be lower, and people would hear just as well. So why do people shout?

The problem involves the difference between individual incentives and group incentives. Suppose everyone starts by speaking at a normal level. But because of the crowded conditions, conversation partners have difficulty hearing one another, even when no one is shouting. The natural solution, from the point of the individual, is to simply raise one's voice a bit. But that is also the natural solution for everyone else. And when everyone speaks more loudly, the ambient noise level rises, so that no one hears any better than before.

No matter what others do, the individual will do better by speaking more loudly. Doing so is a dominant strategy for everyone, in fact. Yet when everyone follows the dominant strategy, the result is worse (no one can hear well) than if everyone had continued to speak normally. While shouting is wasteful, individuals acting alone have no better option. If anyone were to speak softly while others shout, that person wouldn't be heard. No one wants to go home with raw vocal cords, but people apparently prefer that cost to the alternative of not being heard at all. ●

Example 10.3
THE ECONOMIC NATURALIST

Why do people often have to shout to be heard at parties?

RECAP	**THE PRISONER'S DILEMMA**

The prisoner's dilemma is a game in which each player has a dominant strategy, and in which the payoff to each player when each chooses that strategy is smaller than if each had chosen a dominated strategy. Incentives analogous to those found in the prisoner's dilemma help to explain a broad range of behavior in business and everyday life—among them excessive spending on advertising and cartel instability. The tit-for-tat strategy can help sustain cooperation in two-player repeated prisoner's dilemmas but tends to be ineffective in multiplayer repeated prisoner's dilemmas.

EN 10

GAMES IN WHICH TIMING MATTERS

In the games discussed so far, players were assumed to choose their strategies simultaneously, and which player moved first didn't matter. For example, in the prisoner's dilemma, self-interested players would follow their dominant strategies even if they knew in advance what strategies their opponents had chosen. But in other situations, such as the negotiations between Warner Brothers and Tony Bennett described at the beginning of this chapter, timing is of the essence.

We begin with an example of a game whose outcome cannot be predicted if both players move simultaneously, but whose outcome is clear if one player has the opportunity to move before the other.

Should Dodge build a hybrid Viper?

The Dodge Viper and the Chevrolet Corvette compete for a limited pool of domestic sports car enthusiasts. Each company knows that the other is considering whether to bring out a hybrid version of its car. If both companies bring out hybrids, each will earn $60 million in profit. If neither brings out a hybrid, each company will earn $50 million. If Chevrolet introduces a hybrid and Dodge does not, Chevrolet will earn $80 million and Dodge will earn $70 million. If Dodge brings out a hybrid and Chevrolet does not, Dodge will earn $80 million and Chevrolet will earn $70 million. Does either firm have a dominant strategy in this situation? What will happen in this game if Dodge gets to choose first, with Chevrolet choosing after having seen Dodge's choice?

When both companies must make their decisions simultaneously, the payoff matrix for the example looks like Table 10.6.

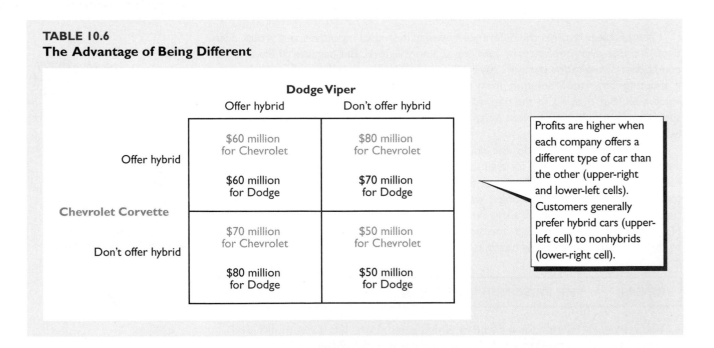

TABLE 10.6
The Advantage of Being Different

	Dodge Viper	
	Offer hybrid	Don't offer hybrid
Chevrolet Corvette Offer hybrid	$60 million for Chevrolet / $60 million for Dodge	$80 million for Chevrolet / $70 million for Dodge
Don't offer hybrid	$70 million for Chevrolet / $80 million for Dodge	$50 million for Chevrolet / $50 million for Dodge

Profits are higher when each company offers a different type of car than the other (upper-right and lower-left cells). Customers generally prefer hybrid cars (upper-left cell) to nonhybrids (lower-right cell).

The logic of the profit figures in Table 10.6 is that although consumers generally like the idea of a hybrid sports car (hence the higher profits when both companies bring out hybrids than when neither does), the companies will have to compete more heavily with one another if both offer the same type of car (and hence the lower profits when both offer the same type of car than when each offers a different type).

In the payoff matrix in Table 10.6, neither company has a dominant strategy. The best outcome for Dodge is to offer a hybrid Viper while Chevrolet does not offer a hybrid Corvette (lower-left cell). The best outcome for Chevrolet is to offer a hybrid Corvette while Dodge does not offer a hybrid Viper (upper-right cell). Both the lower-left and upper-right cells are Nash equilibria of this game because if the companies found themselves in either of these cells, neither would unilaterally want to change its position. Thus, in the upper-right cell, Chevrolet wouldn't want to change (that cell is, after all, the best possible outcome for Chevrolet), and neither would Dodge (since switching to a hybrid would reduce its profit from $70 million to $60 million). But without being told more, we simply cannot predict where the two companies will end up.

If one side can move before the other, however, the incentives for action become instantly clearer. For games in which timing matters, a **decision tree**, or **game tree**, is a more useful way of representing the payoffs than a traditional payoff matrix. This type of diagram describes the possible moves in the sequence in which they may occur, and lists the final payoffs for each possible combination of moves.

If Dodge has the first move, the decision tree for the game is shown in Figure 10.3. At *A*, Dodge begins the game by deciding whether to offer a hybrid. If it chooses to offer one, Chevrolet must then make its own choice at *B*. If Dodge does not offer a hybrid, Chevrolet will make its choice at *C*. In either case, once Chevrolet makes its choice, the game is over.

decision tree (also called a game tree) a diagram that describes the possible moves in a game in sequence and lists the payoffs that correspond to each possible combination of moves

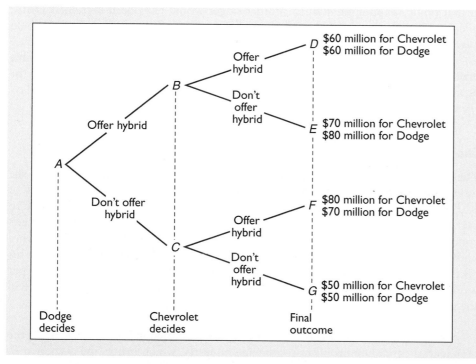

FIGURE 10.3
Decision Tree for Hybrid Example.
This decision tree shows the possible moves and payoffs for the game in the hybrid example, in the sequence in which they may occur.

In thinking strategically about this game, the key for Dodge is to put itself in Chevrolet's shoes and imagine how Chevrolet would react to the various choices it might confront. In general, it will make sense for Dodge to assume that Chevrolet will respond in a self-interested way—that is, by choosing the available option that offers the highest profit for Chevrolet. Dodge knows that if it chooses to offer a hybrid, Chevy's best option at *B* will be not to offer a hybrid (since Chevy's profit is $10 million higher at *E* than at *D*). Dodge also knows that if it chooses not to offer a hybrid, Chevy's best option at *C* will be to offer one (since Chevy's profit is $30 million higher at F than at G). Dodge thus knows that if it offers a hybrid, it will end up at E, where it will earn $80 million, whereas if it does not offer a hybrid, it will end up at F, where it will earn only $70 million. So when Dodge has the first move in this game, its best strategy is to offer a hybrid. And Chevrolet then follows by choosing not to offer one. ◆

CREDIBLE THREATS AND PROMISES

credible threat a threat to take an action that is in the threatener's interest to carry out

Could Chevrolet have deterred Dodge from offering a hybrid by threatening to offer a hybrid of its own, no matter what Dodge did? The problem with this strategy is such a threat would not have been credible. In the language of game theory, a **credible threat** is one that will be in the threatener's interest to carry out when the time comes to act. As the Incentive Principle suggests, people are likely to be skeptical of any threat if they know there will be no incentive to follow through when the time comes. The problem here is that Dodge knows that it would not be in Chevrolet's interest to carry out its threat in the event that Dodge offered a hybrid. After all, once Dodge has already offered the hybrid, Chevy's best option is to offer a nonhybrid.

> **Incentive**

The concept of a credible threat figured prominently in the negotiations between Warner Brothers' managers and Tony Bennett over the matter of Mr. Bennett's fee for performing in *Analyze This*. Once most of the film had been shot, managers knew they couldn't threaten credibly to refuse Mr. Bennett's salary demand because at that point adapting the film to another singer would have been extremely costly. In contrast, a similar threat made before production of the movie had begun would have been credible.

credible promise a promise to take an action that is in the promiser's interest to keep

Just as in some games credible threats are impossible to make, in others **credible promises** are impossible. A credible promise is one that is in the interests of the promiser to keep when the time comes to act. In the following example, both players suffer because of the inability to make a credible promise.

Should the business owner open a remote office?

The owner of a thriving business wants to start up an office in a distant city. If she hires someone to manage the new office, she can afford to pay a weekly salary of $1,000—a premium of $500 over what the manager would otherwise be able to earn—and still earn a weekly economic profit of $1,000 for herself. The owner's concern is that she will not be able to monitor the manager's behavior. The owner knows that by managing the remote office dishonestly, the manager can boost his take-home pay to $1,500 while causing the owner an economic loss of $500 per week. If the owner believes that all managers are selfish income-maximizers, will she open the new office?

The decision tree for the remote-office game is shown in Figure 10.4. At A, the managerial candidate promises to manage honestly, which brings the owner to B, where she must decide whether to open the new office. If she opens it, they reach C, where the manager must decide whether to manage honestly. If the manager's only goal is to make as much money as he can, he will manage dishonestly (bottom branch at C) since that way he will earn $500 more than by managing honestly (top branch at C).

So if the owner opens the new office, she will end up with an economic loss of $500. If she had not opened the office (bottom branch at B), she would have realized an economic profit of zero. Since zero is better than −$500, the owner will choose not to open the remote office. In the end, the opportunity cost of the manager's inability to make a credible promise is $1,500: the manager's forgone $500 salary premium and the owner's forgone $1,000 return.

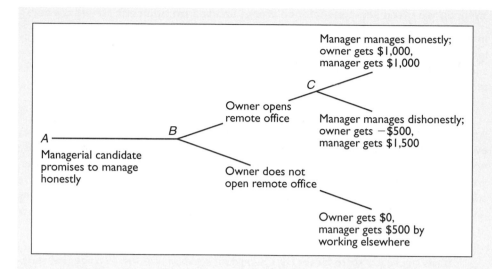

FIGURE 10.4
Decision Tree for the Remote Office Game.
The best outcome is for the manager to open the office at *B* and for the manager to manage the office honestly at *C*. But if the manager is purely self-interested and the owner knows it, this path will not be an equilibrium outcome.

EXERCISE 10.3

Smith and Jones are playing a game in which Smith has the first move at *A* in the decision tree shown below. Once Smith has chosen either the top or bottom branch at *A*, Jones, who can see what Smith has chosen, must choose the top or bottom branch at *B* or *C*. If the payoffs at the end of each branch are as shown, what is the equilibrium outcome of this game? If before Smith chose, Jones could make a credible commitment to choose either the top or bottom branch when his turn came, what would he do?

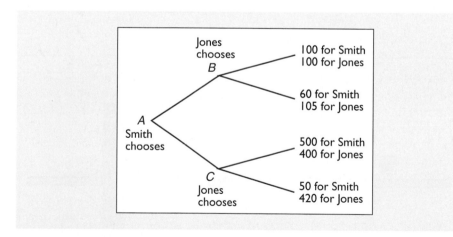

MONOPOLISTIC COMPETITION WHEN LOCATION MATTERS

In many sequential games, the player who gets to move first enjoys a strategic advantage. That was the case, for instance, in the decision of whether to produce a hybrid sports car. In that example, the first mover did better because he was able to exploit the knowledge that both firms do better if each one's product is different from the other's rather than similar to it. But that won't always be true. When the feature that differentiates one seller's product from another's is temporal or spatial location, the firm with the last move in a game sometimes enjoys the upper hand, as Example 10.4 illustrates.

Example 10.4

THE ECONOMIC NATURALIST

Why do retail merchants tend to locate in clusters?

Why do we often see convenience stores located on adjacent street corners?

In many cities, it is common to see convenience stores located in clusters, followed by long stretches with no stores at all. If the stores were more spread out, almost all consumers would enjoy a shorter walk to the nearest convenience store. Why do stores tend to cluster in this fashion?

In Figure 10.5, suppose that when the convenience store located at A first opened, it was the closest store for the 1,200 shoppers who live in identical apartment houses evenly distributed along the road between A and the freeway one mile to the east.[3] Those who live to the east of the freeway shop elsewhere because they cannot cross the freeway. Those who live to the west of the store at A shop either at A or at some other store still further to the west, whichever is closer. In this setting, why might a profit-maximizing entrepreneur planning to open a new store between A and the freeway choose to locate at B rather than at some intermediate location such as C?

It turns out that a store located at C would in fact minimize the distance that shoppers living between A and the freeway would have to walk to reach the nearest store. If there were a store at C, no shopper on this stretch of road would have to walk more than 1/3 of a mile to reach the nearest store. The 800 people who live between point D (which is halfway between A and C) and the freeway would shop at C, while the 400 who live between D and A would shop at A.

Despite the fact that C is the most attractive location for a new store from the perspective of consumers, it is not the most advantageous for the store's owner. The reason is that the owner's profit depends on how many people choose to shop at his store, not on how far they have to walk to get there. Given that consumers shop at the store closest to where they live, the best option from the entrepreneur's perspective is to locate his store at B, on the street corner just east of A. That way, his store will be closer to all 1,200 people who live between A and the freeway. It is this logic that helps explain the clustering of convenience stores, gas stations, and other monopolistically competitive firms whose most important differentiating feature is geographic location.

FIGURE 10.5
The Curious Tendency of Monopolistic Competitors to Cluster.
As a group, consumers would enjoy a shorter walk if the store at B were instead located at C, or even at D. But a second store will attract more customers by locating at B.

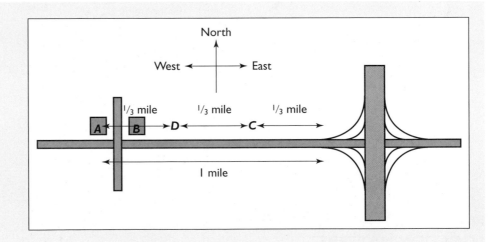

The insight that helped answer the question posed in Example 10.4 is due to the economist Harold Hotelling.[4] Hotelling employed this insight to explain why

[3]"Evenly distributed" means that the number of shoppers who live on any segment of the road between A and the freeway is exactly proportional to the length of that segment. For example, the number who live along a segment one-tenth of a mile in length would be 1/10 × 1,200 = 120.
[4]Harold Hotelling, "Stability and Competition," *Economic Journal* 39, no. 1 (1929), pp. 41–57.

two hot dog vendors on a stretch of beach almost invariably locate next to one another midway between the endpoints of the beach.

For many oligopolistic or monopolistically competitive firms, an important dimension of product differentiation is location in time rather than in physical space. The timing of flight departures for different airlines in the New York–Los Angeles market is one example. The timing of film showings by different local movie theaters is another. In these cases, too, we often see product clustering. Thus, in the New York–Los Angeles market, both United and American have flights throughout the afternoon departing exactly on the hour. And in many local movie markets, the first evening showing starts at 7:15 p.m. in dozens of different theaters.

In other examples, the differentiating features that matter most might be said to describe the product's location in a more abstract "product space." With soft drinks, for example, we might array different products according to their degrees of sweetness or carbonation. Here, too, it is common to see rival products that lie very close to one another such as Coca-Cola and Pepsi. Clustering occurs in these cases for the reasons analogous to those discussed by Hotelling in his classic paper.

RECAP	GAMES IN WHICH TIMING MATTERS

The outcomes in many games depend on the timing of each player's move. For such games, the payoffs are best summarized by a decision tree rather than a payoff matrix. Sometimes the second mover does best to offer a product that differs markedly from existing products. Other times the second mover does best to mimic existing products closely.

COMMITMENT PROBLEMS

Games like the one in Exercise 10.3, as well as the prisoner's dilemma, the cartel game, and the remote-office game, confront players with a **commitment problem**— a situation in which they have difficulty achieving the desired outcome because they cannot make credible threats or promises. If both players in the original prisoner's dilemma could make a binding promise to remain silent, both would be assured of a shorter sentence, hence the logic of the underworld code of *Omerta*, under which the family of anyone who provides evidence against a fellow mob member is killed. A similar logic explains the adoption of military-arms-control agreements, in which opponents sign an enforceable pledge to curtail weapons spending.

The commitment problem in the remote office game could be solved if the managerial candidate could find some way of committing himself to manage honestly if hired. The candidate needs a **commitment device**—something that provides the candidate with an incentive to keep his promise.

Business owners are well aware of commitment problems in the workplace and have adopted a variety of commitment devices to solve them. Consider, for example, the problem confronting the owner of a restaurant. She wants her table staff to provide good service so that customers will enjoy their meals and come back in the future. Since good service is valuable to her, she would be willing to pay waiters extra for it. For their part, waiters would be willing to provide good service in return for the extra pay. The problem is that the owner cannot always monitor whether the waiters do provide good service. Her concern is that, having been paid extra for it, the waiters may slack off when she isn't looking. Unless the owner can find some way to solve this problem, she will not pay extra, the waiters

commitment problem a situation in which people cannot achieve their goals because of an inability to make credible threats or promises

commitment device a way of changing incentives so as to make otherwise empty threats or promises credible

will not provide good service, and she, they, and the diners will suffer. A better outcome for all concerned would be for the waiters to find some way to commit themselves to good service.

Restaurateurs in many countries have tried to solve this commitment problem by encouraging diners to leave tips at the end of their meals. The attraction of this solution is that the diner is *always* in a good position to monitor service quality. The diner should be happy to reward good service with a generous tip since doing so will help to assure good service in the future. And the waiter has a strong incentive to provide good service because he knows that the size of his tip may depend on it.

The various commitment devices just discussed—the underworld code of *Omerta*, military-arms-control agreements, the tip for the waiter—all work because they change the incentives facing the decision makers. But as the next example illustrates, changing incentives in precisely the desired way is not always practical.

Will Sylvester leave a tip when dining on the road?

Sylvester has just finished a $100 steak dinner at a restaurant that is 500 miles from where he lives. The waiter provided good service. If Sylvester cares only about himself, will he leave a tip?

Once the waiter has provided good service, there is no way for him to take it back if the diner fails to leave a tip. In restaurants patronized by local diners, failure to tip is not a problem because the waiter can simply provide poor service the next time a nontipper comes in. But the waiter lacks that leverage with out-of-town diners. Having already received good service, Sylvester must choose between paying $100 and paying $115 for his meal. If he is an essentially selfish person, the former choice may be a compelling one. ◆

Will leaving a tip at an out-of-town restaurant affect the quality of service you receive?

EXERCISE 10.4

A traveler dines at a restaurant far from home. Both he and the waiter who serves him are rational and self-interested in the narrow sense. The waiter must first choose between providing good service and bad service, whereupon the diner must choose whether or not to leave a tip. The payoffs for their interaction are as summarized on the accompanying game tree. What is the most the diner would be willing to pay for the right to make a binding commitment (visible to the waiter) to leave a tip at the end of the meal in the event of having received good service?

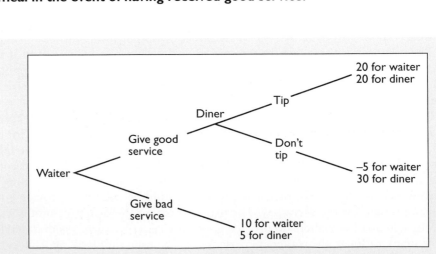

RECAP	COMMITMENT PROBLEMS

Commitment problems arise when the inability to make credible threats and promises prevents people from achieving desired outcomes. Such problems can sometimes be solved by employing commitment devices—ways of changing incentives to facilitate making credible threats or promises.

THE STRATEGIC ROLE OF PREFERENCES

In all the games we have discussed so far, players were assumed to care only about obtaining the best possible outcome for themselves. Thus, each player's goal was to get the highest monetary payoff, the shortest jail sentence, the best chance to be heard, and so on. The irony, in most of these games, is that players do not attain the best outcomes. Better outcomes can sometimes be achieved by altering the material incentives selfish players face, but not always.

If altering the relevant material incentives is not possible, commitment problems can sometimes be solved by altering people's psychological incentives. As the next example illustrates, in a society in which people are strongly conditioned to develop moral sentiments—feelings of guilt when they harm others, feelings of sympathy for their trading partners, feelings of outrage when they are treated unjustly—commitment problems arise less often than in more narrowly self-interested societies.

In a moral society, will the business owner open a remote office?

Consider again the owner of the thriving business who is trying to decide whether to open an office in a distant city. Suppose the society in which she lives is one in which all citizens have been strongly conditioned to behave honestly. Will she open the remote office?

Suppose, for instance, that the managerial candidate would suffer guilt pangs if he embezzled money from the owner. Most people would be reluctant to assign a monetary value to guilty feelings. But for the sake of discussion, let's suppose that those feelings are so unpleasant, the manager would be willing to pay at least $10,000 to avoid them. On this assumption, the manager's payoff if he manages dishonestly will be not $1,500, but $1,500 − $10,000 = −$8,500. The new decision tree is shown in Figure 10.6.

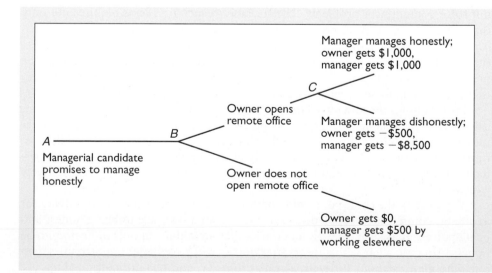

FIGURE 10.6
The Remote Office Game with an Honest Manager.
If the owner can identify a managerial candidate who would choose to manage honestly at C, she will hire that candidate at B and open the remote office.

In this case, the best choice for the owner at B will be to open the remote office because she knows that at C the manager's best choice will be to manage honestly. The irony, of course, is that the honest manager in this example ends up richer than the selfish manager in the previous example, who earned only a normal salary. ◆

ARE PEOPLE FUNDAMENTALLY SELFISH?

As the preceding example suggests, the assumption that people are self-interested in the narrow sense of the term does not always capture the full range of motives that govern choice in strategic settings. Think, for example, about the last time you had a meal at an out-of-town restaurant. Did you leave a tip? If so, your behavior was quite normal. Researchers have found that tipping rates in restaurants patronized mostly by out-of-town diners are essentially the same as in restaurants patronized mostly by local diners.

Indeed, there are many exceptions to the outcomes predicted on the basis of the assumption that people are self-interested in the most narrow sense of the term. People who have been treated unjustly often seek revenge even at ruinous cost to themselves. Every day, people walk away from profitable transactions whose terms they believe to be "unfair." In these and countless other ways, people do not seem to be pursuing self-interest narrowly defined. And if motives beyond narrow self-interest are significant, we must take them into account in attempting to predict and explain human behavior.

PREFERENCES AS SOLUTIONS TO COMMITMENT PROBLEMS

Economists tend to view preferences as ends in themselves. Taking them as given, they calculate what actions will best serve those preferences. This approach to the study of behavior is widely used by other social scientists, and by game theorists, military strategists, philosophers, and others. In its standard form, it assumes purely self-interested preferences for present and future consumption goods of various sorts, leisure pursuits, and so on. Concerns about fairness, guilt, honor, sympathy, and the like typically play no role.

Yet such concerns clearly affect the choices people make in strategic interactions. Sympathy for one's trading partner can make a businessperson trustworthy even when material incentives favor cheating. A sense of justice can prompt a person to incur the costs of retaliation, even when incurring those costs will not undo the original injury.

Preferences can clearly shape behavior in these ways; however, this alone does not solve commitment problems. The solution to such problems requires not only that a person *have* certain preferences, but also that others have some way of *discerning* them. Unless the business owner can identify the trustworthy employee, that employee cannot land a job whose pay is predicated on trust. And unless the predator can identify a potential victim whose character will motivate retaliation, that person is likely to become a victim.

From among those with whom we might engage in ventures requiring trust, can we identify reliable partners? If people could make *perfectly* accurate character judgments, they could always steer clear of dishonest persons. That people continue to be victimized at least occasionally by dishonest persons suggests that perfectly reliable character judgments are either impossible to make or prohibitively expensive.

Vigilance in the choice of trading partners is an essential element in solving (or avoiding) commitment problems, for if there is an advantage in being honest and being perceived as such, there is an even greater advantage in only *appearing* to be honest. After all, a liar who appears trustworthy will have better opportunities than one who glances about furtively, sweats profusely, and has difficulty making eye contact. Indeed, he will have the same opportunities as an honest person but will get higher payoffs because he will exploit them to the fullest.

In the end, the question of whether people can make reasonably accurate character judgments is an empirical one. Experimental studies have shown that even on the basis of brief encounters involving strangers, subjects are adept at predicting who will cooperate and who will defect in prisoner's dilemma games. For example, in one experiment in which only 26 percent of subjects defected, the accuracy rate of predicted defections was more than 56 percent. One might expect that predictions regarding those we know well would be even more accurate.

Do you know someone who would return an envelope containing $1,000 in cash to you if you lost it at a crowded concert? If so, then you accept the claim that personal character can help people to solve commitment problems. As long as honest individuals can identify at least some others who are honest, and can interact selectively with them, honest individuals can prosper in a competitive environment.

RECAP	THE STRATEGIC ROLE OF PREFERENCES

Most applications of the theory of games assume that players are self-interested in the narrow sense of the term. In practice, however, many choices—such as leaving tips in out-of-town restaurants—appear inconsistent with this assumption.

The fact that people seem driven by a more complex range of motives makes behavior more difficult to predict, but also creates new ways of solving commitment problems. Psychological incentives often can serve as commitment devices when changing players' material incentives is impractical. For example, people who are able to identify honest trading partners, and interact selectively with them, are able to solve commitment problems that arise from lack of trust.

■ SUMMARY ■

- Economists use the theory of games to analyze situations in which the payoffs of one's actions depend on the actions taken by others. Games have three basic elements: the players; the list of possible actions, or strategies, from which each player can choose; and the payoffs the players receive for those strategies. The payoff matrix is the most useful way to summarize this information in games in which the timing of the players' moves is not decisive. In games in which timing matters, a decision tree provides a much more useful summary of the information. **LO1, LO5**

- Equilibrium in a game occurs when each player's strategy choice yields the highest payoff available, given the strategies chosen by the other. **LO2**

- A dominant strategy is one that yields a higher payoff regardless of the strategy chosen by the other player. In some games such as the prisoner's dilemma, each player has a dominant strategy. The equilibrium

occurs in such games when each player chooses his or her dominant strategy. In other games, not all players have a dominant strategy. **LO3**

- Equilibrium outcomes are often unattractive from the perspective of players as a group. The prisoner's dilemma has this feature because it is each prisoner's dominant strategy to confess, yet each spends more time in jail if both confess than if both remain silent. The incentive structure of this game helps explain such disparate social dilemmas as excessive advertising, military arms races, and failure to reap the potential benefits of interactions requiring trust. **LO4**

- Individuals often can resolve these dilemmas if they can make binding commitments to behave in certain ways. Some commitments—such as those involved in military-arms-control agreements—are achieved by altering the material incentives confronting the players. Other commitments can be achieved by relying on psychological incentives to counteract material payoffs. Moral sentiments such as guilt, sympathy, and a sense of justice often foster better outcomes than can be achieved by narrowly self-interested players. For this type of commitment to work, the relevant moral sentiments must be discernible by one's potential trading partners. **LO6**

▪ KEY TERMS ▪

basic elements of a game (270)
cartel (275)
commitment device (285)
commitment problem (285)
credible promise (282)

credible threat (282)
decision tree (281)
dominant strategy (271)
dominated strategy (272)
game tree (281)

Nash equilibrium (272)
payoff matrix (271)
prisoner's dilemma (274)
repeated prisoner's dilemma (277)
tit-for-tat (277)

▪ REVIEW QUESTIONS ▪

1. Explain why a military arms race is an example of a prisoner's dilemma. **LO4**

2. Why did Warner Brothers make a mistake by waiting until the filming of *Analyze This* was almost finished before negotiating with Tony Bennett to perform in the final scene? **LO5**

3. Suppose General Motors is trying to hire a small firm to manufacture the door handles for Pontiac sedans. The task requires an investment in expensive capital equipment that cannot be used for any other purpose. Why might the president of the small firm refuse to undertake this venture without

a long-term contract fixing the price of the door handles? **LO6**

4. How is your incentive to defect in a prisoner's dilemma altered if you learn that you will play the game not just once but rather indefinitely many times with the same partner? **LO4**

5. Describe the commitment problem that narrowly self-interested diners and waiters would confront at restaurants located on interstate highways. Given that in such restaurants tipping does seem to assure reasonably good service, do you think people are always selfish in the narrowest sense? **LO6**

▪ PROBLEMS ▪

1. In studying for his economics final, Sam is concerned about only two things: his grade and the amount of time he spends studying. A good grade will give him a benefit of 20; an average grade, a benefit of 5; and a poor grade, a benefit of 0. By studying a lot, Sam will incur a cost of 10; by studying a little, a cost of 6. Moreover, if Sam studies a lot and all other students study a little, he will get a good grade and they will get poor ones. But if they study a lot and he studies a little, they will get good grades and he will get a poor one. Finally, if he and all other students study the same amount of time, everyone will get average grades. Other students share Sam's preferences regarding grades and study time. **LO1, LO2, LO4**
   a. Model this situation as a two-person prisoner's dilemma in which the strategies are to study a little and to study a lot, and the players are Sam and all other students. Include the payoffs in the matrix.
   b. What is the equilibrium outcome in this game? From the students' perspective, is it the best outcome?

2. Consider the following "dating game," which has two players, A and B, and two strategies, to buy a movie ticket or a baseball ticket. The payoffs, given in points, are as shown in the matrix below. Note that the highest payoffs occur when both A and B attend the same event.

	B	
	Buy movie ticket	Buy baseball ticket
Buy movie ticket	2 for A 3 for B	0 for A 0 for B
Buy baseball ticket	1 for A 1 for B	3 for A 2 for B

A (row label)

Assume that players A and B buy their tickets separately and simultaneously. Each must decide what to do knowing the available choices and payoffs but not what the other has actually chosen. Each player believes the other to be rational and self-interested.   **LO2, LO3, LO4, LO5**

a. Does either player have a dominant strategy?

b. How many potential equilibria are there? (Hint: To see whether a given combination of strategies is an equilibrium, ask whether either player could get a higher payoff by changing his or her strategy.)

c. Is this game a prisoner's dilemma? Explain.

d. Suppose player A gets to buy his or her ticket first. Player B does not observe A's choice but knows that A chose first. Player A knows that player B knows he or she chose first. What is the equilibrium outcome?

e. Suppose the situation is similar to part d, except that player B chooses first. What is the equilibrium outcome?

3. Blackadder and Baldrick are rational, self-interested criminals imprisoned in separate cells in a dark medieval dungeon. They face the prisoner's dilemma displayed in the matrix.

	Blackadder	
	Confess	Deny
Confess	5 years for each	0 for Baldrick 20 years for Blackadder
Deny	20 years for Baldrick 0 for Blackadder	1 year for each

Baldrick (row label)

Assume that Blackadder is willing to pay $1,000 for each year by which he can reduce his sentence below 20 years. A corrupt jailer tells Blackadder that before he decides whether to confess or deny the crime, she can tell him Baldrick's decision. How much is this information worth to Blackadder?   **LO4**

4. The owner of a thriving business wants to open a new office in a distant city. If he can hire someone who will manage the new office honestly, he can afford to pay that person a weekly salary of $2,000 ($1,000 more than the manager would be able to earn elsewhere) and still earn an economic profit of $800. The owner's concern is that he will not be able to monitor the manager's behavior and that the manager would therefore be in a position to embezzle money from the business. The owner knows that if the remote office is managed dishonestly, the manager can earn $3,100, while causing the owner an economic loss of $600 per week.   **LO2, LO5**

a. If the owner believes that all managers are narrowly self-interested income maximizers, will he open the new office?

b. Suppose the owner knows that a managerial candidate is a devoutly religious person who condemns dishonest behavior, and who would be willing to pay up to $15,000 to avoid the guilt she would feel if she were dishonest. Will the owner open the remote office?

5. Imagine yourself sitting in your car in a campus parking lot that is currently full, waiting for someone to pull out so that you can park your car. Somebody pulls out, but at the same moment a driver who has just arrived overtakes you in an obvious attempt to park in the vacated spot before you can. Suppose this driver would be willing to pay up to $10 to park in that spot and up to $30 to avoid getting into an argument with you. (That is, the benefit of parking is $10 and the cost of an argument is $30.) At the same time he guesses, accurately, that you too would be willing to pay up to $30 to avoid a confrontation and up to $10 to park in the vacant spot.   **LO2, LO5, LO6**

a. Model this situation as a two-stage decision tree in which his bid to take the space is the opening move and your strategies are (1) to protest and (2) not to protest. If you protest (initiate an argument), the rules of the game specify that he has to let you take the space. Show the payoffs at the end of each branch of the tree.

b. What is the equilibrium outcome?

c. What would be the advantage of being able to communicate credibly to the other driver that your *failure* to protest would be a significant psychological cost to you?

6. Newfoundland's fishing industry has recently declined sharply due to overfishing, even though fishing companies were supposedly bound by a quota agreement. If all fishermen had abided by the agreement, yields could have been maintained at high levels.   **LO4**

a. Model this situation as a prisoner's dilemma in which the players are Company A and Company B and the strategies are to keep the quota and break the quota. Include appropriate payoffs in the matrix. Explain why overfishing is inevitable in the absence of effective enforcement of the quota agreement.

b. Provide another environmental example of a prisoner's dilemma.

c. In many potential prisoner's dilemmas, a way out of the dilemma for a would-be cooperator is to make reliable character judgments about the trustworthiness of potential partners. Explain why this solution is not available in many situations involving degradation of the environment.

7. Consider the following game, called matching pennies, which you are playing with a friend. Each of you has a penny hidden in your hand, facing either heads up or tails up (you know which way the one in your hand is facing). On the count of "three," you simultaneously show your pennies to each other. If the face-up side of your coin matches the face-up side of your friend's coin, you get to keep the two pennies. If the faces do not match, your friend gets to keep the pennies.   **LO1, LO2, LO3**

a. Who are the players in this game? What are each player's strategies? Construct a payoff matrix for the game.

b. Is there a dominant strategy? If so, what?

c. Is there an equilibrium? If so, what?

8. Consider the following game. Harry has four quarters. He can offer Sally from one to four of them. If she accepts his offer, she keeps the quarters Harry offered her and Harry keeps the others. If Sally declines Harry's offer, they both get nothing ($0). They play the game only once, and each cares only about the amount of money he or she ends up with. **LO1, LO2, LO5**

   a. Who are the players? What are each player's strategies? Construct a decision tree for this game.

   b. Given their goal, what is the optimal choice for each player?

9. Two airplane manufacturers are considering the production of a new product, a 150-passenger jet. Both are deciding whether to enter the market and produce the new planes. The payoff matrix is as follows (payoff values are in millions of dollars):

Airbus

		Produce	Don't produce
Boeing	Produce	−5 for each	100 for Boeing 0 for Airbus
	Don't produce	0 for Boeing 100 for Airbus	0 for each

The implication of these payoffs is that the market demand is large enough to support only one manufacturer. If both firms enter, both will sustain a loss. **LO2**

a. Identify two possible equilibrium outcomes in this game.

b. Consider the effect of a subsidy. Suppose the European Union decides to subsidize the European producer, Airbus, with a check for $25 million if it enters the market. Revise the payoff matrix to account for this subsidy. What is the new equilibrium outcome?

c. Compare the two outcomes (pre- and post-subsidy). What qualitative effect does the subsidy have?

10. Jill and Jack both have two pails that can be used to carry water down from a hill. Each makes only one trip down the hill, and each pail of water can be sold for $5. Carrying the pails of water down requires considerable effort. Both Jill and Jack would be willing to pay $2 each to avoid carrying one bucket down the hill, and an additional $3 to avoid carrying a second bucket down the hill. **LO2, LO6**

   a. Given market prices, how many pails of water will each child fetch from the top of the hill?

   b. Jill and Jack's parents are worried that the two children don't cooperate enough with one another. Suppose they make Jill and Jack share equally their revenues from selling the water. Given that both are self-interested, construct the payoff matrix for the decisions Jill and Jack face regarding the number of pails of water each should carry. What is the equilibrium outcome?

■ ANSWERS TO IN-CHAPTER EXERCISES ■

10.1 No matter what American does, United will do better to leave ad spending the same. No matter what United does, American will do better to raise ad spending. So each player will play its dominant strategy: American will raise its ad spending and United will leave its ad spending the same. **LO2, LO3**

American's Choice

	Raise ad spending	Leave ad spending the same
Raise ad spending	United gets $3,000 American gets $8,000	United gets $4,000 American gets $5,000
Leave ad spending the same	United gets $8,000 American gets $4,000	United gets $5,000 American gets $2,000

(*United's Choice* labels the rows.)

10.2 In game 1, no matter what Chrysler does, GM will do better to invest, and no matter what GM does, Chrysler will do better to invest. Each has a dominant strategy, but in following it, each does worse than if it had not invested. So game 1 is a prisoner's dilemma. In game 2, no matter what Chrysler does, GM again will do better to invest; but no matter what GM does, Chrysler will do better *not* to invest. Each has a dominant strategy, and in following it, each gets a payoff of 10—5 more than if each had played its dominated strategy. So game 2 is not a prisoner's dilemma. **LO2, LO3**

10.3 Smith assumes that Jones will choose the branch that maximizes his payoff, which is the bottom branch at either *B* or *C*. So Jones will choose the bottom branch when his turn comes, no matter what Smith chooses. Since Smith will do better (60) on the bottom branch at *B* than on the bottom branch at *C* (50), Smith will choose the top branch at *A*. So equilibrium in this game is for Smith to choose the top branch at *A* and Jones to choose the bottom branch at *B*. Smith gets 60 and Jones gets 105. **LO2, LO5**

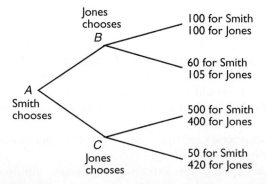

If Jones could make a credible commitment to choose the top branch no matter what, both would do better. Smith would choose the bottom branch at *A* and Jones would choose the top branch at *C*, giving Smith 500 and Jones 400.

10.4 The equilibrium of this game in the absence of a commitment to tip is that the waiter will give bad service because if he provides good service, he knows that the diner's best option will be not to tip, which leaves the waiter worse off than if he had provided good service. Since the diner gets an outcome of 20 if he can commit to leaving a tip (15 more than he would get in the absence of such a commitment), he would be willing to pay up to 15 for the right to commit.   **LO2, LO5, LO6**

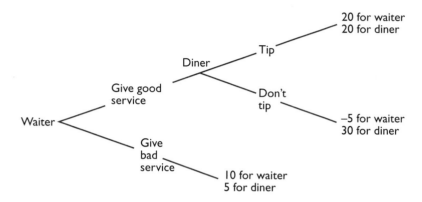

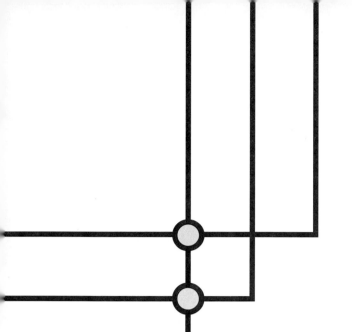

CHAPTER

11

Externalities and Property Rights

LEARNING OBJECTIVES

After reading this chapter, you should be able to:

1. Define negative and positive externalities, and analyze their effect on resource allocation.

2. Explain how the effects of externalities can be remedied.

3. Discuss why the optimal amount of an externality is not equal to zero.

4. Characterize the tragedy of the commons, and show how private ownership is a way of preventing it.

5. Define positional externalities and their effects, and show how they can be remedied.

 droll television ad for a British brand of pipe tobacco opens with a distinguished-looking gentleman sitting quietly on a park bench, smoking his pipe and reading a book of poetry. Before him lies a pond, unrippled except for a mother duck swimming peacefully with her ducklings. Suddenly a raucous group of teenage boys bursts onto the scene with a remote-controlled toy warship. Yelling and chortling, they launch their boat and maneuver it in aggressive pursuit of the terrified ducks.

Interrupted from his reverie, the gentleman looks up from his book and draws calmly on his pipe as he surveys the scene before him. He then reaches into his bag, pulls out a remote control of his own, and begins manipulating the joystick. The scene shifts underwater, where a miniature submarine rises from the depths of the pond. Once the boys' boat is in the sub's sights, the gentleman pushes a button on his remote control. Seconds later, the boat is blown to smithereens by a torpedo. The scene fades to a close-up of the tobacco company's label.

EXTERNAL COSTS AND BENEFITS

external cost (or negative externality) a cost of an activity that falls on people other than those who pursue the activity

external benefit (or positive externality) a benefit of an activity received by people other than those who pursue the activity

externality an external cost or benefit of an activity

External costs and benefits—externalities, for short—are activities that generate costs or benefits that accrue to people not directly involved in those activities. These effects are generally unintended. From the pipe smoker's point of view, the noise generated by the marauding boys was an external cost. Had others been disturbed by the boys' rowdiness, they may well have regarded the pipe smoker's retaliatory gesture as an external benefit.

This chapter focuses on how externalities affect the allocation of resources. Adam Smith's theory of the invisible hand applies to an ideal marketplace in which externalities do not exist. In such situations, Smith argued, the self-interested actions of individuals would lead to socially efficient outcomes. We will see that when the parties affected by externalities can easily negotiate with one another, the invisible hand will still produce an efficient outcome.

But in many cases, such as the scene depicted in the tobacco ad, negotiation is impractical. In those cases, the self-serving actions of individuals will not lead to efficient outcomes. The need to deal with externalities is one of the most important rationales for the existence of government along with a variety of other forms of collective action.

HOW EXTERNALITIES AFFECT RESOURCE ALLOCATION

The following examples illustrate the ways in which externalities distort the allocation of resources.

Does the honeybee keeper face the right incentives? (Part 1)

Phoebe earns her living as a keeper of honeybees. Her neighbors on all sides grow apples. Because bees pollinate apple trees as they forage for nectar, the more hives Phoebe keeps, the larger the harvests will be in the surrounding orchards. If Phoebe takes only her own costs and benefits into account in deciding how many hives to keep, will she keep the socially optimal number of hives?

Phoebe's hives constitute an external benefit, or a positive externality for the orchard owners. If she takes only her own personal costs and benefits into account, she will add hives only until the added revenue she gets from the last hive just equals the cost of adding it. But since the orchard owners also benefit from additional hives, the total benefit of adding another hive at that point will be greater than its cost. Phoebe, then, will keep too few hives. ◆

As we will discuss later in the chapter, problems like the one just discussed have several possible solutions. One is for orchard owners to pay beekeepers for keeping additional hives. But such solutions often require complex negotiations between the affected parties. For the moment, we assume that such negotiations are not practical.

Does the honeybee keeper face the right incentives? (Part 2)

As in the previous example, Phoebe earns her living as a keeper of honeybees. But now her neighbors are not apple growers but an elementary school and a nursing home. The more hives Phoebe keeps, the more students and nursing home residents will be stung by bees. If Phoebe takes only her own costs and benefits into account in deciding how many hives to keep, will she keep the socially optimal number of hives?

For the students and nursing home residents, Phoebe's hives constitute an external cost, or a negative externality. If she considers only her own costs and benefits in deciding how many hives to keep, she will continue to add hives until the added revenue from the last hive is just enough to cover its cost. But since Phoebe's neighbors also incur costs when she adds a hive, the benefit of the last hive at that point will be smaller than its cost. Phoebe, in other words, will keep too many hives. ◆

Every activity involves costs and benefits. When all the relevant costs and benefits of an activity accrue directly to the person who carries it out—that is, when the activity generates no externalities—the level of the activity that is best for the individual will be best for society as a whole. But when an activity generates externalities, be they positive or negative, individual self-interest does not produce the best allocation of resources. Individuals who consider only their own costs and benefits will tend to engage too much in activities that generate negative externalities and too little in activities that generate positive externalities. When an activity generates both positive and negative externalities, private and social interests will coincide only in the unlikely event that the opposing effects offset one another exactly.

HOW DO EXTERNALITIES AFFECT SUPPLY AND DEMAND?

The effects of externalities on resource allocation can be shown in a supply and demand diagram. Consider first the case of negative externalities. Figure 11.1(a) depicts the supply (Private *MC*) and demand curves for a product whose production involves no external costs or benefits. Imagine, say, that the energy that powers the factories in this market comes from nonpolluting hydroelectric generators. The resulting equilibrium price and quantity in the market for this product will then be socially optimal, for the reasons discussed in Chapters 3 and 7: The value to buyers of the last unit of the product consumed (as measured on the demand curve) will be exactly equal to the marginal cost of producing it (as measured on the supply curve), leaving no further possible gains from exchange.

But now suppose that a protracted drought has eliminated hydroelectric power generation, forcing factories to rely instead on electric power produced by coal-burning generators. Now each unit of output produced is accompanied by an external pollution cost of *XC*, as shown in Figure 11.1(b). Since the external pollution cost falls not on firm owners but on others who live downwind from their factories, Private *MC* is still the supply curve for this product, and its demand curve is again

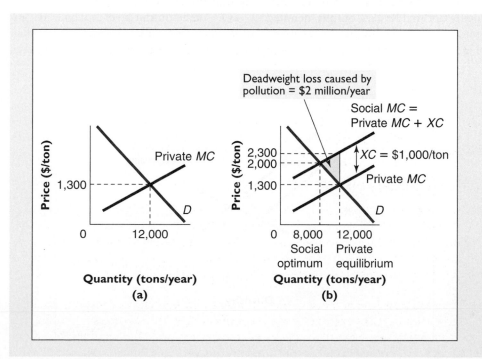

FIGURE 11.1
How External Costs Affect Resource Allocation.
(a) When a market has no external costs or benefits, the resulting equilibrium quantity and price are socially optimal. (b) By contrast, when production of a good is accompanied by an external cost, the market equilibrium price ($1,300 per ton) is too low and the market equilibrium quantity (12,000 tons per year) is too high. The deadweight loss from the negative externality is the area of the blue-shaded triangle, $2 million per year.

as before, so the equilibrium price and quantity will be exactly the same as in Figure 11.1(a). But this time the private market equilibrium is not socially optimal. As before, the market equilibrium level of output is 12,000 tons per year, the output level at which the demand curve (D) intersects Private MC. Note, however, that at that output level, the value to consumers of the last unit of output produced is only $1,300 per ton, while the true cost of producing that last unit (including the external cost) is $2,300 per ton.

This means that society could gain additional economic surplus by producing fewer units of the product. Indeed, the same conclusion will continue to hold whenever the current output exceeds 8,000 tons per year, the output level at which the demand curve intersects Social MC. Social MC, which includes all relevant marginal costs of producing the product, is constructed by adding the external pollution cost, XC, to every value along Private MC. The socially optimal level of output of the good occurs where Social MC intersects the demand curve. As shown in Figure 11.1(b), it is 8,000 tons per year. This is the level of output that exhausts all possibilities from exchange. At that quantity, the marginal benefit of the product, as measured by what buyers are willing to pay for it, is exactly equal to the marginal cost of producing it, which is the private marginal cost MC plus the marginal pollution cost XC. The market equilibrium quantity thus will be higher than the socially optimal quantity for a good whose production generates external costs.

By how much does the presence of pollution reduce total economic surplus from its maximum value, which occurs at an output level of 8,000 tons per year in Figure 11.1(b)? Note in the diagram that as output expands past 8,000, the marginal cost of each successive unit (as measured on the Social MC curve) is greater than the marginal benefit of that unit (as measured on the demand curve). Expanding output from 8,000 tons per year to the private equilibrium level, 12,000 tons per year, thus entails a cumulative reduction in total economic surplus equal to the area of the blue-shaded triangle in Figure 11.1(b), or $2 million per year. The deadweight loss from pollution is $2 million per year in this market.

What about a good whose production generates external benefits? In Figure 11.2, Private demand is the demand curve for a product whose production generates an external benefit of XB per unit. The market equilibrium quantity of this good, Q_{pvt}, is the output level at which Private demand intersects the supply curve of the product (MC). This time, market equilibrium quantity is smaller than the socially optimal level of output, denoted Q_{soc}. Q_{soc} is the output level at which MC intersects the socially optimal demand curve (the curve labeled Social demand in Figure 11.2), which is constructed by adding the external benefit, XB, to every

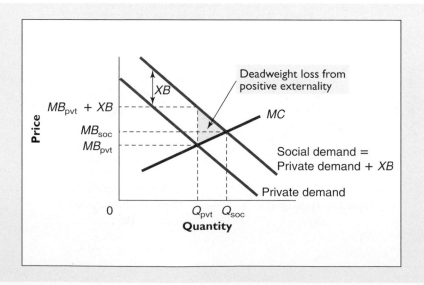

FIGURE 11.2
A Good Whose Production Generates a Positive Externality for Consumers.
For such goods, the market equilibrium quantity, Q_{pvt}, is smaller than the socially optimal quantity, Q_{soc}, because individual buyers are willing to pay only for the benefits they reap from directly consuming the product. The deadweight loss from the positive externality is the area of the blue-shaded triangle.

value along Private demand. Note that the private market equilibrium again fails to exhaust all possible gains from exchange. Thus, at Q_{pvt}, the marginal cost of producing an additional unit of output is only MB_{pvt}, which is smaller than the marginal benefit of an additional unit by the amount XB. The market equilibrium quantity thus will be lower than the socially optimal quantity for a good whose production generates external benefits.

In comparison with the maximum attainable total economic surplus in this market, how much does the total economic surplus associated with the private equilibrium fall short? In Figure 11.2, note that at Q_{pvt}, the marginal benefit of the product (as measured on the curve labeled Social demand) is XB units larger than its marginal cost (as measured on MC). Total economic surplus will continue to increase by successively smaller increments as output grows from Q_{pvt} to Q_{soc}, the socially optimal quantity. The total deadweight loss associated with the positive externality is thus the area of the blue-shaded triangle in Figure 11.2.

If the production of a product generates a positive externality, why do we say that this product causes a reduction in total economic surplus? To say that there is a deadweight loss in this market does not mean that the positive externality causes harm. Rather, it means that failure to take the positive externality into account makes the economic surplus associated with private equilibrium smaller than it could have been. Failure to reap an economic benefit is the same thing as sustaining an economic loss.

To summarize; whether externalities are positive or negative, they distort the allocation of resources in otherwise efficient markets. When externalities are present, the individual pursuit of self-interest will not result in the largest possible economic surplus. This outcome is thus inefficient by definition.

THE COASE THEOREM

To say that a situation is inefficient means that it can be rearranged in a way that would make at least some people better off without harming others. Such situations, we have seen, are a source of creative tension. The existence of inefficiency, after all, means that there is cash on the table, which usually triggers a race to see who can capture it. For example, we saw in Chapter 9 that because monopoly pricing results in an inefficiently low output level, the potential for gain gave monopolists an incentive to make discounts available to price-sensitive buyers. As the next examples illustrate, the inefficiencies that result from externalities create similar incentives for remedial action.

Equilibrium

Will Abercrombie dump toxins in the river? (Part I)

Abercrombie's factory produces a toxic waste by-product. If Abercrombie dumps it in the river, he causes damage to Fitch, a fisherman located downstream. The toxins are short-lived and cause no damage to anyone other than Fitch. At a cost, Abercrombie can filter out the toxins, in which case Fitch will suffer no damage at all. The relevant gains and losses for the two individuals are listed in Table 11.1.

TABLE 11.1
Costs and Benefits of Eliminating Toxic Waste (Part I)

	With filter	Without filter
Gains to Abercrombie	$100/day	$130/day
Gains to Fitch	$100/day	$50/day

If the law does not penalize Abercrombie for dumping toxins in the river, and if Abercrombie and Fitch cannot communicate with one another, will Abercrombie operate with or without a filter? Is that choice socially efficient?

Abercrombie has an incentive to operate without a filter since he earns $30 per day more than if he operates with a filter. But the outcome when he does so is socially inefficient. Thus, when Abercrombie operates without a filter, the total daily gain to both parties is only $130 + $50 = $180, compared to $100 + $100 = $200 if Abercrombie had operated with a filter. The daily cost of the filter to Abercrombie is only $130 − $100 = $30, which is smaller than its daily benefit to Fitch of $100 − $50 = $50. The fact that Abercrombie does not install the filter implies a squandered daily surplus of $20. ◆

Will Abercrombie dump toxins in the river? (Part 2)

Suppose the costs and benefits of using the filter are as in the previous example except that Abercrombie and Fitch can now communicate with one another at no cost. Even though the law does not require him to do so, will Abercrombie use a filter?

This time, Abercrombie will use a filter. Recall from the observation that when the economic pie grows larger, everyone can have a larger slice (the Efficiency Principle). Because use of a filter would result in the largest possible economic surplus, it would enable both Abercrombie and Fitch to have a larger net gain than before. Fitch thus has an incentive to *pay* Abercrombie to use a filter. Suppose, for instance, that Fitch offers Abercrombie $40 per day to compensate him for operating with a filter. Both Abercrombie and Fitch will then be exactly $10 per day better off than before, for a total daily net gain of $20. ◆

> **Efficiency**

EXERCISE 11.1

In the example above, what is the largest whole-dollar amount by which Fitch could compensate Abercrombie for operating with a filter and still be better off than before?

Ronald Coase, a professor at the University of Chicago Law School, was the first to see clearly that if people can negotiate with one another at no cost over the right to perform activities that cause externalities, they will always arrive at an efficient solution. This insight, which is often called the **Coase theorem**, is a profoundly important idea, for which Coase (rhymes with "dose") was awarded the 1991 Nobel Prize in Economics.

Why, you might ask, should Fitch pay Abercrombie to filter out toxins that would not be there in the first place if not for Abercrombie's factory? The rhetorical force of this question is undeniable. Yet Coase points out that externalities are reciprocal in nature. The toxins do harm Fitch, to be sure, but preventing Abercrombie from emitting them would penalize Abercrombie, by exactly $30 per day. Why should Fitch necessarily have the right to harm Abercrombie? Indeed, as the next example illustrates, even if Fitch had that right, he would exercise it only if filtering the toxins proved the most efficient outcome.

> **Coase theorem** if at no cost people can negotiate the purchase and sale of the right to perform activities that cause externalities, they can always arrive at efficient solutions to the problems caused by externalities

Will Abercrombie dump toxins in the river? (Part 3)

Suppose the law says that Abercrombie may *not* dump toxins in the river unless he has Fitch's permission. If the relevant costs and benefits of filtering the toxins are as shown in Table 11.2, and if Abercrombie and Fitch can negotiate with one another at no cost, will Abercrombie filter the toxins?

TABLE 11.2
Costs and Benefits of Eliminating Toxic Waste (Part 3)

	With filter	Without filter
Gains to Abercrombie	$100/day	$150/day
Gains to Fitch	$100/day	$70/day

Note that this time the most efficient outcome is for Abercrombie to operate without a filter, for the total daily surplus in that case will be $220 as compared to only $200 with a filter. Under the law, however, Fitch has the right to insist that Abercrombie use a filter. We might expect him to exercise that right since his own gain would rise from $70 to $100 per day if he did so. But because this outcome would be socially inefficient, we know that each party can do better.

Suppose, for example, that Abercrombie gives Fitch $40 per day in return for Fitch's permission to operate without a filter. Each would then have a net daily gain of $110, which is $10 better for each of them than if Fitch had insisted that Abercrombie use a filter. Abercrombie's pollution harms Fitch, sure enough. But failure to allow the pollution would have caused even greater harm to Abercrombie. ◆

The Coase theorem tells us that regardless of whether the law holds polluters liable for damages, the affected parties will achieve efficient solutions to externalities if they can negotiate costlessly with one another. Note carefully that this does not imply that affected parties will be indifferent about whether the law holds polluters responsible for damages. If polluters are liable, they will end up with lower incomes and those who are injured by pollutants will end up with higher incomes than if the law does not hold polluters liable—even though the same efficient production methods are adopted in each case. When polluters are held liable, they must remove the pollution at their own expense. When they are not held liable, those who are injured by pollution must pay polluters to cut back.

Externalities are hardly rare and isolated occurrences. On the contrary, finding examples of actions that are altogether free of them is difficult. And because externalities can distort the allocation of resources, it is important to recognize them and deal intelligently with them. Consider the following example of an externality that arises because of shared living arrangements.

Will Ann and Betty share an apartment?

Ann and Betty can live together in a two-bedroom apartment for $600 per month, or separately in 2 one-bedroom apartments, each for $400 per month. If the rent paid were the same for both alternatives, the two women would be indifferent between living together or separately, except for one problem: Ann talks constantly on the telephone. Ann would pay up to $250 per month for this privilege. Betty, for her part, would pay up to $150 per month to have better access to the phone. If the two cannot install a second phone line, should they live together or separately?

Ann and Betty should live together only if the benefit of doing so exceeds the cost. The benefit of living together is the reduction in their rent. Since 2 one-bedroom apartments would cost a total of $800 per month, compared to $600 for a two-bedroom unit, their benefit from living together is $200 per month. Their cost of living together is the least costly accommodation they can make to Ann's objectionable telephone habits. Since Ann would be willing to pay up to $250 per month to avoid changing her behavior, the $200 rent saving is too small to persuade her to change. But Betty is willing to put up with Ann's behavior for a compensation payment of only $150 per month. Since that amount is smaller than the total saving in rent, the least costly solution to the problem is for Betty to live with Ann and simply put up with her behavior.

Table 11.3 summarizes the relevant costs and benefits of this shared living arrangement. The Cost-Benefit Principle tells us that Ann and Betty should live together if and only if the benefit of living together exceeds the cost. The cost of the shared living arrangement is not the sum of all possible costs but the least costly accommodation to the problem (or problems) of shared living. Since the $200 per month saving in rent exceeds the least costly accommodation to the phone problem, Ann and Betty can reap a total gain in economic surplus of $50 per month by sharing their living quarters.

Cost-Benefit ◯

TABLE 11.3
The Gain in Surplus from Shared Living Arrangements

Benefits of Shared Living		
Total cost of separate apartments	**Total cost of shared apartment**	**Rent savings from sharing**
(2)($400/month) $800/month	$600/month	$200/month

Costs of Shared Living			
Problem	**Ann's cost of solving problem**	**Betty's cost of solving problem**	**Least costly solution to the problem**
Ann's phone usage	Curtailed phone usage: $250/month	Tolerate phone usage: $150/month	Betty tolerates Ann's phone usage: $150/month

Gain in Surplus from Shared Living		
Rent savings ($200/month) −	Least costly accommodation to shared living problems ($150/month) =	Gain in surplus: ($50/month)

Some people might conclude that Ann and Betty should not live together because if the two share the rent equally, Betty will end up paying $300 per month—which when added to the $150 cost of putting up with Ann's phone behavior comes to $50 more than the cost of living alone. As persuasive as that argument may sound, however, it is mistaken. The source of the error, as the following example illustrates, is the assumption that the two must share the rent equally.

What is the highest rent Betty would be willing to pay for the two-bedroom apartment?

In the previous example, Betty's alternative is to live alone, which would mean paying $400 per month, her reservation price for a living arrangement with no phone problem. Since the most she would be willing to pay to avoid the phone problem is $150 per month, the highest monthly rent she would be willing to pay for the shared apartment is $400 − $150 = $250. If she pays that amount, Ann will have to pay the difference, namely, $350 per month, which is clearly a better alternative for Ann than paying $400 to live alone. ◆

How much should Ann and Betty pay if they agree to split their economic surplus equally?

As we saw in Table 11.3, the total rent saving from the shared apartment is $200, and since the least costly solution to the phone problem is $150, the monthly gain in economic surplus is $50. We know from the previous example that Ann's reservation price for living together is $400 per month and Betty's is $250. So if the two women want to split the $50 monthly surplus equally, each should pay $25 less than her reservation price. Ann's monthly rent will thus be $375 and Betty's, $225. The result is that each is $25 per month better off than if she had lived alone. ◆

EXERCISE 11.2

As in the preceding examples, Ann and Betty can live together in a two-bedroom apartment for $600 per month or separately in 2 one-bedroom apartments, each for $400 per month. Ann would pay up to $250 per month rather than moderate her telephone habits, and Betty would pay up to $150 per month to achieve reasonable access to the telephone. Now, suppose Betty would also be willing to pay up to $60 per month to avoid the loss of privacy that comes with shared living space. Should the two women live together?

LEGAL REMEDIES FOR EXTERNALITIES

We have seen that efficient solutions to externalities can be found whenever the affected parties can negotiate with one another at no cost. But negotiation is not always practical. A motorist with a noisy muffler imposes costs on others, yet they cannot flag him down and offer him a compensation payment to fix his muffler. In recognition of this difficulty, most governments simply require that cars have working mufflers. Indeed, the explicit or implicit purpose of a large share—perhaps the lion's share—of laws is to solve problems caused by externalities. The goal of such laws is to help people achieve the solutions they might have reached had they been able to negotiate with one another.

When negotiation is costless, the task of adjustment generally falls on the party who can accomplish it at the lowest cost. For instance, in our examples, Betty put up with Ann's annoying phone habits because doing so was less costly than asking Ann to change her habits. Many municipal noise ordinances also place the burden of adjustment on those who can accomplish it at the lowest cost. Consider, for example, the restrictions on loud party music, which often take effect at a later hour on weekends than on weekdays. This pattern reflects both the fact that the gains from loud music tend to be larger on weekends and the fact that such music is more likely to disturb people on weekdays. By setting the noise curfew at different hours on different days of the week, the law places the burden on partygoers during the week and on sleepers during the weekend. Similar logic explains why noise ordinances allow motorists to honk their horns in most neighborhoods, but not in the immediate vicinity of a hospital.

The list of laws and regulations that may be fruitfully viewed as solutions to externalities is a long one. When a motorist drives his car at high speed, he endangers not just his own life and property, but also the lives and property of others. Speed limits, no-passing zones, right-of-way rules, and a host of other traffic laws may be seen as reasoned attempts to limit the harm one party inflicts on another. Many jurisdictions even have laws requiring that motorists install snow tires on their cars by the first of November. These laws promote not just safety, but also the smooth flow of traffic: if one motorist can't get up a snow-covered hill, he delays not only himself, but also the motorists behind him.

Similar reasoning helps us understand the logic of zoning laws that restrict the kinds of activities that take place in various parts of cities. Because many residents place a high value on living in an uncongested neighborhood, some cities have enacted zoning laws specifying minimum lot sizes. In places like Manhattan, where a shortage of land encourages developers to build very large and tall buildings, zoning laws limit both a building's height and the proportion of a lot it may occupy. Such restrictions recognize that the taller a building is, and the greater the proportion of its lot that it occupies, the more it blocks sunlight from reaching surrounding properties. The desire to control external costs also helps to explain why many cities establish separate zones for business and residential activity. Even within business districts, many cities limit certain kinds of commercial activity. For example, in an effort to revitalize the Times Square neighborhood, New York City enacted a zoning law banning adult bookstores and pornographic movie theaters from the area.

Limitations on the discharge of pollutants into the environment are perhaps the clearest examples of laws aimed at solving problems caused by externalities. The details of these laws reflect the principle of placing the burden of adjustment on those who can accomplish it at least costs. The discharge of toxic wastes into rivers, for example, tends to be most strictly regulated on those waterways whose commercial fishing or recreational uses are most highly valued. On other waterways, the burden of adjustment is likely to fall more heavily on fishermen, recreational boaters, and swimmers. Similarly, air-quality regulations tend to be strictest in the most heavily populated regions of the country, where the marginal benefit of pollution reduction is the greatest.

The following examples suggest additional ways in which Coase's insights about how societies deal with externalities provide rich fodder for the economic naturalist.

Example 11.1
THE ECONOMIC NATURALIST

Why does the U.S. Constitution protect the right of free speech?

What is the purpose of free speech laws?

The First Amendment's protection of free speech and the pattern of exceptions to that protection are another illustration of how legal remedies are used to solve the problems caused by externalities. The First Amendment acknowledges the decisive value of open communication, as well as the practical difficulty of identifying and regulating acts of speech that cause more harm than good. Yet there are some important exceptions. The Supreme Court has ruled, for instance, that the First Amendment does not allow someone to yell "fire" in a crowded theater if there is no fire, nor does it allow someone to advocate the violent overthrow of the government. In those instances, the external benefits of free speech are far too small to justify the external costs. ●

Example 11.2
THE ECONOMIC NATURALIST

Why does the government subsidize scientific research?

Why does government subsidize private property owners to plant trees on their hillsides?

Societies use laws not only to discourage activities that generate negative externalities, but also to encourage activities that generate positive externalities. The planting of trees on hillsides, for example, benefits not just the landowner, but also his neighbors by limiting the danger of flooding. In recognition of this fact, many jurisdictions subsidize the planting of trees. Similarly, Congress budgets millions of dollars each year in support of basic research—an implicit acknowledgment of the positive externalities associated with the generation of new knowledge. ●

THE OPTIMAL AMOUNT OF NEGATIVE EXTERNALITIES IS NOT ZERO

Curbing pollution and other negative externalities entails both costs and benefits. As we saw in Chapter 6, when we analyzed how many cans should be recycled, the best policy is to curtail pollution until the cost of further abatement just equals the marginal benefit. In general, the marginal cost of abatement rises with the amount of pollution eliminated. (Following the Low-Hanging-Fruit Principle, polluters use the cheapest cleanup methods first and then turn to more expensive ones.) And the law of diminishing marginal utility suggests that beyond some point, the marginal benefit of pollution reduction tends to fall as more pollution is removed. As a result, the marginal cost and marginal benefit curves almost always intersect at less than the maximum amount of pollution reduction.

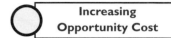

The intersection of the two curves marks the socially optimal level of pollution reduction. If pollution is curtailed by any less than that amount, society will gain more than it will lose by pushing the cleanup effort a little further. But if regulators push beyond the point at which the marginal cost and benefit curves intersect, society will incur costs that exceed the benefits. The existence of a socially optimal level of pollution reduction implies the existence of a socially optimal level of pollution, and that level will almost always be greater than zero.

We saw in Chapter 6 that because people have been conditioned to think of pollution as bad, many cringe when they hear the phrase "socially optimal level of pollution." How can any positive level of pollution be socially optimal? *But to speak of a socially optimal level of pollution is not the same as saying that pollution is good.* It is merely to recognize that society has an interest in cleaning up the environment, but only up to a certain point. The underlying idea is no different from the idea of an optimal level of dirt in an apartment. After all, even if you spent the whole day, every day, vacuuming your apartment, there would be *some* dirt left in it. And because you have better things to do than vacuum all day, you probably tolerate substantially more than the minimal amount of dirt. A dirty apartment is not good, nor is pollution in the air you breathe. But in both cases, the cleanup effort should be expanded only until the marginal benefit equals the marginal cost.

COMPENSATORY TAXES AND SUBSIDIES

As noted, when transaction costs prohibit negotiation among affected parties, negative externalities lead to excessive output levels because activities that produce negative externalities are misleadingly attractive to those who engage in them. One solution to this problem, proposed by the British economist A. C. Pigou, is to make such activities less attractive by taxing them. Figure 11.3(a) reproduces Figure 11.1's portrayal of a market in which each unit of output generates an external cost of XC equal to $1,000 per ton. Because producers fail to take this external cost into account, the private equilibrium is 12,000 tons per year, or 4,000 tons per year more than the socially optimal level of 8,000 tons per year.

Figure 11.3(b) portrays that same market after the imposition of a tax of $1,000 per unit of output. This tax has the effect of raising each producer's marginal cost curve by $1,000, so the industry supply curve shifts upward by $1,000 at every quantity. Note that the resulting private equilibrium output, 8,000 tons per year, is now exactly equal to the socially optimal output. Although many critics insist that taxes always reduce economic efficiency, here we have an example of a tax that actually makes the economy *more* efficient. The tax has that effect because it forces producers to take explicit account of the fact that each additional unit of output they produce imposes an external cost of $1,000 on the rest of society.

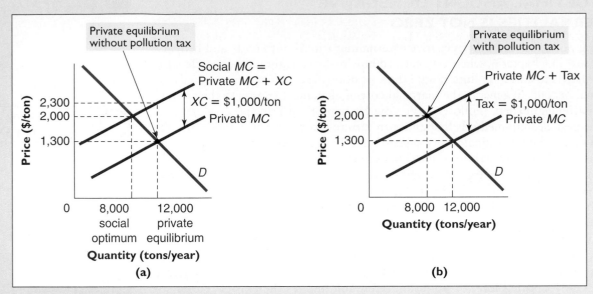

FIGURE 11.3
Taxing a Negative Externality.
(a) Negative externalities lead to an equilibrium with more than the socially optimal level of output. (b) Imposing a tax equal to the external cost leads to an equilibrium in which the output level is socially optimal. The tax makes the economy more efficient because it leads producers to take account of a relevant cost that they would otherwise ignore.

Similar reasoning suggests that a subsidy to producers can serve to counteract misallocations that result from positive externalities. Figure 11.4(a) portrays a market in which each unit of output generates an external benefit $XB = \$6$ per ton. In this market, the socially optimal output level occurs at the intersection of the supply curve (MC) and the Social demand curve, which is constructed by adding $XB = \$6$ per ton to the height of Private demand at each level of output. The

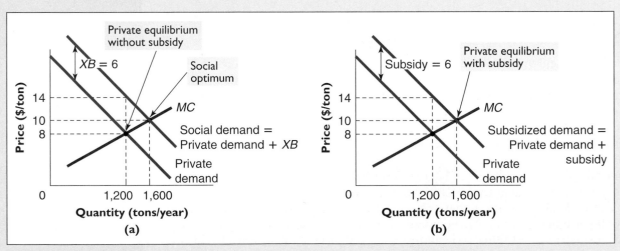

FIGURE 11.4
Subsidizing a Positive Externality.
(a) Positive externalities lead to an equilibrium with less than the socially optimal level of output. (b) Paying producers a subsidy equal to the external benefit of the activity leads to an equilibrium in which the output level is socially optimal. The subsidy makes the economy more efficient because it leads producers to take account of a relevant benefit that they would otherwise ignore.

socially optimal level of output is thus 1,600 tons per year. But private equilibrium in this market will occur at the intersection of Private demand and *MC,* which means that the equilibrium output, 1,200 tons per year, falls short of the social optimum by 400 tons per year.

Figure 11.4(b) shows the effect of paying a subsidy to producers of $6 per ton, the amount of the external benefit. In the presence of this subsidy, the new private equilibrium is 1,600 tons per year, exactly the socially optimal level. The subsidy makes the economy more efficient because it induces producers to take account of a relevant benefit that they otherwise would have ignored.

RECAP	EXTERNAL COSTS AND BENEFITS

Externalities occur when the costs or benefits of an activity accrue to people other than those directly involved in the activity. The Coase theorem says that when affected parties can negotiate with one another without cost, activities will be pursued at efficient levels, even in the presence of positive or negative externalities. But when negotiation is prohibitively costly, inefficient behavior generally results. Activities that generate negative externalities are pursued to excess, while those that generate positive externalities are pursued too little. Laws and regulations, including taxes and subsidies, are often adopted in an effort to alter inefficient behavior that results from externalities.

PROPERTY RIGHTS AND THE TRAGEDY OF THE COMMONS

People who grow up in industrialized nations tend to take the institution of private property for granted. Our intuitive sense is that people have the right to own any property they acquire by lawful means and to do with that property as they see fit. In reality, however, property laws are considerably more complex in terms of the rights they confer and the obligations they impose.

THE PROBLEM OF UNPRICED RESOURCES

To understand the laws that govern the use of property, let's begin by asking why societies created the institution of private property in the first place. The following examples, which show what happens to property that nobody owns, suggest an answer.

How many steers will villagers send onto the commons?

A village has five residents, each of whom has accumulated savings of $100. Each villager can use the money to buy a government bond that pays 13 percent interest per year or to buy a year-old steer, send it onto the commons to graze, and sell it after 1 year. The price the villager will get for the 2-year-old steer depends on the amount of weight it gains while grazing on the commons, which in turn depends on the number of steers sent onto the commons, as shown in Table 11.4.

The price of a 2-year-old steer declines with the number of steers grazing on the commons because the more steers, the less grass available to each. The villagers make their investment decisions one at a time, and the results are public. If each villager decides how to invest individually, how many steers will be sent onto the commons, and what will be the village's total income?

TABLE 11.4
The Relationship between Herd Size and Steer Price

Number of steers on the commons	Price per 2-year-old steer ($)	Income per steer ($/year)
1	126	26
2	119	19
3	116	16
4	113	13
5	111	11

If a villager buys a $100 government bond, he will earn $13 of interest income at the end of 1 year. Thus, he should send a steer onto the commons if and only if that steer will command a price of at least $113 as a 2-year-old. When each villager chooses in this self-interested way, we can expect four villagers to send a steer onto the commons. (Actually, the fourth villager would be indifferent between investing in a steer or buying a bond since he would earn $13 either way. For the sake of discussion, we'll assume that in the case of a tie, people choose to be cattlemen.) The fifth villager, seeing that he would earn only $11 by sending a fifth steer onto the commons, will choose instead to buy a government bond. As a result of these decisions, the total village income will be $65 per year—$13 for the one bondholder and 4($13) = $52 for the four cattlemen. ◆

Has Adam Smith's invisible hand produced the most efficient allocation of these villagers' resources? We can tell at a glance that it has not since their total village income is only $65—precisely the same as it would have been had the possibility of cattle raising not existed. The source of the difficulty will become evident in the following example.

What is the socially optimal number of steers to send onto the commons?

Suppose the five villagers in the previous example confront the same investment opportunities as before, except that this time they are free to make their decisions as a group rather than individually. How many steers will they send onto the commons, and what will be their total village income?

This time the villagers' goal is to maximize the income received by the group as a whole. When decisions are made from this perspective, the criterion is to send a steer onto the commons only if its marginal contribution to village income is at least $13, the amount that could be earned from a government bond. As the entries in the last column of Table 11.5 indicate, the first steer clearly meets this criterion since it contributes $26 to total village income. But the second steer does not. Sending that steer onto the commons raises the village's income from cattle raising from $26 to $38, a gain of just $12. The $100 required to buy the second steer would thus have been better invested in a government bond. Worse, the collective return from sending a third steer is only $10; from a fourth, only $4; and from a fifth, only $3.

In sum, when investment decisions are made with the goal of maximizing total village income, the best choice is to buy four government bonds and send only a single steer onto the commons. The resulting village income will be $78: $26 from sending the single steer and $52 from the four government bonds. That amount is $13 more than the total income that resulted when villagers made their investment

TABLE 11.5
Marginal Income and the Socially Optimal Herd Size

Number of steers on the commons	Price per 2-year-old steer ($)	Income per steer ($/year)	Total cattle income ($/year)	Marginal income ($/year)
1	126	26	26	26
2	119	19	38	12
3	116	16	48	10
4	113	13	52	4
5	111	11	55	3

decisions individually. Once again, the reward from moving from an inefficient allocation to an efficient one is that the economic pie grows larger. And when the pie grows larger, everyone can get a larger slice. For instance, if the villagers agree to pool their income and share it equally, each will get $15.60, or $2.60 more than before. ◆

EXERCISE 11.3

How would your answers to the grazing examples change if the interest rate was 11 percent per year rather than 13 percent?

Why do the villagers in these examples do better when they make their investment decisions collectively? The answer is that when individuals decide alone, they ignore the fact that sending another steer onto the commons will cause existing steers to gain less weight. Their failure to consider this effect makes the return from sending another steer seem misleadingly high to them.

The grazing land on the commons is a valuable economic resource. When no one owns it, no one has any incentive to take the opportunity cost of using it into account. And when that happens, people will tend to use it until its marginal benefit is zero. This problem, and others similar to it, are known as the **tragedy of the commons**. The essential cause of the tragedy of the commons is the fact that one person's use of commonly held property imposes an external cost on others by making the property less valuable. The tragedy of the commons also provides a vivid illustration of the Equilibrium Principle. Each individual villager behaves rationally by sending an additional steer onto the commons, yet the overall outcome falls far short of the attainable ideal.

tragedy of the commons the tendency for a resource that has no price to be used until its marginal benefit falls to zero

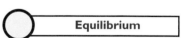

THE EFFECT OF PRIVATE OWNERSHIP

As the following examples illustrate, one solution to the tragedy of the commons is to place the village grazing land under private ownership.

How much will the right to control the village commons sell for?

Suppose the five villagers face the same investment opportunities as before, except that this time they decide to auction off the right to use the commons to the highest bidder. Assuming that villagers can borrow as well as lend at an annual interest rate of 13 percent, what price will the right to use the commons fetch? How will the owner of that property right use it, and what will be the resulting village income?

To answer these questions, simply ask yourself what you would do if you had complete control over how the grazing land were used. As we saw earlier, the most profitable way to use this land is to send only a single steer to graze on it. If you do so, you will earn a total of $26 per year. Since the opportunity cost of the $100 you spent on the single yearling steer is the $13 in interest you could have earned from a bond, your economic profit from sending a single steer onto the commons will be $13 per year, provided you can use the land for free. But you cannot; to finance your purchase of the property right, you must borrow money (since you used your $100 savings to buy a year-old steer).

What is the most you would be willing to pay for the right to use the commons? Since its use generates an income of $26 per year, or $13 more than the opportunity cost of your investment in the steer, the most you would pay is $100 (because that amount used to purchase a bond that pays 13 percent interest would also generate income of $13 per year). If the land were sold at auction, $100 is precisely the amount you would have to pay. Your annual earnings from the land would be exactly enough to pay the $13 interest on your loan and cover the opportunity cost of not having put your savings into a bond.

Note that when the right to use the land is auctioned to the highest bidder, the village achieves a more efficient allocation of its resources because the owner has a strong incentive to take the opportunity cost of more intensive grazing fully into account. Total village income in this case will again be $78. If the annual interest on the $100 proceeds from selling the land rights is shared equally among the five villagers, each will again have an annual investment income of $15.60. ◆

The logic of economic surplus maximization helps to explain why the most economically successful nations have all been ones with well-developed private property laws. Property that belongs to everyone belongs, in effect, to no one. Not only is its potential economic value never fully realized; it usually ends up being of no value at all.

Bear in mind, however, that in most countries the owners of private property are not free to do *precisely* as they wish with it. For example, local zoning laws may give the owner of a residential building lot the right to build a three-story house but not a six-story house. Here, too, the logic of economic surplus maximization applies, for a fully informed and rational legislature would define property rights so as to create the largest possible total economic surplus. In practice, of course, such ideal legislatures never really exist. Yet the essence of politics is the cutting of deals that make people better off. If a legislator could propose a change in the property laws that would enlarge the total economic surplus, she could also propose a scheme that would give each of her constituents a larger slice, thus enhancing her chances for reelection.

As an economic naturalist, challenge yourself to use this framework when thinking about the various restrictions you encounter in private property laws: zoning laws that constrain what you can build and what types of activities you can conduct on your land; traffic laws that constrain what you can do with your car; employment and environmental laws that constrain how you can operate your business. Your understanding of these and countless other laws will be enhanced by the insight that everyone can gain when the private property laws are defined so as to create the largest total economic surplus.

WHEN PRIVATE OWNERSHIP IS IMPRACTICAL

Do not be misled into thinking that the law provides an *ideal* resolution of all problems associated with externalities and the tragedy of the commons. Defining and enforcing efficient property rights entails costs, after all, and sometimes, as in the following examples, the costs outweigh the gains.

Why do blackberries in public parks get picked too soon?

Wild blackberries grow profusely at the edge of a wooded area in a crowded city park. The blackberries will taste best if left to ripen fully, but they still taste reasonably good if picked and eaten a few days early. Will the blackberries be left to ripen fully?

Obviously, the costs of defining and enforcing the property rights to blackberries growing in a public park are larger than the potential gains, so the blackberries will remain common property. That means that whoever picks them first gets them. Even though everyone would benefit if people waited until the berries were fully ripe, everyone knows that those who wait are likely to end up with no berries at all. And that means that the berries will be eaten too soon. ●

Example 11.3
THE ECONOMIC NATURALIST

Why does fruit that grows in public places get picked too soon?

Why are shared milkshakes consumed too quickly?

Sara and Susan are identical twins who have been given a chocolate milkshake to share. If each has a straw and each knows that the other is self-interested, will the twins consume the milkshake at an optimal rate?

Because drinking a milkshake too quickly chills the taste buds, the twins will enjoy their shake more if they drink it slowly. Yet each knows that the other will drink any part of the milkshake she doesn't finish herself. The result is that each will consume the shake at a faster rate than she would if she had half a shake all to herself. ●

Example 11.4
THE ECONOMIC NATURALIST

Why are shared milkshakes drunk too quickly?

Here are some further examples in which the tragedy of the commons is not easily solved by defining private ownership rights.

Harvesting timber on remote public land On remote public lands, enforcing restrictions against cutting down trees may be impractical. Each tree cutter knows that a tree that is not harvested this year will be bigger, and hence more valuable, next year. But he also knows that if he doesn't cut the tree down this year, someone else might do so. In contrast, private companies that grow trees on their own land have no incentive to harvest timber prematurely and a strong incentive to prevent outsiders from doing so.

Harvesting whales in international waters Each individual whaler knows that harvesting an extra whale reduces the breeding population, and hence the size of the future whale population. But the whaler also knows that any whale that is not harvested today may be taken by some other whaler. The solution would be to define and enforce property rights to whales. But the oceans are vast, and the behavior of whalers is hard to monitor. And even if their behavior could be monitored, the concept of national sovereignty would make the international enforcement of property rights problematic.

More generally, the animal species that are most severely threatened with extinction tend to be those that are economically valuable to humans but that are not privately owned by anyone. This is the situation confronting whales as well as elephants. Contrast this with the situation confronting chickens, which are also economically valuable to humans but which, unlike whales, are governed by traditional laws of private property. This difference explains why no one worries that Colonel Sanders might threaten the extinction of chickens.

Controlling multinational environmental pollution Each individual polluter may know that if he and all others pollute, the damage to the environment will be greater than the cost of not polluting. But if the environment is common property into which all are free to dump, each has a powerful incentive to pollute. Enforcing laws and regulations that limit the discharge of pollution may be practical if all polluters live under the jurisdiction of a single government. But if polluters come from many different countries, solutions are much more difficult to implement. Thus, the Mediterranean Sea has long suffered serious pollution since none of the many nations that border it has an economic incentive to consider the effects of its discharges on other countries.

As the world's population continues to grow, the absence of an effective system of international property rights will become an economic problem of increasing significance.

RECAP	**PROPERTY RIGHTS AND THE TRAGEDY OF THE COMMONS**

When a valuable resource has a price of zero, people will continue to exploit it as long as its marginal benefit remains positive. The tragedy of the commons describes situations in which valuable resources are squandered because users are not charged for them. In many cases, an efficient remedy is to define and enforce rights to the use of valuable property. But this solution is difficult to implement for resources such as the oceans and the atmosphere because no single government has the authority to enforce property rights for these resources.

POSITIONAL EXTERNALITIES

Former tennis champion Steffi Graf received more than $1.6 million in tournament winnings in 1992; her endorsement and exhibition earnings totaled several times that amount. By any reasonable measure, the quality of her play was outstanding, yet she consistently lost to archrival Monica Seles. But in April of 1993, Seles was stabbed in the back by a deranged fan and forced to withdraw from the tour. In the ensuing months, Graf's tournament winnings accumulated at almost double her 1992 pace, despite little change in the quality of her play.

PAYOFFS THAT DEPEND ON RELATIVE PERFORMANCE

In professional tennis and a host of other competitive situations, the rewards people receive typically depend not only on how they perform in absolute terms but also on how they perform relative to their closest rivals. In these situations, competitors have an incentive to take actions that will increase their odds of winning. For example, tennis players can increase their chances of winning by hiring personal fitness trainers and sports psychologists to travel with them on the tour. Yet the simple mathematics of competition tells us that the sum of all individual payoffs from such investments will be larger than the collective payoff. In any tennis match, for example, each contestant will get a sizable payoff from money spent on fitness trainers and sports psychologists, yet each match will have exactly one winner and one loser, no matter how much players spend. The overall gain to tennis spectators is likely to be small, and the overall gain to players as a group must be zero. To the extent that each contestant's payoff depends on his or her relative performance, then, the incentive to undertake such investments will be excessive, from a collective point of view.

Consider the following example.

Why do football players take anabolic steroids?

The offensive linemen of many National Football League teams currently average more than 330 pounds. In the 1970s, by contrast, offensive linemen in the league averaged barely 280 pounds, and the all-decade linemen of the 1940s averaged only 229 pounds. One reason that today's players are so much heavier is that players' salaries have escalated sharply over the last two decades, which has intensified competition for the positions. Size and strength are the two cardinal virtues of an offensive lineman, and other things being equal, the job will go to the larger and stronger of two rivals.

Size and strength, in turn, can be enhanced by the consumption of anabolic steroids. But if all players consume these substances, the rank ordering of players by size and strength—and hence the question of who lands the jobs—will be largely unaffected. And since the consumption of anabolic steroids entails potentially serious long-term health consequences, as a group football players are clearly worse off if they consume these drugs. So why do football players take steroids?

The problem here is that contestants for starting berths on the offensive line confront a prisoner's dilemma, like the ones analyzed in the preceding chapter. Consider two closely matched rivals—Smith and Jones—who are competing for a single position. If neither takes steroids, each has a 50 percent chance of winning the job and a starting salary of $1 million per year. If both take steroids, each again has a 50 percent chance of winning the job. But if one takes steroids and the other doesn't, the first is sure to win the job. The loser ends up selling insurance for $60,000 per year. Neither likes the fact that the drugs may have adverse health consequences, but each would be willing to take that risk in return for a shot at the big salary. Given these choices, the two competitors face a payoff matrix like the one shown in Table 11.6.

Example 11.5
THE ECONOMIC NATURALIST

Why do so many football players take steroids?

EN 11

TABLE 11.6
Payoff Matrix for Steroid Consumption

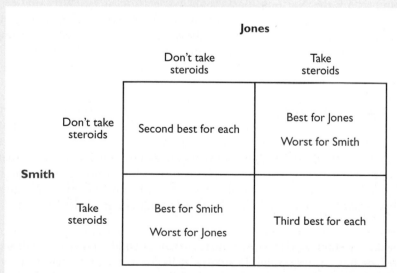

		Jones	
		Don't take steroids	Take steroids
Smith	Don't take steroids	Second best for each	Best for Jones Worst for Smith
	Take steroids	Best for Smith Worst for Jones	Third best for each

---

Clearly, the dominant strategy for both Smith and Jones is to take steroids. Yet when they do, each gets only the third-best outcome, whereas they could have gotten the second-best outcome by not taking the drugs—hence the attraction of rules that forbid the consumption of anabolic steroids. ●

POSITIONAL ARMS RACES AND POSITIONAL ARMS CONTROL AGREEMENTS

positional externality occurs when an increase in one person's performance reduces the expected reward of another in situations in which reward depends on relative performance

The steroid problem is an example of a **positional externality.** Whenever the payoffs to one contestant depend at least in part on how he or she performs relative to a rival, any step that improves one side's relative position must necessarily worsen the other's. The shouting-at-parties example discussed in Chapter 10 is another instance of a positional externality. Just as the invisible hand of the market is weakened by the presence of standard externalities, it is also weakened by positional externalities.

We have seen that positional externalities often lead contestants to engage in an escalating series of mutually offsetting investments in performance enhancement. We call such spending patterns **positional arms races.**

positional arms race a series of mutually offsetting investments in performance enhancement that is stimulated by a positional externality

Because positional arms races produce inefficient outcomes, people have an incentive to curtail them. Steps taken to reduce positional arms races such as blue laws and rules against anabolic steroids may therefore be thought of as **positional arms control agreements.**

positional arms control agreement an agreement in which contestants attempt to limit mutually offsetting investments in performance enhancement

Once you become aware of positional arms races, you will begin to see them almost everywhere. You can hone your skills as an economic naturalist by asking these questions about every competitive situation you observe: What form do the investments in performance enhancement take? What steps have contestants taken to limit these investments? Sometimes positional arms control agreements are achieved by the imposition of formal rules or by the signing of legal contracts. Some examples of this type of agreement follow.

Campaign spending limits In the United States, presidential candidates routinely spend more than $100 million on advertising. Yet if both candidates double their spending on ads, each one's odds of winning will remain essentially the same. Recognition of this pattern led Congress to adopt strict spending limits for presidential candidates. (That those regulations have proved difficult to enforce does not call into question the logic behind the legislation.)

Roster limits Major League Baseball permits franchises to have only 25 players on the roster during the regular season. The National Football League sets its roster limit at 53; the National Basketball Association at 12. Why these limits? In their absence, any team could increase its chance of winning by simply adding players. Inevitably, other teams would follow suit. On the plausible assumption that, beyond some point, larger rosters do not add much to the entertainment value for fans, roster limits are a sensible way to deliver sports entertainment at a more reasonable cost.

Arbitration agreements In the business world, contracting parties often sign a binding agreement that commits them to arbitration in the event of a dispute. By doing so, they sacrifice the option of pursuing their interests as fully as they might wish to later, but they also insulate themselves from costly legal battles. Other parties in the legal system may sometimes take steps to limit spending on litigation. For example, a federal judge in South Dakota announced—presumably to the approval of litigants—that he would read only the first 15 pages of any brief submitted to his court.

Mandatory starting dates for kindergarten A child who is a year or so older than most of her kindergarten classmates is likely to perform better, in relative terms, than if she had entered school with children her own age. And since most parents are aware that admission to prestigious universities and eligibility for top jobs upon graduation depend largely on *relative* academic performance, many are tempted to keep their children out of kindergarten a year longer than necessary. Yet there is no social advantage in holding *all* children back an extra year since their relative performance would essentially be unaffected. In most jurisdictions, therefore, the law requires children who reach their fifth birthday before December 1 of a given year to start kindergarten the same year.

SOCIAL NORMS AS POSITIONAL ARMS CONTROL AGREEMENTS

In some cases, social norms may take the place of formal agreements to curtail positional arms races. Some familiar examples follow.

Is being on fashion's cutting edge more valuable now than in the 1950s?

Nerd norms Some students care more—in the short run, at least—about the grades they get than how much they actually learn. When such students are graded on the curve—that is, on the basis of their performance relative to other students— a positional arms race ensues because if all students were to double the amount of time they studied, the distribution of grades would remain essentially the same. Students who find themselves in this situation are often quick to embrace "nerd norms," which brand as social misfits those who "study too hard."

Fashion norms Social norms regarding dress and fashion often change quickly because of positional competitions. Consider, for instance, the person who wishes to be on the cutting edge of fashion. In some American social circles during the 1950s, that goal could be accomplished by having pierced ears. But as more and more people adopted the practice, it ceased to communicate avant-garde status. At the same time, those who wanted to make a conservative fashion statement gradually became freer to have their ears pierced.

For a period during the 1960s and 1970s, one could be on fashion's cutting edge by wearing two earrings in one earlobe. But by the 1990s multiple ear piercings had lost much of their social significance, the threshold of cutting-edge status having been raised to upward of a dozen piercings of each ear, or a smaller number of piercings of the nose, eyebrows, or other body parts. A similar escalation has taken place in the number, size, and placement of tattoos.

The increase in the required number of tattoos or body piercings has not changed the value of avant-garde fashion status to those who desire it. Being on the outer limits of fashion has much the same meaning now as it once did. To the extent that there are costs associated with body piercings, tattoos, and other steps required to achieve avant-garde status, the current fashions are wasteful compared to earlier ones. In this sense, the erosion of social norms against tattoos and body piercings has produced a social loss. Of course, the costs associated with this loss are small in most cases. Yet since each body piercing entails a small risk of infection, the costs will continue to rise with the number of piercings. And once those costs reach a certain threshold, support may mobilize on behalf of social norms that discourage body mutilation.

Norms of taste Similar cycles occur with respect to behaviors considered to be in bad taste. In the 1950s, for example, prevailing norms prevented major national magazines from accepting ads that featured nude photographs. Naturally, advertisers had a powerful incentive to chip away at such norms in an effort to capture the reader's limited attention. And indeed, taboos against nude photographs have eroded in the same way as taboos against body mutilation.

Consider, for instance, the evolution of perfume ads. First came the nude silhouette; then, increasingly well-lighted and detailed nude photographs; and more recently, photographs of what appear to be group sex acts. Each innovation achieved just the desired effect: capturing the reader's instant and rapt attention. Inevitably, however, other advertisers followed suit, causing a shift in our sense of what is considered attention-grabbing. Photographs that once would have shocked readers now often draw little more than a bored glance.

Opinions differ, of course, about whether this change is an improvement. Many believe that the earlier, stricter norms were ill-advised, the legacy of a more prudish and repressive era. Yet even people who take that view are likely to believe that *some* kinds of photographic material ought not to be used in magazine advertisements. Obviously, what is acceptable will differ from person to person, and each person's threshold of discomfort will depend in part on current standards. But as advertisers continue to break new ground in their struggle to capture attention, the point may come when people begin to mobilize in favor of stricter standards of

"We're looking for the kind of bad taste that will grab—but not appall."

"public decency." Such a campaign would provide yet another case of a positional arms control agreement.

Norms against vanity   Cosmetic and reconstructive surgery has produced dramatic benefits for many people, enabling badly disfigured accident victims to recover a normal appearance. It also has eliminated the extreme self-consciousness felt by people born with strikingly unusual features. Such surgery, however, is by no means confined to the conspicuously disfigured. Increasingly, "normal" people are seeking surgical improvements to their appearance. Some 2 million cosmetic "procedures" were done in 1991—six times the number just a decade earlier[1]—and demand has continued to grow steadily in the years since. Once a carefully guarded secret, these procedures are now offered as prizes in southern California charity raffles.

In individual cases, cosmetic surgery may be just as beneficial as reconstructive surgery is for accident victims. Buoyed by the confidence of having a straight nose or a wrinkle-free complexion, patients sometimes go on to achieve much more than they ever thought possible. But the growing use of cosmetic surgery also has had an unintended side effect: It has altered the standards of normal appearance. A nose that once would have seemed only slightly larger than average may now seem jarringly big. The same person who once would have looked like an average 55-year-old may now look nearly 70. And someone who once would have tolerated slightly thinning hair or an average amount of cellulite may now feel compelled to undergo hair transplantation or liposuction. Because such procedures shift people's frame of

[1]*The Economist,* January 11, 1992, p. 25.

reference, their payoffs to individuals are misleadingly large. From a social perspective, therefore, reliance on them is likely to be excessive.

Legal sanctions against cosmetic surgery are difficult to imagine. But some communities have embraced powerful social norms against cosmetic surgery, heaping scorn and ridicule on the consumers of face-lifts and tummy tucks. In individual cases, such norms may seem cruel. Yet without them, many more people might feel compelled to bear the risk and expense of cosmetic surgery.

RECAP	POSITIONAL EXTERNALITIES

Positional externalities occur when an increase in one person's performance reduces the expected reward of another person in situations in which reward depends on relative performance. Positional arms races are a series of mutually offsetting investments in performance enhancement that are stimulated by a positional externality. Positional arms control agreements are sometimes enacted in an attempt to limit positional arms races. In some cases, social norms can act as positional arms control agreements.

■ SUMMARY ■

- Externalities are the costs and benefits of activities that accrue to people who are not directly involved in those activities. When all parties affected by externalities can negotiate with one another at no cost, the invisible hand of the market will produce an efficient allocation of resources. According to the Coase theorem, the allocation of resources is efficient in such cases because the parties affected by externalities can compensate others for taking remedial action. **LO1, LO2**

- Negotiation over externalities is often impractical, however. In these cases, the self-serving actions of individuals typically will not lead to an efficient outcome. The attempt to forge solutions to the problems caused by externalities is one of the most important rationales for collective action. Sometimes collective action takes the form of laws and government regulations that alter the incentives facing those who generate, or are affected by, externalities. Such remedies work best when they place the burden of accommodation on the parties who can accomplish it at the lowest cost. Traffic laws, zoning laws, environmental protection laws, and free speech laws are examples. **LO2**

- Curbing pollution and other negative externalities entails costs as well as benefits. The optimal amount of pollution reduction is the amount for which the marginal benefit of further reduction just equals the marginal cost. In general, this formula implies that the socially optimal level of pollution, or of any other negative externality, is greater than zero. **LO3**

- When grazing land and other valuable resources are owned in common, no one has an incentive to take into account the opportunity cost of using those resources. This problem is known as the tragedy of the commons. Defining and enforcing private rights governing the use of valuable resources is often an effective solution to the tragedy of the commons. Not surprisingly, most economically successful nations have well-developed institutions of private property. Property that belongs to everyone belongs, in effect, to no one. Not only is its potential economic value never fully realized; it usually ends up having no value at all. **LO4**

- The difficulty of enforcing property rights in certain situations explains a variety of inefficient outcomes such as the excessive harvest of whales in international waters and the premature harvest of timber on remote public lands. The excessive pollution of seas that are bordered by many countries also results from a lack of enforceable property rights. **LO4**

- Situations in which people's rewards depend on how well they perform in relation to their rivals give rise to positional externalities. In these situations, any step that improves one side's relative position necessarily worsens the other's. Positional externalities tend to spawn positional arms races—escalating patterns of mutually offsetting investments in performance enhancement. Collective measures to curb positional arms races are known as positional arms control agreements. These collective actions may take the form of formal regulations or rules such as rules against anabolic steroids in sports, campaign spending limits, and binding arbitration agreements.

Informal social norms can also curtail positional arms races. **LO5**

▪ KEY TERMS ▪

Coase theorem (302)
external benefit (298)
external cost (298)
externality (298)

negative externality (298)
positional arms control
 agreement (316)
positional arms race (316)

positional externality (316)
positive externality (298)
tragedy of the commons (311)

▪ REVIEW QUESTIONS ▪

1. What incentive problem explains why the freeways in cities like Los Angeles suffer from excessive congestion? **LO1**

2. How would you explain to a friend why the optimal amount of freeway congestion is not zero? **LO3**

3. If Congress could declare any activity that imposes external costs on others illegal, would such legislation be advisable? **LO2**

4. Why does the Great Salt Lake, which is located wholly within the state of Utah, suffer lower levels of pollution than Lake Erie, which is bordered by several states and Canada? **LO4**

5. Explain why the wearing of high-heeled shoes might be viewed as the result of a positional externality. **LO5**

▪ PROBLEMS ▪

1. Determine whether the following statements are true or false, and briefly explain why: **LO2**
   a. A given total emission reduction in a polluting industry will be achieved at the lowest possible total cost when the cost of the last unit of pollution curbed is equal for each firm in the industry.
   b. In an attempt to lower their costs of production, firms sometimes succeed merely in shifting costs to outsiders.

2. Phoebe keeps a bee farm next door to an apple orchard. She chooses her optimal number of beehives by selecting the honey output level at which her private marginal benefit from beekeeping equals her private marginal cost. **LO1, LO2**
   a. Assume that Phoebe's private marginal benefit and marginal cost curves from beekeeping are normally shaped. Draw a diagram of them.
   b. Phoebe's bees help to pollinate the blossoms in the apple orchard, increasing the fruit yield. Show the social marginal benefit from Phoebe's beekeeping in your diagram.
   c. Phoebe's bees are Africanized killer bees that aggressively sting anyone who steps into their flight path. Phoebe, fortunately, is naturally immune to the bees' venom. Show the social marginal cost curve from Phoebe's beekeeping in your diagram.
   d. Indicate the socially optimal quantity of beehives on your diagram. Is it higher or lower than the privately optimal quantity? Explain.

3. Suppose the supply curve of boom box rentals in Golden Gate Park is given by $P = 5 + 0.1Q$, where P is the daily rent per unit in dollars and Q is the volume of units rented in hundreds per day. The demand curve for boom boxes is $20 - 0.2Q$. If each boom box imposes $3 per day in noise costs on others, by

how much will the equilibrium number of boom boxes rented exceed the socially optimal number?   **LO1**

4. Refer to problem 3. How would the imposition of a tax of $3 per unit on each daily boom box rental affect efficiency in this market?   **LO2**

5. Suppose the law says that Jones may *not* emit smoke from his factory unless he gets permission from Smith, who lives downwind. If the relevant costs and benefits of filtering the smoke from Jones's production process are as shown in the following table, and if Jones and Smith can negotiate with one another at no cost, will Jones emit smoke?   **LO2**

	Jones emits smoke	Jones does not emit smoke
Surplus for Jones	$200	$160
Surplus for Smith	$400	$420

6. John and Karl can live together in a two-bedroom apartment for $500 per month, or each can rent a single-bedroom apartment for $350 per month. Aside from the rent, the two would be indifferent between living together and living separately, except for one problem: John leaves dirty dishes in the sink every night. Karl would be willing to pay up to $175 per month to avoid John's dirty dishes. John, for his part, would be willing to pay up to $225 to be able to continue his sloppiness. Should John and Karl live together? If they do, will there be dirty dishes in the sink? Explain.   **LO2, LO3**

7. How, if at all, would your answer to problem 6 differ if John would be willing to pay up to $30 per month to avoid giving up his privacy by sharing quarters with Karl?   **LO2, LO3**

8. Barton and Statler are neighbors in an apartment complex in downtown Manhattan. Barton is a concert pianist, and Statler is a poet working on an epic poem. Barton rehearses his concert pieces on the baby grand piano in his front room, which is directly above Statler's study. The following matrix shows the monthly payoffs to Barton and Statler when Barton's front room is and is not soundproofed. The soundproofing will be effective only if it is installed in Barton's apartment.   **LO2, LO3**

	Soundproofed	Not soundproofed
Gains to Barton	$100/month	$150/month
Gains to Statler	$120/month	$80/month

a. If Barton has the legal right to make any amount of noise he wants and he and Statler can negotiate with one another at no cost, will Barton install and maintain soundproofing? Explain. Is his choice socially efficient?
b. If Statler has the legal right to peace and quiet and can negotiate with Barton at no cost, will Barton install and maintain soundproofing? Explain. Is his choice socially efficient?
c. Does the attainment of an efficient outcome depend on whether Barton has the legal right to make noise, or Statler the legal right to peace and quiet?

9. Refer to problem 8. Barton decides to buy a full-sized grand piano. The new payoff matrix is as follows: **LO2, LO3**

	Soundproofed	**Not soundproofed**
Gains to Barton	$100/month	$150/month
Gains to Statler	$120/month	$60/month

a. If Statler has the legal right to peace and quiet and Barton and Statler can negotiate at no cost, will Barton install and maintain soundproofing? Explain. Is this outcome socially efficient?

b. Suppose that Barton has the legal right to make as much noise as he likes and that negotiating an agreement with Barton costs $15 per month. Will Barton install and maintain soundproofing? Explain. Is this outcome socially efficient?

c. Suppose Statler has the legal right to peace and quiet, and it costs $15 per month for Statler and Barton to negotiate any agreement. (Compensation for noise damage can be paid without incurring negotiation cost.) Will Barton install and maintain soundproofing? Is this outcome socially efficient?

d. Why does the attainment of a socially efficient outcome now depend on whether Barton has the legal right to make noise?

10.* A village has six residents, each of whom has accumulated savings of $100. Each villager can use this money either to buy a government bond that pays 15 percent interest per year or to buy a year-old llama, send it onto the commons to graze, and sell it after 1 year. The price the villager gets for the 2-year-old llama depends on the quality of the fleece it grows while grazing on the commons. That in turn depends on the animal's access to grazing, which depends on the number of llamas sent to the commons, as shown in the following table:

Number of llamas on the commons	Price per 2-year-old llama ($)
1	122
2	118
3	116
4	114
5	112
6	109

The villagers make their investment decisions one after another, and their decisions are public. **LO4**

a. If each villager decides individually how to invest, how many llamas will be sent onto the commons, and what will be the resulting net village income?

b. What is the socially optimal number of llamas for this village? Why is that different from the actual number? What would net village income be if the socially optimal number of llamas were sent onto the commons?

c. The village committee votes to auction the right to graze llamas on the commons to the highest bidder. Assuming villagers can both borrow and lend at 15 percent annual interest, how much will the right sell for at auction? How will the new owner use the right, and what will be the resulting village income?

*Problems marked with an asterisk (*) are more difficult.

■ ANSWERS TO IN-CHAPTER EXERCISES ■

11.1 Since Fitch gains $50 per day when Abercrombie operates with a filter, he could pay Abercrombie as much as $49 per day and still come out ahead. **LO2**

11.2 If the two were to live together, the most efficient way to resolve the telephone problem would be as before, for Betty to give up reasonable access to the phone. But on top of that cost, which is $150, Betty would also bear a $60 cost from the loss of her privacy. The total cost of their living together would thus be $210 per month. Since that amount is greater than the $200 saving in rent, the two should live separately. **LO2**

11.3 The income figures from the different levels of investment in cattle would remain as before, as shown in the table. What is different is the opportunity cost of investing in each steer, which is now $11 per year instead of $13. The last column of the table shows that the socially optimal number of steers is now 2 instead of 1. And if individuals still favor holding cattle, all other things being equal, they will now send 5 steers onto the commons instead of 4, as shown in the middle column. **LO4**

Number of steers on the commons	Price per 2-year-old steer ($)	Income per steer ($/year)	Total village income ($/year)	Marginal income ($/year)
				26
1	126	26	26	
				12
2	119	19	38	
				10
3	116	16	48	
				4
4	113	13	52	
				3
5	111	11	55	

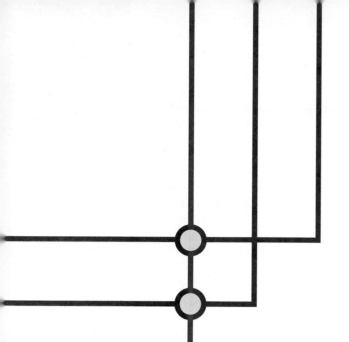

The Economics
of Information

LEARNING OBJECTIVES

After reading this chapter, you should be able to:

1. Explain how middlemen add value to market transactions.

2. Use the concept of rational search to find the optimal amount of information market participants should obtain.

3. Define asymmetric information and describe how it leads to the lemons problem.

4. Discuss how advertising, conspicuous consumption, statistical discrimination, and other devices are responses to asymmetric information problems.

Years ago, a naive young economist spent a week in Kashmir on a houseboat on scenic Dal Lake, outside the capital city of Srinagar. Kashmir is renowned for its woodcarvings, and one afternoon a man in a gondola stopped by to show the economist some of his wooden bowls. When the economist expressed interest in one of them, the woodcarver quoted a price of 200 rupees. The economist had lived in that part of Asia long enough to realize that the price was more than the woodcarver expected to get, so he made a counteroffer of 100 rupees.

The woodcarver appeared to take offense, saying that he couldn't possibly part with the bowl for less than 175 rupees. Suspecting that the woodcarver was merely feigning anger, the young economist held firm. The woodcarver appeared to become even angrier, but quickly retreated to 150 rupees. The economist politely restated his unwillingness to pay more than 100 rupees. The woodcarver then tried 125 rupees, and again the economist replied that 100 was his final offer. Finally, they struck a deal at 100 rupees, and with cash in hand, the woodcarver left in a huff.

Pleased with his purchase, the economist showed it to the houseboat's owner later that evening. "It's a lovely bowl," he agreed, and asked how much the economist had paid for it. The economist told him, expecting praise for his negotiating prowess. The host's failed attempt at suppressing a laugh was the economist's first clue that he had paid too much. When asked how much such a bowl would normally sell for, the houseboat owner was reluctant to respond. But the economist pressed him, and the host speculated that the seller had probably hoped for 30 rupees at most.

Adam Smith's invisible hand theory presumes that buyers are fully informed about the myriad ways in which they might spend their money—what goods and services are available, what prices they sell for, how long they last, how frequently they break down, and so on. But, of course, no one is ever really *fully* informed about anything. And sometimes, as in the transaction with the woodcarver, people are completely ignorant of even the most basic information. Still, life goes on, and most people muddle through somehow.

Consumers employ a variety of strategies for gathering information, some of which are better than others. They read *Consumer Reports*, talk to family and friends, visit stores, kick the tires on used cars, and so on. But one of the most important aspects of choosing intelligently without having complete information is having at least some idea of the extent of one's ignorance. Someone once said that there are two kinds of consumers in the world: those who don't know what they're doing and those who don't know that they don't know what they're doing. As in the case of the wooden bowl, the people in the second category are the ones who are most likely to choose foolishly.

Basic economic principles can help you to identify those situations in which additional information is most likely to prove helpful. In this chapter, we will explore what those principles tell us about how much information to acquire and how to make the best use of limited information.

HOW THE MIDDLEMAN ADDS VALUE

One of the most common problems consumers confront is the need to choose among different versions of a product whose many complex features they do not fully understand. As the following example illustrates, in such cases consumers can sometimes rely on the knowledge of others.

How should a consumer decide which pair of skis to buy?

You need a new pair of skis, but the technology has changed considerably since you bought your last pair and you don't know which of the current brands and models would be best for you. Skis R Us has the largest selection, so you go there and ask for advice. The salesperson appears to be well informed; after asking about your experience level and how aggressively you ski, he recommends the Salomon X-Scream 9. You buy a pair for $600, then head back to your apartment and show them to your roommate, who says that you could have bought them on the internet for only $400. How do you feel about your purchase? Are the different prices charged by the two suppliers related to the services they offer? Were the extra services you got by shopping at Skis R Us worth the extra $200?

Internet retailers can sell for less because their costs are much lower than those of full-service retail stores. Those stores, after all, must hire knowledgeable salespeople, put their merchandise on display, rent space in expensive shopping malls, and so on. Internet retailers and mail-order houses, by contrast, typically employ unskilled telephone clerks, and they store their merchandise in cheap warehouses. If you are a consumer who doesn't know which is the right product for you, the extra expense of shopping at a specialty retailer is likely to be a good investment. Spending $600 on the right skis is smarter than spending $400 on the wrong ones. ◆

Many people believe that wholesalers, retailers, and other agents who assist manufacturers in the sale of their products play a far less important role than the one played by those who actually make the products. In this view, the production worker

*"On the one hand, eliminating the middleman would result in lower
costs, increased sales, and greater consumer satisfaction;
on the other hand, we're the middleman."*

is the ultimate source of economic value added. Sales agents are often disparaged as
mere middlemen, parasites on the efforts of others who do the real work.

On a superficial level, this view might seem to be supported by the fact that
many people go to great lengths to avoid paying for the services of sales agents.
Many manufacturers cater to them by offering consumers a chance to "buy direct"
and sidestep the middleman's commission. But on closer examination, we can see
that the economic role of sales agents is essentially the same as that of production
workers. Consider this example.

How does better information affect economic surplus?

Ellis has just inherited a rare Babe Ruth baseball card issued during the great slugger's rookie year. He'd like to keep the card but has reluctantly decided to sell it to
pay some overdue bills. His reservation price for the card is $300, but he is hoping
to get significantly more for it. He has two ways of selling it: He can place a classified ad in the local newspaper for $5 or he can list the card on eBay. If he sells the
card on eBay, the fee will be 5 percent of the winning bid.

Because Ellis lives in a small town with few potential buyers of rare baseball
cards, the local buyer with the highest reservation price is willing to pay $400 at
most. If Ellis lists the card on eBay, however, a much larger number of potential
buyers will see it. If the two eBay shoppers who are willing to pay the most for Ellis's card have reservation prices of $900 and $800, respectively, by how much will
the total economic surplus be larger if Ellis sells his card on eBay? (For the sake of
simplicity, assume that the eBay commission and the classified ad fee equal the respective costs of providing those services.)

In an eBay auction, each bidder reports his or her reservation price for an item.
When the auction closes, the bidder with the highest reservation price wins, and the
price he or she pays is the reservation price of the second highest bidder. So in this
example, the Babe Ruth baseball card will sell for $800 if Ellis lists it on eBay. Net
of the $40 eBay commission, Ellis will receive a payment of $760, or $460 more
than his reservation price for the card. Ellis's economic surplus will thus be $460.
The winning bidder's surplus will be $900 − $800 = $100, so the total surplus
from selling the card on eBay will be $560.

If Ellis instead advertises the card in the local newspaper and sells it to the local
buyer whose reservation price is $400, then Ellis's surplus (net of the newspaper's

$5 fee) will be only $95 and the buyer's surplus will be $0. Thus, total economic surplus will be $560 − $95 = $465 larger if Ellis sells the card on eBay than if he lists it in the local newspaper.

eBay provides a service by making information available to people who can make good use of it. A real increase in economic surplus results when an item ends up in the hands of someone who values it more highly than the person who otherwise would have bought it. That increase is just as valuable as the increase in surplus that results from manufacturing cars, growing corn, or any other productive activity. ◆

RECAP	HOW THE MIDDLEMAN ADDS VALUE

In a world of incomplete information, sales agents and other middlemen add genuine economic value by increasing the extent to which goods and services find their way to the consumers who value them most. For example, when a sales agent causes a good to be purchased by a person who values it by $20,000 more than the person who would have bought it in the absence of a sales agent, that agent augments total economic surplus by $20,000, an achievement on a par with the production of a $20,000 car.

THE OPTIMAL AMOUNT OF INFORMATION

Without a doubt, having more information is better than having less. But information is generally costly to acquire. In most situations, the value of additional information will decline beyond some point. And because of the Low-Hanging-Fruit Principle, people tend to gather information from the cheapest sources first before turning to more costly ones. Typically, then, the marginal benefit of information will decline, and its marginal cost will rise, as the amount of information gathered increases.

Increasing Opportunity Cost

THE COST-BENEFIT TEST

Cost-Benefit

Information gathering is an activity like any other. The Cost-Benefit Principle tells us that a rational consumer will continue to gather information as long as its marginal benefit exceeds its marginal cost. Suppose, for the sake of discussion, that analysts had devised a scale that permits us to measure units of information, as on the horizontal axis of Figure 12.1. If the relevant marginal cost and marginal benefit curves are as shown in the diagram, a rational consumer will acquire I^* units of information, the amount for which the marginal benefit of information equals its marginal cost.

Another way to think about Figure 12.1 is that it shows the optimal level of ignorance. When the cost of acquiring information exceeds its benefits, acquiring

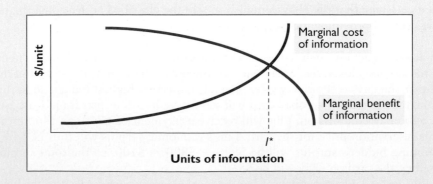

FIGURE 12.1
The Optimal Amount of Information.
For the marginal cost and benefit curves shown, the optimal amount of information is I^*. Beyond that point, information costs more to acquire than it is worth.

additional information simply does not pay. If information could be acquired at no cost, decision makers would, of course, be glad to have it. But when the cost of acquiring the information exceeds the gain in value from the decision it will facilitate, people are better off to remain ignorant.

THE FREE-RIDER PROBLEM

Does the invisible hand assure that the optimal amount of advice will be made available to consumers in the marketplace? The next example suggests one reason why it might not.

Why is finding a knowledgeable salesclerk often difficult?

People can choose for themselves whether to bear the extra cost of retail shopping. Those who value advice and convenience can pay slightly higher prices, while those who know what they want can buy for less from a mail-order house. True or false: It follows that private incentives lead to the optimal amount of retail service.

Why are there so few knowledgeable salesclerks?

The market would provide the optimal level of retail service except for one practical problem, namely, that consumers can make use of the services offered by retail stores without paying for them. After benefiting from the advice of informed salespersons and after inspecting the merchandise, the consumer can return home and buy the same item from an internet retailer or mail-order house. Not all consumers do so, of course. But the fact that customers can benefit from the information provided by retail stores without paying for it is an example of the **free-rider problem,** an incentive problem that results in too little of a good or service being produced. Because retail stores have difficulty recovering the cost of providing information, private incentives are likely to yield less than the socially optimal level of retail service. So the statement above is false. ●

Example 12.1

THE ECONOMIC NATURALIST

free-rider problem an incentive problem in which too little of a good or service is produced because nonpayers cannot be excluded from using it

Why did Rivergate Books, the last bookstore in Lambertville, New Jersey, go out of business?

Small independent bookstores often manage to survive competition from large chains like Borders and Barnes and Noble by offering more personalized service. Janet Holbrooke, the proprietor of Rivergate Books, followed this strategy successfully for more than a decade before closing her doors in 1999. What finally led her to quit?

According to Mrs. Holbrooke, a retired English teacher, "When Barnes and Noble came in, a few people were curious, went to look, and bought some books. But they came back and said they wanted to be able to find things more easily and have clerks that had an idea of what their grandchildren might like to read, and we held our own."[1] Customers also were drawn in by special

Why are so many independent booksellers going out of business?

Example 12.2

THE ECONOMIC NATURALIST

[1]Quoted by Iver Peterson, "A Bookseller Quits Battle with Internet," *New York Times*, June 27, 1999, p. 21.

"In reply to your inquiry regarding the Burke garden hoe, please visit our Worldwide Web home page at: http://www.burke1903.com."

events such as readings and book signings by authors. But during one of these events, Mrs. Holbrooke saw that her store's days were numbered:

> I found out that Gerald Stern, who won the National Book Award for poetry, was a Lambertville man, and I asked him if he would come in and do a reading. He gave a wonderful presentation, and we had a good turnout, but we sold very few books, and then I overheard one of the women who were presenting a book for his signature say that she had bought hers through Amazon.com. Here I thought we were bringing something special to the town. But if people are going to bring in books that they got from the internet, then we don't have a chance.[2] ●

EXERCISE 12.1

Apart from its possible contribution to free-rider problems, how is increased access to the internet likely to affect total economic surplus?

TWO GUIDELINES FOR RATIONAL SEARCH

In practice, of course, the exact value of additional information is difficult to know, so the amount of time and effort one should invest in acquiring it is not always obvious. But as the following examples suggest, the Cost-Benefit Principle provides a strong conceptual framework for thinking about this problem.

Cost-Benefit ○

[2]Ibid.

Should a person living in Paris, Texas, spend more or less time searching for an apartment than someone living in Paris, France?

Suppose that rents for one-bedroom apartments in Paris, Texas, vary between $300 and $500 per month, with an average rent of $400 per month. Rents for similar one-bedroom apartments in Paris, France, vary between $2,000 and $3,000 per month, with an average rent of $2,500. In which city should a rational person expect to spend a longer time searching for an apartment?

In both cities, visiting additional apartments entails a cost, largely the opportunity cost of one's time. In both cities, the more apartments someone visits, the more likely it is that he or she will find one near the lower end of the rent distribution. But because rents are higher and are spread over a broader range in Paris, France, the expected saving from further time spent searching will be greater there than in Paris, Texas. A rational person will expect to spend more time searching for an apartment in France. ◆

This example illustrates the principle that spending additional search time is more likely to be worthwhile for expensive items than for cheap ones. For example, one should spend more time searching for a good price on a diamond engagement ring than for a good price on a stone made of cubic zirconium; more time searching for a low fare to Sydney, Australia, than for a low fare to Sidney, New York; and more time searching for a car than for a bicycle. By extension, hiring an agent—someone who can assist with a search—is more likely to be a good investment in searching for something expensive than for something cheap. For example, people typically engage real estate agents to help them find a house, but they seldom hire agents to help them buy a gallon of milk.

Who should expect to search longer for a good price on a used piano?

Both Tom and Tim are shopping for a used upright piano. To examine a piano listed in the classified ads, they must travel to the home of the piano's current owner. If Tom has a car and Tim does not and both are rational, which one should expect to examine fewer pianos before making his purchase?

The benefits of examining an additional piano are the same in both cases, namely, a better chance of finding a good instrument for a low price. But because it is more costly for Tim to examine pianos, he should expect to examine fewer of them than Tom. ◆

The preceding example makes the point that when searching becomes more costly, we should expect to do less of it. And as a result, the prices we expect to pay will be higher when the cost of a search is higher.

THE GAMBLE INHERENT IN SEARCH

Suppose you are in the market for a one-bedroom apartment and have found one that rents for $400 per month. Should you rent it or search further in hopes of finding a cheaper apartment? Even in a large market with many vacant apartments, there is no guarantee that searching further will turn up a cheaper or better apartment. Searching further entails a cost, which might outweigh the gain. In general, someone who engages in further search must accept certain costs in return for unknown benefits. Thus, further search invariably carries an element of risk.

In thinking about whether to take any gamble, a helpful first step is to compute its expected value—the average amount you would win (or lose) if you played that gamble an infinite number of times. To calculate the **expected value of a gamble** with more than one outcome, we first multiply each outcome by its corresponding probability of occurring, and then add. For example, suppose you win $1 if a coin flip comes up heads and lose $1 if it comes up tails. Since 1/2 is the probability of

expected value of a gamble the sum of the possible outcomes of the gamble multiplied by their respective probabilities *fair gamble* a gamble whose expected value is zero

better-than-fair gamble one whose expected value is positive

risk-neutral person someone who would accept any gamble that is fair or better

risk-averse person someone who would refuse any fair gamble

heads (and also the probability of tails), the expected value of this gamble is $(1/2)(\$1) + (1/2)(-\$1) = 0$. A gamble with an expected value of zero is called a **fair gamble.** If you played this gamble a large number of times, you wouldn't expect to make money, but you also wouldn't expect to lose money.

A **better-than-fair gamble** is one with a positive expected value. (For instance, a coin flip in which you win \$2 for heads and lose \$1 for tails is a better-than-fair gamble.) A **risk-neutral person** is someone who would accept any gamble that is fair or better. A **risk-averse person** is someone who would refuse to take any fair gamble.

EXERCISE 12.2

Consider a gamble in which you win \$4 if you flip a coin and it comes up heads and lose \$2 if it comes up tails. What is the expected value of this gamble? Would a risk-neutral person accept it?

In the next example, we apply these concepts to the decision of whether to search further for an apartment.

Should you search further for an apartment?

You have arrived in San Francisco for a one-month summer visit and are searching for a one-bedroom sublet for the month. There are only two kinds of one-bedroom apartments in the neighborhood in which you wish to live, identical in every respect except that one rents for \$400 and the other for \$360. Of the vacant apartments in this neighborhood, 80 percent are of the first type and 20 percent are of the second type. The only way you can discover the rent for a vacant apartment is to visit it in person. The first apartment you visit is one that rents for \$400. If you are risk-neutral and your opportunity cost of visiting an additional apartment is \$6, should you visit another apartment or rent the one you've found?

If you visit one more apartment, you have a 20 percent chance of it being one that rents for \$360 and an 80 percent chance of it being one that rents for \$400. If the former, you'll save \$40 in rent, but if the latter, you'll face the same rent as before. Since the cost of a visit is \$6, visiting another apartment is a gamble with a 20 percent chance to win $\$40 - \$6 = \$34$ and an 80 percent chance of losing \$6 (which means "winning" $-\$6$). The expected value of this gamble is thus $(0.20)(\$34) + (0.80)(-\$6) = \$2$. Visiting another apartment is a better-than-fair gamble, and since you are risk-neutral, you should take it. ◆

EXERCISE 12.3

Refer to the apartment search example above. Suppose you visit another apartment and discover it, too, is one that rents for \$400. If you are risk-neutral, should you visit a third apartment?

THE COMMITMENT PROBLEM WHEN SEARCH IS COSTLY

When most people search for an apartment, they want a place to live not for just a month but for a year or more. Most landlords, for their part, are also looking for long-term tenants. Similarly, few people accept a full-time job in their chosen field unless they expect to hold the job for several years. Firms, too, generally prefer employees who will stay for extended periods. Finally, when most people search for mates, they are looking for someone with whom to settle down.

Because in all these cases search is costly, examining every possible option will never make sense. Apartment hunters don't visit every vacant apartment, nor do landlords interview every possible tenant. Job seekers don't visit every employer, nor do employers interview every job seeker. And not even the most determined searcher can manage to date every eligible mate. In these and other cases, people are rational to end their searches, even though they know a more attractive option surely exists out there somewhere.

But herein lies a difficulty. What happens when, by chance, a more attractive option comes along after the search has ceased? Few people would rent an apartment if they thought the landlord would kick them out the moment another tenant came along who was willing to pay higher rent. Few landlords would be willing to rent to a tenant if they expected her to move out the moment she discovers a cheaper apartment. Employers, job seekers, and people who are looking for mates would have similar reservations about entering relationships that could be terminated once a better option happened to come along.

This potential difficulty in maintaining stable matches between partners in ongoing relationships would not arise in a world of perfect information. In such a world, everyone would end up in the best possible relationship, so no one would be tempted to renege. But when information is costly and the search must be limited, there will always be the potential for existing relationships to dissolve.

In most contexts, people solve this problem not by conducting an exhaustive search (which is usually impossible, in any event) but by committing themselves to remain in a relationship once a mutual agreement has been reached to terminate the search. Thus, landlords and tenants sign a lease that binds them to one another for a specified period, usually one year. Employees and firms enter into employment contracts, either formal or informal, under which each promises to honor his obligations to the other, except under extreme circumstances. And in most countries a marriage contract penalizes those who abandon their spouses. Entering into such commitments limits the freedom to pursue one's own interests. Yet most people freely accept such restrictions because they know the alternative is failure to solve the search problem.

RECAP	THE OPTIMAL AMOUNT OF INFORMATION

Additional information creates value, but it is also costly to acquire. A rational consumer will continue to acquire information until its marginal benefit equals its marginal cost. Beyond that point, it is rational to remain uninformed.

Markets for information do not always function perfectly. Free-rider problems often hinder retailers' efforts to provide information to consumers.

Search inevitably entails an element of risk because costs must be incurred without any assurance that search will prove fruitful. A rational consumer can minimize this risk by concentrating search efforts on goods for which the variation in price or quality is relatively high and on those for which the cost of search is relatively low.

ASYMMETRIC INFORMATION

One of the most common information problems occurs when the participants in a potential exchange are not equally well informed about the product or service that is offered for sale. For instance, the owner of a used car may know that the car is in excellent mechanical condition, but potential buyers cannot know that merely by inspecting it or taking it for a test drive. Economists use the term **asymmetric information** to describe situations in which buyers and sellers are not equally well informed about the characteristics of products or services. In these situations, sellers are typically much better informed than buyers, but sometimes the reverse will be true.

The problem of asymmetric information can easily prevent exchanges that would benefit both parties. Here is a classic example.

asymmetric information situations in which buyers and sellers are not equally well informed about the characteristics of goods and services for sale in the marketplace

Will Jane sell her car to Tom?

Jane's 2001 Miata has 70,000 miles on the odometer, but most of these are highway miles driven during weekend trips to see her boyfriend in Toronto. (Highway driving causes less wear and tear on a car than city driving.) Moreover, Jane has maintained the car precisely according to the manufacturer's specifications. In short, she knows her car to be in excellent condition. Because she is about to start graduate school in Boston, however, Jane wants to sell the car. On average, 2001 Miatas sell for a price of $8,000, but because Jane knows her car to be in excellent condition, her reservation price for it is $10,000.

Tom wants to buy a used Miata. He would be willing to pay $13,000 for one that is in excellent condition but only $9,000 for one that is not in excellent condition. Tom has no way of telling whether Jane's Miata is in excellent condition. (He could hire a mechanic to examine the car, but doing so is expensive, and many problems cannot be detected even by a mechanic.) Will Tom buy Jane's car? Is this outcome efficient?

Because Jane's car looks no different from other 2001 Miatas, Tom will not pay $10,000 for it. After all, for only $8,000, he can buy some other 2001 Miata that is in just as good condition, *as far as he can tell*. Tom therefore will buy someone else's Miata, and Jane's will go unsold. This outcome is not efficient. If Tom had bought Jane's Miata for, say, $11,000, his surplus would have been $2,000 and Jane's another $1,000. Instead, Tom ends up buying a Miata that is in average condition (or worse), and his surplus is only $1,000. Jane gets no economic surplus at all. ◆

THE LEMONS MODEL

We can't be sure, of course, that the Miata Tom ends up buying will be in worse condition than Jane's—since *someone* might have a car in perfect condition that must be sold even if the owner cannot get what it is really worth. Even so, the economic incentives created by asymmetric information suggest that most used cars that are put up for sale will be of lower-than-average quality. One reason is that people who mistreat their cars, or whose cars were never very good to begin with, are more likely than others to want to sell them. Buyers know from experience that cars for sale on the used car market are more likely to be "lemons" than cars that are not for sale. This realization causes them to lower their reservation prices for a used car.

But that's not the end of the story. Once used car prices have fallen, the owners of cars that are in good condition have an even stronger incentive to hold onto them. That causes the average quality of the cars offered for sale on the used car market to decline still further. Berkeley economist George Akerlof, a Nobel laureate, was the first to explain the logic behind this downward spiral.[3] Economists use the term **lemons model** to describe Akerlof's explanation of how asymmetric information affects the average quality of the used goods offered for sale.

lemons model George Akerlof's explanation of how asymmetric information tends to reduce the average quality of goods offered for sale

The next example suggests that the lemons model has important practical implications for consumer choice.

Should you buy your aunt's car?

You want to buy a used Honda Accord. Your Aunt Germaine buys a new car every four years, and she has a four-year-old Accord that she is about to trade in. You believe her report that the car is in good condition, and she is willing to sell it to you for $10,000, which is the current blue book value for four-year-old Accords. (The blue book value of a car is the average price for which cars of that age and model sell in the used car market.) Should you buy your aunt's Honda?

---

[3]George Akerlof, "The Market for Lemons," *Quarterly Journal of Economics* 84 (1970), pp. 488–500.

Akerlof's lemons model tells us that cars for sale in the used car market will be of lower average quality than cars of the same vintage that are not for sale. If you believe your aunt's claim that her car is in good condition, then being able to buy it for its blue book value is definitely a good deal for you, since the blue book price is the equilibrium price for a car that is of lower quality than your aunt's. ◆

The following two examples illustrate the conditions under which asymmetric information about product quality results in a market in which *only* lemons are offered for sale.

How much will a naive buyer pay for a used car?

Consider a world with only two kinds of cars: good ones and lemons. An owner knows with certainty which type of car she has, but potential buyers cannot distinguish between the two types. Ten percent of all new cars produced are lemons. Good used cars are worth $10,000 to their owners, but lemons are worth only $6,000. Consider a naive consumer who believes that the used cars currently for sale have the same quality distribution as new cars (i.e., 90 percent good, 10 percent lemons). If this consumer is risk-neutral, how much would he be willing to pay for a used car?

Buying a car of unknown quality is a gamble, but a risk-neutral buyer would be willing to take the gamble provided it is fair. If the buyer can't tell the difference between a good car and a lemon, the probability that he will end up with a lemon is simply the proportion of lemons among the cars from which he chooses. The buyer believes he has a 90 percent chance of getting a good car and a 10 percent chance of getting a lemon. Given the prices he is willing to pay for the two types of car, his expected value of the car he buys will thus be $0.90(\$10,000) + 0.10(\$6,000) = \$9,600$. And since he is risk-neutral, that is his reservation price for a used car. ◆

EXERCISE 12.4

How would your answer to the question posed in the last example differ if the proportion of new cars that are lemons had been 20 percent?

Who will sell a used car for what the naive buyer is willing to pay?

Continuing with the previous example: If you were the owner of a good used car, what would it be worth to you? Would you sell it to a naive buyer? What if you owned a lemon?

Since you know your car is good, it is worth $10,000 to you, by assumption. But since a naive buyer would be willing to pay only $9,600, neither you nor any other owner of a good car would be willing to sell to that buyer. If you had a lemon, of course, you would be happy to sell it to a naive buyer, since the $9,600 the buyer is willing to pay is $3,600 more than the lemon would be worth to you. So the only used cars for sale will be lemons. In time, buyers will revise their naively optimistic beliefs about the quality of the cars for sale on the used car market. In the end, all used cars will sell for a price of $6,000, and all will be lemons. ◆

In practice, of course, the mere fact that a car is for sale does not guarantee that it is a lemon because the owner of a good car will sometimes be forced to sell it, even at a price that does not reflect its condition. The logic of the lemons model explains this owner's frustration. The first thing sellers in this situation want a prospective buyer to know is the reason they are selling their cars. For example, classified ads often announce, "Just had a baby, must sell my 2005 Corvette" or

Why do new cars lose a significant fraction of their value as soon as they are driven from the showroom?

"Transferred to Germany, must sell my 2006 Toyota Camry." Any time you pay the blue book price for a used car that is for sale for some reason unrelated to its condition, you are beating the market.

THE CREDIBILITY PROBLEM IN TRADING

Why can't someone with a high-quality used car simply *tell* the buyer about the car's condition? The difficulty is that buyers' and sellers' interests tend to conflict. Sellers of used cars, for example, have an economic incentive to overstate the quality of their products. Buyers, for their part, have an incentive to understate the amount they are willing to pay for used cars and other products (in the hope of bargaining for a lower price). Potential employees may be tempted to overstate their qualifications for a job. And people searching for mates have been known to engage in deception.

That is not to say that most people *consciously* misrepresent the truth in communicating with their potential trading partners. But people do tend to interpret ambiguous information in ways that promote their own interests. Thus, 92 percent of factory employees surveyed in one study rated themselves as more productive than the average factory worker. Psychologists call this phenomenon the "Lake Wobegon effect," after Garrison Keillor's mythical Minnesota homestead, where "all the children are above average."

Notwithstanding the natural tendency to exaggerate, the parties to a potential exchange can often gain if they can find some means to communicate their knowledge truthfully. In general, however, mere statements of relevant information will not suffice. People have long since learned to discount the used car salesman's inflated claims about the cars he is trying to unload. But as the next example illustrates, though communication between potential adversaries may be difficult, it is not impossible.

How can a used car seller signal high quality credibly?

Jane knows her Miata to be in excellent condition, and Tom would be willing to pay considerably more than her reservation price if he could be confident of getting such a car. What kind of signal about the car's quality would Tom find credible?

Again, the potential conflict between Tom's and Jane's interests suggests that mere statements about the car's quality may not be persuasive. But suppose Jane offers a warranty, under which she agrees to remedy any defects the car develops over the next six months. Jane can afford to extend such an offer because she knows her car is unlikely to need expensive repairs. In contrast, the person who knows his car has a cracked engine block would never extend such an offer. The warranty is a credible signal that the car is in good condition. It enables Tom to buy the car with confidence, to both his and Jane's benefit. ◆

THE COSTLY-TO-FAKE PRINCIPLE

costly-to-fake principle to communicate information credibly to a potential rival, a signal must be costly or difficult to fake

The preceding examples illustrate the **costly-to-fake principle,** which holds that if parties whose interests potentially conflict are to communicate credibly with one another, the signals they send must be costly or difficult to fake. If the seller of a defective car could offer an extensive warranty just as easily as the seller of a good car, a warranty offer would communicate nothing about the car's quality. But warranties entail costs that are significantly higher for defective cars than for good cars—hence their credibility as a signal of product quality.

To the extent that sellers have an incentive to portray a product in the most flattering light possible, their interests conflict with those of buyers, who want the most accurate assessment of product quality possible. Note that in the following example, the costly-to-fake principle applies to a producer's statement about the quality of a product.

Why do firms insert the phrase "As advertised on TV" when they advertise their products in magazines and newspapers?

Company *A* sponsors an expensive national television advertising campaign on behalf of its compact disc player, claiming it has the clearest sound and the best repair record of any CD player in the market. Company *B* makes similar claims in a sales brochure but does not advertise its product on television. If you had no additional information to go on, which company's claim would you find more credible? Why do you suppose Company *A* mentions its TV ads when it advertises its CD player in print media?

Accustomed as we are to discounting advertisers' inflated claims, the information given might seem to provide no real basis for a choice between the two products. On closer examination, however, we see that a company's decision to advertise its product on national television constitutes a credible signal about the product's quality. The cost of a national television campaign can run well into the millions of dollars, a sum a company would be foolish to spend on an inferior product.

For example, in 2002 Pepsi paid Britney Spears $8 million to appear in its two 30-second Super Bowl ads, and it paid more than $3.5 million to Fox TV for broadcasting those ads. National TV ads can attract the potential buyers' attention and persuade a small fraction of them to try a product. But these huge investments pay off only if the resulting initial sales generate other new business—either repeat sales to people who tried the product and liked it or sales to others who heard about the product from a friend.

Because ads cannot persuade buyers that a bad product is a good one, a company that spends millions of dollars advertising a bad product is wasting its money. An expensive national advertising campaign is therefore a credible signal that the producer *thinks* its product is a good one. Of course, the ads don't guarantee that a product *is* a winner, but in an uncertain world, they provide one more piece of information. Note, however, that the relevant information lies in the expenditure on the advertising campaign, not in what the ads themselves say.

These observations may explain why some companies mention their television ads in their print ads. Advertisers understand the costly-to-fake principle and hope that consumers will understand it as well. ●

As the next example illustrates, the costly-to-fake principle is also well known to many employers.

Why do many companies care so much about elite educational credentials?

Microsoft is looking for a hardworking, smart person for an entry-level managerial position in a new technical products division. Two candidates, Cooper and Duncan, seem alike in every respect but one: Cooper graduated with the highest honors from MIT, while Duncan graduated with a C+ average from Somerville College. Whom should Microsoft hire?

If you want to persuade prospective employers that you are both hardworking and intelligent, there is perhaps no more credible signal than to have graduated with distinction from a highly selective educational institution. Most people would like potential employers to think of them as hardworking and intelligent. But unless you actually have both those qualities, graduating with the highest honors from a school like MIT will be extremely difficult. The fact that Duncan graduated from a much less selective institution and earned only a C+ average is not proof positive that he is not diligent and talented, but companies are forced to play the percentages. In this case, the odds strongly favor Cooper. ●

CONSPICUOUS CONSUMPTION AS A SIGNAL OF ABILITY

Some individuals of high ability are not highly paid. (Remember the best elementary school teacher you ever had.) And some people—such as the multibillionaire investor Warren Buffet—earn a lot, yet spend very little. But such cases run counter to general tendencies. In competitive markets, the people with the most ability tend

Example 12.3
THE ECONOMIC NATURALIST

Why should buyers care whether a product is advertised on TV?

EN 12

Example 12.4
THE ECONOMIC NATURALIST

Why do some employers care so much about elite degrees?

to receive the highest salaries. And as suggested by the Cost-Benefit Principle, the more someone earns, the more he or she is likely to spend on high-quality goods and services. As the following example suggests, these tendencies often lead us to infer a person's ability from the amount and quality of the goods he consumes.

Cost-Benefit

Example 12.5
THE ECONOMIC NATURALIST

If you were on trial for a serious crime, which lawyer would you hire?

Why do many clients seem to prefer lawyers who wear expensive suits?

You have been unjustly accused of a serious crime and are looking for an attorney. Your choice is between two lawyers who appear identical in all respects except for the things they buy. One of them wears a cheap polyester suit and arrives at the courthouse in a 10-year-old rust-eaten Dodge Neon. The other wears an impeccably tailored suit and drives a new BMW 750i. If this were the *only* information available to you at the time you chose, which lawyer would you hire?

The correlation between salary and the abilities buyers value most is particularly strong in the legal profession. A lawyer whose clients usually prevail in court will be much more in demand than one whose clients generally lose, and their fees will reflect the difference. The fact that one of the lawyers consumes much more than the other does not *prove* that he is the better lawyer, but if that is the only information you have, you can ill afford to ignore it. ●

If the less able lawyer loses business because of the suits he wears and the car he drives, why doesn't he simply buy better suits and a more expensive car? His choice is between saving for retirement or spending more on his car and clothing. In one sense, he cannot afford to buy a more expensive car, but in another sense, he cannot afford *not* to. If his current car is discouraging potential clients from hiring him, buying a better one may simply be a prudent investment. But because *all* lawyers have an incentive to make such investments, their effects tend to be mutually offsetting.

When all is said and done, the things people consume will continue to convey relevant information about their respective ability levels. The costly-to-fake principle tells us that the BMW 750i is an effective signal precisely because the lawyer of low ability cannot afford one, no matter how little he saves for retirement. Yet from a social perspective, the resulting spending pattern is inefficient, for the same reason that other positional arms races are inefficient. (We discussed positional arms races in Chapter 11.) Society would be better off if everyone spent less and saved more for retirement.

The problem of conspicuous consumption as an ability signal does not arise with equal force in every environment. In small towns, where people tend to know one another well, a lawyer who tries to impress people by spending beyond her means is likely to succeed only in demonstrating how foolish she is. Thus, the wardrobe a professional person "needs" in towns like Dubuque, Iowa, or Athens, Ohio, costs less than half as much as the wardrobe the same person would need in Manhattan or Los Angeles.

STATISTICAL DISCRIMINATION

In a competitive market with perfect information, the buyer of a service would pay the seller's cost of providing the service. In many markets, however, the seller does not know the exact cost of serving each individual buyer.

In such cases, the missing information has an economic value. If the seller can come up with even a rough estimate of the missing information, she can improve her position. As the following example illustrates, firms often do so by imputing characteristics to individuals on the basis of the groups to which they belong.

Why do males under 25 years of age pay more than other drivers for auto insurance?

Gerald is 23 years old and is an extremely careful and competent driver. He has never had an accident, or even a moving traffic violation. His twin sister Geraldine has had two accidents, one of them serious, in the last three years and has accumulated three speeding tickets during that same period. Why does Gerald pay $1,600 per year for auto insurance, while Geraldine pays only $800?

The expected cost to an insurance company of insuring any given driver depends on the probability that the driver will be involved in an accident. No one knows what that probability is for any given driver, but insurance companies can estimate rather precisely the proportion of drivers in specific groups who will be involved in an accident in any given year. Males under 25 are much more likely than older males and females of any age to become involved in auto accidents. Gerald pays more than his sister because even those males under 25 who have never had an accident are more likely to have one than females the same age who have had several accidents.

Of course, females who have had two accidents and accumulated several tickets in the last three years are more likely to have an accident than a female with a spotless driving record. The insurance company knows that and has increased Geraldine's premium accordingly. Yet it is still less than her brother's premium. That does not mean that Gerald is in fact more likely to have an accident than Geraldine. Indeed, given the twins' respective driving skills, Geraldine clearly poses the higher risk. But because insurance companies lack such detailed information, they are forced to set rates according to the information they possess.

To remain in business, an insurance company must collect enough money from premiums to cover the cost of the claims it pays out, plus whatever administrative expenses it incurs. Consider an insurance company that charges lower rates for young males with clean driving records than for females with blemished ones. Given that the former group is more likely to have accidents than the latter, the company cannot break even unless it charges females more, and males less, than the respective costs of insuring them. But if it does so, rival insurance companies will see cash on the table: They can offer females slightly lower rates and lure them away from the first company. The first company will end up with only young male policyholders and thus will suffer an economic loss at the low rates it charges. That is why, in equilibrium, young males with clean driving records pay higher insurance rates than young females with blemished records. ●

Example 12.6

THE ECONOMIC NATURALIST

Why do male teens pay so much more for auto insurance?

The insurance industry's policy of charging high rates to young male drivers is an example of **statistical discrimination.** Other examples include the common practice of paying higher salaries to people with college degrees than to people without them and the policy of favoring college applicants with high SAT scores. Statistical discrimination occurs whenever people or products are judged on the basis of the groups to which they belong.

Competition promotes statistical discrimination, even though everyone knows that the characteristics of specific individuals can differ markedly from those of the group to which they belong. For example, insurance companies know perfectly well that *some* young males are careful and competent drivers. But unless they can identify *which* males are the better drivers, competitive pressure forces them to act on their knowledge that, as a group, young males are more likely than others to generate insurance claims.

Similarly, employers know that many people with only a high school diploma are more productive than the average college graduate. But because employers usually cannot tell in advance who those people are, competitive pressure leads them to offer higher wages to college graduates, who are more productive, on average, than high school graduates. Universities, too, realize that many applicants with low SAT scores will earn higher grades than applicants with high scores. But if two applicants

statistical discrimination the practice of making judgments about the quality of people, goods, or services based on the characteristics of the groups to which they belong

look equally promising except for their SAT scores, competition forces universities to favor the applicant with higher scores since, on average, that applicant will perform better than the other.

Statistical discrimination is the *result* of observable differences in group characteristics, not the cause of those differences. Young males, for example, do not generate more insurance claims because of statistical discrimination. Rather, statistical discrimination occurs because insurance companies know that young males generate more claims. Nor does statistical discrimination cause young males to pay insurance rates that are high in relation to the claims they generate. Among any group of young male drivers, some are careful and competent, and others are not. Statistical discrimination means the more able males will pay high rates relative to the volume of claims they generate, but it also means the less able male drivers will pay low rates relative to the claims they generate. On average, the group's rates will be appropriate to the claims its members generate.

Still, these observations do little to ease the frustration of the young male who knows himself to be a careful and competent driver, or the high school graduate who knows herself to be a highly productive employee. Competitive forces provide firms an incentive to identify such individuals and treat them more favorably whenever practical. When firms succeed in this effort, however, they have often discovered some other relevant information on group differences. For example, many insurance companies offer lower rates to young males who belong to the National Honor Society or make the dean's list at school. Members of those groups generate fewer claims, on average, than other young males. But even these groups include risky drivers, and the fact that companies offer discounts to their members means that all other young males must pay higher rates.

ADVERSE SELECTION

adverse selection the pattern in which insurance tends to be purchased disproportionately by those who are most costly for companies to insure

Since insurance companies routinely practice statistical discrimination, each individual within a group pays the same rate, even though individuals within the group often differ sharply in terms of their likelihood of filing claims. Within each group, buying insurance is thus most attractive to those individuals with the highest likelihood of filing claims. As a result, high-risk individuals are more likely to buy insurance than low-risk individuals, a pattern known as **adverse selection.** Adverse selection forces insurance companies to raise their premiums, which makes buying insurance even less attractive to low-risk individuals, which raises still further the average risk level of those who remain insured. In some cases, only those individuals faced with extreme risks may continue to find insurance an attractive purchase.

MORAL HAZARD

moral hazard the tendency of people to expend less effort protecting those goods that are insured against theft or damage

Moral hazard is another problem that makes buying insurance less attractive for the average person. This problem refers to the fact that some people take fewer precautions when they know they are insured. Someone whose car is insured, for example, may take less care to prevent it from being damaged or stolen. Driving cautiously and searching for safe parking spaces require effort, after all, and if the losses from failing to engage in these precautions are covered by insurance, some people will become less vigilant.

Insurance companies help many of their potential clients soften the consequences of problems like moral hazard and adverse selection by offering policies with deductible provisions. Under the terms of an automobile collision insurance policy with, say, a $1,000 deductible provision, the insurance company covers only those collision repair costs in excess of $1,000. For example, if you have an accident in which $3,000 in damage occurs to your car, the insurance company covers only $2,000, and you pay the remaining $1,000.

How does the availability of such policies mitigate the negative effects of adverse selection and moral hazard? Since the policies are cheaper for insurance companies to provide, they sell for lower prices. The lower prices represent a much better bargain, however, for those drivers who are least likely to file insurance claims since those drivers are least likely to incur any uncovered repair costs. Policies with deductible provisions also confront careless drivers with more of the extra costs for which they are responsible, giving them additional incentives to take precautions.

These policies benefit insurance buyers in another way. Because the holder of a policy with a deductible provision will not file a claim at all if the damage to his car in an accident is less than the deductible threshold, insurance companies require fewer resources to process and investigate claims, savings that get passed along in the form of lower premiums.

RECAP	ASYMMETRIC INFORMATION

Asymmetric information describes situations in which not all parties to a potential exchange are equally well informed. In the typical case, the seller of a product will know more about its quality than the potential buyers. Such asymmetries often stand in the way of mutually beneficial exchange in the markets for high-quality goods because buyers' inability to identify high quality makes them unwilling to pay a commensurate price.

Information asymmetries and other communication problems between potential exchange partners can often be solved through the use of signals that are costly or difficult to fake. Product warranties are such a signal because the seller of a low-quality product would find them too costly to offer.

Buyers and sellers also respond to asymmetric information by attempting to judge the qualities of products and people on the basis of the groups to which they belong. A young male may know he is a good driver, but auto insurance companies must nonetheless charge him high rates because they know only that he is a member of a group that is frequently involved in accidents.

DISAPPEARING POLITICAL DISCOURSE

An intriguing illustration of statistical discrimination arises when a politician decides what to say about controversial public issues. Politicians have an interest in supporting the positions they genuinely believe in, but they also have an interest in winning reelection. As the next examples illustrate, the two motives often conflict, especially when a politician's statements about one subject convey information about her beliefs on other subjects.

Why do opponents of the death penalty often remain silent?

Quite apart from the question of whether execution of convicted criminals is morally legitimate, there are important practical arguments against capital punishment. For one thing, it is extremely expensive relative to the alternative of life without parole. Execution is costly because of judicial safeguards against execution of innocent persons. In each capital case prosecuted in the United States, these safeguards consume thousands of person-hours from attorneys and other officers of the court, at a cost that runs well into the millions of dollars.[4] Such efforts notwithstanding, the record is replete with examples of executed persons who are later shown to be innocent. Another argument against capital

Example 12.7
THE ECONOMIC NATURALIST

[4]See Philip J. Cook and Donna B. Slawson, "The Costs of Processing Murder Cases in North Carolina," The Sanford Institute of Public Policy, Duke University, Durham, NC, 1993.

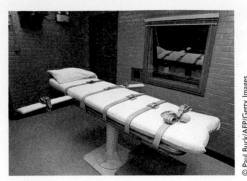

Why do many politicians who oppose the death penalty refuse to speak out against it?

punishment is that many statistical studies find that it does not deter people from committing capital crimes. Though many political leaders in both parties find these and other arguments against capital punishment compelling, few politicians voice their opposition to capital punishment publicly. Why not?

A possible answer to this puzzle is suggested by the theory of statistical discrimination. Voters in both parties are concerned about crime and want to elect politicians who take the problem seriously. Suppose there are two kinds of politicians: some who in their heart of hearts take the crime issue seriously and others who merely pay lip service to it. Suppose also that voters classify politicians in a second way: those who publicly favor the death penalty or remain silent and those who publicly oppose it. Some politicians will oppose the death penalty for the reasons just discussed, but others will oppose it because they are simply reluctant to punish criminals—perhaps because they believe that crime is ultimately more society's fault than the criminal's. (Politicians in the latter category are the ones voters think of as being "not serious about crime"; they are the ones most voters want to get rid of.) These two possible motives for opposing the death penalty suggest that the proportion of death penalty opponents who take the crime issue seriously, in the public's view, will be somewhat smaller than the corresponding proportion among proponents of the death penalty. For the sake of discussion, imagine that 95 percent of politicians who favor the death penalty and only 80 percent of politicians who oppose the death penalty are "serious about crime."

If you are a voter who cares about crime, how will your views about a politician be affected by hearing that he opposes the death penalty? If you knew nothing about that politician to begin with, your best guess on hearing his opposition to the death penalty would be that there is an 80 percent chance that he is serious about crime. Had he instead voiced support for the death penalty, your best guess would be that there is a 95 percent chance that he is serious about crime. And since voters are looking for politicians who are serious about crime, the mere act of speaking out against the death penalty will entail a small loss of political support even for those politicians who are extremely serious about crime.

Knowing this tendency on the part of voters, some politicians who are only marginally opposed to the death penalty may prefer to keep their views to themselves. As a result, the composition of the group that speaks out publicly against the death penalty will change slightly so that it is more heavily weighted with people reluctant to punish criminals in any way. Suppose, for example, that the proportion of death penalty opponents who are serious about crime falls from 80 to 60 percent. Now the political cost of speaking out against the death penalty rises, leading still more opponents to remain silent. Once the dust settles, very few opponents of capital punishment will risk stating their views publicly. In their desire to convince voters that they are tough on crime, some may even become outspoken proponents of the death penalty. In the end, public discourse will strongly favor capital punishment. But that is no reason to conclude that most leaders—or even most voters—genuinely favor it. ●

disappearing political discourse the theory that people who support a position may remain silent because speaking out would create a risk of being misunderstood

The economist Glenn Loury was the first to call attention to the phenomenon described in the preceding example. We call it the problem of **disappearing political discourse.** Once you understand it, you will begin to notice examples not just in the political sphere but in everyday discourse as well.

Example 12.8
THE ECONOMIC NATURALIST

Why do proponents of legalized drugs remain silent?

That addictive drugs like heroine, cocaine, and methamphetamines cause enormous harm is not a matter of dispute. The clear intent of laws that ban commerce in these drugs is to prevent that harm. But the laws also entail costs. By making the drugs illegal, they substantially increase their price, leading many addicts to commit crimes to pay for drugs. The high incomes of many illicit drug dealers also divert people from legitimate careers and result in turf battles that often have devastating consequences for both participants and bystanders. If these drugs were legal, drug-related crime would vanish completely. Drug use would also rise, how significantly we do not know. In short, it is at least *conceivable* that legalizing addictive drugs might be sound public policy. Why, then, do virtually no politicians publicly favor such a policy?

Many politicians may simply believe that legalizing drugs is a bad idea. Theoretically, legalization could lead to such a steep rise in drug consumption that the cost of the policy might far outweigh its benefits. This concern, however, is not supported by experience in countries such as England and the Netherlands, which have tried limited forms of legalization. A second explanation is that politicians who favor legalization are reluctant to speak out for fear that others will misinterpret them. Suppose that some people favor legalization based on careful analysis of the costs and benefits, while other proponents are merely crazy. If the proportion of crazies is higher among supporters than among opponents of legalization, someone who speaks out in favor of legalization may cause those who do not know her to increase their estimate of the likelihood she is crazy. This possibility deters some proponents from speaking out, which raises the proportion of crazies among the remaining public supporters of legalization—and so on in a downward spiral, until most of the remaining public supporters really are crazy. •

The disappearing political discourse problem helps to explain why the United States had difficulty reestablishing normal diplomatic relations with China, which were severed in the wake of the communist revolution. One could oppose communist expansionism and yet still favor normalized relations with China on the grounds that war is less likely when antagonists communicate openly. In the Cold War environment, however, American politicians were under enormous pressure to demonstrate their steadfast opposition to communism at every opportunity. Fearing that support for the normalization of relations with China would be misinterpreted as a sign of softness toward communism, many supporters of the policy remained silent. Not until Richard Nixon—whose anticommunist credentials no one could question—was elected president were diplomatic relations with China finally reopened.

Why did the task of reestablishing normal diplomatic relations with China fall to President Richard Nixon, the lifelong communist basher?

The problem of disappearing discourse also helps explain the impoverished state of public debate on issues such as the reform of Social Security, Medicare, and other entitlement programs.

■ SUMMARY ■

- Retailers and other sales agents are important sources of information. To the extent that they enable consumers to find the right products and services, they add economic value. In that sense they are no less productive than the workers who manufacture goods or perform services directly. Unfortunately, the free-rider problem often prevents firms from offering useful product information. **LO1**

- Virtually every market exchange takes place on the basis of less-than-complete information. More information is beneficial both to buyers and to sellers, but information is costly to acquire. The rational individual therefore acquires information only up to the point at which its marginal benefit equals its marginal cost. Beyond that point, one is rational to remain ignorant. **LO2**

- Several principles govern the rational search for information. Searching more intensively makes sense when the cost of a search is low, when quality is highly variable, or when prices vary widely. Further search is always a gamble. A risk-neutral person will search whenever the expected gains outweigh the expected costs. A rational search will always terminate before all possible options have been investigated. Thus, in a search for a partner in an ongoing bilateral relationship, there is always the possibility that a better partner will turn up after the search is over. In most contexts, people deal with this problem by entering into contracts that commit them to their partners once they have mutually agreed to terminate the search. **LO2**

• Many potentially beneficial transactions are prevented from taking place by asymmetric information—the fact that one party lacks information that the other has. For example, the owner of a used car knows whether it is in good condition, but potential buyers do not. Even though a buyer may be willing to pay more for a good car than the owner of such a car would require, the fact that the buyer cannot be sure he is getting a good car often discourages the sale. More generally, asymmetric information often prevents sellers from supplying the same quality level that consumers would be willing to pay for. **LO3**

• Both buyers and sellers often can gain by finding ways of communicating what they know to one another. But because of the potential conflict between the interests of buyers and sellers, mere statements about the relevant information may not be credible. For a signal between potential trading partners to be credible, it must be costly to fake. For instance, the owner of a high-quality used car can credibly signal the car's quality by offering a warranty—an offer that the seller of a low-quality car could not afford to make. **LO4**

• Firms and consumers often try to estimate missing information by making use of what they know about the groups to which people or things belong. For example, insurance firms estimate the risk of insuring individual young male drivers on the basis of the accident rates for young males as a group. This practice is known as statistical discrimination. Other examples include paying college graduates more than high school graduates and charging higher life insurance rates to 60-year-olds than to 20-year-olds. Statistical discrimination helps to explain the phenomenon of disappearing political discourse, which occurs when opponents of a practice such as the death penalty remain silent when the issue is discussed publicly. **LO4**

▪ KEY TERMS ▪

adverse selection (340)
asymmetric information (333)
better-than-fair gamble (332)
costly-to-fake principle (336)
disappearing political
   discourse (342)

expected value of a
   gamble (331)
fair gamble (332)
free-rider problem (329)
lemons model (334)

moral hazard (340)
risk-averse person (332)
risk-neutral person (332)
statistical discrimination (339)

▪ REVIEW QUESTIONS ▪

1. Can it be rational for a consumer to buy a Chevrolet without having first taken test drives in competing models built by Ford, Chrysler, Honda, Toyota, and others? **LO2**

2. Explain why a gallery owner who sells a painting might actually create more economic surplus than the artist who painted it. **LO1**

3. Explain why used cars offered for sale are different, on average, from used cars not offered for sale. **LO3**

4. Explain why the used-car market would be likely to function more efficiently in a community in which moral norms of honesty are strong than in a community in which such norms are weak. **LO4**

5. Why might leasing a new Porsche be a good investment for an aspiring Hollywood film producer, even though he can't easily afford the monthly payments? **LO4**

▪ PROBLEMS ▪

1. State whether the following are true or false, and briefly explain why: **LO4**
   a. Companies spend billions of dollars advertising their products on network TV primarily because the texts of their advertisements persuade consumers that the advertised products are of high quality.

b. You may not get the optimal level of advice from a retail shop when you go in to buy a lamp for your bike because of the free-rider problem.

c. If you need a lawyer, and all your legal expenses are covered by insurance, you should *always* choose the best-dressed lawyer with the most expensive car and the most ostentatiously furnished office.

d. The benefit of searching for a spouse is affected by the size of the community you live in.

2. Consumers know that some fraction x of all new cars produced and sold in the market are defective. The defective ones cannot be identified except by those who own them. Cars do not depreciate with use. Consumers are risk-neutral and value nondefective cars at $10,000 each. New cars sell for $5,000 and used ones for $2,500. What is the fraction x? **LO3**

3. Carlos is risk-neutral and has an ancient farmhouse with great character for sale in Slaterville Springs. His reservation price for the house is $130,000. The only possible local buyer is Whitney, whose reservation price for the house is $150,000. The only other houses on the market are modern ranch houses that sell for $125,000, which is exactly equal to each potential buyer's reservation price for such a house. Suppose that if Carlos does not hire a Realtor, Whitney will learn from her neighbor that Carlos's house is for sale and will buy it for $140,000. However, if Carlos hires a Realtor, he knows that the Realtor will put him in touch with an enthusiast for old farmhouses who is willing to pay up to $300,000 for the house. Carlos also knows that if he and this person negotiate, they will agree on a price of $250,000. If Realtors charge a commission of 5 percent of the selling price and all Realtors have opportunity costs of $2,000 for negotiating a sale, will Carlos hire a Realtor? If so, how will total economic surplus be affected? **LO1**

4. Ann and Barbara are computer programmers in Nashville who are planning to move to Seattle. Each owns a house that has just been appraised for $100,000. But whereas Ann's house is one of hundreds of highly similar houses in a large, well-known suburban development, Barbara's is the only one that was built from her architect's design. Who will benefit more by hiring a Realtor to assist in selling her house, Ann or Barbara? **LO1**

5. For each pair of occupations listed, identify the one for which the kind of car a person drives is more likely to be a good indication of how good she is at her job. **LO4**

a. Elementary school teacher, real estate agent

b. Dentist, municipal government administrator

c. Engineer in the private sector, engineer in the military

6. Brokers who sell stocks over the internet can serve many more customers than those who transact business by mail or over the phone. How will the expansion of internet access affect the average incomes of stockbrokers who continue to do business in the traditional way? **LO1**

7. Whose income do you predict will be more affected by the expansion of internet access: **LO1**

a. Stockbrokers or lawyers?

b. Doctors or pharmacists?

c. Bookstore owners or the owners of galleries that sell original oil paintings?

8. How will growing internet access affect the number of film actors and musicians who have active fan clubs? **LO2**

9. Fred, a retired accountant, and Jim, a government manager, are 63-year-old identical twins who collect antique pottery. Each has an annual income of $100,000 (Fred's from a pension, Jim's from salary). One buys most of his pottery at local auctions, and the other buys most of his from a local dealer. Which

brother is more likely to buy at an auction, and does he pay more or less than his brother who buys from the local dealer?   **LO2**

10. Female heads of state (e.g., Israel's Golda Meir, India's Indira Gandhi, Britain's Margaret Thatcher) have often been described as more bellicose in foreign policy matters than the average male head of state. Using Loury's theory of disappearing discourse, suggest an explanation for this pattern.   **LO4**

■ ANSWERS TO IN-CHAPTER EXERCISES ■

12.1 Internet search is a cheap way to acquire information about many goods and services, so the effect of increased internet access will be a downward shift in the supply curve of information. In equilibrium, people will acquire more information, and the goods and services they buy will more closely resemble those they would have chosen in an ideal world with perfect information. These effects will cause total economic surplus to grow. Some of these gains, however, might be offset if the internet makes the free-rider problem more serious.   **LO2**

12.2 The probability of getting heads is 0.5, the same as the probability of getting tails. Thus, the expected value of this gamble is $(0.5)(\$4) + (0.5)(-\$2) = \$1$. Since the gamble is better than fair, a risk-neutral person would accept it.   **LO3**

12.3 Since you still have a 20 percent chance of finding a cheaper apartment if you make another visit, the expected outcome of the gamble is again $2, and you should search again. The bad outcome of any previous search is a sunk cost and should not influence your decision about whether to search again.   **LO3**

12.4 The expected value of a new car will now be $0.8(\$10,000) + 0.2(\$6,000) = \$9,200$. Any risk-neutral consumer who believed that the quality distribution of used cars for sale was the same as the quality distribution of new cars off the assembly line would be willing to pay $9,200 for a used car.   **LO3**

PART

4

ECONOMICS OF PUBLIC POLICY

■

Why do some people earn so much more money than others? No other single question in economics has stimulated nearly as much interest and discussion. Our aim in Chapter 13 will be to apply simple economic principles in an attempt to answer this question. We'll first discuss the human capital model, which emphasizes the importance of differences in personal characteristics. We then focus on why people with similar personal characteristics often earn sharply different incomes. Among the factors we will consider are labor unions, winner-take-all markets, discrimination, and the effect of nonwage conditions of employment. We also will explore whether income inequality is something society should be concerned about, and if so, whether practical remedies exist for it. We will see that government programs to redistribute income have costs as well as benefits.

In Chapter 14 we will explore economic policies for dealing with specific problems in the environmental, safety, and health domains, showing how careful application of basic economic principles can help society design policies that both expand the economic pie and make everyone's slice larger. The unifying thread running through the examples we will consider is the problem of scarcity. In each case, we will explore how the cost-benefit principle can help to resolve the resulting trade-offs.

In Chapter 15 we consider how big government should be, what sorts of goods and services it should provide, and how it should raise the revenue to pay for them. We also will investigate circumstances under which rational citizens might vest in government the power to constrain their behavior in various ways, and how such powers should be apportioned among local, state, and federal levels.

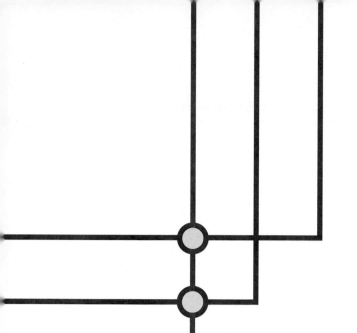

CHAPTER

13

Labor Markets, Poverty, and Income Distribution

LEARNING OBJECTIVES

After reading this chapter, you should be able to:

1. Understand the relationship between wages and the marginal productivity of workers.

2. Analyze how wages and employment are determined in competitive labor markets.

3. Compare and contrast the various hypotheses economists have proposed to explain earnings differences.

4. Discuss recent trends in U.S. income inequality and philosophical justifications for income redistribution.

5. Describe and analyze some of the methods used to reduce poverty in the United States.

B y only the slimmest of margins, Mary Lou Retton won the individual all-around gold medal in women's gymnastics at the Los Angeles Summer Olympic Games in 1984. In the years since, she has remained in the spotlight, continuing to earn millions of dollars from product endorsements and motivational speeches. In contrast, the silver medalist from 1984 has dropped completely from view. (Can you name her?) She is Ecaterina Szabo, one of the most talented Romanian gymnasts of her era, and although she came within a hairbreadth of beating Retton, wealth and international recognition were not to be hers.

Many physicians in Szabo's homeland are likewise every bit as talented and hardworking as physicians in the United States. But while American physicians

Why do small differences in performance sometimes translate into enormous differences in pay?

earn an average annual income of almost $200,000, Romanian physicians earn so little that some of them supplement their incomes by cleaning the Bucharest apartments of expatriate Americans for just $10 a day.

Why do some people earn so much more than others? No other single question in economics has stimulated nearly as much interest and discussion. American citizenship, of course, is neither necessary nor sufficient for receiving high income. Many of the wealthiest people in the world come from extremely poor countries, and many Americans are homeless and malnourished.

Our aim in this chapter will be to employ simple economic principles in an attempt to explain why different people earn different salaries. We'll first discuss the human capital model, which emphasizes the importance of differences in personal characteristics. Next, we will focus on why people with similar personal characteristics often earn sharply different incomes. Among the factors we will consider are labor unions, discrimination, the effect of nonwage conditions of employment, and winner-take-all markets. Finally, we will explore whether income inequality is something society should be concerned about, and if so, whether practical remedies for it exist. As we will see, government programs to redistribute income have costs as well as benefits. As always, policymakers must compare an imperfect status quo with the practical consequences of imperfect government remedies.

THE ECONOMIC VALUE OF WORK

In some respects, the sale of human labor is profoundly different from the sale of other goods and services. For example, although someone may legally relinquish all future rights to the use of her television set by selling it, the law does not permit people to sell themselves into slavery. The law does, however, permit employers to "rent" our services. And in many ways the rental market for labor services functions much like the market for most other goods and services. Each specific category of labor has a demand curve and a supply curve. These curves intersect to determine both the equilibrium wage and the equilibrium quantity of employment for each category of labor.

What is more, shifts in the relevant demand and supply curves produce changes analogous to those produced by shifts in the demand and supply curves for other goods and services. For instance, an increase in the demand for a specific category of labor will generally increase both the equilibrium wage and the equilibrium quantity of employment in that category. By the same token, an increase in the supply of labor to a given occupation will tend to increase the level of employment and lower the wage rate in that occupation.

As in our discussions of other markets, our strategy for investigating how the labor market works will be to go through a series of examples that shed light on different parts of the picture. In the first example, we focus on how the Equilibrium Principle helps us to understand how wages will differ among workers with different levels of productive ability.

Equilibrium ⟶ ◯

How much will the potters earn?

Mackintosh Pottery Works is one of numerous identical companies that hire potters who mold clay into pots. These companies sell the pots for $1.10 each to a finishing company that glazes and fires them, and then sells them in the retail marketplace. Clay, which is available free of charge in unlimited quantities, is the only input used by the potters. Rennie and Laura are currently the only two potters who work for Mackintosh, whose only cost other than potters' salaries is a 10-cent handling cost for each pot it delivers to the finisher. Rennie delivers 100 pots per week and Laura delivers 120. If the labor market for potters is perfectly competitive, how much will each be paid?

We begin with the assumption that Rennie and Laura have decided to work full time as potters, so our focus is not on how much they will work but on how much they will be paid. After taking handling costs into account, the value of the pots that Rennie delivers is $100 per week, and that is the amount Mackintosh will pay him. To pay him less would risk having him bid away by a competitor. For example, if Mackintosh paid Rennie only $90 per week, the company would then enjoy an economic profit of $10 per week as a result of hiring him. Seeing this cash on the table, a rival firm could then offer Rennie $91, thus earning an additional economic profit of $9 per week by bidding him away from Mackintosh. So under the bidding pressure from rival employers, Mackintosh will have difficulty keeping Rennie if it pays him less than $100 per week. And the company would suffer an economic loss if it paid him more than $100 per week. Similarly, the value of the pots delivered each week by Laura is $120, and this will be her competitive equilibrium wage. ◆

In the preceding example, the number of pots each potter delivered each week was that potter's **marginal physical product**, or **marginal product (MP)** for short. More generally, a worker's marginal product is the extra output the firm gets as a result of hiring that worker. When we multiply a worker's marginal product by the net price for which each unit of the product sells, we get that worker's **value of marginal product**, or **VMP**. (In the preceding example the "net price" of each pot was $1.00—the difference between the $1.10 sale price and the $0.10 handling charge.) The general rule in competitive labor markets is that *a worker's pay in long-run equilibrium will be equal to his or her VMP—the net contribution he or she makes to the employer's revenue.* Employers would be delighted to pay workers less than their respective VMPs, to be sure. But if labor markets are truly competitive, they cannot get away with doing so for long.

In the pottery example, each worker's VMP was independent of the number of other workers employed by the firm. In such cases, we cannot predict how many workers a firm will hire. Mackintosh could break even with 2 potters, with 10, or even with 1,000 or more. In many other situations, however, we can predict exactly how many workers a firm will hire. Consider the following example.

marginal product of labor **(MP)** the additional output a firm gets by employing one additional unit of labor

value of marginal product of labor **(VMP)** the dollar value of the additional output a firm gets by employing one additional unit of labor

How many workers should Adirondack hire?

The Adirondack Woodworking Company hires workers in a competitive labor market at a wage of $350 per week to make kitchen cutting boards from scrap wood that is available free of charge. If the boards sell for $20 each and the company's weekly output varies with the number of workers hired as shown in Table 13.1, how many workers should Adirondack hire?

TABLE 13.1

Employment and Productivity in a Woodworking Company (when cutting boards sell for $20 each)

Number of workers	Total number of cutting boards/week	MP (extra cutting boards/week)	VMP ($/week)
0	0		
		30	600
1	30		
		25	500
2	55		
		21	420
3	76		
		18	360
4	94		
		14	280
5	108		

In the pottery example, our focus was on wage differences for employees whose productive abilities differed. In contrast, we assume here that all workers are equally productive and the firm faces a fixed market wage for each. The fact that the marginal product of labor declines with the number of workers hired is a consequence of the law of diminishing returns. (As discussed in Chapter 6, this law says that when a firm's capital or other productive inputs are held fixed in the short run, adding workers beyond some point results in ever smaller increases in output.) The third column of the table reports the marginal product for each additional worker, and the last column reports the value of each successive worker's marginal product—the number of cutting boards he or she adds times the selling price of $20. Adirondack should keep hiring as long as the next worker's *VMP* is at least $350 per week (the market wage). The first four workers have *VMP*s larger than $350, so Adirondack should hire them. But since hiring the fifth worker would add only $280 to weekly revenue, Adirondack should not hire that worker. ◆

Note the similarity between the perfectly competitive firm's decision about how many workers to hire and the perfectly competitive firm's output decision we considered in Chapter 6. When labor is the only variable factor of production, the two decisions are essentially the same. Because of the unique correspondence between the firm's total output and the total number of workers it hires, deciding how many workers to hire is the same as deciding how much output to supply.

The worker's attractiveness to the employer depends not only on how many cutting boards he or she produces, but also on the price of cutting boards and on the wage rate. For example, because *VMP* rises when product price rises, an increase in product price will lead employers to hire more workers. Employers also will increase hiring when the wage rate falls.

EXERCISE 13.1

In the woodworking example, how many workers should Adirondack hire if the price of cutting boards rises to $26?

EXERCISE 13.2

In the woodworking example, how many workers should Adirondack hire if the wage rate falls to $275 per week?

RECAP	THE ECONOMIC VALUE OF WORK

In competitive labor markets, employers face pressure to pay each worker the value of his or her marginal product. When a firm can hire as many workers as it wishes at a given market wage, it should expand employment as long as the value of marginal product of labor exceeds the market wage.

THE EQUILIBRIUM WAGE AND EMPLOYMENT LEVELS

As we saw in Chapter 3, the equilibrium price and quantity in any competitive market occur at the intersection of the relevant supply and demand curves. The same is true in competitive markets for labor.

THE DEMAND CURVE FOR LABOR

An employer's reservation price for a worker is the most the employer could pay without suffering a decline in profit. As discussed, this reservation price for the

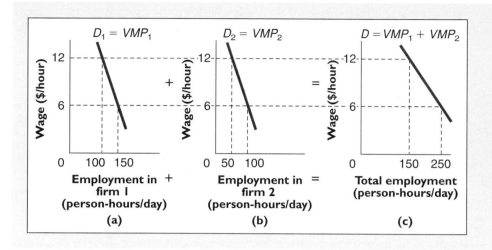

FIGURE 13.1
The Occupational Demand for Labor.
If firm 1 and firm 2 are the only firms that employ labor in a given occupation, we generate the demand curve for labor in that occupation by adding the individual demand curves horizontally.

employer in a perfectly competitive labor market is simply the value of the worker's marginal product (*VMP*). Because of the law of diminishing returns, we know that the marginal product of labor, and hence *VMP*, declines in the short run as the quantity of labor rises. The individual employer's demand curve for labor in any particular occupation—say, computer programmers—may thus be shown, as in Figure 13.1(a), as a downward-sloping function of the wage rate. Suppose firm 1 [part (a)] and firm 2 [part (b)] are the only two firms that employ programmers in a given community. The demand for programmers in that community will then be the horizontal sum of the individual firm demands [part (c)].

THE SUPPLY CURVE OF LABOR

What does the supply curve of labor for a specific occupation look like? Will more labor be offered at high wage rates than at low wage rates? An equivalent way to pose the same question is to ask whether consumers will wish to consume less leisure at high wage rates than at low wage rates. By themselves, the principles of economic theory do not provide an answer to this question because a change in the wage rate exerts two opposing effects on the quantity of leisure demanded. One is the substitution effect, which says that at a higher wage, leisure is more expensive, leading consumers to consume less of it. The second is the income effect, which says that at a higher wage, consumers have more purchasing power, leading them to consume more leisure. Which of these two opposing effects dominates is an empirical question.

For the economy as a whole during the past several centuries, the workweek has been declining and real wages have been rising. This pattern might seem to suggest that the supply curve of labor is downward-sloping, and for the economy as a whole it may be. There is also evidence that individual workers may sometimes work fewer hours when wage rates are high than when they are low. A study of taxicab drivers in New York City, for example, found that drivers quit earlier on rainy days (when the effective wage is high because of high demand for cab rides) than on sunny days (when the effective wage is lower).[1]

These observations notwithstanding, the supply of labor *to any particular occupation* is almost surely upward-sloping because wage differences among occupations influence occupational choice. It is no accident, for example, that many more people are choosing jobs as computer programmers now than in 1970. Wages of programmers have risen sharply during the past several decades, which has led many people to forsake other career paths in favor of programming. Curve *S* in

---

[1]L. Babcock, C. Camerer, G. Loewenstein, and R. Thaler, "Labor Supply of New York City Cab Drivers: One Day at a Time," *Quarterly Journal of Economics* 111 (1997), pp. 408–441.

FIGURE 13.2
The Effect of an Increase in the Demand for Computer Programmers.
An increase in the demand for programmers from D_1 to D_2 results in an increase in the equilibrium level of employment (from L_1 to L_2) and an increase in the equilibrium wage (from W_1 to W_2).

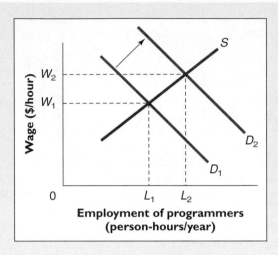

Figure 13.2 represents the supply curve of computer programmers. Its positive slope is typical of the supply curves for most individual occupations.

MARKET SHIFTS

As more tasks have become computerized in recent decades, the demand for programmers has grown, as shown by the shift from D_1 to D_2 in Figure 13.2. Equilibrium in the market for computer programmers occurs at the intersection of the relevant supply and demand curves. The increase in demand has led to an increase in the equilibrium level of programmers from L_1 to L_2 and a rise in the equilibrium wage from W_1 to W_2.

As discussed in Chapter 8, the market for stocks and other financial assets reaches equilibrium very quickly in the wake of shifts in the underlying supply and demand curves. Labor markets, by contrast, are often much slower to adjust. When the demand for workers in a given profession increases, shortages may remain for months or even years, depending on how long it takes people to acquire the skills and training needed to enter the profession.

RECAP	EQUILIBRIUM IN THE LABOR MARKET

The demand for labor in a perfectly competitive labor market is the horizontal sum of each employer's value of marginal product (*VMP*) curve. The supply curve of labor for an individual labor market is upward-sloping, even though the supply curve of labor for the economy as a whole may be vertical or even downward-sloping. In each labor market, the demand and supply curves intersect to determine the equilibrium wage and level of employment.

EXPLAINING DIFFERENCES IN EARNINGS

The theory of competitive labor markets tells us that differences in pay reflect differences in the corresponding *VMP*s. Recall that in the pottery example, Laura earned 20 percent more than Rennie because she made 20 percent more pots each week than he did. This difference in productivity may have resulted from an underlying difference in talent or training, or perhaps Laura simply worked harder than Rennie.

Yet often we see large salary differences even among people who appear equally talented and hardworking. Why, for instance, do lawyers earn so much more than those plumbers who are just as smart as they are and work just as hard? And why do surgeons earn so much more than general practitioners? These wage differences might seem to violate the No-Cash-on-the-Table Principle, which says that only differences in talent, luck, or hard work can account for long-run differences in earnings. For example, if plumbers could earn more by becoming lawyers, why don't they just switch occupations? Similarly, if general practitioners could boost their incomes by becoming surgeons, why didn't they become surgeons in the first place?

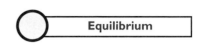

HUMAN CAPITAL THEORY

Answers to these questions are suggested by **human capital theory**, which holds that an individual's *VMP* is proportional to his or her stock of **human capital**—an amalgam of factors such as education, experience, training, intelligence, energy, work habits, trustworthiness, and initiative. According to this theory, some occupations pay better than others because they require larger stocks of human capital. For example, a general practitioner could become a surgeon, but only by extending her formal education by several more years. An even larger investment in additional education is required for a plumber to become a lawyer.

Differences in demand can result in some kinds of human capital being more valuable than others. Consider again the increase in demand for computer programmers that has been occurring for the past several decades. During that same time period, the demand for the services of tax accountants has fallen as more and more taxpayers have used tax-preparation software in lieu of hiring accountants to help them with their taxes. Both occupations require demanding technical training, but the training received by computer programmers now yields a higher return in the labor market.

human capital theory a theory of pay determination that says a worker's wage will be proportional to his or her stock of human capital

human capital an amalgam of factors such as education, training, experience, intelligence, energy, work habits, trustworthiness, and initiative that affect the value of a worker's marginal product

LABOR UNIONS

Two workers with the same amount of human capital may earn different wages if one of them belongs to a **labor union** and the other does not. A labor union is an organization through which workers bargain collectively with employers for better wages and working conditions.

Many economists believe that unions affect labor markets in much the same way that cartels affect product markets. To illustrate, consider a simple economy with two labor markets, neither of which is unionized initially. Suppose the total supply of labor to the two markets is fixed at $S_0 = 200$ workers per day, and that the demand curves are as shown by VMP_1 and VMP_2 in Figure 13.3(a) and (b). The sum of the two demand curves, $VMP_1 + VMP_2$ [part (c)], intersects the supply curve to determine an equilibrium wage of $9 per hour. At that wage, firms in market 1 hire 125 workers per day [part (a)] and firms in market 2 hire 75 [part (b)].

Now suppose workers in market 1 form a union and refuse to work for less than $12 per hour. Because demand curves for labor are downward-sloping, employers of unionized workers reduce employment from 125 workers per day to 100 [Figure 13.4(a)]. The 25 displaced workers in the unionized market would, of course, be delighted to find other jobs in that market at $12 per hour. But they cannot, and so they are forced to seek employment in the nonunionized market. The result is an

labor union a group of workers who bargain collectively with employers for better wages and working conditions

FIGURE 13.3

An Economy with Two Nonunionized Labor Markets.

Supply and demand intersect to determine a market wage of $9 per hour (c). At that wage, employers in market 1 hire 125 workers per day and employers in market 2 hire 75 workers per day. The VMP is $9 in each market.

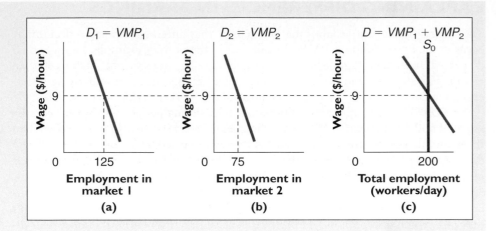

excess supply of 25 workers in the nonunion market at the original wage of $9 per hour. In time, wages in that market decline to $W_N = \$6$ per hour, the level at which 100 workers can find jobs in the nonunionized market [Figure 13.4(b)].

FIGURE 13.4

The Effect of a Union Wage above the Equilibrium Wage.

When the unionized wage is pegged at $W_U = \$12$/hour (a), 25 workers are discharged. When these workers seek employment in the nonunionized market, the wage in that market falls to $W_N = \$6$/hour (b).

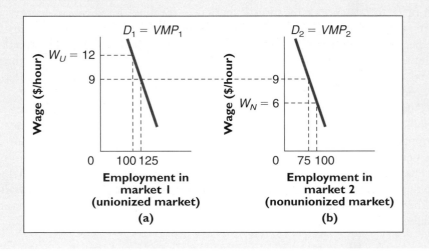

It might seem that the gains of the unionized workers are exactly offset by the losses of nonunionized workers. On closer inspection, however, we see that pegging the union wage above the equilibrium level actually reduces the value of total output. If labor were allocated efficiently between the two markets, its value of marginal product would have to be the same in each. Otherwise, the total value of output could be increased by moving workers from the low-*VMP* market to the high-*VMP* market. With the wage set initially at $9 per hour in both markets, the condition for efficient allocation was met because labor's *VMP* was $9 per hour in both markets. But because the collective bargaining process drives wages (and hence *VMP*s) in the two markets apart, the value of total output is no longer maximized. To verify this claim, note that if a worker is taken out of the nonunionized market, the reduction in the value of output there will be only $6 per hour, which is less than the $12 per hour gain in the value of output when that same worker is added to the unionized market.

EXERCISE 13.3

In Figure 13.4, by how much would the value of total output be increased if the wage rate were $9 per hour in each market?

Wages paid to workers in a unionized firm are sometimes 50 percent or more above the wages paid to their nonunionized counterparts. To the alert economic naturalist, this difference prompts the following question:

Example 13.1

THE ECONOMIC NATURALIST

If unionized firms have to pay more, how do they manage to survive in the face of competition from their nonunionized counterparts?

In fact, nonunionized firms sometimes do drive unionized firms out of business, as when the American textile industry moved to the South in the late nineteenth and early twentieth centuries to escape the burden of high union wages in New England. Even so, unionized and nonunionized firms often manage to compete head-to-head for extended periods. If their costs are significantly higher, how do the unionized firms manage to survive?

The observed pay differential actually overstates the difference between the labor costs of the two types of firm. Because the higher union wage attracts an excess supply of workers, unionized employers can adopt more stringent hiring requirements than their nonunionized counterparts. As a result, unionized workers tend to be more experienced and skilled than nonunionized workers. Studies estimate that the union wage premium for workers with the same amount of human capital is only about 10 percent.

Another factor is that unions may actually boost the productivity of workers with any given amount of human capital, perhaps by improving communication between management and workers. Similarly, the implementation of formal grievance procedures, in combination with higher pay, may boost morale among unionized workers, leading to higher productivity. Labor turnover is also significantly lower in unionized firms, which reduces hiring and training costs. Studies suggest that union productivity may be sufficiently high to compensate for the premium in union wages. So even though wages are higher in unionized firms, these firms may not have significantly higher labor costs per unit of output than their nonunionized counterparts. •

How do firms that employ higher-paid union labor remain competitive?

Only 12 percent of American workers belonged to a labor union in 2006, about half the union membership rate during the 1950s. Because the union wage premium is small and applies to only a small fraction of the labor force, union membership in the United States is probably not an important explanation for why workers with similar qualifications often earn sharply different incomes.

COMPENSATING WAGE DIFFERENTIALS

If people are paid the value of what they produce, why do garbage collectors earn more than lifeguards? Picking up the trash is important, to be sure, but is it more valuable than saving the life of a drowning child? Similarly, we need not question the value of a timely plumbing repair to wonder why plumbers get paid more than fourth-grade teachers. Is replacing faucet washers really more valuable than educating children? As the next example illustrates, the wage for a particular job depends not only on the value of what workers produce, but also on how attractive they find its working conditions.

Do tobacco company CEOs get paid extra for testifying that cigarette smoking does not cause cancer?

Example 13.2

THE ECONOMIC NATURALIST

Why do some ad–copy writers earn more than others?

You plan to pursue a career in advertising and have two job offers: one to write ad copy for the American Cancer Society, the other to write copy for Camel cigarette ads aimed at the youth market. Except for the subject matter of the ads, working conditions are identical in the two jobs. If each job paid $30,000 per year and offered the same prospects for advancement, which would you choose?

When this question was recently posed to a sample of graduating seniors at Cornell University, almost 90 percent of them chose the American Cancer Society job. When asked how much more they would have to be paid to induce them to switch to the Camel

EN 13

compensating wage differential a difference in the wage rate—negative or positive—that reflects the attractiveness of a job's working conditions

cigarettes job, their median response was a premium of $15,000 per year. As this sample suggests, employers who offer jobs with less attractive working conditions cannot hope to fill them unless they also offer higher salaries. ●

Other things being equal, jobs with attractive working conditions will pay less than jobs with less attractive conditions. Wage differences associated with differences in working conditions are known as **compensating wage differentials.** Economists have identified compensating differentials for a host of specific working conditions. Studies have found, for example, that safe jobs tend to pay less than otherwise similar jobs that entail greater risks to health and safety. Studies also have found that wages vary in accord with the attractiveness of the work schedule. For instance, working night shifts commands a wage premium, and teachers must accept lower wages in part because many of those with children value having hours that coincide with the school calendar.

DISCRIMINATION IN THE LABOR MARKET

Women and minorities continue to receive lower wage rates, on average, than white males with similar measures of human capital. This pattern poses a profound challenge to standard theories of competitive labor markets, which hold that competitive pressures will eliminate wage differentials not based on differences in productivity. Defenders of standard theories attribute the wage gap to unmeasured differences in human capital. Many critics of these theories reject the idea that labor markets are effectively competitive, and instead attribute the gap to various forms of discrimination.

Discrimination by Employers

employer discrimination an arbitrary preference by an employer for one group of workers over another

Employer discrimination is the term used to describe wage differentials that arise from an arbitrary preference by an employer for one group of workers over another. An example occurs if two labor force groups, such as males and females, are equally productive, on average, yet some employers ("discriminators") prefer hiring males and are willing to pay higher wages to do so.

Most consumers are not willing to pay more for a product produced by males than for an identical one produced by females (if indeed they even *know* which type of worker produced the product). If product price is unaffected by the composition of the workforce that produces the product, a firm's profit will be smaller the more males it employs because males cost more yet are no more productive (on the assumption that discrimination is the cause of the wage gap). Thus, the most profitable firms will be ones that employ only females.

Arbitrary wage gaps are an apparent violation of the No-Cash-on-the-Table Principle. The initial wage differential provides an opportunity for employers who hire mostly females to grow at the expense of their rivals. Because such firms make an economic profit on the sale of each unit of output, their incentive is to expand as rapidly as they possibly can. And to do that, they would naturally want to continue hiring only the cheaper females.

But as profit-seeking firms continue to pursue this strategy, the supply of females at the lower wage rate will run out. The short-run solution is to offer females a slightly higher wage. But this strategy works only if other firms do not pursue it. Once they too start offering a higher wage, females will again be in short supply. The only stable outcome occurs when the wage of females reaches parity with the wage of males. The wage for both males and females will thus settle at the common value of their *VMP.*

Any employer who wants to voice a preference for hiring males must now do so by paying males a wage in excess of *VMP.* Employers can discriminate against females if they wish, but only if they are willing to pay premium wages to males out of their own profits. Not even the harshest critics of the competitive model seem willing to impute such behavior to the owners of capitalist enterprises.

| Equilibrium |

Discrimination by Others

If employer discrimination is not the primary explanation of the wage gap, what is? In some instances, **customer discrimination** may provide a plausible explanation. For example, if people believe that juries and clients are less likely to take female or minority attorneys seriously, members of these groups will face a reduced incentive to attend law school, and law firms will face a reduced incentive to hire those who do.

Another possible source of persistent wage gaps is discrimination and socialization within the family. For example, families may provide less education for their female children, or they may socialize them to believe that lofty career ambitions are not appropriate.

customer discrimination the willingness of consumers to pay more for a product produced by members of a favored group, even if the quality of the product is unaffected

Other Sources of the Wage Gap

Part of the wage gap may be explained by compensating wage differentials that spring from differences in preferences for other nonwage elements of the compensation package. Jobs that involve exposure to physical risk, for example, command higher wages, and if men are relatively more willing to accept such risks, they will earn more than females with otherwise identical stocks of human capital. (The same difference would result if employers felt constrained by social norms not to assign female employees to risky jobs.)

Elements of human capital that are difficult to measure also may help to explain earnings differentials. For example, productivity is influenced not only by the quantity of education an individual has, which is easy to measure, but also by its quality, which is much harder to measure. Part of the black–white differential in wages may thus be due to the fact that schools in black neighborhoods have not been as good, on average, as those in white neighborhoods.

Differences in the courses people take in college appear to have similar implications for differences in productivity. For instance, students in math, engineering, or business—male or female—tend to earn significantly higher salaries than those who concentrate in the humanities. The fact that males are disproportionately represented in the former group gives rise to a male wage premium that is unrelated to employer discrimination.

"English lit—how about you?"

As economists have grown more sophisticated in their efforts to measure human capital and other factors that influence individual wage rates, unexplained wage differentials by sex and race have grown steadily smaller, and have even disappeared altogether in some studies.[2] Other studies, however, continue to find significant unexplained differentials by race and sex. Debate about discrimination in the workplace will continue until the causes of these differentials are more fully understood.

WINNER-TAKE-ALL MARKETS

Differences in human capital do much to explain observed differences in earnings. Yet earnings differentials have also grown sharply in many occupations within which the distribution of human capital among workers seems essentially unchanged. Consider the following example.

Example 13.3

THE ECONOMIC NATURALIST

Why does Renée Fleming earn millions more than sopranos of only slightly lesser ability?

Although the best sopranos have always earned more than others with slightly lesser talents, the earnings gap is sharply larger now than it was in the nineteenth century. Today, top singers like Renée Fleming earn millions of dollars per year—hundreds or even thousands of times what sopranos only marginally less talented earn. Given that listeners in blind hearings often have difficulty identifying the most highly paid singers, why is this earnings differential so large?

The answer lies in a fundamental change in the way we consume most of our music. In the nineteenth century, virtually all professional musicians delivered their services in concert halls in front of live audiences. (In 1900, the state of Iowa alone had more than 1,300 concert halls!) Audiences of that day would have been delighted to listen to the world's best soprano, but no one singer could hope to perform in more than a tiny fraction of the world's concert halls. Today, in contrast, most of the music we hear comes in recorded form, which enables the best soprano to be literally everywhere at once. As soon as the master recording has been made, Renée Fleming's performance can be burned onto compact discs at the same low cost as for a slightly less talented singer's.

Tens of millions of buyers worldwide are willing to pay a few cents extra to hear the most talented performers. Recording companies would be delighted to hire those singers at modest salaries, for by so doing they would earn an enormous economic profit. But that would unleash bidding by rival recording companies for the best singers. Such bidding assures that the top singers will earn multimillion-dollar annual salaries (most of which constitute economic rents, as discussed in Chapter 8). Slightly less talented singers earn much less because the recording industry simply does not need them. ●

Why does Renée Fleming earn so much more than sopranos who are only slightly less able?

winner-take-all labor market
one in which small differences in human capital translate into large differences in pay

The market for sopranos is an example of a **winner-take-all market,** one in which small differences in ability or other dimensions of human capital translate into large differences in pay. Such markets have long been familiar in entertainment and professional sports. But as technology has enabled the most talented individuals to serve broader markets, the winner-take-all reward structure has become an increasingly important feature of modern economic life, permeating such diverse fields as law, journalism, consulting, medicine, investment banking, corporate management, publishing, design, fashion, even the hallowed halls of academe.

Contrary to what the name seems to imply, a winner-take-all market does not mean a market with literally only one winner. Indeed, hundreds of professional musicians earn multimillion-dollar annual salaries. Yet tens of thousands of others, many of them nearly as good, struggle to pay their bills.

[2]S. Polachek and M. Kim, "Panel Estimates of the Male–Female Earnings Functions," *Journal of Human Resources* 29, no. 2 (1994), pp. 406–28.

The fact that small differences in human capital often give rise to extremely large differences in pay might seem to contradict human capital theory. Note, however, that the winner-take-all reward pattern is completely consistent with the competitive labor market theory's claim that individuals are paid in accordance with the contributions they make to the employer's net revenue. The leverage of technology often amplifies small performance differentials into very large ones.

RECAP	EXPLAINING DIFFERENCES IN EARNINGS AMONG PEOPLE

Earnings differ among people in part because of differences in their human capital, an amalgam of personal characteristics that affect productivity. But pay often differs substantially between two people with the same amount of human capital. This can happen for many reasons: one may belong to a labor union while the other does not; one may work in a job with less pleasant conditions; one may be the victim of discrimination; or one may work in an arena in which technology or other factors provide greater leverage to human capital.

RECENT TRENDS IN INEQUALITY

In the United States, as in most other market economies, most citizens receive most of their income from the sale of their own labor. An attractive feature of the free-market system is that it rewards initiative, effort, and risk taking. The harder, longer, and more effectively a person works, the more she will be paid.

Yet relying on the marketplace to distribute income also entails an important drawback: Those who do well often end up with vastly more money than they can spend, while those who fail often cannot afford even basic goods and services. Hundreds of thousands of American families are homeless, and still larger numbers go to bed hungry each night. Many distinguished philosophers have argued that such poverty in the midst of plenty is impossible to justify on moral grounds. It is thus troubling that income inequality has been growing rapidly in recent decades.

The period from the end of World War II until the early 1970s was one of balanced income growth in the United States. During that period, incomes grew at almost 3 percent a year for rich, middle-class, and poor Americans alike. In the ensuing years, however, the pattern of income growth has been dramatically different.

In the first row of Table 13.2, for example, notice that families in the bottom 20 percent of the income distribution saw their real incomes grow by about 10 percent

TABLE 13.2
Mean Income Received by Families in Each Income Quintile and by the Top 5 Percent of Families, All Races, 1980–2000 (2005 dollars)

Quintile	1980	1990	2000
Bottom 20 percent	$ 14,386	$ 14,241	$ 16,008
Second 20 percent	31,316	33,217	36,602
Middle 20 percent	47,308	51,157	57,525
Fourth 20 percent	65,634	73,569	84,781
Top 20 percent	110,507	136,725	177,879
Top 5 percent	157,094	214,527	315,205

SOURCE: U.S. Census Bureau, Table F-3. (http://www.census.gov/hhes/www/income/histinc/f03ar.html).

from 1980 to 2000 (a growth rate of less than one-half of 1 percent per year). The third row of the table indicates that the real incomes of families in the middle quintile grew by about 18 percent during the same 20-year period (a growth rate of less than 1 percent per year). In contrast, real incomes jumped almost 40 percent for families in the top quintile between 1980 and 2000, while those for families in the top 5 percent jumped by more than 50 percent. Even for these families, however, income growth rates were low relative to those of the immediate post–World War II decades.

The only people whose incomes have grown substantially faster than in that earlier period are those at the very pinnacle of the income ladder. Real earnings of the top 1 percent of U.S. earners, for example, have more than doubled since 1980, and those even higher up have taken home paychecks that might have seemed unimaginable just two decades ago. The CEOs of America's largest companies, who earned 42 times as much as the average worker in 1980, now earn more than 500 times as much.

It is important to emphasize that being near the bottom of the income distribution in one year does not necessarily mean being stranded there forever. On the contrary, people in the United States have always experienced a high degree of economic mobility by international standards. Many CEOs now earning multimillion-dollar paychecks, for example, were struggling young graduate students in 1980, and were hence among those classified in the bottom 20 percent of the income distribution for that year in Table 13.2. We must bear in mind, too, that not all economic mobility is upward. Many blue-collar workers, for instance, had higher real incomes in 1980 than they do today.

On balance, then, the entries in Table 13.2 tell an important story. In contrast to the economy a quarter-century ago, those near the top of the income ladder today are prospering as never before, while those further down have seen their living standards grow much more slowly.

RECAP	**RECENT TRENDS IN INEQUALITY**

From 1945 until the mid-1970s, incomes grew at almost 3 percent a year for rich, middle-class, and poor families alike. In contrast, most of the income growth since the mid-1970s has been concentrated among top earners.

IS INCOME INEQUALITY A MORAL PROBLEM?

John Rawls, a moral philosopher at Harvard University, constructed a cogent ethical critique of the marginal productivity system, one based heavily on the economic theory of choice itself.[3] In thinking about what constitutes a just distribution of income, Rawls asks us to imagine ourselves meeting to choose the rules for distributing income. The meeting takes place behind a "veil of ignorance," which conceals from participants any knowledge of what talents and abilities each has. Because no individual knows whether he is smart or dull, strong or weak, fast or slow, no one knows which rules of distribution would work to his own advantage.

Rawls argues that the rules people would choose in such a state of ignorance would necessarily be fair; and if the rules are fair, the income distribution to which they give rise will also be fair.

What sort of rules would people choose from behind a veil of ignorance? If the national income were a fixed amount, most people would probably give everyone an equal share. That scenario is likely, Rawls argues, because most people are

---

[3]John Rawls, *A Theory of Justice* (Cambridge, MA: Harvard University Press, 1971).

strongly risk-averse. Since an unequal income distribution would involve not only a chance of doing well but a chance of doing poorly, most people would prefer to eliminate the risk by choosing an equal distribution. Imagine, for example, that you and two friends have been told that an anonymous benefactor donated $300,000 to divide among you. How would you split it? If you are like most people, you would propose an equal division, or $100,000 for each of you.

Yet the attraction of equality is far from absolute. Indeed, the goal of absolute equality is quickly trumped by other concerns when we make the rules for distributing wealth in modern market economies. Wealth, after all, generally doesn't come from anonymous benefactors; we must produce it. In a large economy, if each person were guaranteed an equal amount of income, few would invest in education or the development of special talents; and as the next example illustrates, the incentive to work would be sharply reduced.

Does income sharing affect labor supply?

Sue is offered a job reshelving books in the University of Montana library from noon until 1 p.m. each Friday. Her reservation wage for this task is $10 per hour. If the library director offers Sue $100 per hour, how much economic surplus will she enjoy as a result of accepting the job? Now suppose the library director announces that the earnings from the job will be divided equally among the 400 students who live in Sue's dormitory. Will Sue still accept?

When the $100 per hour is paid directly to Sue, she accepts the job and enjoys an economic surplus of $100 − $10 = $90. If the $100 were divided equally among the 400 residents of Sue's dorm, however, each resident's share would be only 25 cents. Accepting the job would thus mean a negative surplus for Sue of $0.25 − $10 = −$9.75, so she will not accept the job. ◆

EXERCISE 13.4

What is the largest dorm population for which Sue would accept the job on a pay-sharing basis?

In a country without rewards for hard work and risk taking, national income would be dramatically smaller than in a country with such rewards. Of course, material rewards for effort and risk taking necessarily lead to inequality. Rawls argues, however, that people would be willing to accept a certain degree of inequality as long as these rewards produced a sufficiently large increase in the total amount of output available for distribution.

But how much inequality would people accept? Much less than the amount produced by purely competitive markets, Rawls argues. The idea is that behind the veil of ignorance, each person would fear ending up in a disadvantaged position, so each would choose rules that would produce a more equal distribution of income than exists under the marginal productivity system. And since such choices *define* the just distribution of income, he argues, fairness requires at least some attempt to reduce the inequality produced by the market system.

RECAP	IS INCOME INEQUALITY A MORAL PROBLEM?

John Rawls argues that the degree of inequality typical of unregulated market systems is unfair because people would favor substantially less inequality if they chose distributional rules from behind a veil of ignorance.

METHODS OF INCOME REDISTRIBUTION

Although we as a society have an interest in limiting income inequality, programs for reducing it are often fraught with practical difficulties. The challenge is to find ways to raise the incomes of those who cannot fend for themselves, without at the same time undermining their incentive to work, and without using scarce resources to subsidize those who are not poor. Of course, some people simply cannot work, or cannot find work that pays enough to live on. In a world of perfect information, the government could make generous cash payments to those people, and withhold support from those who can fend for themselves. In practice, however, the two groups are often hard to distinguish from each other. And so we must choose among imperfect alternative measures.

WELFARE PAYMENTS AND IN-KIND TRANSFERS

in-kind transfer a payment made not in the form of cash, but in the form of a good or service

Cash transfers and in-kind transfers are at the forefront of antipoverty efforts around the globe. **In-kind transfers** are direct transfers of goods or services to low-income individuals or families, such as food stamps, public housing, subsidized school lunches, and Medicaid.

From the mid-1960s until 1996, the most important federal program of cash transfers was Aid to Families with Dependent Children (AFDC), which in most cases provided cash payments to poor single-parent households. Critics of this program charged that the program ignored the Incentive Principle. AFDC created incentives that undermined family stability because a poor mother was ineligible for AFDC payments in many states if her husband or other able-bodied adult male lived with her and her children. This provision confronted many long-term unemployed fathers with an agonizing choice. They could leave their families, making them eligible for public assistance; or they could remain, making them ineligible. Even many who deeply loved their families understandably chose to leave.

Personal Responsibility Act the 1996 federal law that transferred responsibility for welfare programs from the federal level to the state level and placed a five-year lifetime limit on payment of AFDC benefits to any given recipient

Concern about work incentives led Congress to pass the **Personal Responsibility Act** in 1996, abolishing the federal government's commitment to provide cash assistance to low-income families. The new law requires the federal government to make lump-sum cash grants to the states, which are then free to spend it on AFDC benefits or other income-support programs of their own design. For each welfare recipient, the new law also sets a five-year lifetime limit on receipt of benefits under the AFDC program.

Supporters of the Personal Responsibility Act argue that it has already reduced the nation's welfare rolls substantially and that it will encourage greater self-reliance over the long run. Skeptics fear that denial of benefits may eventually impose severe hardships on poor children if overall economic conditions deteriorate even temporarily. Debate continues about the extent to which the observed rise in homelessness and malnutrition among the nation's poorest families during the economic downturn of 2001 was attributable to the Personal Responsibility Act. What is clear, however, is that abolition of a direct federal role in the nation's antipoverty effort does not eliminate the need to discover efficient ways of providing assistance to people in need.

MEANS-TESTED BENEFIT PROGRAMS

means-tested a benefit program whose benefit level declines as the recipient earns additional income

Many welfare programs, including AFDC, are **means-tested**, which means that the more income a family has, the smaller are the benefits it receives under these programs. The purpose of means testing is to avoid paying benefits to those who don't really need them. But because of the way welfare programs are administered, means testing often has a pernicious effect on work incentives.

Consider, for example, an unemployed participant in four welfare programs: food stamps, rent stamps, energy stamps, and day care stamps. Each program

Incentive

gives him $100 worth of stamps per month, which he is then free to spend on food, rent, energy, and day care. If he gets a job, his benefits in each program are reduced by 50 cents for each dollar he earns. Thus, if he accepts a job that pays $50 weekly, he will lose $25 in weekly benefits from each of the four welfare programs, for a total benefit reduction of $100 per week. Taking the job thus leaves him $50 per week worse off than before. Low-income persons need no formal training in economics to realize that seeking gainful employment does not pay under these circumstances.

What is more, means-tested programs of cash and in-kind transfers are extremely costly to administer. If the government were to eliminate all existing welfare and social service agencies that are involved in these programs, the resulting savings would be enough to lift every poor person out of poverty. One proposal to do precisely this is the negative income tax.

THE NEGATIVE INCOME TAX

Under the **negative income tax** (NIT), every man, woman, and child—rich or poor—would receive a substantial income tax credit, say $4,500 per year. A person who earns no income would receive this credit in cash. People who earn income would receive the same initial credit, and their income would continue to be taxed at some rate less than 100 percent.

The negative income tax would do much less than current programs to weaken work incentives because, unlike current programs, it would ensure that someone who earned an extra dollar would keep at least a portion of it. And because the program would be administered by the existing Internal Revenue Service, administrative costs would be far lower than under the current welfare system.

Despite these advantages, however, the negative income tax is by no means a perfect solution to the income-transfer problem. Although the incentive problem under the program would be less severe than under current welfare programs, it would remain a serious difficulty. To see why, note that if the negative income tax were the *sole* means of insulating people against poverty, the payment to people with no earned income would need to be at least as large as the government's official **poverty threshold**.

The poverty threshold is the annual income level below which a family is officially classified as "poor" by the government. The threshold is based on government estimates of the cost of the so-called economy food plan, the least costly of four nutritionally adequate food plans designed by the Department of Agriculture. The department's 1955 Household Food Consumption Survey found that families of three or more people spent approximately one-third of their after-tax income on food, so the government pegs the poverty threshold at three times the cost of the economy food plan. In 2005, that threshold was approximately $19,000 for a family of four.

For a family of four living in a city, $19,000 a year is scarcely enough to make ends meet. But suppose a group of, say, eight families were to pool their negative tax payments and move to the mountains of northern New Mexico. With a total of $144,000 per year to spend, plus the fruits of their efforts at gardening and animal husbandry, such a group could live very nicely indeed.

Once a small number of experimental groups demonstrated the feasibility of quitting their jobs and living well on the negative income tax, others would surely follow suit. Two practical difficulties would ensue. First, as more and more people left their jobs to live at government expense, the program would eventually become prohibitively costly. And second, the political cost of the program would almost surely force supporters to abandon it long before that point. Reports of people living lives of leisure at taxpayers' expense would be sure to appear on the nightly news. People who work hard at their jobs all day long would wonder why their tax dollars were being used to support those who are capable of holding paying jobs,

negative income tax (NIT) a system under which the government would grant every citizen a cash payment each year, financed by an additional tax on earned income

poverty threshold the level of income below which the federal government classifies a family as poor

yet choose not to work. If the resulting political backlash did not completely eliminate the negative income tax program, it would force policymakers to cut back the payment so that members of rural communes could no longer afford to live comfortably. And that would mean the payment would no longer support an urban family. This difficulty has led policymakers to focus on other ways to increase the incomes of the working poor.

MINIMUM WAGES

The United States and many other industrialized countries have sought to ease the burden of low-wage workers by enacting minimum wage legislation—laws that prohibit employers from paying workers less than a specified hourly wage. The federal minimum wage in the United States is currently set at $5.85 per hour, and several states have set minimum wage levels significantly higher. For example, the minimum wage in the state of Washington is $8.07 per hour for 2008.

How does a minimum wage affect the market for low-wage labor? In Figure 13.5, note that when the law prevents employers from paying less than W_{min}, employers hire fewer workers (a decline from L_0 to L_1). Unemployment results: The L_1 workers who keep their jobs earn more than before, but the $L_0 - L_1$ workers who lose their jobs earn nothing. Whether workers together earn more or less than before depends on the elasticity of demand for labor. If elasticity of demand is less than 1, workers as a group will earn more than before. If it is more than 1, workers as a group will earn less.

FIGURE 13.5
The Effect of Minimum Wage Legislation on Employment.
If minimum wage legislation requires employers to pay more than the equilibrium wage, the result will be a decline in employment for low-wage workers.

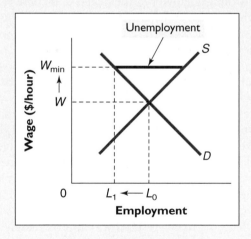

At one point, economists were almost unanimous in their opposition to minimum wage laws, arguing that those laws reduce total economic surplus, as do other regulations that prevent markets from reaching equilibrium. In recent years, however, some economists have softened their opposition to minimum wage laws, citing studies that have failed to show significant reductions in employment following increases in minimum wage levels. These studies may well imply that, as a group, low-income workers are better off with minimum wage laws than without them. But as we saw in Chapter 7, any policy that prevents a market from reaching equilibrium causes a reduction in total economic surplus—which means society ought to be able to find a more effective policy for helping low-wage workers.

THE EARNED-INCOME TAX CREDIT

One such policy is the **earned-income tax credit** (EITC), which gives low-wage workers a credit on their federal income tax each year. The EITC was enacted into law in 1975, and in the years since has drawn praise from both liberals and conservatives. The program is essentially a wage subsidy in the form of a credit against the amount a family owes in federal income taxes. For example, a family of four with total earned income of $15,000 in 2007 would have received an annual tax credit of approximately $4,700 under this program. That is, the program would have reduced the annual federal income tax payment of this family by roughly that amount. Families who earned less would have received a larger tax credit, and those who earned more would have received a smaller one. Families whose tax credit exceeds the amount of tax owed actually receive a check from the government for the difference. The EITC is thus essentially the same as a negative income tax, except that eligibility for the program is confined to people who work.

earned-income tax credit (EITC) a policy under which low-income workers receive credits on their federal income tax

Like both the negative income tax and the minimum wage, the EITC puts extra income into the hands of workers who are employed at low wage levels. But unlike the minimum wage, the earned-income tax credit creates no incentive for employers to lay off low-wage workers.

The following examples illustrate how switching from a minimum wage to an earned-income tax credit can produce gains for both employers and workers.

By how much will a minimum wage reduce total economic surplus?

Suppose the demand and supply curves for unskilled labor in the Tallahassee labor market are as shown in Figure 13.6. By how much will the imposition of a minimum wage at $7 per hour reduce total economic surplus? By how much do worker surplus and employer surplus change as a result of adopting the minimum wage?

In the absence of a minimum wage, the equilibrium wage for Tallahassee would be $5 per hour, and employment would be 5,000 person-hours per day. Both employers and workers would enjoy economic surplus equal to the area of the shaded triangles in Figure 13.6, $12,500 per day.

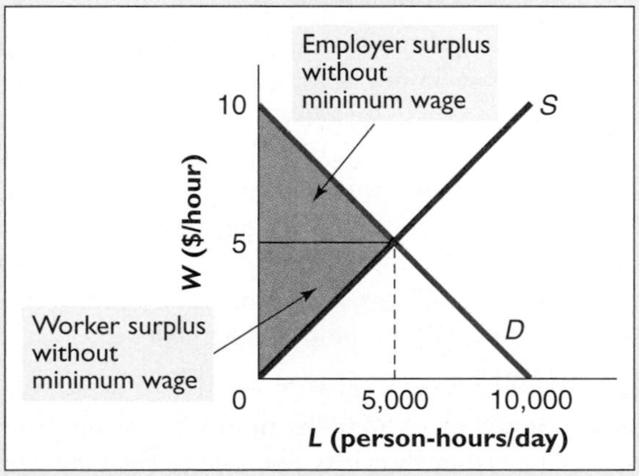

**FIGURE 13.6
Worker and Employer Surplus in an Unregulated Labor Market.**
For the demand and supply curves shown, worker surplus is the area of the lower shaded triangle, $12,500 per day, the same as employer surplus (upper shaded triangle).

With a minimum wage set at $7 per hour, employer surplus is the area of the cross-hatched triangle in Figure 13.7, $4,500 per day, and worker surplus is the area of the green shaded figure, $16,500 per day. The minimum wage thus reduces employer surplus by $8,000 per day and increases worker surplus by $4,000 per day. The net reduction in surplus is the area of the blue shaded triangle shown in Figure 13.7, $4,000 per day.

FIGURE 13.7
The Effect of a Minimum Wage on Economic Surplus.
A minimum wage of $7 per hour reduces employment in this market by 2,000 person-hours per day, for a reduction in total economic surplus of $4,000 per day (area of the blue shaded triangle). Employer surplus falls to $4,500 per day (area of cross-hatched triangle), while worker surplus rises to $16,500 per day (green shaded area).

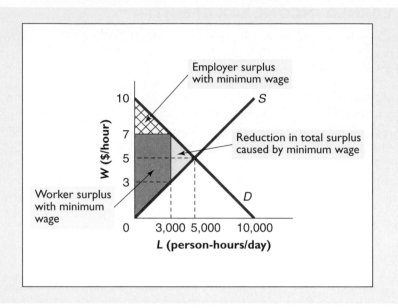

EXERCISE 13.5

In the minimum wage example above, by how much would total economic surplus have been reduced by the $7 minimum wage if labor demand in Tallahassee had been perfectly inelastic at 5,000 person-hours per day?

Efficiency

The following example illustrates the central message of the Efficiency Principle, which is that if the economic pie can be made larger, everyone can have a larger slice.

Suppose that, instead of imposing a minimum wage, the government enacts an earned-income tax credit program. How much would it cost the government each day to provide an earned-income tax credit under which workers as a group receive the same economic surplus as they do under the $7 per hour minimum wage? (Assume for simplicity that the earned-income tax credit has no effect on labor supply.)

With an earned-income tax credit in lieu of a minimum wage, employment will be 5,000 person-hours per day at $5 per hour, just as in the unregulated market. Since worker surplus in the unregulated market was $4,000 per day less than under the minimum wage, the government would have to offer a tax credit worth $0.80 per hour for each of the 5,000 person-hours of employment to restore worker surplus to the level obtained under the $7 minimum wage. With an EITC of that amount in effect, worker surplus would be the same as under the $7 minimum wage. If the EITC were financed by a $4,000 tax on employers, employer surplus would be $4,000 greater than under the $7 minimum wage. ◆

We stress that our point is not that the minimum wage produces no gains for low-income workers, but rather that it is possible to provide even larger gains for these workers if we avoid policies that try to prevent labor markets from reaching equilibrium.

PUBLIC EMPLOYMENT FOR THE POOR

The main shortcoming of the EITC is that it does nothing for the unemployed poor. The negative income tax lacks that shortcoming but may substantially weaken work incentives. There is yet another method of transferring income to the poor that avoids both shortcomings. Government-sponsored jobs could pay wages to the unemployed poor for useful work. With public service employment, the specter of people living lives of leisure at public expense simply does not arise.

But public service employment has difficulties of its own. Evidence shows that if government jobs pay the same wages as private jobs, many people will leave their private jobs in favor of government jobs, apparently because they view government jobs as being more secure. Such a migration would make public service employment extremely expensive. Other worrisome possibilities are that such jobs might involve make-work tasks, and that they would prompt an expansion in government bureaucracy.

Acting alone, government-sponsored jobs for the poor, the EITC, or the negative income tax cannot solve the income-transfer problem. But a combination of these programs might do so.

A COMBINATION OF METHODS

Consider a negative income tax whose cash grant is far too small for anyone to live on, but that is supplemented if necessary by a public service job at below minimum wage. Keeping the wage in public service jobs well below the minimum wage would eliminate the risk of a large-scale exodus from private jobs. And while living well on either the negative income tax or the public service wage would be impossible, the two programs together could lift people out of poverty (see Figure 13.8).

To prevent an expansion of the bureaucracy, the government could solicit bids from private management companies to oversee the public service employment program. The fear that this program would inevitably become a make-work project is allayed by evidence that unskilled workers can, with proper supervision, perform many valuable tasks that would not otherwise be performed in the private sector. They can, for example, do landscaping and maintenance in public parks; provide transportation for the elderly and those with disabilities; fill potholes in city streets and replace burned-out street lamps; transplant seedlings in erosion control projects; remove graffiti from public places and paint government buildings; recycle newspapers and containers; staff day care centers; and so on.

Can unskilled workers perform useful public service jobs?

© David Young-Wolff/PhotoEdit, Inc.

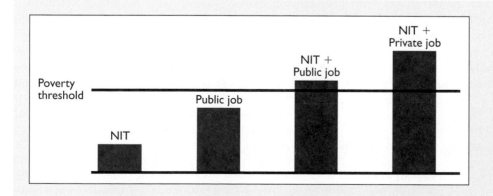

FIGURE 13.8
Income by Source in a Combination NIT–Jobs Program.
Together, a small negative income tax and a public job at below minimum wage would provide a family enough income to escape poverty, without weakening work incentives significantly.

This combination of a small negative income tax payment and public service employment at a subminimum wage would not be cheap. But the direct costs of existing welfare programs are also large, and the indirect costs, in the form of perverse work incentives and misguided attempts to control prices, are even larger. In economic terms, dealing intelligently with the income-transfer problem may in fact prove relatively inexpensive, once society recognizes the enormous opportunity cost of failing to deal intelligently with it.

RECAP	METHODS OF INCOME REDISTRIBUTION

Minimum wage laws reduce total economic surplus by contracting employment. The earned-income tax credit boosts the incomes of the working poor without that drawback, but neither policy provides benefits for those who are not employed.

Other instruments in the battle against poverty include in-kind transfers such as food stamps, subsidized school lunches, Medicaid, and public housing as well as cash transfers such as Aid to Families with Dependent Children. Because benefits under most of these programs are means-tested, beneficiaries often experience a net decline in income when they accept paid employment.

The negative income tax is an expanded version of the earned-income tax credit that includes those who are not employed. Combining this program with access to public service jobs would enable government to ensure adequate living standards for the poor without significantly undermining work incentives.

▪ SUMMARY ▪

- A worker's long-run equilibrium pay in a competitive labor market will be equal to the value of her marginal product (*VMP*)—the market value of whatever goods and services she produces for her employer. The law of diminishing returns says that when a firm's capital and other productive inputs are held fixed in the short run, adding workers beyond some point results in ever smaller increases in output. Firms that purchase labor in competitive labor markets face a constant wage, and they will hire labor up to the point at which *VMP* equals the market wage. **LO1, LO2**

- Human capital theory says that an individual's *VMP* is proportional to his stock of human capital—an amalgam of education, experience, training, intelligence, and other factors that influence productivity. According to this theory, some occupations pay better than others simply because they require larger stocks of human capital. **LO3**

- Wages often differ between individuals whose stocks of human capital appear nearly the same, as when one belongs to a labor union and the other does not. Compensating wage differentials—wage differences associated with differences in working conditions—are another important explanation for why individuals with similar human capital might earn different salaries. They help to explain why garbage collectors earn more than lifeguards and, more generally, why individuals with a given stock of human capital tend to earn more in jobs that have less-attractive working conditions. **LO3**

- Many firms pay members of certain groups—notably blacks and females—less than they pay white males who seem to have similar personal characteristics. If such wage gaps are the result of employer discrimination, their existence implies profit opportunities for firms that do not discriminate. Several other factors, including discrimination by customers and institutions other than firms, may explain at least part of the observed wage gaps. **LO3**

- Technologies that allow the most productive individuals to serve broader markets can translate even small differences in human capital into enormous differences in pay. Such technologies give rise to winner-take-all markets, which have long been common in sports and entertainment, and which are becoming common in other professions. **LO3**

- Although incomes grew at almost 3 percent a year for all income classes during the three decades following World War II, the lion's share of income growth in the years since has been concentrated among top earners. **LO4**

- Philosophers have argued that at least some income redistribution is justified in the name of fairness, because if people chose society's distributional rules without knowing their own personal circumstances, most would favor less inequality than would be produced by market outcomes. **LO4**

- Policies and programs for reducing poverty include minimum wage laws, the earned-income tax credit, food stamps, subsidized school lunches, Medicaid, public housing, and Aid to Families with Dependent Children. Of these, all but the earned-income tax credit fail to maximize total economic surplus, either by interfering with work incentives or by preventing markets from reaching equilibrium. **LO5**

• The negative income tax works much like the earned-income tax credit, except that it includes those who are not employed. A combination of a small negative income tax and access to public service jobs at sub-minimum wages could ensure adequate living standards for the poor without significantly undermining work incentives. **LO5**

▪ KEY TERMS ▪

compensating wage
  differential (358)
customer discrimination (359)
earned-income tax credit
  (EITC) (367)
employer discrimination (358)

human capital (355)
human capital theory (355)
in-kind transfer (364)
labor union (355)
marginal product (*MP*) (351)
means-tested (364)

negative income tax (NIT) (365)
Personal Responsibility Act (364)
poverty threshold (365)
value of marginal product
  (*VMP*) (351)
winner-take-all market (360)

▪ REVIEW QUESTIONS ▪

1. Why is the supply curve of labor for any specific occupation likely to be upward-sloping, even if, for the economy as a whole, people work fewer hours when wage rates increase? **LO2**

2. True or false: If the human capital possessed by two workers is nearly the same, their wage rates will be nearly the same. Explain. **LO3**

3. How might recent changes in income inequality be related to the proliferation of technologies that enable the most productive individuals to serve broader markets? **LO3, LO4**

4. Mention two self-interested reasons that a top earner might favor policies to redistribute income. **LO4**

5. Why is exclusive reliance on the negative income tax unlikely to constitute a long-term solution to the poverty problem? **LO5**

▪ PROBLEMS ▪

1. Mountain Breeze supplies air filters to the retail market and hires workers to assemble the components. An air filter sells for $26, and Mountain Breeze can buy the components for each filter for $1. Sandra and Bobby are two workers for Mountain Breeze. Sandra can assemble 60 air filters per month and Bobby can assemble 70. If the labor market is perfectly competitive, how much will Sandra and Bobby be paid? **LO1, LO2**

2. Stone, Inc., owns a clothing factory and hires workers in a competitive labor market to stitch cut denim fabric into jeans. The fabric required to make each pair of jeans costs $5. The company's weekly output of finished jeans varies with the number of workers hired, as shown in the following table: **LO2, LO3, LO5**

Number of workers	Jeans (pairs/week)
0	0
1	25
2	45
3	60
4	72
5	80
6	85

a. If the jeans sell for $35 a pair and the competitive market wage is $250 per week, how many workers should Stone hire? How many pairs of jeans will the company produce each week?

b. Suppose the Clothing Workers Union now sets a weekly minimum acceptable wage of $230 per week. All the workers Stone hires belong to the union. How does the minimum wage affect Stone's decision about how many workers to hire?

c. If the minimum wage set by the union had been $400 per week, how would the minimum wage affect Stone's decision about how many workers to hire?

d. If Stone again faces a market wage of $250 per week but the price of jeans rises to $45, how many workers will the company now hire?

3. Acme, Inc., supplies rocket ships to the retail market and hires workers to assemble the components. A rocket ship sells for $30,000, and Acme can buy the components for each rocket ship for $25,000. Wiley and Sam are two workers for Acme. Sam can assemble 1/5 of a rocket ship per month and Wiley can assemble 1/10. If the labor market is perfectly competitive and rocket components are Acme's only other cost, how much will Sam and Wiley be paid? **LO1, LO2**

4. Carolyn owns a soda factory and hires workers in a competitive labor market to bottle the soda. Her company's weekly output of bottled soda varies with the number of workers hired, as shown in the following table: **LO2, LO3, LO5**

Number of workers	Cases/week
0	0
I	200
2	360
3	480
4	560
5	600

a. If each case sells for $10 more than the cost of the materials used in producing it and the competitive market wage is $1,000 per week, how many workers should Carolyn hire? How many cases will be produced per week?

b. Suppose the Soda Bottlers Union now sets a weekly minimum acceptable wage of $1,500 per week. All the workers Carolyn hires belong to the union. How does the minimum wage affect Carolyn's decision about how many workers to hire?

c. If the wage is again $1,000 per week but the price of soda rises to $15 per case, how many workers will Carolyn now hire?

5. Suppose the equilibrium wage for unskilled workers in New Jersey is $7 per hour. How will the wages and employment of unskilled workers in New Jersey change if the state legislature raises the minimum wage from $5.15 per hour to $6 per hour? **LO5**

6. Jones, who is currently unemployed, is a participant in three means-tested welfare programs: food stamps, rent stamps, and day care stamps. Each program grants him $150 per month in stamps, which can be used like cash to purchase the good or service they cover. **LO5**

a. If benefits in each program are reduced by 40 cents for each additional dollar Jones earns in the labor market, how will Jones's economic position change if he accepts a job paying $120 per week?

b. In light of your answer to part a, explain why means testing for welfare recipients has undesirable effects on work incentives.

7. Sue is offered a job reshelving books in the University of Montana library from noon until 1 p.m. each Friday. Her reservation wage for this task is $10 per hour. **LO4**

   a. If the library director offers Sue $100 per hour, how much economic surplus will she enjoy as a result of accepting the job?

   b. Now suppose the library director announces that the earnings from the job will be divided equally among the 400 students who live in Sue's dormitory. Will Sue still accept?

   c. Explain how your answers to parts a and b illustrate one of the incentive problems inherent in income redistribution programs.

8.* Suppose the demand and supply curves for unskilled labor in the Corvallis labor market are as shown in the accompanying figure. By how much will the imposition of a minimum wage at $12 per hour reduce total economic surplus? Calculate the amounts by which employer surplus and worker surplus change as a result of the minimum wage. **LO5**

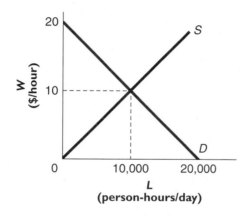

9.* Refer to problem 8. How much would it cost the government each day to provide an earned-income tax credit under which workers as a group receive the same economic surplus as they do under the $12 per hour minimum wage? (Assume for simplicity that the earned-income tax credit has no effect on labor supply.) **LO5**

10.* Suppose employers and workers are risk-neutral, and Congress is about to enact the $12 per hour minimum wage described in problem 8. Congressional staff economists have urged legislators to consider adopting an earned-income tax credit instead. Suppose neither workers nor employers would support that proposal unless the expected value of each party's economic surplus would be at least as great as under the minimum wage. Describe an earned-income tax credit (and a tax that would raise enough money to pay for it) that would receive unanimous support from both workers and employers. **LO5**

■ ANSWERS TO IN-CHAPTER EXERCISES ■

13.1 At a price of $26 per cutting board, the fifth worker has a *VMP* of $364 per week, so Adirondack should hire five workers. **LO1, LO2**

13.2 Since the *VMP* of each worker exceeds $275, Adirondack should hire five workers. **LO1, LO2**

*Problems marked with an asterisk (*) are more difficult.

13.3 When the wage rate is $9 per hour in each market, 25 fewer workers will be employed in the nonunionized market and 25 more in the unionized market. The loss in output from removing 25 workers from the nonunionized market is the sum of the *VMP*s of those workers, which is the shaded area in the right panel of the figure below. This area is $187.50 per hour. (*Hint:* To calculate this area, first break the figure into a rectangle and a triangle.) The gain in output from adding 25 workers to the unionized market is the shaded area in the left panel, which is $262.50 per hour. The net increase in output is thus $262.50 − $187.50 = $75 per hour. **LO3**

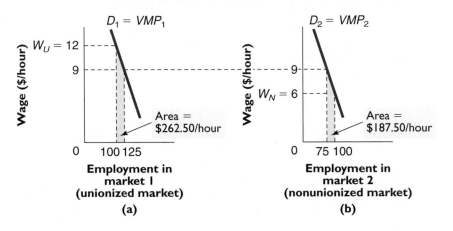

13.4 Since Sue's reservation wage is $10 per hour, she must be paid at least that amount before she will accept the job. The largest dorm population for which she will accept is thus 10 residents, since her share in that case would be exactly $10 per hour. **LO4**

13.5 With perfectly inelastic demand, employment would remain at 5,000 person-hours per day, so the minimum wage would cause no reduction in economic surplus. **LO5**

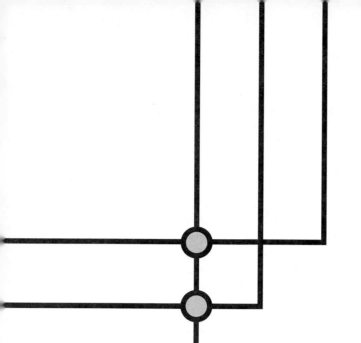

The Environment, Health, and Safety

LEARNING OBJECTIVES

After reading this chapter, you should be able to:

1. Use economic analysis to show how the U.S. health care system can be improved.

2. Compare and contrast the ways in which taxes and tradable permits can be used to reduce pollution.

3. Apply the cost-benefit principle to improve workplace safety.

4. Show how economic analysis contributes to debates regarding public health and domestic security spending.

In 1979, in the wake of the second major oil supply interruption in a decade, officials in the Carter administration met to discuss policies for reducing the risks to domestic security inherent in U.S. dependence on foreign oil. The proposal they ultimately put forward was a gasoline tax of 50 cents per gallon. Anticipating objections that the tax would impose an unacceptable hardship on the poor, policymakers proposed to return the revenues from the tax to the citizenry by reducing the payroll tax—the tax on wages that supports the Social Security system.

Proponents of the gasoline tax argued that in addition to reducing the nation's dependence on foreign oil, the tax would reduce air pollution and ease highway congestion. But critics ridiculed the proposal, charging that if the revenues from the tax were returned to the people, the quantity of gasoline demanded would remain essentially the same. Their argument tipped the debate, and officials never managed to implement the proposal.

Whatever the ultimate merits of the administration's proposal, there was no merit at all in the argument the critics used to attack it. True, the proposed tax rebate meant that people *could* have bought just as much gasoline as before the tax. Yet the tax would have given them a powerful incentive not to do so. As we saw in Chapter 5, consumers can change their behavior to escape the effects of a steep rise in the after-tax price of gasoline—by switching to cars with smaller, more fuel-efficient engines; forming carpools; and so on. Such changes free up money to spend on other goods and services, which become relatively more attractive because they are not taxed.

No society can hope to formulate and implement intelligent economic policies unless its citizens and leaders share an understanding of basic economic principles. Our aim in this chapter is to explore how careful application of these principles can help us design policies that both expand the economic pie and make everyone's slice larger. Specifically, we examine the economics of health care delivery, environmental regulation, and public health and safety regulation. The unifying thread running through these issues is the problem of scarcity. In each case, we will explore how the Cost-Benefit Principle can help to resolve the resulting trade-offs.

Scarcity ○

Cost-Benefit ○

THE ECONOMICS OF HEALTH CARE DELIVERY

In the United States, real health care expenditures per capita have grown more rapidly than real income per capita for as long as the relevant data have been available. As a share of national income, health care costs have risen from only 4 percent in 1940 to roughly 16 percent in 2005. Part of this increase is the result of costly new health care technologies and procedures. Diagnostic tests have grown more expensive and sophisticated, and procedures like coronary bypass surgery and organ transplantation have grown far more common. Yet a great deal of medical expenditure inflation has nothing to do with these high-tech developments. Rather, it is the result of fundamental changes in the way we pay for medical services.

The most important change has been the emergence of the so-called third-party payment system. Earlier in this century, many people insured themselves against catastrophic illness but purchased routine medical care out of their own pockets, just as they did food, clothing, and other consumer goods. Starting after World War II, and increasingly since the mid-1960s, people have come to depend on insurance for even routine medical services. Some of this insurance is provided privately by employers; some, by the government. In the latter category, Medicaid covers the medical expenses of the poor and Medicare covers those of the elderly and disabled.

The spread of medical insurance, especially government-financed medical insurance, owes much to the belief that an inability to pay should not prevent people from receiving medical care they need. Indeed, medical insurance has surely done much to shelter people from financial hardship. The difficulty is that in its most common form, it also has spawned literally hundreds of billions of dollars of waste each year.

APPLYING THE COST-BENEFIT CRITERION

Cost-Benefit ○

To understand the nature of this waste, we must recognize that although medical services differ from other services in many ways, they are in one fundamental respect the same: The cost-benefit test is the only sensible criterion for deciding which services ought to be performed. The fact that a medical procedure has *some* benefit does not, by itself, imply that the procedure should be performed. Rather, it should be performed only if its marginal benefit, broadly construed, exceeds its marginal cost.

The costs of medical procedures are relatively easy to measure, using the same methods applied to other goods and services. But the usual measure of the benefit of a good or service, a person's willingness to pay, may not be acceptable in the case of many medical services. For example, most of us would not conclude that a life-saving appendectomy is unjustified merely because the person who needs it can afford to pay only half of its $2,000 cost. When someone lacks the resources to pay for what most of us would consider an essential medical service, society has at least some responsibility to help. Hence the proliferation of government-sponsored medical insurance.

Many other medical expenditures are not as pressing as an emergency appendectomy, however. Following such surgery, for example, the patient requires a period of recuperation in the hospital. How long should that period last—2 days? 5? 10? The Cost-Benefit Principle is critically important to thinking intelligently about such questions. But as the following example illustrates, the third-party payment system has virtually eliminated cost-benefit thinking from the medical domain.

How long should David stay in the hospital?

To eliminate recurrent sore throats, David plans to have his tonsils removed. His surgeon tells him that the average hospital stay after this procedure is two days (some people stay only one day, while others stay three, four, or even five days). Hospital rooms cost $300 per day. If David's demand curve for days in the hospital is as shown in Figure 14.1, how many days will he stay if he must pay for his hospital room himself? How many days will he stay if his medical insurance fully covers the cost of his hospital room?

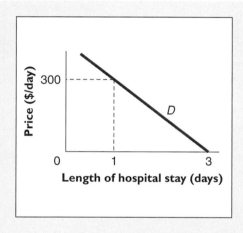

FIGURE 14.1
The Demand for Hospital Care.
The demand curve for postoperative hospital care is downward-sloping, just like any other demand curve. At higher prices, people choose shorter hospital stays, not because there is no benefit to a longer stay, but because they prefer to spend their money in other ways.

If David must pay for his hospital room himself, his best option will be to stay for just one day. But if the cost of his hospital room is completely covered by insurance, the marginal cost *to him* will be zero. In that case, he will stay for three days. ◆

EXERCISE 14.1

In the example above, how long would David choose to stay in the hospital if his health insurance covered 50 percent of the cost of his hospital room?

Should we be concerned that people choose longer hospital stays when their expenses are fully insured? The Cost-Benefit Principle tells us that a hospital stay should be extended another day only if the benefit of doing so would be at least as great as the cost of the resources required to extend the stay. But when hospital costs are fully covered by insurance, the decision maker sees a marginal cost of zero, when in fact the marginal cost is several hundred dollars. According to the cost-benefit criterion, then, full insurance coverage leads to wastefully long hospital stays. This is not to say that the additional days in the hospital do no good at all. Rather, their benefit is less than their cost. As the next example illustrates, a shorter hospital stay would increase total economic surplus.

How much waste does full insurance coverage cause?

Using the demand and cost information from the hospital stay example, how much waste results from full insurance coverage of David's hospital room?

If the marginal cost of an additional day in the hospital is $300, the supply curve of hospital room days in an open market would be horizontal at $300. If David had to pay that price, he would choose a one-day stay, which would result in the largest possible economic surplus. If he extends his stay past one day, cost continues to accumulate at the rate of $300 per day, but the benefit of additional care—as measured by his demand curve—falls below $300. If he stays three days, as he will if he has full insurance coverage, the two extra days cost society $600 but benefit David by only $300 (the area of the lower shaded triangle under David's demand curve in Figure 14.2). The amount by which the extra cost exceeds the extra benefit will thus be $300 (the area of the upper shaded triangle).

FIGURE 14.2
The Waste That Results from Full Insurance Coverage.
The area of the lower shaded triangle ($300) represents the benefit of extending the hospital stay from one day to three days. Since the cost of the extra two days is $600, the area of the upper shaded triangle ($300) represents the loss in economic surplus that results from the longer stay.

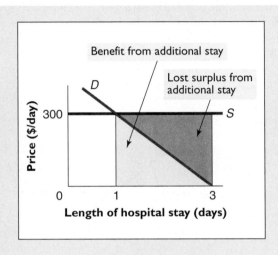

EXERCISE 14.2

In the last example, how much waste would be caused by an insurance policy that reimbursed hospital room expenses at the rate of $150 per day?

DESIGNING A SOLUTION

In circumstances in which economic surplus has not been maximized, a transaction can always be found that will make both the patient *and* the insurance company better off. Suppose, for instance, that the insurance company in the previous example gives David a cash payment of $700 toward hospital expenses and lets him decide for himself how long to stay in the hospital. Confronted with a price of $300 per day, David would choose to stay only a single day. The $400 cash he would have left after paying his hospital bill is $100 more than enough to compensate him for the benefit he would lose by not staying an extra two days. (Again, that benefit is $300, the area of the lower shaded triangle in Figure 14.2.) A $700 cash payment also would leave his insurance company better off by $200 than if it had provided unlimited hospital coverage at no extra charge (since David would have stayed three days in that case, at a cost of $900 to his insurance company). And since no one else is harmed by this transaction, it represents a *Pareto improvement* over unlimited coverage, meaning a change that makes some people better off without harming others (see Chapter 7).

The amount of waste caused by full insurance coverage depends on the price elasticity of demand for medical services—the more elastic the demand, the greater the waste. Proponents of full coverage believe that the demand for medical services is almost completely inelastic with respect to price and that the resulting waste is therefore negligible. Critics of full coverage argue that the demand for medical services is actually quite sensitive to price and that the resulting waste is significant.

Who is right? One way to determine this is to examine whether people who lack full insurance coverage spend significantly less than those who have it. The economist W. G. Manning and several co-authors did so by performing an experiment in which they assigned subjects randomly to one of two different kinds of medical insurance policy.[1] The first group of subjects received **first-dollar coverage,** meaning that 100 percent of their medical expenses was covered by insurance. The second group got "$1,000-deductible" coverage, meaning that only expenses beyond the first $1,000 a year were covered. (For example, someone with $1,200 of medical bills would receive $1,200 from his insurance company if he belonged to the first group, but only $200 if he belonged to the second.) In effect, since most people incur less than $1,000 a year in medical expenses, most subjects in the second group effectively paid full price for their medical services, while subjects in the first group paid nothing. Manning and his colleagues found that *people with $1,000-deductible policies spent between 40 and 50 percent less on health care than subjects with first-dollar coverage. More important, there were no measurable differences in health outcomes between the two groups.*

Taken at face value, the results of the Manning study suggest that a large share of the inflation in medical expenditures since World War II has been caused by growth in first-dollar medical insurance. The problem with first dollar coverage is that it completely ignores the Incentive Principle. Why not simply abandon first-dollar coverage in favor of high deductibles? People would still be protected against financial catastrophe but would have a strong incentive to avoid medical services whose benefit does not exceed their cost.

Some would say that Medicaid and Medicare should not carry high deductibles because the resulting out-of-pocket payments would impose too great a burden on poor families. But as in other instances in which concern for the poor is offered in defense of an inefficient policy, an alternative can be designed that is better for rich and poor alike. For example, all health insurance could be written to include high deductibles, and the poor could be given an annual stipend to defray the initial medical expenses not covered by insurance. At year's end, any unspent stipend would be theirs to keep. Here again, concern for the well-being of the poor is no reason for not adopting the most efficient policy. As the Efficiency Principle reminds us, when the economic pie grows larger, it is possible for everyone to have a larger slice.

THE HMO REVOLUTION

During the 1990s, the high cost of conventional health insurance led many people to switch to **health maintenance organizations (HMOs).** An HMO is a group of physicians that provides its patients with medical services in return for a fixed annual fee. As the next example illustrates, the incentive to provide any given medical service is weaker under the standard HMO contract than under conventional health insurance.

Why is a patient with a sore knee more likely to receive an MRI exam if he has conventional health insurance than if he belongs to a health maintenance organization?

When a patient visits his physician complaining of a sore knee, the physician has several options. After hearing the patient describe his symptoms and examining the knee manually, the physician may prescribe anti-inflammatory drugs and advise the patient to abstain from vigorous physical activity for a period; or she may advise the patient to undergo a

first-dollar insurance coverage insurance that pays all expenses generated by the insured activity

Incentive

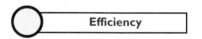
Efficiency

health maintenance organization (HMO) a group of physicians that provides health services to individuals and families for a fixed annual fee

Example 14.1
THE ECONOMIC NATURALIST

[1]W. G. Manning, J. P. Newhouse, E. B. Keeler, A. Liebowitz, and M. S. Marquis, "Health Insurance and the Demand for Medical Care," *American Economic Review* 77 (June 1987), pp. 251–77.

magnetic resonance imaging (MRI) exam, a costly diagnostic procedure that generates images of the inner workings of the injured joint. The physician in an HMO receives no additional revenue if she orders the MRI because all services are covered by the patient's fixed annual fee. Under conventional health insurance, in contrast, the physician will be reimbursed at a fixed rate, usually well above her marginal cost, for each additional service performed.

*"Well, Bob, it looks like a paper cut, but just
to be sure let's do lots of tests."*

In many instances, the most prudent course of treatment is unambiguous, and in such cases physicians will make the same recommendation despite this striking difference in incentives. But in many other cases, it may not be obvious which decision is best. And in these cases, HMO physicians are less likely to order expensive tests. ●

People who switch to HMOs pay less for their health plans than those who stick with conventional health insurance since the HMO contract provides a strong incentive for doctors not to prescribe nonessential services. Many people fear, however, that the very same incentive may sometimes result in their not receiving valuable care. These concerns have led to proposed legislation granting patients rights of appeal when they are denied care by an HMO.

PAYING FOR HEALTH INSURANCE

It is troubling, but perhaps not surprising, that access to medical care is extremely limited in many of the world's poorest nations. After all, citizens of those nations lack enough income to buy adequate food, shelter, and many other basic goods and services. What *is* surprising, however, is that despite the movement to less expensive HMO plans, some 47 million Americans had no health coverage of any kind in 2007. Politicians in both parties agree that something must be done to expand health coverage. But before an intelligent solution to this problem can be implemented, we must first understand why so many are without coverage in the first place.

In the richest country on Earth, why do so many people lack basic health insurance?

Although the incomes of most Americans are higher than ever, millions of American families continue to experience day-to-day financial distress. For example, at the height of the economic boom in 1998, one of every 68 families filed for bankruptcy, more than the number of families with children graduating from college that year. Under the circumstances, it is easy to see why many families in generally good health might be tempted to press their luck. After all, health coverage for a family of four with no preexisting medical conditions costs upwards of $5,000 a year, which is almost always far more than what such a family spends on medical services. The extra cash could help pay for a move into a better school district, for example, or at least keep creditors at bay.

As more people cancel their health coverage, going without insurance becomes more socially acceptable. Parents who didn't buy health insurance for their families were once viewed as irresponsible, but this stigma loses some of its sting as the number of uninsured grows. Making matters worse is the changing composition of the pool of the insured. As more healthy families forgo coverage, those left tend to be sicker and more costly to treat, forcing up premiums (an example of *adverse selection*, discussed in Chapter 12). In short, our health insurance system is in a long-term downward spiral. And as more people become uninsured, the problem will get worse because the costs borne by those who remain insured will continue to escalate. ●

Why do 47 million Americans have no health insurance?

Example 14.2
THE ECONOMIC NATURALIST

Government could eliminate the downward spiral by simply reimbursing each family up to $5,000 a year for health insurance. Government bureaucrats would not need to prescribe which doctors we see or micromanage any of the other details. They would simply process insurance receipts and send out reimbursement checks. This plan sounds expensive but would actually be less costly than the current system. The principal savings would come from delivering more cost-effective care to those who are now uninsured.

As it stands now, the untreated minor illnesses of the uninsured often develop into major illnesses, which are far more costly to treat. And when such illnesses befall the uninsured, we almost always treat them, often in costly emergency rooms. The resulting burden on hospitals leads to higher fees and increased government support—both of which now come largely out of the pockets of high-income taxpayers with health insurance.

The total budget needed to finance a $5,000 health insurance reimbursement for every American family—some $350 billion a year—would obviously require higher taxes. But for those whose employers currently provide health insurance, these taxes would be offset by an increase in salaries. After all, companies offer insurance not because they are charitable, but because they find doing so an effective way to compete for workers. Any company that did not offer higher salaries to previously insured workers would risk losing them to a company that did.

A universal reimbursement program would impose no net burden on taxpayers because of both salary adjustments and reductions in the high cost of care for the uninsured. And by providing a powerful incentive for all families to buy insurance, it would reverse the current downward spiral.

Critics of health care reform may say that if some people want to save money by going without health insurance, that's their problem or their choice. Perhaps, but it's a problem for the rest of society as well, one that if left untended will grow steadily worse.

RECAP	**THE ECONOMICS OF HEALTH CARE DELIVERY**

The rapid escalation in medical expenditures since World War II is attributable in large part to the spread of first-dollar insurance coverage, which encourages people to behave as if medical services were free of charge. Total economic surplus would be larger if we switched to insurance coverage with high deductibles because such policies provide an incentive to use only those services whose benefit exceeds their cost.

The switch to HMOs addresses this problem because the standard HMO contract provides a strong incentive for physicians not to prescribe nonessential services. Some voice concern, however, that HMO contracts may lead physicians to withhold services that satisfy the cost-benefit test.

Mounting insurance premiums have caused many people in good health to do without health coverage, resulting in higher premiums for those who remain insured. Government reimbursement for health coverage is one way to stop the downward spiral in health coverage.

USING PRICE INCENTIVES IN ENVIRONMENTAL REGULATION

As we saw in Chapter 11, goods whose production generates negative externalities, such as atmospheric pollution, tend to be overproduced whenever negotiation among private parties is costly. Suppose we decide, as a society, that the best attainable outcome would be to have half as much pollution as would occur under completely unregulated conditions. In that case, how should the cleanup effort be distributed among those firms that currently discharge pollution into the environment?

The most efficient—and hence best—distribution of effort is the one for which each polluter's marginal cost of abatement is exactly the same. To see why, imagine that under current arrangements, the cost to one firm of removing a ton of pollution from the air is larger than the cost to another firm. Society could then achieve the same total reduction in pollution at lower cost by having the first firm discharge 1 ton more into the air and the second firm 1 ton less.

Unfortunately, government regulators seldom have detailed information on how the cost of reducing pollution varies from one firm to another. Many pollution laws therefore require all polluters simply to cut back their emissions by the same proportion or to meet the same absolute emissions standards. If different polluters have different marginal costs of pollution abatement, however, these approaches will not be efficient.

TAXING POLLUTION

Fortunately, alternative policies can distribute the cleanup more efficiently, even if the government lacks detailed information about how much it costs different firms to curtail pollution. One method is to tax pollution and allow firms to decide for themselves how much pollution to emit. The following example illustrates the logic of this approach.

What is the least costly way to cut pollution by half?

Two firms, Sludge Oil and Northwest Lumber, each has access to five production processes, each of which has a different cost and produces a different amount of pollution. The daily costs of the processes and the number of tons of smoke emitted are as shown in Table 14.1. Pollution is currently unregulated, and negotiation

TABLE 14.1
Costs and Emissions for Different Production Processes

Process (smoke)	A (4 tons/day)	B (3 tons/day)	C (2 tons/day)	D (1 ton/day)	E (0 tons/day)
Cost to Sludge Oil ($/day)	100	200	600	1,300	2,300
Cost to Northwest Lumber ($/day)	300	320	380	480	700

between the firms and those who are harmed by pollution is impossible, which means that each firm uses process A, the least costly of the five. Each firm emits 4 tons of pollution per day, for a total of 8 tons of pollution per day.

The government is considering two options for reducing total emissions by half. One is to require each firm to curtail its emissions by half. The other is to set a tax of $T per ton of smoke emitted each day. How large must T be to curtail emissions by half? What would be the total cost to society under each alternative?

If each firm is required to cut pollution by half, each must switch from process A to process C. The result will be 2 tons per day of pollution for each firm. The cost of the switch for Sludge Oil will be $600 per day − $100 per day = $500 per day. The cost to Northwest Lumber will be $380 per day − $300 per day = $80 per day, for a total cost of $580 per day.

Consider now how each firm would react to a tax of $T per ton of pollution. If a firm can cut pollution by 1 ton per day, it will save $T per day in tax payments. Whenever the cost of cutting a ton of pollution is less than $T, then, each firm has an incentive to switch to a cleaner process. For example, if the tax were set at $40 per ton, Sludge Oil would stick with process A because switching to process B would cost $100 per day extra but would save only $40 per day in taxes. Northwest Lumber, however, would switch to process B because the $40 saving in taxes would be more than enough to cover the $20 cost of switching.

The problem is that a $40 per day tax on each ton of pollution results in a reduction of only 1 ton per day, 3 short of the 4-ton target. Suppose instead that the government imposed a tax of $101 per ton. Sludge Oil would then adopt process B because the $100 extra daily cost of doing so would be less than the $101 saved in taxes. Northwest Lumber would adopt process D because, for every process up to and including C, the cost of switching to the next process would be less than the resulting tax saving.

Overall, then, a tax of $101 per ton would result in the desired pollution reduction of 4 tons per day. The total cost of the reduction would be only $280 per day ($100 per day for Sludge Oil and $180 per day for Northwest Lumber), or $300 per day less than when each firm was required to cut its pollution by half. (The taxes paid by the firms do not constitute a cost of pollution reduction because the money can be used to reduce whatever taxes would otherwise need to be levied on citizens.) ◆

EXERCISE 14.3

In the example above, if the tax were $61 per ton of pollution emitted each day, which production processes would the two firms adopt?

The advantage of the tax approach is that it concentrates pollution reduction in the hands of the firms that can accomplish it at least cost. Requiring each firm to cut emissions by the same proportion ignores the fact that some firms can reduce pollution much more cheaply than others. Note that under the tax approach, the cost of the last ton of smoke removed is the same for each firm, so the efficiency condition is satisfied.

One problem with the tax approach is that unless the government has detailed knowledge about each firm's cost of reducing pollution, it cannot know how high to set the pollution tax. A tax that is too low will result in too much pollution, while a tax that is too high will result in too little. Of course, the government could start by setting a low tax rate and gradually increase the rate until pollution is reduced to the target level. But because firms often incur substantial sunk costs when they switch from one process to another, that approach might be even more wasteful than requiring all firms to cut their emissions by the same proportion.

AUCTIONING POLLUTION PERMITS

Another alternative is to establish a target level for pollution and then auction off permits to emit that level. The virtues of this approach are illustrated in the following example.

How much will pollution permits sell for?

Two firms, Sludge Oil and Northwest Lumber, again have access to the production processes described earlier (which are reproduced in Table 14.2). The government's goal is to cut the current level of pollution, 8 tons per day, by half. To do so, the government auctions off four permits, each of which entitles the bearer to emit 1 ton of smoke per day. No smoke may be emitted without a permit. What price will the pollution permits fetch at auction, how many permits will each firm buy, and what will be the total cost of the resulting pollution reduction?

TABLE 14.2
Costs and Emissions for Different Production Processes

Process (smoke)	A (4 tons/day)	B (3 tons/day)	C (2 tons/day)	D (1 ton/day)	E (0 tons/day)
Cost to Sludge Oil ($/day)	100	200	600	1,300	2,300
Cost to Northwest Lumber ($/day)	300	320	380	480	700

If Sludge Oil has no permits, it must use process E, which costs $2,300 per day to operate. If it had one permit, it could use process D, which would save it $1,000 per day. Thus, the most Sludge Oil would be willing to pay for a single 1-ton pollution permit is $1,000 per day. With a second permit, Sludge Oil could switch to process C and save another $700 per day; with a third permit, it could switch to process B and save another $400; and with a fourth permit, it could switch to process A and save another $100. Using similar reasoning, we can see that Northwest Lumber would pay up to $220 for one permit, up to $100 for a second, up to $60 for a third, and up to $20 for a fourth.

Suppose the government starts the auction at a price of $90. Sludge Oil will then demand four permits and Northwest Lumber will demand two, for a total demand of six permits. Since the government wishes to sell only four permits, it will keep raising the price until the two firms together demand a total of only four permits. Once the price reaches $101, Sludge Oil will demand three permits and Northwest Lumber will demand only one, for a total quantity demanded of four permits. Compared to the unregulated alternative, in which each firm used process

A, the daily cost of the auction solution is $280: Sludge Oil spends $100 switching from process *A* to process *B,* and Northwest Lumber spends $180 switching from *A* to *D.* This total is $300 less than the cost of requiring each firm to reduce its emissions by half. (Again, the permit fees paid by the firms do not constitute a cost of cleanup because the money can be used to reduce taxes that would otherwise have to be collected.) ◆

The auction method has the same virtue as the tax method: It concentrates pollution reduction in the hands of those firms that can accomplish it at the lowest cost. But the auction method has other attractive features that the tax approach does not. First, it does not induce firms to commit themselves to costly investments that they will have to abandon if the cleanup falls short of the target level. And second, it allows private citizens a direct voice in determining where the emission level will be set. For example, any group that believes the pollution target is too lenient could raise money to buy permits at auction. By keeping those permits locked away in a safe, the group could ensure that they will not be used to emit pollution.

Several decades ago, when economists first proposed the auctioning of pollution permits, reactions of outrage were widely reported in the press. Most of those reactions amounted to the charge that the proposal would "permit rich firms to pollute to their hearts' content." Such an assertion betrays a total misunderstanding of the forces that generate pollution. Firms pollute not because they *want* to pollute but because dirty production processes are cheaper than clean ones. Society's only real interest is in keeping the total amount of pollution from becoming excessive, not in *who* actually does the polluting. And in any event, the firms that do most of the polluting under an auction system will not be rich firms, but those for whom pollution reduction is most costly.

Economists have argued patiently against these misinformed objections to the auction system, and their efforts have finally borne fruit. The sale of pollution permits is now common in several parts of the United States, and there is growing interest in the approach in other countries.

RECAP	USING PRICE INCENTIVES IN ENVIRONMENTAL REGULATION

An efficient program for reducing pollution is one for which the marginal cost of abatement is the same for all polluters. Taxing pollution has this desirable property, as does the auction of pollution permits. The auction method has the advantage that regulators can achieve a desired abatement target without having detailed knowledge of the abatement technologies available to polluters.

WORKPLACE SAFETY REGULATION

Most industrialized countries have laws that attempt to limit the extent to which workers are exposed to health and safety risks on the job. These laws often are described as necessary to protect workers against exploitation by employers with market power. Given the working conditions we saw in the early stages of the industrial revolution, the idea that such exploitation pervades unregulated private markets has intuitive appeal. Witness Upton Sinclair's vivid account of life in the Chicago meat-packing factories at the turn of the twentieth century:

> Some worked at the stamping machines, and it was very seldom that
> one could work long there at the pace that was set, and not give out
> and forget himself, and have a part of his hand chopped off. There
> were the "hoisters," as they were called, whose task it was to press

the lever which lifted the dead cattle off the floor. They ran along a rafter, peering down through the damp and the steam; and as old Durham's architects had not built the killing room for the convenience of the hoisters, at every few feet they would have to stoop under a beam, say four feet above the one they ran on; which got them into the habit of stooping, so that in a few years they would be walking like chimpanzees. Worst of any, however, were the fertilizer men, and those who served in the cooking rooms. These people could not be shown to the visitors—for the odor of the fertilizer-man would scare any ordinary visitor at a hundred yards, and as for the other men, who worked in tank-rooms full of steam, and in which there were open vats near the level of the floor, their peculiar trouble was that they fell into the vats; and when they were fished out, there was never enough of them left to be worth exhibiting—sometimes they would be overlooked for days, till all but the bones of them had gone out to the world as Durham's Pure Leaf Lard.[2]

The miserable conditions of factory workers, juxtaposed with the often opulent lifestyle enjoyed by factory owners, seemed to affirm the idea that owners were exploiting workers. But if conditions in the factories were in fact too dangerous, how much safer should they have been?

Consider the question of whether to install a specific safety device—say, a guard rail on a lathe. Many people are reluctant to employ the Cost-Benefit Principle to answer such a question. To them, safety is an absolute priority, so the guard rail should be installed regardless of its cost. Yet most of us do not make personal decisions about our own health and safety that way. No one you know, for example, gets the brakes on his car checked every day, even though doing so would reduce the likelihood of being killed in an accident. The reason, obviously, is that daily brake inspections would be very costly and would not reduce the probability of an accident significantly compared to annual or semiannual inspections.

The same logic can be applied to installing a guard rail on a lathe. If the amount one is willing to pay to reduce the likelihood of an accident exceeds the cost of the guard rail, it should be installed; otherwise, it should not be. And no matter how highly we value reducing the odds of an accident, we will almost surely settle for less than perfect safety. After all, to reduce the risk of an accident to nearly zero, one would have to enclose the lathe in a thick Plexiglas case and operate it with remote-controlled mechanical arms. Faced with the prohibitive cost of such an alternative, most of us would decide that the best approach is to add safety equipment whose benefit exceeds its cost and then use caution while operating the machine.

But will unregulated employers offer the level of workplace safety suggested by the cost-benefit principle? Most nations appear to have decided that they will not. As noted, virtually every industrial country now has comprehensive legislation mandating minimum safety standards in the workplace—laws usually described as safeguards against exploitation of workers.

Yet explaining safety regulation as an antidote for exploitation raises troubling questions. One difficulty stems from the economist's argument that competition for workers prods firms to provide the socially optimal level of amenities. For example, if an amenity—say, a guard rail on a lathe—costs $50 per month to install and maintain, and workers value it at $100 per month, then the firm must install the device or risk losing workers to a competitor

Cost-Benefit

"Not enough money is being spent on safety, so be careful."

[2]Upton Sinclair, *The Jungle* (New York: Doubleday, Page, and Co., 1906), p. 106.

that does. After all, if a competing firm were to pay workers $60 per month less than they currently earn, it could cover the cost of the device with $10 to spare, while providing a compensation package that is $40 per month more attractive than the first employer's.

To this argument, critics respond that in practice there is very little competition in the labor market. They argue that incomplete information, worker immobility, and other frictions create situations in which workers have little choice but to accept whatever conditions employers offer. But even if a firm were the *only* employer in the market, it would still have an incentive to install a $50 safety device that is worth $100 to the worker. Failure to do so would be to leave cash on the table.

Other defenders of regulation suggest that workers may not know about safety devices they lack. But that explanation, too, is troubling because competing firms would have a strong incentive to call the devices to workers' attention. If the problem is that workers cannot move to the competing firm's location, then the firm can set up a branch near the exploited workers. Collusive agreements to restrain such competition should prove difficult to maintain because each firm can increase its profit by cheating on the agreement.

In fact, worker mobility between firms is high, as is entry by new firms into existing markets; as noted in Chapter 10, cartel agreements have always been notoriously unstable. Information may not be perfect, but if a new employer in town is offering a better deal, sooner or later word gets around.

Finally, if, despite these checks, some firms still manage to exploit their workers, we should expect those firms to earn a relatively high profit. But in fact we observe just the opposite. Year in and year out, firms that pay the *highest* wages are the most profitable. And so we are left with a puzzle. The fear of exploitation by employers with market power has led governments to adopt sweeping and costly safety regulations; yet the evidence suggests that exploitation cannot be a major problem. As the following example suggests, however, safety regulation might prove useful even in a perfectly competitive environment with complete information.

Will Don and Michael choose the optimal amount of safety?

Suppose Don and Michael are the only two members of a hypothetical community. They get satisfaction from three things: their income, safety on the job, and their position on the economic ladder. Suppose Don and Michael must both choose between two jobs, a safe job that pays $50 per week and a risky job that pays $80 per week. The value of safety to each is $40 per week. Having more income than one's neighbor is worth $40 per week to each; having less income than one's neighbor means a $40 per week reduction in satisfaction. (Having the same income as one's neighbor means no change in satisfaction.) Will Don and Michael make the best job choices possible in this situation?

EN 14

Viewed in isolation, each person's decision should be to take the safe job. Granted, it pays $30 per week less than the risky job, but the extra safety it offers is worth $40 per week. So aside from the issue of relative income, the value of the safe job is $90 per week (its $50 salary plus $40 worth of safety), or $10 per week more than the risky job.

Once we incorporate concerns about relative income, however, the logic of the decision changes in a fundamental way. Now the attractiveness of each job depends on the job chosen by the other. The four possible combinations of choices and their corresponding levels of satisfaction are shown in Table 14.3. If each man chooses a safe job, he will get $50 of income, $40 worth of satisfaction from safety, and—because each will have the same income—zero satisfaction from relative income. So if each man chooses the safe job, each will get a total of $90 worth of satisfaction. If instead each man chooses the risky job, each will get $80 of income, zero satisfaction from safety, and because each has the same income as the other, zero satisfaction

TABLE 14.3
The Effect of Concern about Relative Income on Worker Choices Regarding Safety

		Michael	
		Safe job @ $50/week	Risky job @ $80/week
Don	Safe job @ $50/week	$90 for Don $90 for Michael	$50 for Don $120 for Michael
	Risky job @ $80/week	$120 for Don $50 for Michael	$80 for Don $80 for Michael

from relative income. If we compare the upper-left cell of the table to the lower-right cell, then, we can say unequivocally that Don and Michael would be happier if each took a safe job at lower income than if each chose a risky job with more income.

But consider how the choice plays out once the two men recognize their interdependency. Suppose, for example, that Michael chooses the safe job. If Don then chooses the unsafe job, he ends up with a total of $120 of satisfaction—$80 in salary plus $40 from having more income than Michael. Michael, for his part, ends up with only $50 worth of satisfaction—$50 in salary plus $40 from safety, minus $40 from having lower income than Don. Alternatively, suppose Michael chooses the risky job. Then Don will again do better to accept the risky job, for by doing so he gets $80 worth of satisfaction rather than $50.

In short, no matter which job Michael chooses, Don will get more satisfaction by choosing the risky job. Likewise, no matter which job Don chooses, Michael will do better by choosing the risky job. Yet when each follows his dominant strategy, they end up in the lower-right cell of the table, which provides only $80 per week of satisfaction to each—$10 less than if each had chosen the safe job. Thus their job-safety choice confronts them with a prisoner's dilemma (see Chapter 10). As in all such situations, when the players choose independently, they fail to make the most of their opportunities. ◆

EXERCISE 14.4

How would your answer to the question posed in the above example have differed if the value of safety had been not $40 per week, but $20?

This example suggests an alternative explanation for safety regulation, one that is not based on the need to protect workers from exploitation. If Don and Michael could choose collectively, they would pick the safe job and maximize their combined satisfaction. Thus, each might support legislation that establishes safety standards in the workplace.

We stress that concern about relative income need not mean that people care only about having more or better goods than their neighbors. In our society, a person's relative income is important for reasons that everyone recognizes. For example, if you want to send your child to a good school, in most cases you must buy a house in a good school district. But who gets a house in a good school district? Those who have high relative income. Similarly, if everyone wants a house with a view, and only 10 percent of home sites have views, who gets them? The people in the top 10 percent of the income distribution, of course, and only those people. Many important outcomes in life depend on where a person stands on the economic ladder. And when people care about their relative income, rational, self-interested actions will not always lead to efficient outcomes in the labor market.

Regulation, however, does not always improve matters. The labor market may not be perfect, but government regulators aren't perfect either. Safety in the workplace is overseen by the Occupational Safety and Health Administration (OSHA), an agency that has drawn considerable criticism, much of it justified. Consider, for example, the following passage on safety requirements for ladders, taken verbatim from an early OSHA manual:

> The general slope of grain in flat steps of minimum dimension shall not be steeper than 1 in 12, except that for ladders under 10 feet in length the slope shall not be steeper than 1 in 10. The slope of grain in areas of local deviation shall not be steeper than 1 in 12 or 1 in 10 as specified above. For all ladders, cross grain not steeper than 1 in 10 are permitted in lieu of 1 in 12, provided the size is increased to afford at least 15 percent greater strength than for ladders built to minimum dimensions. Local deviations of grain associated with otherwise permissible irregularities are permitted.[3]

This befogged passage appears in a section devoted to ladders that is 30 pages long, two columns to the page. One can easily imagine the managers of a firm deciding that their best course of action is simply to abandon any activities requiring ladders.

As an alternative to OSHA-style prescriptive safety regulation, many economists favor programs that increase employers' financial incentives to reduce workplace injuries. The **workers' compensation** system provides a mechanism through which such a change might be achieved. Workers' compensation is a government insurance system that provides benefits to workers who are injured in the workplace. As currently administered, the program does not adjust each individual employer's premiums fully to reflect the claims generated by its workers. Employers with low injury rates thus pay premiums higher than needed to cover the claims generated by their workers, while those with high injury rates pay premiums too small to cover the claims generated by their workers.

workers' compensation a government insurance system that provides benefits to workers who are injured on the job

Economists argue that revising insurance premiums to reflect the full social cost of the injuries sustained by each employer's workers would provide the optimal incentive to curtail injuries in the workplace. In effect, premiums set at this level would be an optimal tax on injuries, and this would be efficient for the same reason that a properly chosen tax on pollution is efficient. An injury tax set at the marginal cost of injury would encourage employers to adopt all safety measures whose benefits exceed their costs.

As in other domains, we are far more likely to achieve optimal safety levels in the workplace if we choose among policies on practical cost-benefit grounds rather than on the basis of slogans about the merits or flaws of the free market.

As the following example illustrates, costs and benefits play a pivotal role in decisions about whether the government chooses to constrain individual choice in the safety domain and, if so, how.

Why does the government require safety seats for infants who travel in cars but not for infants who travel in airplanes?

A mother cannot legally drive her six-month-old son to a nearby grocery store without first strapping him into a government-approved safety seat. Yet she can fly with him from Miami to Seattle with no restraining device at all. Why this difference?

In case of an accident—whether in a car or an airplane—an infant who is strapped into a safety seat is more likely to escape injury or death than one who is unrestrained.

Example 14.3
THE ECONOMIC NATURALIST

---

[3]Quoted by Robert S. Smith, "Compensating Wage Differentials and Public Policy: A Review," *Industrial and Labor Relations Review* 32 (1977), pp. 339–52.

Cost-Benefit

Why are child safety seats required in cars but not in airplanes?

But the probability of being involved in a serious accident is hundreds of times higher when traveling by car than when traveling by air, so the benefit of having safety seats is greater for trips made by car. Using safety seats is also far more costly on plane trips than on car trips. Whereas most cars have plenty of extra room for a safety seat, parents might need to purchase an extra ticket to use one on an airplane. Most parents appear unwilling to pay $600 more per trip for a small increment in safety, for either themselves or their children. The difference in regulations is thus a straightforward consequence of the Cost-Benefit Principle. ●

RECAP	WORKPLACE SAFETY REGULATION

Most countries regulate safety in the workplace, a practice often defended as needed to protect workers from being exploited by employers with market power. Yet safety regulation might be attractive even in perfectly competitive labor markets because the social payoff from investment in safety often exceeds the private payoff. An injury tax set at the marginal cost of injury would encourage optimal investment in workplace safety.

PUBLIC HEALTH AND SECURITY

Because public health and law enforcement officials are charged with protecting our health and safety, political leaders are often reluctant to discuss expenditures on public health and law enforcement in cost-benefit terms. But because we live in a world of scarcity, we cannot escape the fact that spending more in these areas means spending less on other things of value.

Illnesses, like accidents, are costly to prevent. The socially optimal expenditure on a health measure that reduces a specific illness is that amount for which the marginal benefit to society of the measure exactly equals its marginal cost. For example, in deciding how much to spend on vaccinating against measles, a rational public health policy would expand the proportion of the population vaccinated until the marginal cost of an additional vaccination was exactly equal to the marginal value of the illnesses thus prevented.

As the following example illustrates, however, the decision of whether to become vaccinated looks very different from each individual's perspective.

Example 14.4
THE ECONOMIC NATURALIST

Why do many states have laws requiring students to be vaccinated against childhood illnesses?

Proof of immunization against diphtheria, measles, poliomyelitis, and rubella is now universally required for entry into American public schools. Most states also require immunization against tetanus (49 states), pertussis (44 states), mumps (43 states), and hepatitis B (26 states). Why these requirements?

Being vaccinated against a childhood illness entails a small but potentially serious risk. The vaccine against pertussis (whooping cough), for example, is believed to cause some form of permanent brain damage in 1 out of every 110,000 children vaccinated. Contracting the disease itself also poses serious health risks, and in an environment in which infections were sufficiently likely to occur, individuals would have a compelling reason to bear the risk of being vaccinated in order to reduce the even larger risk from infection. The problem is that in an environment in which most children were vaccinated, infection rates would be low, making the risk of vaccination loom understandably large in the eyes of individual families. The ideal situation from the perspective of any individual family would be to remain unvaccinated in an environment in which all other families were vaccinated. But as more and more families decided to forgo vaccination, infection rates would mount. Eventually the vaccination rate would stabilize at the point at which the additional risk to the individual family of becoming vaccinated would be exactly equal to the risk from remaining unvaccinated. But this calculation ignores the fact that a decision to remain unvaccinated poses risk not just to the individual decision maker, but also to others who have decided to become vaccinated (since no vaccine affords 100 percent protection against infection).

Relegating the vaccination decision to individuals results in a suboptimally low vaccination rate because individual decision makers fail to take adequate account of the cost that their becoming infected will impose on others. It is for this reason that most states require vaccinations against specific childhood illnesses.

Even these laws, however, allow parents to apply for exemptions on religious or philosophical grounds. Communities vary in the extent to which parents avail themselves of these exemptions. In Colorado, for example, Boulder County heads the list of parents who opt to exempt their children from taking the pertussis vaccine (with an exemption rate of 8.4 percent, more than four times the rate statewide). Not surprisingly, the incidence of whooping cough is much higher in Boulder (34.7 cases per year per 100,000 people) than in the state as a whole (9.4 cases per year per 100,000 people).[4] ●

Why are vaccinations against many childhood illnesses required by law?

Crimes, like childhood illnesses, are also costly to prevent. The socially optimal amount to spend on avoiding any specific type of crime is that amount for which the marginal benefit of reducing that crime exactly equals its marginal cost. As the next example illustrates, the Cost-Benefit Principle helps to explain why society invests so much more heavily in preventing some crimes than in preventing others.

Cost-Benefit

Why do more Secret Service agents guard the president than the vice president, and why do no Secret Service agents guard college professors?

When the president of the United States flies to Cleveland to give a speech, hundreds of federal agents are assigned to protect him against attack by an assassin. But when the vice president flies to Cleveland to give a speech, many fewer agents are assigned, and when a college professor goes to Cleveland for the same purpose, no agents are assigned at all. Why this difference?

According to the cost-benefit principle, the government should keep assigning agents in each case until the cost of an additional agent equals the value of the extra protection provided. In each of the three cases, the marginal cost of assigning agents is essentially the same. As shown in Figure 14.3, marginal cost (*MC*) is likely to be upward-sloping because of the Low-Hanging-Fruit Principle, according to which the most effective agents should be assigned first.

Example 14.5

THE ECONOMIC NATURALIST

Increasing Opportunity Cost

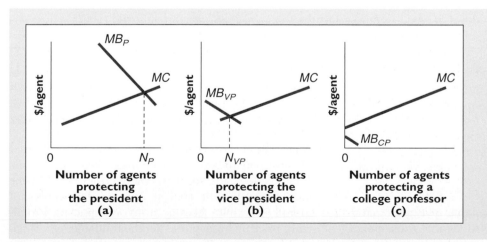

FIGURE 14.3
Differential Investment in Crime Prevention.
Because of differences in the marginal benefit of protection, more Secret Service agents are assigned to protect the president (a) than to protect the vice president (b), and none are assigned to protect an ordinary citizen (c).

[4]Colorado Department of Public Health and Environment, *Vaccine Preventable Diseases in Colorado* (http://www.cdphe.state.co.us/de/Epidemiology/vaccinepreventable2000.pdf).

Should college professors receive Secret Service protection when they give out-of-town lectures?

© The Everett Collection

The important difference among these three cases lies in the value of assigning additional agents. The marginal benefit of an agent assigned to the president [MB_P, part (a)] is much higher than the marginal benefit of an agent assigned to the vice president [MB_{VP}, part (b)], for at least two reasons. First, opponents of the government have a stronger motive to attack the president than the vice president because the president's role is so much more important than the vice president's. Thus, assigning an additional agent to the president is more likely to prevent an attack. And second, the benefit of preventing an attack against the president is much higher than that of preventing an attack against the vice president—again, because the president's role is so much more important. These observations imply that the optimal number of agents to assign to the president [N_P, part (a)] is much greater than the optimal number of agents to assign to the vice president [N_{VP}, part (b)]. Finally, the optimal number of agents to assign to a traveling professor is zero [part (c)] because the marginal benefit of such an assignment (MB_{CP}) is so small. After all, few people have any reason to attack a professor, and in the unlikely event of an attack, the consequences would be far less serious than if a prominent government leader were attacked. •

Many critics of the cost-benefit approach complain that when applied in examples like the one just discussed, it gives short shrift to the dignity of human life. On closer inspection, however, this complaint is difficult to support. The recommendation to assign no Secret Service agents to protect a traveling college professor does not imply that the lives of ordinary citizens are not to be cherished. Rather, it simply acknowledges that even without Secret Service protection, not even a single traveling professor is likely to be assassinated in the course of the next 100 years. For the same money that we would spend to send agents on largely pointless assignments, we could install guard rails on dangerous mountain roads, purchase additional mobile coronary care units, or make any number of other investments that would save thousands of lives. The logic of the Scarcity Principle does not cease to apply whenever the choices we must make involve human health or safety.

Scarcity ◯

RECAP	PUBLIC HEALTH AND SECURITY

The cost-benefit principle applies to public health and safety measures just as in other areas of public policy. Society's efforts to promote security should be expanded only to the point at which their marginal benefits equal their marginal costs.

▪ SUMMARY ▪

• Basic microeconomic principles can be applied to a variety of government policy questions. These principles help to show how different methods of paying for health care affect the efficiency with which medical services are delivered. In the case of health care, the gains from marginal cost pricing can often be achieved through insurance policies with large deductibles.   **LO1**

• An understanding of the forces that give rise to environmental pollution can help to identify those policy measures that will achieve a desired reduction in pollution at the lowest possible cost. Both the taxing of

pollution and the sale of transferable pollution rights promote this goal. Each distributes the cost of the environmental cleanup effort so that the marginal cost of pollution abatement is the same for all polluters.   **LO2**

• A perennially controversial topic is the application of the cost-benefit principle to policies involving public health, safety, and security. Many critics feel that the use of cost-benefit analysis in this domain is not morally legitimate because it involves putting a monetary price on human life. Yet the fundamental principle of scarcity applies to human health and safety, just as it does to other issues. Spending more on public health and safety necessarily means spending less on other things of value. Failure to weigh the relevant costs and benefits means that society will be less likely to achieve its stated goals. **LO3, LO4**

▪ KEY TERMS ▪

first-dollar insurance coverage (379)

health maintenance organization (HMO) (379)

workers' compensation (389)

▪ REVIEW QUESTIONS ▪

1. Why is vaccination against many childhood illnesses a legal requirement for entry into public schools? **LO4**

2. Why do economists believe that pollution taxes and effluent permits are a more efficient way to curb pollution than laws mandating across-the-board cutbacks? **LO2**

3. Why is first-dollar health care coverage inefficient? **LO1**

4. How would you explain to a skeptical bank manager why the socially optimal number of bank robberies is not zero? **LO4**

5. Does it make sense for the Federal Aviation Administration to require more sophisticated and expensive safety equipment in large commercial passenger jets than in small private planes? **LO4**

▪ PROBLEMS ▪

1. In the event he requires an appendectomy, David's demand for hospital accommodations is as shown in the diagram. David's current insurance policy fully covers the cost of hospital stays. The marginal cost of providing a hospital room is $150 per day. If David's only illness this year results in an appendectomy, how many days will he choose to stay in the hospital? **LO1**

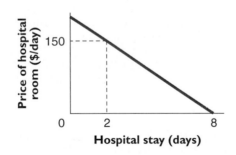

2. Refer to problem 1. By how much would total economic surplus have been higher this year if David's hospital insurance covered only the cost of hospital stays that exceed $1,000 per illness? **LO1**

3. Refer to problems 1 and 2. Suppose David's employer adopts a new health care plan that pays 50 percent of all medical expenses up to $1,000 per illness, with full coverage thereafter. How will economic surplus under this plan compare with economic surplus with the policy in problem 2? **LO1**

4. In Los Angeles, the demand for Botox injections (a procedure that removes wrinkles and smoothes the skin) is as shown in the diagram. The marginal cost of a Botox injection is $1,000 and the procedure is not currently covered by health insurance. By how much will total economic surplus change if the city council passes a law requiring employers to include full reimbursement for Botox injections in their employees' health coverage? **LO1**

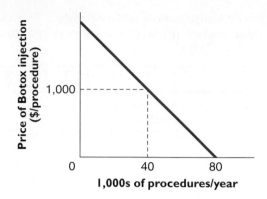

5. Refer to problem 4. How would the change in total economic surplus be affected if the law instead required health insurance to pay only $500 per procedure? **LO1**

6. Two firms, Sludge Oil and Northwest Lumber, have access to five production processes, each one of which has a different cost and gives off a different amount of pollution. The daily costs of the processes and the corresponding number of tons of smoke emitted are as shown in the following table: **LO2**

Process (smoke)	A (4 tons/day)	B (3 tons/day)	C (2 tons/day)	D (1 ton/day)	E (0 tons/day)
Cost to Sludge Oil ($/day)	50	70	120	200	500
Cost to Northwest Lumber ($/day)	100	180	500	1,000	2,000

a. If pollution is unregulated, which process will each firm use, and what will be the daily smoke emission?

b. The City Council wants to curb smoke emissions by 50 percent. To accomplish this, it requires each firm to curb its emissions by 50 percent. What will be the total cost to society of this policy?

7. The City Council in the previous problem again wants to curb emissions by half. This time, it sets a tax of T per day on each ton of smoke emitted. How large will T have to be to effect the desired reduction? What is the total cost to society of this policy? **LO2**

8. Refer to problem 7. Instead of taxing pollution, the city council decides to auction off four permits, each of which entitles the bearer to emit 1 ton of smoke per day. No smoke may be emitted without a permit. Suppose the government conducts the auction by starting at $1 and asking how many permits each firm wants to buy at that price. If the total is more than four, it then raises the price by $1 and asks again, and so on, until the total quantity of demanded permits falls to four. How much will each permit sell for in this auction? How many permits will each firm buy? What will be the total cost to society of this reduction in pollution? **LO2**

9. Tom and Al are the only two members of a household. Each gets satisfaction from three things: his income, his safety at work, and his income relative to his roommate's income. Suppose Tom and Al must each choose between two jobs: a safe job that pays $100 per week and a risky job that pays $130 per week. The value of safety to each is $40 per week. Each person evaluates relative income as follows: Having more income than his roommate provides the equivalent of $30 per week worth of satisfaction; having less implies a reduction of

$30 per week worth of satisfaction; and earning the same income as his roommate means no change in satisfaction. Will Tom and Al choose optimally between the two jobs?   **LO3**

10. Refer to problem 9. If Tom and Al could negotiate binding agreements with one another at no cost, which job would each choose? Suppose negotiation is impractical, and that the only way Tom and Al can achieve greater workplace safety is for the government to adopt safety regulations. If enforcement of the regulations costs $25 per week, would Tom and Al favor their adoption?   **LO3**

▪ ANSWERS TO IN-CHAPTER EXERCISES ▪

14.1 With 50 percent coverage, David would have to pay $150 for each additional day in the hospital, so he would choose to stay for two days.   **LOI**

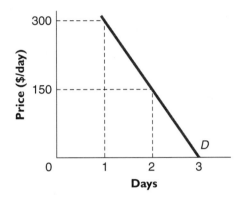

14.2 The optimal stay is still one day. If insurance reimburses $150 per day, then the marginal charge seen by David will be the remaining $150 per day, so he will stay two days. The cost to society of the additional day is $300 and the benefit to David of the extra day is only $225 (the area of the lower shaded figure). The loss in surplus from the additional day's stay is thus $75.   **LOI**

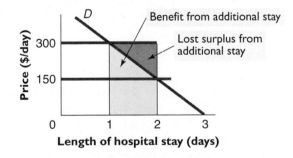

14.3 With a tax of $61 per ton each day, Sludge Oil would adopt process *A* and Northwest Lumber would adopt process *C*.   **LO2**

Process (smoke)	*A* (4 tons/day)	*B* (3 tons/day)	*C* (2 tons/day)	*D* (1 ton/day)	*E* (0 tons/day)
Cost to Sludge Oil ($/day)	100	200	600	1,300	2,300
Cost to Northwest Lumber ($/day)	300	320	380	480	700

14.4 The payoff matrix would now be as shown below, and the best choice, both individually and collectively, would be the risky job. **LO3**

		Michael	
		Safe job @ $50/week	Risky job @ $80/week
Don	Safe job @ $50/week	$70 for Don $70 for Michael	$30 for Don $120 for Michael
	Risky job @ $80/week	$120 for Don $30 for Michael	$80 for Don $80 for Michael

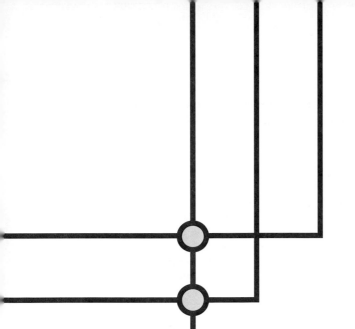

CHAPTER 15

Public Goods and Tax Policy

LEARNING OBJECTIVES

After reading this chapter, you should be able to:

1. Use the concepts of rivalry and excludability to distinguish among private goods, public goods, collective goods, and commons goods.

2. Show how economic concepts can be used to find the optimal quantity of a public good.

3. Describe the ways in which private firms can supply public goods.

4. Analyze the types of efficiencies and inefficiencies that are associated with the provision of public goods.

5. Discuss the criteria that should be applied to taxation in order to promote efficiency.

Government has the power to tax. Unlike a private business, which can get our money only if we voluntarily buy its product, the government can take our money even if we don't want the particular mix of goods and services provided.

Government also has a monopoly on the legitimate use of force. If people break the law, government has the power to restrain them, using force if necessary. It also has the power to deprive lawbreakers of their liberty for extended periods, and, in some places, even to execute them. Government can draft law-abiding citizens into the armed forces and send them into situations in which they must kill others and risk being killed themselves.

These are awesome powers. And although they are often used in the pursuit of noble ends, the historical record abounds with illustrations of their abuse. Voters and politicians of both parties are keenly aware of these abuses. Indeed, contemporary political rhetoric almost invariably entails criticism of bloated, out-of-control government bureaucracy. Even mainstream Democrats—ostensibly the party of activist government in the United States—have conceded the need to curb government's role. For example, former president Clinton remarked in his 1996 State of the Union Message, "the era of big government is over."

Others advocate even more radical retrenchment. For instance, Harry Browne, the 1996 Libertarian Party presidential candidate, called for abolition of the Internal Revenue Service, the agency responsible for collecting the federal income tax. This step would be tantamount to abolishing the federal government itself, for without tax revenues, there would be no way to pay for public goods and services.

Browne is right, of course, that a sure way to prevent government abuse of power is simply to have no government. But since virtually no society on earth lacks a government, we may suspect that governments, on balance, do more good than harm.

But how big, exactly, should government be? What goods and services should it provide? How should it raise the revenue to pay for them? What other powers should it have to constrain the behavior of its citizens? And how should the various powers we assign to government be apportioned among local, state, and federal levels? Our goal in this chapter will be to employ the principles of microeconomics in an attempt to answer these pragmatic questions.

GOVERNMENT PROVISION OF PUBLIC GOODS

public good a good or service that, to at least some degree, is both nonrival and nonexcludable

One of the primary tasks of government is to provide what economists call **public goods** such as national defense and the criminal justice system.

PUBLIC GOODS VERSUS PRIVATE GOODS

nonrival good a good whose consumption by one person does not diminish its availability for others

nonexcludable good a good that is difficult, or costly, to exclude nonpayers from consuming

Public goods are those goods or services that are, in varying degrees, **nonrival** and **nonexcludable**. A nonrival good is one whose consumption by one person does not diminish its availability for others. For example, if the military prevents a hostile nation from invading your city, your enjoyment of that protection does not diminish its value to your neighbors. A good is nonexcludable if it is difficult to exclude nonpayers from consuming it. For instance, even if your neighbors don't pay their share of the cost of maintaining an army, they will still enjoy its protection.

Another example of a nonrival and nonexcludable good is an over-the-air broadcast of *The Late Show with David Letterman*. The fact that you tune in one evening does not make the program any less available to others, and once the broadcast has been beamed out over the airwaves, it is difficult to prevent anyone from tuning in. Similarly, if the City of New York puts on a fireworks display in New York harbor to celebrate a special occasion, it cannot charge admission because the harbor may be viewed from many different locations in the city. And the fact that additional persons view the display does not in any way diminish its value to other potential viewers.

In contrast, the typical private good is diminished one-for-one by any individual's consumption of it. For instance, when you eat a cheeseburger, it is no longer available for anyone else. Moreover, people can be easily prevented from consuming cheeseburgers they don't pay for.

EXERCISE 15.1

Which of the following, if any, is nonrival?

a. **The Web site of the Bureau of Labor Statistics at 3 a.m.**

b. **The World Cup soccer championship game watched in person.**

c. **The World Cup soccer championship game watched on television.**

pure public good a good or service that, to a high degree, is both nonrival and nonexcludable

Goods that are both highly nonexcludable and nonrival are often called **pure public goods.** Two reasons favor government provision of such goods. First, for-profit private companies would have obvious difficulty recovering their cost of production. Many people might be willing to pay enough to cover the cost of producing the good, but if it is nonexcludable, the company cannot easily charge for it (an example of the free-rider problem discussed in Chapter 12). And second, if the marginal cost of serving additional users is zero once the good has been produced, then charging for the good would be inefficient, even if there were some practical way to do so. This inefficiency often characterizes the provision of **collective goods**— nonrival goods for which it is possible to exclude nonpayers. Pay-per-view cable television is an example. People who don't pay to get HBO don't get to watch programs shown only on HBO, a restriction that excludes many viewers who would have benefited from watching. Since the marginal cost to society of their tuning in is literally zero, excluding these viewers is wasteful.

A **pure private good** is one from which nonpayers can easily be excluded and for which one person's consumption creates a one-for-one reduction in the good's availability for others. The theory of perfectly competitive supply developed in Chapter 6 applies to pure private goods, of which basic agricultural products are perhaps the best examples. A **pure commons good** is a rival good that is also nonexcludable, so-called because goods with this combination of properties almost always result in a tragedy of the commons (see Chapter 11). Fish in ocean waters are an example.

The classification scheme defined by the nonrival and nonexcludable properties is summarized in Table 15.1. The columns of the table indicate the extent to which one person's consumption of a good fails to diminish its availability for others. Goods in the right column are nonrival and those in the left column are not. The rows of the table indicate the difficulty of excluding nonpayers from consuming the good. Goods in the top row are nonexcludable; those in the bottom row, excludable. Private goods (lower-left cell) are rival and excludable. Public goods (upper-right cell) are nonrival and nonexcludable. The two hybrid categories are commons goods (upper-left cell), which are rival but nonexcludable, and collective goods (lower-right cell), which are excludable but nonrival.

collective good a good or service that, to at least some degree, is nonrival but excludable

pure private good one for which nonpayers can easily be excluded and for which each unit consumed by one person means one less unit available for others

pure commons good one for which nonpayers cannot easily be excluded and for which each unit consumed by one person means one less unit available for others

TABLE 15.1
Private, Public, and Hybrid Goods

		Nonrival	
		Low	High
Nonexcludable	High	Commons good (fish in the ocean)	Public good (national defense)
	Low	Private good (wheat)	Collective good (pay-per-view TV)

Collective goods are provided sometimes by government, sometimes by private companies. Most pure public goods are provided by government, but even private companies can sometimes find profitable ways of producing goods that are both nonrival *and* nonexcludable. An example is broadcast radio and television, which covers its costs by selling airtime to advertisers.

The mere fact that a good is a pure public good does not necessarily mean that government ought to provide it. On the contrary, the only public goods the government should even *consider* providing are those whose benefits exceed their costs. The cost of a public good is simply the sum of all explicit and implicit costs incurred to provide it. The benefit of a public good is measured by asking how much people would be willing to pay for it. Although that sounds similar to the way we measure

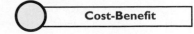

Cost-Benefit

the benefit of a private good, an important distinction exists. The benefit of an additional unit of a private good such as a cheeseburger is the highest sum that any individual buyer would be willing to pay for it. In contrast, the benefit of an additional unit of a public good such as an additional broadcast episode of *Sesame Street* is the sum of the reservation prices of all people who will watch that episode.

Even if the amount that all beneficiaries of a public good would be willing to pay exceeds its cost, government provision of that good makes sense only if there is no other less costly way of providing it. For example, whereas city governments often pay for fireworks displays, they almost invariably hire private companies to put on these events. Finally, if the benefit of a public good does not exceed its cost, we are better off without it.

PAYING FOR PUBLIC GOODS

Not everyone benefits equally from the provision of a given public good. For example, some people find fireworks displays highly entertaining, but others simply don't care about them, and still others actively dislike them. Ideally, it might seem that the most equitable method of financing a given public good would be to tax people in proportion to their willingness to pay for the good. To illustrate this approach, suppose Jones values a public good at $100, Smith values the same good at $200, and the cost of the good is $240. Jones would then be taxed $80 and Smith would be taxed $160. The good would be provided, and each taxpayer in this example would reap a surplus equal to 25 percent of his tax payment: $20 for Jones, $40 for Smith.

In practice, however, government officials usually lack the information they would need to tax people in proportion to their willingness to pay for specific public goods. (Think about it: If an IRS agent asked you how much you would be willing to pay to have a new freeway and you knew you would be taxed in proportion to the amount you responded, what would you say?) The following three examples illustrate some of the problems that arise in financing public goods and suggests possible solutions to these problems.

Will Prentice and Wilson buy a water filter?

Prentice and Wilson own adjacent summer cottages along an isolated stretch of shoreline on Cayuga Lake. Because of a recent invasion of zebra mussels, each must add chlorine to his water intake valve each week to prevent it from becoming clogged by the tiny mollusks. A manufacturer has introduced a new filtration device that eliminates the nuisance of weekly chlorination. The cost of the device, which has the capacity to serve both houses, is $1,000. Both owners feel equally strongly about having the filter. But because Wilson earns twice as much as Prentice, Wilson is willing to pay up to $800 to have the filter, whereas its value to Prentice, a retired schoolteacher, is only $400. Would either person be willing to purchase the device individually? Is it efficient for them to share its purchase?

Neither will purchase the filter individually because each has a reservation price that is below its selling price. But because the two together value the filter at $1,200, sharing its use would be socially efficient. If they were to do so, total economic surplus would be $200 higher than if they did not buy the filter. ◆

Since sharing the filter is the efficient outcome, we might expect that Prentice and Wilson would quickly reach agreement to purchase it. Unfortunately, however, the joint purchase and sharing of facilities is often easier proposed than accomplished. One hurdle is that people must incur costs merely to get together to discuss joint purchases. With only two people involved, those costs might not be significant. But if hundreds or thousands of people were involved, communication costs could be prohibitive.

With large numbers of people, the free-rider problem also emerges (see Chapter 12). After all, everyone knows that the project will either succeed or fail independently of any one person's contribution to it. Everyone thus has an incentive to withhold contributions—or get a free ride—in the hope that others will give.

Finally, even when only a few people are involved, reaching agreement on a fair sharing of the total expense may be difficult. For example, Prentice and Wilson might be reluctant to disclose their true reservation prices to one another for the same reason that you might be reluctant to disclose your reservation price for a public good to an IRS agent.

These practical concerns may lead us to empower government to buy public goods on our behalf. But as the next example makes clear, this approach does not eliminate the need to reach political agreement on how public purchases are to be financed.

Will government buy the water filter if there is an "equal tax" rule?

Suppose Prentice and Wilson could ask the government to help broker the water filter purchase. And suppose that the government's tax policy must follow a "nondiscrimination" rule that prohibits charging any citizen more for a public good than it charges his or her neighbor. Another rule is that public goods can be provided only if a majority of citizens approve of them. Will a government bound by these rules provide the filter that Prentice and Wilson want?

A tax that collects the same amount from every citizen is called a **head tax.** If the government must rely on a head tax, it must raise $500 from Prentice and $500 from Wilson. But since the device is worth only $400 to Prentice, he will vote against the project, thus denying it a majority. So a democratic government cannot provide the water filter if it must rely on a head tax. ◆

head tax a tax that collects the same amount from every taxpayer

A head tax is a **regressive tax,** one for which the proportion of a taxpayer's income that is paid in taxes declines as the taxpayer's income rises.

The point illustrated by this example is not confined to the specific public good considered. It applies whenever taxpayers place significantly different valuations on public goods, as will almost always happen whenever people earn significantly different incomes. An equal-tax rule under these circumstances will almost invariably rule out the provision of many worthwhile public goods.

regressive tax a tax under which the proportion of income paid in taxes declines as income rises

As our third example suggests, one solution to this problem is to allow taxes to vary by income.

Will the government buy the filter if there is a proportional tax on income?

Suppose that Prentice proposes that the government raise revenue by imposing a proportional tax on income to finance the provision of the water filter. Will Wilson, who earns twice as much as Prentice, support this proposal?

proportional income tax one under which all taxpayers pay the same proportion of their incomes in taxes

A **proportional income tax** is one under which all taxpayers pay the same percentage of their incomes in taxes. Under such a tax, Wilson would support Prentice's proposal because if he didn't, each would fail to enjoy a public good whose benefit exceeds his share of its cost. Under the proportional tax on income, Prentice would contribute $333 toward the $1,000 purchase price of the filter and Wilson would contribute $667. The government would buy the filter, resulting in additional surpluses of $67 for Prentice and $133 for Wilson. ◆

The following example makes the point that just as equal contributions are often a poor way to pay for public goods, they are also often a poor way to share expenses within the household.

Example 15.1

THE ECONOMIC NATURALIST

Why do married couples usually pool their incomes?

Why don't most married couples contribute equally to joint purchases?

Suppose Hillary earns $2,000,000 per year while her husband Bill earns only $20,000. Given her income, Hillary as an individual would want to spend much more than Bill would on housing, travel, entertainment, education for their children, and the many other items they consume jointly. What will happen if the couple adopts a rule that each must contribute an equal amount toward the purchase of such items?

This rule would constrain the couple to live in a small house, take only inexpensive vacations, and skimp on entertainment, dining out, and their children's education. It is therefore easy to see why Hillary might find it attractive to pay considerably more than 50 percent for jointly consumed goods because doing so would enable *both* of them to consume in the manner their combined income permits. ●

Public goods and jointly consumed private goods are different from individually consumed private goods in the following important way: *Different individuals are free to consume whatever quantity and quality of most private goods they choose to buy, but jointly consumed goods must be provided in the same quantity and quality for all persons.*

As in the case of private goods, people's willingness to pay for public goods is generally an increasing function of income. Wealthy individuals tend to assign greater value to public goods than low-income people do, not because the wealthy have different tastes but because they have more money. A head tax would result in high-income persons getting smaller amounts of public goods than they want. By increasing the total economic surplus available for all to share, a tax system that assigns a larger share of the tax burden to people with higher incomes makes possible a better outcome for both rich and poor alike. Indeed, virtually all industrialized nations have tax systems that are at least mildly **progressive**, which means that the proportion of income paid in taxes actually rises with a family's income.

progressive tax one in which the proportion of income paid in taxes rises as income rises

Progressive taxation and even proportional taxation often have been criticized as being unfair to the wealthy, who are forced to pay more than others for public goods that all consume in common. The irony in this charge, however, is that exclusive reliance on head taxes, or even proportional taxes, would curtail the provision of public goods and services that are of greatest value to high-income families. Studies have shown, for instance, that the income elasticity of demand for public goods such as parks and recreation facilities, clean air and water, public safety, un-congested roads, and aesthetically pleasing public spaces is substantially greater than 1. Failure to rely on progressive taxation would result in gross underprovision of such public goods and services.

RECAP	PUBLIC GOODS

A public good is both nonrival and nonexcludable. Private firms typically cannot recover the costs of producing such goods because they cannot exclude nonpayers from consuming them. Nor would charging for a public good promote efficiency, since one person's consumption of the good does not diminish its availability for others.

Both obstacles can be overcome by creating a government with the power to levy taxes. Even high-income citizens often favor progressive taxes because proportional or regressive taxes may generate insufficient revenue to pay for the public goods those taxpayers favor.

THE OPTIMAL QUANTITY OF A PUBLIC GOOD

In the examples considered thus far, the question was whether to provide a particular public good and, if so, how to pay for it. In practice, we often confront additional questions about what level and quality of a public good to provide.

Standard cost-benefit logic also applies to these questions. For example, New York City should add another rocket to a fireworks display if and only if the amount that citizens would collectively be willing to pay to see the rocket is at least as great as its cost.

(Cost-Benefit)

THE DEMAND CURVE FOR A PUBLIC GOOD

To calculate the socially optimal quantity of a public good, we must first construct the demand curve for that public good. The process for doing so differs in an important way from the one we use to generate the market demand curve for a private good.

For a private good, all buyers face the same price and each chooses the quantity he or she wishes to purchase at that price. Recall from Chapter 5 to construct the demand curve for a private good from the demand curves for individual consumers, we place the individual demand curves side by side and add them horizontally. That is, for each of a series of fixed prices, we add the resulting quantities demanded on the individual demand curves. In Figure 15.1, for example, we add the individual demand curves for a private good, D_1 and D_2 [parts (a) and (b)], horizontally to obtain the market demand curve for the good D [part (c)].

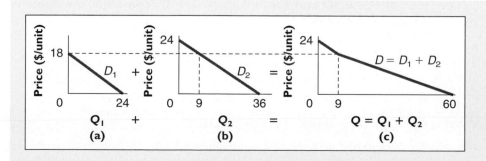

FIGURE 15.1
Generating the Market Demand Curve for a Private Good.
To construct the market demand curve for a private good (c), we add the individual demand curves (a) and (b) horizontally.

For a public good, all buyers necessarily consume the same quantity, although each may differ in terms of willingness to pay for additional units of the good. Constructing the demand curve for a public good thus entails not horizontal summation of the individual demand curves but vertical summation. That is, for each of a series of quantity values, we must add the prices that individuals are willing to pay for an additional unit of the good. The curves D_1 and D_2 in Figure 15.2(b) and (c) show individual demand curves for a public good by two different people. At each quantity, these curves tell how much the individual would be willing to pay for an additional unit of the public good. If we add D_1 and D_2 vertically, we obtain the total demand curve D for the public good [part (a)].

FIGURE 15.2

Generating the Demand Curve for a Public Good.

To construct the demand curve for a public good (a), we add the individual demand curves (b) and (c) vertically.

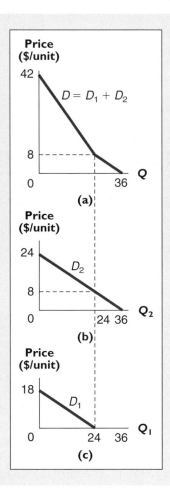

EXERCISE 15.2

Bill and Tom are the only demanders of a public good. If Bill's demand curve is $P_B = 6 - 0.5Q$ and Tom's is $P_T = 12 - Q$, construct the demand curve for this public good.

In the following example, we see how the demand curve for a public good might be used in conjunction with information about costs to determine the optimal level of parkland in a city.

What is the optimal quantity of urban parkland?

The city government of a new planned community must decide how much parkland to provide. The marginal cost curve and the public demand curve for urban parkland are as shown in Figure 15.3. Why is the marginal cost curve upward-sloping and the demand curve downward-sloping? Given these curves, what is the optimal quantity of parkland?

The marginal cost schedule for urban parkland is upward-sloping because of the Low-Hanging-Fruit Principle: The city acquires the cheapest parcels of land first, and only then turns to more expensive parcels. Likewise, the marginal willingness-to-pay curve is downward-sloping because of the law of diminishing marginal utility. Just as people are generally willing to pay less for their fifth hot dog than for their first, they are also willing to pay less for the 101st acre of parkland than for the 100th acre. Given these curves, A^* is the optimal quantity of parkland. For any quantity less than A^*, the benefit of additional parkland exceeds its cost, which means that total economic surplus can be made larger by expanding the amount of parkland. For example, at A_0, the community would be willing to pay $200,000 for an additional acre of urban parkland, but its cost is only $80,000. Similarly, for any quantity of parkland in excess of A^*, the community would gain more than it would lose by selling off some parkland.

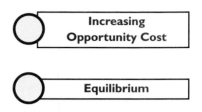

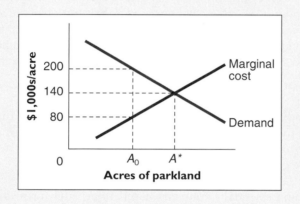

FIGURE 15.3
The Optimal Quantity of Parkland.
The optimal number of acres of urban parkland is A^*, the quantity at which the public's willingness to pay for additional parkland is equal to the marginal cost of parkland.

PRIVATE PROVISION OF PUBLIC GOODS

One advantage of using the government to provide public goods is that once a tax collection agency has been established to finance a single public good, it can be expanded at relatively low cost to generate revenue for additional public goods. Another advantage is that because government has the power to tax, it can summarily assign responsibility for the cost of a public good without endless haggling over who bears what share of the burden. And in the case of goods for which nonpayers cannot be excluded, the government may be the only feasible provider.

But exclusive reliance on government also entails disadvantages. Most fundamentally, the government's one-size-fits-all approach invariably requires many people to pay for public goods they don't want, while others end up having to do without public goods they want desperately. For example, many people vehemently oppose the provision of *any* sex education in the public schools, while others fervently believe that far more such instruction should be provided than is currently offered in most current public school curriculums. Mandatory taxation strikes many people as coercive, even if they approve of the particular public goods being provided.

It is no surprise, then, that governments are not the exclusive providers of public goods in any society. Indeed, many public goods are routinely provided through private channels. The challenge, in each case, is to devise a scheme for raising the required revenues. Here are some methods that seem to work.

Funding by donation In 2001 Americans gave more than $200 billion to private charities, many of which provide public goods to their communities. People also volunteer their time on behalf of organizations that provide public goods. When you paint your house, mow your lawn, or plant a flower garden, you are enhancing the quality of life in your neighborhood, and in that sense you are voluntarily providing a public good to your neighbors.

Development of new means to exclude nonpayers New electronic technology makes it possible to exclude nonpayers from many goods that in the past could not be thus restricted. For instance, broadcast television stations now have the ability to scramble their signals, making them available only to those consumers who purchase descrambling devices.

Private contracting More than 8 million Americans now live in gated private communities—private homeowners' associations that wall off contiguous properties and provide various services to residents. Many of these associations provide security services, schools, and fire protection and in other ways function much like ordinary local governments. Recognizing that individual incentives may not be strong enough to assure socially optimal levels of maintenance and landscaping, these associations often bill homeowners for those services directly. Many of the rules imposed by these associations are even more restrictive than those imposed by local governments, a distinction that is defended on the grounds that people are always free to choose some other neighborhood if they don't like the rules of any particular homeowners' association. Many people would be reluctant to tolerate a municipal ordinance that prevents people from painting their houses purple, yet such restrictions are common in the bylaws of homeowners' associations.

Sale of by-products Many public goods are financed by the sale of rights or services that are generated as by-products of the public goods. For instance, as noted earlier, radio and television programming is a public good that is paid for in many cases by the sale of advertising messages. Internet services are also underwritten in part by commercial messages that pop up or appear in the headers or margins of Web pages.

Given the quintessentially voluntary nature of privately provided public goods, it might seem that reliance on private provision might be preferred whenever it proved feasible. But as the following example makes clear, private provision often entails problems of its own.

Example 15.2
THE ECONOMIC NATURALIST

Why do television networks favor *Jerry Springer* over *Masterpiece Theater*?

In a given time slot, a television network faces the alternative of broadcasting either the *Jerry Springer Show* or *Masterpiece Theater*. If it chooses *Springer*, it will win 20 percent of the viewing audience, but only 18 percent if it chooses *Masterpiece Theater*. Suppose those who would choose *Springer* would collectively be willing to pay $10 million for the right to see that program, while those who choose *Masterpiece Theater* would be willing to pay $30 million. And suppose, finally, that the time slot is to be financed by a detergent company. Which program will the network choose? Which program would be socially optimal?

A detergent maker cares primarily about the number of people who will see its advertisements and will thus choose the program that will attract the largest audience—here, the *Springer Show*. The fact that those who prefer *Masterpiece Theater* would be willing to pay a lot more to see it is of little concern to the sponsor. But to identify the optimal result from society's point of view, we must take this difference into account. Because the people who prefer *Masterpiece Theater* could pay the *Springer* viewers more than enough to compensate them for relinquishing the time slot, *Masterpiece Theater* is the efficient outcome. But unless its supporters happen to buy more soap in total than the *Springer* viewers, the latter will prevail. In short, reliance on advertising and other indirect mechanisms for financing public goods provides no assurance that the goods chosen will maximize economic surplus. ●

Of course, the fact that the programs that best suit advertisers' needs may not be socially optimal does not mean that government decisions would necessarily be better. One can imagine, for example, a cultural affairs ministry that would choose television programming that would be "good for us" but that few of us would want to watch.

One way to avoid the inefficiency that arises when advertisers choose programming is to employ pay-per-view methods of paying for television programming. These methods allow viewers to register not just which programs they prefer but also the strength of their preferences, as measured by how much they are willing to pay.

But although pay-per-view TV is more likely to select the programs the public most values, it is also less efficient than broadcast TV in one important respect. As noted earlier, charging each household a fee for viewing discourages some households from tuning in. And since the marginal social cost of serving an additional household is exactly zero, limiting the audience in this way is inefficient. Which of the two inefficiencies is more important—free TV's inefficiency in choosing among programs or pay TV's inefficiency in excluding potential beneficiaries—is an empirical question.

In any event, the mix between private and public provision of public goods and services differs substantially from society to society and from arena to arena within any given society. These differences depend on the nature of available technologies for delivering and paying for public goods, and also on people's preferences.

Why do detergent companies care more about audience size than about how much people would be willing to pay to see the programs they sponsor?

By how much is economic surplus reduced by a pay-per-view charge?

If *Mystery Theater* is shown on pay-per-view television at 10 p.m. on Thursdays, the demand curve for each episode is as given in Figure 15.4. If the regulated pay-per-view charge is $10 per household, by how much would economic surplus rise if the same episode were shown instead on "free" broadcast public TV?

With a fee of $10 per episode, 10 million households will watch (see Figure 15.4). But if the same episode were shown instead on broadcast public TV, 20 million households would watch. The additional economic surplus reaped by the extra 10 million households is the area of the blue triangle, which is $50 million. The marginal cost of permitting these additional households to watch the episode is zero, so the total gain in surplus is $50 million.

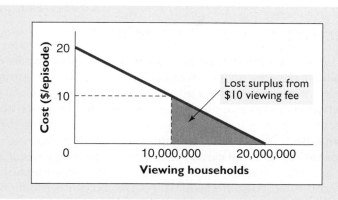

FIGURE 15.4
The Loss in Surplus from a Pay-per-View Fee.
Twice as many households would watch the program if its price were zero instead of $10. The additional economic surplus is the area of the blue triangle, or $50 million.

In general, charging a positive price for a good whose marginal cost is zero will result in a loss in surplus. As we saw in Chapter 7, the size of the loss that results when price is set above marginal cost depends on the price elasticity of demand. When demand is more elastic, the loss in surplus is greater. Exercise 15.3 provides an opportunity to see that principle at work.

EXERCISE 15.3

How would your answer to the previous example have been different if the demand curve had instead been as shown below?

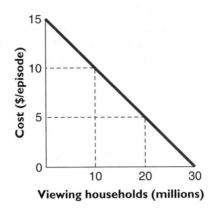

RECAP	**THE OPTIMAL QUANTITY OF A PUBLIC GOOD**

Because the quantity of a public good must be the same for every consumer, the total demand curve for a public good is constructed by adding individual demand curves vertically. Optimal production of a public good occurs at the quantity for which the demand curve intersects the marginal cost curve for the public good.

Government need not always be the best way to provide public goods. Such goods can be provided by private organizations that rely on charitable contributions or the sale of by-products. Private for-profit companies also can become providers when new technologies such as pay-per-view television convert public goods into collective goods.

ADDITIONAL FUNCTIONS OF GOVERNMENT

The provision of public goods is not the only rationale for the existence of government. Government also creates and enforces the rules without which the efficient production of private goods would not be possible.

EXTERNALITIES AND PROPERTY RIGHTS

As we saw in Chapter 11, externalities often stand in the way of socially optimal resource allocation in private activities. We saw, too, that optimal allocations are unlikely to result whenever property rights are poorly defined (for example, the tragedy of the commons). These observations suggest the existence of two additional important roles for government: the regulation of activities that generate externalities and the definition and enforcement of property rights.

These rationales for government action explain why most governments regulate activities that generate pollution, subsidize education (on the grounds that an educated public creates positive externalities), control access to fishing waters and public timber lands, and enforce zoning laws. Most laws, in fact, represent attempts to define property rights or to control externalities. The law requiring motorists to drive on the right, for example, is an attempt to prevent the activities of one motorist from causing harm to others.

Proponents of minimalist government often object that the government unjustly curtails our freedom when it uses zoning laws to limit the size of the houses we build or imposes fines on motorists who violate highway speed limits. Yet the justification for such regulations is precisely the same as for the laws that prohibit your fist from occupying the same physical space as your neighbor's nose. You are free to swing your fists as you please, provided you cause no harm to others. But if your fist strikes your neighbor's nose, you become a violator of the law and subject to punishment. If the proponents of minimalist government approve of restricting behavior in this way, why do they disapprove of other attempts to discourage behaviors that cause harm to others?

Perhaps their fear is that because externalities are so pervasive, governments that were empowered to regulate them might quickly get out of control. This is by no means an idle fear, and we emphasize that the mere fact that an externality exists does not necessarily mean that the best outcome is for the government to regulate it. As we will see in the next section, regulation entails costs of its own. The ultimate question is therefore a practical one: Will government regulation of the externality in question do more good than harm? Slogans about being free to live without government interference provide little help in answering such questions.

LOCAL, STATE, OR FEDERAL?

Framers of the U.S. Constitution were deeply skeptical of centralized government power. In drafting the Constitution, therefore, they explicitly tried to limit the powers of the federal government as much as possible, delegating most important powers to the states, who in turn delegated many of their powers to governments at the local level.

EN 15

It is no surprise that the dangers of remote, centralized government ranked high among the founding fathers' concerns. After all, fresh in their memories was the autocratic treatment received by the American colonies at the hands of the monarchy in England. The founding fathers recognized that government will be more responsive the shorter the distance between officeholders and the voters who elect them.

Another obvious advantage of giving as much authority to local governments as possible is that different communities often have markedly different preferences about how much to spend on public goods, and even on what kinds of public goods to provide. When such decisions are made at the local level, people can shop for a community whose voters' preferences largely coincide with their own. Those who like high levels of public goods and services can band together and authorize high taxes to pay for them. Others who place less value on public services can choose communities in which both services and taxes are lower.

Why, given the many attractions of decisions made at the local level, did the founding fathers create federal and state governments at all? One reason is economies of scale in defense. For a country to survive politically, it must be able to deter aggression by hostile governments. A country consisting only of, say, Concord, New Hampshire, would be ill-equipped to do that. Large, well-equipped armies and navies cost a lot of money, and countries without sufficient population simply cannot afford them.

Defense, however, is not the only reason to empower governments beyond the local or state level. The problem of pollution, for example, is difficult to solve when the various sources of pollution are not subject to regulatory control by a single government. Much of the acid rain experienced in Canada, for instance, is the result of sulfur dioxide emissions from industrial sources in the upper Midwest of the United States. These emissions are beyond the reach of Canadian environmental regulations. In many instances, as with the discharge of greenhouse gases, not even a coalition of all the governments in North, Central, and South America would have power to take effective action. Carbon dioxide emitted anywhere on the planet disperses to uniform concentrations around the globe in a matter of months.

The choice between different levels of government, then, often confronts us with difficult trade-offs. Ceding the power of taxation to a federal government often entails painful compromises for voters in individual states. But the loss of political autonomy is an even less attractive option. Similarly, nations are understandably reluctant to cede any of their sovereign powers to a higher authority, but failure to take such steps may entail unacceptable environmental costs in the long run.

RECAP	ADDITIONAL FUNCTIONS OF GOVERNMENT

Government creates economic surplus not only by providing public goods but also by regulating activities that generate externalities and by defining and enforcing property rights. These rationales explain why most governments regulate pollution, subsidize education, control access to fishing waters and public timber lands, and enforce zoning laws.

Although the framers of the Constitution disliked centralized government power, they recognized that some government functions are not best performed at the local or even state level. Economies of scale argue for provision of defense at the national level. Externalities that transcend local boundaries provide an additional rationale for national or even international government.

SOURCES OF INEFFICIENCY IN THE POLITICAL PROCESS

In most countries, expenditures on public goods, tax policy, and laws regulating behavior are determined in large part by the votes of democratically elected representatives. This process is far from perfect. (Winston Churchill called democracy "the worst form of government, except for any other.") Inefficiencies often arise in the public sphere not because of incompetent or ignorant legislators but because of structural incentive problems.

PORK BARREL LEGISLATION

The following example, drawn not from the public sector but from everyday private life, illustrates one of the important incentive gaps.

Example 15.3
THE ECONOMIC NATURALIST

Why does check-splitting make the total restaurant bill higher?

Sven Torvaldsen and nine friends are having dinner at La Maison de La Casa House, a four-star restaurant in Minneapolis. To simplify the task of paying for their meal, they have agreed in advance to split the cost of their meal equally, with each paying one-tenth of the total check. Having cleared the entree dishes, the waiter arrives with the dessert menu, on which Sven's two favorite items are pumpkin bread pudding ($10) and chocolate mousse ($6). Sven's reservation prices for these items are $4 and $3, respectively. Will he order dessert, and, if so, which one? Would he order dessert if he were dining by himself?

When Sven and his friends split the total check equally, Sven's payment goes up by one-tenth of the menu price of any dessert he orders. Thus, the prices—to him—of the bread pudding and chocolate mousse are $1 and 60 cents, respectively. Because he gets $4 − $1 = $3 of consumer surplus from the bread pudding and only $3 − $0.60 = $2.40 from the chocolate mousse, he will order the bread pudding. If Sven were dining alone, however, his bill would increase dollar for dollar with the menu price of any dessert he ordered. And since the menu prices exceed his corresponding reservation prices, he would not order dessert at all.

The irony, of course, is that if Sven's nine friends have the same preferences regarding dessert, each will order bread pudding and each person's share of the total bill will rise not by $1 but by the full $10. Compared to the alternative of no one having dessert, each diner suffers a $6 loss in consumer surplus. Still, it made sense for each to order bread pudding, since failure to do so would have reduced each diner's bill by only $1. ●

Does check-splitting make people more likely to order dessert?

EXERCISE 15.4

In the preceding example, would Sven have ordered dessert if there had been only 5 people splitting the check instead of 10?

Alert readers will have noticed the similarity between the problem posed in the preceding example and the one posed in Chapter 11, Example 11.7, in which identical twins had a single milkshake to share with two straws. The same incentive problem leads to the inefficient outcome in both cases.

The following example illustrates how the very same incentive problem rears its head in the legislative process.

Why do legislators often support one another's pork barrel spending programs?

Pork barrel programs are government programs that benefit local areas but are of questionable value from a national perspective. Why do voters seem to support legislators who initiate such projects even when the total effect of all such projects on local tax bills far exceeds the local benefits?

Consider a voter in a congressional district that contains one one-hundredth of the country's taxpayers. Suppose that voter's representative is able to deliver a public project that generates benefits of $100 million for the district but that costs the federal government $150 million. Since the district's share of the tax bill for the project will be only $150 million/100 = $1.5 million, residents of the district are $98.5 million better off with the project than without it. And that explains why so many voters favor legislators with a successful record of "bringing home the bacon."

But why would legislator A support such a project in legislator B's home district? After all, B's project will cause A's constituents' taxes to rise—albeit by a small amount—yet they will get no direct benefit from the project. The answer is that if A does not support B's project, then B will not support A's. The practice whereby legislators support one another's pet projects is known as **logrolling**. This practice creates a bias toward excessive spending, much like the bias created when a dinner check is split equally. •

RENT-SEEKING

A related source of inefficiency in the public sphere occurs because the gains from government projects are often concentrated in the hands of a few beneficiaries, while the costs are spread among many. This means that beneficiaries often have a powerful incentive to organize and lobby in favor of public projects. Individual taxpayers, by contrast, have little at stake in any public project and therefore have little incentive to incur the cost of mobilizing themselves in opposition.

Suppose, for example, that a price support bill for sugar will raise the price of sugar by 10 cents per pound and that the average American family currently consumes 100 pounds of sugar per year. How will this legislation affect the average family's consumption of sugar? Recall from the chapter on demand that a good such as salt or sugar whose share in most family budgets is small is likely to have a low price elasticity of demand. Hence, each family's sugar consumption will decline only slightly as a result of the 10-cent price hike. The resulting increase in each family's annual expenditures on sugar—slightly less than $10—is scarcely a noticeable burden, and surely not enough to induce many people to complain to their representatives. The same legislation, however, will raise sugar industry revenues by nearly $1 billion annually. With a sum that large at stake, it is certain that the industry will lobby vigorously in its favor.

Why don't citizens vote against those legislators who support such bills? One reason is the problem of rational ignorance, discussed in Chapter 12. Most voters have no idea that a price support bill for sugar and other special-interest bills even

Example 15.4
THE ECONOMIC NATURALIST

pork barrel spending a public expenditure that is larger than the total benefit it creates but that is favored by a legislator because his or her constituents benefit from the expenditure by more than their share of the resulting extra taxes

logrolling the practice whereby legislators support one another's legislative proposals

exist, much less how individual legislators vote on them. If all voters became well-informed about such bills, the resulting increase in the quality of legislation might well be sufficient to compensate each voter for the cost of becoming informed. But because of the free-rider problem, each voter knows that the outcome of votes in Congress will not be much affected by whether he or she becomes well-informed.

Still other sources of inefficiency arise even in the case of projects whose benefits exceed their costs. In the 1980s, for example, the federal government announced its decision to build a $25 billion high-energy physics research facility (the "superconducting supercollider"), which ignited an intense competition among more than 20 states vying to be chosen as the site for this facility. Hundreds of millions of dollars were spent on proposal preparation, consultants' fees, and various other lobbying activities. Such investments are known as **rent-seeking,** and they tend to be inefficient for the same reason that investments by contestants in other positional arms races are inefficient (see Chapter 11).

rent-seeking the socially unproductive efforts of people or firms to win a prize

Efforts devoted to rent-seeking are socially unproductive because of the simple incentive problem illustrated in the following example.

Why would anyone pay $50 for a $20 bill?

Suppose a $20 bill is to be auctioned off to the highest bidder. The rules of this particular auction require an initial bid of at least 50 cents, and succeeding bids must exceed the previous high bid by at least 50 cents. When the bidding ceases, both the highest bidder and the second-highest bidder must give the amounts they bid to the auctioneer. The highest bidder then receives the $20, and the second-highest bidder gets nothing. For example, if the highest bid is $11 and the second-highest bid is $10.50, the winner earns a net payment of $20 − $11 = $9, and the runner-up loses $10.50. How high will the winning bid be, on average?

Auctions like this one have been extensively studied in the laboratory. And although subjects in these experiments have ranged from business executives to college undergraduates, the pattern of bidding is almost always the same. Following the opening bid, offers proceed quickly to $10, or half the amount being auctioned. A pause then occurs as the subjects appear to digest the fact that with the next bid the sum of the two highest bids will exceed $20, thus taking the auctioneer off the hook. At this point, the second-highest bidder, whose bid stands at $9.50, invariably offers $10.50, apparently preferring a shot at winning $9.50 to a sure loss of $9.50.

In most cases, all but the top two bidders drop out at this point, and the top two quickly escalate their bids. As the bidding approaches $20, a second pause occurs, this time as the bidders appear to recognize that even the highest bidder is likely to come out behind. The second-highest bidder, at $19.50, is understandably reluctant to offer $20.50. But consider the alternative. If he drops out, he will lose $19.50 for sure. But if he offers $20.50 and wins, he will lose only 50 cents. So as long as he thinks there is even a small chance that the other bidder will drop out, it makes sense to continue. Once the $20 threshold has been crossed, the pace of the bidding quickens again, and from then on it is a war of nerves between the two remaining bidders. It is common for the bidding to reach $50 before someone finally yields in frustration. ◆

One might be tempted to think that any intelligent, well-informed person would know better than to become involved in an auction whose incentives so strongly favor costly escalation. But many of the subjects in these auctions have been experienced business professionals; many others have had formal training in the theory of games and strategic interaction. For example, psychologist Max Bazerman reports that during a recent 10-year period, he earned more than $17,000 by auctioning $20 bills to his MBA students at Northwestern University's Kellogg Graduate School of Management, which is consistently among the top-rated MBA programs in the world. In the course of almost 200 of his auctions, the top two bids never totaled less than $39, and in one instance they totaled $407.

The incentives that confront participants in the $20 bill auction are strikingly similar to those that confront companies that are vying for lucrative government contracts. Consider the following example.

How much will cellular phone companies bid for an exclusive license?

The State of Wyoming has announced its intention to grant an exclusive license to provide cellular phone services within its borders. Two firms have met the deadline for applying for this license. The franchise lasts for exactly one year, during which time the franchisee can expect to make an economic profit of $20 million. The state legislature will choose the applicant that spends the most money lobbying legislators. If the applicants cannot collude, how much will each spend on lobbying?

If both spend the same, each will have a 50-50 chance at the $20 million prize, which means an expected profit of $10 million minus the amount spent lobbying. If the lobbyists could collude, each would agree to spend the same small, token amount on lobbying. But in the absence of a binding agreement, each will be strongly tempted to try to outspend the other. Once each firm's spending reaches $10 million, each will have an expected profit of zero (a 50-50 chance to earn $20 million, minus the $10 million spent on lobbying).

Further bidding would guarantee an expected loss. And yet, if one firm spent $10,000,001 while the other stayed at $10 million, the first firm would get the franchise for sure and earn an economic profit of $9,999,999. The other firm would have an economic loss of $10 million. Rather than face a sure loss of $10 million, it may be tempted to bid $10,000,002. But then, of course, its rival would face a similar incentive to respond to that bid. No matter where the escalation stops, it is sure to dissipate much of the gains that could have been had from the project. And perhaps, as in the $20 bill auction, the total amount dissipated will be even more than the value of the franchise itself. ◆

From the individual perspective, it is easy to see why firms might lobby in this fashion for a chance to win government benefits. From society's perspective, however, this activity is almost purely wasteful. Lobbyists are typically intelligent, well-educated, and socially skilled. The opportunity cost of their time is high. If they were not lobbying government officials on behalf of their clients, they could be producing other goods or services of value. Governments can discourage such waste by selecting contractors not according to the amount they spend lobbying but on the basis of the price they promise to charge for their services. Society will be more successful the more its institutions encourage citizens to pursue activities that create wealth rather than activities that merely transfer existing wealth from one person or company to another.

STARVE THE GOVERNMENT?

Nobel laureate Milton Friedman said that no bureaucrat spends taxpayers' money as carefully as those taxpayers themselves would have. And indeed, there can be little doubt that many government expenditures are wasteful. Beyond the fact that log-rolling often results in pork barrel programs that would not satisfy the cost-benefit test, we must worry that government employees may not always face strong incentives to get the most for what they spend. The Pentagon, for example, once purchased a coffeemaker for $7,600 and on another occasion paid $600 for a toilet seat. Such expenditures may have been aberrations, but there seems little doubt that private contractors often deliver comparable services at substantially lower costs than their public counterparts.

In their understandable outrage over government waste, many critics have urged major cutbacks in the volume of public goods and services. These critics reason that if we let the government spend more money, there will be more waste. This is true, of course, but only in the trivial sense that there would be more of *everything* the government does—good and bad—if public spending were higher.

One of our most extensive experiences with the consequences of major reductions in government spending comes from the Proposition 13 movement in California. This movement began with the passage of State Proposition 13 in 1978, which mandated large reductions in property taxes. As Californians have belatedly recognized, this remedy for government waste is like trying to starve a tapeworm by not eating. Fasting does harm the tapeworm, sure enough, but it harms the host even more. Residents of the Golden State, who once proudly sent their children to the nation's best schools, are now sending them to some of its worst.

The physician treats an infected patient by prescribing drugs that are toxic to the parasite but not to the host. A similar strategy should guide our attack on government waste. For example, we might consider the adoption of campaign-finance reform laws that would prevent legislators from accepting campaign contributions from the tobacco industry and other special interests whose government subsidies they support.

The question, then, isn't whether bureaucrats know best how to spend our money. Rather, it's "How much of our money do *we* want to spend on public services?" Although we must remain vigilant against government waste, we also must remember that many public services deliver good value for our money.

RECAP	SOURCES OF INEFFICIENCY IN THE POLITICAL PROCESS

Government does much to help the economy function more efficiently, but it also can be a source of waste. For example, legislators may support pork barrel projects, which do not satisfy the cost-benefit criterion but which benefit constituents by more than their share of the extra taxes required to pay for the projects.

Rent-seeking, a second important source of inefficiency, occurs when individuals or firms use real resources in an effort to win favors from the government. Voters often fail to discipline legislators who abet rent-seeking because the free-rider problem gives rise to rational ignorance on the part of many voters.

Concern about government waste has led many to conclude that the best government is necessarily the smallest one. The solution favored by these critics is to starve government by reducing the amount of money it can collect in taxes. Yet starving the government reduces one kind of waste only to increase another by curtailing public services whose benefit exceeds their cost.

WHAT SHOULD WE TAX?

Although the primary purpose of the tax system is to generate the revenue needed to fund public goods and other government expenditures, taxes also have many other consequences, some intended, others not. For example, taxes alter the relative costs and benefits of engaging in different activities. They also affect the distribution of real purchasing power in the economy. The best tax system is one that raises the needed revenues while at the same time having the most beneficial, or least deleterious, side effects.

On the first criterion, the federal tax system has not performed particularly well. Although the federal budget began to show a modest surplus in the late 1990s, until then it had been in continuous deficit since 1969, during which time the federal government had to borrow trillions of dollars to pay its bills. And now, early in the twenty-first century, the federal budget is again in deficit.

crowding out government borrowing that leads to higher interest rates, causing private firms to cancel planned investment projects

The fact that governments and private corporations borrow money in the same capital market explains the phenomenon economists call **crowding out.** When government increases its demand in the market for borrowed funds, interest rates rise, causing firms to cancel some of their planned investment projects. When the government fails to raise enough revenue from taxes to cover the amount it spends on public goods and services, it thus diverts funds from investments that would have helped the economy to grow.

What about the effect of taxes on incentives? As discussed in Chapter 7, taxes will hold production and consumption below socially optimal levels in markets in which the private costs and benefits coincide exactly with all relevant social costs and benefits. Suppose, for example, that the long-run private marginal cost of producing cars is $20,000 per unit and that the demand curve for cars is as shown in Figure 15.5. The equilibrium quantity and price will be 6 million per year and $20,000, respectively. If no externalities accompany the production or consumption of cars, these will be the socially optimal levels for quantity and price. But if we now add a tax of $2,000 per car, the new equilibrium price and quantity will be $22,000 and 4 million, respectively. The loss in economic surplus will be equal to the area of the blue triangle ($2 billion per year), which is the cumulative sum of the differences between what excluded buyers would have been willing to pay for extra cars and the marginal cost of producing those cars.

Economists who write for the popular press have long focused on the loss in surplus caused by taxes like the one shown in Figure 15.5. These economists argue that the economy would perform better if taxes were lower and total government expenditures were smaller.

But arguments for that claim are far from compelling. As discussed in Chapter 7, for example, even if a tax in a market like the one shown in Figure 15.5 did produce a loss in surplus for participants in that market, it might nonetheless be justified if it led to an even larger gain in surplus from the public expenditures it financed. We also saw in Chapter 7 that the deadweight loss from taxing a good (or activity) will be smaller the smaller is the elasticity of demand or supply for the good. This principle suggests that deadweight losses could be minimized by concentrating taxes on goods with highly inelastic supply or demand curves.

Another difficulty with the argument that taxes harm the economy is more fundamental—namely, that taxes need not cause any loss in surplus at all, even in the markets in which they are directly applied. Suppose, for example, that in the market for cars considered earlier, private marginal cost is again $20,000 but that the production and use of cars now generates air pollution and congestion, negative externalities that sum to $2,000 per car each year. The socially optimal quantity of cars would then be not 6 million per year but only 4 million (see Figure 15.5). Without a tax on cars, the market would reach equilibrium at a price of $20,000 and a quantity of 6 million per year. But with a tax of $2,000 per car, the equilibrium quantity would shrink to 4 million per year, precisely the socially optimal number. Here, the direct effect of the tax is not only to reduce total economic surplus but actually to augment it by $2 billion per day.

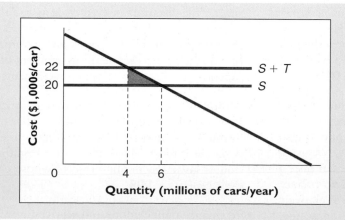

FIGURE 15.5
The Loss in Surplus from a Tax on Cars.
If the supply and demand curves for cars embody all relevant cost benefits of producing and consuming cars, then placing a tax on cars will lead to underproduction of them and a corresponding reduction in economic surplus.

Could we raise enough tax revenue to run the government if we limited ourselves to taxing only those activities that generate negative externalities? No one knows for sure, but it might be possible, for the list of such activities is a long one.

For instance, when someone enters a congested freeway, he creates additional delays for the motorists already there. Existing technology would enable us to levy road-use taxes that reflect these congestion externalities. Each time fossil fuels are burned, they emit greenhouse gases into the atmosphere, which will accelerate the trend toward global warming. A tax on carbon would increase economic surplus by causing decision makers to take this external cost into account. Taxes on other forms of air and water pollution would have similarly benign effects on resource allocation. Recent experience with refundable taxes on food and beverage containers demonstrates that taxes like these can raise needed revenue while at the same time contributing to a cleaner environment.

■ SUMMARY ■

- Our aim in this chapter was to apply principles of microeconomics to the study of the government's role in modern society. One of government's principal tasks is to provide public goods such as national defense and the criminal justice system. Such goods are, in varying degrees, nonrival and nonexcludable. The first property describes goods for which one person's consumption does not diminish the amount available for others, while the second refers to the difficulty of preventing nonpayers from consuming certain goods. **LO1**

- Goods that are both highly nonexcludable and nonrival are often called pure public goods. A collective good—such as pay-per-view cable television—is nonrival but excludable. Commons goods are goods that are rival but nonexcludable. **LO1**

- Because not everyone benefits equally from the provision of any given public good, charging all taxpayers equal amounts for the provision of public goods will generally not be either feasible or desirable. As in the case of private goods, people's willingness to pay for public goods generally increases with income, and most governments therefore levy higher taxes on the rich than on the poor. Tax systems with this property have been criticized on the grounds that they are unfair to the wealthy, but this criticism ignores the fact that alternative tax schemes generally lead to worse outcomes for both rich and poor alike. **LO2**

- The criterion for providing the optimal quantity or quality of a public good is to keep increasing quantity or quality as long as the marginal benefit of doing so exceeds the marginal cost. One advantage of using the government to provide public goods is that once a tax collection agency has been established to finance a single public good, it can be expanded at relatively low cost to generate revenue to finance additional public goods. A second advantage is that because

government has the power to tax, it can easily assign responsibility for the cost of a public good. And in the case of goods for which nonpayers simply cannot be excluded, the government may be the only feasible provider. **LO2**

- One disadvantage to exclusive reliance on government for public goods provision is the element of coercion inherent in the tax system, which makes some people pay for public goods they don't want, while others do without public goods they do want. Many public goods are provided through private channels, with the necessary funding provided by donations, by sale of by-products, by development of new means to exclude nonpayers, and in many cases by private contract. A loss in surplus results, however, whenever monetary charges are levied for the consumption of a nonrival good. **LO3**

- In addition to providing public goods, government serves two other important roles: the regulation of activities that generate externalities and the definition and enforcement of property rights. Despite a general view that government is more responsive the shorter the distance between citizens and their elected representatives, factors such as economies of scale in the provision of public goods and externalities with broad reach often dictate the assignment of important functions to state or national governments. **LO4**

- Although history has shown that democracy is the best form of government, it is far from perfect. For example, practices such as logrolling and rent-seeking, common in most democracies, often result in the adoption of laws and public projects whose costs exceed their benefits. **LO4**

- To finance public goods and services, governments at all levels must tax. But a tax on any activity not only generates revenue, it also creates an incentive to reduce the activity. If the activity would have been pursued at the optimal level in the absence of a tax, taxing it will result in too little of the activity. This observation has led many critics to denounce all taxes as harmful to the economy. Yet the negative effects of taxes on incentives must be weighed against the benefits of the public goods and services financed by tax revenue. Furthermore, taxes on inelastically supplied or demanded activities may generate only small deadweight losses, while taxes on activities that create negative externalities may actually increase economic efficiency.   **LO5**

■ KEY TERMS ■

collective good (399)
crowding out (414)
head tax (401)
logrolling (411)
nonexcludable good (398)

nonrival good (398)
pork barrel spending (411)
progressive tax (402)
proportional income tax (402)
public good (398)

pure commons good (399)
pure private good (399)
pure public good (398)
regressive tax (401)
rent-seeking (412)

■ REVIEW QUESTIONS ■

1. a. Which of the following goods are nonrival?   **LO1**
   Apples
   Stephen King novels
   Street lighting on campus
   NPR radio broadcasts
   b. Which of these goods are nonexcludable?

2. Give examples of goods that are, for the most part: **LO1**
   a. Rival but nonexcludable
   b. Nonrival but excludable
   c. Both nonrival and nonexcludable

3. Why might even a wealthy person prefer a proportional income tax to a head tax?   **LO2**

4. True or false: A tax on an activity that generates negative externalities will improve resource allocation in the private sector and also generate revenue that could be used to pay for useful public goods. Explain.   **LO2, LO5**

5. Consider a good that would be provided efficiently by private market forces. Why is the direct loss in surplus that would result from a tax on this good an overstatement of the loss in surplus caused by the tax?   **LO2, LO5**

■ PROBLEMS ■

1. Jack and Jill are the only two residents in a neighborhood, and they would like to hire a security guard. The value of a security guard is $50 per month to Jack and $150 per month to Jill. Irrespective of who pays the guard, the guard will protect the entire neighborhood.   **LO2, LO5**
   a. What is the most a guard can charge per month and still be assured of being hired by at least one of them?
   b. Suppose the competitive wage for a security guard is $120 per month. The local government proposes a plan whereby Jack and Jill each pays 50 percent of this monthly fee, and asks them to vote on this plan. Will the plan be voted in? Would economic surplus be higher if the neighborhood had a guard?

2. Refer to problem 1. Suppose Jack earns $1,000 per month and Jill earns $11,000 per month.   **LO2, LO5**
   a. Suggest a proportional tax on income that would be accepted by majority vote and would pay for the security guard.
   b. Suppose instead that Jack proposes a tax scheme under which Jack and Jill would each receive the same net benefit from hiring the guard. How much would Jack and Jill pay now? Would Jill agree to this scheme?
   c. What is the practical problem that prevents ideas like the one in part b from working in real-life situations?

3. The following table shows all the marginal benefits for each voter in a small town whose town council is considering a new swimming pool with capacity for at least three citizens. The cost of the pool would be $18 per week and would not depend on the number of people who actually used it. **LO2, LO5**

Voter	Marginal benefit ($/week)
A	12
B	5
C	2

    a. If the pool must be financed by a weekly head tax levied on all voters, will the pool be approved by majority vote? Is this outcome socially efficient? Explain.

    b. The town council instead decides to auction a franchise off to a private monopoly to build and maintain the pool. If it cannot find such a firm willing to operate the pool, then the pool project will be scrapped. If all such monopolies are constrained by law to charge a single price to users, will the franchise be sold, and if so, how much will it sell for? Is this outcome socially efficient? Explain.

4. Refer to problem 3. Suppose now that all such monopolies can perfectly price-discriminate. **LO2, LO5**

    a. Will the franchise be sold, and if so, how much will it sell for? Is this outcome socially efficient? Explain.

    b. The town council decides that, rather than auction off the franchise, it will give it away to the firm that spends the most money lobbying council members. If there are four identical firms in the bidding and they cannot collude, what will happen?

5. Two consumers, Smith and Jones, have the following demand curves for Podunk Public Radio broadcasts of recorded opera on Saturdays:

$$\text{Smith:} \qquad P_S = 12 - Q$$

$$\text{Jones:} \qquad P_J = 12 - 2Q,$$

where P_S and P_J represent marginal willingness-to-pay values for Smith and Jones, respectively, and Q represents the number of hours of opera broadcast each Saturday. **LO2**

    a. If Smith and Jones are the only public radio listeners in Podunk, construct the demand curve for opera broadcasts.

    b. If the marginal cost of opera broadcasts is $15 per hour, what is the socially optimal number of hours of broadcast opera?

6. Suppose the demand curves for hour-long episodes of the *Jerry Springer Show* and *Masterpiece Theater* are as shown in the following diagram. A television network is considering whether to add one or both programs to its upcoming fall lineup. The only two time slots remaining are sponsored by Colgate, which is under contract to pay the network 10 cents for each viewer who watches the program, out of which the network would have to cover its production costs of $400,000 per episode. (Viewership can be estimated accurately with telephone surveys.) Any time slot the network does not fill with *Springer* or *Masterpiece Theater* will be filled by infomercials for a weight-loss program, for which the network incurs no production costs and for which it receives a fee of $500,000. Viewers will receive $5 million in economic surplus from watching each installment of the infomercial. **LO2**

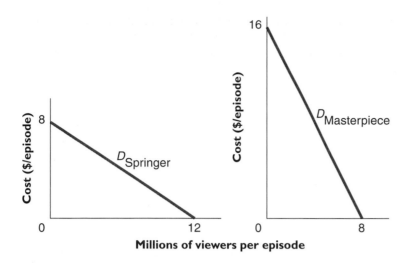

a. How will the network fill the two remaining slots in its fall lineup?

b. Is this outcome socially efficient?

7. Refer to problem 6. By how much would total economic surplus be higher if each episode of *Masterpiece Theater* were shown on PBS free of charge than if it were shown by a profit-maximizing pay-per-view network?   **LO2**

8. When a TV company chooses a pay-per-view scheme to pay for programming, which of the following statements is true? Explain.   **LO2, LO3**

a. The outcome is socially efficient.

b. The programs selected will maximize advertising revenue.

c. The marginal cost to an additional viewer of watching the programs is lower than when advertising is used to finance programming.

d. The outcome is always more socially efficient than when advertising is used to finance programming.

e. The variety of programs provided is likely to rise.

9. When a group of people must decide whether to buy a shared public good or service, the free-rider problem frequently occurs because   **LO4**

a. People have an incentive to understate how much the facility is really worth to them if they have to pay taxes to finance it.

b. Each individual's needed contribution is an insignificant amount of the total required.

c. People have an incentive to overstate how much the facility is worth to them if they don't have to pay taxes to finance it.

d. People hope that others will value the facility enough to pay for it entirely.

e. Only one of the above statements is not a reason for the existence of the free-ride problem.

10. The town of Smallsville is considering building a museum. The interest on the money Smallsville will have to borrow to build the museum will be $1,000 per year. Each citizen's marginal benefit from the museum is shown in the following table, and this marginal benefit schedule is public information.   **LO2, LO4**

a. Assuming each citizen voted his or her private interests, would a referendum to build the museum and raise each citizen's annual taxes by $200 pass?

b. A citizen proposes that the city let a private company build the museum and charge the citizens a lump-sum fee each year to view it as much as they like. Only citizens who paid the fee would be allowed to view the museum. If the private company were allowed to set a single fee, would any company offer to build the museum?

c. A second citizen proposes allowing the private company to charge different prices to different citizens and auctioning the right to build the museum to the highest bidding company. Again, only the citizens who pay the fee may view the museum. What is the highest bid a private company would make to supply the museum to Smallsville?

Citizen	Marginal benefit from museum ($/year)
Anita	340
Brandon	290
Carlena	240
Dallas	190
Eloise	140

■ ANSWERS TO IN-CHAPTER EXERCISES ■

15.1 a. The BLS Web site at 3 in the morning has the capacity to serve far more users than it attracts, so an additional user calling up the site does not prevent some other user from doing so. Other Web sites, however, do not show the nonrival property, at least during certain hours, because they attract more users than their servers can accommodate. **LO1**

b. The stadium at the championship game is always full, so anyone who watches the game in person prevents someone else from doing so.

c. Additional people can watch the game on television without diminishing the availability of the telecast for others.

15.2 To construct the demand curve (a), we first graph Bill's demand curve (c) and Tom's demand curve (b) and then add the two individual demand curves vertically. The equation for the demand curve is $P = 18 - 1.5Q$. **LO2**

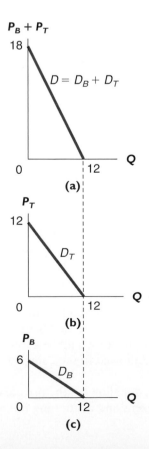

15.3 Whereas elasticity of demand was 1 at a price of $10 on the original demand curve, it is 2 on the new demand curve. As a result, the $10 fee now excludes 20 million viewers, and the resulting loss in surplus (again the area of the blue triangle) is now $100 million. **LO2, LO4**

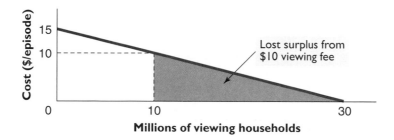

15.4 If Sven orders bread pudding, his share of the bill would now go up by $2 instead of $1. If he orders chocolate mousse, his share of the bill would go up by $1.20 instead of $0.60. So he would still order the bread pudding (surplus = $4 − $2 = $2) rather than the chocolate mousse (surplus = $3 − $1.20 − $1.80). **LO4**

GLOSSARY

A

Absolute advantage. One person has an absolute advantage over another if he or she takes fewer hours to perform a task than the other person.

Accounting profit. The difference between a firm's total revenue and its explicit costs.

Adverse selection. The pattern in which insurance tends to be purchased disproportionately by those who are most costly for companies to insure.

Allocative function of price. Changes in prices direct resources away from overcrowded markets and toward markets that are underserved.

Asymmetric information. Situations in which buyers and sellers are not equally well informed about the characteristics of goods and services for sale in the marketplace.

Attainable point. Any combination of goods that can be produced using currently available resources.

Average benefit. Total benefit of undertaking n units of an activity divided by n.

Average cost. Total cost of undertaking n units of an activity divided by n.

Average total cost (*ATC*). Total cost divided by total output.

Average variable cost (*AVC*). Variable cost divided by total output.

B

Barrier to entry. Any force that prevents firms from entering a new market.

Basic elements of a game. The players, the strategies available to each player, and the payoffs each player receives for each possible combination of strategies.

Better-than-fair gamble. A gamble whose expected value is positive.

Buyer's reservation price. The largest dollar amount the buyer would be willing to pay for a good.

Buyer's surplus. The difference between the buyer's reservation price and the price he or she actually pays.

C

Cartel. A coalition of firms that agree to restrict output for the purpose of earning an economic profit.

Cash on the table. Economic metaphor for unexploited gain from exchange.

Change in demand. A shift of the entire demand curve.

Change in supply. A shift of the entire supply curve.

Change in the quantity demanded. A movement along the demand curve that occurs in response to a change in price.

Change in the quantity supplied. A movement along the supply curve that occurs in response to a change in price.

Coase theorem. If at no cost people can negotiate the purchase and sale of the right to perform activities that cause externalities, they can always arrive at efficient solutions to the problems caused by externalities.

Collective good. A good or service that, to at least some degree, is nonrival but excludable.

Commitment device. A way of changing incentives so as to make otherwise empty threats or promises credible.

Commitment problem. A situation in which people cannot achieve their goals because of an inability to make credible threats or promises.

Comparative advantage. One person has a comparative advantage over another if his or her opportunity cost of performing a task is lower than the other person's opportunity cost.

Compensating wage differential. A difference in the wage rate—negative or positive—that reflects the attractiveness of a job's working conditions.

Complements. Two goods are complements in consumption if an increase in the price of one causes a leftward shift in the demand curve for the other (or if a decrease causes a rightward shift).

Constant (or parameter). A quantity that is fixed in value.

Constant returns to scale. A production process is said to have constant returns to scale if, when all inputs are changed by a given proportion, output changes by the same proportion.

Consumer surplus. The economic surplus gained by the buyers of a product as measured by the cumulative difference between their respective reservation prices and the price they actually paid.

Cost-plus regulation. A method of regulation under which the regulated firm is permitted to charge a price equal to its explicit costs of production plus a markup to cover the opportunity cost of resources provided by the firm's owners.

Costly-to-fake principle. To communicate information credibly to a potential rival, a signal must be costly or difficult to fake.

Credible promise. A promise to take an action that is in the promiser's interest to keep.

Credible threat. A threat to take an action that is in the threatener's interest to carry out.

Cross-price elasticity of demand. The percentage by which the quantity demanded of the first good changes in response to a 1 percent change in the price of the second.

Crowding out. Government borrowing that leads private firms to cancel planned investment projects because of higher interest rates.

Customer discrimination. The willingness of consumers to pay more for a product produced by members of a favored group, even if the quality of the product is unaffected.

D

Deadweight loss. The deadweight loss caused by a policy is the reduction in economic surplus that results from adoption of that policy.

Decision tree (or game tree). A diagram that describes the possible moves in a game in sequence and lists the payoffs that correspond to each possible combination of moves.

Demand curve. A schedule or graph showing the quantity of a good that buyers wish to buy at each price.

Dependent variable. A variable in an equation whose value is determined by the value taken by another variable in the equation.

Disappearing political discourse. The theory that people who support a position may remain silent because speaking out would create a risk of being misunderstood.

Dominant strategy. One that yields a higher payoff no matter what the other players in a game choose.

Dominated strategy. Any other strategy available to a player who has a dominant strategy.

E

Earned-income tax credit (EITC). A policy under which low-income workers receive credits on their federal income tax.

Economic efficiency. *See* **Efficiency.**

Economic loss. An economic profit that is less than zero.

Economic profit. The difference between a firm's total revenue and the sum of its explicit and implicit costs; also called *excess profit.*

Economic rent. That part of the payment for a factor of production that exceeds the owner's reservation price, the price below which the owner would not supply the factor.

Economic surplus. The economic surplus from taking any action is the benefit of taking the action minus its cost.

Economics. The study of how people make choices under conditions of scarcity and of the results of those choices for society.

Efficiency (or economic efficiency). Condition that occurs when all goods and services are produced and consumed at their respective socially optimal levels.

Efficient (or Pareto-efficient). A situation is efficient if no change is possible that will help some people without harming others.

Efficient markets hypothesis. The theory that the current price of stock in a corporation reflects all relevant information about its current and future earnings prospects.

Efficient point. Any combination of goods for which currently available resources do not allow an increase in the production of one good without a reduction in the production of the other.

Elastic. The demand for a good is elastic with respect to price if its price elasticity of demand is greater than 1.

Employer discrimination. An arbitrary preference by an employer for one group of workers over another.

Equation. A mathematical expression that describes the relationship between two or more variables.

Equilibrium. A balanced or unchanging situation in which all forces at work within a system are canceled by others.

Equilibrium price and equilibrium quantity. The price and quantity of a good at the intersection of the supply and demand curves for the good.

Excess demand (or shortage). The difference between the quantity supplied and the quantity demanded when the price of a good lies below the equilibrium price; buyers are dissatisfied when there is excess demand.

Excess supply (or surplus). The difference between the quantity supplied and the quantity demanded when the price of a good exceeds the equilibrium price; sellers are dissatisfied when there is excess supply.

Expected value of a gamble. The sum of the possible outcomes of the gamble multiplied by their respective probabilities.

Explicit costs. The actual payments a firm makes to its factors of production and other suppliers.

External benefit (or positive externality). A benefit of an activity received by people other than those who pursue the activity.

External cost (or negative externality). A cost of an activity that falls on people other than those who pursue the activity.

Externality. An external cost or benefit of an activity.

F

Factor of production. An input used in the production of a good or service.

Fair gamble. A gamble whose expected value is zero.

First-dollar insurance coverage. Insurance that pays all expenses generated by the insured activity.

Fixed cost. A cost that does not vary with the level of an activity; the sum of all payments made to the firm's fixed factors of production.

Fixed factor of production. An input whose quantity cannot be altered in the short run.

Free-rider problem. An incentive problem in which too little of a good or service is produced because nonpayers cannot be excluded from using it.

G

Game tree. *See* **Decision tree.**

H

Head tax. A tax that collects the same amount from every taxpayer.

Health maintenance organization (HMO). A group of physicians that provides health services to individuals and families for a fixed annual fee.

Human capital. An amalgam of factors such as education, training, experience, intelligence, energy, work habits, trustworthiness, initiative, and others that affect the value of a worker's marginal product.

Human capital theory. A theory of pay determination that says a worker's wage will be proportional to his or her stock of human capital.

Hurdle method of price discrimination. The practice by which a seller offers a discount to all buyers who overcome some obstacle.

I

Imperfectly competitive firm. A firm that has at least some control over the market price of its product.

Implicit costs. The opportunity costs of the resources supplied by the firm's owners.

Income effect. The change in the quantity demanded of a good that results because a change in the price of a good changes the buyer's purchasing power.

Income elasticity of demand. The percentage by which a good's quantity demanded changes in response to a 1 percent change in income.

Increasing returns to scale. A production process is said to have increasing returns to scale if, when all inputs are changed by a given proportion, output changes by more than that proportion; also called *economies of scale.*

Independent variable. A variable in an equation whose value determines the value taken by another variable in the equation.

Inefficient point. Any combination of goods for which currently available resources enable an increase in the production of one good without a reduction in the production of the other.

Inelastic. The demand for a good is inelastic with respect to price if its price elasticity of demand is less than 1.

Inferior good. A good whose demand curve shifts leftward when the incomes of buyers increase.

In-kind transfer. A payment made not in the form of cash but in the form of a good or service.

Invisible hand theory. Adam Smith's theory stating that the actions of independent, self-interested buyers and sellers will often result in the most efficient allocation of resources.

L

Labor union. A group of workers who bargain collectively with employers for better wages and working conditions.

Law of demand. People do less of what they want to do as the cost of doing it rises.

Law of diminishing marginal utility. The tendency for the additional utility gained from consuming an additional unit of a good to diminish as consumption increases beyond some point.

Law of diminishing returns. A property of the relationship between the amount of a good or service produced and the amount of a variable factor required to produce it; the law says that when some factors of production are fixed, increased production of the good eventually requires ever larger increases in the variable factor.

Lemons model. George Akerlof's explanation of how asymmetric information tends to reduce the average quality of goods offered for sale.

Logrolling. The practice whereby legislators support one another's legislative proposals.

Long run. A period of time of sufficient length that all the firm's factors of production are variable.

M

Macroeconomics. The study of the performance of national economies and the policies that governments use to try to improve that performance.

Marginal benefit. The marginal benefit of an activity is the increase in total benefit that results from carrying out one additional unit of the activity.

Marginal cost. The marginal cost of an activity is the increase in total cost that results from carrying out one additional unit of the activity; as output changes from one level to another, the change in total cost divided by the corresponding change in output.

Marginal product of labor (MP). The additional output a firm gets by employing one additional unit of labor.

Marginal revenue. The change in a firm's total revenue that results from a one-unit change in output.

Marginal utility. The additional utility gained from consuming an additional unit of a good.

Market. The market for any good consists of all buyers or sellers of that good.

Market equilibrium. Occurs when all buyers and sellers are satisfied with their respective quantities at the market price.

Market power. A firm's ability to raise the price of a good without losing all its sales.

Means-tested. A benefit program is means-tested if its benefit level declines as the recipient earns additional income.

Microeconomics. The study of individual choice under scarcity and its implications for the behavior of prices and quantities in individual markets.

Monopolistic competition. Industry structure in which a large number of firms produce slightly differentiated products that are reasonably close substitutes for one another.

Moral hazard. The tendency of people to expend less effort protecting those goods that are insured against theft or damage.

N

Nash equilibrium. Any combination of strategy choices in which each player's choice is his or her best choice, given the other players' choices.

Natural monopoly. A monopoly that results from economies of scale (increasing returns to scale).

Negative externality. *See* **External cost.**

Negative income tax (NIT). A system under which the government would grant every citizen a cash payment each year, financed by an additional tax on earned income.

Nominal price. Absolute price of a good in dollar terms.

Nonexcludable good. A good that is difficult, or costly, to exclude nonpayers from consuming.

Nonrival good. A good whose consumption by one person does not diminish its availability for others.

Normal good. A good whose demand curve shifts rightward when the incomes of buyers increase.

Normal profit. The opportunity cost of the resources supplied by the firm's owners; Normal profit = Accounting profit − Economic profit.

Normative economic principle. One that says how people should behave.

O

Oligopoly. An industry structure in which a small number of large firms produce products that are either close or perfect substitutes.

Opportunity cost. The opportunity cost of an activity is the value of what must be forgone to undertake the activity.

Optimal combination of goods. The affordable combination that yields the highest total utility.

Outsourcing. A term increasingly used to connote having services performed by low-wage workers overseas.

P

Parameter. *See* **Constant.**

Pareto-efficient. *See* **Efficient.**

Payoff matrix. A table that describes the payoffs in a game for each possible combination of strategies.

Perfect hurdle. One that completely segregates buyers whose reservation prices lie above some threshold from others whose reservation prices lie below it, imposing no cost on those who jump the hurdle.

Perfectly competitive market. A market in which no individual supplier has significant influence on the market price of the product.

Perfectly discriminating monopolist. A firm that charges each buyer exactly his or her reservation price.

Perfectly elastic demand. The demand for a good is perfectly elastic with respect to price if its price elasticity of demand is infinite.

Perfectly elastic supply curve. A supply curve whose elasticity with respect to price is infinite.

Perfectly inelastic demand. The demand for a good is perfectly inelastic with respect to price if its price elasticity of demand is zero.

Perfectly inelastic supply curve. A supply curve whose elasticity with respect to price is zero.

Personal Responsibility Act. The 1996 federal law that transferred responsibility for welfare programs from the federal level to the state level and placed a five-year lifetime limit on payment of AFDC benefits to any given recipient.

Pork barrel spending. A public expenditure that is larger than the total benefit it creates but that is favored by a legislator because his or her constituents benefit from the expenditure by more than their share of the resulting extra taxes.

Positional arms control agreement. An agreement in which contestants attempt to limit mutually offsetting investments in performance enhancement.

Positional arms race. A series of mutually offsetting investments in performance enhancement that is stimulated by a positional externality.

Positional externality. Occurs when an increase in one person's performance reduces the expected reward of another in situations in which reward depends on relative performance.

Positive economic principle. One that predicts how people will behave.

Positive externality. *See* **External benefit.**

Poverty threshold. The level of income below which the federal government classifies a family as poor.

Present value of a perpetual annual payment. For an annual interest rate r, the present value (PV) of a perpetual annual payment (M) is the amount that would have to be deposited today at that interest rate to generate annual interest earnings of M: $PV = M/r$.

Price ceiling. A maximum allowable price, specified by law.

Price discrimination. The practice of charging different buyers different prices for essentially the same good or service.

Price elasticity of demand. The percentage change in the quantity demanded of a good or service that results from a 1 percent change in its price.

Price elasticity of supply. The percentage change in the quantity supplied that will occur in response to a 1 percent change in the price of a good or service.

Price setter. A firm with at least some latitude to set its own price.

Price taker. A firm that has no influence over the price at which it sells its product.

Prisoner's dilemma. A game in which each player has a dominant strategy, and when each plays it, the resulting payoffs are smaller than if each had played a dominated strategy.

Producer surplus. The economic surplus gained by the sellers of a product as measured by the cumulative difference between the price received and their respective reservation prices.

Production possibilities curve. A graph that describes the maximum amount of one good that can be produced for every possible level of production of the other good.

Profit. The total revenue a firm receives from the sale of its product minus all costs—explicit and implicit—incurred in producing it.

Profit-maximizing firm. A firm whose primary goal is to maximize the difference between its total revenues and total costs.

Profitable firm. A firm whose total revenue exceeds its total cost.

Progressive tax. One in which the proportion of income paid in taxes rises as income rises.

Proportional income tax. One under which all taxpayers pay the same proportion of their incomes in taxes.

Public good. A good or service that, to at least some degree, is both nonrival and nonexcludable.

Pure commons good. One for which nonpayers cannot easily be excluded and for which each unit consumed by one person means one less unit available for others.

Pure monopoly. The only supplier of a unique product with no close substitutes.

Pure private good. One for which nonpayers can easily be excluded and for which each unit consumed by one person means one less unit available for others.

Pure public good. A good or service that, to a high degree, is both nonrival and nonexcludable.

R

Rational person. Someone with well-defined goals who tries to fulfill those goals as best he or she can.

Rational spending rule. Spending should be allocated across goods so that the marginal utility per dollar is the same for each good.

Rationing function of price. Changes in prices distribute scarce goods to those consumers who value them most highly.

Real price. Dollar price of a good relative to the average dollar price of all other goods and services.

Regressive tax. A tax under which the proportion of income paid in taxes declines as income rises.

Rent-seeking. The socially unproductive efforts of people or firms to win a prize.

Repeated prisoner's dilemma. A standard prisoner's dilemma that confronts the same players repeatedly.

Rise. *See* **Slope.**

Risk-averse person. Someone who would refuse any fair gamble.

Risk-neutral person. Someone who would accept any gamble that is fair or better.

Run. *See* **Slope.**

S

Seller's reservation price. The smallest dollar amount for which a seller would be willing to sell an additional unit, generally equal to marginal cost.

Seller's surplus. The difference between the price received by the seller and his or her reservation price.

Short run. A period of time sufficiently short that at least some of the firm's factors of production are fixed.

Shortage. *See* **Excess demand.**

Slope. In a straight line, the ratio of the vertical distance the straight line travels between any two points (*rise*) to the corresponding horizontal distance (*run*).

Socially optimal quantity. The quantity of a good that results in the maximum possible economic surplus from producing and consuming the good.

Statistical discrimination. The practice of making judgments about the quality of people, goods, or services based on the characteristics of the groups to which they belong.

Substitutes. Two goods are substitutes in consumption if an increase in the price of one causes a rightward shift in the demand curve for the other (or if a decrease causes a leftward shift).

Substitution effect. The change in the quantity demanded of a good that results because buyers switch to or from substitutes when the price of the good changes.

Sunk cost. A cost that is beyond recovery at the moment a decision must be made.

Supply curve. A graph or schedule showing the quantity of a good that sellers wish to sell at each price.

Surplus. *See* **Excess supply.**

T

Time value of money. The fact that a given dollar amount today is equivalent to a larger dollar amount in the future because the money can be invested in an interest-bearing account in the meantime.

Tit-for-tat. A strategy for the repeated prisoner's dilemma in which players cooperate on the first move, then mimic their partner's last move on each successive move.

Total cost. The sum of all payments made to the firm's fixed and variable factors of production.

Total expenditure = Total revenue. The dollar amount consumers spend on a product is equal to the dollar amount sellers receive.

Total revenue. *See* **Total expenditure.**

Total surplus. The difference between the buyer's reservation price and the seller's reservation price.

Tragedy of the commons. The tendency for a resource that has no price to be used until its marginal benefit falls to zero.

U

Unattainable point. Any combination of goods that cannot be produced using currently available resources.

Unit elastic. The demand for a good is unit elastic with respect to price if its price elasticity of demand is equal to 1.

V

Value of marginal product of labor (VMP). The dollar value of the additional output a firm gets by employing one additional unit of labor.

Variable. A quantity that is free to take a range of different values.

Variable cost. A cost that varies with the level of an activity; the sum of all payments made to the firm's variable factors of production.

Variable factor of production. An input whose quantity can be altered in the short run.

Vertical intercept. In a straight line, the value taken by the dependent variable when the independent variable equals zero.

W

Winner-take-all labor market. One in which small differences in human capital translate into large differences in pay.

Workers' compensation. A government insurance system that provides benefits to workers who are injured on the job.

INDEX

Page numbers followed by n indicate material found in notes.

A

Absolute advantage, 36
Absolute dollar amount, 9
Abstract models, 7–8
Accountants, definition of profit, 204
Accounting profit
    of best-managed companies, 223
    definition, 204
    versus economic profit, 204–207
Adams, Walter, 101
Ad–copy writers, 357–358
Adverse selection, 340
Advertisers, inefficiency avoided
    by, 407
Advertising
    by airlines, 270–273
    of cigarettes regulated, 278–279
    and norms of taste, 317–318
    Super Bowl ads, 337
Aerobics instructors, 212–214
Aid to Families with Dependent Children
    (AFDC), 364
Airline fares, 84
Airline industry
    and Aviation Consumer Action
        Project, 187
    compensation policy, 185–187
    first-come, first-served policy, 185–187
    in invisible hand theory, 219
    price discrimination by, 256
Air quality regulations, 306
Akerlof, George, 334
Algebra, 30–31
    of marginal revenue curve, 244–245
    of profit maximization, 267–268
    of supply and demand, 93–94
Allocative function of prices, 207–208
    and free entry or exit, 214
Amazon.com, 330
American Airlines, 270–273
American Cancer Society, 357–358
Anabolic steroids, 315
Analyze This, 269, 282
Antipoverty programs, invisible hand
    in, 220
Antitrust laws, 248
    vigorous enforcement of, 259–260
Apple Macintosh, 78, 238
Arbitration agreements, 316
Aristotle, 64
Asymmetric information
    and adverse selection, 340
    conspicuous consumption as signal of ability,
        337–338
    costly-to-fake principle, 336–337
    credibility problem in trading, 336
    definition, 333
    example, 333–334
    lemons model, 334–336
    and moral hazard, 340–341
    statistical discrimination, 338–340
ATMs, 18–19
AT&T, 235, 258
Attainable point, 43–44
Auction process, 412–413
Automobile accessories, 18
Automobile engine size, 140
Automobile industry, time factor in production,
    280–282
Automobile insurance costs, 339
Automobiles
    gas prices and size of, 138–139
    prices of, 116–117
Average benefit, 12–14
    irrelevance of, 14–15
Average cost, 12–14
    irrelevance of, 14–15
Average total cost, 159
    of bottle production, 160
    and economic profit/loss, 208–211
    with economies of scale, 239–240
    of natural monopoly, 257
    and negative profit, 162–163
    video game producers, 240–241
Average total cost curve, 160–161
Average variable cost, 159
    of bottle production, 160
Average variable cost curve, 160
Aviation Consumer Action project, 187
Avocado market
    with taxes, 192–194
    without taxes, 192
Axelrod, Robert, 277

B

Babcock, L., 353n
Banifoot, Kösten, 12–13
Barnes and Noble, 329
Barriers to entry, 214
Barriers to exit, 214
Basic elements of games, 270–272
Basketball team roster limits, 316
Baskin-Robbins, 140
Bazerman, Max, 412
Beautiful Mind, A, 272n
Benefits, relevant, 299
Bennett, Danny, 269
Bennett, Tony, 269–270, 280, 282
Bentham, Jeremy, 128–129
Better-than-fair gamble, 332

Bidding
  by cellular phone companies, 413
  for exclusive contracts, 258–259
BMW, 18, 140, 338
Boating industry job losses, 102
Boeing 747s, 219
Border patrols, 98
Borders, 329
Braille ATMs, 18–19
Bread market subsidies, 183–185
Break-even calling volume, 30
Browne, Harry, 398
Budget deficit, 414
Budget share, 100
Buffett, Warren, 224–225, 337
Burlington, Vermont, 166
Business negotiations, 269–270
Buyers, 64–67
  asymmetric information, 333–341
  cost-benefit principle, 150
  and credibility problem, 336
  fully informed, 325–326
  obstacles to charging highest price, 252–253
  in perfectly competitive markets, 154
  taxes paid by, 190–192
Buyer's reservation price, 66, 79, 85
Buyer's surplus, 85

C

Cable television companies, 257
Cadillac, 256
California
  electricity market, 117
  gasoline prices, 116–117
  Proposition 13, 414
  water shortages, 127–128
Camel cigarettes, 235, 357–358
Camerer, C., 353n
Cameron, James, 127
Capital equipment investments, 205
Capital investment per worker, 50
Capitalism, 64
Capital punishment, 341–342
Carbon tax, 416
Carnegie, Andrew, 259
Carpenters' wage rates, 80
Carrey, Jim, 118
Cartels, 259
  compared to unions, 355–356
  definition, 275
  economics of, 275–277
  Organization of Petroleum Exporting
    Countries, 277
  temptation to violate agreements, 276
  tit-for-tat strategy, 278
  unstable agreements, 275–277
Carter administration, 375
Cash-on-the-table metaphor, 85–86
Cellular phone companies, 413
Centralized government, dangers of, 409
Central planning, 63–64
CEOs, compensation of, 362
Chamberlin, Edward, 235n
Change in demand, 75
Change in quantity demanded, 75
Change in quantity supplied, 75, 164

Change in supply, 75, 164
Chaplin, Charlie, 52
Character judgments, 289
Charitable contributions, 405–406
Check-splitting, 410–411
Chevrolet, 235, 256, 280–282
Chicago meat-packing factories, 385–386
China, 63
  United States diplomatic relations, 343
Chrysler Corporation, 275
Cigarette advertising, 278–279
Cigarette tax, effect on teenage smoking, 102
Civil Aeronautics Board, 219
Clayton Antitrust Act, 259
Clinton, Bill, 53, 398
Coase, Ronald, 302
Coase theorem, 301–306
Coca-Cola Company, 285
Cold War, 343
Collective bargaining, 356
Collective goods, 399
Commitment device, 285
Commitment problem, 285–287
  with costly information search, 332–333
  preferences as solution to, 288–289
Communication, complex, 55
Communist economies, 63
Comparative advantage, 35–56
  versus absolute advantage, 36
  definition, 36
  exchange and opportunity cost, 36–41
  gains from, 39
  gains from specialization and exchange, 46–47
  and international trade
    free-trade agreements, 53
    and outsourcing, 53–55
  principle of, 1–2, 37–40
  production possibilities, 41–46
  production possibilities curve
    factors that shift, 49–51
    many-person economy, 47–49
  and slow specialization, 51–52
  sources
    individual, 40
    national, 40
    noneconomic, 40–41
  and too much specialization, 52–53
Compensating wage differentials, 357–358
Competition
  effect on economic profit, 215
  Internet vs. retail stores, 326
  promoting statistical discrimination, 339–340
  union vs. nonunion workers, 357
Complements, 75–76
Complex communication, 55
Computer models, 7–8
Conspicuous consumption, 337–338
Constant, 24
Constant returns to scale, 238
Consumer Reports, 326
Consumers
  asymmetric information, 333–341
  changes in behavior, 375–376
  information gathering, 326
  information search by
    commitment problem, 332–333
    cost-benefit test, 328–329

free-rider problem, 329–330
  gamble inherent in, 331–332
  guidelines for, 330–331
  reliance on middlemen, 326–328
Consumer surplus
  calculating, 142–145
  compared to producer surplus, 168
  definition, 142
  effect of price ceilings on, 181
  effect of price subsidies, 183–184
  enhanced by hurdle method, 255
  total, 144
  at zero for perfectly discriminating
    monopolist, 252
Consumption
  effect of taxation on, 415
  at subsistence level, 127
Convenience store locations, 284
Cook, Philip J., 341n
Copernicus, N., 64
Copyright law, 214
Copyrights, 234
  source of market power, 237
Corporate earnings forecasters, 225
Cosmetic surgery, 318–319
Cost(s)
  and demand curve, 126
  explicit, 204
  implicit, 204
  influencing decisions, 11
  of medical procedures, 376–378
  of providing public goods, 399–400
  relevant, 299
  of taxi medallions, 218
Cost advantage
  of oligopoly, 235–236
  video game producers, 240–241
Cost-benefit analysis, 4–5
Cost-benefit principle
  applied to health care delivery, 376–378
  applying, 6–8
  for buyers and sellers, 150
  and conspicuous consumption, 337–338
  for consumer surplus, 142
  on crime prevention, 391–392
  for decision making, 8
  decision pitfalls, 8–15
    failure to think at the margin, 11–15
    ignoring implicit costs, 9–10
    proportions vs. absolute dollar amounts, 9
    summary of, 14
  definition, 1
  and economic surplus, 6–7
  effect on demand curve, 78
  on expansion of firms, 161–162
  guidelines for information search, 330–331
  for hospital stay, 373–379
  for hurdle method, 253
  and incentive principle, 15
  on information search, 328–329
  and law of demand, 126
  for level of output, 157–158
  and marginal utility, 131
  for natural monopoly, 260
  nature of, 4–5
  as normative economics, 15
  and opportunity cost, 7

output of monopolist, 245
  and price elasticity of demand, 100
  rationality assumption, 6
  and rational spending rule, 135
  for recycling, 151
  role of economic models, 7–8
  safety seats for infants, 390
  in shared living arrangements, 303–305
  and socially optimal quantity, 86
  and taxation, 193
  workplace safety, 386–389
Cost curves, 160–161
Costly-to-fake principle, 336–337
Cost-plus regulation, 258
Cost-saving innovations, 217
  with cost-plus regulation, 258
Costs of production
  average total cost, 159
  average variable cost, 159
  effect on supply curve, 78–80
  fixed costs, 156–157
  input prices, 164
  marginal cost, 156–157
  pollution costs, 86–87
  start-up costs, 239–242
  technology, 164
  total cost, 156–157
  variable costs, 156–157
Credibility problem in trading, 336
Credible promises, 282
Credible threats, 282
Crime prevention, 391–392
Cross-price elasticity of demand, 111–112
Crowding out, 414–415
Crystal, Billy, 269
Cuba, 63
Customer discrimination, 359

D
Davidson, Richard, 128–129
Deadweight loss
  of monopoly, 248
  of negative externalities, 299
  from taxation, 193
    and elasticity of demand, 194–195
    and elasticity of supply, 194–195
Death penalty opponents, 341–342
Decision making
  with cost-benefit principle, 8
  costs that influence, 11
Decision tree
  for automobile industry, 281
  definition, 281
  for remote-office game, 282–283
Deductibles, health insurance, 379
Demand; see also Cross-price elasticity of
    demand; Income elasticity of demand;
    Price elasticity of demand
  elastic, 99
  inelastic, 99
  for mineral water, 276
  for needs vs. wants, 127–128
  shifts in, 75–78
  translating wants into
    allocating fixed income, 132–135
    income effect, 135–137

Demand—*Cont.*
    rational spending rule, 135
    substitution effect, 135–137
    utility concept, 127–131
  unit elastic, 99
Demand consumer surplus, 142–145
Demand curve, 65–66
  effect of externalities on, 299–300
  effect of technology changes, 80–81
  to find equilibrium, 68
  horizontal addition, 141
  horizontal interpretation, 66, 145
  for illicit drugs, 97–98
  income effect, 65
  individual, 140–142
  market, 140–142
  with market power, 237
  midpoint formula, 124
  for milk, 176–177
  for monopolist, 243–246
  movement along, 75
  and operation of invisible hand, 212–214
  for perfectly competitive firms, 154–155
  perfectly elastic, 106
  perfectly inelastic, 106–107
  perfect vs. imperfect competition, 236
  for pizza market, 70–71
  and price elasticity of demand, 104–106
  for private goods, 403
  for public goods, 403–405
  quantity demanded and all costs, 126
  for rental housing, 71
  and reservation price, 66
  shift factors
    expectations, 78
    income, 77–78
    preferences and tastes, 78
    price of complements, 75–76
    price of substitutes, 76–77
    rules governing, 81–84
    with supply curve shift, 83–84
  for skate boards, 79
  straight-line, 105–106
  substitution effect, 65
  and total expenditure, 107–111
  for urban parkland, 404–405
  vertical interpretation, 66, 145
  and wage rates, 80
Demand curve for labor, 350, 352–353
Demand-side of markets, 150
DeNiro, Robert, 269
Department of Agriculture Household Food
    Consumption Survey, 365
Dependent variables, 24
Diagnostic tests, 376
Diminishing marginal utility, 131
  and fixed-income allocation, 132–135
  of urban parkland, 405
Diminishing returns, 156
Disappearing public discourse
  death penalty opponents, 341–342
  definition, 342
  legalized drug proponents, 342–343
Discount pricing, 259
Discounts; *see* Price discrimination
Discrimination in labor market
  by customers, 359

  by employers, 358
  from family ambition, 359
Dodge Neon, 338
Dodge Viper hybrid, 280–282
Dominant strategy, 271–272
  in prisoner's dilemma, 274
  taking steroids, 315
Dominated strategy, 273
Domingo, Placido, 127
Donation of public goods, 405–406
Downsizing, 175

E

Earned-Income Tax Credit, 183, 368
Earnings; *see* Income; Income inequality;
    Wage Rates; Wages
East Germany, 52
eBay, 327–328
Economic efficiency; *see* Efficiency
Economic growth, 49–51
  from knowledge improvements, 50
  from population growth, 50
  from saving and investment, 50
  from technological improvements, 50
Economic loss, 162–163, 206
  firm's responses to, 208–214
  of monopolist, 246
  in monopolistic competition, 235
  reduced by hurdle method, 256
  and resource allocation, 207–208
  short-run, 210
Economic mobility, 362
Economic models, 7–8
Economic naturalism
  ATM example, 18–19
  auto heater example, 18
  and cost-benefit-analysis, 19
  definition, 17
  software example, 17–18
Economic principles, need to understand, 376
Economic profit
  versus accounting profit, 204–207
  calculating, 205
  central role of, 204–207
  of cigarette makers, 278
  definition, 204
  effect of entry on, 208–209
  firm's responses to, 208–214
  and long-run equilibrium, 211
  in monopolistic competition, 235
  of natural monopoly, 259–260
  negative, 206
  not guaranteed to monopolist, 246–247
  of oligopoly, 236
  and operation of invisible hand, 212–214
  and resource allocation, 207–208
  in short run, 208
  from taxi medallions, 218
  when entry ceases, 209–210
Economic rent; *see also* Rent-seeking
  definition, 215
  versus economic profit, 215–216
  for talented chefs, 215–216
Economics
  characteristics of, 1
  core principles of, 1–2

cost-benefit principle, 4–5
definition, 4
incentive principle, 15
micro and macro, 15–16
normative vs. positive, 15
scarcity principle, 4–5
Economics class sizes, 3–5
Economic surplus, 6–7; *see also* Consumer
surplus; Producer surplus
from compensation policy, 187–187
effect of better information, 327–328
effect of externalities, 300–301
effect of price subsidies on, 183–185
effect of tax collected from sellers, 192–194
from equilibrium price, 178
in health care delivery, 378–379
largest, 177
lost by taxation, 415
maximized by perfectly discriminating
monopolist, 252
of monopolist not realized, 247–248
with price controls, 181–183
without price controls, 180–181
and property rights and maximization of, 312
reduced by minimum wage, 366, 367–368
reduced by pay-per-view TV, 407–408
reduced by positive externalities, 301
Economic systems based on specialization,
35–36
Economic value of work
hiring and output decision, 351–352
wages and productivity, 350–351
Economies of scale
average total cost, 239–240
examples, 240–241
importance for start-up costs, 239–242
marginal cost, 239–240
for natural monopoly, 238, 257, 259
total cost, 239–240
Economists
definition of profit, 204
opposed to minimum wage, 366
opposition to rent controls, 64, 73
view of preferences, 288
on workers' compensation, 389
on workplace safety, 386–387
Economy food plan, 365
Efficiency
basis of, 179
definition, 86
and equilibrium, 84–87
as first goal, 179
loss from single-price monopoly, 256
and market equilibrium, 176–179
other goals than, 179
as social goal, 86
and taxation, 190–196
Efficiency principle, 2
and Coase theorem, 302
earned-income tax credit, 368
in health insurance, 379
versus monopoly inefficiency, 249
and socially optimal quantity, 86–87
Efficient, 176
Efficient market hypothesis, 221–222
Efficient point, 44
Eight Crossings, 54

Elastic demand, 99
and substitution possibilities, 100
Elasticity
cross-price elasticity of demand, 111–112
definition, 98
income elasticity of demand, 111–112
point elasticity, 124
price elasticity of demand, 98–107
price elasticity of supply, 112–118
and taxation and efficiency, 194–195
and total expenditure, 107–111
Elasticity estimates, 101
Elasticity of demand for labor, 366
Electricity market, 117
Elzinga, K., 101
Employer discrimination, 358
Employment
effect of minimum wage, 366
public employment for the poor, 368–369
Employment levels
demand curve for labor, 352–353
and labor market shifts, 354
supply curve for labor, 353–354
English-speaking nations, 40
Entrepreneurs, and invisible hand, 204
Environmental regulation using price incentives
auctioning pollution permits, 384–385
taxation of pollution, 382–384
Equality, attraction of, 363
Equations
constructed from tables, 28–30
definition, 24
demand curve, 93
derived from graph, 26
for equilibrium price/quantity, 93–94
graph of, 25
simultaneous, 30–31
supply curve, 93
from verbal description, 24
Equilibrium
definition, 68
and efficiency, 84–87
Equilibrium price
definition, 68
and economic profit, 209–210
economic surplus from, 178
effect of demand shifts, 75–78
effect of price controls, 73–74
effect of rent controls, 71–73
effect of supply curve shifts, 78–81
effects of demand and supply shifts, 83–84
equations for solving, 93–94
market functions, 84
without subsidies, 183
and surplus-enhancing transactions, 178
with taxes, 191
tendency to gravitate toward, 69–70
Equilibrium principle, 2
in demand for urban parkland, 405
effect of free entry and exit, 211
examples of, 216–217
and inefficiency, 301
and opportunities for gain, 224–225
and recycling, 167
and tragedy of the commons, 311
wages and productivity, 350–351

Equilibrium quantity
    definition, 68
    effect of demand shifts, 75–78
    effect of price controls, 73–74
    effect of rent controls, 71–73
    effect of supply curve shifts, 78–81
    effect of taxes on, 190–191
    effects of demand and supply shifts, 83–84
    efficiency principle, 86–87
    equations for solving, 93–94
    and equilibrium principle, 87
    reduced by taxation, 195
    tendency to gravitate toward, 69–70
    and total surplus, 86–87
Equilibrium quantity of labor, 350
Equilibrium wage, 350
    effect of unions on, 356
    and employment levels
        demand curve of labor, 352–353
        market shifts, 354
        supply curve for labor, 353–354
Europe, automobile engine size, 140
Excess demand, 69
    from rent controls, 72
    for surplus-enhancing transactions, 177
Excess profit; see Economic profit
Excess supply, 69
    for surplus-enhancing transactions, 178
Exchange
    and cash-on-the-table metaphor, 85–86
    gains from, 46–47
    and opportunity cost, 36–41
    voluntary nature of, 85
Exclusive contracting, 258–259
Expectations, 78
    determinant of supply, 165
Expected value of a gamble, 331–332
Explicit costs, 204, 205
External benefits, 298; see also Externalities
External costs, 298; see also Externalities
    and taxation, 195
Externalities; see also Pollution entries;
        Positional externalities
    burden of adjustment, 305–306
    Coase theorem, 301–306
    compensatory taxes or subsidies, 307–309
    effect on resource allocation, 298–299
    effect on supply and demand, 299–301
    examples of, 297
    and government regulation, 408–409
    legal remedies, 305–306
    negative, 298–299
    optimal negative amount, 307
    pollution costs, 299–300
    positive, 298

F

Fabrikant, Geraldine, 269n
Factors of production, 155
    fixed or variable, 156
Fair gamble, 332
Families
    poverty threshold, 365
    source of labor discrimination, 359
Fashion norms, 317
Federal government powers, 409

Finder's fees, 72
First Amendment, 306
First-come, first-served policy
    airline industry, 185–187
    overbooking policy, 187–188
First-dollar insurance coverage, 379
First impressions, 127
Fiscal policy, crowding-out effect, 414–415
Fisher, Ronald, 101
Fixed costs, 239
    definition, 156–157
    and level of output, 157–158
    in software industry, 241
    video game producers, 240–241
Fixed factors, 156
Fixed income allocation
    between goods, 132–135
    income effect, 135–137
    and rational spending rule, 135
    substitution effect, 135–137
Fleming, Renée, 360
Flexibility of inputs, 115
Florida Power and Light Company, 234
Food distribution system, 61–63
Football players
    on steroids, 315
    team roster limits, 316
Ford, 235
Ford Excursion, 139
Franchises, government, 237–238
Free enterprise/market system, 64, 175–176
    functions of price, 207–208
    rewards from work, 361
Free entry
    effect on profit and price, 208–209
    importance of, 214
    in monopolistic competition, 235
    and zero economic profit, 211
Free exit
    effect on profit and price, 210
    importance of, 214
    and zero economic profit, 211
Free-rider problem
    in information search, 329–330
    with public goods, 401
Free speech laws, 306
Free-trade agreements, 53
Freeways, 217
Friedman, Milton, 413
Fuel shortages, 138
Full-coverage health insurance
    critics of, 378–379
    waste from, 377–378
Funding by donation, 405–406

G

Gainesville, Florida, 188–189
Gains from exchange, 41, 46–47
Gains from specialization, 46–47
    real-world, 50–51
Gamble inherent in information search, 331–332
Game theory/Games
    commitment device, 285
    commitment problems, 285–287
    credible threats or promises, 282–283
    decision tree, 281–282, 283

dominant strategy, 271–272
dominated strategy, 272
economics of cartels, 275–277
elements of games, 270–272
location game, 283–285
movie industry example, 269–270
Nash equilibrium, 272–273
original prisoner's dilemma, 274–275
payoff matrix, 271
repeated prisoner's dilemma, 277–279
role of preferences, 287–289
for strategic decision making, 270–273
timing factor, 280–285
tit-for-tat strategy, 277–279
Game tree, 281
Gandhi, Indira, 346
Gasoline prices
and car size, 138–139
and engine size, 140
real vs. nominal, 139
volatility, 116–117
Gasoline tax, 375
Gated communities, 406
Gates, Bill, 5, 54–55, 138, 215
Gemstone makers, 115–116
General Motors, 256, 275
George, Henry, 195
Global warming, 416
Goods
allocating fixed income between, 132–135
collective, 399
complements, 75–76
hybrid, 399
inferior, 78
needs vs. wants, 127–128
normal, 78
public vs. private, 398–400
substitutes, 76–77
Gould, Stephen Jay, 40n
Government
abuses of power, 397–398
additional functions, 408–410
disadvantages of reliance on, 405
marginal cost pricing by, 188–190
monopoly in use of force, 397
policy toward natural monopoly
enforcement of antitrust laws, 259–260
exclusive contracting, 258–259
ignore the problem, 259
state ownership, 257
state regulation, 258
power to tax, 397
provision of public goods, 398–403
role in paying for health insurance, 381
sources of inefficiency
critics of waste, 413–414
pork barrel legislation, 410–411
rent-seeking, 411–413
workers' compensation, 389
Government franchises, 237–238
Government licenses, 237–238
bidding for, 413
Government regulation, 408–410
of cigarette advertising, 278–279
cost-plus, 258
of externalities, 305–306, 408–409
local, state, and federal differences, 409

of natural monopolies, 258
price incentives in pollution control
auctioning pollution permits, 384–385
taxing pollution, 382–384
of property rights, 408–409
safety seats for infants, 389–390
of workplace safety, 385–390
zoning laws, 305–306
Government-sponsored jobs, 368–369
Graf, Steffi, 314
Graphs
changes in vertical intercept and slope, 27–28
constructed from tables, 28–30
deriving equilibrium, 26
equation of straight line, 25
marginal revenue curve, 244
to measure profit, 162–163
price elasticity of demand, 103–105
profit maximization, 159–161
ratio rise/run, 25
slope, 25
total expenditure and demand curve, 108–110
vertical intercept, 25
Greenspan, Alan, 193

H

Hair stylists, 212–214
HBO network, 399
Head tax, 401, 402
Health care delivery
cost-benefit criteria, 376–378
designing a solution to, 378–379
diagnostic tests, 376
economics of, 376–382
HMO revolution, 379–380
hospital stay, 377–379
paying for health insurance, 380–381
price elasticity of demand for, 378–379
public health services, 390–391
third-party payment system, 376
waste from full-coverage insurance, 377–379
Health care expenditures, 376
Health insurance
critics of full coverage, 378–379
deductibles, 379
first-dollar coverage, 379
government reimbursements for, 381
vs. HMOs, 379–380
number of uninsured in U.S., 380–381
paying for, 380–381
waste from full coverage, 377–379
Health insurance providers, 376
Health maintenance organizations, 379–380
Heating oil, effect of price ceilings on, 180–181
Heston, Alan, 50n
High-income countries, 47n
Hiring policy, 352
Honda Civic, 139
Honeybee keeper, 298–299
Horizontal addition, 141
Horizontal interpretation
of demand curve, 66, 145
of supply curve, 67, 79, 169
Hospital stay, 377–379
Hotelling, Harold, 284–285
Household Food Consumption Survey, 365

Housing market
   New York vs. Seattle, 138
   regulated vs. unregulated, 71–73
   and wage rates of carpenters, 80
Houthakker, H. S., 101
Human capital, 355
   and earnings differentials, 359–360
   in winner-take-all labor market, 360–361
Human capital theory, 347, 355
Hurdle method of price discrimination
   examples of, 255–256
   fairness and efficiency in, 260
   obstacles to charging highest price, 252–253
   perfect hurdle, 253
Hybrid automobiles, 280–282
Hybrid goods, 399

I

IBM, 259
Illicit drug users, 97–98
Imperfect competition
   compared to perfectly competitive firms,
      236–237
   monopolistic competition, 234–235
   oligopoly, 235–236
Imperfectly competitive firms, 155, 234
   responses of rivals, 270
Imperfect price discrimination, 252
Implicit costs, 204
   ignoring, 9–10
Incentive principle, 1–2
   and cash-on-the-table metaphor, 86
   for cost-saving innovations, 217
   and credible threats, 282
   effect of taxation on, 415
   effect on rent controls, 72
   and efficient market hypothesis, 223
   and equality of income, 363
   ignored by first-dollar coverage, 379
   and income, 78
   and marginal cost pricing, 189–190
   in Nash equilibrium, 273
   and negative income tax, 365
   and price controls, 182–183
   in regulated markets, 217–219
   undermined by AFDC, 364
Income
   of families by quintiles, 360–362
   growth in U.S. 1980–2000, 361
   importance of differences in, 140
   and incentive principle, 78
   poverty threshold, 365
   and shifts in demand, 77
   of top one percent of earners, 362
   and willingness to pay for public goods, 402
Income allocation, 132–137
Income distribution
   and economic mobility, 362
   by quintiles, 361–362
   rules for justice in, 362–363
Income effect, 65
   and marginal utility, 135–137
   and rational spending rule, 136–137
   work-leisure decision, 353
Income elasticity of demand, 111–112
   for public goods, 402–403

Income inequality, 347
   economic value of work, 350–352
   equilibrium wage and employment
      levels, 352–354
   examples, 349–350
   explaining differences in
      compensating wage differentials, 357–358
      human capital theory, 355
      labor market discrimination, 358–360
      labor unions, 355–357
      winner-take-all labor market, 360–361
   and income redistribution, 364–370
   as moral problem, 362–363
   recent trends in, 361–362
Income redistribution methods, 364–370
   combination of methods, 369
   earned-income tax credit, 367–368
   in-kind transfers, 364
   means-tested programs, 364–365
   minimum wage, 366
   negative income tax, 365–366
   public employment, 368–369
   welfare payments, 364
Income sharing, 363
Income tax
   progressive, 402–403
   proportional, 402
Income tax credit, 365
Income transfers
   and price ceilings, 182–183
   and price subsidies, 184–185
Increasing marginal utility, 131
Increasing opportunity cost
   in crime prevention, 391
   in demand for urban parkland, 405
Increasing returns to scale, 238
Independent variable, 24
Individual demand curve, 140–142
   and market efficiency, 178
Individual marginal cost curve, 178
Individual sources of comparative
      advantage, 40
Individual supply curve, 152–153
Inefficiency
   avoided by advertisers, 407
   of natural monopoly, 257
   in political process
      critics of waste, 413–414
      pork barrel legislation, 410–411
      rent-seeking, 411–413
   of profit-maximizing monopolist, 247–248
   in provision of collective goods, 399
   resulting from externalities, 302
Inefficient point, 44
Inelastic demand, 99
   and total expenditure, 110
Inferior goods, 78
Inflation in medical expenses, 379
Information; see also Asymmetric information
   effect on economic surplus, 327–328
   and efficient market hypothesis, 221–222
   marginal benefit, 328–329
   marginal cost, 328–329
   middlemen as source of, 326–328
   optimal amount of
      commitment problem with costly
         search, 332–333

cost-benefit test, 328–329
free-rider problem, 329–330
gamble inherent in search, 331–332
guidelines for rational search, 330–331
increasing opportunity cost, 328
in perfectly competitive markets, 154
versus political discourse, 341–343
value to buyers, 325–326
Information search by consumers, 326
In-kind transfers, 364
Innovations, 217
Input prices, 164
Inputs
exclusive control over, 237
flexibility, 115
mobility, 115
substitutes, 115
unique and essential, 117–118
Insurance companies
adverse selection, 340
auto insurance costs, 339
moral hazard, 340–341
statistical discrimination by, 340
Intel Corporation, 241
Interest rates, present value of perpetual annual
payment, 218–219
Internal Revenue Service, abolition called
for, 398
International trade, and comparative
advantage
free-trade agreements, 53
and outsourcing, 53–55
Internet retailers, 326
Introductory economics course, 3–5
Intuit Corporation, 17
Investment, 50
Investment decisions
collective, 310–311
individual, 309–310
Invisible hand, *204*
in antipoverty programs, 220
breakdown under monopoly, 47–249
and consumer information, 329
cost-saving innovations, 217
economic rent vs. economic profit,
215–216
equilibrium vs. social optimum, 224–226
examples of, 216–224
and externalities, 298
multilane freeways, 217
operation of, 212–214
in regulated markets, 217–219
and resource allocation, 310
role of economic profit, 204–207
self-interest vs. society's interest, 225
in stock market, 220–223
supermarket checkout lines, 216
weakened by positional externalities, 316
Invisible hand theory
efficient market outcomes, 211–212
fair market outcomes, 212
on flow of resources, 219
free entry or exit, 214
functions of price, 207–208
responses to profit or loss, 208–214
Irrational choices, 15
Irrigation project, 220

J
Jamail, Joe, 36
James, Bill, 40
Jerry Springer Show, 406
Jeter, Derek, 226
Jevons, Stanley, 65
Jobs
government-sponsored, 368–369
lost in boating industry, 102
outsourcing, 53–55
with physical risk, 359
rules-based, 55
Joint Economic Committee on Taxation, 102
Jurassic Park, 78

K
Kahneman, Daniel, 8n
Keeler, E. B., 379n
Keeler, Wee Willie, 39–40
Keillor, Garrison, 336
Key deposits, 72
Kim, M., 360n
Kindergarten stating date, 316–317
Knowledge, improvements in, 50
Koromvokis, Lee, 54

L
Labor
demand curve for, 350, 352–353
elasticity of demand for, 366
marginal product of, 351
occupational demand for, 353
rental market for, 350
supply curve of, 350, 353–354
value of marginal product of, 351
Labor force, size of, 55
Labor market
discrimination in
by customers, 359
by employers, 358
from family ambitions, 359
effect of minimum wage, 366
effect of unions on, 355–357
shifts in, 354
winner-take-all, 360–361
Labor supply, and income sharing, 363
Labor unions
definition, 355
membership in 2006, 357
reasons for earnings differences,
355–357
Lake Wobegon effect, 336
Land prices, New York City vs. Seattle, 138
Land supply, 113
Late Show with David Letterman, 398
Law enforcement, 390
differential investment in crime
prevention, 391
Secret Service agents, 391–392
Law of demand, 163
and cost-benefit principle, 126
definition, 126
needs vs. wants, 127–128
and price increases, 108
sources of demand, 126–127

Law of diminishing marginal utility, 131
   and curbing pollution, 307
   and fixed-income allocation, 132–135
Law of diminishing returns, 156
   and demand for labor, 353
   in long run, 163
   and marginal cost, 158
Law of supply, 163–164
Lawyers, 338
Legalized drug proponents, 342–343
Lemons model, 334–336
Levy, Frank, 54–55
Libertarian Party, 398
Licenses
   bidding for, 413
   government-issued, 237–238
Liebowitz, A., 379n
Lobbyists, 413
Local government powers, 409
Location game, 283–285
Loewenstein, G., 353n
Logrolling, 411, 413
London Philharmonic Orchestra, 149
Long run, 155
   law of diminishing returns in, 163
Long-run average cost, 211
Long-run competitive equilibrium
   efficient outcomes, 211–212
   fair outcomes, 212
Long-run marginal cost, 211
Long-run supply curve, 191
   and economic profit, 211
Los Angeles Summer Olympic Games of
   1984, 349
Loss; *see* Economic loss
Loury, Glenn, 342, 346
Low-hanging-fruit principle, 48–49, 152–153
   and crime prevention, 391
   and curbing pollution, 307
   and supply curve, 67
   for water supply, 189
Luxury tax, 102

M

Macintax, 17
Macroeconomics, 15
Magic Cards, 233–234
Major League Baseball roster limits, 316
Manhattan land supply, 113
Manning, W. G., 379
Manufacturers
   buying direct from, 327
   productivity growth, 149
Marginal analysis, failure to do, 11–15
Marginal benefit, 12–14
   of crime prevention, 392
   of information, 328–329
   and output level, 158
   of private vs. public goods, 400
   to society of monopolist's output, 247–248
Marginal cost, 12–14
   of crime prevention, 391
   definition, 156–157
   and economic profit/loss, 208–211
   with economies of scale, 239–240
   effect of externalities, 299–301

   equal to marginal revenue, 248
   of information, 328–329
   for microprocessors, 241
   of natural monopoly, 257
   and output level, 158
   of pollution abatement, 382
   price equal to, 161–163
   video game producers, 240–241
   and wage rates, 164
Marginal cost curve, 160
   for urban parkland, 404–405
   for water, 188–189
Marginal cost pricing by public utilities,
   188–190
Marginal cost schedule for urban parkland, 405
Marginal physical product, 351
Marginal product of labor, 351
Marginal revenue
   definition, 242
   equal to marginal cost, 248
   less than monopolist's price, 248
   for monopolist, 242–245
   and price discrimination, 250–251
Marginal revenue curve for monopolist, 244–245
Marginal utility, 130–131
   and allocation of fixed income, 132–135
   increasing, 131
   and rational spending rule, 135
Marginal utility curve, 134
Market(s)
   barriers to entry, 214
   buyers and sellers, 64–67
   for cars vs. gasoline, 116–117
   versus central planning, 63–64
   changing nature of, 203–204
   critics of, 179
   definition, 64
   demand curve, 65–66
   demand-side, 150
   efficient outcomes, 211–212
   fair outcomes, 212
   functions of equilibrium price, 84
   versus government agency, 63
   imperfections in, 178
   importance of free entry/exit, 214
   and income inequality, 361
   and political coordination, 176
   problems not solved by, 175–176
   regulated
     airline industry, 219
     taxi industry, 217–219
   supply-side, 150
   in 21st century, 64
Market demand curve, 140–142, 163–164
Market equilibrium
   buyer's surplus, 85
   and cash on the table, 85–86
   contribution to economic surplus, 84–87
   definition, 68
   effect of externalities on, 300–301
   effect of monopoly on, 47–249
   effect of price controls, 73–74
   effect of rent controls, 71–73
   effect of taxes on sellers, 192–194
   and efficiency, 176–179
   equilibrium price, 68
   equilibrium quantity, 68

excess supply or demand, 69
hair stylists and aerobics instructors, 212–214
seller's surplus, 85
versus social optimum, 224–226
total surplus, 85
when exit ceases, 210
Market power
    definition, 237
    sources of, 237–239
        control over inputs, 237
        copyrights, 237
        economies of scale, 238
        government licenses or franchises, 237–238
        natural monopoly, 238
        network economies, 237
        patents, 237
Market supply curve, 152–153, 163–164
Marlboro, 234
Marquis, M. S., 379n
Marshall, Alfred, 65, 75
Marx, Karl, 52n, 64
Masterpiece Theater, 406
Maximum-profit condition, 161–163
Means-tested benefit programs, 364–365
Medicaid, 379
Medicare, 379
Mediterranean Sea pollution, 314
Meir, Golda, 346
Mellon, Andrew, 259
Merchant marine companies, 217
Method of simultaneous equations, 31
Miami Heat, 118
Microeconomics, 15–16
Microsoft Corporation, 54, 154, 155, 214, 215
Microsoft Windows, 238
Middlemen, value added by, 326–328
Midpoint formula, 123–124
Minimum wage, 66
    versus earned-income tax credit, 368
    effect on low-wage labor, 366
    opposed by economists, 366
    reducing economic surplus, 366, 367–368
Minorities, wage rates, 358
Mixed economies, 64
Mobility of inputs, 115
Modern Times, 52
Money, time value of, 221
Monopolist
    definition, 236
    inefficiency of profit-maximizing, 247–248
    marginal revenue less than price, 248
    perfectly discriminating, 252
    price discrimination by, 249–256
    profit maximization for
        decision rule, 245–246
        economic profit, 246–247
        marginal revenue, 242–245
        output level, 242–246
    profit-maximizing output level,
        245–246, 247
    socially efficient level of output, 248
Monopolistic competition; *see also* Game theory
    characteristics, 234–235
    definition, 234
    location decisions, 283–285
    product differentiation by time, 285
    tendency to cluster, 284–285

Monopoly; *see also* Natural monopoly
    algebra of profit maximization, 267–268
    and antitrust laws, 248, 259–260
    breakdown of invisible hand, 47–249
    deadweight loss from, 248
    definition, 234
    in Magic Cards, 233–234
    from patent protection, 248
    single-price, 256
    as socially inefficient, 248–249
Moral hazard, 340–341
Moral problem, income inequality as, 362–363
Morton salt, 100
Movement along a demand curve, 75
Movement along a supply curve, 75
Movie industry, 118
    business negotiations, 269–270
    hurdle method of, 256
Movie price tickets, 107–110
Movie theaters, price discrimination by, 250
Multinational environmental pollution, 314
Multiplayer prisoner's dilemmas, 275
Murnane, Richard, 54–55
Musicians, 360

N

Nash, John, 272
Nash equilibrium, 272–273
National Aeronautics and Space Administration,
    12–14
National Basketball Association, 118
    roster limits, 316
National Football League
    roster limits, 316
    steroid use, 315
National income, health care costs in, 376
National sources of comparative
    advantage, 40
Natural monopoly
    definition, 238
    economic profit, 259–260
    economies of scale, 238, 257, 259
    inefficiency of, 257
    versus many small firms, 249
    public policy toward
        enforcement of antitrust laws,
            259–260
        exclusive contracting, 258–259
        ignore the problem, 259
        state ownership, 257
        state regulation, 258
Needs vs. wants, 127–128
Negative economic profit, 206; *see also*
        Economic loss
Negative externalities, 298–299, 382; *see also*
        Pollution *entries*
    optimal amount, 307
Negative income tax, 365–366
    combined with public employment, 326
Negative profit, 162–163
Nepal, 35–36, 51–52
Nerd norms, 317
Network economies, 238
Newhouse, J. P., 379n
News Hour with Jim Lehrer, 54
Newton, Isaac, 64

New York City
    food distribution system, 61–63
    rental housing market, 62–73, 71–73
    rent controls, 62–73
    taxi medallion costs, 218
    zoning laws, 306
New York Times, 115, 127
Nintendo, 240–241
Nixon, Richard M., 343
No-cash-on-the-table principle, 87
    and anti-poverty programs, 220
    effect of free entry and exit, 211
    examples, 216–217
    and opportunities for gain, 224–225
    and wage differences, 355
    on wage gap, 358
No-free-lunch principle, 4–5
Nominal price, 139
Noneconomic sources of comparative
        advantage, 40–41
Nonexcludable goods, 398
    pure common good, 399
Nonpayers, means of excluding from public
        goods, 406
Nonrival goods, 398
    collective goods, 399
Normal goods, 78
Normal profit, 205
    cost of doing business, 208
Normative economics, 15
Norms against vanity, 318–319
Norms of taste, 317–318
North American Free Trade Agreement, 53
North Korea, 52, 63

O

Occupational demand for labor, 353
Occupational Safety and Health
        Administration, 389
Oil production cartel, 277
Oligopoly; *see also* Game theory
    cartels, 275–277
    characteristics, 235–236
    definition, 235
    product differentiation by time, 285
Omerta, 285, 286
O'Neal, Shaquille, 118
Opportunity cost
    and absolute advantage, 36–37
    in calculating economic profit, 205
    and comparative advantage, 37–41
    and cost-benefit principle, 7
    and crime prevention, 391
    of curbing pollution, 307
    of different resources, 48–49
    and economic profit, 208–209
    and exchange, 36–41
    and implicit costs, 10
    and increased production, 48–49
    increasing, 152–153
    of information search, 331
    of operating and taxes, 218
    principle of, 2, 49
    in production possibilities curve, 43
    of pursuing occupations, 149
    of resources, 150

scarcity principle, 36–37
    and supply curve, 66–67, 150–152
    of time, 253
Optimal amount of negative externalities, 307
Organization of Petroleum Exporting
        Countries, 117
    as cartel, 277
Output
    and cost-benefit principle, 157, 158
    effect of price discrimination on, 250–252
    and hiring policy, 352
    monopolist's profit-maximizing level,
        245–246, 247
    profit-maximizing level, 157–158
    in short-run production, 155–156
    socially efficient level of, 248
    variable vs. fixed costs, 239
Outsourcing
    job candidates for, 54–55
    of service jobs, 53–54
Overbooking problem, 187–188

P

Parameter, 24
Pareto, Vilfredo, 176
Pareto efficient, 176
Pareto improvement, 378
Patent protection, 238, 248
Patents, source of market power, 237
Payoff, 269–270
    for performance, 314–315
    in positional externalities, 316
    in prisoner's dilemma, 274–275
Payoff matrix
    for advertising game, 272
    in auto industry, 280
    for cartel agreements, 277
    for cigarette advertisers, 279
    definition, 271
    and Nash equilibrium, 273
    in prisoner's dilemma, 274
    for steroid use, 315
Pay-per-view cable TV, 399, 407–408
Payroll tax, 375
Peer influence, 127
Pentagon attack of 2001, 117
Pentagon spending, 413
PepsiCo, 285, 337
Perfect hurdle, 253
Perfectly competitive firms
    compared to imperfectly competitive
        firms, 236–237
    compared to monopolistic competition, 234
    hiring policy and output decision, 352
    marginal revenue, 242, 245
    price takers, 217
Perfectly competitive markets
    average total cost, 159
    average variable cost, 159
    characteristics of, 154
    cost concepts, 156–157
    definition, 154
    demand curve, 154–155
    effect of taxes on sellers, 192–194
    and law of supply, 163–164
    maximum profit condition, 161–163

output level, 157–158
price takers, 154
profit maximization, 153–154, 159–161, 248
short-run production, 155–156
shutdown condition, 159
socially efficient, 248
Perfectly discriminating monopolist, 252
Perfectly elastic demand curve, 106
Perfectly elastic supply, 114
Perfectly inelastic demand curve, 106–107
Perfectly inelastic supply, 113
Perfect price discrimination, 252
Perot, Ross, 53
Personal Responsibility Act of 1996, 364
Peterson, Iver, 329n
Pharmaceutical companies, 237
Philip Morris, 278–279
Picasso, Pablo, 64
Pigou, A. C., 307
Plato, 64
Players, 270–271
Playstation, 240–241
Point elasticity, 124
Polachek, S., 360n
Political discourse; *see* Disappearing political discourse
Political process, sources of inefficiency
critics of waste, 413–414
pork barrel legislation, 410–411
rent-seeking, 411–413
Pollock, Jackson, 64
Pollution
and Coase theorem, 301–303
costs and benefits of avoiding, 307
limits on discharge of, 306
multinational, 314
socially optimal level of, 307
sources not subject to control, 409
Pollution abatement, marginal cost of, 382
Pollution costs, 86–87, 299–300
Pollution tax, 195, 382–384, 416
Poor, the
effect of rent controls on, 71–73
health insurance for, 379
income redistribution to, 364–370
poverty threshold, 365
public employment for, 368–369
ways of helping, 73
Poor nations, 50
Population density, 52
Population growth, 50
Pork barrel legislation, 410–411, 413
Positional arms control agreements, 316
Positional arms race
definition, 316
social norms as, 317–319
Positional externalities
arbitration agreements, 316
arms control agreements, 316
arms race, 316
campaign spending limits, 316
definition, 316
dependent on relative performance, 314–315
kindergarten starting date, 316–317

professional sports roster limits, 316
social norms, 317–319
weakening invisible hand, 316
Positive economics, 15
Positive externalities, 298
reduction in economic surplus, 301
Poverty threshold, 365
Preferences, 78, 126–127
character judgments, 289
of local communities, 409
remote-office game, 287–288
role in game theory, 287–289
and self-interest, 288
as solution to commitment problems, 288–289
Present value
of future costs and benefits, 221
of a perpetual annual payment, 218–219
President, Secret Service protection, 391–392
Price(s); *see also* Equilibrium price
allocative function, 207–208, 214
buyer's reservation price, 66
and change in quantity demanded, 75
and consumer surplus, 142–145
and demand curve, 65–66
determination of, 64–65
effect of entry on, 208–209
effect of patents on, 237
equal to marginal cost, 161–163
with excess demand, 69–70
with excess supply, 69–70
expectations of change in, 165
explaining changes in, 74–84
shifts in demand, 75–78
shifts in supply, 78–81
of gasoline vs. cars, 116–117
and invisible hand, 207–208
and law of demand, 163–164
less than average variable cost, 159
marginal cost pricing, 188–190
marginal revenue less than, 248
with market power, 237
in monopolistic competition, 235
obstacles to charging highest, 252–253
and opportunity cost of resources, 150
in perfectly competitive markets, 155
and producer surplus, 168–169
rationing function, 207–208
real vs. nominal, 139
seasonal movements, 84
seller's reservation price, 67
and shutdown condition, 159
and supply and demand, 176–178
and supply curve, 66–67
total expenditure as function of, 108–110
when entry ceases, 209–210
Price adjustments, costs of preventing
first-come, first-served policy, 185–188
price ceilings, 180–183
price subsidies, 183–185
Price ceilings
economic surplus with, 181–182
economic surplus without, 180–181
on heating oil, 180–183
and income transfers, 181–182
justifications for, 182
waste caused by, 181

Price changes
    and budget share, 100
    and demand curve for movie tickets,
        107–110
    determinant of supply, 165
    effect on total expenditure, 110, 111
    expectations of, 81
    and income effect, 65, 135–137
    and price elasticity of demand, 103–105
    and substitution effect, 65, 135–137,
        138–140
    and substitution possibilities, 100
Price controls, 85
    effects of, 73–74
    on gasoline, 73
    rent regulations, 63
Price discrimination
    definition, 249
    effectiveness of, 249
    effect on output, 250–252
    examples, 255–256
    hurdle method, 252–254
    imperfect, 252
    merits of, 255
    by movie theaters, 250
    perfect, 252
Price elasticity of demand, 98–99, 411
    applications
        cigarette tax and teenage smoking, 102
        luxury tax on yachts, 102
    calculating, 104
    for cars vs. gasoline, 116–117
    changes along straight-line demand curve,
        105–106
    and demand curve, 104–106
    determinants
        budget share, 100
        substitution possibilities, 100
        time, 100
    effect of taxes, 102, 194–195
    exceptions to general rule, 106–107
    graphical interpretation, 103–105
    for medical services, 378–379
    midpoint formula, 123–124
    and quantity demanded, 99
    representative estimates, 101
    and total expenditure, 110–111
Price elasticity of supply
    car prices vs. gasoline prices, 116–117
    definition, 112
    determinants, 114–117
        ability to produce substitute
          inputs, 115
        flexibility of inputs, 115
        mobility of inputs, 115
        time factor, 115–116
    effect of taxes on sellers, 191
    formula, 112
    perfectly elastic supply curve, 114
    perfectly inelastic supply curve, 113
    straight-line supply curve, 113
    with unique and essential inputs, 117–118
Price incentives in environmental regulation
    auctioning pollution permits, 384–385
    taxation of pollution, 382–384
Price-quantity pair, 123–124, 163
Price setters, 234

Price setting
    by cartels, 275–277
    with cost-plus regulation, 258
    by natural monopoly, 257
Price subsidies
    effect on economic surplus, 183–185
    versus income transfers, 184–185
Price support legislation, 411–412
Price takers, 154, 217
Price volatility
    electricity market, 117
    gasoline prices, 116–117
Principle of comparative advantage, 1–2, 37–40
Principle of increasing opportunity cost, 2, 49
    and supply curve, 152–153
Prisoner's dilemma
    multiplayer, 275
    original game, 274–275
    predicted defectors, 289
    repeated, 277–279
    tit-for-tat strategy, 277–279
Private contracting for public goods, 406
Private goods
    generating demand curve for, 403
    jointly or individually consumed, 402
    marginal benefit, 400
    versus public goods, 398–400
Private marginal cost, 299–300
Private ownership; *see also* Property rights
    effect of, 311–312
    when impractical, 312–314
Private provision of public goods
    exclusion of nonpayers, 406
    funding by donation, 405–406
    private contracting, 406
    problems with, 406–407
    and reduced economic surplus, 407–408
    versus reliance on government, 405
    sale of by-products, 406
Producer surplus
    calculating, 168–169
    definition, 168
    effect of price ceilings on, 181
    effect of price subsidies, 183–184
    enhanced by hurdle method, 255
Product compatibility, 214
Product differentiation
    in monopolistic competition, 235
    by time or scheduling, 285
Production; *see also* Costs of production
    constant returns to scale, 238
    economies of scale, 238
    effect of taxation on, 415
    flexibility of inputs, 115
    increasing returns to scale, 238
    law of diminishing returns, 156
    mobility of inputs, 115
    profit-maximizing output level, 157–158
    in short run, 155–156
    shutdown condition, 159
    start-up costs, 239–242
    substitute inputs, 115
    unique and essential inputs, 117–118
Production possibilities curve, 41–44
    attainable point, 43–44
    definition, 36, 41
    economic growth, 49–51

effect of productivity on, 44–46
    efficient point, 44
    factors that shift, 49–53
    gains from specialization and exchange, 46–47
    high-income countries, 47n
    inefficient point, 44
    many-person economy, 47–49
    one-worker economy, 42–44
    and scarcity principle, 43
    unattainable point, 43–44
Productive ability, 350–351
Productivity
    boosted by unions, 357
    effect on production possibilities curve, 44–46
    and specialization, 35–36
Productivity growth, and wage rates, 149
Products
    changes in price of other, 165
    costly-to-fake principle, 336–337
    in monopolistic competition, 234–235
    in perfectly competitive markets, 154
    undifferentiated, 235
    value added by middlemen, 326–328
Professional sports
    baseball, 39–40
    basketball, 117–118
    football, 315–316
    roster limits, 316
Profit
    accounting profit, 204
    and average total cost, 159
    and average variable cost, 159
    definition, 153
    economic profit vs. accounting
        profit, 204–207
    firm's responses to, 208–214
    graphical measurement, 162–163
    normal profit, 205
    revenue vs. explicit costs, 204
Profitable firms, 159
Profit maximization
    algebra of, 267–268
    by cartels, 275–277
    for monopolist, 248
        demand curve, 243–246
        economic profit, 246–247
        marginal revenue, 242–245
        output level, 245–246
    in perfectly competitive markets
        average total cost, 159
        average variable cost, 159
        chosen level of output, 157–158
        cost concepts, 156–157
        demand curve, 154–155
        graphical approach to, 159–161
        and law of supply, 163–164
        maximum profit condition, 161–163
        short-run production, 155–156
        shutdown condition, 159
        terminology, 153–154
Profit-maximizing decision rule, 245–246
Profit-maximizing firm, 154
Profit-maximizing output level, 157–158
    of monopolist, 245–246, 247
Profit-maximizing rule, 209
Profit opportunities, 203–204
Progressive tax, 402–403

Property rights
    effect of private ownership, 311–312
    and government regulation, 408–409
    legal limits on, 312
    and logic of economic surplus
        maximization, 312
    problem of unpriced resources, 309–311
    tragedy of the commons, 311
    when private ownership impractical,
        312–314
Property tax, California Proposition 13, 414
Proportional income tax, 401
Proportion vs. absolute dollar amount, 9
Proposition 13, California, 414
Public employment for the poor, 368–369
Public goods
    collective, 399
    cost of, 399–400
    definition, 398
    demand curve for, 403–405
    disadvantages of reliance on government, 405
    and equal tax rule, 401–402
    free-rider problem, 401
    and income, 402
    income elasticity of demand for, 402–403
    marginal benefit, 400
    nonrival and nonexcludable, 398
    optimal quantity of, 403–408
    paying for, 400–403
    preferences of local communities, 409
    versus private goods, 398–400
    private provision of
        excluding nonpayers, 406
        funding by donation, 405–406
        loss of economic surplus, 407–408
        private contracting, 406
        problems with, 406–407
        versus reliance on government, 405
        sale of by-products, 406
    and proportional tax, 402
    pure, 398–399
    reservation price for, 400–401
Public health services, 390–391
Public service employment, 368–369
Public utilities, marginal cost pricing,
    188–190
Pure common good, 399
Pure monopoly, 234
Pure private good, 399
Pure public goods, 398–399

Q

Quality
    costly-to-fake principle, 336–337
    desire for, 127
Quantities
    and demand curve, 65–66
    determination of, 64–65
    socially optimal, 86–87
    and supply curve, 66–67
Quantity demanded
    and all costs, 126
    and income elasticity of demand, 111
    and price elasticity of demand, 99
Quantity supplied, 152–153
    and price elasticity of supply, 112

Quicken software, 17
Quintiles of income, 360–362

R

Rational choice, 15
Rational information search, 330–331
Rational person, 6
Rational spending rule
    definition, 135
    formula, 135
    and income differences, 140
    and income effect, 135–137
    role of substitutes, 138–140
    and substitution effect, 135–137
Rationing function of price, 207–208
Rawls, John, 362
Real price, 139
Rebate coupons, 253–254
Recycling, 150–152, 165–168
    redemption price, 151–152, 166
    socially optimal amount, 166
Red Cross, 153
Redemption price, 151–152, 166
Refundable taxes, 416
Regressive tax, 401
Regulated markets
    airline industry, 219
    taxi industry, 217–219
Regulation; see Government regulation
Relevant costs and benefits, 299
Remote-office game, 282–283, 287–288
Rental housing market, 62–73
Rent controls
    economists' view of, 64
    versus market equilibrium, 71–73
    negative effects of, 72
    in New York City, 62–63
Rent-seeking by/from government,
        411–413
    in auction process, 412–413
    definition, 412
    government contracts, 412
    lobbyists, 413
    price supports, 411–412
Repeated prisoner's dilemma, 277–279
Research and development, 241
Reservation price
    of buyers, 66, 79
    buyers and sellers, 85
    and economic rent, 215
    of employers, 352–353
    of low-income buyers, 253
    and perfect hurdle, 253
    and perfectly discriminating monopolist, 252
    of potential customers, 252
    for public goods, 400–401
    of sellers, 67
    and wants, 126
Resource allocation
    effect of externalities on, 298–299
    and invisible hand, 310
Resource mobility, 154
Resources
    allocative function of price, 207–208
    in invisible hand theory, 219
    unpriced, 309–310

Retail stores
    competition from Internet retailers, 326
    costs of shopping at, 329
Retton, Mary Lou, 349
Revenue, and explicit costs, 204
Rich nations, 50
Rise, 25
Risk-averse person, 332, 363
Risk-neutral person, 332
Risk taking, 363
Rival products, 234
Rivergate Books, Lambertville, NJ, 329–330
RJR Corporation, 278–279
Road use tax, 416
Robber barons, 259
Robinson, Joan, 235n
Rockefeller, John D., 259
Roster limits, professional sports, 316
Rules-based jobs, 55
Run, 25

S

Safety seats for infants, 389–390
Sale of by-products, 406
Sales agents, 326–327
Savings rate, 50
Scarcity, 4
    and trade-offs, 4, 5
Scarcity principle, 4–5
    definition, 1
    and income allocation, 137
    and litter reduction, 167
    and opportunity cost, 36–37
    and production possibilities curve, 43
Sears, 256
Sears Tower, 237
Seasonal price movements, 84
Secret Service, 391–392
Seles, Monica, 314
Self-interest, 225
    and preferences, 288
Selfishness, 288
Sellers, 64–67
    asymmetric information, 333–341
    cost-benefit principle, 150
    and credibility problem, 336
    obstacles to charging highest price, 252–253
    in perfectly competitive markets, 154
    producer surplus, 168–169
    taxes and economic surplus, 192–194
    taxes paid by, 190–192
Seller's reservation price, 67, 85
Seller's surplus, 85
Service jobs, outsourcing, 53–54
Shared living arrangements, 303–305
Sherman Antitrust Act, 259
Shift in entire demand curve, 75
Shift in entire supply curve, 75
Shifts in demand, 75–78
Shortages from price ceilings, 181–182
Short run, 155
    law of supply in, 163
Short-run economic loss, 210
Short-run economic profit, 208
Short-run production, 155–156
Short-run shutdown condition, 159

Shutdown condition, 159
Silver Blaze (Conan Doyle), 9
Simultaneous equations, 30–31
Sinclair, Upton, 385–386
Single tax proposal, 195
Skateboard prices, 79
Slawson, Donna B., 341n
Slope, 25
    changes in, 27–28
Smart for one, dumb for all, 86–87
    and self interest vs. society, 225
Smith, Adam, 51, 64, 204, 207, 212, 214, 225,
        226, 231, 298, 310, 326
Smith, Robert S., 389n
Social influences, 126–127
Socially efficient level of output
    of monopolist, 248
    in perfect competition, 248
    with price discrimination, 251–252
Socially optimal expenditure on health, 390
Socially optimal level of pollution, 307
Socially optimal quantity, 86–87
Social marginal cost, 299–300
Social norms
    fashion norms, 317
    nerd norms, 317
    norms against vanity, 318–319
    norms of taste, 317–318
Social optimum vs. market equilibrium, 224–226
Soft-drink container recycling, 150–152
Software industry, 17–18
Solman, Paul, 54–55
South Korea, 52
Soviet Union, 63
Space shuttle program, 12–14
Spears, Britney, 337
Specialization, 1–2
    Adam Smith on, 51
    danger of too much, 52–53
    economies based on, 35–36
    gains from, 46–47
    gains from comparative advantage, 39
    and population density, 52
    real-world gains from, 50–51
    reasons for slowness in, 51–52
Spielberg, Steven, 78
Sprint, 235
Standardized products, 154
Standard of living
    gains from specialization and exchange, 47
    rich vs. poor nations, 50
Start-up costs, 50–51
    and economies of scale, 239–242
State government
    laws on vaccination, 390–391
    powers of, 409
State ownership and management, 257
Statistical discrimination
    adverse selection, 340
    definition, 339
    and insurance industry, 339
    moral hazard, 340–341
    promoted by competition, 339–340
    results of observable differences, 340
    and value of missing information, 338–339
Stern, Gerald, 330
Steroids, 315

Stock
    in best-managed companies, 223
    calculating present value of future
        costs/benefits, 221
    calculating value of, 220–221
    and time value of money, 221
Stock analysts, 225
Stock market
    calculating share value, 220–221
    corporate earnings forecasters, 225
    efficient market hypothesis, 221–222
    invisible hand in, 220–223
    stock performance, 223
Stock prices, 220–221
    response to new information, 225
Straight-line demand curve, 105–106
Straight-line supply curve, 113
Strategic decisions, using game theory
    elements of games, 270–272
    Nash equilibrium, 272–273
Subsidies
    to deal with negative externalities, 307–309
    for planting trees, 306
    for scientific research, 306
Subsistence level of consumption, 127
Substitute inputs, 115
Substitutes, 76–77
    and budget share, 100
    and cross-price elasticity of demand, 111
    foreign-built yachts, 102
    and time factor, 100
Substitution effect, 65
    car engine sizes, 140
    in energy use, 138–139
    in housing market, 138
    and marginal utility, 135–137
    and rational spending rule, 136–137, 138–140
    work-leisure decision, 353
Substitution possibilities, 100
Sugar price supports, 411–412
Summers, Robert, 50n
Sunk cost, 11
    irrelevance of, 14–15
Super Bowl ads, 337
Supermarket checkout lines, 216
Supply; *see also* Price elasticity of supply
    applying theory of, 165–168
    determinants of
        expectations, 165
        input prices, 164
        number of suppliers, 165
        price changes on other goods, 165
        technology, 164
    law of, 163–164
    and producer surplus, 168–169
Supply and demand, 61–88
    algebraic analysis, 93–94
    demand curve, 65–66
    effect of externalities on, 299–301
    effect of price controls, 73–74
    effect of rent controls, 71–73
    and equilibrium price, 84
    excess, 69
    to explain price/quantity changes, 74–84
    food distribution system, 61–63
    market equilibrium, 68–74
    in market for milk, 168–169

Supply and demand—*Cont.*
  markets vs. central planning, 63–64
  and operation of invisible hand, 212–214
  and price, 176–178
  rental housing market, 62–63
  socially optimal quantity, 86–87
  supply curve, 66–67
Supply bottleneck, 117–118
Supply curve
  car market vs. gasoline market, 116–117
  container recycling services, 166
  and cost side of market, 163
  effect of externalities on, 299–300
  effect of number of suppliers, 165
  effect of technology on, 164
  to find equilibrium, 68
  horizontal interpretation, 65, 79, 169
  for illicit drugs, 97–98
  individual, 152–153
  market, 152–153
  for milk, 176–177
  movement along, 75
  and operation of invisible hand,
      212–214
  and opportunity cost, 150–152
  perfectly elastic, 114
  perfectly inelastic, 113
  for pizza market, 70–71
  for price elasticity, 112–113
  for recycling services, 151–152
  for rental housing, 71
  shift factors
      decline in costs of production, 79–80
      with demand curve shift, 83–84
      increased costs of production, 78–79
      number of sellers, 81
      price change expectations, 81
      rules governing, 81–84
      technology changes, 80–81
      weather, 81
  shift in, 75
  straight-line, 113
  vertical interpretation, 67, 79, 169
Supply curve of labor, 350, 353–354
Supply-side of markets, 150
Surplus-enhancing transactions
  from excess demand, 177
  from excess supply, 178
SUVs (sport utility vehicles), 139
Switching costs, 50–51
Szabo, Ecaterina, 349–350

T

Tables, constructing graphs from, 28–30
Taste, 78, 126–127
  norms of, 317–318
Taxation
  and budget deficit, 414
  California Proposition 13, 414
  carbon tax, 416
  cigarette tax, 102
  critics of waste, 43–414
  crowding-out effect, 414–415
  deadweight loss from, 193, 194–195
  to deal with negative externalities, 307–309
  earned-income tax credit, 368

  effect on incentives, 415
  effect on production and consumption, 415
  and efficiency, 190–196
      actual payers, 190–192
      effect on economic surplus, 192–194
      and elasticity, 194–195
      external costs, 195
  gasoline tax, 375
  head tax, 401
  justification for, 415–416
  loss of economic surplus, 415
  luxury tax mistake, 102
  of monopolist's economic profit, 259
  negative income tax, 365–366
  objects of, 414–416
  to pay for public goods, 401–403
  pollution tax, 195, 382–384, 416
  progressive tax, 402–403
  proportional income tax, 402
  regressive tax, 401
  road use tax, 416
  single tax proposal, 195
  unintended consequences, 414
Taxi industry, cost of medallions, 217–219
Taylor, Lester, 101
Technological improvements, 50
Technology
  determinant of supply, 164
  effect on supply curve, 80–81
Teenage smoking, 102
Television, 41
  broadcast preferences of networks, 406–407
  cable networks, 257
Tennis matches, 314–315
Terrorist attack of 2001, 117
Thaler, Richard, 11n, 353n
Thatcher, Margaret, 346
Theory of market exchange, 177
Theory of supply, 165–168
Third-party payment system, 376
Tierney, John, 62n
Timber harvesting, 313–314
Time factor
  in auto industry, 280–282
  in game theory, 280–285
  in information search, 331
  in price elasticity of demand, 100
  in price elasticity of supply, 115–116
Time value of money, 221
Titanic, 126–127
Tit-for-tat strategy, 277–279
Tjoa, Bill, 19
Total consumer surplus, 144
Total cost
  definition, 156–157
  with economies of scale, 239–240
  video game producers, 240–241
Total expenditure
  definition, 107
  and demand curve for movie tickets, 107–110
  effect of price changes, 110, 111
  and elasticity, 107–111
  as function of price, 108–110
  with inelastic demand, 110
  and price elasticity of demand, 110–111
  product of price and quantity, 110
  and total revenue, 107–108

Total revenue
 equal to total expenditure, 107–108
 and explicit costs, 204
 factors governing, 108
 and price discrimination, 250–251
Total surplus, 85
 and equilibrium quantity, 86–87
 from socially optimal quantity, 86
Total utility, 129–130
Toxic waste, 301–303
Toyota Prius, 139
Trade-offs, 4, 5
Tragedy of the commons
 definition, 309–310
 and lack of private property solutions,
  313–314
Transfer payments, 364; *see also* Income
  redistribution; Income transfers
Trial lawyers, 36
Trump, Donald, 238
Turbo Tax, 17
Tversky, Amos, 8n
Twain, Mark, 1

U

Unattainable point, 43–44
Undifferentiated products, 234
Unemployment from minimum wage, 366
United Airlines, 270–273
United States
 automobile engine size, 140
 contributions to private charities, 405–406
 dependence on foreign oil, 375
 diplomatic relations with China, 343
 failure in TV/video recorder market, 41
 health care expenditures, 376
 labor force size, 55
 median income by quintiles, 361–362
 minimum wage legislation, 366
 trends in income inequality, 361–362
United States Constitution, 409
Unit elastic demand, 99
Urban parkland, 404–405
Used car sales
 credibility problem, 336
 lemons model, 334–336
Utility
 concept of, 128–131
 definition, 128
 diminishing marginal utility, 132
 marginal utility, 130–131
 measured electronically, 128–129
 total utility, 129–130
Utility maximization, 128
 with fixed income, 132–135
Utilometer, 128–129
Utils, 129–130

V

Vaccination laws, 390–391
Value added by middlemen, 326–328
Value of marginal product of labor
 definition, 351
 demand curve for labor, 353
 and earnings differences, 355

effect of unions on, 355–356
and hiring policy, 352
in human capital theory, 355
wages in excess of, 358
Vanity, norms against, 318–319
Variable costs, 239
 definition, 156–157
Variable factors, 156
Variables, 24
Verizon Communications, 235
Vertical intercept, 25
 changes in, 27–28
Vertical interpretation
 of demand curve, 66, 145
 of supply curve, 67, 79, 169
Vice president, protection of, 391–392
Videocassette recorders, 41
Video game producers, 240–241
Videotape recorder formats, 238
Village commons
 decisions on using, 309–311
 private ownership, 311–312
VMP; *see* Value of marginal product of labor

W

Wage differences; *see* Income inequality
Wage gap
 arbitrary, 358
 compensating differentials, 357–358
 from differences in preferences, 359
 effect of labor unions, 355–357
 human capital differences, 359–360
 in human capital theory, 355
 from labor market discrimination, 358–359
Wage rates
 of carpenters, 80
 and marginal cost, 164
 and productivity growth, 149
 of women and minorities, 358
 in relation to workplace safety, 387–389
Wages
 compensating differentials, 357–358
 and declining workweek, 353
 and firm's profitability, 387
 minimum wage, 66
 and productive ability, 350–351
 reservation price of employers, 352–353
Wall Street Journal, 223
Wants
 law of diminishing marginal utility, 131
 marginal utility, 130–131
 versus needs, 127–128
 origin of, 126–127
 translated into demand, 138–137
 utility concept, 128–131
Warner Brothers, 269–270, 280, 282
Waste
 from full-coverage health insurance,
  373–379
 by government, 413–414
 in health care delivery, 376–378
Water shortages, 127–128
Wealth of Nations (Smith), 64, 204
Welfare payments, 364
Welfare reform of 1996, 364
West Germany, 52

Whale harvesting, 313–314
Williams, Ted, 39–40
Winner-take-all labor market, 360–361
Women, wage rates, 358
Work
    economic value of, 350–352
    in free-market system, 361
Worker mobility, 387
Workers, capital investment in, 50
Workers' compensation, 389
Work-leisure decision, 353
Workplace fragmentation, 52
Workplace safety regulation
    cost-benefit analysis, 386–387
    critics and defenders of, 387
    in early industrial revolution, 385–386
    and fear of employer exploitation, 387
    Occupational Safety and Health
        Administration, 389

optimal amount of safety, 387–389
relative income and worker choices, 387–389
and wage rates, 387–389
workers' compensation, 389
Workweek, 353
World Trade Center attack, 117

Y

Yachts, luxury tax on, 102
Yosemite Concession Services Corporation,
    237–238

Z

Zero economic profit, 211
    in monopolistic competition, 235
Zimmerman, Dennis, 102n
Zoning laws, 305–306, 312, 408–409